D1597326

Battles that Changed History

Battles that Changed History

An Encyclopedia of World Conflict

Spencer C. Tucker

 ABC-CLIO

Santa Barbara, California • Denver, Colorado • Oxford, England

Library of Congress Cataloging-in-Publication Data

Tucker, Spencer, 1937–
  Battles that changed history : an encyclopedia of world conflict / Spencer C. Tucker.—1st ed.
        p. cm.
  Includes bibliographical references and index.
  ISBN 978-1-59884-429-0 (hard copy : alk. paper)
  ISBN 978-1-59884-430-6 (ebook)
  1. Battles—Encyclopedias.   2. Battles—History—Encyclopedias.   3. Military history—Encyclopedias.   I. Title.
  D25.A2T83   2010
  355.4'8—dc22

                                                          2010032810

15 14 13 12 11   1 2 3 4 5

This book is also available on the World Wide Web as an eBook.
Visit www.abc-clio.com for details.

ABC-CLIO, LLC
130 Cremona Drive, P.O. Box 1911
Santa Barbara, California 93116-1911

This book is printed on acid-free paper ∞
Manufactured in the United States of America

To Timothy C. Dowling
Scholar, colleague, friend

Contents

List of Battles

Preface

Important battles fascinate us. What constitutes an important battle? What can it teach us about the influence of leadership, motivation and morale, technology, and such factors as terrain and climate? What are the consequences for the war in which it has occurred, and what if the battle had gone the other way?

Numerous books have sought to identify and dissect the important military battles in human history. The classic work is Sir Edward Creasy's *The Fifteen Decisive Battles of the World* (originally published in 1851). Usually these books present 50 or 100 or so battles. Jeremy Black's edited work *The Seventy Great Battles in History* (2005) is one example. More recently, Tony Jacques has assembled a three-volume *Dictionary of Battles and Sieges: A Guide to 8,500 Battles of Antiquity through the Twenty-first Century* (2007), but most are dealt with in only a few sentences.

This study falls between the two extremes. It was to be limited to 200 battles, but others crept in. I have sought to include a wide chronological and geographical range of engagements, although most are modern (half are drawn from the 19th, 20th, and 21st centuries). I have sought to include not only those battles that most would agree are decisive but also those that are influential or interesting because of generalship, because of the play of chance, or perhaps because they witness the introduction of new weapons or tactics.

Clearly, some battles are truly decisive. The First Battle of the Marne in 1914, for example, denied Germany its best—and perhaps only—chance to win World War I. The outcome of the Battle of Britain (1940) prompted Adolf Hitler's decision to invade the Soviet Union. The Battle of the Somme (1916), the greatest battle in terms of casualties of World War I, while not in itself decisive was certainly influential for its great human cost and for the consequences this held for both the British and Germans in 1917. The Battle of the Somme also saw the introduction of the tank in warfare and helped bring changes in tactics.

The American Revolutionary War Battle of Saratoga (1777) and the World War II Pacific theater Battle of Midway (1942) are both turning-point battles. The Battle of Saratoga saw the surrender of an entire British army and brought France into the war openly on the American side, while the Battle of Midway largely wiped out the trained Japanese naval air arm and was, in the words of Pacific Fleet commander Admiral Chester Nimitz, "the engagement that made everything else possible." Both of these battles also illustrate the dangers inherent in an overly complicated polycentric plan, as does the Battle of Leyte Gulf (1944). The Battle of Midway also clearly shows the role played by chance.

Some battles reveal the importance of charismatic leadership, such as that of Edward III at Crécy (1346) or Joan of Arc in the siege of Orléans (1428–1429); others hinge on technological innovation or ingenuity, such as Alexander the Great's siege of Tyre (332 BCE), the Battle of Hampton Roads (1862), the Battle of Cambrai (1917), and the Battle of the Atlantic in World War II. Some battles demonstrate tremendous human will and sacrifice, such as the sieges of Rhodes (1522) and Leningrad (1941–1944). Others may truly be described as the birthright of a nation, such as the siege of Pleven (1877) for Bulgaria. Small battles can have exaggerated impact, such as two engagements on Lake Champlain (1776 and 1814) and Guernica (1937). Some battles have unforeseen salutary consequences. Thus, the bloody Battle of Solferino (1859) is notable not only for its impact on Italian unification but also because the suffering of the wounded after the battle prompted the establishment of the International Red Cross.

For the most part I have tried to let the facts speak for themselves, but on occasion I have indulged in "what if" speculation. While each battle entry stands on its own, I have tried to place each in the context of the war in which it occurs so that the reader might indeed be able to construct a rough outline of world military history from reading the whole work chronologically.

I have endeavored to provide alternate names and spellings for geographic locations. Strength figures for armies as well as casualties in battles are often difficult to establish, especially for the earlier battles. I have tried to utilize the latest scholarship as well as to provide possible ranges. I have retained the German ranks for flag officers in World War I and World War II because, while easily translated into English, they do not necessarily equate to U.S. equivalents. Thus generalmajor, or major general in the German system, is actually equivalent to brigadier general; generalleutnant is equivalent to major general; general der infanterie (artillery, cavalry, etc.) is equivalent to lieutenant general; generaloberst is equivalent to full general; and generalfeldmarschall (general field marshal) is equivalent to general of the army.

I am especially grateful to Dr. Timothy C. Dowling, associate professor of history at the Virginia Military Institute. In addition to teaching Central and East European history, Tim is a military historian specializing in the Eastern Front in World War I. I have known him since he was an undergraduate in several of my courses at Texas Christian University, and I have followed his career with interest and pride. Tim is also an uncommonly fine editor. He has graciously read this entire manuscript and made numerous editorial suggestions. I accept full responsibility for the final product, however.

I would also like to thank Pat Carlin, military history editor at ABC-CLIO, for agreeing that this project had merit and my wife Dr. Beverly B. Tucker for her continued and great patience and support.

Spencer C. Tucker

Battles that Changed History

Battle of Megiddo

Date	May 1479 BCE	
Location	Near Megiddo, present-day Palestine	
Opponents (* winner)	*Egypt	Kadesh
Commander	Pharaoh Thutmose III	King of Kadesh
Approx. # Troops	10,000–30,000	Unknown
Importance	First battle in history recorded by eyewitnesses	

The first battle in history to be recorded by eyewitnesses, this engagement was fought near the city of Megiddo (Armageddon in Hebrew) in central Palestine in May 1479 BCE. Egyptian power was declining, and following the death of the Egyptian co-regent Hatshepsut in 1482, Durusha, the king of Kadesh, led a revolt of cities of Palestine and Syria.

Pharaoh Thutmose III was anxious to assert his power and restore Egyptian authority in the Levant. After ordering the removal of Hatshepsut's name from all public buildings, Thutmose rebuilt the Egyptian Army, which had been dormant for decades, and led a rapid advance into Palestine. The size of his army has been estimated at 10,000–30,000 men; it is believed to have consisted largely of infantry, with some chariots. The infantrymen were armed with swords and axes and carried shields. The nobility fought from the chariots, probably as archers.

Thutmose's adversaries, who were similarly armed, were led by the king of Kadesh. He assembled a large force at the fortified city of Megiddo, north of Mount Carmel. Disregarding the advice of his generals, who feared an ambush, Thutmose chose the most direct route north to Megiddo, through a narrow pass. Apparently the king of Kadesh believed that the Egyptians would consider this route too risky, for he had deployed the bulk of his forces along another road to the east. Leading in person in a chariot, Thutmose pushed through Megiddo Pass, scattering its few defenders. He then consolidated his forces while the king of Kadesh withdrew his covering troops back on Megiddo.

Thutmose drew up his army in a concave formation of three main groups southwest of Megiddo and athwart the small Kina River. Both flanks were on high ground, with the left flank extending to the northwest of Megiddo to cut off any enemy escape along a road from the city. The rebel force was drawn up on high ground near Megiddo.

While the southern wing of his army held his adversary, Thutmose personally led the northern wing in an attack that sliced between the rebel left flank and Megiddo itself, enveloping the enemy force and winning the battle. The surviving enemy soldiers fled; they were momentarily saved by the fact that the Egyptian soldiers halted their pursuit to loot the enemy camp, something that greatly displeased Thutmose.

Thutmose then subjected Megiddo to a siege that lasted at least three months. On the surrender of Megiddo, Thutmose took most of the rebel kings prisoner, although the king of Kadesh escaped. Thutmose did capture the king's son and took him back to Egypt as a hostage along with the sons of other captured kings. Among the spoils of war the Egyptians recorded more than 900 chariots and 2,200 horses as well as 200 suits of armor. Reportedly, in the entire campaign Thutmose acquired 426 pounds of gold and silver.

References

Benson, Douglas. *Ancient Egypt's Warfare.* Ashland, OH: Book Masters, 1995.

Gabriel, Richard, and Donald Boose. *The Great Battles of Antiquity.* Westport, CT: Greenwood, 1994.

Steindorff, George, and Keith Seele. *When Egypt Ruled the East.* Chicago: University of Chicago Press, 1957.

Battle of Kadesh

Date	1298 BCE	
Location	Northwestern Syria	
Opponents (* winner)	*Hittites	Egypt
Commander	King Muwatallish	Pharaoh Ramses II
Approx. # Troops	Unknown	Unknown
Importance	Hittites retain control of Syria in one of the largest chariot battles in history	

Fought near Kadesh (believed to be Carchemish on the Euphrates River in northwestern Syria) in 1298 BCE, the Battle of Kadesh was waged between Egyptian forces led by Pharaoh Ramses II and a Hittite army led by King Muwatallish.

Almost everything about this battle is in dispute, including the exact date, the location, the strength of the forces involved, and the performance of the Egyptian troops. It is, however, mentioned in both Egyptian and biblical accounts, so its occurrence is fairly certain. Apparently Ramses was campaigning in Syria, with his army in four separate divisions and advancing against Hittite forces whom he believed to be to the north. Ramses was with the Amon division and decided to camp northwest of Kadesh, which he had bypassed. The main Hittite army was secreted behind Kadesh. No sooner had the Egyptians begun to set up camp than the Hittite leader Muwatallish appeared from the south, sending a reported 2,500 chariots (some across the Euphrates, probably by means of a dam) to attack the Re division, which was unprepared for battle. The Egyptians fled to the north away from their supply bases.

Meanwhile, Ramses and the Amon division came under attack in their camp from another Hittite force from south of Kadesh. Ramses sent messengers by a side route to the west to speed the arrival from the south of the two other Egyptian divisions, the Ptah and Sutekh.

Deserted by many if not most of his troops, who fled northward, Ramses was saved by his bravery in standing his ground but also by the timely arrival of elite auxiliary forces—probably mercenaries from Judah who were not part of the four Egyptian divisions—who cut through the Hittites surrounding the pharaoh. This saved him from death or captivity and brought him out to the Ptah and Sutekh divisions, which had not participated in the battle. Ramses' generals urged him to return to Egypt with his remaining forces, which he did.

Although the Hittites had inflicted a serious setback on Ramses and retained control of Syria, they found themselves under pressure from both the Assyrians and the Egyptians and ultimately sought a peace treaty with Egypt.

References

Goedicke, Hans, ed. *Perspectives on the Battle of Kadesh.* Baltimore: Halgo, 1985.

Kitchen, Kenneth A. *Pharaoh Triumphant: The Life and Times of Ramses II.* Warminster, UK: Aris and Philips, 1982.

Murnane, William J. *The Road to Kadesh.* Chicago: Oriental Institute, 1990.

Velikovsky, Immanuel. *Ramses II and His Time.* New York: Doubleday, 1978.

Siege of Troy

Date	1194–1184 BCE	
Location	Southern entrance to the Dardanelles	
Opponents (* winner)	*Greek city states	Troy
Commander	King Agamemnon	King Priam
Approx. # Troops	Unknown	Unknown
Importance	Greeks secure control of an important trade route	

The chief source on the siege of Troy is Homer's great epic, the *Iliad.* Its 24 chapters treat the last year of the siege; however, it was composed two or three centuries after the siege. Modern archaeological excavations have revealed a series of strata that identify a number of different cities built on the site. The one associated with the siege is the seventh stratum (from the bottom). It bears traces of a fire, and according to Homer, a great fire ended the siege. Scientific experts agree that the fire in the seventh stratum occurred in 1184 BCE. Homer tells us that the siege of Troy by the Mycenaeans (the mainland Greeks) went on for 10 years, hence the starting date of 1194 BCE.

The siege was undoubtedly motivated by economics. Located at the southern entrance to the Hellespont (present-day Dardanelles), Troy controlled the important trade between East and West, that is, from the Black Sea to the Mediterranean. Along this route flowed such commodities as grain, precious metals, and timber to construct ships. Troy was allied with a number of other neighboring city-states, and the Mycenaeans saw this as a threat to their position in the Mediterranean. Homer tells us that the cause of the conflict was the rape of Helen, wife of King Menelaus of Sparta, by Paris, the son of King Priam of Troy. Helen fled to Troy with Paris, possibly taking part of Menelaus's treasure. Another account has the Trojans turning an official visit to Sparta into a raid of revenge for something done to them by the Greeks.

In any case, according to Homer the city-states of Greece were outraged and provided both contingents of troops and 1,200 ships, which then came under the command of Agamemnon, king of Mycenae and the brother of Menelaus. Homer tells us that on the Greek side the greatest heroes of the fighting were Achilles, king of the Myrmidons of Thessaly, and Ulysses, king of Ithaca. On the Trojan side there were Hector, son of Priam, and Aeneas, son of Venus and Anchises.

Following an unsuccessful effort to take Troy by assault, the Greeks settled in for a siege, which apparently was not complete. The Trojans were able to communicate by land to the interior most of the time. Homer indicates that the ships were brought up on land, where they were protected by entrenchments. Quarreling between Agamemnon and Achilles served to divide the Greeks, allowing Hector and the Trojans to attack and destroy a number of the beached Greek ships. Following the deaths of a number of prominent figures on each side (including Hector and Achilles), the Greeks found themselves in desperate straits. Both sides, however, were exhausted by the long siege.

At this point Ulysses came up with the ruse of an enormous wooden horse. Left on the field, it contained Ulysses and a number of other Greek warriors. The remaining Greeks boarded their ships and sailed away. The Trojans, believing that the Greeks had given up, thought that the trophy had religious significance and brought it inside the city. At night Ulysses and his warriors climbed down out of the horse, signaled to the fleet offshore, and opened the city gates. The Trojans were taken by surprise, and the city was burned.

Some have suggested that the alleged Trojan horse that ended the siege was instead a great movable siege tower of wood covered by horse hides for the protection of those working it, which the Greeks set against the western, and weakest, part of the great wall that protected the fortress. Others believe that the wooden horse refers to some type of battering ram or to the image of a horse painted on one of the gates of the city, which was opened by a Trojan traitor. In any case, as a consequence of their victory, the Greeks secured control of the important trade through the Dardanelles and the Black Sea.

References

Melegari, Vezio. *The Great Military Sieges.* New York: Crowell, 1972.
Pope, Alexander, trans. *The Iliad of Homer.* New York: Heritage, 1943.

Battle of Thymbra

Date	546 BCE	
Location	Plain of Thymbra near Sardis in eastern present-day Turkey	
Opponents (* winner)	*Persia	Lydia
Commander	King Cyrus II	King Croesus
Approx. # Troops	20,000–50,000	Unknown, but larger than the Persians
Importance	Adds significantly to Persian resources, making possible the subsequent defeat of Babylonia	

In 612 BCE a coalition of Medes, Babylonians, and Scythians destroyed the city of Nineveh, ending the Assyrian Empire. The Babylonians took over the southern part of the empire, while the Medes ruled the north. Medea was then the area of present-day northwestern Iran south of the Caspian Sea and into Armenia. The Medes also extended their control west to the borders of Asia Minor and east to Afghanistan.

Around 553 BCE Cyrus, son of Medean king Astyages, took up arms against his father. Cyrus was supported by powerful members of the aristocracy who resented Astyages' tyrannical policies. The ensuing civil war went on for four years, but in 550 Cyrus won the Battle of Pasargadai in which he captured the Persian capital. He went on to take the Medean capital of Ecbatana in 550–549 and then spent several years consolidating his authority, winning over many former enemies by giving them positions of authority in the army and the government. Ruling as Cyrus II and known as Cyrus the Great, he became one of the most important of Persian rulers.

The increasing Persian power alarmed King Croesus of Lydia in Asia Minor, who appealed for assistance to Egypt, Babylon, and Sparta. Lydia was known for its excellent cavalry, which Cyrus rightly considered a threat to his own position. In 547 Croesus sent his troops across the Halys River into Medea, and Cyrus gathered an army to meet them. His army moved west along the frontier between Medea and Babylonia, crossing the Tigris River at Arbela. Gathering reinforcements in Armenia and Kurdistan, Cyrus gained the Cappadocian plain of Medea in late 547.

The two sides fought an inconclusive winter battle near Pteria. Because his forces had already stripped Cappadocia of much of its food, Croesus decided to withdraw for the winter to his capital of Sardis in western Anatolia. There he dismissed his Greek mercenaries and sent messages to his allies, informing them what forces he would require for a spring campaign. Cyrus's advisers urged him to return home with his army as well and resume combat in the spring. Cyrus rejected what seemed to be wise counsel and decided to fight while Croesus was bereft of the mercenaries. Cyrus also knew that Croesus's allies would not be able to reinforce him for at least several months.

After allowing sufficient time for Croesus to return to Sardis and dismiss the bulk of his forces, Cyrus followed, marching across Anatolia. Although Croesus received reports of the Persian advance, he dismissed them as untrue. Not until Cyrus had arrived with his army before Sardis did Croesus realize what had happened. Croesus still had reason for optimism, however. His forces were significantly larger than those of Cyrus, which numbered perhaps 20,000 to 50,000 men.

In early 546 the two armies came together on the Plain of Thymbra just outside of Sardis. Cyrus deployed his army in a large square, holding back his chariots and cavalry on the flanks, while Croesus deployed his forces in the traditional long ranks. Croesus opened the battle by sending his cavalry to envelop the Persian square. This created gaps in the Lydian line, and Cyrus sent against them cavalry men mounted on camels. One of his generals had noted that at Pteria, the Lydian horses were terrified of the camels the Persians used for supply purposes, and Cyrus now sought to take advantage of this. At the scent of the approaching camels, the Lydian horses bolted. Although the Lydian cavalrymen dismounted, they could not fight effectively on foot with their heavy lances.

Meanwhile, archers in the great Persian square launched volleys of arrows at the Lydian line, further breaking it apart. Cyrus then ordered his cavalry and infantry on the flanks to charge through the gaps in the opposing line, routing it. The remnants of the Lydian army withdrew into Sardis, which Cyrus promptly besieged.

After 14 days the Persians took advantage of a weak point in the city wall where it joined a cliff. Cyrus dispatched a force to secure the high ground there and capture a portion of the wall as well as Croesus. Sardis surrendered the next day.

His victory at Thymbra gave Cyrus the great resources of Lydia. (Croesus's very name was synonymous with wealth.) The victory cut off Babylonia from an important military ally and thus helped Cyrus to defeat the new Babylonian Empire in 539.

References

Cook, J. M. *The Persian Empire.* New York: Schocken Books, 1983.

Lamb, Harold. *Cyrus the Great.* Garden City, NY: Doubleday, 1960.

Xenophon. *Cyropaedia.* Translated by Walter Miller. Cambridge: Harvard University Press, 1979.

Siege of Babylon

Date	539–538 BCE	
Location	Mesopotamia; present-day Iraq	
Opponents (* winner)	*Persia	Babylonia
Commander	King Cyrus II	Nabonidus
Approx. # Troops	Unknown	Unknown
Importance	Brings the destruction of Babylon	

Having absorbed Lydia, it was natural that King Cyrus II (also known as Cyrus the Great) of Persia would eventually move against Lydia's ally, Babylon. King Nabonidus's authority in Babylon was weak because he had secured the throne as a successful general rather than by right of inheritance, and he had further alienated his people by advancing the worship of Sin, the moon goddess, over Marduk, the national deity. Nabonidus also spent years away from his capital campaigning in distant lands including Harran, where he established a temple to Sin. In Arabia Nabonidus secured a number of oases, and his journey reached as far as Medina.

Cyrus meanwhile seems to have established contact with Babylon's alienated religious leaders, assuring them of his support for their traditional religious practices. Too late, Nabonidus embraced Marduk and ordered all statues of the god to be assembled at Babylon to fortify it spiritually.

There are two very different accounts of how Cyrus secured Babylon. One has him defeating the Babylonians at Opis, the former capital of Akkadia, and then destroying that city. Learning this, the city of Sippar surrendered to Cyrus, whereupon Nabonidus fled Babylon and Cyrus made a peaceful entry into the city in October.

The second account is put forward by the Greek historian Herodotus and is supported by the books of Daniel and Jeremiah in the Bible, although Daniel incorrectly identifies Darius as king of Persia and Belshazzar as king of Babylon. (The latter was the son of Nabonidus and ruled the city while his father was away on campaign.) This version tells of a great siege during 539–538 BCE. In it, Cyrus arrived and quickly encircled the city with his army under the walls, cutting off Babylon from assistance. Riding on horseback, he personally inspected the troop dispositions and concluded that the city could not be taken by direct assault. He then ordered his troops to set up for a siege.

Cyrus was either advised to take the city or came up on his own with a stratagem to do so. He ordered the construction of a circular system of trenches around the city and ditches to be dug to a sufficient depth to accommodate the water of the Euphrates River, which bisected Babylon through a break in the city walls. This work, supervised by Persian engineers, went forward into the winter. The Euphrates was separated from the ditches by only a simple dam that could be easily opened. The Persians also constructed towers made of palm trees, which led the

Nineteenth-century engraving depicting the capture of Babylon by Persian king Cyrus II (the Great) in 538 BCE, following what was most likely a siege during 539–538 BCE (Ridpath, John Clark, *Ridpath's History of the World,* 1901)

Babylonians to believe that their enemies intended to starve them out. The authorities in the city were not worried though, as they had gathered sufficient food stocks to last for many years.

Early in 538 Cyrus was ready to unleash his attack, which he timed to coincide with the beginning of an important Babylonian festival. That evening, with the Babylonian rituals under way and the inhabitants distracted, Cyrus ordered the dam broken and the Euphrates diverted. Normally the river was so deep that the breaks in the walls where it flowed through Babylon did not represent a serious threat from outside enemies. When the river was diverted, however, the flow was so low that it was possible for Persian infantry and even cavalry to traverse the newly formed riverbanks into Babylon itself.

The Persian attack caught the Babylonians by surprise, and the city was soon taken. Cyrus was known for sparing the lives of kings he had defeated, and this may have been the case with Nabonidus. Cyrus, however, ordered that Babylon be destroyed. As the prophet Jeremiah notes in the Bible: "And the land shall tremble and sorrow: for every purpose of the Lord shall be performed against Babylon to make the land of Babylon a desolation without an inhabitant. . . . And Babylon shall become heaps, a dwelling place for dragons, an astonishment, and an hissing, without an inhabitant" (Jeremiah 51:29 and 51:37).

Following the reduction of Babylon, Cyrus took Jerusalem. He allowed those Jews of Babylon who wished to do so to return home to Jerusalem, ending the Babylonian captivity of the Jews.

References

Cook, J. M. *The Persian Empire.* New York: Schocken Books, 1983.

Herodotus. *The History of Herodotus.* Edited by Manuel Komroff. Translated by George Rawlinson. New York: Tudor Publishing, 1956.

Lamb, Harold. *Cyrus the Great.* Garden City, NY: Doubleday, 1960.

Melegari, Vezio. *The Great Military Sieges.* New York: Crowell, 1972.

Xenophon. *Cyropaedia.* Translated by Walter Miller. Cambridge: Harvard University Press, 1979.

Battle of Marathon

Date	August 12 (?), 490 BCE	
Location	Plain of Marathon on the northeast Greek coast, 26 miles northeast of Athens	
Opponents (* winner)	*Athens and Plataea	Persia
Commander	Miltiades	Artaphernes and Datia
Approx. # Troops	10,000 Athenians; 1,000 Plateans	15,000
Importance	Greek city states remain independent of Persian control	

At the beginning of the fifth century BCE the Persian Empire exercised hegemony over the western coast of Asia Minor, then known as Ionia. In 499 BCE, however, the rich Greek commercial cities of Ionia revolted against King Darius I of Persia, who had imposed heavy taxes on them, restricted their trade with the Black Sea, and refused to allow changes toward more democratic government.

The leader of this revolt, Aristagoras, traveled to Greece to solicit aid. Sparta refused, but Athens responded with 20 ships, and Eretria (a city on the island of Euboea) responded with 5 ships. As Herodotus notes, when this small Greek naval force sailed, it marked the beginning of trouble for mainland Greece. Although the rebels took and burned Sardis, the principal Persian city of western Anatolia, Greek disunity and the desertion of the Samians and Lesbians led to the defeat of the Greek fleet in a battle off the island of Lade in 494. Darius then set out to punish the mainland Greeks. Although it is true that Athenian aid to the Ionian Greeks prompted his decision, Darius had long sought to control Greece.

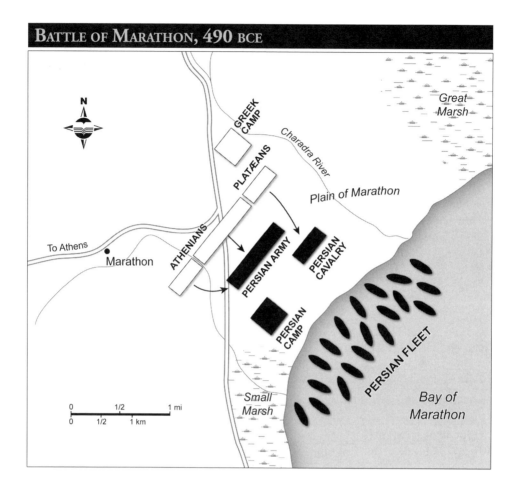

BATTLE OF MARATHON, 490 BCE

In 492 Darius dispatched an army under his son-in-law Mardonius across the Dardanelles into Thrace, bringing about the subjugation of that area. The Persians were in position to invade Greece from the north, but a great storm wrecked much of the Persian fleet as it rounded the Mount Athos peninsula, forcing the Persian army to return home.

In 491 Darius demanded of the mainland Greeks earth and water as symbols of submission. The Greek city-states must have been in a panic at the news that Persia was again preparing to invade. Persia was the greatest empire in terms of area that the world had yet known, and its army appeared invincible. Strong pro-Persian factions existed in virtually all the city-states, including Athens. Even the oracle at Delphi was pro-Persian. How could the Greeks, so divided and so relatively weak, expect to triumph? Nonetheless, both Athens and Sparta refused to submit.

In 490 Darius mounted his second invasion, this time commanded by his nephew Artaphernes and a Medean noble, Datia. The invasion fleet of some 200 triremes and 400 transports, carrying perhaps 25,000 infantry and 1,000 cavalry, assembled at Tarsus on the Cilician coast and then proceeded westward to Ionia and through the Cyclades. The Persians took and sacked Naxos, which had resisted capture 10 years before. The fleet proceeded from island to island across the Aegean, picking up conscripts and taking children as hostages. By the time the Persians landed on Euboea they had perhaps 80,000 men, including rowers and conscripts.

Euboea refused to surrender, and the Persians destroyed the countryside and laid siege to the city. The city held out for a week until the defenders were betrayed. In reprisal for Sardis, the Persian burned all the city's temples. The fleet then sailed west from Eritrea and made landfall on the Greek mainland in the Bay of Marathon, some 26 miles northeast of Athens. The Persians selected this site because Hippias, who had been deposed as the tyrant of Athens in 510 and fled to Persia, told the Persians that the plain there would allow them to employ their cavalry, in which they were overwhelmingly superior to the Greeks. Hippias was with the Persian force and, following their anticipated victory, was to work with the pro-Persian faction in Athens and be installed as Persian governor of all Greece.

The Persians hoped that by landing at Marathon they might draw the Athenian army away from the city's great protective walls and destroy it or else hold the smaller Athenian force there while sending part of their army south to Athens by ship. Athens sent an appeal to Sparta, probably carried by the famed runner Pheidippides; reportedly he once covered 140 miles in two days. The Spartan leaders agreed to assist, but they refused to suspend a religious festival that would delay their army's march north until the next full moon, on the night of August 11–12. It was then August 5.

News of the fall of Eretria brought fierce debate in Athens. Some wanted to simply prepare for a siege, but others, including Miltiades, urged that the army be sent out to fight. Miltiades hailed from Ionia, and in 512 he had fought with Darius against the Scythians in the Danube region. When the Scythians defeated the Persians in a battle and Darius withdrew his Persians toward a key bridge that Miltiades and the Greeks were holding, Miltiades reportedly suggested that the Greeks destroy the bridge and cut off the Persians, allowing the Scythians to destroy them. He was overruled by the other Ionian generals. Darius found out about Miltiades' treachery and vowed revenge, whereupon Miltiades fled to Athens and became active in politics there.

Reportedly Miltiades pointed out that allowing the Persians to besiege would cut Athens off from Spartan aid (the Long Walls were not yet built) and increase the chances of treachery. Miltiades won the day. He argued that the city's only hope once the Persians landed at Marathon with their cavalry was to destroy them on the beachhead. In the city, slaves were freed; they and other freedmen and citizens traversed the mountains to Marathon. The Athenian force numbered some 10,000 hoplites (infantrymen). The little city-state of Plataea sent unexpected aid of as many as 1,000 hoplites. Callimachus commanded as war archon (*polemarchos*). Each of the 10 tribes of Athens had its own general, and Miltiades was only one of these.

The Athenians positioned themselves on high ground west of the plain in position to block a Persian advance overland toward Athens, and they set about felling trees to inhibit the Persian cavalry. Not only did the Persians vastly outnumber the Greeks, but they had cavalry and archers, whereas the Greeks had none. For several days (August 7–11) the two armies simply sat in place, some two miles apart. Both sides were waiting: the Athenians were waiting for the Spartans to arrive, and the Persians were waiting for conspirators in touch with Hippias to seize power in Athens.

The Persians must have known that Spartan reinforcements would soon arrive, and with no word that pro-Persian conspirators in Athens had been successful, they evidently decided to send the bulk of their fleet to Phaleron Bay on the night of August 11–12 along with a substantial land force, including the cavalry. They left behind a land force of perhaps 15,000 men.

If the Persians had hoped to win by treachery, it was the Greeks who actually did so. Ionian deserters got word to the Greeks before dawn on August 12, including information that the cavalry had departed. Miltiades realized that the one hope the Athenians had was to attack swiftly, defeat the Persian land force, and then march to the relief of Athens before the other Persian force could disembark, perhaps in late afternoon.

Miltiades formed the Greek line about a mile long so that its flanks rested on two small streams flowing to the sea. Beyond these were marshes north and south. The disposition of the Greek force thinned the center of the line, which contained the best troops, to perhaps only three or four men, but Miltiades kept the flanks, which had his least reliable troops, at full phalanx depth. The Greeks thus had a weak center with powerful striking forces on either side. The Greeks were better armed, with long spears against javelins and short swords against daggers or scimitars. They were also better protected with bronze body armor, and they were more highly motivated, fighting for their homeland.

Battle was joined that morning. The Greeks advanced slowly toward the Persian camp and the beach until they were 150–200 yards away and within bow range of the Persian archers, who were in front. They charged the center of the Persian line to minimize the time that they would be under arrow attack. The Greeks easily broke through the ranks of lightly armed Persian bowmen, who only had time to get off a few arrows each before seeking safety behind the main Persian formation. The Persian infantry easily threw back the Greek center, but Greek discipline held as the line became concave. The heavy Greek flanks folded on the lightly armed Persian flanks, compressing the Persians in a double envelopment. Authorities differ as to whether this was planned or simply accidental.

The Persian flanks and center now gave way as the troops fled for the beach and their transports, being cut down by the Greeks as they tried to get away. Some sort of Persian rear guard was organized to cover their embarkation, and most of the force escaped. It was then about 9:00 a.m. The Greek historian Herodotus claims that the Greeks only lost 192 men killed, while 6,400 Persians fell. The Greeks also destroyed seven Persian ships.

Miltiades sent word of the Greek victory to Athens by a runner, reportedly Pheidippedes, on the first Marathon run. The Athenians could not pause to celebrate, for the two Persian naval forces were now making for Phaleron Bay. Leaving a detachment to guard the Persian prisoners and booty, the remainder of the Athenian army marched to Athens. They arrived in late afternoon just as the Persian fleet was approaching shore for a landing. Realizing they were too late, the Persians withdrew. The Spartans did not arrive at Athens until several days later. They praised the victors and returned home.

The Greeks had won one of the important battles of history. The Battle of Marathon allowed the continuation of Greek independence. The victory was not conclusive, but it did hold the Persians at bay for a decade. Marathon, at least, allowed the Greeks to imagine that they might triumph a second time.

References
Burn, A. R. *Persia and the Greeks: The Defence of the West, c. 546–478 BC.* Stanford, CA: Stanford University Press, 1984.

Creasy, Edward S. *The Fifteen Decisive Battles of the World: From Marathon to Waterloo.* New York: Heritage, 1969.

Green, Peter. *The Greco-Persian Wars.* Berkeley: University of California Press, 1996.

Herodotus. *The History of Herodotus.* Edited by Manuel Komroff. Translated by George Rawlinson. New York: Tudor Publishing, 1956.

Battle of Thermopylae

Date	August 19(?), 490 BCE	
Location	Pass of Thermopylae in northeast Greece	
Opponents (* winner)	*Persia	Allied Greek states
Commander	King Xerxes I of Persia	King Leonidas of Sparta
Approx. # Troops	180,000 (estimated total army strength)	4,000?
Importance	Held up as an example of patriots defending their homeland and of sacrificial courage	

Those Athenians who believed that their victory at Marathon in 490 BCE meant that the war with Persia was over were mistaken. Persian king Darius I immediately set about raising a new and far larger force. To pay for it, he raised taxes. This led to a revolt in Egypt in the winter of 486–485 BCE that disrupted grain deliveries and diverted Persian military resources to restore order in that important province. Darius died in late 486. His son and successor, Xerxes, was temporarily distracted by the Egyptian revolt, but once it had been crushed, he returned to the invasion of Greece.

News of the Persian preparations reached Athens, and the Athenian leader Themistocles urged that the city build the largest possible naval force. Athens then had only 50 triremes in commission. Themistocles wanted 200, but the conservatives in power, led by Miltiades, who had distinguished himself at Marathon, opposed such a step.

In 489 the Assembly voted to send Miltiades with 70 ships (20 of them purchased from Corinth) to attack the island city-states that had assisted the Persians. After pressuring some of the other islands back into the fold, Miltiades moved against the Cycladic island of Pardos, which had provided one trireme to the Persians. The city refused to pay the 100 talents he demanded to sail away, and Miltiades commenced siege operations. Following a month-long effort, however, he was forced to admit defeat and returned with the fleet to Athens. This humiliation led to Miltiades' arrest and trial on a charge of treason. He was sentenced to death, but this was subsequently reduced to a fine of 50 talents. Unable to pay this large sum, he was sent to prison, where he died of gangrene from a leg wound sustained in the siege.

The disgrace of Miltiades and his faction left Themistocles the dominant political figure in Athens. Themistocles did what he could to prepare the city-state for war. He reformed the government to allow long-term war planning and then secured approval to increase the fleet to 200 triremes.

When he at last set out for Greece in 481, Xerxes commanded one of the largest invasion forces in history. Its exact size has been debated ever since. Modern reckoning puts it at perhaps 600 ships and three Persian army corps of 60,000 men each. This was a Persian advantage of at least 3 to 1 on land and 2 to 1 at sea.

In the spring of 480 the Persian host reached the Hellespont (present-day Dardanelles). There Egyptian and Phoenician engineers had constructed a bridge that was among the most-admired mechanical achievements of antiquity. Herodotus tells us that they distributed 674 boats in two rows athwart the strait, each vessel facing the current and moored with a heavy anchor. The engineers then stretched flaxen cables across the ships from bank to bank. These cables were bound to every ship and were made taut by the use of capstans on shore. Wooden planks were then laid across the cables and were fastened to them and to one another. The planks were covered with brushwood, which was then covered with earth, and the whole was tamped down to resemble a road. A bulwark was erected on each side of this causeway to keep animals from becoming frightened of the sea. In seven days and nights the Persian forces passed over the bridge and entered Europe.

The Persian army quickly occupied Thrace and Macedonia. The northern Greek city-states were completely intimidated, surrendering to fear or bribery and allowing their troops to be added to those of Xerxes. Only Plataea and Thespiae in the north prepared to fight.

For once, however, Athens and Sparta worked together. Athens provided the principal naval force, while Sparta furnished the main contingent of land forces sent north to resist the Persians. The land force was under the command of King

Leonidas of Sparta. The Greek plan was for the land forces to hold the Persians just long enough for the fleet to force a Persian withdrawal. Themistocles led the Athenian fleet. Joined by other Greek vessels to make 271 frontline ships, it sailed north to meet the Persian force of more than 650 ships. A storm reduced the Persian naval forces to around 500 serviceable warships, but this was still a comfortable advantage in numbers.

On an afternoon in mid-August the Greek fleet attacked the Persian ships off the northern coast of Euboea at Artemisium. The battle was inconclusive, although the Greeks managed to capture some 30 Persian vessels.

The allied Greek land force of about 4,000 men under Leonidas had meanwhile taken up position at the Pass of Thermopylae, some 135 miles north of Athens. Because of sedimentation in the Gulf of Malis, today the pass of Thermopylae is several miles inland, but at the time of the Persian invasion it was a narrow track between the waters of the Gulf of Malis to the south and cliffs to the north. Leonidas selected the site because here a small force could hold off a much larger one. Three hundred Spartan men-at-arms formed the nucleus of Leonidas's force, accompanied by perhaps 900 helots. Leonidas had chosen only fathers with sons so that no Spartan family line would be extinguished.

The same day that the fleets clashed at Artemisium, Xerxes launched his first attack against the Greek defenders at Thermopylae. They were driven back. Xerxes committed his famous Guards Division, the Ten Thousand Immortals, but they too were forced back in disorder. The pass was piled high with corpses. Xerxes tried again the next day, but the defenders repelled this assault as well.

Leonidas and his troops were eventually overwhelmed, however, not by the bravery of the Persians but by the treachery of Hellenes. On August 19 a Greek, Ephialtes of Malis, betrayed to Xerxes, apparently for reward, the secret of an indirect route over the mountains. Ephialtes then led a Persian force by that approach, routing a lightly held Phocian outpost that Leonidas had in position to block this route and turning the Greek position.

On the night of the second day of battle upon learning from Ionian Greek deserters from Xerxes' army that they were going to be cut off, Leonidas permitted the allied Greeks to withdraw. Herodotus wrote, "I incline to think that Leonidas gave the order, because he perceived the allies to be out of heart and unwilling to encounter the danger to which his own mind was made up. He therefore commanded them to retreat, but said that he himself could not draw back with honor; knowing that, if he stayed, glory awaited him, and that Sparta in that case would not lose her prosperity" (Herodotus, *The History of Herodotus,* 424–425). An oracle had foretold that either Sparta would be overthrown by the barbarians or one of its kings had to perish.

Seven hundred Thespians and 300 Thebans refused the order to withdraw and remained with the Spartans. Only 2 Spartans are said to have survived: 1 fell at the Battle of Plataea a year later, and the other hanged himself in shame. Over the tomb of the Spartans was placed the most famous of Greek epitaphs: "Go, stranger, and tell the Lacedamonians [Spartans] we lie here in obedience to their laws."

This battle, which is also said to have claimed two younger brothers of Xerxes, had far more psychological than military importance. While some Greeks saw it as an excuse to ally with the Persians, others admired the Spartan example and re-doubled their efforts to resist the Asian tide.

References

Bradford, Ernie. *Thermopylae: Battle for the West.* New York: McGraw-Hill, 1980.

Green, Peter. *The Greco-Persian Wars.* Berkeley: University of California Press, 1996.

Hignett, C. *Xerxes' Invasion of Greece.* Oxford: Oxford University Press, 1963.

Herodotus. *The History of Herodotus.* Edited by Manuel Komroff. Translated by George Rawlinson. New York: Tudor Publishing, 1956.

Battle of Salamis

Date	September 20(?), 480 BCE	
Location	Bay of Salamis off Athens, Greece	
Opponents (* winner)	*Athens and allied Greek states	Persia
Commander	Themistocles	King Xerxes I of Persia
Approx. # Troops	310 triremes	500 triremes
Importance	Ends the year's campaign and assures survival of Greek independence	

The Battle of Salamis was the most important naval engagement of the Greco-Persian Wars. When news came of the Greek defeat at Thermopylae, the remaining Greek triremes sailed south to Salamis to provide security for the city of Athens. With no barrier remaining between Athens and the Persian land force, the proclamation was made that every Athenian should save his family as best he could. Some citizens fled to Salamis or the Peloponnese, and some men joined the crews of the returning triremes. When Xerxes and his army arrived at Athens the city was devoid of civilians, although some troops remained to stage a defense (largely symbolic) of the Acropolis. The Persians soon secured it and destroyed it by fire.

Xerxes now had to contend with the remaining Greek ships. He would have to destroy them or at least leave a sufficiently large force to contain Themistocles' ships before he could force the Peloponnese and end the Greek campaign. Every-thing suggested the former, for if Xerxes left the Greek force behind, his ships remained vulnerable to a flanking attack. On August 29 the Persian fleet of per-haps 500 ships appeared off Phaleron Bay, east of the Salamis Channel, and en-tered the Bay of Salamis.

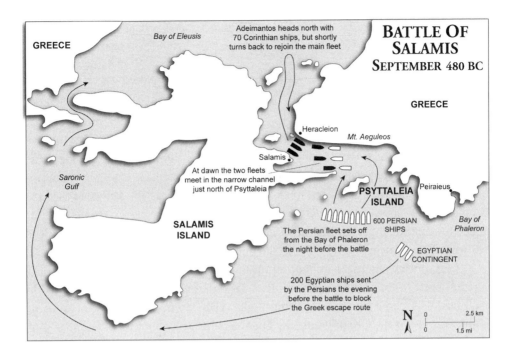

The Greeks had added the reserve fleet at Salamis. Triremes from other states joined, giving them about 100 additional ships. The combined fleet at Salamis was thus actually larger than it had been at Artemisim: about 310 ships.

Xerxes and his admirals did not wish to fight the Greek fleet in the narrow waters of the Salamis Channel, and for about two weeks the Persians busied themselves constructing causeways across the channel so that they might take the island without having to engage the Greek ships. Salamis then contained most of the remaining Athenian population and government officials, and the Persians reasoned that their capture would bring the fleet's surrender. Massed Greek archers, however, gave the workers such trouble that the Persians abandoned the effort.

On September 16 or 17 Xerxes met with his generals and chief advisers at Phalerum. Herodotus tells us that all except Queen Artemisia of Halicarnassus, the commander of its squadron in the Persian fleet, favored engaging the Greek fleet in a pitched battle. Xerxes then brought advance elements of his fleet from Phalerum, off Salamis. He also put part of his vast army in motion toward the Peloponnese in the hope that this action would cause the Greeks of that region to order their ships from the main Greek fleet to return home, allowing him to destroy them at his leisure. Failing that, Xerxes sought a battle in the open waters of the Saronic Gulf (Gulf of Aegina) that forms part of the Aegean Sea. There his superior numbers would have the advantage.

Themistocles wanted a battle in the Bay of Salamis. Drawing on the lessons of the Battle of Artemisium, he pointed out that a fight in close conditions would be to the advantage of the better-disciplined Greeks. With his captains in an uproar at this and with the likely possibility that the Peloponnesian ships would bolt from the coalition, Themistocles resorted to one of the most famous stratagems in all military history. Before dawn on September 19 he sent a trusted slave, an Asiatic Greek named Sicinnus, to the Persians with a letter informing Xerxes that Themistocles had changed sides. Themistocles gave no reason for this decision but said that he now sought a Persian victory. The Greeks, he said, were bitterly divided and would offer little resistance; indeed, there would be pro-Persian factions fighting the remainder. Furthermore, Themistocles claimed, elements of the fleet intended to sail away during the next night and link up with Greek land forces defending the Peloponnese. The Persians could prevent this only by not letting the Greeks escape. This letter contained much truth and was, after all, what Xerxes wanted to hear. It did not tell Xerxes what Themistocles wanted him to do: engage the Greek ships in the narrows.

Xerxes, not wishing to lose the opportunity, acted swiftly. He ordered Persian squadrons patrolling off Salamis to block all possible Greek escape routes while the main fleet came into position that night. The Persians held their stations all night waiting for the Greek breakout. Themistocles was counting on Xerxes' vanity. As Themistocles expected, the Persian king chose not to break off the operation that he had begun.

The Greeks then stood out to meet the Persians. Xerxes, seated on a throne at the foot of nearby Mount Aegaleus on the Attic shore across from Salamis, watched the action. Early on the morning of September 20 the entire Persian fleet went on the attack, moving up the Salamis Channel in a crowded mile-wide front that precluded any organized withdrawal should that prove necessary. The details of the actual battle are obscure, but the superior tactics and seamanship of the Greeks allowed them to take the Persians in the flank. The confusion of minds, languages, and too many ships in narrow waters combined to decide the issue in favor of the Greeks.

The Persians, according to one account, lost some 200 ships, while the defenders lost only 40. However, few of the Greeks, even from the lost ships, died; they were for the most part excellent swimmers and swam to shore when their ships floundered. The Greeks feared that the Persians might renew the attack but awoke the next day to find the Persian ships gone. Xerxes had ordered them to the Hellespont to protect the bridge there.

The Battle of Salamis meant the end of the year's campaign. Xerxes left two-thirds of his forces in garrison in central and northern Greece and marched the remainder to Sardis. A large number died of pestilence and dysentery on the way. The Greco-Persian Wars concluded a year later in the Battle of Plataea and the Battle of Mycale.

References

Green, Peter. *The Greco-Persian Wars*. Berkeley: University of California Press, 1996.

Herodotus. *The History of Herodotus*. Edited by Manuel Komroff. Translated by George Rawlinson. New York: Tudor Publishing, 1956.

Nelson, Richard B. *The Battle of Salamis.* London: William Luscombe, 1975.

Strauss, Barry. *The Battle of Salamis: The Naval Encounter That Saved Greece—and Western Civilization.* New York: Simon and Schuster, 2004.

Battles of Plataea and Mycale

Date	September 479 BCE	
Location	About 25 miles northwest of Athens, Greece (Plataea); Mycale Peninsula of Asia Minor, across from the island of Samos (Mycale)	
Opponents (* winner)	*Allied Greek states	Persia
Commander	King Pausanias of Sparta (Plataea); Leotychidas (Mycale)	Mardonius (Plataea); Tigranes (Mycale)
Approx. # Troops	40,000 (Plataea); more than 3,500 men (Mycale)	50,000 (Plataea); 10,000 men (Mycale)
Importance	Effectively ends the Persian wars, preserving Greek independence and civilization	

In 479 BCE a year after the Battle of Salamis, the garrisoning Persian forces in northern Greece again invaded Attica. Commanded by Mardonius, brother-in-law of King Xerxes, they advanced from central Greece and again occupied Athens. Most of the buildings were burned, and those that survived were razed. Sparta and some other Greek city-states, however, answered the Athenian appeal for assistance.

The Battle of Plataea took place near the city of Plataea in Boeotia. The Persian force numbered about 50,000 men, including 15,000 from northern and central Greece. The opposing Greek army, led by King Pausanias of Sparta, totaled about 40,000 men, including 10,000 Spartans and 8,000 Athenians. The Persians not only had the advantage in total numbers but also had more cavalry and archers.

When Pausanias threatened Mardonius from the flank, the latter withdrew his army north behind the Asopus River. The Greeks followed and set up defensive positions on the other side of the river, about 25 miles northwest of Athens. Mardonius found it difficult to employ his cavalry and archers against the more heavily armed Greek hoplites. The two sides faced one another for several days. The Greeks were confident that they could defeat the Persians in a shock-action battle, but they were unable to entice their enemy into an attack. While the standoff lasted, the Persian cavalry harried Greek forage and water parties.

Finally, with the Greeks running out of supplies, Pausanias developed a plan to bring Mardonius to battle by withdrawing closer to Plataea. The Greek change of position was to be carried out entirely at night, but by dawn only about half the forces had departed. The Persians could see the much smaller Athenian and Spartan forces in march.

Noting the disorder, Mardonius immediately ordered an attack, hoping to prevail with his archers against the remaining hoplites. Although the outcome was in doubt for some time, the attackers approached the Greeks too closely, and the Greeks mounted a countercharge. Greek reinforcements also came up, although Persian and allied cavalry proved effective against them.

The battle was fierce, but the archers, who had only wicker armor and leather helmets, were unable to defend themselves at close quarters against the better-disciplined Greek hoplites, who had bronze spears and metal breastplates and helmets. The Persians were simply overwhelmed. The Greeks may have lost 1,360 men, but the Persians lost 10,000 or more, including some 1,000 allied Greeks. Mardonius and his personal guard were among those slain in the wild retreat. The remaining 40,000 men were scattered in every direction. For all practical purposes, the Persian field army ceased to exist.

In the simultaneous Battle of Mycale (according to Greek tradition, the battle occurred on the same day as the Battle of Plataea), the Greeks engaged the Persians on the slopes of Mount Mycale, on the coast of Ionia, opposite the island of Samos. Unbeknownst to the Persian-backed ruler of Samos, a number of Samian envoys had appealed to King Leotychidas of Sparta, who led the combined Greek fleet of some 250 triremes from a base at Delos. The Samians told Leotychidas that the Persians had detached their powerful Phoenician contingent and, with little more than 100 triremes remaining, were vulnerable to attack.

Leotychidas departed Delos and sailed east to Samos. Afraid to risk a naval engagement with the Greeks, the Persians had drawn their ships up on land on the Mycale Peninsula of Asia Minor, across the narrow channel from Samos. There they had land communications with Sardis and a line of retreat. They also had the support of Persian general Tigranes and 6,000 Persian troops detached to keep watch over Ionia. The Persians had thrown up land defensive works, including a stockade of wood, to protect the ships. In all, counting the troops under Tigranes, the Persians and their Ionian Greek allies numbered about 10,000 men.

Leotychidas had at best 2,500 marines and 1,000 archers in addition to his rowers and sailors, but a number of the rowers may have been hoplites, drafted in the emergency. Despite the disparity in numbers, the Greeks decided to attack the Persians on land and destroy their ships.

Leotychidas could not hope to take the Persian fortification by storm with his small force and no heavy equipment. He therefore decided to tempt Tigranes into attacking. Leotychidas detached a group of Athenians and other Greek forces, while he took the majority of his men and secretly worked overland to strike the Persians in the flank. The plan worked perfectly.

The Athenians attacked directly along the beach, in full view of the Persians. Seeing the small size of the Greek force, Tigranes launched an attack from the defenses. Some of the Ionian Greeks abandoned the Persians, however, and switched sides. The battle hung in the balance, and Leotychidas and the Spartans arrived only just in time. After hard fighting, the Persians were routed. Perhaps 4,000 lost their lives, including Tigranes and his second-in-command. Greek losses must have also been heavy. The Greeks then seized what booty they could, set fire to the Persian ships in the stockade, and sailed to Samos.

These two battles effectively ended the Greco-Persian Wars. The outcome was momentous. The Greeks were able to continue their civilization, and their control of the sea enabled them to export ideas as well as goods throughout the Mediterranean world. Greece now entered its Golden Age.

References

Green, Peter. *The Greco-Persian Wars.* Berkeley: University of California Press, 1996.

Herodotus. *The History of Herodotus.* Edited by Manuel Komroff. Translated by George Rawlinson. New York: Tudor Publishing, 1956.

Siege of Plataea

Date	428–427 BCE	
Location	Plataea in southeast Boeotia, central Greece	
Opponents (* winner)	*Sparta	Plataea
Commander	Archidamos	Unknown
Approx. # Troops	Unknown	480
Importance	Ends Plataean independence	

The long Second Peloponnesian War (431–404 BCE) between the Greek city-states was marked by cruelties and breaches of honor on both sides, particularly for the small states caught between the major powers in the conflict. The historian Thucydides, a contemporary, provides ample record of this in his chronicling of the war and especially his telling of the Spartan reduction of Plataea.

In 428 BCE, having already laid waste to Attica and fearing infection from the great plague that had swept Athens, the leaders of Sparta decided to attack Plataea. This Athenian ally and small Boeotian city-state was of no strategic value and had done nothing to invite attack. The invasion was undertaken instead on the insistence of Thebes, Sparta's ally.

Plataea had been the only other Greek city-state to aid Athens during the Battle of Marathon against Persia in 490. Following the Battle of Plataea in 479 that ended the Greco-Persian Wars, the Spartans had administered an oath to all the Greeks who had taken part by which they restored to the Plataeans "their land and their city, holding them in independence," and swore to see to it "that no one should march against them unjustly or for their enslavement; if any one did the allies who were present should defend them with all their might." Thus, the Spartan attack on Plataea was a considerable embarrassment to and stain on the honor of the Spartans. King Archidamos of Sparta offered the Plaeaeans the choice of abandoning their alliance with Athens and joining Sparta or at least pledging neutrality. But Spartan promises rang hollow, for Thebes was determined to acquire Plataea.

The Plataeans asked for a truce so that they might request permission to surrender from Athens. Plataea hoped that Athens might allow it to strike some arrangement with the Spartans, since the city could not be rescued without an infantry battle that Athens could not win. Athens refused, urging the Plataeans to remain true to their alliance and promising assistance. Plataea therefore refused the Spartan demands, whereupon Archidamos announced that Plataea was responsible for what would ensue because it had rejected a reasonable offer.

A series of Spartan attempts to take Plataea by storm failed. Plataea was defended by only 400 of its own men and 80 Athenians, with 110 women to cook for them. The remainder of its citizenry, including all the children and the elderly, had been sent to Athens for safety. Despite the small number of defenders, Plataea's walls were formidable and were sufficient to hold off a large enemy force.

Thus, in September 428 the Spartans laid siege, building a palisade around the city and manning it with troops. Archidamos ordered construction of an embankment behind the palisade that would equal the walls in height. Over a 70-day period, the Spartans created the embankment with earth, stones, and logs sufficient to support siege machines. During this time, however, the Plataeans used wood to add to the height of their own walls that faced the embankment. Most materials for the construction came from structures in the city, but at least some were secured from the enemy by means of a tunnel. The defenders also built a second wall inside the first so that if the latter was breached the attackers would have to begin the process anew.

The Spartans sent their battering rams against the outer wall but were unsuccessful; the defenders damaged a number by dropping large chained beams on the long metal-tipped rams. Archidamos then tried filling the short space between the embankment and wall with combustible materials and setting them afire. The Plataeans thought that the walls were lost, but a providential rain extinguished the flames.

In September 428 with winter coming on, Archidamos had his men build a more substantial double wall around the city and then ordered half his force home for the winter. That winter on a stormy night, 200 of the Plataeans managed to get across the Spartan wall by means of ladders without being detected. After a brief skirmish, they broke free and made their way to Athens.

The remaining defenders were simply starved into surrender in the summer of 427. The Spartans might easily have taken the city earlier by force, but they did not do so because if peace was to be concluded with Athens, Sparta could hold on to Plataea by claiming that defenders had gone over of their own free will.

The Spartans therefore promised that each of the defenders would receive a fair trial by a panel of 5 Spartan judges. The question put to each defender, however, was whether he had rendered assistance to Sparta or its allies in the war. All had to answer no. At least 200 Plataeans and 25 Athenian men were subsequently put to death. All of the women were sold into slavery.

Eventually the Spartans turned Plataea over to Thebes, which leveled it entirely and divided the land among its own citizens. Thereafter Thebes considered what had been Plataea to be part of its own territory. The siege of Plataea offered plenty of embarrassment for all sides. The Athenians might have released their loyal ally to conclude reasonable terms with the Spartans or rendered the military assistance promised but did neither. Granting Athenian citizenship to the surviving Plataeans was hardly adequate compensation.

References

Kagan, Donald. *The Peloponnesian War.* New York: Viking, 2003.

Melegari, Vezio. *The Great Military Sieges.* New York: Crowell, 1972.

Thucydides. *History of the Peloponnesian War.* Translated by Rex Warner. New York: Penguin, 1984.

Siege of Syracuse

Date	415–413 BCE	
Location	Syracuse in Sicily	
Opponents (* winner)	*Syracuse and Sparta	Athens and its allies
Commander	Gylippus	Alcibiades, Lamachus, Nicias, Demosthenes
Approx. # Troops	Sparta: 4,400; Syracuse: Unknown but probably equal to Athens and allies	42,000
Importance	Leads to revolts against Athens from within its empire	

The siege of the city-state of Syracuse in Sicily by Athens and its allies during 415–413 BCE initiated the final phase of the Second Peloponnesian War (431–404 BCE). Alcibiades, a nephew of Pericles, convinced Athenians that if they could secure Sicily they would have the resources to defeat their enemies. The grain of Sicily was immensely important to the people of the Peloponnese, and cutting it off could turn the tide of war. The argument was correct, but securing Sicily was the problem.

The Athenians put together a formidable expeditionary force. A contemporary historian, Thucydides, described the expeditionary force that set out in June 415 as "by far the most costly and splendid Hellenic force that had ever been sent out by

A nineteenth-century engraving of the naval battle in Syracuse harbor in September 413 BCE, in which the Athenians attempted to break free but suffered defeat during the Second Peloponnesian War. (Ridpath, John Clark, *Ridpath's History of the World*, 1901)

a single city up to that time" (Finley, *The Greek Historians,* 314). The naval force consisted of 134 triremes (100 of them from Athens and the remainder from Chios and other Athenian allies), 30 supply ships, and more than 100 other vessels. In addition to sailors, rowers, and marines, the force included some 5,100 hoplites and 1,300 archers, javelin men, and slingers as well as 300 horses. In all, the expedition numbered perhaps 27,000 officers and men. Three generals—Alcibiades, Lamachus, and Nicias—commanded.

The original plan was for a quick demonstration in force against Syracuse and then a return of the expeditionary force to Greece. Alcibiades considered this a disgrace. He urged that the expeditionary force stir up political opposition to Syracuse in Sicily. In a council of war, Lamachus pressed for an immediate descent on Syracuse while the city was unprepared and its citizens afraid, but Alcibiades prevailed.

The expedition's leaders then made a series of approaches to leaders of the other Sicilian cities; all ended in failure, with no city of importance friendly to Athens. Syracuse used this time to strengthen its defenses. Alcibiades meanwhile was recalled to stand trial in Athens for impiety.

Nicias and Lamachus then launched an attack on Syracuse and won a battle there, but the arrival of winter prevented further progress, and they suspended offensive operations. What had been intended as a lightning campaign now became a prolonged siege that sapped Athenian energies.

Alicibades, fearing for his life, managed to escape Athens and find refuge in Sparta. He not only betrayed the Athenian plan of attack against Syracuse but also spoke to the Spartan assembly and strongly supported a Syracusan plea for aid. The Spartans then sent out a force of their own commanded by Gylippus, one of their best generals.

In the spring of 414 the Athenians renewed offensive operations at Syracuse. Despite Syracuse's work during the winter, the Athenians captured the fortifications at Euryalus close to Syracuse and drove the Syracusans behind their city's walls. The Athenians then constructed a fortification, known as the Circle, along with other protective walls. They also destroyed several Syracusan counterwalls. Unfortunately for the Athenians, Lamachus was killed in the fighting, and leadership devolved on the ineffective Nicias.

Syracuse was now in despair, with the city on the brink of defeat. At this point a Corinthian ship made its way into the harbor with news that help was coming. Fortified by this development, the leaders of Syracuse vowed to fight on. Gylippus's expeditionary force then landed in northern Sicily and marched to Syracuse; Nicias failed to challenge it en route. Gylippus's men strengthened the defenses of Syracuse and, in the spring of 413, won a stunning victory over the Athenian Navy, capturing its base.

Rather than lose prestige by abandoning the siege, the Athenians decided to send out a second expedition. Led by Demosthenes, one of Athens's most distinguished generals, it consisted of 73 triremes carrying 5,000 hoplites and 3,000 bowmen, slingers, and javelin throwers—in all some 15,000 men—and arrived at Syracuse in July 413.

Demosthenes attempted to destroy one of the Syracusan counterwalls; when this proved unsuccessful, he mounted a night attack. It caught the defenders by surprise, and the Athenians took Euryalus and much of the Epipolaen plateau. Enough of Gylippus's troops held fast, and the Syracusans mounted an immediate counterattack that caught the Athenians disorganized and inflicted heavy casualties. Cut off from supplies and prey to enemy cavalry, the Athenians attempted a breakout from the harbor of Syracuse in September 413 with 110 ships—both fit and unfit for action—but were contained by a great boom of block ships across the mouth of the Great Harbor as well as some 76 Corinthian and Syracuse ships. The naval battle ended in Athenian defeat, with Athens losing 50 ships to its enemy's 26.

The Athenians still had 60 triremes to their enemy's 50, and the generals wanted to try another breakout. The crews refused and demanded an overland retreat. Instead of setting out at once in the midst of Syracusan victory celebrations, the Athenians paused for 36 hours because of a false report (which had been spread to gain time until the victory celebrations had ended) that the retreat route was blocked.

Once the retreat was under way, 6,000 Athenian men under Demosthenes were offered freedom if they would desert. They refused and fought on until the situation was hopeless. On receiving a guarantee that his men's lives would be spared, however, the Athenian commander surrendered. Another group of 1,000 men was also forced to surrender. Nicias and Demosthenes were butchered, against the will of Gylippus. These 7,000 men—out of 45,000–50,000 who had taken part in the expedition on the Athenian side—were sent off to the stone quarries of Syracuse. The expedition also cost Athens some 200 triremes. Thucydides concluded, "This was the greatest Hellenic achievement of any in this war, or, in my opinion in, Hellenic history; at once most glorious to the victors, and most calamitous to the conquered" (Finley, *The Greek Historians,* 379).

The annihilation of the Athenian fleet and army in Sicily shook the Athenian Empire to its core. The islands of Euboea, Lesbos, and Chios now revolted against Athens. Sparta built 100 warships, and Persia set out to regain its lost Ionian dominions.

Athens might have had peace in 410, but its people were buoyed by a naval victory that year and rejected Spartan overtures. In 405 an Athenian fleet of 170 ships was taken while beached in the "Battle" of Aegospotami at the Hellespont while taking on supplies. Lysander, the Spartan naval commander, then captured the remaining Athenian garrisons at the Hellespont and severed Athenian access to Ukrainian wheat supplies. The Spartans permitted their Athenian prisoners to return to Athens in order to increase the strain on its scant food stocks. Pausanias, the second Spartan king, then brought a large land force to Athens and laid siege to the city by land, while Lysander arrived with 150 ships and blockaded it by sea. Starved into submission, Athens surrendered in 404. Corinth and Thebes urged that the city should be utterly destroyed and its people sold into slavery. To their credit the Spartans rejected these proposals, insisting that the city's Long Walls and fortifications all be demolished. Athens also had to give up all its foreign possessions and its fleet, and the city was forced to enter into alliance with Sparta and accept its leadership. The Peloponnesian Wars were over, and so too was the period of Athenian supremacy.

References

Finley, M. I., ed. *The Greek Historians: The Essence of Herodotus, Thucydides, Xenophon, Polybius.* New York: Viking, 1959.

Green, Peter. *Armada from Athens.* Garden City, NY: Doubleday, 2003.

Kagan, Donald. *The Peloponnesian War.* New York: Viking, 2003.

Siege of Veii

Date	404–396 BCE	
Location	Central Italy, north of Rome	
Opponents (* winner)	*Rome	Veii
Commander	Appius Claudius; later Marcus Furius Camillus	Unknown
Approx. # Troops	Unknown	Unknown
Importance	First expansion of Roman territory beyond that occupied by the original Latin people	

In the fifth century BCE, Veii was an important Italian city. Located in central Etruria and situated on high ground about two and a half hours' march from Rome, this rich and powerful republic was well protected with high walls. Veii's territory reached the Tiber River, blocking Roman expansion to the north. The Romans regarded Veii as the most important threat to their expanding power. Both Veii and Rome claimed the town of Fidenae (Castel Giubileo) on the south (Latin) bank of the Tiber. The hill on which Fidenae stood controlled the lowest river ford above Rome and apparently changed hands a number of times. Apparently Veii broke a truce with Rome to seize Fidenae.

Believing conflict inevitable and desiring the Veii lands for farming, Rome carried out governmental reforms to prepare for war and then captured Fidenae. The inhabitants of Veii meanwhile worked to strengthen their city's defenses against an anticipated Roman attack. Where possible, the cliffs on which the city stood were cut back to make them steeper and, around other portions of the periphery of the 480 acres of the city, the inhabitants built earthen ramparts with a stone breastwork.

Renewed warfare began between the two cities in 404 BCE on Roman initiative. Veii appealed in vain for assistance to the Etruscan confederation, which blamed it for the renewal of fighting. The war marked a number of firsts for Rome. It was the first conflict for Rome beyond the area occupied by the original Latin people, the first time the Romans campaigned year-round without interruptions for the harvest, and the first occasion on which Roman soldiers received regular pay. It was also perhaps the most important war in Roman history, as the city's survival depended on a successful outcome.

The Romans soon placed Veii under siege. The fighting went on for eight years, from 404 to 396. At one point a Veientine force sortied from the city at night and destroyed siege works that had taken the Romans months to build. This only strengthened Roman resolve.

The Romans succeeded, over the course of the siege, in occupying the northern neck of land that provided the only level access to Veii. This contained one of the large tunnels used for irrigation purposes. The tunnel went under the city walls and opened into Veii itself. Marcus Furius Camillus set a large number of sappers to work, in shifts of six hours at a time, to enlarge the tunnel. Camillus, who was made dictator of Rome and directed the latter stages of the operation, was so confident of victory that he requested a decision by the Senate on how to divide the spoils. The Senate decided to allow the troops to take what they could. This brought out a large portion of the population of Rome to participate in the final assault in 396.

While the vast majority of his forces loudly assaulted Veii's walls, Camillus sent a force of handpicked shock troops through the tunnel into the city center. This smaller force did its work well and managed to open the gates. Not until the city was entirely in Roman hands did Camillus issue orders to spare the defenseless and begin the pillage. Once the city was sacked, the Romans partially destroyed it, razing its defenses and forcing many of the inhabitants to leave. Rome's elimination of the independent existence of another city-state was both a radical departure and an ominous precedent, an indication of the importance of the conflict. The Romans also took over the city's deity of Juno, the symbol of vitality and youthfulness, as one of their own. Now she watched not over Veii but instead over Rome.

References
Grant, Michael. *History of Rome*. New York: Scribner, 1978.

Melegari, Vezio. *The Great Military Sieges*. New York: Crowell, 1972.

Battle of Leuctra

Date	July 371 BCE	
Location	Central Greece	
Opponents (* winner)	*Thebes and Boeotian League	Sparta and Peloponnesian League
Commander	Epaminondas	Cleombrotus
Approx. # Troops	6,000 hoplites and 1,500 cavalry	10,000 hoplites and 1,000 cavalry
Importance	Marks the end of Spartan military invincibility and the beginning of Theban hegemony; also leads to changes in military tactics	

The Battle of Leuctra, between Thebes and Sparta, was one of many in the wars for Greek hegemony. Following its victory over Athens in 404 BCE in the Peloponnesian Wars, Sparta became the dominant power in Greece but used its position to pursue an expansionary policy. In 383 in an act of blatant aggression, Sparta seized Thebes. Theban exiles liberated their city in 379, but Sparta's action had made a staunch enemy of Thebes, which was at first assisted by Athens. Thebes and Athens now worked together to expel Spartan forces from central Greece and also defeated the Spartans at sea off Naxos in the Aegean in 376.

Thebes reclaimed its position of leadership in Boeotia, bullying some city-states and destroying others in order to revive the Boeotian League under its leadership. Athens viewed this with alarm, however, and in these circumstances Sparta proposed a peace conference in 371. The talks deadlocked, and the Theban representatives, led by Epaminondas, walked out. Not wishing to give Thebes time to gather forces, King Cleombrotus of Sparta opted for a quick invasion.

The two sides met at Leuctra in Boeotia, some eight miles southwest of Thebes, sometime in July 371. Cleombrotus commanded some 10,000 Spartan and Peloponnesian League hoplites and 1,000 cavalry, while Epaminondas commanded the Boeotian League's 6,000 hoplites and 1,500 cavalry. The Spartans used their cavalry basically as a reconnaissance force, while the Thebans employed theirs in combat. Given Cleombrotus's nearly twofold advantage in manpower, all of Greece expected a Spartan victory.

Epaminondas had the advantage of being able to choose the battlefield, and he established a fortified camp to block the Spartan approach to Thebes. As he would undoubtedly lose to the Spartans in the shoving contest that typified phalanx warfare, he developed tactics that, while they had been seen before, were new in their degree. Epaminondas expected that the Spartans would place their best troops on the right flank. He therefore deliberately weakened his right flank and strengthened the left flank to meet the Spartans in oblique attack formation, with a left flank 48 ranks deep instead of the customary 8–12 ranks deep. The 300-man Theban Sacred Band, formed of 150 homosexual couples as the elite force of the army, held the Boeotian League's extreme left flank. The plan was both bold and innovative.

The oblique order allowed Epaminondas to refuse (i.e., hold back from the direct line of battle) his right flank, which was to act, with cavalry, as a holding force against the numerically superior Spartan left flank. Epaminondas hoped that he could win the battle with his powerful left flank before his weakened right flank could lose it.

Both sides were drawn up in linear formation, separated by about a mile of open plain. The Spartan cavalry was in front of its army's right flank, while the Theban cavalry was split between the flanks. Epaminondas attacked, first sending in his cavalry, which easily drove the Spartan horsemen from the field. The Theban hoplites then advanced, the powerful Theban left flank crashing into the Spartan right flank. Despite heavy resistance, the Spartans could not withstand the overwhelming Theban pressure. The Spartan left flank took no part in the battle, as the refused Theban right-flank infantry and cavalry were too far away.

Epaminondas's forces moved to the right and advanced on the remaining Spartan line. The Spartan ranks broke and the men fled, leaving the Thebans in possession of the field and victory. Theban casualties in the battle were light, while the Spartans lost perhaps 2,000 men. After the battle, both sides were open to negotiations. Spartan forces were permitted to withdraw back into the Peloponnese.

This battle amazed all of Greece. Not only did it lead to changes in tactics, but it marked the end of Spartan military invincibility and the beginning of a period of Theban hegemony. Thebes raised up Messenia as an independent state after centuries of helotism, an action that deprived Sparta of the economic means to maintain the traditional state structure on which its military supremacy had rested. Sparta sank to second-class status. Thebes, however, proved incapable of leadership, and Athens combined with Sparta against Thebes. The continuation of inter-Greek warfare made the Greek city-states susceptible to outside invasion, and in 338 Philip II of Macedon won the Battle of Chaeronea, ending the warfare that had plagued Greece for centuries but also bringing to a close Greek independence.

References

Buckley, John. *The Theban Hegemony.* Cambridge: Harvard University Press, 1980.

Delbruck, Hans. *Warfare in Antiquity.* Translated by Walter J. Renfore Jr. Lincoln: University of Nebraska Press, 1990.

Warry, John. *Warfare in the Classical World.* New York: Salamander Books, 1993.

Battle of Chaeronea

Date	August 4, 338 BCE	
Location	Boeotia in central Greece	
Opponents (* winner)	*Macedon	Athens, Thebes, and other allied Greeks and mercenaries
Commander	King Philip II	Chares
Approx. # Troops	30,000 infantry and 10,000 cavalry	35,000 infantry and 2,000 cavalry
Importance	Philip becomes master of all Greece	

This land battle, fought between the forces of King Philip II of Macedon and those of Athens, Thebes, and other allied Greeks and mercenaries, occurred in Boeotia in central Greece. Philip had hoped to campaign against Persia at the head of an army that would include an allied Greek force, but the leading Greek city-states stole a march on him and concluded an alliance with King Artaxerxes of Persia. Philip thus found that he had to move quickly against the Greeks before he could invade Persia.

Athens's strength remained its powerful navy of some 300 triremes. Sending the fleet north into the Thermaic Gulf would have forced Philip to withdraw from central Greece. Athenian leader Demosthenes, however, was caught up in the myth of the Greek hoplite and chose to meet Philip on land, playing to the Macedonian's strength.

Philip advanced faster than the Greeks anticipated. He first fell on and destroyed a force of some 10,000 Greek mercenaries at Amphissa, turning the flank of the remaining Greek forces holding the passes of northwestern Boeotia in central Greece. This forced Greek troops there to abandon the passes and withdraw south. Philip commanded perhaps 30,000 infantry and 2,000 cavalry. The Greek force now opposing him, commanded by Chares, was probably marginally larger: about 35,000 infantry and 2,000 cavalry.

The Greeks took up a strong position near Chaeronea in Boeotia. To the east, west, and south they were protected by mountains. In order to triumph, Philip would have to attack them head-on. Philip was an experienced military commander who faced in Chares a mediocre general at best. However, Philip was sufficiently impressed with the strength of the Greek position to make a last effort at a peace settlement with Athens and Thebes. Although the Delphic Oracle issued gloomy predictions for the allied side, Demosthenes overruled those who favored accepting the king's offer, forcing Philip to attack.

The battle took place probably on August 4 in 338 BCE on a front extending over about two miles. Some 12,000 Boeotians occupied the allied right, anchored by the Theban Sacred Band, the army's elite unit comprised of 150 pairs of male lovers who had shattered the hitherto invincible Spartan Army at Leuctra in 371. Perhaps 10,000 Athenian hoplites held the Greek left wing, while on the extreme left some lightly armed Greek troops stretched east to the Chaeronea citadel. Remaining Greek contingents, stiffened by some 5,000 mercenaries, occupied the Greek center.

Philip knew that the Theban forces posed the major allied threat. Thebes had broken an alliance with Macedon to side with Athens and had the most to fear from a Macedonian victory. The Theban men were exceptionally well trained; indeed, Theban forces had been the model for Philip's military reforms after he had taken the throne of Macedon. Athenian forces, on the other hand, were not well trained. Athens had not fought a major land battle for 20 years, and its men were basically citizen volunteers. Philip held to one cardinal principle in battle: the quickest and most economical way to win a victory is to attack and defeat not the weakest but the strongest portion of an enemy force. Crushing the Theban Sacred Band would be the key to a Macedonian victory.

Philip took up position on the Macedonian right, commanding the Guards Brigade (the Hypaspists), with a strong but lightly armed force protecting his flank. In the center he placed the regiments of the Macedonian phalanx. On the Macedonian left opposite the Theban Sacred Band, the position of greatest responsibility, Philip placed his son Alexander (later Alexander III, also known as Alexander the Great) in command of the Macedonian cavalry, an awesome responsibility for an 18-year-old and a measure of the confidence that Philip had in his son's military ability.

The Macedonians then began their advance. When the two armies came together, Philip's right wing slightly outflanked the allied left. His Guards Brigade engaged the Athenians first, Philip's center and left being refused (i.e., slightly echeloned back from the Greek center and right). As the Guards Brigade and Athenians came together, the Athenians, followed by the Greek center, drifted slightly to the left.

The Athenian commander on the left, Stratocles, ordered his men to charge the Macedonians. Although the Athenians drove the Macedonians back, the Guards Brigade's withdrawal was a planned move, not a rout. Still facing their enemy, they moved back step by step up a slight incline, keeping the advancing Greeks at bay.

At this point a gap developed between the Greek center and the Theban forces to the right. The superior discipline of the Thebans, who had held their position while the force to their left had not, would bring their doom. Into the gap Alexander led one division of Macedonian cavalry, while another got in around the Thebans on the other side. The 300-man Sacred Band was completely surrounded.

Philip, probably not wishing to concede the victory to his son, now ordered the Guards Division to charge. It swiftly reversed direction downhill, and the Athenian line, disorganized because of its own charge, swiftly broke. The Macedonians killed some 1,000 Athenians and took double that number prisoner. The remainder, including Demosthenes, who was present on the field that day, escaped.

The Macedonian phalanx meanwhile engaged the Greek center; it too broke and fled. Only the Sacred Band held. As with Leonidas's Spartans at Thermopylae, the Sacred Bank stood firm in perfect formation and was wiped out on the spot. Only 46 of its number were taken alive; the remaining 254 were subsequently buried on the spot in a common grave where they remain today, marked by the Lion of Chaeronea. Reportedly Philip subsequently ridiculed the performance of the Athenians but wept for the Sacred Band.

The Battle of Chaeronea demonstrated the superiority of the Macedonian 13-foot pike over the 6-foot Greek spear. One of the most decisive battles in Greek history, it extinguished the independence of the city-states and made Philip master of all Greece. He went on to establish a federal system that united the many city-states and ended the struggles that had distracted them for so long.

References

Ashley, James R. *Macedonian Empire: The Era of Warfare under Philip II and Alexander the Great, 359–323 B.C.* Jefferson City, NC: McFarland, 1998.

Bradford, Alfred S., ed. *Philip II of Macedon.* Westport, CT: Praeger, 1992.

Green, Peter. *Alexander of Macedon, 336–323 B.C.: A Historical Biography.* Berkeley: University of California Press, 1991.

Hammond, Nicholas G. L. *Philip of Macedon.* London: Duckworth, 1994.

Battle of the Granicus

Date	May 334 BCE	
Location	Along the Granicus River in northwestern Asia Minor	
Opponents (* winner)	*Macedonians and allied Greeks	Persian Empire and Greek mercenaries
Commander	King Alexander III	Arsames
Approx. # Troops	35,000?	20,000–40,000?
Importance	First major victory for Alexander the Great in Persian territory; enables him to liberate the Greek city-states in Asia Minor and establish a base for further operations	

In 336 BCE the aristocrat Pausanias, a member of the king's bodyguard and reportedly also his former lover, assassinated Philip II, king of Macedon. Pausanias was almost immediately slain. Philip's 20-year-old son Alexander III (356–323) succeeded to the throne.

Two years before, Philip had defeated the principal Greek city-states in the Battle of Chaeronea in 338 and made himself master of all Greece through the Hellenic League, an essential step prior to his planned great enterprise of invading and conquering the Persian Empire. On ascending the throne, Alexander quickly crushed a rebellion of the southern Greek city-states and mounted a short and successful operation against Macedon's northern neighbors. He then took up his father's plan to conquer the Persian Empire.

Leaving his trusted general Antipater and an army of 10,000 men to hold Macedonia and Greece, in the spring of 334 Alexander set out from Pella and marched by way of Thrace for the Hellespont (Dardanelles) at the head of an army of some 30,000 infantry and 5,000 cavalry. Among his forces were men from the Greek city-states. His army reached the Hellespont in just three weeks and crossed without Persian opposition. His fleet numbered only about 160 ships supplied by the allied Greeks. The Persian fleet included perhaps 400 Phoenician triremes, and its crews were far better trained; however, not a single Persian ship appeared.

Alexander instructed his men that there was to be no looting in what was now, he said, their land. The invaders soon received the submission of a number of Greek towns in Asia Minor. King Darius III was, however, gathering forces to oppose Alexander. Memnon, a Greek mercenary general in the employ of Darius, knew that Alexander was short of supplies and cash. Memnon therefore favored a scorched-earth policy that would force Alexander to withdraw. At the same time Darius should use his fleet to transport the army and invade Macedonia. Unfortunately, Memnon also advised that the Persians should avoid a pitched battle at all costs. This wounded Persian pride and influenced Darius to reject the proffered advice.

The two armies met in May. The Persian force, which was approximately the same size as Alexander's force, took up position on the east bank of the swift

Granicus River in western Asia Minor. The Persians were strong in cavalry but weak in infantry, with perhaps as many as 6,000 Greek hoplite mercenaries. Memnon and the Greek mercenaries were in front, forming a solid spear wall and supported by men with javelins. The Persian cavalry was on the flanks, to be employed as mounted infantry.

When Alexander's army arrived, Parmenio and the other Macedonian generals recognized the strength of the Persian position and counseled against an attack. The Greek infantry would have to cross the Granicus in column and would be vulnerable while they were struggling to re-form. The generals urged that since it was already late afternoon, they should camp for the night. Alexander was determined to attack but eventually followed their advice.

That night, however, probably keeping his campfires burning to deceive the Persians, Alexander located a ford downstream and led his army across the river. The Persians discovered Alexander's deception the next morning. The bulk of the Macedonian army was already across the river and easily deflected a Persian assault. The rest of the army then crossed.

With Alexander having turned their position, the Persians and their Greek mercenaries were forced to fight in open country. Their left was on the river, and their right was anchored by foothills. The Persian cavalry was now in front, with the Greek mercenary infantry to the rear. Alexander placed the bulk of his Greek cavalry on the left flank, the heavy Macedonian infantry in the center, and the light Macedonian infantry, the Paeonian light cavalry, and his own heavy cavalry (the Companions) on the right flank. Alexander was conspicuous in magnificent armor and shield with an extraordinary helmet with two white plumes. He stationed himself on the right wing, and the Persians therefore assumed that the attack would come from that quarter.

Alexander initiated the battle. Trumpets blared, and Alexander set off with the Companions in a great wedge formation aimed at the far left of the Persian line. This drew Persian cavalry off from the center, whereupon Alexander wheeled and led the Companions diagonally to his left, against the weakened Persian center. Although the Companions had to charge uphill, they pushed their way through a hole in the center of the Persian line. Alexander was in the thick of the fight as the Companions drove back the Persian cavalry, which finally broke.

Surrounded, the Greek mercenaries were mostly slaughtered. Alexander sent the 2,000 who surrendered to Macedonia in chains, probably to work in the mines. It would have made sense to have incorporated them into his own army, but Alexander intended to make an example of them for having fought against fellow Greeks.

References

Green, Peter. *Alexander of Macedon, 356–323 B.C.: A Historical Biography.* Berkeley: University of California Press, 1991.

Hammond, Nicholas G. L. *Alexander the Great: King, Commander, and Statesman.* 3rd ed. London: Bristol Classical Press, 1996.

Sekunda, Nick, and John Warry. *Alexander the Great: His Armies and Campaigns, 332–323 B.C.* London: Osprey, 1988.

Battle of Issus

Date	November (5?) 333 BCE	
Location	Southeastern Turkey	
Opponents (* winner)	*Macedonians and allied Greeks	Persian Empire and Greek mercenaries
Commander	King Alexander III	King Darius III
Approx. # Troops	30,000?	As many as 100,000
Importance	Second major victory for Alexander the Great in Persian territory; it enables him to campaign to the south and conquer Egypt	

Following his victory in the May 334 BCE Battle of the Granicus River, Macedonian king Alexander III (Alexander the Great) marched south, continuing the liberation of the Greek coastal cities of Asia Minor. He met real opposition only at Miletus, which he captured following a brief siege.

Alexander then took the momentous decision of disbanding his fleet of some 160 triremes. He kept only the Athenian detachment, to serve as transports and provide hostages, and a squadron in the Hellespont. With the Persian fleet of more than 400 triremes dominating the eastern Mediterranean, Alexander could not hope to win a sea battle, and maintaining the fleet was expensive. His commanders opposed this decision. The Persians might now easily cut off the army in Asia Minor and prevent both its resupply and its return to Macedonia and Greece. They could also raid Greece and stir up revolts against Alexander there. Alexander, however, believed that his men would fight harder knowing that retreat was not possible. He also seems to have profoundly distrusted his Greek allies, so much so that he was prepared to risk his entire campaign rather than entrust its safety to a Greek fleet.

Alexander told his generals that he intended to move against the Persian fleet from the land instead, taking the Persian and Phoenician naval bases along the eastern Mediterranean coast. During 334–333 he conquered much of the coast of Asia Minor. Alexander's early military successes owed much to his reputation for mercy, justice, and toleration. It certainly helped his cause that his rule brought improved administration, lower taxes, and public works projects. The only difficult operation occurred at Halicarnassus, where the defenders were led by the Greek mercenary Memnon. Alexander took the city after a siege.

While Alexander secured the remaining coastal cities, Persian king Darius III now loosed Memnon, his only first-class general, against Alexander's lines of communication. However, Memnon soon took sick and died. Darius was gathering yet

Mosaic depicting Macedonian king Alexander III's victory over Persian king Darius III at Issus in 333 BCE. The youthful Alexander (left) leads the charge of retreating Persian troops commanded by Darius (right). It was Alexander's second defeat of a Persian army. (Jupiterimages)

another army for another military test with the invader when he learned that Alexander had moved south into Syria. Darius therefore moved before he was fully ready. Crossing the Amarnus Mountains, he positioned his forces behind Alexander, cutting off his line of communications. With the potentially hostile cities of Phoenicia to the south, Alexander had no choice but to turn and fight.

The two armies came together at Issus in early November 333 BCE (possibly November 5). The numbers are in dispute. Darius probably had more men, perhaps as many as 100,000 (Macedonian reports of 600,000 are complete propaganda). Alexander had only 30,000 men. Darius positioned his army on the narrow coastal plain on the north side of the steep-banked Pinarus River, a front of about three miles. This meant that only part of his force could engage at any one time. Largely untrained troops held the Persian left and right; Darius placed archers to their fronts to buttress them. In the center of the Persian line were the 2,000 Royal Bodyguards, the elite force in the army. Darius was with them in a great ornamental chariot. As many as 30,000 Greek mercenaries were on either side of the Royal Bodyguards, while Persian cavalry anchored the far right flank on the Gulf of Issus. If the Persians could at least hold, Alexander's days would be numbered.

Alexander arrived before the Persian line in late afternoon. The Persian cavalry screen that had been south of the Pinarus masking Darius's dispositions and intent now withdrew across the river. Alexander halted to reorganize his line. Seeing Darius massing his cavalry on his right flank near the seashore against the Macedonian left wing under Parmenio, Alexander shifted his Thessalonian cavalry there, placing it behind the phalanx so as to conceal their movement. He sent a mixed force of light-armed troops to deal with a Persian detachment in the hills that had worked its way behind his right wing. He also detached cavalry from the center to strengthen his right wing, but the Persians on his far right made no attempt to attack and were soon routed. Alexander then recalled most of his troops sent against them, leaving only 300 cavalry to protect his far right flank.

Having completed his dispositions, Alexander resumed the advance. His forces were also on a three-mile front. He halted just out of bowshot, hoping that the Persians would attack. As he occupied a strong prepared defensive position, Darius understandably refused. Alexander then ordered his own men forward. Determining that the infantry on the Persian left was the weak part of the enemy line, Alexander had his Macedonian heavy cavalry (the Companions) on the right of his line.

Battle was joined when the Persian archers let loose a volley of arrows said to be so thick that they collided with one another in air. The archers then withdrew back into the mass of infantry as Alexander led the Companions in an assault against the light infantry on the Persian left. It almost immediately broke.

The Macedonian attack in the center did not go as well. The men had difficulty getting across the river and then encountered a steep bank and stake palisades placed by the Persians. Desperate hand-to-hand fighting ensued, pitting the Macedonian infantrymen against equally tough Greek mercenaries. Alexander meanwhile rolled up the Persian left.

Alexander then shifted his cavalry to strike the rear of the Greek mercenaries and the Royal Bodyguards in an effort to kill or capture Darius. Alexander was wounded in the thigh during the fighting, some reports say by Darius himself. Wounded, the horses on Darius III's chariot suddenly reared and bolted. Darius managed to control them but, in danger of capture, shifted to a smaller chariot and fled the field.

Things were not going well for Alexander elsewhere, however. The Macedonian center was hard-pressed, as were the Thessalonians on the left, by the Persian heavy cavalry. Alexander therefore had to break off his pursuit of Darius. Alexander swung his right wing into the Persian army's Greek mercenaries from the flank, rolling them up. When the men of the Persian heavy cavalry saw this and learned of the flight of Darius, they too decamped. Retreat became rout. Alexander pursued but was forced to break this off due to darkness.

Persian losses may have been as high as half of the force, or 50,000 men, while Alexander reported some 450 dead. Among the captives were Darius's wife, mother, and two daughters. The loot included some 3,000 talents in gold. Alexander also recovered Darius's royal mantle and insignia, which he had stripped off in flight.

The Battle of Issus was a glorious victory for Alexander, but it was not decisive. More than 10,000 Greek mercenaries escaped and would form the nucleus of yet another army. Darius still lived, and as long as this was the case the fight would continue.

References

Green, Peter. *Alexander of Macedon, 356–323 B.C.: A Historical Biography.* Berkeley: University of California Press, 1991.

Hammond, Nicholas G. L. *Alexander the Great: King, Commander, and Statesman.* 3rd ed. London: Bristol Classical Press, 1996.

Sekunda, Nick, and John Warry. *Alexander the Great: His Armies and Campaigns, 332–323 B.C.* London: Osprey, 1988.

Sieges of Tyre and Gaza

Date	332 BCE	
Location	Eastern Mediterranean coast	
Opponents (* winner)	*Macedonians and allied Greeks	Tyre and Gaza
Commander	King Alexander III	Unknown
Approx. # Troops	Unknown	40,000–50,000
Importance	Two of the most masterful operations in the history of siege warfare	

Alexander the Great's sieges of Tyre and Gaza in 332 BCE are two of the great military operations in history. In the summer of 334 Alexander (353–326), ruler of Macedon and master of all Greece, led some 35,000 men across the Hellespont in an invasion of Asia Minor. Alexander defeated the Persian army on the Granicus River and conquered much of Asia Minor. In 333 he defeated Persian king Darius III at Issus, then turned south to conquer Egypt. This secured his southern flank prior to resuming his eastward march to the extremities of the Persian Empire. Securing the Phoenician coastal city-states of Syria would also open those ports for his own triremes and deny them to the Persian fleet, preventing a Persian naval descent on Greece.

Tyre was the most important of the Phoenician coastal city-states. Ruled by King Azemilk and located in present-day Lebanon, Tyre was actually two cities. Old Tyre was located on an island about three miles in circumference, separated from the mainland city by a half mile of water. The channel between the island and mainland was more than 20 feet deep. The island citadel was protected by massive walls up to 150 feet high on the land side that were reputedly impregnable. Alexander wanted to bypass Tyre, but he had to reduce it before he could move against Egypt, lest it be used as a base for Darius's fleet. Alexander predicted that once Tyre fell the Phoenician ships, deprived of their bases, would desert to the winning side.

Determined to hold out, the Tyrians rejected Alexander's overtures. They were confident in their defenses and believed that a protracted siege would purchase time for Darius to mobilize a new army and campaign in Asia Minor. Alexander had second thoughts about the task ahead and sent heralds to the Tyrians to urge a peaceful resolution. The Tyrian leaders, however, saw this as a sign of weakness; they killed the heralds and threw their bodies over the walls. This foolish act cemented Alexander's resolve and won him solid support from his generals.

Alexander took mainland Old Tyre without difficulty and initiated siege operations against the island in January 332. He ordered Dyadis the Thessalian, head of the Macedonian Army's corps of engineers, to construct a great mole, about 200 feet wide, out from the land and to reach the island and bring up siege engines. The Macedonians secured wood from the forests of Lebanon for the piles of the mole, while the structures of mainland Tyre were demolished for the fill. Alexander reportedly worked alongside his men on the project.

The Tyrians sent ships from the island filled with archers to attack the Macedonians working on the mole. To counter such forays, Alexander ordered his men to construct two great siege towers, each 150 feet in height. As the mole advanced, the towers moved with it. One night with a favorable wind the Tyrians sent an old horse transport rigged as a fireship and laden with combustibles against the towers and causeway. The towers caught fire and were destroyed. At the same time, a flotilla of smaller Tyrian craft arrived; men from them attacked Alexander's men on the mole and destroyed other siege equipment that had escaped destruction in the fire. They then withdrew.

Alexander responded by ordering construction of two more towers. Leaving operations at Tyre in the hands of trusted lieutenants, he then traveled to Sidon to secure ships to operate against the island and protect those working on the mole. Soon he had gathered 223 ships from Sidon, Cyprus, Rhodes, and other eastern Mediterranean city-states. Alexander placed in them some 4,000 hoplites recruited from the Peloponnese by Cleander. This flotilla then sailed for Tyre. Alexander commanded its right wing, and Pinitagoras commanded its left wing.

The Tyrians learned of Alexander's activities and planned to give battle at sea, but noting the size of the approaching fleet, the Tyrian admiral changed his mind; he chose instead to protect the two narrow entrances to the island's harbor. A number of ships sunk side by side were sufficient to block both. Alexander concentrated offensive actions against Sidonian Harbor, the smaller of these entrances and about 200 feet wide, but he was unsuccessful. Subsequently the Tyrians substituted heavy iron chains for their block ships.

Thanks to the presence of Alexander's flotilla, it was no longer possible for the Tyrians to attack the mole with their ships. Instead, they employed catapults against both it and the Macedonian siege towers as the latter came within range. Alexander's catapults replied. Although the Macedonians suffered setbacks, the mole gradually advanced and ultimately reached the island. Under the protection of the towers, the Macedonians employed battering rams against the citadel's walls, but the Tyrian defenses stood firm.

Alexander had also ordered construction of naval battering rams. Each was mounted on a large platform lashed between two barges. Other barges carried catapults. Finally, this naval assault opened a breach in the walls; unfortunately, a gale then arose. Some of Alexander's vessels were sunk, and others were badly damaged.

During this respite, the Tyrians demolished a number of buildings and dropped the masonry over the walls to keep Alexander's naval rams at a distance. They also devised drop beams, which could be swung out against the ships by derricks, and, at the end of lines, grappling irons or barbed hooks known as crows that could be dropped on the Macedonians, hooking and hoisting them up to a tortured death in front of their colleagues.

Alexander's men now had to remove the debris in the water around the walls, allowing the assault craft to close on the island. The Tyrians replied by tipping onto the attackers bowls of red-hot sand. Finally, Alexander's naval rams broke down a section of the wall. Infantry were sent into the breach on boarding ramps as the defenders continued their resistance in the city center.

Tyre fell at the end of July. Frustration over the length and ferocity of the siege gave way to rage, and the Macedonian troops extended no quarter to the inhabitants. Reportedly 8,000 Tyrians died during the siege; the Macedonians slew another 7,000 afterward as the city became one large abattoir. Another 30,000 inhabitants, including women and children, were sold into slavery.

With Tyre destroyed, the Macedonian Army set out on foot in July or early August for Egypt. Some 160 miles from Tyre, the army encountered the fortress city of Gaza, situated on a rocky hill on the sole route between Egypt and Syria. The city's governor, Batis, rejected calls for surrender. Siege operations were quite difficult, as the siege engines sank in the sand. On occasion the defenders sallied to destroy the Macedonian siege equipment. On one such foray Alexander was badly wounded in the shoulder by an arrow.

Alexander again called on Dyadis, this time to build an earthen rampart around the city. In two months the Macedonians had built an earthen rampart topped by a wooden platform encircling Gaza, a mammoth undertaking. A breach was finally made in the walls, and Macedonian troops entered the city. The Macedonians had also carried out mining operations, and another group went in by a tunnel.

After heavy fighting, the city fell. Reportedly the Macedonians slew 10,000 defenders, and the women and children were all sold as slaves. Batis was among the captured. Alexander ordered him lashed by his ankles behind a chariot and dragged around the city walls until he was dead.

Although it was fortunate for Alexander that during these operations Darius III did not move against the Macedonian lines of communication, the successful sieges of both Tyre and Gaza thoroughly demonstrated Alexander's mastery of this type of warfare and greatly added to his mystique of invincibility. In 1627 Cardinal

Richelieu of France drew inspiration from Alexander's tactics at Tyre for his own reduction of La Rochelle.

References

Green, Peter. *Alexander of Macedon, 356–323 B.C.: A Historical Biography.* Berkeley: University of California Press, 1991.

Kern, Paul Bentley. *Ancient Siege Warfare.* Bloomington: Indiana University Press, 1999.

Sekunda, Nick, and John Warry. *Alexander the Great: His Armies and Campaigns, 332–323 B.C.* London: Osprey, 1988.

Battle of Gaugamela

Date	October 1, 331 BCE	
Location	Plain of Gaugamela, east of the city of Mosul in modern northern Iraq	
Opponents (* winner)	*Macedonians and allied Greeks	Persian Empire and Greek mercenaries
Commander	King Alexander III	King Darius III
Approx. # Troops	31,000 infantry; 7,000 cavalry	Up to 100,000 men (as many as 40,000 of them cavalry)
Importance	Alexander's decisive victory leads to the collapse of the Persian Empire	

Following his successful siege operations against Tyre and Gaza in 332 BCE, Alexander the Great temporarily turned aside from further conquest to organize his new territories and to solidify his lines of communication. The conquered peoples of Babylon and other places welcomed Alexander as a liberator because of his reputation for leniency to those who surrendered and because he restored the temples that the Persians had destroyed. During December 332 to March 331 BCE Alexander absorbed Egypt and laid plans for the new city of Alexandria.

Alexander then marched back across the empire he had carved out of Asia Minor. This time, however, he moved directly against the distant cities of Persia, crossing the Euphrates on a bridge constructed by a detachment of his men under his general and lover, Hephaestion.

Persian king Darius III had not been idle. Since his defeat at Issus in 333, he had assembled a new army. Alexander had a maximum of 47,000 men: 31,000 heavy infantry (Phalangists) and 9,000 light infantry (Peltists) along with 7,000 cavalry. Ancient sources credit Darius with a force of between 200,000 and 1 million men. This is almost certainly an exaggeration, for maintaining a force this large would have been almost impossible given the primitive logistics of the time. Modern estimates place the total size of his army at no more than 100,000 men, of whom up to 40,000 were cavalry. By whatever measurement, Alexander's army was greatly outnumbered, but to him numbers meant little. Alexander's force was well trained, well organized, and disciplined, while Darius's was a polyglot force drawn chiefly from the eastern provinces that included Persians, Medes, Babylonians, Syrians, Armenians, and Hindus.

Darius and his great host awaited Alexander on the plain at Gaugamela, some 60 miles from the city of Arbela (present-day Erbil). The clash is sometimes erroneously known as the Battle of Arbela, since that was the nearest settlement. Most probably it took place east of the city of Mosul in northern Iraq.

Darius chose not to oppose Alexander's approach, trusting in superior numbers. Darius had selected the location so that he could make effective use of his superior numbers and employ his chariots, which had scythes mounted on their wheel hubs to cut down Alexander's forces. Some sources contend that Darius had the plain cleared of vegetation for ease of maneuver. He was confident that his preparations would bring him victory.

Alexander moved slowly to Gaugamela, hoping to wear down the defenders and exhaust their food stocks. When he finally arrived, his chief of staff, Parmenio, urged a night attack to offset the numerical disadvantage, but Alexander refused. Apart from the difficulty of maintaining control at night, he is reported to have said, "Alexander does not steal victories." As it turned out, Darius had feared a night assault and had kept his troops awake all night. The next morning the men were exhausted, while Alexander's men were well rested.

Battle was joined on October 1, 331. Alexander, who fought with his Companion cavalry, commanded the right flank of his army, while Parmenio had charge of the left flank. Macedonian and Greek cavalry protected the two flanks. Alexander arranged the army in oblique formation, refusing his left and moving the army laterally to the right across the Persian front. His plan was to draw the Persians to the flanks, opening a weak point in the center of the Persian line. Everything depended on his flanks holding until Alexander could detect this weakness and strike a decisive blow.

Darius positioned himself in the center of the Persian line with his best infantry. Bessus commanded the cavalry on the Persian left wing with chariots in front, while Mazaeus commanded the right flank of other cavalry. With their vast superior numbers of cavalry and much longer line, it appeared that the Persians must inevitably flank Alexander's army.

Darius ordered Bessus to release cavalry to ride around the Macedonian right wing and arrest Alexander's movement. Bessus committed some 11,000 cavalry to the effort, but they were halted by the numerically far inferior force of Macedonian cavalry and Greek mercenary infantry. Clearly Alexander's cavalry was far better disciplined and more closely knit than Persia's local detachments, which had never trained together.

Darius ordered the 100 chariots positioned in front of his left wing to attack Alexander's elite force of Companion cavalry on the Macedonian right. Alexander's infantry screen of javelin throwers, archers, and light infantrymen somewhat blunted the Persian chariot charge before it reached the Companions. The Companions then wheeled aside, allowing the remaining chariots to pass through unopposed, when they came up against the lances of the infantry. The gap then closed, and the Persian charioteers were annihilated in the Macedonian rear.

Darius then ordered a general advance. Mazaeus, who commanded the Persian right wing, advanced against the Macedonian left led by Parmenio. Mazaeus also sent cavalry in an attempt to get around the Macedonian line. At the same time, Bessus sought to push men around the Macedonian right wing to envelop it. These efforts by Bessus and Mazaeus elongated the Persian line as Alexander had hoped, weakening its center. Mazaeus's job was especially difficult, as his men had to travel a greater distance to engage Alexander's refused left wing.

Alexander watched for weakness in the Persian line, bringing up his reserves. Once he detected it, he led his Companion cavalry and light infantry in a great wedge-shaped formation into the breach. Twice the Macedonians burst through gaps in the Persian line and drove close to where Darius's chariot stood. Both Persian flanks were now threatened by the great gap that the Macedonians had torn in the center of the line.

The possibility of encirclement led Bessus to retreat, his forces suffering heavy casualties at the hands of the pursuing Macedonians. Darius, now himself in danger of being cut off, panicked and fled. With the Persians in wild retreat, the Macedonians vigorously pressed their advance, scattering the vast Persian host.

Alexander's left wing, heavily engaged with Mazaeus's men, could not keep pace with the rest of the Macedonian advance. Alexander's attempt to encircle Mazaeus failed, however, because his own cavalry drove the Persians back too quickly. The victory was nonetheless sweeping. The Macedonians reported their casualties in the battle at some 500 killed and up to 3,000 wounded while setting Persian losses at close to 50,000.

Bessus and other Persian generals murdered Darius. Alexander later caught such regicides as he could and executed them. He did not rest but instead after the battle advanced rapidly toward the Persian capital of Persepolis so as not to allow the Persian generals time to reorganize their forces.

Alexander sent most of his men by the long route, while he led about a third of his force through the mountains on a short route through the Persian Gates (the strategic pass now known as Tang-e Meyran in present-day Iran), held by a Persian army under Ariobarzan. The Persians halted the Macedonians at the narrow pass and reportedly inflicted heavy casualties on them. Either through a shepherd or prisoners, Alexander learned of a path that flanked the Persian position. In a highly dangerous move, he and a number of his men traversed it at night and turned the Persian position. As a result, Alexander reached Persepolis before the guards of the treasury could secret its reputed

3,000 tons of gold and silver, the greatest treasury in the world. He then destroyed the great palace, perhaps as a sign of the end of Persian power.

Alexander was now 25 years old. In 4 years he had broken the power of Persia forever and ruled an empire of 1 million square miles. No one in the world could come close to him in wealth or power. The speed of what he accomplished stands unequaled before or since. He had no intention of resting on his laurels, though. He continued his conquests, reaching the steppes of Russia to the north and India to the south before his soldiers would go no farther. Alexander died in Babylon, following a drinking bout, in 323 BCE.

Among the many riddles of Alexander's life is his failure to provide for a successor. Only in the last year of his life did he beget an heir, who was too young to prevent a struggle for the throne. As Alexander lay dying, one of his generals asked to whom he left the throne. Reportedly Alexander whispered "*Kratisto*" ("to the strongest"). His empire was divided among his generals, and his vision of a universal commonwealth was lost.

References

Arrian [Lucius Flavius Arrianus]. *The Campaigns of Alexander.* Translated by Aubrey de Selincourt. East Rutherford, NJ: Penguin, 1976.

Creasy, Edward S. *The Fifteen Decisive Battles of the World: From Marathon to Waterloo.* New York: Heritage, 1969.

Fox, Robin Lane. *The Search for Alexander.* Boston: Little, Brown, 1980.

Fuller, J. F. C. *A Military History of the Western World,* Vol. 1. New York: Funk and Wagnalls, 1954.

Marsden, E. W. *The Campaign of Gaugamela.* Liverpool: Liverpool University Press, 1964.

Tarn, W. W. *Alexander the Great.* Cambridge: Cambridge University Press, 1948.

Battle of Ipsus

Date	Spring 301 BCE	
Location	Near Ipsus (present-day Sipsin, Turkey) in eastern Asia Minor	
Opponents (* winner)	*Macedonians, Seleucids	Antigonids
Commander	Seleucus, Lysimachus	Antigonus, Demetrius
Approx. # Troops	64,000 infantry, 15,000 light cavalry, 400 war elephants	70,000 infantry, 10,000 heavy Macedonian cavalry, 75 war elephants
Importance	This battle of the successors of Alexander the Great marks the definitive end of his empire	

Ipsus was fought in the spring of 301 BCE between the successors of Alexander the Great to see who would control his empire. Legend has it that when Alexander the Great lay dying in Babylon in 323, he was asked to whom he left his vast empire. He is reported to have said "*Kratisto*" ("To the strongest"). Predictably, a struggle soon ensued among Alexander's chief lieutenants, known as the Diadochi (Successors). The so-called Diadochi Wars occurred during 322–275.

A number of Alexander's lieutenants hoped to inherit his empire. They included Perdiccas (d. 331), whom Alexander named his regent; Eumenes (360?–316), Alexander's staff secretary; Lysimachus (361?–281), a staff officer; Craterus (d. 321), a division commander and son-in-law of Antipater; and Demetrius (d. 283), a cavalry commander and son of Antigonus. The most powerful of Alexander's former subordinates, however, were Ptolemy (367?–283) in Egypt, Antipater (398?–319) in Macedonia, Antigonus (382–301) in Asia Minor, and Seleucus (358–280) in Mesopotamia. All of these men had been trained by Alexander and were highly skilled professionals. However, they lacked both his vision and his daring. Certainly they did not share his genius for war.

Ptolemy was perhaps the best placed. He had the wealth of Egypt to pay for a large army, and he also had Alexander's body, which he had secured to bury at the temple of Amon. Antipater not only controlled Alexander's base of operations in Macedonia but also dominated Greece during the period 334–323. Antipater soon died though and was followed by his son Cassander (350–297). Antigonus, who was both ambitious and a skilled general, controlled the central portion of Alexander's former empire, while Seleucus, who had risen to be governor of Babylon, could draw on the resources of much of the former Persian Empire.

War began in earnest in 316. It was a shifting struggle, marked by guile and bribery. During most of the period Antigonus was fighting the other three principal lieutenants. In the spring of 316 Antigonus defeated Eumenes, chancellor of Macedon, at Gabiene near Susa. This victory gave Antigonus the largest number of Alexander's veteran troops. He now also controlled upper Asia Minor. Antigonus's success drove Seleucus into alliance with Ptolemy, who then appealed to Cassander in Macedon for assistance. In 315 Antigonus demanded an armistice on the basis of recognition of the then-existing territorial arrangement. His rivals rejected such an arrangement that would have confirmed Antigonus as the most powerful of them; they demanded instead that Alexander's empire be divided equitably between them.

The war continued, and occasionally the allied leaders fought one another. The struggle was both opaque and complicated. In 322 in the so-called Lamian War at Crannon, Antipater and Craterus crushed a revolt by Athens. The Macedonian Navy then obliterated the Athenian Navy in the Battle of Amorgos. Demosthenes, who had led the revolt, committed suicide. Perdiccas died in 321, murdered on Ptolemy's order, while Eumenes killed Craterus in 321, and Antipater died in 319. In 317 in the Battle of Paraetakena in present-day Iran, Antigonus and Eumenes fought an inconclusive battle. The next year following another inconclusive battle, Antigonus bribed some of Eumenes' own men to kill him.

In 310 Cassander killed Alexander's wife Roxana and their son and the legitimate heir, Alexander IV, when he came of age, thus wiping out Alexander's line. In 308 Antigonus secured Cyprus, thanks to a naval battle off Salamis in Cyprus by Demetrius over Ptolemy's brother Menelius. This victory gave Antigonus control over the eastern Mediterranean. Antigonus proclaimed himself king and demanded that the others acknowledge this, which would have made him successor to Alexander. Ptolemy replied by naming himself king of Egypt and encouraging his allies to name themselves kings of Greece and Babylon, thus in effect confirming the end of Alexander's empire.

In 307 Demetrius invaded and conquered most of Greece before taking Palestine. Ptolemy repulsed him from Egypt in 305. During 305–304 Demetrius laid siege to the island of Rhodes, held by Ptolemy, but Ptolemy was able to resupply it by sea, and Demetrius eventually gave up and retired to Greece.

In 301 Seleucus and Lysimachus, allied to Cassander, engaged Antigonus and Demetrius in the Battle of Ipsus (present-day Sipsin, Turkey) in Asia Minor. Antigonus and his son had some 70,000 infantry, 10,000 heavy Macedonian cavalry, and perhaps 75 war elephants. Seleucus and Lysimachus fielded 64,000 infantry and 15,000 light cavalry, but Seleucus had secured 500 elephants in return for a pledge not to invade India, and he had 400 of these with him.

Accounts of the battle are sketchy, but apparently both armies deployed their infantry in phalanx formation, facing one another, with the cavalry on the flanks and war elephants as a screen in front. Seleucus, however, committed only about 100 of his war elephants in front, holding the other 300 in reserve. Antigonus attacked, with Demetrius commanding the heavy cavalry to break the opposing cavalry and wheel in behind his enemy.

The battle initially unfolded as Antigonus intended, but Demetrius was so successful that he drove the opposing cavalry from the field and took himself out of the battle. Seleucus then deployed his reserve elephants as a screen to block Demetrius from returning. Accounts differ as to whether these events were by design on the part of Seleucus or mere happenstance.

Meanwhile, the Seleucid light cavalry on the other flank advanced against Antigonus's phalanx and broke it with arrows. Antigonus, then 81 years old, was determined to stand and fight, awaiting the return of his son. Antigonus was killed, and Demetrius never did attempt to return. Informed of the results of the fighting, Demetrius escaped with some 9,000 men back to Ephesus.

The Battle of Ipsus marked the definitive end to Alexander's empire. Had Antignous won, no doubt that empire would have been largely reconstituted. Only Ptolemy would have remained of Antigonus's opponents, and he could have soon been defeated. Such an empire would have presented a serious obstacle to Roman expansion. As it worked out, the eastern empire now broke into a series of smaller states, none of which could stand alone against Rome.

References

Billows, Richard A. *Antigonos the One-Eyed and the Creation of the Hellenistic State.* Berkeley: University of California Press, 1990.

Cary, M. *The History of the Greek World: From 323 to 146 B.C.* London: Methuen, 1932.

Plutarch. *The Lives of the Nobles Grecians and Romans.* Translated by John Dryden, revised by Arthur Hugh Clough. New York: Modern Library, 1979.

Battle of Cannae

Date	August 2, 216 BCE	
Location	Cannae in south Italy	
Opponents (* winner)	*Carthage and allies	Rome
Commander	Hannibal Barca	Lucius Aemilius Paullus, Gaius Terentius Varro
Approx. # Troops	50,000	87,000
Importance	Hannibal destroys two Roman legions but is unable to change the outcome of the Second Punic War	

In the Battle of Cannae on August 2, 216 BCE, Hannibal Barca's Carthaginians destroyed two Roman armies in perhaps the most famous double envelopment in history. In 264 Roman troops crossed the Strait of Messina between Italy and the island of Sicily to aid Messina against Carthage, initiating the First Punic War (264–241). The war saw Rome take to the sea, winning naval battles over Carthage at Mylae in 260 and over Economus in 256. The tide of battle shifted several times, but after another Roman victory off Sicily, Carthage surrendered. By the terms of the Peace of Catulus, Carthage agreed to return all Roman prisoners and deserters, pay a heavy indemnity, and surrender its possessions in Sicily to Rome.

An uneasy peace of 23 years followed, during which Carthage's great general Hamilcar Barca consolidated Carthaginian power in Spain. Hannibal (247–183), Hamilcar's son, continued his father's efforts. The Second Punic War (218–201) has been called the contest of one man against a nation, for it was Hannibal, largely unaided, who carried the war to Rome. The treaty ending the First Punic War had divided Spain into spheres of influence, with Rome to be dominant north of the Ebro River and Carthage to be dominant below the river. A bone of contention between the two arose in Saguntum, a city south of the Ebro River on the Mediterranean coast and thus in Carthaginian-assigned territory but with a government that favored Rome. The 28-year-old Hannibal took Saguntum after a eight-month siege in 218. Its leaders appealed to Rome, which declared war. Putting together a large force, in the spring of 218 Hannibal crossed the Pyrenees into southern Gaul and fought his way east through the Gallic tribes. In an amazing feat, Hannibal

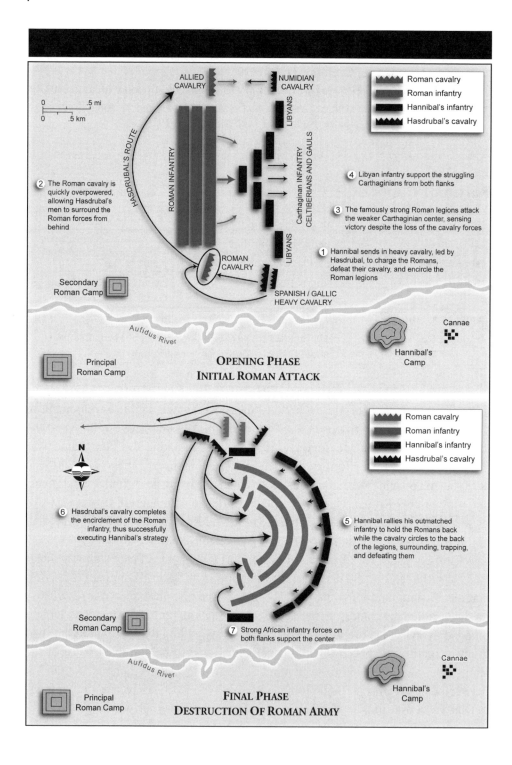

OPENING PHASE
INITIAL ROMAN ATTACK

Roman cavalry
Roman infantry
Hannibal's infantry
Hasdrubal's cavalry

ALLIED CAVALRY
NUMIDIAN CAVALRY
LIBYANS
ROMAN INFANTRY
HASDRUBAL'S ROUTE
Carthaginian INFANTRY CELTIBERIANS AND GAULS
LIBYANS
ROMAN CAVALRY
SPANISH / GALLIC HEAVY CAVALRY

2 The Roman cavalry is quickly overpowered, allowing Hasdrubal's men to surround the Roman forces from behind

4 Libyan infantry support the struggling Carthaginians from both flanks

3 The famously strong Roman legions attack the weaker Carthaginian center, sensing victory despite the loss of the cavalry forces

1 Hannibal sends in heavy cavalry, led by Hasdrubal, to charge the Romans, defeat their cavalry, and encircle the Roman legions

Secondary Roman Camp

Principal Roman Camp

Aufidus River

Cannae

Hannibal's Camp

0 .5 mi
0 .5 km

FINAL PHASE
DESTRUCTION OF ROMAN ARMY

Roman cavalry
Roman infantry
Hannibal's infantry
Hasdrubal's cavalry

N

6 Hasdrubal's cavalry completes the encirclement of the Roman infantry, thus successfully executing Hannibal's strategy

5 Hannibal rallies his outmatched infantry to hold the Romans back while the cavalry circles to the back of the legions, surrounding, trapping, and defeating them

7 Strong African infantry forces on both flanks support the center

Secondary Roman Camp

Principal Roman Camp

Aufidus River

Cannae

Hannibal's Camp

battled hostile tribes and the elements to cross the Alps with his army in October 218. He arrived in Italy with perhaps 26,000 men and 15 war elephants. For the next 16 years, Hannibal campaigned in Italy.

His strength bolstered by disaffected Gauls in northern Italy who joined his army, Hannibal marched through the Po Valley and throughout southern Italy, destroying all Roman armies sent against him. Following a series of Roman defeats (at Ticinus and Trebia in 218 and at Lake Trasimene in 217), Rome selected Quintus Fabius Maximus as dictator for six months. He chose to avoid decisive battles in which he might come up against Hannibal's superior cavalry, for which he came to be known as "Cunctator" (the delayer).

Impatient, in 216 the Romans replaced Fabius with two consuls, Gaius Terentius Varro and Lucius Aemilius Paullus. Normally Varro and Paullus would have had independent commands. This time the Senate ordered them to combine their forces in order to meet and defeat Hannibal once and for all. Together they commanded eight enlarged legions (5,000 infantry and 300 cavalry rather than 4,000 infantry and 200 cavalry). The troops first underwent a period of training, but by late summer they moved near to Hannibal at Cannae, in northern Apulia on the Adriatic coast. Counting their allied forces, Varro and Paullus commanded some 87,000 men, one of the largest land armies of antiquity. Against them Hannibal had 50,000 Carthaginian and allied troops (40,000 infantry and 10,000 cavalry).

The consuls alternated command daily, and on August 2 Varro, who then had the command, ordered both armies to engage the Carthaginians. Paullus reluctantly complied. The consuls led their forces onto an open plain on the right bank of the Aufidus River, Paullus having detached some 10,000 of his men to guard his camp. Varro positioned the Roman cavalry on both flanks, and since his forces were far superior in numbers, he arranged the infantry in a more compact center mass than was the custom, with short distances between the maniples in deep formation. Varro's intention was to launch a powerful drive through the Carthaginian center, smashing a wide hole. He would then use his superior numbers to annihilate first one Carthaginian wing and then the other.

Hannibal drew up his army in a linear formation. His cavalry, which was superior to the Romans, was on the flanks, with his brother Hasdrubal commanding the Spanish and Gallic cavalry on the left and the Numidian cavalry on the right. The infantry was in the center, and Hannibal placed his best-trained African heavy infantry on either side, with the center formed of Spanish and Gallic infantry in a convex position. Hannibal personally supervised its slow planned withdrawal before the heavy Roman pressure.

While he lured the Romans forward, Hannibal ordered his flanking cavalry to destroy their counterpart Roman cavalry units. The Roman center pinched out the forward bulge in the Carthaginian line, collapsing it inward. With the Romans apparently having broken through, Hannibal ordered his African infantry on each side of the line to wheel in.

Hannibal's cavalry then returned from their pursuit of the Roman cavalry and closed behind the close-packed Roman infantry, who were blinded by the dust kicked up on the dry plain. Over the next several days the Carthaginians attacked both Roman camps and killed or captured many more Romans; only about 14,500 men got away, Varro among them. The Carthaginian side lost 5,700 dead of whom 4,000 were Celts, but two or three times this number were probably wounded. Hannibal's daring double envelopment of a numerically superior enemy was one of the greatest tactical masterpieces of all military history. Never again did Roman commanders allow a full army to be drawn into open battle with Hannibal. Instead, those forces that remained in the field harassed Hannibal's supply lines and inhibited the provisioning of his forces. Cannae was a disaster for Rome, but the fact that Rome was able to recover from it says much for the Roman state.

Hannibal was later criticized for not having marched on Rome after the victory, but Rome was a large fortified city, and Hannibal could not have besieged it effectively. Instead, he sought to induce revolts against Rome. Much of southern Italy, including Capua, did indeed revolt, as did Syracuse in Sicily. The Gauls also rose in the north and wiped out a Roman army sent to reconquer them. Yet most Roman subjects in central Italy remained loyal. Many decades of effective Roman government and extensive grants of citizenship outweighed the catastrophes, and the Romans continued the fight.

References

Caven, Brian. *The Punic Wars*. New York: Barnes and Noble, 1980.

De Beer, Gavin. *Hannibal: The Struggle for Power in the Mediterranean*. London: Thames and Hudson, 1969.

Healy, Mark. *Cannae, 216 B.C.: Hannibal Smashes Rome's Army*. London: Osprey Military, 1994.

Lazenby, J. F. *Hannibal's War: A Military History of the Second Punic War*. Norman: University of Oklahoma Press, 1998.

Siege of Syracuse

Date	213–212 BCE	
Location	City of Syracuse, Sicily	
Opponents (* winner)	*Rome	Syracuse
Commander	Marcus Claudius Marcellus	Hippocrates, Epicydes
Approx. # Troops	16,000	Unknown
Importance	Gives Rome control of all Sicily	

Following his victory in the 216 BCE Battle of Cannae, Carthaginian general Hannibal Barca appeared to have the military advantage. The Romans avoided pitched battle with him unless on favorable terms, however, and Hannibal lacked the re-

Illustration of the Roman Siege of Syracuse during 213–212 BCE. The cranes protruding from the walls were used to drop grapples, known as "claws," into the Roman ships. The ships could then be lifted up and suddenly released, destroying them. (Photos.com)

sources to take the Roman cities and to protect those cities that rallied to him. Not until 214 did he receive significant reinforcements, when a Punic fleet managed to land men, elephants, and supplies at Locri. Consul Marcus Claudius Marcellus defeated Hannibal's repeated efforts to take Nola in the interim and then sailed with a Roman army to Sicily, where Propraetor Appius Claudius Pulcher was attempting to keep Syracuse from joining with Carthage.

Sicily was effectively divided in two. Rome controlled the west and north, while the staunchly pro-Roman tyrant of Syracuse, Hiero, controlled the remainder. Hiero died in late 216 or early 215, however. His young grandson Hieronymus succeeded him and immediately opened negotiations with Carthage. After little more than a year Hieronymus was murdered in a coup, and Syracuse became a democratic republic where the Carthaginian faction dominated. Hippocrates and Epicydes, two brothers of Syracusan extraction but natives of Carthage, led the pro-Carthage group and hoped to make all Sicily a Carthaginian stronghold. The government therefore sent Hippocrates and 4,000 men, many of them deserters from the Roman Army, to garrison the city of Leontini. From there Hippocrates began to raid the Roman portion of the island.

On his arrival in Sicily, Marcellus immediately seized Leontini and ordered all Roman deserters taken prisoner there to be beaten with rods and then beheaded. Hippocrates and Epicydes, who had joined his brother at Leontini, escaped and subsequently spread the story that the Romans had massacred all inhabitants of the city, including women and children. They exploited this lie to bring Syracusan soldiers over to their side and seize power in Syracuse.

Marcellus commenced military operations against Syracuse, probably in the spring of 213, supported by Appius Claudius Pulcher. The latter led troops against the city from the land side, while Marcellus utilized 68 quinqueremes to blockade and attack Syracuse from the sea. The Roman land force may have numbered 16,000 men.

Both sides employed a number of novel devices. For instance, Marcellus had four pairs of galleys specially prepared. He ordered removal of the starboard oars from one side and the port oars from the other. The two ships were then lashed together. Solid scaling ladders were mounted in their bows. These could be raised by means of ropes attached to pulleys at the tops of masts in the center of the ships. The resulting craft was known as a *sambuca* because it somewhat resembled a harplike instrument of the same name. The *sambuca* enabled troops in the ships to reach the top of the city walls.

On the land side, the Romans employed *tolleni*. These assault machines consisted of a boom and counterweight mounted on a mast. A large wicker or wooden basket was attached to the far end of the boom. This basket, loaded with men, could be lifted by soldiers pulling down the other end of the boom by means of ropes wound around a capstan.

The Syracusans, on the other hand, had a formidable asset in the celebrated geometrician Archimedes. Then in his seventies, he developed a number of innovative military devices. To attack the Roman ships, Archimedes arranged catapults and ballistas situated in batteries according to required range. He also came up with a type of crane that extended over the walls and employed a grapple, known as a claw, to hook onto a ship. A counterbalance enabled the crane to lift the ship. Letting it go again would dash the vessel to pieces. Another technique was to drop heavy stones on the ships that would crash through their hulls and sink them. A number of these boulders, one of which was said to weigh 10 talents (670 pounds), were dropped on the *sambucas,* destroying them. Archimedes also used smaller shorter-range catapults, known as Scorpions, to hurl boulders and stones at the attackers. The most controversial story of the siege concerns Archimedes' supposed invention of "burning mirrors" whereby the sun's rays were reflected to set fire to the Roman ships.

All Roman attempts to overcome the city, by land and by sea, were failures, including a night attack from the sea against a section of the wall that seemed to offer maximum protection from the Syracusan war machines. With only heavy casualties to show for his efforts, Marcellus settled in for a siege and blockade. In the meantime, he sent some Roman troops to defeat the other rebel Sicilian cities, in one instance surprising a force under Hippocrates near Acila and inflicting 8,000 casualties. Reportedly, only Hippocrates and 500 cavalry escaped.

Both sides reinforced in Sicily. The Romans built their strength up to three or four legions in addition to the allied troops. The Carthaginians sent an expeditionary force of 25,000 men, 3,000 cavalry, and 12 war elephants under the command of Himilco. They also broke through the blockade with 55 galleys commanded by Bomilcar.

The siege continued through the winter, and early in 212 Marcellus decided on a surprise attack. Outside Syracuse near a tower known as Galeagra while negotiations over prisoner exchange were under way, one of the Romans carefully calculated the height of the tower based on its even blocks of stone. Shortly thereafter, taking advantage of the distraction of a major festival in Syracuse dedicated to the goddess Artemis, Marcellus sent at night 1,000 men with scaling ladders against the Galeagra tower. The ladders proved to be the correct height, and the assaulting troops took the defenders by surprise.

Before the night was over, the Romans had opened the Hexapylon Gate to other troops and captured much of the city. Other portions of the city continued to hold out but suffered greatly from the ravages of disease, which seems to have hit the Romans less hard. Carthaginian ships continued to penetrate the blockade, but Marcellus confronted and turned back a massive Carthaginian convoy of 700 merchantmen protected by 150 warships.

With all hope gone, Epicydes fled the city. (Hippocrates had earlier died of disease.) In the summer of 212 Roman forces took the remainder of Syracuse. The Romans then gave the city over to pillage and fire. Although Marcellus had ordered that Archimedes be taken alive, he died with his city. Reportedly he was working on a mathematical problem when the Romans burst in upon him. The soldiers were ignorant of the identity of the old man who demanded that they not disturb his "circles" in the dirt, whereupon a soldier dispatched him with a single sword thrust.

References

Craven, Brian. *The Punic Wars*. New York: Barnes and Noble, 1992.
Goldsworthy, Adrian. *The Punic Wars*. London: Cassell, 2000.
Melegari, Vezio. *The Great Military Sieges*. New York: Crowell, 1972.

Battle of the Metaurus River

Date	207 BCE	
Location	Metaurus River in northern Italy	
Opponents (* winner)	*Rome	Carthage
Commander	Livius Salinator, Caius Claudius Nero	Hasdrubal Barca
Approx. # Troops	40,000	Far less than 40,000
Importance	The Romans prevent Hasdrubal from joining forces with Hannibal	

The Roman victory in the Battle of the Metaurus River in northern Italy in 207 BCE during the Second Punic War (218–202) prevented Carthaginian reinforcements from reaching Hannibal Barca to the south. In 218, 28-year-old Hannibal led

Carthaginian forces against Saguntum in Spain, the leaders of which appealed to Rome for aid. Following an eight-month siege Hannibal was victorious, but this action began the Second Punic War. In the spring of 218 Hannibal set out to invade Italy. Crossing the Pyrenees, he pushed through southern Gaul and then across the Alps, reaching northern Italy by October. For the next 16 years Hannibal campaigned throughout Italy. Even his brilliant success at Cannae in 216, however, could not bring him victory.

While Hannibal defeated all the Roman armies sent out against him, he was also desperately short of manpower and, in effect, was pinned in southern Italy, where he could not bring about the defeat of Rome. To win the war he would need substantial reinforcements, and he therefore called on his brother Hasdrubal in Spain to join him.

Although Roman galleys controlled much of the Mediterranean, Carthage was able to send supplies across the Strait of Gibraltar and through Spain. As a consequence, Rome sent men to Spain under Publius Cornelius Scipio in the hopes of severing the Carthaginian supply line. Scipio managed to regain territory lost earlier to Carthage north of the Ebro and then moved south of that river to engage Hasdrubal. In 208 the two fought a battle near Baecula (Bailén) that was a tactical victory for Scipio. Hasdrubal, mindful of the need to reinforce his brother, managed to withdraw.

Even though it meant abandoning Spain to Scipio, Hasdrubal crossed the Pyrenees with about 10,000 men and spent the winter in southern Gaul gathering reinforcements. In April 207 he crossed into northern Italy over the Alps via the Cenis Pass. The exact size of his force is unknown but may have been as many as 50,000 men, certainly too small to oppose the 15 Roman legions (perhaps 150,000 men) that now lay between the Barca brothers.

Hasdrubal initiated a siege of Placentia, probably to placate the Gauls in his army, but this was unsuccessful, and he then proceeded south to Fanum Fortunae (Fano) on the Adriatic Sea, where he encountered Roman forces under Consul Livius Salinator. Hannibal, having learned of his brother's siege of Placentia, moved slowly north to join him, closely watched by a Roman army of four legions under Consul Caius Claudius Nero. Unaware of the threat to his brother, Hannibal established camp at Canusium (Canora); Nero interposed his army between the two Carthaginian forces. Fortunately for the Romans, they captured two Carthaginian couriers proceeding south and learned of Hasdrubal's intention to link up with Hannibal in Umbria.

Leaving a force to keep watch on Hannibal, Nero struck north with his best troops—some 6,000 infantry and 1,000 cavalry—to join Livius. Moving quickly and instructing towns in advance of his troops to render all possible assistance, Nero reached Fanum Fortunae in about a week's march and secretly joined Livius at night. Nero convinced Livius that they should attack Hasdrubal before he learned of the arrival of the Roman reinforcements. Both armies were drawn up for battle when Hasdrubal sensed the increase in Roman numbers and decided to withdraw up the Via Flanania. Hasdrubal's local guides may have deserted during this difficult night movement, which delayed him in gaining the road. Nero caught up with the Carthaginians near the Metaurus River.

Hasdrubal hastily deployed his forces for battle. He placed his Gauls on the left (northern) flank behind a deep ravine. His Ligurian troops held the center with 10–15 war elephants in front, while Spanish troops were on the right. The Romans were also in three bodies. Nero commanded the Roman right, opposite the Gauls. The three bodies of troops on both sides were somewhat separated from one another and thus were not able to offer mutual support. The Romans probably had 40,000 men, and the Carthaginians had far fewer.

The battle began with an attack on the Roman left by the Spaniards. To the north meanwhile Nero discovered that the ravine kept him from closing with Hasdrubal. Nero therefore made a bold decision. Leaving only a small part of his force to hold his opponent in place, he marched most of his men southward behind the Roman lines and then turned into the rear of the attacking Spaniards. Hasdrubal's men could not hold against this Roman pincer. Sensing defeat, Hasdrubal drove directly at the Romans to die fighting, which occurred. His army was largely destroyed. The battle probably claimed some 10,000 Carthaginian dead, while the Romans lost only 2,000. Six elephants were also killed and the remainder captured.

Nero wasted no time but swiftly retraced his steps, in only six days. News of the victory, the first time the Carthaginians had been defeated in Italy, was received with joy in Rome, the Senate decreeing three days of public thanksgiving. Legend has it that Hannibal first heard of the battle when a Roman horseman approached the Carthaginian camp and hurled a sack at their lines. It was found to contain the head of Hasdrubal. However he learned of events, Hannibal broke camp on the news and took his army south to the port of Bruttium.

The Carthaginian defeat on the Metaurus River meant that Hannibal had little hope of actually defeating Rome. Although Mago, his remaining brother, landed near Genoa in 205 with 12,000 infantry and 2,000 cavalry, Mago seems to have made no real effort to link up with Hannibal. Wounded in battle, Mago was ordered home to defend Carthage but died of his wound en route.

Hannibal remained in Italy, undefeated, for six years after the Battle of Metaurus River, but even his brilliance could not compensate for his dwindling resources. Eventually he was ordered home. Scipio meanwhile defeated all Carthaginian forces sent against him and secured Spain. Rome would control Spain for the next 600 years.

References

Caven, Brian. *The Punic Wars.* New York: Barnes and Noble, 1980.

Dodge, Theodore Ayrault. *Hannibal: A History of the Art of War among the Carthaginians and the Romans Down to the Battle of Pydna, 168 B.C.* Mechanicsburg, PA: Stackpole Books, 1994.

Goldsworthy, Adrian. *The Punic Wars.* London: Cassell, 2000.

Lazenby, J. F. *Hannibal's War: A Military History of the Second Punic War.* Norman: University of Oklahoma Press, 1998.

Battle of Zama

Date	October? 202 BCE	
Location	Zama, southwest of Carthage in Numidia, North Africa	
Opponents (* winner)	*Rome and allied Numidians	Carthage
Commander	Publius Cornelius Scipio	Hannibal Barca
Approx. # Troops	30,000 Romans, 10,000 Numidians	40,000
Importance	Marks the end of the Second Punic War	

The Battle of Zama, fought in Numidia in North Africa, ended the Second Punic War. One of the most famous conflicts in history, the Second Punic War (218–202 BCE) pitted the great Carthaginian general Hannibal Barca against Rome. After Hannibal's destruction of two Roman legions in the Battle of Cannae in 216, one Roman army kept Hannibal under constant observation while others reconquered cities that had rebelled against Rome. Syracuse fell to the Romans in 212. In 210 at age 25, the brilliant Publius Scipio became commander of Roman forces in Spain. He quickly secured the upper hand. In 209 Scipio captured the Carthaginian stronghold of Cartagena, and in 206 in the Battle of Ilipa he ended Carthaginian influence in Spain.

Despite military victories in Spain and Sicily, Rome was sorely pressed by the long war. Finally, in 204, Scipio sailed with 30,000 well-trained and well-equipped troops to Africa. There in the Battle of the Great Plains he defeated a Carthaginian force of equal size. Carthage sued for peace and, at the same time, recalled Hannibal from Italy. In 203 Hannibal and 18,000 men returned to Carthage. Never defeated in battle in Italy, he had not been sufficiently supplied to win the war there.

The scene was set for the final struggle between Hannibal and Scipio, the two ablest generals of the war. More confident with Hannibal's return, Carthage broke the peace by seizing Roman supply ships scattered in a great storm. The final battle took place in 202, probably in October and at Zama, five days' march southwest of Carthage.

Hannibal moved west from Hadrumetum to near Zama and encamped less than four miles from the Romans. He proposed a parlay, to which Scipio agreed. The two men talked with only an interpreter present. Hannibal apparently sought peace, but Scipio refused. Because of the recent Carthaginian treachery in attacking the Roman supply ships, Scipio would not agree to peace without a battle.

That battle took place the next day, and Scipio held the upper hand. Just before the battle, Numidian king Masinissa joined him with 4,000 cavalry and 6,000 infantry, a fact unknown to Hannibal. Each side then had about 40,000 men. Probably Hannibal enjoyed a slight overall numerical advantage, but Scipio had more cavalry.

Hannibal positioned more than 80 war elephants in front. Behind these he placed his infantry, in Roman fashion, in a series of three separate linear formations (although not in maniples). The first body consisted of 12,000 seasoned mercenary troops: Ligurian and Gallic swordsmen, Balearic slingers, and Mauretanian archers. The second rank consisted of the less experienced Carthaginian and Libyan troops, while the third grouping was of Hannibal's best troops, the seasoned veterans who had campaigned with him in Italy. Numidian cavalry protected Hannibal's left flank, and Carthaginian cavalry protected his right flank. Hannibal expected the first two bodies of infantry to absorb the initial Roman assault, whereupon he would fall on the Romans with his veterans.

Scipio placed his infantry facing the Carthaginian line of battle. His Italian cavalry was on the left flank, and his Numidian cavalry under Masinissa was on the right flank. Scipio's infantry was not in solid ranks but instead was subdivided into smaller maniples, with spaces between the lines to help absorb the shock of the Carthaginian war elephants. Fearing these, Scipio placed the maniples one behind the other, abandoning the usual Roman checkerboard formation. At the beginning of the battle these gaps of the hastati (the youngest infantrymen), each armed with two pila (throwing spears) and the famous short sword or gladius, were filled by velites (light infantry), armed with javelins and the gladius.

The battle began with Hannibal advancing his elephants toward the Roman lines. The elephants were not well trained, however, and many of them soon became disoriented by Roman trumpets and bugles and bolted to their left, causing Hannibal's Numidian cavalry to stampede and greatly assisting in their rout by Masinissa's cavalry. Meanwhile, Scipio's Roman cavalry attacked and defeated the Carthaginian cavalry on Hannibal's right, driving it from the field. The situation now resembled the Battle of Cannae in reverse, with the Romans poised to envelop the Carthaginian flanks.

Although the first body of Hannibal's infantry fought well, the second failed to come up on time, leading the mercenaries in the first rank to believe that they had been deserted, whereupon they withdrew. Hannibal then brought up his seasoned veterans but earlier than he had planned. These now clashed with the retreating mercenaries. Scipio re-formed his infantry before Hannibal could strike, and his cavalry fell on Hannibal's veterans from the flanks, cutting them to pieces. Scipio's horsemen pursued and killed many of those attempting to flee.

The Romans won a decisive victory. Carthaginian losses are variously estimated at 20,000–25,000 killed and 8,500–20,000 captured. Only Hannibal and some of the cavalry escaped to Hadrumetum. Roman losses were perhaps 1,500–2,500 killed, while Masinissa may have lost 2,500 men killed. Zama was payback for Cannae. Well-trained Roman infantry, supported by a superior cavalry force, had annihilated a larger poorly trained infantry force that was weak in cavalry.

Hannibal urged the Carthaginians to sue for peace. According to the terms dictated by Scipio, Carthage retained its autonomy but had to give up all its elephants and all but 10 of its triremes. Carthage also ceded Spain to Rome as well as the Mediterranean islands that Carthage had held and was obliged to pay a large indemnity of 10,000 talents over a 50-year span. Furthermore, Carthage was forced to agree not to wage war, even in Africa, without Roman approval. Hannibal, however, took charge of the Carthaginian state and re-formed the government, paying the heavy tribute demanded by Rome. In 195 Rome demanded that he be surrendered. Hannibal fled to Syria, where he received asylum. Learning that he was about to be turned over to Rome, however, he committed suicide in 183.

The Battle of Zama gave Rome control of the Mediterranean world. A grateful Rome accorded Scipio the title of "Africanus." Rome also meted out harsh treatment to the allied states that had revolted and scarcely acknowledged the services of loyal states. During the course of the conflict, the Senate had also greatly increased its power. One other consequence of the war was the creation of a standing Roman army of four legions to hold the two new provinces in Spain. The men enlisted for long terms and were paid, but this standing professional army had ominous consequences for the Roman political system.

References

Caven, Brian. *The Punic Wars.* New York: Barnes and Noble, 1980.

Dodge, Theodore Ayrault. *Hannibal: A History of the Art of War among the Carthaginians and the Romans Down to the Battle of Pydna, 168 B.C.* Mechanicsburg, PA: Stackpole Books, 1994.

Lazenby, J. F. *Hannibal's War: A Military History of the Second Punic War.* Norman: University of Oklahoma Press, 1998.

Liddell Hart, Basil. *Scipio Africanus: Greater Than Napoleon.* New York: Da Capo, 1994.

Nardo, Don. *The Battle of Zama: Battles of the Ancient World.* San Diego: Lucent Books, 1996.

Battle of Gaixia

Date	December 202 BCE	
Location	Gaixia (Kai-hsia) (today's Anhui (Anhwei) Province), China	
Opponents (* winner)	*Principality of Han	Chu
Commander	Liu Bang	Xiang Yu
Approx. # Troops	300,000	100,000
Importance	Establishes the Han dynasty in China	

The Battle of Gaixia (Kai-hsia) in China in December 202 BCE established the Han dynasty in power. In 256 BCE a new ruler, Zheng (Cheng), had come to power in the westernmost Chinese state of Qin (Ch'in). He took the ruling name of Qin Shi Huangdi (Ch'in Shih-huang-ti) and between 230 and 221 conquered his rivals in the remaining seven Chinese states. He then united China under the Qin (Ch'in) dynasty, which gave its name to China. The emperor divided China into administrative districts, standardized weights and measures, ordered a widespread disarmament, and melted down the weapons. "The First Emperor," as he is known, died in 210. His tomb, with its 7,000 thousand life-size terra-cotta soldiers (discovered in 1974), is an important source of information about the period.

With no strong hand at the seat of power, rebellions soon overtook the Qin dynasty; two individuals emerged as chief claimants to replace the Qin. They were Liu Bang (Liu Pang), a former peasant who had risen to be a bureaucrat under Qin Shi Huangdi, and Xiang Yu (Hsiang Yü), a professional soldier from Chu (Ch'u), the largest of the previous states and located in east-central China. Xiang established his military reputation leading Chu forces against the Qin beginning in 209 BCE. Liu meanwhile raised forces in northern China, in present-day Hubei (Hupeh) Province, against the Qin. In 208 he joined Xiang in establishing a new ruler in Chu as a rival to the Qin. Xiang then marched to the city of Ju Lu (Chu-lu) to raise a siege by Qin forces. Xiang's victory there gave him command of all forces opposing the Qin.

The new Chu ruler meanwhile dispatched Liu to attack territory around the Qin capital of Xianyang (Hsien-yang). There Liu Bang won a number of victories, the most important being at Lantian (Lan-t'ien) in late 206. As a consequence, Liu captured the last Qin ruler and secured the capital. Liu then set up a new administration, winning the support of the peasants through reforms.

A few months later Xiang arrived at Xianyang. He promptly executed the last Qin ruler, seized the treasury for his own benefit, and allowed his soldiers to loot. Liu opposed these actions but kept quiet. Xiang reorganized China, eschewing the strongly centralized Qin state in favor of a confederation of 19 kingdoms. Xiang cemented his position by ordering the execution of the Chu ruler he had recently installed in power. Xiang assigned Liu one of the 19 new kingdoms, the most remote of the 3 kingdoms carved from former Qin territory. It was known as the Western Han region, and Liu styled himself the "King of Han."

Liu decided to challenge his former colleague, however, because he believed that he had not been adequately compensated for his services and because there were rumors that Xiang sought his assassination. In mid-206 Liu took up arms against Xiang. Liu first conquered the other two kingdoms of the former Qin territory. He used the murder of the Chu king to brand Xiang a regicide and to rally the other kingdoms against him. Liu then advanced on Xiang's capital of Pengcheng (P'eng-ch'eng), only to have his army virtually annihilated. Liu escaped with only several dozen cavalry. He suffered another major defeat along the Huang He (Huang Ho, Hwang Ho, Yellow River), again escaping with only a few of his men.

The only positives for Liu were victories achieved by his generals in the eastern provinces.

The two opposing armies then encamped for some months on opposite sides of the river at Guangwu (Kwangwu). Although Liu rejected Xiang's call for single combat, Xiang did wound Liu with a crossbow bolt, whereupon Liu withdrew to nearby Xingyang (Hsing-yang). Xiang laid siege to the city. Liu's generals were so successful in harassing Xiang's supply lines, however, that Xiang was forced to take much of his force to deal with them. This allowed Liu to defeat the remainder of Xiang's troops at Xingyang, whereupon Xiang returned. Liu again refused battle and withdrew into the mountains. Xiang then offered to split China with Liu Bang, who agreed. Ziang took the west, and Liu took the east.

This arrangement did not last. Liu's advisers convinced him that he had the support of most provincial leaders. That and reports of the weakening of Chu forces led Liu to take up arms again. The decisive confrontation occurred at Gaixia (Kai-hsia), in present-day Anhui (Anhwei) Province, beginning in December 202. There Xiang and some 100,000 men constructed a walled camp, which Liu and a reported 300,000 men surrounded. Over the ensuing weeks a series of attacks at different points along the defenses brought success.

Early one morning at the end of December, Xiang and 800 cavalry broke out, hoping to avoid defeat and capture. Liu sent 5,000 horsemen in pursuit. Xiang reached the Wujiang (Wu-kiang or Wu) River with only 100 men and was cornered by the Han cavalry. Xiang then led a series of forays against his enemy. Although he and his men killed a number of the Han each time, his own force grew steadily smaller. Knowing that the end was near, Xiang committed suicide.

All Chu territory now surrendered to Liu except the city of Lu. Liu invested that city, which refused to submit until Liu rode out with the head of Xiang. Impressed with the courage of the defenders, Liu treated the city honorably, allowed Xiang's body to be buried with full honors, and refused to execute any of the family of his defeated foe.

Liu's victory removed the last threat to his power and enabled him to establish the Han dynasty under the imperial name of Gaozu (Kao Tsu). A highly effective emperor, Gaozu ruled until 195 BCE, reforming the administration and embracing Confucianism. He and his successors also expanded the territory of the empire.

References

Davis, Paul K. *100 Decisive Battles: From Ancient Times to the Present.* Santa Barbara, CA: ABC-CLIO, 1999.

Sima Qian. *Record of the Great Historian: Han Dynasty I.* Translated by Barton Watson. New York: Columbia University Press, 1993.

Twitchett, Denis, and Michael Lewis. *The Cambridge History of China,* Vol. 1. New York: Cambridge University Press, 1986.

Battle of Pydna

Date	June 22, 168 BCE	
Location	Leucus River, south of the city of Pydna	
Opponents (* winner)	*Rome	Macedon
Commander	Lucius Aemilius Paullus	Perseus
Approx. # Troops	38,000	4,000 cavalry, 40,000 infantry
Importance	Ends the Third Macedonian War and the Macedonian threat to Greece and secures Roman control over the Near East	

The Battle of Pydna, which took place in Greece during the Third Macedonian War (171–167 BCE), ended the Macedonian threat to Greece and solidified Roman control over the Near East. Rome first intervened in Greece in 215 during the Second Punic War. The great Carthaginian general Hannibal Barca, hoping to siphon off some Roman forces, concluded an alliance with King Philip V of Macedon, ushering in the First Macedonian War (215–205 BCE). Rome dispatched troops to Greece and, operating in conjunction with forces from the various Greek city-states, over the next decade helped prevent the Macedonians from again conquering the peninsula.

Despite their failure in this decade-long war, the Macedonian kings were determined to reestablish Macedonian control over Greece. In 200 Philip concluded an alliance with King Antiochus III of the Seleucid Empire (present-day Syria), one of the successor kingdoms formed from Alexander the Great's empire, whereupon Rome declared war. The Second Macedonian War (200–196 BCE) ended with Philip V's defeat by Rome in the Battle of Cynoscephalae in 197. Philip V died in 179; his son Perseus succeeded him and renewed the effort to conquer Greece. Rome therefore allied with Pergamum against Perseus in the Third Macedonian War (171–167 BCE).

Initially the Romans did poorly. The troops they sent to Greece landed on the east coast of Illyria and marched to Macedon, only to be defeated in three separate campaigns during 171–170. Finally, in 168, Rome sent out a capable commander in Lucius Aemilius Paullus along with reinforcements. After taking command, Paullus retrained his forces and then set out in June 168. Paullus planned a hammer-and-anvil battle. He would hold Perseus in camp with part of his force while sending most of his troops around in a flanking attack from the northwest against the Macedonian rear. Perseus learned of the flanking movement, however; he extricated his army in time and then moved north. Paullus quickly reunited his forces at Dium and set out in pursuit. The Romans caught up with the Macedonians at the Leucus River, south of the city of Pydna. Paullus established his camp to the west of the Macedonians, in the foothills of Mount Olocrus.

On the night of June 21–22, 168, a lunar eclipse occurred. A Roman officer had predicted the event, so the Romans were forewarned and chose to regard it as a good omen. The Macedonians were surprised and troubled by the eclipse, believing it to be a bad omen. The exact effect of this on the resulting battle is unclear, however.

On the afternoon of June 22, 168, both sides were observing a truce to allow them to draw water from the Leucus when a misunderstanding led to a rush for weapons. Perseus organized his forces first and crossed the Leucus probably with two phalanxes in the center, mercenaries on his left flank and cavalry on his right. Reportedly he had at his disposal some 4,000 cavalry and 40,000 infantry. Paullus probably had two legions in the center, with cavalry on his left flank facing that of the Macedonians and some Italian allied light infantry, along with a few war elephants, on his right.

At first Perseus enjoyed success as his phalanxes crashed into the forming Roman legions. The mercenaries on his left also beat back a Roman counterattack by Paullus's allied infantry. The phalanx could only operate effectively on flat ground, however, and as they advanced the Macedonian formations broke up in the foothills of the Roman camp. Paullus seized the opportunity of openings in the Macedonian line to insert his troops and war elephants.

The Romans exacted a terrible price, reportedly killing up to 20,000 men and taking another 11,000 prisoner. The victors reported their losses at 100 killed and 400 wounded. Perseus fled the field with his cavalry.

The Battle of Pydna ended the Third Macedonian War. It also extinguished Macedonia as a threat to its neighbors. Rome disarmed the Macedonians and sought out and killed or sent to Italy all those who had aided Perseus. Rome also divided Macedonia into four unrelated republics that were forced to pay a moderate tribute. Perseus died in captivity in Italy. Rome now took control of Illyria and stripped Rhodes of its fleet.

References

Adcock, Frank Ezra. *The Roman Art of War under the Republic.* 1940; reprint, New York: Barnes and Noble, 1960.

Gabba, Emilio. *Republican Rome, the Army, and the Allies.* Translated by P. J. Cuff. Oxford: Basil Blackwell, 1976.

Keppie, L. J. F. *The Making of the Roman Army.* London: Batsford, 1984.

Siege of Carthage

Date	149–146 BCE	
Location	The city of Carthage, on the Gulf of Tunis in present-day Tunisia, North Africa	
Opponents (* winner)	*Rome	Carthage
Commander	Publius Scipio Aemilianus	Hasdrubal Barca
Approx. # Troops	40,000–50,000	Unknown
Importance	City of Carthage is destroyed and Africa becomes a Roman province	

After its defeat at Zama, Carthage observed the terms of its treaty with Rome and abstained from any provocation. Hannibal Barca, the legendary Carthaginian general, put Carthaginian finances in good order and paid off the indemnity. When Carthage began to prosper again, Roman fears and hatred were again aroused. No Roman could forget that it had taken 25 legions to subdue Hannibal.

Roman leaders therefore schemed with Masinissa, the ruler of neighboring Numidia, encouraging him to encroach on what remained of Carthage's territory. Finally after many vain appeals to Rome, Carthage was goaded into an attempt at self-defense. In 150 BCE Carthage declared war, sending an army under Hasdrubal against Masinissa. This was a violation of the peace that had ended the Second Punic War whereby Carthage could declare war only with Roman consent. The Roman Senate agreed that Carthage had to be destroyed and dispatched a sizable force to Utica in North Africa. This city had been Carthage's most important ally but rallied to Rome just before the war. This provided Rome with an important base less than 30 miles from Carthage.

The Roman expeditionary force to North Africa was under two consuls, Manlius Manilus, who had command of four legions of some 40,000–50,000 men, and Lucius Marcius Censorinus, who had charge of the fleet with 50 quinqueremes. Thus began the Third Punic War (149–146 BCE), which was basically the siege of Carthage. The Romans fully expected a short, profitable, and virtually bloodless campaign.

The Carthaginians opened negotiations with the two consuls and were informed that they must surrender their fleet, arms, and missile weapons. The Roman position was that since Carthage would pass under Roman protection, the city would have no need of weapons. The Carthaginians agreed. They surrendered their fleet, which was burned in the harbor, as well as a reported 200,000 sets of infantry weapons and 2,000 catapults. The consuls then announced that the inhabitants would have to leave the city, as the Romans intended to destroy it. They could rebuild at any location so long as it was at least 80 *stades* (10 miles) from the sea.

The Carthaginian envoys returned to the city with the Roman demand. Following initial shock and despair, the Carthaginian Council rejected the Roman demand, declared war on Rome, shut the gates of the city, and commenced the manufacture of weapons. The Romans were surprised, having assumed that with Carthage virtually disarmed its leaders would have no choice but to accept their demands.

The Romans then mounted an assault, led by Manilus from the land side and Censorinus from the sea, on the city. Carthage had excellent defenses, being surrounded by three walls that were almost 50 feet high and sufficiently wide to contain stalls for elephants and horses as well as troop quarters. The Carthaginians easily repelled the first two assaults. When the Romans sent troops to find timber to build additional catapults, they were surprised by Carthaginian forces under Hamilcon that had been harassing their base camps. In one engagement a cavalry force led by Himilco Phameas inflicted some 500 casualties on the Romans and seized a number of weapons.

Despite this setback the Romans located the timber to build a number of new siege machines, including two large ones equipped with battering rams. The Romans employed these to make a breach in the wall, but the Carthaginians quickly repaired it and then mounted sorties from the city, setting fire to and destroying both machines. Scipio Aemilianus, tribune of the Fourth Legion, distinguished himself in the fighting both by rescuing some trapped legionnaires and in subsequent engagements against Hasdrubal.

In the spring of 148 Himilco defected, bringing over a reported 2,200 Carthaginian cavalry to the Romans. Two new Roman consuls, L. Calpurnius Piso Ceasonibus for the army and Lucius Hostilius Mancinus for the navy, arrived at Carthage. They concentrated their resources against minor cities close to Carthage and destroyed most of them. Piso then retired for the winter to Utica.

In Rome meanwhile Scipio was elected at age 37 as consul and set sail for Africa with additional forces in 147. He landed at Utica and then proceeded to Carthage, rescuing Mancinus and a number of his men who had been cut off by the Carthaginians. Mancinus returned to Italy, and Scipio undertook the construction of extensive siege works.

The Carthaginians secretly built 50 triremes. Instead of using the element of surprise to launch an attack on the unprepared Roman fleet, the Punic admiral paraded his ships (to give his crews practice) and returned to port. When he sallied out to do battle several days later the Roman fleet was ready, and the Carthaginians were soundly beaten.

At the beginning of the spring of 146 Scipio launched his major offensive. Employing Carthaginian deserters as guides, the Romans managed to overcome the three lines of Carthaginian defenses and penetrate the city itself, with vicious fighting in the narrow streets and in the six-story buildings along them. Fighting was house to house and room to room, and the Romans laid plank bridges from houses already taken to the remainder, eventually reaching the slopes of the Byrsa, where the citadel was situated. Once the buildings had been taken, Scipio ordered that the city be fired. The flames raged for six days and nights. Many Carthaginians were trapped in the buildings and died. Roman engineers then leveled what remained of the structures.

The Carthaginian leaders at Byrsa appealed to Scipio to spare the lives of those who wished to leave. He agreed except for any Roman deserters. Reportedly 50,000 people departed the Byrsa, to be held under guard. This left only some 900 Roman deserters and Hasdrubal and his wife and sons. Hasdrubal turned traitor, however, opening the gates to the Romans and begging Scipio for mercy. Hasdrubal's wife then came out on the roof of the temple, which the defenders had set on fire; she denounced Hasdrubal for his treachery and leapt with her sons into the flames.

The Romans plundered the city (Scipio took nothing for himself) and utterly demolished it. The 50,000 survivors of Carthage, all that remained of a presiege population of 500,000, were sold as slaves. The terrible destruction gave rise to the term "Carthaginian Peace." Africa now became a Roman province.

References
Craven, Brian. *The Punic Wars.* New York: Barnes and Noble, 1992.
Goldsworthy, Adrian. *The Punic Wars.* London: Cassell, 2000.

Siege of Alesia

Date	July-October 52 BCE	
Location	Alesia (today Alise-Sainte Reine) on Mount Auxois, near the source of the Seine in east central Gaul, today France	
Opponents (* winner)	*Romans	Gauls
Commander	Julius Caesar	Vercingetorix
Approx. # Troops	55,000	90,000
Importance	Ends the Gallic revolt; pacified Gaul becomes a rich Roman province	

The Roman First Triumvirate (60–51 BCE) gave Julius Caesar the consulship in 59 BCE and then a military command for 5 years (later increased to 10 years) in Illyricum (area of the former Yugoslavia) and in Gaul on both sides of the Alps (France and northern Italy). During 58–57 Caesar reduced the disunited tribes of northern France and Belgium. He also undertook amphibious operations along the Atlantic seaboard in 56. In June the next year Caesar caused a great bridge to be built across the Rhine near present-day Bonn and marched his army over it into Germany. After receiving the submission of several German tribes, Caesar returned to Gaul and destroyed the bridge.

After campaigning for three months in Britain, Caesar returned to Gaul again in 55. He planned to split up his legions and station them in different parts of Gaul for the winter. Gaul was by no means subjugated, as Caesar soon discovered, for a formidable coalition of central Gallic tribes developed against Roman rule. The uprising began in the area of present-day Orléans, a particularly important area as a meeting place of the Druids who dominated affairs throughout Gaul. This was followed by outbreaks elsewhere, including the Belgae in the northern part of Gaul. Caesar faced the distinct possibility that his legions might be destroyed piecemeal; indeed, one of his garrisons (more than a legion in size) was massacred. Another legion, at Samarobriva (Amiens), was narrowly saved from destruction.

In 53 Caesar held a series of conferences with the Gallic chiefs at Samarobriva and elsewhere in an effort to end disaffection. In 52, however, the tribes of Gaul rose in general revolt. They selected as their leader the only talented military commander produced by the Gauls in the wars against Rome, young Vercingetorix of the Arverni tribe in central Gaul. He adopted a scorched-earth strategy, destroying all Gallic settlements that might aid the Romans. A series of battles and sieges followed. Caesar proved to be a master of both siege warfare and rapid offensive movement and showed himself to be one of the greatest military commanders in history.

The culmination of the fighting in Gaul came in the great siege of Alesia in 52. Caesar concentrated his efforts against the principal Arverni stronghold of Gergovia but was obliged to break off the siege with the revolt of the Aedui, the other principal tribe of the region. Caesar therefore recalled his deputy Labienus, whom he had sent to the north, and the two of them mounted a siege of Alesia (present-day Alise-Sainte Reine, France), where Vercingetorix had retired following a defeat. Alesia was situated on the top of Mount Auxois near the source of the Seine.

The siege of Alesia lasted from July to October 52. Vercingetorix commanded more than 90,000 men. Caesar had only 55,000 men, and of this number some 40,000 were legionnaires, with the remainder Gallic cavalry and auxiliaries. Caesar ordered his legionnaires to construct both a wall of contravallation and one of circumvallation; each was roughly 10 miles in circumference and incorporated a ditch 20 feet wide and deep, backed by two additional trenches 15 feet wide and deep. Behind these the Romans constructed ramparts with 12-foot-high palisades and towers every 130 yards. The Romans placed sharpened stakes facing outward in front of and in the ditches.

Caesar's foresight in having a defensive works facing outward as well as inward was soon manifest. Responding to appeals from Vercingetorix, a vast Gallic relief force numbering as many as 250,000 men and 8,000 cavalry gathered around Alesia and besieged the besiegers. Caesar had laid in considerable stocks of food and had an assured water supply, so he calmly continued his own siege operations, repulsing two relief attempts and a breakout sortie with heavy losses.

To win time Vercingetorix tried to send out the women and children from Alesia, but Caesar refused to allow them through the lines. With the situation hopeless, Vercingetorix surrendered. Taken to Rome for Caesar's triumph, Vercingetorix was then executed.

The defeat at Alesia broke Gallic resistance to Rome. The Gauls' failure to unite had cost them dearly. At least a third of their men of military age had been killed in the fighting, and another third were sold into slavery. The vast majority of Gauls hastened to renew their fealty to Rome. After a few mopping-up operations the next year, the Gallic Wars were over. Gaul would be an integral part of the Roman Empire for the next 500 years. The newly conquered territories, with a population of perhaps 5 million people, proved immensely important to Rome because of their vast resources of agriculture, stock breeding, mining, and metallurgy as well as the production of pottery and glass. During the conquest of Gaul, however, Caesar's army had grown from 2 to 13 legions, making Caesar a threat to Rome itself.

References

Caesar, Gaius Julius. *Seven Commentaries on the Gallic War.* New York: Oxford University Press, 1996.

Grant, Michael. *Julius Caesar.* New York: M. Evans, 1992.

Battle of Pharsalus

Date	August 9, 48 BCE	
Location	North of the Enipeus River, on the Plain of Pharsalus near Cynoscephalae in Thessaly	
Opponents (* winner)	Roman legions (Rome)	Roman legions (Spain)
Commander	Julius Caesar	Gnaeus Pompeius (Pompey)
Approx. # Troops	22,000 infantry, 1,000 cavalry	45,000 infantry, 7,000 cavalry
Importance	Caesar controls the Balkans, and much of the remainder of Roman territories now declares for him	

Following the Punic Wars the Roman republic was on its deathbed. Slavery had concentrated wealth in the hands of a few, and latifundia (great estates worked by slaves) took the place of small freehold farms. Landless peasants flocked to Rome, where candidates for public office bought their votes. Increasingly, the senators came to think of the state as their private property. The army too became corrupt. Ordinary citizens raised private armies. No longer were soldiers drawn into the military from a sense of duty; instead, they joined the military as a means of making a living. These professional soldiers recognized neither the Senate nor the law but rather only the authority of their generals.

Key figures arose in the ambitious millionaire Licinus Crassus and the arrogant young Gnaeus Pompeius, known as Pompey. Both had established their military reputations under Lucius Cornelius Sulla, who had defeated King Mithradates of Pontus and made himself dictator in Rome in 81 BCE, only to retire three years later. As consuls, Crassus and Pompey soon demonstrated their independence of Senate control. Pompey commanded Roman forces against Mithradates, who was again at war with Rome. An outstanding general, Pompey during 68–62 defeated Mithradates, captured Judea, and annexed the city-states of Syria. In 60 Pompey allied himself with the aristocratic Gaius Julius Caesar and Crassus in an unofficial partnership known as the First Triumvirate (60–51 BCE), cemented by Pompey's marriage to Caesar's daughter Julia.

The division of spoils under the First Triumvirate made Caesar consul in 59, followed by a military command for 5 years (later increased to 10 years) in Illyricum (Yugoslavia) and in Gaul on both sides of the Alps (France and northern Italy). Pompey received the governorship of Spain for 5 years, which he exercised by proxy from Rome. Pompey's wife Julia died in 54, and a group of senators talked Pompey into a breach with Caesar to limit the tenure of Caesar's command in Gaul and prevent him from again becoming consul. In 53 Crassus was killed in fighting in Parthia across the Euphrates, and the First Triumvirate was over. The next year amid increasing civil unrest, Pompey became sole consul where there had always been two, a precedent for emperors. Caesar's term in Gaul came to an end in 49. If he wanted to run for consul again, he would have to give up his military command. When Pompey would not do the same, Caesar decided on military action.

Caesar and Pompey (and their legions) now fought for control of the Roman state. Outnumbered by Pompey's potential force, Caesar relied on boldness. Announcing that "the die is cast," he broke Roman law by bringing his legions across the Rubicon River into Italy proper. Caesar quickly occupied Italy, while Pompey withdrew to the Balkans. Following rapid expeditions to subdue Corsica and Sardinia, Caesar sailed to Spain and secured the surrender of two armies loyal to Pompey at Ilerda and Gades (Cádiz). He also took Massilia (Marseilles) in southern Gaul. Caesar then returned to Italy and had the Senate declare him dictator.

In January 48 after assembling sufficient shipping for half of his army, Caesar pursued Pompey into the Balkans. Caesar sailed across the Adriatic to Dyrrachium (Durrës), where Pompey was building his forces, and laid siege to it. When Caesar's subordinate Mark Antony (Marcus Antonius) arrived in March with reinforcements, Pompey sallied from Dyrrachium and drove Caesar away. Leaving a strong detachment at Dyrrachium, Pompey then cautiously pursued Caesar into Thessaly in northern Greece while another army loyal to Pompey secured Macedonia. Caesar hoped that by threatening to attack this latter force he could draw Pompey into an attack. Pompey, who now had Caesar heavily outnumbered and could thus wear him down, was reluctant to risk his advantage in pitched battle but was apparently goaded into it by advisers who convinced him that Romans would want to see Caesar crushed in actual combat.

Pompey and Caesar and their armies came together at the Plain of Pharsalus, near Cynoscephalae in Thessaly, in August 48. Both armies were camped next to the Epineus River a few miles from each other. Each day the armies deployed, only to return to camp; gradually Caesar moved his forces closer to Pompey, hoping to entice him into an attack. Pompey had some 45,000 infantry and 7,000 cavalry, while Caesar commanded only 22,000 infantry and 1,000 cavalry. Caesar's left flank rested on the steep banks of the Enipeus River. His right flank was the weak point. Here his cavalry was outnumbered 7 to 1. Caesar formed his troops in three lines, but he held back six cohorts, about 2,000 men, in the so-called fourth line to cover his right rear. He extended the intervals between his cohorts to match the frontage of Pompey's line, which was drawn up in normal formation. Caesar's third line, as usual, was a reserve to the other two. Caesar took his own position with the fourth line to the right rear.

Pompey refused to allow his men to attack, holding them in a compact mass to break Caesar's charge. Pompey thought that enemy javelins would be less effective if the men were stationary rather than running forward. Caesar therefore ordered an attack on Pompey's stationary force. Caesar's men rushed forward, javelins leveled. When they saw that Pompey's men were not running out to meet them, Cesar's veterans knew immediately to halt their charge so as not to wear themselves out. After a short interval they resumed the charge, hurling their javelins and drawing their swords. Pompey's side threw their own javelins and then resorted to their swords.

At the moment of the infantry impact Pompey launched his cavalry on his left flank, supported by archers and slingers, against Caesar's horsemen. Although Caesar's cavalry fought well, they fell back from Pompey's vastly superior numbers. Then Caesar wheeled out with his six reserve cohorts. They charged with such force that Pompey's cavalry were scattered. This left Pompey's archers and slingers exposed, and they were overwhelmed and slain. Caesar then turned the fourth line against the left flank of Pompey's more numerous army and drove it in from the rear.

At the same time Caesar ordered forward his third line, which had been inactive to this point. This fresh force and the fourth line attacking from the rear set Pompey's army to flight. Caesar would not allow his men to stop to plunder and instead pressed the pursuit. Pompey escaped with only a handful of followers, reaching the coast and sailing for Egypt. Caesar's superior military leadership and bold innovation had carried the day against a capable yet unimaginative commander who had failed to divine Caesar's intentions. The Battle of Pharsalus cost Pompey 15,000 killed and 24,000 prisoners; Caesar lost 230 killed and perhaps 2,000 wounded. Greece and Asia now declared for Caesar.

In Egypt, Pompey's remaining troops mutinied, and he was murdered. Caesar then campaigned in Egypt and Asia Minor in the company of the beautiful 22-year-old Cleopatra, whom he confirmed as queen of Egypt. Cleopatra bore Caesar a son, Caesarion. Caesar returned to Rome and, in further lightning wars, crushed Pompey's sons in North Africa in 46 and in Spain in 45. In 46 Caesar was appointed dictator for 10 years. The republic was over.

References

Caesar, Julius. *War Commentaries of Caesar.* Translated by Rex Warner. New York: New American Library, 1960.

Grant, Michael. *The Army of the Caesars.* New York: Scribner, 1974.

———. *Julius Caesar.* New York: M. Evans, 1992.

Suetonius. *The Twelve Caesars.* Translated by Michael Graves. London: Penguin, 1957.

Battle of Actium

Date	September 2, 31 BCE	
Location	Off Actium in western Greece, just south of the entrance to the Gulf of Ambracia in Epirus	
Opponents (* winner)	Roman Western provinces	Roman Eastern provinces
Commander	Gaius Julius Caesar Octavianus (Octavian), Marcus Vipsanius Agrippa	Mark Antony, Cleopatra
Approx. # Troops	60,000 men? 200 ships	60,000 men? 170 ships
Importance	Octavian is able to invade Egypt and defeats Antony and Cleopatra there	

The Battle of Actium in 31 BCE ended the civil wars of the late Roman Republic and allowed Octavian (later Augustus) to establish the Roman Empire. On March 15, 44 BCE, in Rome, assassins stabbed to death Julius Caesar shortly after he had extended his dictatorship to life. Caesar's lieutenant, Mark Antony (Marcus Antonius), turned the Senate against the murderers, who then fled for their lives. Encouraged by Cicero, the Senate rallied against Antony's effort to succeed Caesar, and its forces defeated him in pitched battle in 43.

Antony, however, had allied himself with the 20-year-old Octavian, who had been adopted in his great-uncle Caesar's will as his principal heir and probably also as his son. They formed a partnership to "reform the state" and avenge Caesar's murder. Among some 2,000 executed were 300 senators and Cicero. Antony and Octavian also defeated the republican forces in the Battle of Philippi in Macedonia in 42, after which both Brutus and Cassius, two of the principal conspirators in the death of Caesar, committed suicide.

Octavian and Antony then battled to see who would hold power. Octavian controlled Italy and the western provinces, while Antony's strength was in the eastern provinces. Antony ignored his wife Octavia (Octavian's sister) and withdrew into Egypt with a large army. While there he fell in love with the beautiful Queen Cleopatra, which allowed Octavian to portray Antony as sacrificing Roman interests to those of Egypt. Octavian also induced the Senate to declare war on Cleopatra.

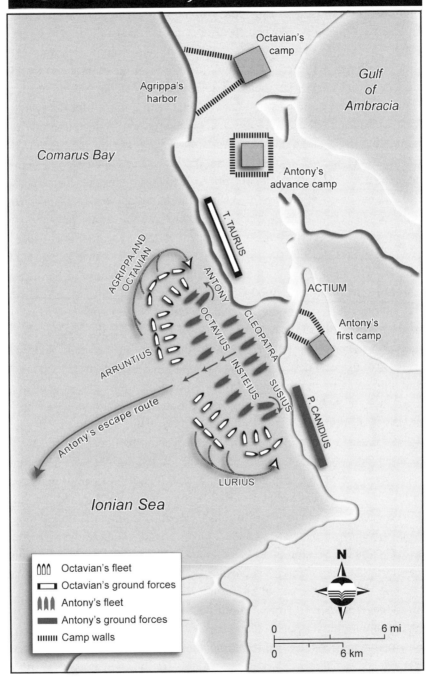

NAVAL BATTLE OF ACTIUM
SEPTEMBER 2, 31 BCE

Octavian's camp

Gulf of Ambracia

Agrippa's harbor

Comarus Bay

Antony's advance camp

T. TAURUS

AGRIPPA AND OCTAVIAN

ANTONY

ACTIUM

OCTAVIUS

CLEOPATRA

Antony's first camp

ARRUNTIUS

INSTEIUS

SUSIUS

P. CANIDIUS

Antony's escape route

LURIUS

Ionian Sea

Octavian's fleet
Octavian's ground forces
Antony's fleet
Antony's ground forces
Camp walls

N

0   6 mi
0   6 km

Gathering their forces in Antioch, in 32 Antony and Cleopatra brought some 500 ships (including transports) and a large land force to northwestern Greece, apparently planning an invasion of Italy. Octavian was fortunate in having as his naval commander Marcus Vispanius Agrippa, probably the greatest naval tactician of the era. In a series of actions, Agrippa secured important coastal bases in Greece and used these to disrupt Antony's sea routes of supply and communication.

Antony stationed his forces at Actium, just south of the entrance to the Gulf of Ambracia in Epirus. Octavian then transferred his army from Italy to north of Actium and, during the summer of 31, established both a naval blockade and a land blockade of Antony's forces. Antony lost so many men to desertion and disease that he could not fully man his ships. Apparently the resulting sea battle was more an effort to extricate his forces than an attempt to secure a victory.

The battle occurred on September 2. Octavian, without his detached light squadrons, had at his disposal perhaps 200 ships, while Antony had perhaps 170. Each commander added legionnaires to bolster the ship crews and thus may have shipped as many as 60,000 or more men. As evidence that Antony's chief goal was escape, however, his crews did not stow their masts and sails on shore but instead kept them on board their galleys so that they might take advantage of the usual later daily breeze and outrun their opponents' galleys powered only by oars. Given that Antony's larger ships were quite fast under sail, this plan appeared to be a wise one. Agrippa's smaller ships, however, enjoyed a speed advantage under oars, and their attacks prevented Antony from fully implementing his plan. Agrippa also made effective use of a new harpoonlike weapon, the harpax. It had a hook at one end and a line attached to the other. Projected by a catapult against an enemy vessel, it was used to draw the ship close so that it could be boarded.

The principal fighting occurred on the northern flank. Antony initially had the upper hand, but his crews in the center and left wing had been sapped by propaganda attacking Cleopatra, and they fell back or failed to fight with much enthusiasm. Antony signaled to Cleopatra to escape and then tried to get to the open sea. When his own vessel was secured with a harpax, he escaped to another ship and broke free with a few of his ships to join Cleopatra. In the end, only Cleopatra's Egyptian squadron of 60 vessels made a clean breakthrough under sail, followed by the few ships led by Antony. Most of Antony's fleet surrendered, as did his land force a short time later. Octavian subsequently ordered the construction of Nicopolis ("Victory City") on the site of his former headquarters.

Antony never recovered from Actium. Octavian invaded Egypt in July 30. Although Antony initially repulsed Octavian's forces before Alexandria, Antony was misinformed that Cleopatra had killed herself and stabbed himself, only to die a lingering death in Cleopatra's presence. Cleopatra held out hope that she might beguile Octavian as she had done with both Caesar and Antony. He was not interested, however. When it became obvious that he intended to exhibit her in a triumphant procession through Rome, Cleopatra too committed suicide, at age 39, by means of a snake smuggled to her in a basket of figs.

Octavian now controlled the immense wealth of Egypt as well as being master of the entire Mediterranean. He secured the Roman eastern provinces largely by confirming Antony's appointments there and returned to Rome to declare the civil wars at an end. In October 27 the Senate proclaimed him *augustus princeps* ("revered first citizen").

References

Adcock, Frank Ezra. *The Roman Art of War under the Republic.* 1940; reprint, New York: Barnes and Noble, 1960.

Carter, John M. *The Battle of Actium: The Rise and Triumph of Augustus Caesar.* London: Hamilton, 1970.

Gurval, Robert Alan. *Actium and Augustus: The Politics and Emotions of Civil War.* Ann Arbor: University of Michigan Press, 1995.

Morrison, J. S. *Greek and Roman Oared Warships.* Oxford: Oxbow Books, 1996.

Starr, Chester G. *The Roman Imperial Navy, 31 B.C.–A.D. 324.* New York: Barnes and Noble, 1960.

Battle of the Teutoburg Forest

Date	Autumn 9 CE	
Location	Kalkriese, Germany	
Opponents (* winner)	*Germans	Romans
Commander	Arminius	Publius Quinctilius Varus
Approx. # Troops	20,000–30,000	15,000–18,000 Romans, 10,000 German auxiliaries
Importance	Marks the end of Roman efforts to expand northward	

In the year 6 CE a major revolt against Roman rule occurred throughout Dalmatia and Pannonia, which comprised the Roman province of Illyricum. It seemed to Romans the worst crisis they had experienced since the Second Punic War. The revolt was finally put down after three years, but a worse shock was to come with the annihilation of three Roman legions in Germany in the year 9.

The recently conquered area of Germany from the Rhine to the Elbe seemed peaceful, and the Roman legate of lower Germany, Publius Quinctilius Varus, was assigned to integrate it into the empire. Varus had been governor in Syria, and his talents lay in administration rather than as a field commander. His appointment to the German post strongly suggests that Emperor Augustus was unaware of the state of affairs there.

The Romans seem not to have appreciated the degree to which their rule—especially the taxes, which had to be paid in metal—was resented by the German tribes. Arminius, prince of the Cherusci, who had commanded German auxiliaries under Rome and had been rewarded with Roman citizenship for his exemplary service, took leadership of the revolt, although he kept his role secret. Arminius even suggested the route of march for the Roman legions to winter quarters, which he said would allow Varus to put down several small revolts en route.

In the summer of 9 CE Varus set out from his camp near the Weser River with three Roman legions (XVII, XVIII, and XIX), all veterans of fighting in Germany and totaling 15,000 to 18,000 men, including some cavalry. Family members and camp followers accompanied them as did German auxiliaries, totaling perhaps another 10,000 people. When the attack came, the unsuspecting Romans and their wagons were strung out over a considerable distance in the Teutoburg Forest (Teutoburger Wald), most probably near Osnabrück.

From archaeological digs at the site and the recovery of numerous Roman coins (none later than 9 CE) over a several-mile stretch, it would appear that the Romans simply marched into an ambush. Arminius had left the Roman column beforehand, allegedly telling Varus that he wanted to scout ahead. The German attackers numbered between 20,000 and 30,000 men and held the high ground on one side. There were marshes on the other side. Traditional Roman tactics could not be applied in the difficult terrain, and the Roman position was made worse by strong wind and rain.

On the first day the Germans engaged in hit-and-run attacks, causing significant Roman casualties. Varus threw up breastworks, however, holding the Germans at bay for the night. He then ordered the wagons burned, hoping that this would increase the speed of the Roman march. It had little effect, and the Romans then retreated to the original fortifications.

Over several days the three legions were slaughtered. Only a handful of soldiers managed to escape to the nearby Roman base at Aliso. Varus and his officers preferred to commit suicide rather than be taken. Indeed, the Germans sacrificed those captured.

Although Arminius brought Aliso under siege, he failed to take it and departed. The Roman garrison at Aliso then abandoned the city. Arminius made no attempt to follow up on his great victory by invading Italy or Gaul. It was impossible, as the tribes soon fell to quarreling among themselves. Prompt Roman action also secured their control of the Rhine bridges, but the loss of three legions with more than 10 percent of Roman military might (from 28 down to 25 legions) severely impacted Roman military options.

On learning of the Battle of the Teutoburg Forest, Emperor Augustus disbanded his German bodyguard, saying that no Germans could be trusted. He was also heard to cry "Quinctilius Varus, give me back my legions!" The numbers of these three legions never were resurrected, even after Roman operations in 14–16 CE and 41 CE recovered their standards.

The Battle of the Teutoburg Forest signaled the end of Roman efforts to expand northward. Augustus was not only jolted to learn that Germany was not pacified but also was forced to rethink his entire suppositions about the military strength required to garrison the empire. He reintroduced conscription by the drawing of lots. These levies were not used to create new legions but rather to augment those already in existence. Augustus also concentrated a third of his strength, eight legions, on the Rhine under his stepson Tiberius, who conducted punitive operations in Germany during 10–12 CE. Germanicus Caesar also campaigned there with four legions during 14–16 CE but made no real attempt at conquest and occupation.

Augustus abandoned plans for a German province between the Rhine and Elbe, thereby fixing Rome's northern boundary on the Rhine and Danube rivers. North-central and Northeastern Europe would not be brought within Latin cultural and legal systems for several hundred years and then only as an enhancement rather than a replacement. Subsequent German leaders, including the Nazis, exploited the Battle of the Teutoburg Forest to build national consciousness and unity, presenting it as an example of Germans defending their "freedom" against foreign invasion.

References

Murdoch, Adrian. *Rome's Greatest Defeat: Massacre in the Teutoburg Forest.* Stroud, Gloucestershire, UK: Sutton, 2006.

Schlüter, W. "The Battle of the Teutoburg Forest: Archaelogical Research at Kalkriese near Osnabrück." *Journal of Roman Archaeology,* Supp. 32 (1999): 125–159.

Tacitus. *The Annals of Imperial Rome.* Translated by Michael Grant. London: Penguin, 1974.

Battle of Beth-Horon

Date	October 66	
Location	Beth-Horon gorge (named for two villages 10 and 12 miles northwest of Jerusalem)	
Opponents (* winner)	*Jews	Romans
Commander	Unknown	Cestius Gallus
Approx. # Troops	Unknown	Unknown
Importance	Unprecedented defeat for the Romans in a provincial revolt leads more Jews to join the rebellion and to full-scale war	

The Hebrew victory over Roman forces in the Battle of Beth-Horon prompted a general Jewish uprising against Rome, with fatal consequences for the Hebrew nation. Modern Israel occupies a small land area, slightly less than the U.S. state of New Jersey. In ancient times the region was poor, bereft of natural resources, and barely able to provide for itself. It could hardly resist Roman power. The area was important because it formed a highway between the larger empires of the Assyrians, Babylonians, and the Persians to the east and the Egyptians and finally the Greeks and Romans to the west.

The unique contribution of the Jews to the West was their development of an exclusive monotheism, the belief in a single all-powerful god, Jehovah, who watched over his chosen people but also demanded a high standard of ethical conduct on pain of severe punishment. No people in history were to fight more tenaciously for their liberty against greater odds. The belief of Jews in their uniqueness along with their intolerance of other religions created in the ancient world a sense of separation and widespread animosity against them.

In 63 BCE Roman consul Pompey Magnus (Pompey the Great), fresh from defeating Mithridates VI of Pontus and Tigranes I of Armenia, moved to annex Syria, making it a Roman province. Pompey next laid siege to Jerusalem and took it. Roman soldiers secured the Temple there, cutting down its priests with the sword. Although he preserved the Temple treasury, Pompey dared to visit the Holy of Holies, where only the high priest was allowed. This typified Roman rule thereafter.

Jews constituted only a small proportion (about 6–9 percent) of the Roman Empire's population, but this did not keep them from being a constant problem. Roman insensitivity, sacrilege, and plain stupidity produced riots and uprisings that brought savage reprisals. Consequently, this part of the empire attracted only the dregs of the Roman civil service. A string of maladroit decrees and a succession of inept Roman administrators fed Jewish extremism and convinced many Jews that a day of reckoning was inevitable. These determined Jews came to be known as Zealots.

Matters came to a head in May 66 CE under Roman procurator Gessius Florus. His tactless decisions led to rioting, and the Zealots seized control of Jerusalem. Promised amnesty, the Roman forces holding the Antonia Fortress that overlooked the Temple precinct were nonetheless slaughtered. Gessius soon lost control of Judea and appealed to the Roman governor of Syria, legate Cestius Gallus at Antioch, who had available a much larger force of four legions.

Cestius took three months to assemble an expeditionary force, however. Centered on the XII Fulminata (Thunderbolt) legion of 4,800 men, it included another 6,000 legionnaires (2,000 from each of the other three legions). Cestius also had some 2,000 cavalry and 5,000 auxiliary infantry in six cohorts. Rome's allies, King Antiochus IV of Commagene and King Sohamemus of Emesa, furnished slingers and javelin throwers, perhaps another 32,000 men. Some 2,000 Greek militias of Syria also joined, eager to participate in any action against Jews.

In October 66 Cestius easily subdued Galilee. His men unleashed a terror campaign of widespread destruction in the expectation that this would both remove any threat to his rear area and intimidate the Jewish population along the route to Jerusalem. Leaving moderate forces to hold Galilee, Cestius also detached units to secure the seaport of Joppa. The Romans razed Joppa and slew perhaps 8,000 people there. Additional Roman columns secured other potential rebel strongholds.

These coastal columns rejoined the main force at Caesarea, and Cestius moved against Jerusalem. He expected to conclude the campaign in a few weeks, before the heavy autumnal rains could make quagmires of the roads. To this point, Jewish resistance was sporadic and apparently disorganized.

Cestius believed that his terror campaign had worked. On his approach to Jerusalem through the Beth-Horon gorge (named for two villages 10 and 12 miles northwest of Jerusalem), he therefore failed to follow standard procedure and make an adequate reconnaissance. As a result, the Jews were able to lay an ambush and attack the head of his column before the Romans could deploy from march formation. According to Jewish sources the Romans sustained some 500 dead, while the Jews sustained only 22 dead.

Cestius recovered and resumed the advance. He set up camp on Mount Scopus, less than a mile from the city. The Zealots refused, however, to treat with any emissaries and even put one to death. After several days of waiting, on October 15 Cestius sent his men into Jerusalem. The Jews fell back to the inner city wall. The Romans burned the suburb of Betheza, expecting that this would bring submission. It did not. The Romans then launched full-scale attacks but failed to penetrate the Jewish defenses. Following a week of this, Cestius suddenly withdrew. Stiffer than expected Jewish resistance, the approach of winter, and the shortages of supplies and mules for transport were the factors in his decision.

Cestius decided to move back to the coast through the Beth-Horon gorge. Again he failed to post pickets on the hills, allowing the Jews to attack his forces in the narrow defile. Other Jewish forces moved to block the Roman escape. This running engagement, known as the Battle of Beth-Horon, turned into a rout. Cestius and the bulk of his force escaped but at the cost of all of their baggage and nearly 6,000 men killed. The XII Legion also lost its eagle standard. The equipment that the Jews captured would serve them effectively in combating Roman siege operations four years later.

The battle had serious consequences. One immediate effect was the massacre of Jews in Damascus; the Greek rulers there were now confident that this action would have Cestius's support. The Battle of Beth-Horon meant that the Jewish revolt would not immediately be put down, however. Jews hitherto reluctant to commit themselves now joined the Zealots. Many were convinced that the victory was a sign that God favored their cause. By November the Jews had set up an independent secessionist government in Jerusalem.

The Romans could not allow this. Emperor Nero appointed Vespasian (Titus Flavius Vespasianus) as commander of an expeditionary force to bring Judea to heel. Vespasian moved south from Antioch with two legions, while his son Titus came up with another legion drawn from the garrison of Egypt. The invasion began in 69 CE, and following some delays, in 70 the Romans took Jerusalem without difficulty, thanks to internal divisions among the Jews. The sack of the city was terrible (the Jewish historian Josephus gives a figure of 1.1 million for the number of dead in the siege), and the Romans burned the Temple. Some isolated Jewish fortresses managed to hold out for another several years, but the Jewish state was no more. The Romans renamed it Syria Palestina. It was not until 1948 that there would again be a Jewish nation-state.

References

Grant, Michael. *The Jews in the Roman World.* New York: Scribner, 1973.

Jones, A. H. M. *The Herods of Judea.* Oxford, UK: Clarendon, 1967.

Lendon, J. E. "Roman Siege of Jerusalem." *MHQ: Quarterly Journal of Military History* 17(4) (Summer 2005): 6–15.

————. *Soldiers and Ghosts: A History of Battle in Classical Antiquity.* New Haven, CT: Yale University Press, 2005.

Battle of the Milvian Bridge

Date	October 28, 312	
Location	North of the Tiber River near Rome	
Opponents (* winner)	*Eastern Roman Empire	Western Roman Empire
Commander	Constantine	Marcus Aurelius Valerius Maxentius
Approx. # Troops	50,000	75,000
Importance	Constantine is confirmed as emperor of the western Roman Empire	

The Battle of the Milvian Bridge on October 28, 312, took place just north of the Tiber River, about a mile and a half north of Rome. It confirmed Constantine as augustus (emperor) of the western portion of the Roman Empire. It also led to his becoming the first Christian leader of Rome.

For most of the third century the Roman Empire had experienced considerable chaos, including a rapid succession of emperors. Diocletian, who became emperor in 284, temporarily halted the decay. He also concluded that the empire was too vast to be ruled effectively by one man, so he instituted a tetrarchy, or rule by four men. He installed Maximian in the west, while Diocletian himself ruled in the east. Each held the title of augustus, and each appointed a subordinate to assist in ruling his half of the empire. These men—Galerius in the east and Constantius in the west—had the title of caesar. On the death or retirement of the augustus, the caesar was to succeed him and then name a caesar in his turn. This system was supposed to provide both an orderly transition to power and a training period for the most powerful position in the empire.

In 305 Diocletian retired and persuaded Maximian to do the same, whereupon Galerius and Constantius received the title of augustus. They named as caesars Flavius Severus in the west and Maximinus Daia in the east. These actions, however, angered two people who thought that position should be theirs: Constantine, the son of Constantius, and Marcus Aurelius Valerius Maxentius, son of Maximian.

In 306 Constantius died. His legions in Britain and Gaul proclaimed Constantine as augustus, although Constantine declined the title. Constantine was duly confirmed as caesar, but Severus became augustus in the west. The legions in Italy, however, refused to recognize Severus, proclaiming Maxentius as augustus. This led to civil war in the west during 306–307, ending with the execution of Severus and the proclamation of Maxentius as augustus. Maxentius acceded to his father Maximian, however, who came out of retirement and reclaimed the throne.

Galerius, in the eastern empire, refused to recognize either Constantine or Maximian as augustus. Galerius named one of his generals, Licianus Licinius, to replace Severus and invaded the western empire to enforce this decision. If all this was not already sufficiently complicated, Maxentius then forced his father from power again and assumed the title of western augustus. Galerius's nephew Maximinus Daia also claimed the title.

To settle the issue, Diocletian called a conference in 308 at Carnuntum (present-day Hainburg, Austria). It confirmed all the claimants, except Maximian, in the title of augustus and gave each a portion of the empire to administer. This arrangement lasted only two years. In 310 Maximian fled from his son to Constantine's court in Gaul. There Maximian intrigued to overthrow Constantine but was taken prisoner and forced to commit suicide. In 311 Galerius died, leaving four augusti: Constantine in Gaul, Maxentius in Italy, Licinius in the Balkans, and Maximinus Daia in the east.

The tyrannical Maxentius, convinced that Constantine was plotting against him, prepared for an invasion of Gaul. Learning of this, Constantine decided to strike first. Although he commanded some 100,000 men, Constantine was obliged to leave the majority of them to protect the frontiers. Constantine did conclude a pact with Licinius in the east, however, that included the pledge of the marriage of Constantine's sister to Licinius in return for the latter's neutrality.

With about 40,000 men Constantine moved swiftly through the Alps into northern Italy, where he won hard-fought battles against Maxentius's legions at Susa, Turin, Milan, and Verona. As Constantine moved south his support increased, the result of both volunteers from the countryside and defections from Maxentius's legions. By the time Constantine arrived just north of Rome he probably commanded about 50,000 men, while Maxentius had some 75,000 men. Maxentius sallied from Rome, positioning his men on the plain across the Tiber River near the village of Saxa Rubra.

On October 27 the day before the climactic battle, Constantine allegedly saw a sign in the sky that he and those around him interpreted as representing the Christian god. A story has it that during the night Constantine experienced a dream in which a voice told him to order his men to place the Greek letters chi and rho (the sign of Christ) on their shields, assuring him, "In this sign you will conquer." In any case, Constantine ordered the symbols scratched into the shields prior to the battle. There were a number of Christians in Constantine's army, and Eusebius, later bishop of Caesarea in Palestine, related that Constantine later told him that he had vowed before the battle to convert to that faith if he triumphed.

There are few details of the battle, which took place just north of the Tiber. Apparently both Constantine and Maxentius placed their infantry in the center and their cavalry on the flanks. The decisive point came when Constantine led a charge by one of his cavalry wings. Maxentius was utterly defeated. Only the Milvian Bridge was open as an escape route back to Rome, and not all the men could get across it in time. Maxentius and many of his legionnaires drowned in the Tiber. His body, clad in armor, was found the next day.

Following the battle, the Roman Senate recognized Constantine as sole augustus in the west. Constantine duly converted to Christianity, an act that encouraged many of his entourage to do the same. In 313 Constantine met with Licinius at Milan, and the two announced the Edict of Milan that pledged religious tolerance in the empire, to include Christianity. Constantine then fought hostile Germanic tribes while Licinius waged war against Maximinus Daia, defeating him.

Constantine and Licinius were soon quarreling, and in 323 Constantine defeated him. Licinius was executed the next year. In 325 Constantine called the Council of Nicea to define Christian doctrine. It declared some Christian beliefs heretical and blamed the Jews for Christ's death, setting in motion a series of pogroms. Christians now persecuted other religions as Christianity once had been persecuted, and Christianity gradually became the dominant religion of the Roman Empire. Constantine, however, soon founded the city of Constantinople, setting up the formal division of the Roman Empire. The eastern portion, known as the Later Roman Empire or the Byzantine Empire, lasted until 1453.

References

Barnes, Timothy D. *Constantine and Eusebius.* Cambridge: Harvard University Press, 1981.

Cameron, Averil, and Stuart G. Hall. *Eusebius: Life of Constantine.* Oxford, UK: Clarendon, 1999.

Durant, Will. *Caesar and Christ,* Vol. 3, *The Story of Civilization.* New York: Simon and Schuster, 1944.

Ridley, Ronald T., ed. and trans. *Zosimus: New History.* Canberra: Australian Association for Byzantine Studies, 1982.

Battle of Adrianople

Date	August 9, 378	
Location	Adrianople (Hadrianopolis) in Thrace	
Opponents (* winner)	*Goths	Romans
Commander	King Fritigern	Emperor Valens
Approx. # Troops	Up to 100,000	Perhaps 50,000
Importance	Worst Roman military defeat since the Battle of Cannae	

The Battle of Adrianople (Hadrianopolis, Edirne) in Thrace between the Romans and the Goths was one of the worst military defeats sustained by the Roman Empire. Following the death of Constantine the Great in 337, the Roman Empire underwent a series of succession struggles. In 364 Valentian, a successful general, became emperor. Valentian I (r. 364–375) appointed his brother as coemperor and sent him to Constantinople to deal with the Persians while Valentian concentrated on shoring up the empire's Danubian defenses against the Barbarians. Valentian died in 375 and was succeeded by his 16-year-old son Gratian, who proved too young and inexperienced to deal with the incursions of large numbers of Goths in the Balkans.

The movement of the Huns west from China drove other peoples before them. As the Huns forced the Ostrogoths (eastern Goths) west, they in turn pushed against the Visigoths (western Goths), driving them into the Danube River valley, the northern border of the Roman Empire. When the Visigoths arrived in Byzantine territory, they asked to be allowed to settle there. Valens (r. 364–378) agreed but on the condition that they surrender their weapons to Byzantine authorities and give up as hostage all males under military age. Valens held the Visigoths in utter contempt; had he been more accommodating, he might well have won their loyalty and secured a large loyal population from which he could draw soldiers.

In 377 Valens campaigned against the Persians. He left two generals, Luppicinus and Maximus, in charge of disarming the Visigoths. They chose to enrich themselves and, in return for bribes and sexual favors, allowed the Visigoths to keep their weapons. Meanwhile, the Ostrogoths arrived. When their request for sanctuary was denied, they simply crossed into Roman territory anyway and pillaged widely.

King Fritigern, one of the Visigoth leaders pressed too far by Luppicinus and Maximus, made common cause with the Ostrogoths. When the two Roman generals attempted to assassinate Fritigern, the Goths went to war and soon inflicted several defeats on the Romans.

Valens responded by concluding a truce with the Persians and returning to Europe. He then sent a sizable force against Fritigern, pushing the Goths back into a marshy area near the mouth of the Danube. The resulting battle proved inconclusive, with most of the Goths escaping through the marsh. The Goths then raided northern Greece, and Valens pursued, marching into Thrace northeast of Greece.

Valens sought reinforcements from his nephew Gratian in Italy, for the Goths had concluded a series of alliances with German tribes against Rome. German uprisings along the Rhine forced Gratian to campaign there. Defeating the Germanic tribes, he then moved down the Danube River valley to join up with his uncle.

In the summer of 378 Valens' generals drove the Goths back in Thrace toward the city of Adrianople, west of Constantinople on the Maritza River. Valens' principal general, Sebastian, had trained a small reliable force and had conducted a series of successful hit-and-run attacks with it. Sebastian recommended a continuation of this strategy, believing that it would eventually force the Goths to depart. Valens disagreed. He favored a large pitched battle, believing that his forces would have the advantage against poorly trained Goth levies.

Some eight miles from Adrianople, Fritigern and the Visigoths set up camp in an excellent defensive position on high ground with a perimeter circle of wagons. The Visigoths were primarily an infantry force, while the Ostrogoths provided the bulk of the cavalry. The Goth cavalry then departed to forage for provisions to feed the camp population of perhaps 100,000 warriors and 200,000 women and children.

Jealous of Gratian's success and anxious to achieve a glorious victory before his nephew could arrive, Valens decided to press the issue. He departed Adrianople with his legions at dawn on August 9, having left behind under suitable guard his treasury and baggage. After a rapid advance in extreme heat over rough ground, at about 2:00 p.m. Valens and his legions came on Fritigern's camp. Valens commanded some 50,000 men; Fritigern had twice that number, the majority of them cavalry.

Fritigern sent negotiators to Valens to buy time for the Ostrogoth cavalry to return. Valens stalled in order to rest and deploy his men but finally broke off negotiations. Before the Romans had completed their deployment of infantry in the center and cavalry on the wings, however, the Goth cavalry returned and fell on the cavalry on the Roman right wing. Although the Roman cavalry fought well, it was badly outnumbered; when it broke, the cavalry under Ostrogoth chieftains Alatheus and Saphrax drove against the infantry, which was still not completely deployed. Blinded by dust kicked up by the cavalry, the foot soldiers were driven back into a mass so tight that many could not even draw their swords, let alone use them.

The Ostrogoths then subjected the Roman infantry to attack by arrows. Seeing the situation, Fritigern passed his own infantry from inside the ring of wagons. Their long slashing swords and battle-axes exacted a terrible toll on the Romans; some 40,000 reportedly perished in the battle, Valens and Sebastian among them.

Called by one Roman historian the greatest defeat for Rome since the Battle of Cannae (216 BCE), the Battle of Adrianople did not immediately affect the Roman Empire. Although the Goths rampaged through the Balkans for a time, Gratian and a new emperor in the East, Theodosius I (r. 379–395), eventually drove back across the Danube those Goths who would not swear loyalty to the empire. In 382 Theodosius extended official recognition to the German communities within Roman territory in return for a pledge of military service. Influenced by the large number of Goths in the army, the army of the Eastern Roman Empire became predominantly a cavalry force.

References

Burns, Thomas S. *Barbarians within the Gates of Rome.* Bloomington: Indiana University Press, 1994.

Ferrill, Arthur. *The Fall of the Roman Empire: The Military Explanation.* London: Thames and Hudson, 1986.

Gibbon, Edward. *The History of the Decline and Fall of the Roman Empire,* Vol. 3. Edited by J. B. Bury. London: Methuen, 1909.

Grant, Michael. *The Army of the Caesars.* New York: Scribner, 1974.

Whittacker, C. R. *Frontiers of the Roman Empire.* Baltimore: Johns Hopkins University Press, 1994.

Battle of Châlons

Date	Summer (July?) 451	
Location	Some 20 miles northwest of Troyes and 35 miles south of Châlons-sur-Marne in northeastern Gaul (France)	
Opponents (* winner)	*Western Roman Empire and German mercenaries, allied Franks and Visigoths	Huns and allied Ostrogoths, Gelphs
Commander	Aetius, King Theodoric	Attila, Valamer, Ardaric
Approx. # Troops	Unknown	Unknown
Importance	Turns back the Huns, perhaps saving Western civilization	

The Battle of Châlons (also known as the Battle of the Catalaunian Plains) in the summer of 451 resulted in the defeat of the Huns and their withdrawal from Western Europe, quite probably saving Western civilization. The nomadic Huns originated in Asia. Over a period of several centuries they migrated west, defeating all peoples with whom they came into contact. The Huns crossed the Don River in 375, driving east the Alans, the Goths, and others. In the early fifth century the Huns conquered the territory north of the Danube River. They also raided south to Constantinople. After losing an army to them, Emperor Theodosius II of the Eastern Roman Empire agreed to pay the Huns an annual tribute in gold.

Rua, the first recognized ruler of Huns, died in 433 and was succeeded by his two nephews, Bleda and Attila. In 441 Attila led a raid into Southeastern Europe, sacking cities and destroying the countryside. Theodosius was forced to increase his annual tribute to 2,100 pounds of gold.

In 445 Attila murdered his brother and assumed sole leadership of the Huns, then invaded Gaul and the Italian peninsula. Western Europe was disunited; what remained of the Western Roman Empire under Valentinian III was being pressed both by Gaiseric, king of the Vandals in North Africa, and Theodoric, ruler of the Visigoths, who controlled southern Gaul (present-day France). Gaiseric and Theodoric were at odds, with Gaiseric having repudiated his marriage to Theodoric's daughter. The Franks were also in disarray, with the two sons of Frankish king Chlodian vying for the throne. Attila expected to play these groups against one another. Using as his excuse an appeal he had received some years earlier from Valentinian's sister Honoria, who had sought assistance against her brother, Attila claimed that this constituted a marriage proposal and that he was owed half of the Western Roman Empire as a dowry.

In the spring of 451 Attila, known in the West as the "Scourge of God," led a force of at least 100,000 Huns and allied Ostrogoths, Scirians, Heruls, Gepids, and others across the Rhine River into Gaul. The Huns crossed on a wide front in the vicinity of Strasbourg and made their way west, devastating the countryside and attacking and destroying every city they encountered. They turned south before they reached Paris. According to popular belief, the city was saved by the prayers of a young girl who motivated the citizenry. She was later beatified by the Catholic Church as Saint Genevieve.

Arriving at Orléans in May, Attila put that city under siege. Its ruler, Sangiban, king of the Alans, sent word to Attila that he would surrender Orléans. Learning of this, Aetius, commander of the army of the Western Roman Empire, marched his forces north. To oppose Attila, Aetius had perhaps 50,000 German mercenaries. Aetius also worked out a loose alliance with the Franks in the Rhineland and with the Visigoths in Aquitania. These peoples had no love for the Romans, but they regarded the Huns as the greater threat and agreed to join Aetius in a coalition against Attila. Sangiban reluctantly went back on his promise to Attila and joined the coalition against the Huns.

The Huns were on the verge of taking Orléans when the coalition forces appeared. Attila, whose forces were widely scattered, withdrew northward and sent word to the scattered wings of his army to re-form on the main body. Crossing the Seine, Attila left a Gepid force to cover his withdrawal, but Aetius destroyed Attila's rear guard in a night attack, inflicting a reputed 15,000 casualties.

The main battle took place the next day, though the exact date is in dispute. Possibilities range from late June to late September 451. The place is also in dispute, but most historians believe that it occurred on the Mauriac Plain (present-day Mery-sur-Seine), about 20 miles northwest of Troyes and 35 miles south of Châlons-sur-Marne.

Attila's army faced north. Ardaric led the Gepids on the right wing, Attila and the Huns were in the center, and Valamer led the Ostrogoths on the left wing. Aetius positioned his Roman forces on the left wing. He placed Sangiban and the Alans in the center of the coalition line, apparently so they could be kept under surveillance and preventing from bolting or switching sides. King Theodoric and his Visigoths held the coalition's right wing, facing their Ostrogothic kinsmen. The position of the Franks is unknown. They may have sustained such heavy casualties the day before that they did not participate, or they may have been in reserve.

The battle commenced late, perhaps about 5:00 p.m., in a struggle for possession of an important ridge line. Prince Thorismund and the Visigoths reached the ridge first and repelled the advancing Huns. The two sides then closed in bloody combat. The Alans gave good account of themselves before having to withdraw under intense pressure. Aetius and his Germans had little success on his end of the battle line, but the Visigoths held against the Ostrogoths, although old King Theodoric fell from his horse and was trampled to death by his own men. The Visigoths then turned and rolled up the left flank of the Huns, with Attila narrowly escaping death or capture.

In the meantime, Aetius and his men broke through the Gepid line. Attila ordered the Huns to stage a fighting retreat to their camp, which was fortified in the sense that it was encircled with wagons. As darkness fell the Visigoths attempted to storm the camp but were repulsed.

Casualties were such that neither side sought to resume the battle the next day. Contemporary estimates of the dead in the battle range from 165,000 to 300,000, although even the smaller figure is thought to be a gross exaggeration.

Aetius and Thorismund at first decided to besiege the Hunnish camp, but Aetius had second thoughts. Apparently he feared that if the Huns were destroyed completely the Visigoths would have a free hand in Gaul, so he advised Thorismund, who became king on the death of Theodoric, to return home and consolidate his rule. The Franks also withdrew.

The Huns, so weakened as to no longer pose a serious threat to the West, withdrew back across the Rhine. The coalition victory at Châlons probably prevented Attila and the Huns from dominating Western Europe. Attila was not finished, however. In 452 he renewed his vow to marry Honoria and invaded the Italian peninsula. Aetius could not gather sufficient forces to challenge him, and Valentinian sent Pope Leo I to negotiate with the Hun leader. The two men met at the Mincio River, and Attila agreed to depart Italy, probably because he had learned that Marcian, the new emperor of the Eastern Roman Empire, had sent an army to attack Attila's capital. Attila planned to renew his effort in the West but died in 453, and his sons fell to fighting among themselves. The subject peoples broke free, and the Hunnic Empire soon collapsed.

References

Fuller, J. F. C. *A Military History of the Western World,* Vol. 1. New York: Funk and Wagnalls, 1954.

Gregory of Tours. *History of the Franks.* Translated by Ernest Brehaut. New York: Columbia University Press, 1916.

Thompson, E. A. *A History of Attila and the Huns.* Oxford, UK: Clarendon, 1948.

Battle of Tricameron

Date	553	
Location	Near Carthage (close to present-day Tunis), North Africa	
Opponents (* winner)	*Byzantine Empire	Vandals
Commander	Belisarius	Gelimer
Approx. # Troops	5,000 (mostly cavalry)	50,000 (mostly cavalry)
Importance	The Byzantine Empire regains control of North Africa	

The Battle of Tricameron during the Vandal War of 533–534 led to the forces of the Byzantine Empire regaining control of North Africa. The battle also positioned them to launch an invasion of Italy. In 527 Justinian became ruler of the Byzantine Empire. The most illustrious of all the emperors in the Eastern Roman Empire, Justinian was a great lawgiver, builder, and administrator and a devout Christian. His chief foreign policy goals were to recover the lands of the Western Roman Empire from their Germanic conquerors and to reestablish imperial unity in the person of the Eastern Roman Empire emperor. His motto became "one empire, one law, one church."

Justinian became emperor during the First Persian War (524–532). At first the Persians made advances in Mesopotamia, but the later years of the war saw Byzantine victories under the young Thracian general Belisarius (505–563). After rising to command the Byzantine armies in the East, in 530 Belisarius and 25,000 men defeated 40,000 Persians at Dara. He was defeated by a vastly superior Persian army at Callinicum the next year, however. Withdrawing to islands in the Euphrates River, Belisarius won laurels for his skillful defense; the Persians withdrew and concluded peace in 532.

Belisarius was then given command of an expeditionary force to North Africa. The Vandals there had overthrown King Hilderic, who had been friendly with Constantinople. The hostile Gelimer replaced Hilderic. Justinian held that the Germanic kings were his vassals, and he demanded the reinstatement of Hilderic. When this was refused, Justinian concluded an alliance with the Ostrogoths to forestall them coming to the aid of the Vandals and sent Belisarius to North Africa.

In September 533 Belisarius, supported by a fleet of 500 transports and 92 warships, landed at Cape Vada with 15,000 men (10,000 infantry and 5,000 cavalry). The invasion took the Vandals by surprise, and Belisarius immediately moved against the Vandal capital of Carthage. The Vandals were handicapped by the fact that Gelimer had sent his brother Tzazon (Zano) and 7,000 men to crush a revolt in Sardinia. On September 13 at Ad Decimum, the 10th mile marker from Carthage, Gelimer and a Vandal force attempted an ambush, which Belisarius defeated. Two days later the Byzantine forces occupied Carthage without resistance.

With the hasty recall of Tzazon and his men from Sardinia, Gelimer put together about 50,000 troops, mostly cavalry, and advanced on Carthage. Belisarius moved out of the city to meet him. Leading with his cavalry, Belisarius came on Gelimer's forces on the opposite side of a shallow stream. Realizing that Gelimer was not fully prepared for battle, Belisarius chose not to wait for his infantry and instead immediately ordered an attack, although he was outnumbered nearly 10 to 1. Three times the Byzantines advanced, but each time they were repulsed.

The death of Tzazon in the fighting led to a Vandal collapse. Gelimer fell back on his fortified camp, but the Byzantine infantry had now arrived. Although casualties had been light, with only about 50 Byzantine soldiers and 800 Vandals killed, Gelimer decided to withdraw. Seeing their king in flight, the remainder of the Vandals quickly followed. The Byzantines then fell on the Vandal camp and looted it. Had Gelimer been able to regroup his forces and attack at this time, undoubtedly the far more numerous Vandals would have triumphed.

All Vandal resistance ended with Gelimer's surrender in March 534. In addition to the Vandal territory of North Africa, Justinian secured the former Vandal possessions of Sardinia, Corsica, and the Balearic Islands. In 534, jealous of Belisarius's success, Justinian recalled him to Constantinople. Belisarius left behind a small force under Solomon to complete the subjugation of not only the Vandals but also the Moors and Numidians. The Moors were not anxious to pass under Byzantine control, and it was 539 before resistance was at an end. Byzantine authority had now been reestablished over almost all of North Africa. The Byzantines held North Africa until the Saracen invasion a century and a half later.

References

Barker, John. *Justinian and the Later Roman Empire.* Madison: University of Wisconsin Press, 1966.

Gibbon, Edward. *The History of the Decline and Fall of the Roman Empire,* Vol 4. Edited by J. B. Bury. London: Methuen, 1909.

Treadgold, Warren. *Byzantium and Its Army, 284–1081.* Stanford, CA: Stanford University Press, 1995.

Battle of Badr

Date	March 15, 624	
Location	Badr, 80 miles southwest of Medina (in present-day Saudi Arabia)	
Opponents (* winner)	*Medina	Mecca
Commander	Muhammad	Abu Jahl
Approx. # Troops	300	900
Importance	Confirms Muhammad as the leader of Islam and allows its future expansion	

The Battle of Badr was small in terms of numbers of men engaged but had immense repercussions. It confirmed Muhammad as the leader of Islam and allowed the religion's expansion.

A Persian painting depicting a scene from the 624 Battle of Badr. Many saw Muhammad's victory here against much more numerous foes as a sign from God. The battle marked the beginning of Islam's spread across Arabia and the Near East, North Africa, southeastern Europe, and much of Asia. (Bilkent University)

Muhammad (Mohammed, Mahomet, 570?–632) was born in the city of Mecca in Arabia, the son of Abdallah ibn Abd-al-Muttalib (who died before Muhammad was born) and his wife Amina, both of the Koreish tribe that ruled the city. Amina died when Muhammad was about 6 years old, and the young boy was raised by his grandfather and an uncle. Muhammad became a merchant in the caravan trade, and at about age 25 he married a much older wealthy widow, Kadijah.

Muhammad was given to meditation, and Mecca, a major trading center, saw the circulation of numerous intellectual currents. Influenced both by Jewish and Christian traditions and claiming to have heard voices that imparted to him divine will, Muhammad at about age 40 became a prophet. His doctrine included belief in One God (Allah), the Last Judgment, alms, regular prayer, and the surrender of the self to the will of God (Islam) as expressed through His prophet (Muhammad). The teachings of the faith were later expressed in the holy book the Koran (Qur'an, Quran), which Muhammad said had been given to him by God in visions.

Although Muhammad gained a few converts in Mecca, he and his followers aroused the ire of the city elite (probably because of his opposition to usury). Subjected to persecution, they were forced to flee (known as the Hegira [Hijira]) to Medina in July 622. There Muhammad rallied his followers and organized the tribes of Medina into a community under the revealed will of God. At the same time, Muhammad waged war against Mecca.

Muhammad's first military actions were raids on Meccan caravans. In early 624 he ordered a dozen men to attack a small caravan from Yemen to Mecca. Acting as pilgrims bound for Mecca, his followers located the caravan and joined it. They faced one glaring problem: it was a holy month in Arabia during which warfare was forbidden. If they obeyed that stricture, then they would reach the holy city of Mecca, where fighting was forbidden. The raiders decided to violate the first rule and fell on the guards, killing one and capturing two others.

Muhammad was condemned for the raid. His response was that the merchants of Mecca were committing greater sins than any violation of the holy month by his men. The leaders of Mecca, however, were now determined to destroy Muhammad. They used as bait a rich caravan from Sinai to Mecca, tricking Muhammad into a battle in which he would be badly outnumbered.

Muhammad fell into the trap. In early March he led some 300 men from Medina to intercept the caravan. Most of his men were on foot. Reportedly they had only 70 camels and 2 horses. The Meccans meanwhile sent out almost 1,300 men. Led by Abu Jahl, they were far better armed and equipped and had some 700 camels and 100 horses. Half the men were supposedly wearing chain mail.

The caravan leader, Abu Sufyan, discovered the location of Muhammad's ambush force and diverted the caravan to another route. Abu Sufyan then informed Abu Jahl of its safe arrival at Mecca. This news caused some 400 of the Meccans, who now saw no need for battle, to desert. Abu Jahl was determined to destroy Muhammad, however, and told his remaining forces that they would travel to the wells at Badr, about 25 miles southwest of Mecca, and there celebrate the safe passage of the caravan.

Muhammad's men were laying in wait at Badr. Learning of Abu Jahl's approach, Muhammad called a council on the evening of March 14. When representatives of both his Mecca and Medina followers pledged their support, Muhammad announced that they would indeed give battle. On the advice of his second-in-command, Abu Bakr, Muhammad had all the wells except one stopped up; he then positioned his men around this well. On March 15 Abu Jahl's men arrived, nearly out of water. They approached the one serviceable well on rising ground.

Muhammad, seated under a tent, instructed his men to hold their positions and advance only when ordered. In the meantime, they would meet the attackers with arrows. Reportedly a sandstorm struck the Meccans as they advanced; their attack faltered, whereupon Muhammad ordered his force forward. The Meccan force broke and ran, leaving 70 dead and another 70 as prisoners. Abu Jahl was wounded and taken prisoner. He was beheaded when he refused to acknowledge Allah as the real victor.

Many in Arabia saw the victory of Muhammad's badly outnumbered, poorly armed, and badly equipped force as a sign from God. It certainly added immensely to Muhammad's reputation, especially as a military leader. Defeat at Badr would probably have brought his death. Instead, he emerged as the leader of a rapidly growing religion that soon came to dominate North Africa and the Middle East.

References

Balyuzi, H. M. *Mahammed and the Course of Islam.* Oxford: G. Ronald, 1976.

Holt, P. M., Ann K. S. Lambton, and Bernard Lewis. *The Cambridge History of Islam,* Vol. 1. Cambridge: Cambridge University Press, 1970.

Irving, Washington. *Mahamet and His Successors.* Madison: University of Wisconsin Press, 1970.

Battle of Yarmouk River

Date	August 636	
Location	Yarmouk River in Palestine	
Opponents (* winner)	*Rashidun Caliphate	Byzantine Empire
Commander	Abu Ubaidah ibn al-Jarrah, Khalid ibn al-Walid	Mahan of Armenia
Approx. # Troops	7,500–25,000	50,000–100,000
Importance	Marks the beginning of the great wave of Islamic military conquests	

The Battle of the Yarmouk (Yarmük, Yarmuk) River was fought between Arab forces of the Rashidun caliphate, led by Abu Ubaidah ibn al-Jarrah and Khalid ibn al-Walid, and Byzantine Empire forces under Mahan of Armenia. The battle took place in Palestine over the course of six days in August 636 next to the Yarmouk River, the largest tributary of the Jordan River. The battle marks the beginning of the first great wave of Islamic military conquests.

In 634 Caliph Abu Bakr ordered Muslim forces to invade Syria, long a Byzantine Empire preserve. The Arab army captured Damascus and took most of Palestine. Faced with these developments, Byzantine emperor Heraclius assembled a large force at Antioch. Organized as five separate armies, it included native Byzantines as well as Slavs, Franks, Armenians, Georgians, and Christian Arabs. Heraclius sought to take advantage of the fact that the Arab forces were separated into four main armies: at Palestine, in Jordan, at Caesarea, and at Emesa (Homs) in Syria. The emperor planned to concentrate his own forces and defeat the Arabs in detail. In June 636 he sent reinforcements under his son Constantine to Caesarea, hoping to tie down Arab forces there, while sending his remaining four armies on converging axes toward Damascus and Emesa.

The Arabs learned the broad outlines of the Byzantine plan from prisoners, and in a council of war Jarrah accepted the advice of his subordinate, Walid, to withdraw from northern and central Syria and concentrate on the plain of Yarmouk, which was more suitable for cavalry operations. Close to the Rashidun stronghold of Najd, this location also offered an escape route.

The Byzantine army camped just north of the Wadi Raqqad. The two sides conducted protracted negotiations, but these soon collapsed. Muslim accounts place the Byzantine force at 200,000–250,000 men and their own army at only 24,000–40,000 men. Modern estimates are something on the order of 50,000–100,000 for the Byzantines and only 7,500–25,000 for the Arabs. Whatever the numbers, all accounts agree that the Arabs were heavily outnumbered.

Byzantine commander Mahan formed his four armies in a line of battle some 12 miles wide. He distributed the cavalry equally among the armies, situating it in the rear to act as a reserve. He deployed his Arab Christian forces in front. Mounted on camels and horses, they acted as a light screening force and skirmish line.

On the Muslim side, Khalid offered to assume command of the army for the battle; Jarrah, who lacked the experience of his subordinate, accepted. Khalid divided the army into 36 infantry and 4 cavalry units, holding a total front of about 10 miles, with the Muslim left anchored on the Yarmouk River. The cavalry constituted about a quarter of the Muslim strength, and Khalid distributed much of it to his flanks as a reserve to arrest any Byzantine breakthrough there. The remainder he held as a mobile reserve under his personal command in the center. The army thus consisted of 4 subgroups of 9 infantry formations each. Each was organized on the basis of clan or tribe.

The battle opened in mid-August 636, with the two armies less than a mile apart. The Byzantines began with an advance by all four armies in line. The initial assault was not strong, however, as Mahan tried to locate weak points in the Muslim line.

On the second day Mahan attacked at dawn, launching two armies against the Muslim center to fix the Muslim forces in place but with the main thrusts coming on the flanks. The Byzantines made considerable headway in each of their flanking attacks and came close to achieving victory. However, Khalid's cavalry reserve made the difference; it shored up first the Muslim right and then its left.

On the third day the Byzantines attacked again, this time trying to break through where the Muslim right flank joined the center. Again the Muslim mobile reserve made the difference, averting disaster and pushing the Byzantines back to their original position.

On the fourth day the Byzantines again came close to victory. Believing that the previous day's assault had severely weakened the Muslim right wing, Mahan resumed the attack there. The Armenian portion of the Byzantine army broke completely through the Muslim line and drove on their camp. Once again Khalid's cavalry reserve averted disaster. Khalid split it into two main bodies in order to attack the Armenians on each flank. Facing Muslim forces on three sides, the Armenians were forced to withdraw, and the original line was restored. There were significant losses on each side.

Early on the fifth day Mahan dispatched an emissary to the Muslims who asked for a truce of several days to negotiate. Jarrah was willing to accept the proposal, but Khalid was opposed. The battle continued, although there was no major fighting that day.

To this point the Muslims had remained on the defensive. On the sixth day, assuming correctly that Byzantine morale was low, Khalid ordered an attack. He planned to use his cavalry to defeat that of the Byzantines, leaving their infantry without cavalry support and open to attacks from the flanks and rear. He also planned a major simultaneous flanking attack on the Byzantine left that would roll up their line against the river ravine to the west. While Mahan was attempting to organize his cavalry, the Muslim cavalry struck in force, causing the Byzantine horsemen to withdraw to the north and abandon the infantry. Khalid then directed his cavalry to attack the rear of the Armenian infantry on the Byzantine left. Under the pressure of a three-pronged attack of Muslim cavalry the Armenians broke, carrying the rest of the Byzantine army with them. Pinned against the steep ravines of the Yarmouk so closely that they were hardly able to use their weapons, the Byzantines were slaughtered in large numbers. Many others were killed or maimed by falling into the ravines.

The Battle of Yarmouk secured Syria and Palestine for the Muslims. Khalid then recaptured both Damascus and Emesa. Emperor Heraclius returned to Constantinople to consolidate his forces against a Muslim drive in Egypt.

References

Akram, A. I. *The Sword of Allah, Khalid bin al-Waleed: His Life and Campaigns.* Rawalpindi, Pakistan: National Publishing House, 1970.

Donner, Fred. *The Early Islamic Conquests.* Princeton, NJ: Princeton University Press, 1981.

Gil, Moshe, and Ethel Broido. *A History of Palestine, 634–1099.* Cambridge: Cambridge University Press, 1997.

Kaegi, Walter E. *Byzantium and the Early Islamic Conquests.* New York: Cambridge University Press, 1992.

McGraw, Donner F. *The Early Islamic Conquests.* Princeton, NJ: Princeton University Press, 1981.

Nicolle, David. *Yarmuk 636 A.D.: The Muslim Conquest of Syria.* Osprey Campaign Series #31. London: Osprey, 1994.

Siege of Constantinople

Date	August 15, 717–August 15, 718	
Location	Constantinople on the Bosphorus	
Opponents (* winner)	*Byzantine Empire, Bulgar allies	Umayyad Caliphate
Commander	Leo III; Terbelis, king of the Bulgars	Islama ibn Abdal Malik; Suleiman the General
Approx. # Troops	Unknown	Up to 200,000
Importance	Forces the Muslims to withdraw from western Asia Minor	

The chief Muslim goal throughout the seventh and eighth centuries remained the acquisition of Constantinople. That great city controlled the Bosporus and thus access between the Mediterranean and the Black Sea. It also guarded the entrance to Southern and Central Europe. The Muslims first attempted to take the city in 655, when Caliph Othman (r. 644–656) sent out a naval expedition. Although the Byzantine fleet met decisive defeat, the subsequent assassination of Othman and war of succession provided a respite. In 669 the Muslims mounted a second attempt, and thereafter Constantinople came under intermittent attack. Several attempts in the 670s were turned back when the Byzantines defeated the attackers at sea.

The greatest threat to the city, and to Byzantium, came in the siege of 717–718. Caliph Suleiman (r. 715–717) prepared a great effort to attack the city, ending the short reign of Byzantine emperor Theodosius III (r. 716–717) and bringing to the throne a successful general, Leo the Isaurian (Isauria is in Asia Minor, today's Konia). Leo (r. 717–741), who had been born a poor peasant, took the title of Leo III. He immediately ordered the granaries of Constantinople restocked and repairs made to the city's walls. He also secured weapons and ordered siege engines installed.

Constantinople was secure as long as its sea communications remained open. The city was built on a promontory flanked on the north by the so-called Golden Horn, an inlet of the Bosporus forming a natural harbor, and on the south by the Sea of Marmara. The city was protected on its western, or landward, side by both inner and outer walls; the inner wall had been built under Emperor Constantine the Great. The outer wall was constructed under Emperor Theodosius II and was some four miles in length. Normally the city population numbered about half a million people, but in 717 it must have swelled from refugees.

Until the invention of gunpowder, the only practical way to take a strongly held city was by blockading and starving its population. This meant closing both the Bosporus and the Dardanelles, a difficult feat because Constantinople flanked the Bosporus from the south. Everything depended on the Byzantine fleet, which was markedly inferior in numbers to that of the attackers.

Maslama, brother of the caliph, commanded the operation against Constantinople. He took personal command of the land force of some 80,000 men and gave command of the 1,800-ship fleet transporting another 80,000 men to Suleiman the General (not to be confused with the caliph of the same name). The attackers also had some 800 additional ships preparing in African and Egyptian ports, while the caliph was assembling a reserve army at Tarsus.

Maslama crossed over the Dardanelles to Europe, probably in July 717, and then moved overland to Constantinople, arriving there on August 15. Maslama ordered his troops to entrench before the city. He attempted a land attack, but the Byzantines beat it back. Malsama then ordered his men to surround his camp with a deep ditch and decided to reduce the city by blockade. He therefore instructed Suleiman the General to divide his fleet into two squadrons, one to cut off supplies from reaching Constantinople via the Aegean and Dardanelles and the other to move through the Bosporus and sever communications with the city from the Black Sea.

In early September the second fleet got under way to sail north of the Golden Horn, where Leo III had his fleet. The entrance to the harbor was protected by a great chain suspended between two towers that could be raised or lowered. When the blockading squadron approached, the strong current in the Bosporus threw the leading ships into confusion. Leo immediately ordered the chain lowered, stood out with his galleys, and attacked the broken Muslim formation with Greek fire, destroying 20 ships and capturing others before retiring to the Golden Horn on the approach of the main body of Suleiman's fleet.

Suleiman the General made no further attempt to force the strait, and Leo was thus able to bring in supplies and prevent Constantinople's surrender through starvation. To add to Maslama's difficulties, his brother, Caliph Suleiman, suddenly died, and his successor, Omar II, turned out to be a religious bigot but no soldier. Omar continued the siege by land, but then winter set in and was unusually severe with snow. Many of the besiegers died in these conditions, among them Suleiman the General.

In the spring of 718 an Egyptian squadron of 400 ships arrived. Passing Constantinople at night, it closed the Bosporus. The Egyptian squadron was followed by a squadron from Africa of 360 ships and the reserve army to reinforce the land troops, who had reportedly been reduced to cannibalism. Although the closure of the Bosporus would have, in time, forced Constantinople to surrender, a large number of the crewmen on the Egyptian ships were impressed Christians, and many were able to desert and provide accurate intelligence.

Choosing an opportune time when his enemy was unprepared, Leo again ordered the boom lowered and came out of the Golden Horn to engage and defeat the Egyptian ships. The Christian crewmen deserted en masse. Many Muslim vessels were destroyed by Greek fire, and others were captured. This gave Leo control of the Bosporus. He followed it up by ferrying over to the Asiatic side a sizable land force, which trapped and routed a number of Muslim troops.

Leo was also active diplomatically. He arranged an alliance with Terbelis, king of the Bulgars, who then marched against Maslama and defeated him, probably in July 718, somewhere south of Adrianople. Some 22,000 Muslim troops are said to have been killed. Leo made adroit use of disinformation as well, scattering reports that the Franks were preparing to send large forces to the aid of Constantinople.

The caliph finally recalled Maslama, who raised the siege on August 15. It had lasted exactly one year. The fleet embarked the army, landing them on the Asiatic shore of the Sea of Marmara. The ships then sailed for the Dardanelles, but en route they encountered a great storm. Reportedly only 5 galleys out of some 2,560 in the siege returned to Syria and Alexandria. Of the land forces, which some estimates place at more than 200,000 men, no more than 30,000 made it home. In 739 Leo won a land victory that compelled the Muslims to withdraw from western Asia Minor. Leo's leadership was key to the Byzantine victory.

References

Gibbon, Edward. *The History of the Decline and Fall of the Roman Empire,* Vol. 6. Edited by J. B. Bury. London: Methuen, 1912.

Runciman, Steven. *Byzantine Civilization.* New York: Barnes and Noble, 1994.

Vasiliev, Alexander Alexandrovich. *History of the Byzantine Empire, 324–1453.* Madison: University of Wisconsin Press, 1990.

Battle of Tours

Date	October 25, 732	
Location	Near Tours in west central France	
Opponents (* winner)	*Franks	Arabs
Commander	Charles Martel	Abd-ar-Rahmān
Approx. # Troops	Unknown	20,000–80,000
Importance	Franks turn back the deepest penetration of Muslim power in Europe; Charles establishes the Carolingian dynasty	

Even as the Muslims threatened Christian Europe in the east at Constantinople, a similar threat developed in the west. Around the year 710 the tide of Arab conquest reached Morocco and the Atlantic Ocean. The Berbers or Moors (the Numidians of Hannibal's day) supplied the necessary manpower. These peoples were essentially nomadic raiders, and to keep them employed Musa ibn Nusair, Muslim governor of North Africa, turned them toward Spain.

Musa apparently sought to plunder rather than conquer Spain. The caliph gave his permission for a raid only, cautioning Musa not to expose his army in an overseas expedition. Thus, in 710 a force of 400 men crossed the Strait of Gibraltar to Spain, pillaged around Algeciras, and returned to Morocco.

Encouraged by this success and having learned that the Visigothic king of Spain was fighting in the north against the Franks, Musa decided on an extensive expedition. He sent to Spain, in small groups of 400 men at a time, a force of some 7,000 men. These took the Visigoth capital of Toledo, and by the end of 712 they had conquered all of Spain.

No sooner had Spain been overrun than Musa initiated an invasion of Aquitaine across the Pyrenees mountains to eliminate the remnants of the Visigoths, possibly still in 712. In 717–718 Musa's successor ordered a full-scale raid; this failed, apparently because it became an operation of conquest. In 719 the Muslims took Narbonne, but two years later they met defeat at Toulouse. In 725 the Muslims occupied Carcassonne and Nîmes, and the next year they advanced up the Rhône River Valley and ravaged Burgundy.

The Franks were hardly in a position to oppose the Muslim advance. The ruling Merovingian dynasty was in decline, and effective power had passed into the hands of the mayor of the palace. In 714 Charles had assumed this title and was king in all but name.

Frankish leader Charles, known to posterity as Charles Martel (Charles the Hammer), turns back the Muslim advance from Spain in the Battle of Tours in October 732. Painting by French painter Charles Steuben (1788–1856). (Photos.com)

In 732 Muslim governor of Spain Abd-ar-Rahmān launched a full-scale invasion of Aquitaine, then ruled by Duke Eudo. The Muslim invaders defeated Eudo at Bordeaux and sacked and burned that city. From Bordeaux Abd-ar-Rahmān moved north, pillaging and destroying as he advanced. He took Poitiers and moved toward Tours because of reports of that city's wealth. Eudo meanwhile appealed for assistance to Charles, who had been fighting the Germanic tribes along the Danube. Charles agreed to assist if Eudo would submit Aquitaine to Frankish control. Putting together an army, he crossed the Loire, probably at Orléans. Abd-ar-Rahmān's army, now burdened down by plunder, fell back on Poitiers.

Little is known about the composition of Abd-ar-Rahmān's army or its size, which has been variously estimated at 20,000 to 80,000 men. Most were probably mounted Moors. They were armed principally with the lance and sword, and most of the men were without body armor. A mule train followed the troops, probably carrying plunder rather than supplies, for the army lived off the country. Its tactics centered on wild headlong charges.

The Frankish army was basically an infantry force and smaller than that of the invaders. Only the nobles had horses, and these were used only during the march. The Frankish soldiers were armed with swords, daggers, javelins, and two kinds of axes, one for wielding and one for throwing. The men carried shields for protection. The infantry consisted of the general's private army, which had to be constantly employed because it was paid by plunder alone, and a conscript force of poorly armed militia. There was little discipline on either side.

Charles understood the vulnerability of his foe. He had written to Eudo, "If you follow my advice, you will not interrupt their march, nor precipitate your attack. They are like a torrent, which it is dangerous to stem in its career. The thirst of riches and the consciousness of success redouble their valour, and valour is of more avail than arms or numbers. Be patient till they have loaded themselves with the encumbrance of wealth. The possession of wealth will divide their counsels and assure your victory" (Gibbon, *The Decline and Fall of the Roman Empire,* 6:17). Such an approach had the advantage for Charles, of course, of wasting large tracts of land belonging to the rebel duke of Aquitaine.

The sudden appearance of Charles's force caused consternation among the Muslims, who were so heavily weighed down with loot that they were no longer mobile. Abd-ar-Rahmān considered abandoning the plunder but did not, possibly because his men would have refused to obey such an order. The two armies faced one another for seven days, with Charles waiting for the arrival of reinforcements.

Few details exist concerning the actual battle. It most likely occurred at a site later called Moussais-la-Bataille on October 25, 732. Probably the armies first came into contact near Tours, and Abd-ar-Rahmān withdrew toward Poitiers. When he found that the army's booty had not gotten farther south, he decided to accept battle. As the Muslims were solely an offensive force, this meant an attack. Realizing this, Charles drew up his own forces in a solid phalanx formation, centered on his veterans.

The battle opened with a furious Muslim cavalry charge. Although they repeated it again and again, the Muslims were unable to break the Frankish phalanx. Toward dusk Eudo and a force of Aquitanians turned one of the Muslim flanks and launched an attack on Abd-ar-Rahmān's camp, where the bulk of the loot was located. Abd-ar-Rahmān died in the battle, which was over by nightfall.

The next morning scouts reported to Charles that the Muslim troops had fled south, abandoning the bulk of their plunder. Frankish chroniclers provided fantastic figures of 360,000 Muslims killed against only 1,500 for Charles's troops. The losses were more likely along the lines of 2,000 for the Muslims and 500 for the Franks.

There was no pursuit, for Charles on foot could not pursue a retiring mounted force, and the capture of the loot prohibited such an operation. Probably Charles also deemed it wise not to remove all Muslim pressure from Eudo in order to ensure his loyalty, so Charles collected the loot and recrossed the Loire. For his role in the victory, Charles became known to posterity as Charles Martel (Charles the Hammer).

The Battle of Tours saw the deepest Muslim penetration into Europe east and west. It might not have saved Western Europe from Arab rule, but it did make Charles supreme in Gaul and enabled him to establish the Carolinigian dynasty, which reached its zenith under his grandson Charlemagne. In 735 Eudo died. Charles overran Aquitaine and compelled Eudo's two sons to pay homage to him. After this Charles undertook several campaigns against the Muslims in the Rhône Valley, and a few years later the Muslims withdrew south of the Pyrenees for good.

References

Gibbon, Edward. *The History of the Decline and Fall of the Roman Empire,* Vol. 6. Edited by J. B. Bury. London: Methuen, 1912.

Kennedy, Hugh. *Muslim Spain and Portugal: A Political History of al-Andalus.* London: Longman, 1997.

Wallace-Hadrill, J. M. *The Fourth Book of the Chronicle of Fredegar with Its Continuations.* London: Nelson, 1960.

Siege of Pavia

Date	773–774	
Location	Pavia in Lombardy, northern Italy	
Opponents (* winner)	Franks	Lombards
Commander	Charlemagne	Desiderius
Approx. # Troops	Unknown	Unknown
Importance	Charlemagne secures the Lombard cities and becomes king of the Lombards as well as of the Franks	

Following the Battle of Tours in 732, Charles Martel became king of the Franks in all but name. His son, Pepin the Short (Pepin III), was the first of the Carolingian line (751–987) to assume the title "King of the Franks." In 751 Pepin sent the last of the Merovingian rulers, Childeric III, off to a monastery.

Pepin was a highly effective ruler. Implacable in war and a wise and effective administrator, he prepared the foundation upon which his son Charles built. Recognizing the importance of the church, Pepin restored its property and brought religious relics to France. He also rescued the papacy from Lombard control. Pepin died in 768, bequeathing the throne jointly to his two sons, Carloman II and Charles.

Charles, born in 742, became the greatest of all medieval kings, recognized by both the French and Germans as Charles the Great (Charlemagne; Karl der Grosse). In 770, on the advice of his mother, Charles divorced his first wife and married

Desiderata, daughter of Lombard king Desiderius. Desiderata returned to Lombardy a year later possibly because she was infertile, greatly straining the off-and-on relations between the Franks and Lombards.

In 771 Charles became sole king on the death of his brother. Carloman's wife then also departed for Lombardy. Pope Stephen III, who had criticized Charles's marriage to Desiderata, drew closer to the Lombards and appointed a number of Lombard nobles to important posts in Rome. When Stephen died in 772, his successor Adrian I removed the Lombards from their positions, leading Desiderius to send troops into the northern papal territories. Adrian then appealed to Charles for assistance.

While he readied his army, Charles sent letters to both Adrian and Desiderata urging peaceful settlement. In the summer of 773, having received confirmation of Desiderius's invasion of papal territory and refusal of a large monetary settlement to evacuate territories taken, Charles sent his army to northern Italy. The size of Charles's army is unknown, but he divided it for the passage through the Alps. His uncle Bernard led part of the army through the St. Bernard Pass, while Charles led the remainder through the Dora Susa via Mount Cenis.

As they descended the Alps, Charles's contingent found their way blocked by Lombard fortifications. An assault failed, but Charles found a way to attack the Lombards in the flank. The defenders then fled to Pavia, perhaps motivated by news that Bernard was moving in from the east.

In September 773 Charles's combined force arrived before the walled city of Pavia. The Frankish siege of Pavia lasted for the next 10 months. Although Charles did not have siege engines, the defenders had not anticipated the need, and their city was but poorly provisioned. Desiderius was among those trapped at Pavia, although his son Adelchis had fled to the stronger walled city of Verona, there to watch over Carloman's wife and children. Charles must have had a fairly large force, as he had sufficient men to march on Verona, which succumbed without a fight. Adelchis fled to Constantinople. Charles secured Carloman's wife and children.

With famine taking hold and no other city attempting his relief, Desiderius surrendered Pavia in June 774. Having captured Pavia and other Lombard cities, Charles absorbed the Lombard kingdom into the rising Frankish Empire, naming himself king of both the Franks and the Lombards. He sent Desiderius off to France to enter a monastery. Charles's victory made him supreme in northern Italy. He also reached accommodation with Adrian. While Charles recognized Adrian's claim to much of Italy, he failed to oblige the pope by actually conquering it.

Adrian died in 795, and Leo III succeeded him. Leo proved unpopular and fled to Charles's capital of Aachen (Aix-la-Chapelle), where he demanded that Charles restore him to power. Charles sent Leo back to Rome with troops, following himself in December 800. On Christmas Day in Rome at St. Peter's Basilica as Charles knelt in prayer, Leo produced a jeweled crown and placed it on Charles's head, proclaiming him "Charles the Augustus, crowned by God the great and peace-bringing Emperor of the Romans." It might not have been to Charlemagne's liking to receive the crown from the pope, opening a long debate as to the relative authority of the pope and Holy Roman emperor.

Charlemagne went on to expand Frankish power significantly. He already had won part of northeastern Spain, and in the 780s he pushed his authority to the east, invading the old German lands and converting them to Catholicism. Ultimately his territory extended to the Elbe and then south along the Danube to below Vienna. Once more the west was united. Charlemagne established his capital at Aachen near the mouth of the Rhine. Charlemagne died in 814 and was succeeded as emperor by his son, the ineffectual Emperor Louis I (r. 814–840), also known as Louis the Pious. On Louis's death full-scale civil war involving his three sons broke out almost immediately, and the territory was divided among them in the Treaty of Verdun of 843. From these territories emerged modern France and Germany.

References

Durant, Will. *The Age of Faith.* New York: Simon and Schuster, 1940.

Riché, Pierre. *The Carolingians.* Translated by Michael I. Allen. Philadelphia: University of Pennsylvania Press, 1993.

Winston, Richard. *Charlemagne: From the Hammer to the Cross.* Indianapolis: Bobbs-Merrill, 1954.

Battle of Lechfeld

Date	August 10, 955	
Location	Lechfeld, close to the Lech River and Augsburg in south Germany	
Opponents (* winner)	*Coalition of Saxony, Bavaria, Franconia, Swabia, and Bohemia	Magyars
Commander	Saxon Emperor Otto I	Bulcasú and Lél (Lehel)
Approx. # Troops	10,000 cavalry	50,000 horsemen
Importance	Ends Magyar raids into Germany and leads to establishment of the Holy Roman Empire	

In 894 nomadic Magyars raided into the Kingdom of Moravia, north of the Danube. The origin of the Magyars is uncertain. Their language is linked in Europe only with Finnish, and tradition has it that one group of Magyars settled in Finland, while the other went south and established itself on the Hungarian plain. Their own legends have the Magyars entering Hungary with the Huns, leaving it to resettle in the Caucasus and Volga regions and then reentering Hungary at the end of the ninth century. Under their leader Arpád, the Magyars entered Hungary to stay in 896, the year generally given for the founding of the Hungarian state. They easily subdued the scattered population of the central plain and then crushed Moravia in 906 and German forces in 907. A century later they conquered Transylvania.

A long period of warfare followed. The Magyars ravaged Swabia, Bavaria, and Thuringia, obliging German princes to buy them off or incorporate them into their armies. After being defeated by King Henry I in 933, the Magyars shifted their attention elsewhere. In 934 and 942 they raided the Byzantine Empire, reaching Constantinople. In 954 the Magyars struck west, cutting a wide swath of destruction through Bavaria and Burgundy all the way to Aquitaine. This raid gave some urgency to calls by Saxon emperor Otto I for a coalition against them.

In 955 the Magyars again invaded Germany. Their civil leader Bulcasú and military chieftain Lél (Lehel) led a force variously estimated at 50,000–100,000 horsemen. The Magyars were confident but departed from their usual light cavalry tactics to lay siege to the city of Augsburg beginning on August 8. With its walls in poor repair and the defenders badly outnumbered, Augsburg appeared easy prey for the Magyars, but Otto hastily put together a force of some 10,000 men from Saxony, Bavaria, Franconia, Swabia, and Bohemia and hurried to the relief of the city.

Only a day after the siege had begun the Magyars learned of Otto's approach. They abandoned the siege and made camp next to the nearby Lech River. Otto arrived and set up his camp knowing that he was heavily outnumbered. His force consisted largely of heavy cavalry, and he hoped to use his heavier and better-disciplined force to smash through the far more numerous Magyars. This had been the foundation of a victory in 933 against the Magyars at Merseburg by Otto's father, Henry the Fowler.

The battle took place under a scorching sun at Lechfeld, on the Lech River, on August 10, 955. Otto planned to attack in waves by nationality. Bavarians formed the first three waves, and Franks the fourth wave. The fifth wave was Otto's own Saxons, followed by lines of Swabians and a rear guard of Bohemian cavalry. As the Germans rode down the eastern side of the Lech, a force of Magyars rode undetected in the opposite direction on the western side of the river and then crossed it to attack Otto's rear area and supply train. This force of Magyars easily scattered the defending Bohemians and Swabians as well.

The Magyars appeared poised to crush Otto in a great pincer movement, but their lack of coordination (largely the result of their smaller force halting to loot the baggage train) proved their undoing. Otto ordered the Franconians to turn and deal with the attack to his rear; they soon came on the Magyars unhorsed and wiped them out. Otto then turned to deal with the main Magyar body to his front and ordered the charge.

The Germans rode forward in good order. The Magyars managed to get off one volley of arrows before the Germans reached their lines, but shields deflected most of the Magyar missiles. Superior discipline and the bravery of the coalition forces won the day, with Otto, sword in hand, joining the fighting.

The Magyars broke and were annihilated. Most of those who stood and fought were slain, and many others drowned trying to escape across the Lech. The battle extended over a 20-hour period, but for several days the Germans rounded up Magyar survivors. Both Bulcasú and Lél were among those executed. The Germans maimed a number of the prisoners they did not execute before setting them free.

Otto decided not to press his luck by invading the Magyar homeland. His victory had accomplished his aim of ending Magyar raids into Germany, and it convinced the Magyars to accommodate the new Holy Roman Empire, especially in matters of religion. The victory at Lechfeld brought Otto international recognition and led to the formal establishment of the Holy Roman Empire. Otto officially received the title of Holy Roman Emperor from Pope John XII in 962, assuming the mantle of Charlemagne as defender of the faith. Otto visited Rome the same year and reaffirmed the temporal power of the pope but as a vassal of the German king. The struggle of popes versus emperors continued, helping to delay the unification of both Germany and Italy until the second half of the 19th century, with great consequences for European history.

References

Balász, György, and Károly Szelényi. *The Magyars: The Birth of a European Nation.* Budapest: Corvina, 1989.

Falco, Giorgio. *The Holy Roman Empire.* Westport, CT: Greenwood, 1980.

Reuter, Timothy. *Germany in the Early Middle Ages.* London: Longman, 1991.

Battle of Hastings

Date	October 14, 1066	
Location	Hastings in southern England	
Opponents (* winner)	*Normans	Anglo-Saxons
Commander	Duke William of Normandy	King Harold of England
Approx. # Troops	6,000	6,000
Importance	Most important battle on English soil leads to William being crowned king of England with tremendous future consequences that entangle England with France	

The Battle of Hastings (October 14, 1066), arguably the most important land battle in British history, resulted in the Norman conquest of England. By 1066 Duke William of Normandy was probably the most powerful French noble and the potential master of France. William also laid claim to the throne of England. In 1064 Harold Godwinson, Earl of Wessex and chief adviser to English king Edward the Confessor (r. 1042–1066), arrived in Normandy, either as an emissary from Edward to confirm William as his successor or because, as Harold later claimed, his ship had

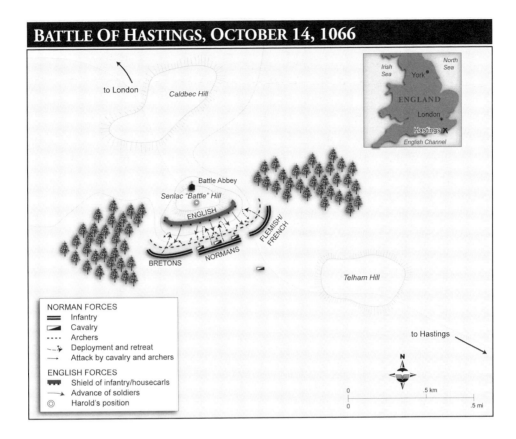

BATTLE OF HASTINGS, OCTOBER 14, 1066

been wrecked on the Norman coast. In any case, William extracted from Harold an oath in which Harold recognized him as Edward's successor and promised to aid William in securing the crown.

On his return to England, Harold was soon forced to side against his brother Tostig, who led a popular uprising against Edward. Tostig was driven into exile and sought refuge with his wife's brother-in-law Baldwin of Flanders, William's father-in-law and ally. In January 1066 Edward died, commending his family and kingdom to Harold. The principal English nobles assembled as the Witan elected Harold king.

When this news reached William he resolved to secure by whatever means necessary his claimed inheritance. He sent emissaries to Harold demanding that he fulfill his oath. Harold's position was weak. England was disunited, and Harold was not of a royal line. Two important earls in northern England refused to acknowledge his rule. Harold won over one emissary by marrying his sister, and in April Harold secured recognition as king.

Still, William's position was much stronger. Not only did he rule the rich duchy of Normandy, but his alliances with other prominent French nobles were strong, and he enjoyed the support of much of European opinion, which regarded Harold as a usurper. William isolated Harold diplomatically and even secured the support of

Pope Alexander II. To weaken Harold further, William encouraged Tostig to lead Norse forces on raids against the English coast. Although Harold defeated Tostig's men and forced them back to their ships, the raids had an important ancillary effect because they led Harold to believe that William's invasion was imminent.

William's army was centered on mounted cavalry and had been well tested in various military campaigns. Its principal weapons were the lance, the sword, and the mace. The men were protected by shields and helmets, and many wore chain mail armor. William would have to requisition ships to transport his men and horses to England. A more serious problem lay in the vagaries of the weather for a channel crossing.

Edward had disbanded the small English fleet, so Harold had to scrape together and transform into warships various fishing and commercial vessels to meet a Norman invasion. Harold could count only on a small force of professionals for his army. Only with difficulty would he be able to assemble a larger citizen force, the fyrd, for which there would be pay for two months. Although many of his professional soldiers were mounted, the major fighting was on foot. The men were armed with spears, javelins, two-edged swords, and long-handled axes. Archery was practiced but was not yet important as an English weapon of war. Judging by the historical record of the Bayeux Tapestry, the Anglo-Saxon soldiers were protected similarly to the Normans.

Harold mobilized both his land and sea forces and kept them on guard throughout the summer. At the end of September their terms of service as well as money and provisions for the troops had all expired. No sooner had the English forces disbanded than Harold received word that Norwegian king Harald Hardrada, accompanied by Tostig, had invaded the north.

Norwegian forces, sailing in some 300 ships, landed near York on September 18, 1066. Two days later at Gate Fulford the invaders defeated English forces under earls Edwin and Morcar. Harold immediately marched north with such forces as had not already been disbanded, and on September 25 at Stamford Bridge he all but wiped out the Norwegians. Both Harald Hardrada and Tostig were among the dead. Harold allowed the survivors (reportedly not more than two dozen boatloads full) to return to Norway. Harold had also sustained heavy losses, and the battle thus had tremendous consequences for the upcoming struggle with William.

William was preparing to sail for England. His forces were ready in early August, but for some reason he did not then sail. He did attempt to depart in mid-September, but contrary winds prevented it. On September 27 the winds finally shifted to the south, and the fleet set out. Landing in England at Pevensey the next day, William soon marched his army to Hastings, the coastal terminus of the road to London. He then set about ravaging the countryside in an effort to draw Harold into battle.

Harold was at York on October 1 celebrating his victory when he learned of William's arrival. Harold immediately hurried south, stopping only briefly in London to gather additional men. He also ordered out some 70 vessels to prevent William's ships from escaping. Harold undoubtedly would have been better served by remaining in London longer to gather more men, but he was by nature impulsive and offensive-minded. He departed London on October 11 to cover the 60 miles to Hastings, probably hoping to catch William by surprise with a night attack, but arrived too late on October 13 and decided to let his men rest. The two armies were about seven miles apart when Harold made camp. Learning of Harold's approach, William decided to strike first.

William advanced on the Saxon forces at dawn on October 14. Although William may have enjoyed a slight numerical advantage, each side probably had about 6,000 men. The fight was also even in terms of training and equipment. Harold's professional forces formed a shield wall and held the high ground, but Harold was short of archers and had no cavalry, whereas William had a mixed force of infantry, cavalry, and archers.

Battle was joined with a Norman attack at about 9:00 a.m. William's Breton left wing soon retreated in confusion, and there was a sense of panic in the army on false news that William had been slain. William did have three horses killed underneath him that day, but he now showed himself to his men, rallied them, and led his troops in cutting down the few Saxons who left the shield wall in the pursuit.

The battle raged for the remainder of the day and might have gone either way. The Normans mounted a series of attacks and feigned retreats but drew few of the Saxons from the protection of the shield wall. Finally William ordered high-angle arrow fire from his archers, followed by a last charge. Harold was struck in the eye with an arrow, probably in this barrage. In any case, the Norman horsemen and infantry managed to crack the shield wall. Harold was cut down fighting under his standard. The English were soon in flight, pursued by the Normans. Harold's death made the battle decisive.

Following the battle William cautiously advanced on London, ravaging the countryside as he went. The death of Harold and his brothers in the battle created a leadership vacuum, and in mid-December most Anglo-Saxon nobles submitted to William. He was formally crowned king of England on Christmas Day 1066, to be known to history ever since as William the Conqueror.

William spent the next three years putting down rebellions and destroying much of the English countryside in the process, but he also created the English nation and an effective state system centered on the king that was of tremendous advantage to England in the centuries to come. William's victory also ended the long Anglo-Saxon connection with Scandinavia and linked Norman England with France, which had tremendous consequences for both nations in ensuing centuries.

References

Bradbury, Jim. *The Battle of Hastings.* Stroud, Gloucestershire, UK: Sutton, 1998.

Freeman, Edward. *The History of the Norman Conquest of England.* Chicago: University of Chicago Press, 1974.

Howarth, David. *1066: The Year of the Conquest.* New York: Viking Penguin, 1977.

Morillo, Stephen, ed. *The Battle of Hastings: Sources and Interpretations.* Rochester, NY: University of Rochester Press, 1996.

Battle of Manzikert

Date	August 19, 1071	
Location	Manzikert (modern Malazgirt), eastern Turkey	
Opponents (* winner)	*Ottomans	Byzantines
Commander	Alp Arslan, Seljuk Sultan of Baghdad	Emperor Romanos IV Diogenes
Approx. # Troops	50,000	35,000–50,000 men
Importance	Byzantine Empire falls into warring factions, allowing the Ottomans to periodically ravage Anatolia	

The Battle of Manzikert (on August 19, 1071), which took place near Lake Van in eastern Anatolia, occurred during the wars between the Byzantine Empire and the Seljuk Ottomans and opened the way for Seljuk domination of Anatolia.

In 1055 Muslim Seljuk leader Tughril Beg captured Baghdad and brought an end to the Buyid dynasty. Initially they did not seek war with the Christian Byzantine Empire, but such a clash became more likely as Seljuk power expanded into the dissident Byzantine border province of Christian Armenia. From Armenia, marauding Turkish forces penetrated central Anatolia and even reached the eastern Aegean Sea.

The Byzantine Empire was already under assault on several fronts. The Normans threatened its control of southern Italy, and Byzantine possessions in the Balkans were also under attack. More ominously, feuds among the noble families of the empire and rebellions frequently forced the emperor to recall forces from the periphery of his empire. When Emperor Constantine X Doukas (r. 1059–1067) died in 1067, the aristocracy insisted that his widow, Eudokia Makrembolitissa (Eudocia Macrembolitissa), take as her new husband and emperor the successful General Romanos. He became Emperor Romanos IV Diogenes (Romanus IV Diogenese, r. 1067–1071).

After rebuilding the Byzantine Army, during 1068–1069 Romanos conducted a series of successful campaigns against Seljuk sultan of Baghdad Alp Arslan (the "Brave Lion"), forcing him back into Armenia and Mesopotamia. Romanos then campaigned in Syria, which had taken advantage of Seljuk successes to rise against Byzantium, but returned to eastern Anatolia to defeat the Ottomans in the Battle of Heraclea (Eregli) in 1069. Alp then withdrew to Aleppo. Romanos again controlled Armenia except for a few Seljuk fortresses.

In 1070 Romanos shifted his efforts to Italy. He enjoyed some success against the Normans, but a renewed Turkish threat against eastern Anatolia forced him to withdraw, and in 1071 the Normans conquered southern Italy completely. The Anatolian threat took the form of two Turkish armies under Alp and his brother-in-law Arisiaghi. Alp took the Byzantine fortress city of Manzikert but was repulsed at Edessa (Urfa). Arisiaghi meanwhile defeated the principal Byzantine force under Manuel Comnenus near Sebastia.

In the spring of 1071 Romanos departed Constantinople to deal with the Seljuks, moving east from Sebastia via Theodosiopolis (Erzerum). Estimates of the size of his army vary from 35,000 to 50,000 men. The army was clearly a polyglot force and included some elite units, especially the emperor's own Varangian Guard, but also a number of pressed Armenian and Syrian forces of dubious quality and loyalty. There were also many mercenaries: Frankish, German, and Norman heavy cavalry and Turkish light cavalry.

Arriving in eastern Anatolia, Romanos dispatched an advance force under General Basilacius to the vicinity of Seljuk-held Akhlat to ravage that area and serve as a screen for his own force. Romanos laid siege to and took Manzikert, then moved to besiege Akhlat. He sent Basilacius toward Khoi, in Media, where Alp was reported to be assembling a large army.

In late July or early August, Alp's army of 50,000 or more men brushed aside Basilacius's covering force of perhaps 10,000–15,000 men. Basilacius then withdrew his men to the southeast without informing Romanos. The reasons for this are obscure but are believed to have been prompted by a treachery including Basilacius; Romanos's second-in-command, Andronicus Ducas; and Empress Eudokia.

In any event, Alp's more powerful force came on Romanos's army unawares. Almost all of the Ottomans were mounted, and the bulk were horse archers. Had Romanos been prepared, his heavy cavalry (cataphracts), which combined missile and shock tactics, would undoubtedly have been more than a match for the Turkish light cavalry. With his forces disorganized, Romanos ordered an immediate withdrawal toward Manzikert to regroup. His mercenary light cavalry, believing that the emperor had been defeated, promptly deserted, leaving Romanos with fewer than 35,000 men.

On August 19, 1071, Romanos formed his remaining men in two lines. He commanded the first line in person, while Andronicus commanded the second line. While the Ottomans were forming for battle, Alp sent a messenger requesting terms, probably a ruse to gain time. In any case, Romanos demanded a full Turkish withdrawal from Byzantine territory.

The battle began shortly thereafter with Turkish arrow attacks, which Romanos met effectively with his own archers and heavy cavalry. By late afternoon Romanos had driven the Ottomans back far enough to take their camp. By dusk, with no decision gained and being some seven miles from his own lightly guarded camp, Romanos decided to withdraw. The Ottomans then harassed the Byzantine withdrawal. With confusion growing in his own force, Romanos decided to turn and counterattack with his first line. Despite the order to halt, Andronicus continued to withdraw his second line, abandoning Romanos. The far more numerous Ottomans easily enveloped Romanos's line and killed or took as prisoner all of the Byzantines, Romanos among the latter.

The Battle of Manzikert, remembered thereafter by the Greeks as the Dreadful Day, had tremendous consequences. Although Alp freed Romanos in return for tribute and the dismantling of some Byzantine fortresses, Romanos's enemies back in Constantinople had seized power. When Romanos attempted to regain his throne, he was captured. Blinded by Andronicus Daccus, Romanos died soon thereafter.

The Byzantine Empire then fell into a series of civil wars and rebellions. Frequently the warring factions called in the Turks, opening the way for these warlords to ravage Anatolia. The Seljuks razed the Byzantine cities there and killed or sold into slavery hundreds of thousands of people. Anatolia never recovered. This state of affairs finally prompted an appeal from Constantinople to Rome that led in 1095 to the First Crusade. The Battle of Manzikert also carried the immense longer-term consequence of the expansion of Muslim power into Eastern Europe.

References

Friendly, Alfred. *The Dreadful Day: The Battle of Manzikert, 1071*. London: Hutchinson, 1981.

Kaegi, Walter E. *Byzantium and the Early Islamic Conquests*. New York: Cambridge University Press, 1992.

Treadgold, Warren. *Byzantium and Its Army, 284–1081*. Stanford, CA: Stanford University Press, 1995.

Siege of Jerusalem

Date	June 7–July 18, 1099	
Location	City of Jerusalem in Palestine	
Opponents (* winner)	*Christian crusaders	Fatimid Caliphate of Cairo
Commander	Godfrey of Bouillon, Duke of Lorraine	Emir Iftikhar ad-Dawla
Approx. # Troops	13,000	20,000
Importance	Makes possible the establishment of the Latin Kingdom of Jerusalem	

At the end of the 11th century, Latin Christendom took the offensive against Islam with the Crusades, a series of wars designed to free the Holy Land from Muslim control. A number of factors were behind the Crusades. In 1070 the Ottomans took Jerusalem from Egypt, and accounts began to reach the West of persecution of Christians visiting the holy places. The schism of 1054 dangerously weakened the Byzantine Empire, which had traditionally barred Turkish expansion into Eastern

Europe, and certain Italian cities (including Genoa, Pisa, and Venice) sought to secure the lucrative trade of the eastern Mediterranean. The final decision rested with Pope Urban II, who in 1095 preached the First Crusade at Clermont. He envisioned it as a holy war to save Europe and the Byzantine Empire from Islam but also a means to end feudal strife between Christians in a grand war against the infidel. Urban hoped that the result would be a unified West under the leadership of the Catholic Church.

The First Crusade lasted from 1096 to 1099. Urban called for the Christian armies to depart in August 1096, but the peasants would not wait. Stirred by religious fervor and a plenary indulgence, some 12,000 peasants set out from France, and another 9,000 set out from Germany. The peasants made their way to Constantinople, where Byzantine emperor Alexius I provided ships to transport them across the Bosporus. He urged them to wait there until the armed knights could arrive, but the peasant soldiers set out alone and were slaughtered in large numbers by Sultan Kilij Arslan's Turkish archers on October 21, 1096, at Dracon.

Meanwhile, the feudal knights assembled in France. No king was among them, and the most notable figure was Godfrey of Bouillon, Duke of Lorraine. The knights and supporting infantry then made their way to Constantinople, where Alexis, fearful of their presence, hurried them across the straits in early 1097. Fortunately for the Crusaders, their opponents were even more divided, and most Turkish forces were off conducting operations to the east.

The Crusaders moved south along the Mediterranean coast so that they might be resupplied from the sea. On their way they were joined by Italian-Norman forces under a certain Taticius. On May 6 Godfrey and his men reached Nicea. Raymond of Saint Giles, Count of Toulouse and Marquis of Provence, joined the force, as did Bohemond of Taranto, uncle of Taticius; Robert, Duke of Normandy (the son of William the Conqueror); and Stephen, Count of Blois and Chartres. On May 21 the Crusaders defeated Turkish forces under Arslan, which then withdrew.

The Crusaders then besieged Nicea. Operations included unsuccessful mining under one of the main towers. Only the appearance of a Byzantine fleet off Nicea induced the leaders to surrender on June 19, 1097, but to the Byzantines. The Crusaders were bent on plunder, but Emperor Alexis plied their leaders with gold and the soldiers with food.

Two weeks later the Crusaders resumed their southward progression in two separate armies under Bohemond and Raymond of Toulouse. At dawn on July 1 the Turks attacked Bohemond's camp on the plains of Dorylaeum (present-day Eskisehir). Bohemond held off the Turks for six hours until Raymond could arrive, whereupon the combined Christian forces utterly defeated the Turks, capturing their camp and Arslan's treasury.

In November 1097 the Crusaders arrived at the rich, well-fortified city of Antioch, governed by Yaghi Siyan. The Crusaders secured the nearest port, Saint Simeon, thanks to the arrival of 13 ships from Genoa bringing men and supplies.

The Crusaders then defeated a Muslim relief force coming from Syria. In early February with defections mounting and conditions fast deteriorating, the Crusaders defeated a second Turkish relief force. Early in March, English ships arrived at Saint Simeon from Constantinople with siege machines. With yet another Turkish relief force en route, however, they were able to capture Antioch only on June 3. The Ottomans arrived several days later, only to discover the Christians in possession of the city. After an unsuccessful effort to take the city by storm, the Ottomans settled in to starve the Christians out. The situation seemed dire, but on June 28 in a bold strike the entire Christian army sortied from Antioch and defeated the Ottomans.

Following six-months' respite, the Crusaders resumed their advance in mid-January 1099. Their objective was Jerusalem, the most holy city for Christians, who believe it to be the site of Christ's death and resurrection. Jerusalem had passed under Muslim control in 638; in 1099 it was ruled by the Fatimid caliphate of Cairo. Following a 400-mile march south from Antioch along the eastern Mediterranean coast through Sidon, Acre, and Caesarea, the Crusaders arrived at Jerusalem on June 7, 1099.

During the siege of Jerusalem, Duke Godfrey commanded some 13,000 men, including 1,300 knights. The Fatimid governor of Jerusalem, Emir Iftikhar ad-Dawla, could count on 20,000 men. The defenders had poisoned nearby wells and cisterns, and the heat was oppressive. The Crusaders knew that they would have to work quickly. As early as June 12 they attempted an assault, but lacking sufficient scaling ladders and war machines, they were easily repulsed. This material arrived on June 17 when six supply ships sailed into the port of Jaffa, which had been abandoned by the Egyptians. Within several weeks the Crusaders had constructed a large number of mangonels and scaling ladders and two large wooden siege towers.

On the night of July 13–14 the Crusaders braved defensive fire to push the towers against the city walls. On the morning of July 15 Duke Godfrey led attackers in one of the towers over a wooden drawbridge; other Crusaders employed scaling ladders in a well-coordinated attack. Many of the Muslims sought refuge in the El Aqsa Mosque. Tancred, one of the Crusader leaders, promised that their lives would be spared and gave them his banner as proof.

Once the Christian forces had taken the city, they embarked on an orgy of destruction, slaughtering all Muslims who could be found regardless of location, including those within the El Aqsa Mosque. The victims included women and children. Some Muslims were beheaded, others were slain with arrows or forced to jump from the towers, and still others were tortured or burned to death. Estimates of the number slain reach as high as 70,000 people.

Jews fared no better; the Christians herded them into a synagogue and burned them alive. Their blood lust at last spent, the victors proceeded to the Church of the Holy Sepulcher, the grotto of which they believed had once held the body of the crucified Christ, and there gave thanks to the God of Mercies for their victory.

On August 2, 1099, in the Battle of Ascalon (Askelon), Duke Godfrey led 10,000 Crusaders against a relief force of 50,000 Egyptians under Emir Al-Afdal. Unlike the Turks, who relied primarily on mounted archers, the Egyptian Fatimids counted on fanaticism and shock action. They were thus at great disadvantage against the heavily armored and well-armed Crusaders. A cavalry charge gave the Christians an overwhelming victory.

The Latin Kingdom of Jerusalem lasted only 50 years, from 1099 to 1148. Its decline was in part due to the death of Godfrey of Bouillon, who was known as Defender of the Holy Sepulcher. He refused to take the title of king in a city where Christ had worn a crown of thorns. Godfrey's successors were far less capable men. The Crusades continued for more than another century with at least seven separate efforts, all of which ultimately failed. By the end of the 12th century, the Muslims again controlled the Holy Land.

References

Armstrong, Karen. *Jerusalem: One City, Three Faiths.* New York: Knopf, 1996.

Asbridge, Thomas. *The First Crusade: A New History.* New York: Oxford University Press, 2005.

Baldwin, Marshall W., ed. *A History of the Crusades,* Vol. 1, *The First Hundred Years,* edited by Kenneth M. Setton. Madison: University of Wisconsin Press, 1969.

Riley-Smith, Jonathan, ed. *The Oxford Illustrated History of the Crusades.* New York: Oxford University Press, 1997.

Tyerman, Christopher. *Fighting for Christendom: Holy War and the Crusades.* New York: Oxford University Press, 2005.

Battle of Hattin

Date	July 4, 1147	
Location	Near Lake Galilee	
Opponents (* winner)	*Muslims	Christian crusaders
Commander	Saladin, ruler of Syria and Egypt	Guy of Lusignan, King of Jerusalem
Approx. # Troops	30,000	20,000
Importance	Leads to the Muslim conquest of most of Palestine	

The Battle of Hattin, fought in the Holy Land during the Second Crusade of 1147–1149, was a major Muslim victory over the Christian forces. Hattin is located in Galilee, seven miles west of Tiberius and the Sea of Galilee.

Crusader Reynald of Châtillon, lord of the castle at Kerak on the road between Damascus and Mecca, carried out a series of attacks on Muslim caravans and towns along the Red Sea. When King Guy de Lusignan, of the Latin Kingdom of Jerusalem, failed to punish Reynald for these actions, the brilliant Muslim military leader Egyptian sultan Saladin (Salan-al-din) vowed to do so and mounted an invasion of Palestine.

On June 26, 1187, Saladin crossed the Jordan River at the head of a force of some 20,000 Ottomans and laid siege to the Crusader stronghold of Tiberius. King Guy's advisers called for an immediate effort to raise the siege. Count Raymond of Tripoli, the ablest of the Crusader generals, whose wife was then in Tiberius, urged Guy to wait. Raymond knew that Tiberius was well supplied and believed it best to delay any relief effort until Saladin's forces experienced supply problems in the countryside. Also, the extreme heat of summer would make campaigning difficult then. Guy ignored this. He ordered Christian castles and strong points to provide much of their garrisons and in late June Guy led a relieving Christian army of approximately 1,200 knights and 18,000 infantry toward Tiberius.

On July 2 the Christian force reached Sephoria, about equidistant between Acre and Tiberius. Again Raymond urged caution, and again he was rebuffed. Although Raymond had warned Guy that there was only one spring accessible to the army along its planned route, the army continued east.

Saladin was pleased. He knew the effects that lack of water would have on the heavily armored Crusader force. Saladin immediately sent light cavalry to attack the Christians, bringing them to a halt on July 3 in the middle of the parched and barren land. The Muslim attackers and the heat of the day forced the Christians to take up position near the village of Hattin and next to two mounds known as the Horns.

The Ottomans surrounded the Crusaders and kept constant arrow fire on their camp during the night of July 3–4. What little water the Christians had was consumed. Saladin also had his men set fire to nearby brush upwind of the Crusader camp, blowing smoke into it and making it even more difficult for the men and horses.

The next morning, July 4, Saladin still refused to close with the heavily armored Christians. Bringing up fresh stocks of arrows, he ordered his bowmen to continue their harassing fire. The Christian cavalry charged the Muslims but this separated the infantry from the cavalry and enabled the Muslims to destroy the latter piecemeal. At the very end of the battle, Raymond and a small force of cavalry cut their way through the Turkish lines, but they were the only ones to escape. The rest of the Crusaders, out of water, their horses dying of thirst, and under constant harassing fire from Turkish archers, were forced to surrender. Guy was among the prisoners.

Exact casualty totals are unknown, but certainly the majority of the Christians were either taken prisoner or killed. While Saladin ordered Reynald executed, he treated Guy well and subsequently released him on the latter's promise that he would not fight again. Raymond later died of wounds sustained in the battle.

Saladin's victory at Hattin led to the Muslim conquest of most of Palestine, the Christian garrisons of which had been so badly depleted to put together the force taken in the battle. Over the next months Saladin captured Tiberius, Acre, and Ascalon, although Crusaders arriving by sea managed to hold off the Ottomans at

Tyre. Saladin laid siege to Jerusalem on September 20, and that city surrendered on October 2, 1187. Unlike the behavior of the Christians in the First Crusade, Saladin treated the defeated well.

Most of the Latin Kingdom of Jerusalem had now been lost to the Muslims, not to be regained. However, the Europeans controlled the Mediterranean Sea, and the Christian states soon mounted a new series of Crusades in the Holy Land. These Crusades, however, were increasingly motivated by secular rather than religious reasons.

References

France, John. *Western Warfare in the Age of the Crusades, 1000–1300.* Ithaca, NY: Cornell University Press, 1999.

Gore, Terry L. *Neglected Heroes: Leadership and War in the Early Medieval Period.* Westport, CT: Praeger, 1995.

Tyerman, Christopher. *Fighting for Christendom: Holy War and the Crusades.* New York: Oxford University Press, 2005.

Siege of Acre

Date	August 28, 1189–July 12, 1191	
Location	City of Acre in Palestine (Akko, Israel) on the eastern Mediterranean	
Opponents (* winner)	*Christian crusaders	Muslims
Commander	Guy, King of the Latin Kingdom of Jerusalem; Henry of Troyes, Count of Champagne; Philippe II Augustus, King of France; and Richard I, King of England	Saladin, Sultan of Egypt
Approx. # Troops	Unknown	Unknown
Importance	Halts the reconquest of the Holy Land by Egyptian sultan Saladin; permits the existence of a truncated Christian kingdom there for another century	

One of the great sieges in history, the two-year-long operation by Christian Crusaders against the port city of Acre in Palestine during 1189–1191 halted the reconquest of the Holy Land by Egyptian sultan Saladin (Salan-al-din) and helped ensure the survival of a truncated Crusader kingdom there for another century.

In the months following Saladin's great victory over the Crusaders in the Battle of Hattin on July 4, 1187, the Muslims reconquered much of the territory of the Latin Kingdom of Jerusalem. Acre surrendered without a fight on July 10; Jerusalem followed on October 2 after resisting for less than two weeks. Saladin had taken as prisoner King Guy, ruler of the Latin Kingdom of Jerusalem since 1186, but had freed Guy on the promise that he would not again fight against the Muslims. Although Guy was able to secure a ruling from the Catholic Church that the oath he had taken in captivity was null and void, he was without a kingdom.

The fall of Jerusalem prompted the Third Crusade, however, and brought Christian reinforcements under Archbishop Ubaldo of Pisa as well as Sicilian mercenaries. On August 28, 1189, Guy began an ineffectual siege of Acre. An assault several days later failed, and Guy appealed to the Christian states for additional assistance. A Danish fleet arrived in September and placed Acre under blockade from the sea. Ships from other European states joined this effort, and Conrad of Monferrat, who had established a kingdom at Tyre, lent troops. In October the Crusaders assaulted Acre again but were halted in bitter fighting.

Saladin sought reinforcements from Muslim powers as far away as Spain. With this support, in both October and December he was able to pass ships through the Christian naval blockade and bring supplies and men into Acre. He also began a land countersiege of King John's forces. Both sides built extensive trench systems and fortifications, with those of the Crusaders facing in two directions. Conrad was nevertheless able to get vital supplies to Guy by sea.

Using these supplies, during the winter of 1189 the Christians built three large siege towers and moved them against the city walls on May 1, 1190. On May 11 Saladin launched an attack on the Christian siege lines. The fighting was intense, and Saladin's attacks forced the Crusaders to fight on both fronts, allowing the defenders of Acre to burn the Crusaders' siege towers.

During the summer of 1190 more Christian reinforcements arrived, chiefly from France. The most important figure among the new Crusaders was Henry of Troyes, Count of Champagne, who took command of siege operations. In October, Germans from the army of Holy Roman Emperor Frederick Barbarossa arrived but without Frederick, who had drowned in June. The besieging Crusaders constructed both rams and trebuchets for another assault on Acre, but the defenders were again able to destroy the siege engines with inflammatory devices, beating back several major assaults.

In November the Crusaders succeeded in opening a land supply route. That winter, however, Saladin was able to close it off and isolate the Crusaders again. The winter of 1190–1191 was especially severe and hard on the Crusaders, now suffering from disease and famine. Among the victims were Guy's wife Sybelle and their daughters. The Christians would have broken off the siege had it not been for the hope of English and French reinforcements that spring.

As promised, additional Christian manpower, ships, supplies, and money arrived under French king Philippe II Augustus on April 20, 1191, and English king Richard I (the Lion-Hearted) on June 8. Their arrival created a new sense of hope and enthusiasm among the Crusaders. With additional warships, the Crusader forces were able at last to cut off Acre entirely from the seaborne resupply. On land the Crusaders constructed a large number of trebuchets and other artillery pieces and a large siege tower. The Crusaders concentrated their attacks on one tower, known as "The Accused."

With Acre in dire straits, Saladin attempted to draw off the Crusaders on July 3. This attack, led by his nephew, failed. The Crusaders had now opened a number of breaches in the city walls. Although the defenders repulsed three assaults, the city finally surrendered on July 12, 1191.

Acre served as the chief military base for King Richard I and his reconquest of much of the coast of Palestine to Jaffa thereafter. Almost exactly 100 years later, there was another siege of Acre. This time the Crusaders defended the city against a Muslim Turkish attack. The Ottomans were victorious, capturing this last Christian enclave in Palestine in May 1291. The victors then filled in the harbor. Acre was again the site of a famous siege in 1799, when Napoleon Bonaparte and his Army of Egypt tried unsuccessfully to take the city. Failure here forced Napoleon to retreat back to Cairo.

References

Gillingham, J. *Richard I.* 2nd ed. New Haven, CT: Yale University Press, 2000.

Lyons, M., and D. Jackson. *Saladin: The Politics of Holy War.* Cambridge: Cambridge University Press, 1982.

Rogers, R. *Latin Siege Warfare in the Twelfth Century.* Oxford, UK: Clarendon, 1992.

Second Battle of Taraori

Date	1192	
Location	Taraori near Panipat, some 90 miles north of Delhi, India	
Opponents (* winner)	*Ghor, with Afghans, Persians, and Ottomans	Rajpatuna
Commander	Muhammad of Ghor	King Prithvaraja
Approx. # Troops	As many as 120,000	Unknown
Importance	Muhammad annexes Rajpatuna, leading to Muslim rule in India until the British end the Moghul dynasty in 1857	

The 1192 Battle of Taraori led to Muslim rule in India. Islam had been known in India through Muslim traders since soon after the death of the Prophet Muhammad in 632. The first Muslim military expedition against India occurred in 637, and in 712 Muhammad ibn Kasim invaded and conquered the impoverished north Indian province of Sind. There was, however, no Arab military move against the interior of the subcontinent.

It would not be the Arabs but rather the steppe Ottomans who, having conquered Persia and Afghanistan, would carry the Muslim faith into India. In 1000 Mahmud of Ghazni launched the first of 16 military expeditions that occurred over a 26-year period into Hindustan, in northern India. His objectives were both monetary and religious. He sought to acquire the wealth of India, but he also wanted to propagate the faith and eradicate what he regarded as the "false" Indian religions. His wanton destruction of Indian temples made him known as the "Idol Breaker." Mahmud looted but did not build, yet for a time his capital of Ghazni was one of the world's wealthiest cities.

Early in the 12th century, Ghazni came under challenge from the Afghan fortress city of Ghor. The struggle between Ghor and Ghazni was at first inconclusive, but in 1174 the soldiers of Ghor triumphed when Ghiyas-ad-Din captured Ghazni and placed his brother Muizz-al-Din on its throne. The latter came to be known as Muhammad of Ghor.

Muhammad of Ghor immediately set out to expand his influence into India. In 1182 he conquered Sind, and three years later he secured control of Punjab, in northwestern India, and westernmost Hindustan. Where his predecessors had relied on Hindu levies, Muhammad employed only Ottomans and Afghans, reliable Muslims who would be zealous in carrying out a religious war against Hindus.

In the winter of 1190–1191 Muhammad invaded south from the Punjab into Rajputana. That state's soldiers were skilled and well-disciplined fighters and were loyal to their ruler, King Prithvaraja, who was also a capable general. Muhammad's troops soon captured the border fortress town of Bhatinda and garrisoned it with 1,200 cavalry. King Prithvaraja immediately responded; the battle between the two sides occurred near Panipat, some 90 miles north of Delhi. Panipat is known variously as Tarain, Narain, and, most recently, Taraori. No precise date for the battle is available, but it took place in 1191. The size of the armies is also not known, although reputedly the Rajputs were the more numerous.

The battle began with Muhammad launching a cavalry attack, firing off arrows, against the Rajput center. The Rajputs stood firm, mounting flanking attacks that forced a Muslim retreat. To save the situation, Muhammad led a charge at the enemy line. Reportedly he fought personally with King Prithvaraja's brother, Govind Tai, Viceroy of Delhi. Govind Tai was mortally wounded but managed to wound Muhammad seriously in the arm. Muhammad escaped and joined his retreating army, which withdrew back to Ghor. Rather than pursue, the Rajputs proceeded to Bhatinda, which they recaptured only after a 13-month siege.

Muhammad recovered from his wound and mounted a new campaign the next year with a large force of Afghans, Persians, and Ottomans that may have totaled 120,000 men. The battle occurred sometime in 1192 on the same battlefield, although this time Muhammad was careful not to close with the well-disciplined Rajputs. He formed his army in five divisions and sent four of these to attack the Rajput flanks and rear. If pressed, they were to feign retreat to try to break the Rajput unit cohesion.

The flanking attacks failed in their design, and the fighting continued for most of the day. When Muhammad ordered his fifth division to pretend to withdraw in panic, the ruse worked. The Rajputs charged, breaking their unit cohesion. Muhammad then threw a fresh cavalry unit of 12,000 men into the battle, and they threw back the Rajput advance. The remaining Muslim forces turned and pursued, sending the Rajputs fleeing in panic.

With the Muslims almost on him, King Prithvanaja abandoned his elephant for a horse in an attempt to escape. He was ridden down and captured some miles from the battlefield and was promptly executed. Most of his subordinate commanders were also killed.

Muhammad annexed Rajputana, but he was not content with this. With the victory at Taraori, there was no armed force in India capable of withstanding him. In 1193 his forces took Bihar Province, the center of Buddhism. They virtually eradicated Buddhism there, forcing its practitioners to flee to Tibet and Nepal and thus ensuring that this religion would spread in China and not India. Over the next several years his armies expanded his control to the east and throughout northern India. In 1202 one of the armies reached Bengal, completing the annexation of Hindustan.

Muhammad also sought to expand his power in Persia and the Middle East but was defeated in his invasion of Khwarizm (Kiva) in 1203. At the end of the 13th century the Mongols arrived, defeating in turn the ruling Muslim dynasty in northern India and establishing the Moghul dynasty that ruled India until the British officially ended it in 1857. The religious divisions of India continued, and in 1948 irreconcilable differences led to the establishment of an independent Hindu India and Muslim Pakistan.

References

Davis, Paul K. *100 Decisive Battles: From Ancient Times to the Present.* Santa Barbara, CA: ABC-CLIO, 1999.

Haig, Wolseley, ed. *The Cambridge History of India,* Vol. 3. Delhi: S. Chand, 1965.

Kar, H. C. *Military History of India.* Calcutta: Firma KLM, 1980.

Battle of Bouvines

Date	July 27, 1214	
Location	Bouvines, near Tournai in Flanders	
Opponents (* winner)	*France	Holy Roman Empire, the County of Flanders, and England
Commander	King of France Philippe II (Philip Augustus)	Holy Roman Emperor Otto IV
Approx. # Troops	11,000 cavalry; 25,000 infantry	11,000 cavalry; 60,000 infantry
Importance	Ends the alliance against France and leads to French control of the Low Countries	

The Battle of Bouvines on July 27, 1214, was the culminating event of the 1213–1214 war between France and a coalition consisting of the Holy Roman Empire, the County of Flanders, and England. The war resulted from conflicting dynastic ambitions. King John of England had inherited large holdings in France as a result of his father Henry II's marriage to Eleanor of Aquitaine. John's so-called Angevin Empire consisted of most of present-day western France. He wanted to expand his holdings in France, while the nominal king of France, Philippe II of the Capetian dynasty in Paris, sought to control nearby territories nominally belonging to England. Upset by John's marriage to Isabella of Angoulême, Philippe summoned his vassal John to Paris (John's ancestor William, Count of Normandy and conqueror of England in 1066, had been a vassal of the French king). When John refused, Philippe went on the offensive.

During 1204–1206 Philippe led French forces in conquering Normandy, Brittany, Anjou, Maine, Touraine, and Poitou. The situation was further complicated by the political machinations of Pope Innocent III, who opposed the ambitions of Holy Roman Emperor Otto IV in Italy. King Philippe, who had his own differences with Innocent, nonetheless supported him against Otto.

The war began in 1212. An English naval victory at Damme in 1213 initially blocked Philippe's effort to control Flanders, and the allies then planned a two-pronged invasion of France. English forces under John were to attack in the southwest, while coalition forces under Otto delivered the main blow from the northeast.

As it worked out John posed no threat, failing to rally support in Aquitaine. Philippe sent forces under his son Louis to contain John, while Philippe took the bulk of his troops against the principal allied thrust in the northeast. There Otto had put together a coalition that included forces of the counts of Flanders and Boulogne as well as the leading feudal nobility of the Netherlands and Lorraine.

To forestall an invasion of his own territory, Philippe moved into Flanders. During March–July 1214 at the head of 11,000 cavalry and 25,000 infantry, Philippe consistently outmaneuvered Otto's larger force (11,000 cavalry and 60,000 infantry). With German and Flemish reinforcements coming up, Otto sought to get astride Philippe's line of communications between Tournai in Flanders and Paris. Philippe staged a withdrawal to bring Otto into a premature battle east of the town of Bouvines, near Tournai. Philippe had selected the terrain as ideally suited for cavalry operations, in which his better-trained horsemen would have the advantage. The infantry on both sides were indifferently trained and armed.

On July 27, 1214, Otto came upon the French already in line of battle and hastily deployed the imperial forces to meet them. Flemish knights under Count Ferrard held the allied left wing, the imperial infantry under Otto IV were in the center, and Count of Boulogne Renaud de Danmartin led the imperial forces on the right wing that included a small English contingent. On the French side, the left consisted of knights and infantry, the center contained the bulk of the infantry under Philippe, and the right was held largely by knights from Champagne.

A 19th-century drawing depicting the Battle of Bouvines in 1214, in which the outnumbered but better disciplined forces of King Philippe II Augustus of France defeated allied forces under King John of England, Holy Roman Emperor Otto IV, and the rulers of Flanders and Holland. The battle gave Philippe control of the Low Countries. (Ridpath, John Clark, *Ridpath's History of the World,* 1901)

The battle began when infantry from Soissons on the French left attacked the imperial right wing. Flemish knights and German pikemen drove back the French, causing the French royal household cavalry to ride to the rescue. A melee ensued, with each side hacking away at the other. The battle seesawed back and forth. Both Philippe and Otto were in the thick of the fight, and on occasion Philippe was in mortal danger.

Superior French discipline and training, especially in the cavalry, proved the difference. While Philippe's right-flank horsemen under Garin the Hospitaller held off the more numerous imperial cavalry, Philippe utilized the bulk of his horsemen to mount converging attacks against the center of the imperial line, eventually causing it to give way.

While the battle was still in doubt, Otto fled the field, hastening a general imperial collapse. Philippe was then able to concentrate on the imperial right under Danmartin. Although the small English force there distinguished itself, the battle was soon over. French casualties are unknown but were said to have been lighter than those of the coalition. The number of imperial infantry killed is unknown, but 170 of their knights died, and 140 other knights and 1,000 infantry were taken prisoner.

The Battle of Bouvines gave France control of the Low Countries. Philippe II, now recognized as Philippe Auguste or Philip Augustus, became the most powerful of European rulers. France now was the leading nation of medieval Europe. Conversely, the war marked the decline of the Holy Roman Empire and revealed the inability of the German states to resist outside incursions. Otto IV was replaced as emperor by Frederick II (Stupor Mundi) of Sicily. Finally, King John of England, already unpopular at home because of his poor leadership, heavy taxes, and unsuccessful wars, was forced to sign the Magna Carta, which restricted royal power.

References

Bradbury, Jim. *Philip Augustus, King of France, 1180–1223.* London: Longman, 1998.

Contamine, Philippe. *War in the Middle Ages.* Translated by Michael Jones. New York: Basil Blackwell, 1984.

Duby, Georges. *The Legend of Bouvines.* Berkeley: University of California Press, 1990.

Verbruggen, J. F. *The Art of Warfare in Western Europe during the Middle Ages.* Amsterdam: North Holland, 1977.

Battle of the Sajó River

Date	April 11, 1241	
Location	Muhi on the Sajó River in northeastern Hungary	
Opponents (* winner)	*Mongols	Hungarians
Commander	Subotai	King Béla IV
Approx. # Troops	As many as 120,000	More than 100,000
Importance	The Mongols ravage eastern Hungary and Transylvania and gain access to all central Europe	

The victory over a Hungarian army led by King Béla IV at Muhi on the Sajó River gave the Mongols access to all of Central Europe. Genghis Khan died in 1227, but his son and successor, Ogatai Khan, continued Mongol expansion. The Mongols conquered Korea in 1231 and defeated the Chin Empire during 1231–1234. In 1235 in the course of a conference with Mongol leaders, Ogatai outlined a plan of expansion in four areas: China, Korea, Southeast Asia, and Eastern Europe.

The offensive against Eastern Europe began in 1236–1237, when Ogatai sent 130,000 Mongols into the region. Batu Khan had nominal command, but Subotai exercised real command. Subotai defeated the Bulgars and then led his army across the frozen Volga River in December 1237. In the course of their winter campaign the Mongols destroyed the northern Russian principalities, culminating in the defeat and death of Grand Prince Yuri II of Vladimir in the Battle of the Sil River on March 4, 1237. At the same time, Mongol forces to the south entered the Ukraine, where they reorganized and reequipped their forces.

During the next two years Subotai consolidated Mongol control over eastern and southern Russia. While the states of Central and Western Europe knew little about Mongol conquests or intentions, the Mongols gathered accurate intelligence about the political situation to their west. Subotai began the offensive in November 1240 with 150,000 men, again campaigning in winter to achieve maximum mobility on horseback in the marshlands and across frozen rivers. When Kiev rejected surrender demands, Subotai captured it on December 6.

Leaving behind 30,000 men to control the conquered territory and maintain his lines of communication, Subotai invaded Central Europe with 120,000 men. The Mongols moved on four axes. Kaidu, grandson of Ogatai, commanded the northern flank; Batu and Subotai had charge of the two central forces; and Kadan, son of Ogatai, protected the southern flank. The two middle forces were to pass through the central Carpathians into Transylvania and then meet at Pest, on the east bank of the Danube.

Kaidu meanwhile moved into Silesia, defeating a Polish army under King Boleslav V at Kraków (Cracow) on March 3, 1241. To meet Kaidu, Prince Henry of Silesia put together a mixed force of some 40,000 Silesians, Germans, Poles, and Teutonic Knights. King Wenceslas of Bohemia marched north with 50,000 men to join them. However, Kaidu struck before the two opposing forces could join. In the hard-fought Battle of Legnica (known as the Battle of Liegnitz in German and also called the Battle of Wahlstatt) on April 9, 1241, Kaidu smashed Prince Henry's army. Kaidu then halted, having achieved his aims of devastating North-Central Europe and preventing its armies from moving south.

The Mongol southern advance had gone well. In mid-April the Mongols secured Transylvania, and Kadan drove north through the Iron Gates to join Subotai. On March 12, 1241, Hungarian king Béla IV, informed of the Mongol advance, called a conference of nobles at Buda, on the west bank of the Danube, to discuss how to meet the threat. On March 15 the conferees learned that the Mongol advance guard had already arrived at Pest, just opposite Buda.

Sure that the Pest defenses could hold the attackers, Béla IV gathered some 100,000 men over the next two weeks. At the beginning of April he set out from Pest to meet the invaders, confident that he had sufficient strength to defeat them. The Mongols withdrew before Béla's cautious advance. Late on April 10 about 100 miles northeast of Pest, the Hungarians encountered and defeated a weak Mongol force defending a bridge at Muhi on the Sajó River, a tributary of the Tisza. Béla IV then established a strong bridgehead on the east bank of the Sajó and camped for the night with the bulk of his force on the west bank in a strong defensive position of wagons chained together.

The Mongols attacked the Hungarians before dawn on April 11, 1241, striking the bridgehead with arrows and with stones hurled by catapults, followed closely by an infantry assault. The defenders fought fiercely, and the Hungarians sortied from the main camp to their aid.

They soon discovered that the attack was only a feint. Subotai had led 30,000 men across the river some distance south of the bridge, and this force now came in from the south and rear of the Hungarians. The Hungarians found themselves packed in a small space and devastated by Mongol arrows, stones, and burning naptha. King Béla IV managed to escape with some of his men to the north toward Pozsony (Bratislava). Although Mongol losses in the battle were heavy, the Hungarian force was virtually destroyed. It suffered between 40,000 and 70,000 dead, including much of the Magyar nobility.

With this Hungarian defeat, only the Danube River prevented a further Mongol advance. The Mongols held Eastern Europe from the Dnieper to the Oder and from the Baltic to the Danube. In a campaign lasting only four months, they had destroyed Christian forces numbering many times their own. Following the victory, the Mongols ravaged all eastern Hungary and Transylvania. With a majority of its settlements having been destroyed and a large portion of the population slain during the Mongol occupation, which lasted until 1242, the Hungarian state had to be completely reconstituted.

References

Allsen, Thomas. *Mongol Imperialism*. Berkeley: University of California Press, 1987.

Grousaset, Rene. *The Empire of the Steppes: A History of Central Asia*. New Brunswick, NJ: Rutgers University Press, 1970.

Nicolle, David. *The Mongol Warlords: Genghis Khan, Kublai Khan, Hulegu, Tamerlane*. London: Brookhampton, 1998.

Battle of Hakata Bay

Date	August 14–15, 1281	
Location	Northern Kyūshū, Japan	
Opponents (* winner)	*Japanese	Mongols, with Chinese and Korean auxiliaries
Commander	Unknown	Kublai Khan
Approx. # Troops	Unknown	170,000 men and 4,500 ships
Importance	Japanese stave off a Mongol invasion and maintain their independence, developing their own institutions	

Under the Kamakura shogunate 13th-century Japan was prosperous and largely peaceful, but in the second half of the century Japan came under increased pressure from the Mongols. The Mongols had come to power in China early in the 13th century as the Yuan dynasty, with the great Kublai Khan ruling China during 1260–1294. Kublai Khan's ambitions included not only the Eurasian landmass but the Japanese archipelago. At first he tried diplomacy, sending five diplomatic missions to the Japanese court during the period 1268–1273. The Japanese killed some of the Chinese emissaries, and Kublai Khan resolved to use force.

The first invasion, in 1274, was most probably a reconnaissance in force. Kublai Khan sent 25,000 soldiers to Korca and pressured the vassal Korean emperor to raise an army of 15,000 men and supply 900 ships to transport the men, their horses, and their equipment to Kyūshū. The Mongols first took the islands of Tsushima and Iki, between Korea and Japan, as staging areas and then landed their army at Hakata Bay (Ajkozaki) in the northwestern part of the island of Kyūshū. The Japanese hastily mobilized all available forces, but their generals had no experience in managing large bodies of troops, and the Mongols were both better armed and more effectively led. The Mongols were defeating the Japanese when a severe storm led the Mongol ship captains to call for the men to be reembarked or risk being marooned on Japanese soil. Although the majority of Mongol ships made it back to Korea, reportedly some 200 were lost at sea, and others were taken by the Japanese. The invaders suffered some 13,000 men killed in the invasion attempt.

Kublai Khan then assembled a far larger expeditionary force in two separate contingents. The Northern Fleet, which numbered as many as 70,000 Mongol and Korean soldiers in perhaps 1,000 ships, sailed from ports in northern China. The Southern Fleet was even larger. It numbered 100,000 men, to be transported in perhaps 3,500 ships. It was not yet ready when the Northern Fleet departed on May 22, 1281.

In early June the Mongols again took Tsushima and Iki as staging areas. The expeditionary force then sailed to northern Kyūshū, arriving in Hakata Bay on June 21. The Southern Fleet had not yet arrived, but the Northern Fleet troops began to go ashore on June 23. This time the Japanese were better prepared. At sea they carried out nighttime harassing attacks against the Mongol ships and destroyed some of them. While unable to defeat the Mongols on land, the Japanese were at least able to check their advance inland.

The Southern Fleet began arriving in mid-July, and its deployment was complete by August 12. The Japanese appeared lost before such a large force, but on the night of August 14–15 a violent storm (the Kamikaze, or Divine Wind) blew in from the north and wrecked most of the Mongol ships in the bay. The Japanese claimed that only about 200 of the Mongol ships survived the storm or the Japanese soldiers waiting for them when they swam ashore. Cut off from their supplies, those Mongols already ashore were easily defeated. Some 120,000 Mongols and Koreans may have perished in the invasion attempt. Reportedly the Japanese made slaves of some 12,000 others.

The indefatigable Kublai Khan made plans for yet another invasion of Japan, but unrest in China diverted his attention. He never launched the third invasion. The following Ming dynasty (1368–1644) sought conciliation and trade with Japan. Thus, the Japanese retained their independence and continued to develop their own institutions free from Chinese control. In the 19th and 20th centuries a modernized Japan sought to reverse the situation and secure control of China.

References

Farris, W. W. *Heavenly Warriors: The Evolution of Japan's Military, 500–1700.* Cambridge: Harvard University Press, 1992.

Mason, R. H. P., and J. G. Caiger. *History of Japan.* New York: Free Press, 1972.

Turnbull, Stephen. *The Samurai: A Military History.* New York: Macmillan, 1977.

Battle of Bannockburn

Date	June 23–24, 1314	
Location	Near Stirling, Scotland	
Opponents (* winner)	*Scots	English
Commander	King Robert I (Robert the Bruce)	King Edward II
Approx. # Troops	8,000, including some 500 light horsemen	20,000, including 2,000 heavily armored knights
Importance	Scotland retains its independence	

Following the execution of William Wallace in 1305, Robert the Bruce, grandson of an earlier claimant to the Scottish throne, took up resistance to English rule. After suffering defeats in 1306 at the hands of the Earl of Pembroke at Methven on June 19 and at Dalry on August 11, Bruce was victorious over Pembroke in the Battle of Loudoun Hill on May 10, 1307. Hardly a major battle, Loudoun Hill nonetheless reversed the negative effects of Bruce's two earlier defeats.

Bruce, now recognized as King Robert I of Scotland (r. 1306–1329), utilized mostly guerrilla tactics and raids to drive out the English. By 1314 he controlled all Scotland except five English-held castles. That spring Edward Bruce, Robert's younger brother, began a siege of the major English stronghold, Stirling Castle, held by Sir Philip Mowbray. Bruce and Mowbray eventually concluded an agreement that if no relief appeared by midsummer, June 24, the castle would surrender.

That arrangement forced English king Edward II to act. Assembling a force of 20,000 men, including 2,000 heavily armored knights, he invaded Scotland in mid-June. His stated goal was to relieve the siege, but his real intent was to reclaim Scotland. His army was probably twice the size of the Scottish force opposing it.

Aware of the English approach, King Robert prepared a defensive position about one mile wide on a slope several miles south of Stirling, behind the stream of Bannockburn. Woods anchored the Scottish right, and a morass flanked the left. The only good approach to the Scottish position was by the old Roman road. Along that approach the Scots blocked paths with branches and dug cavalry traps (pits implanted with stakes and covered with brush). These were intended to prevent any flanking movements and channel the advance, forcing the English to bunch up.

The Scots were armed similarly to the English, primarily with long pikes. They were formed into schiltroms, large circles of men with the pikes pointing outward to form an impenetrable wall. The pikes could be grounded at an angle to blunt a cavalry charge. The Scots numbered only some 8,000 men, however, of whom 500 were cavalry.

Mowbray knew of the Scottish preparations and warned Edward and also informed him that battle was not necessary, for Edward had already met the technical terms of the relief of the castle, which now would not have to surrender. Edward, however, had lost control of his army, and its leaders were eager for battle.

Edward arrived in the vicinity of Bannockburn on June 23. Preliminary skirmishing occurred that day, with the main battle occurring on June 24. The fighting went badly for the English from the beginning. On June 23 Mowbray met with Edward and requested a relief force for Stirling Castle. Edward agreed and allocated 500 cavalry for the purpose. Mowbray attempted to reach the castle undetected via a narrow bridle path, but Robert spotted this and ordered his men to intercept. In the ensuing fight the Scottish schiltroms withstood repeated English cavalry charges, and the knights were forced to retreat with the loss of about 100 of their number.

This small engagement cheered the Scots. That evening a young Scottish knight who had been with the English deserted and informed King Robert that the English were demoralized and unhappy with Edward's leadership. This convinced Robert, even though he was badly outnumbered, to keep his position and fight the next day.

The main battle opened with an English advance on the Scottish positions. Crowded into the narrow front, the English cavalry became disorganized, and the Scottish schiltroms beat back its charges. The English infantry, behind the cavalry with the archers, was not able to deploy properly, and the archers, unable to deploy to the flanks, could not employ their weapons effectively. They hit their own men in the back as often as they hit the Scots.

As the English faltered, the Scots staged a general advance against the disorganized mass of the English army, which began to break. Edward was forcibly taken from the field by his bodyguard, but this ended what remained of army discipline.

The Scots pursued and slew thousands of the English. Although there is no accurate count of English casualties, perhaps only a third of Edward's infantry returned to England. The Scots killed some 700 of the men-at-arms and held another 500 for ransom. Scottish losses in the battle are said to have been light.

The Battle of Bannockburn was decisive. One of the greatest victories in Scottish history, it greatly strengthened Robert's position, although full English recognition of independence for Scotland was still more than a decade away.

References

Barrow, G. W. S. *Robert Bruce and the Community of the Realm of Scotland.* Berkeley: University of California Press, 1965.

Prestwick, Michael. *The Three Edwards: War and State in England, 1272–1377.* New York: St. Martin's, 1980.

Scott, Robert McNair. *Robert the Bruce, King of Scots.* New York: Carroll and Graf, 1996.

Battle of Sluys

Date	June 24, 1340	
Location	off Sluys (Sluis, Ecluse) on the Flemish coast	
Opponents (* winner)	*English	French and Genoese
Commander	King Edward III	Admiral Hughes Quiéret
Approx. # Troops	250 ships (number of men unknown)	200 ships and 25,000–40,000 men
Importance	Most important naval battle of the Hundred Years' War; prevents a French invasion of England and makes possible an English invasion of France	

The Battle of Sluys (Sluis, Ecluse) was the most important naval engagement of the Hundred Years' War between France and England. Actually a series of wars, the Hundred Years' War began in 1337 and lasted until 1453. The chief cause of the war was the desire of the English kings to hold on to and expand their territorial holdings in France, while the French kings sought to liberate their territory from English control. King Edward III of England (r. 1327–1377), for instance, believed that he had better claim to the French throne than did its occupant, King Philippe VI (r. 1330–1350). Other factors were the struggle for control of the seas and international trading markets. Finally, the English resented the assistance provided by the French to the Scots in their wars with the English.

In 1328 Philippe VI marched in troops and established French administrative control over Flanders, where the English had made economic inroads and forced the weavers into dependence on English wool. Edward III responded by embargoing English wool in 1336; this led to a revolt of the Flemings against the French and their conclusion of an alliance with England in 1338. Edward III then declared himself king of France, and the Flemings recognized him as their king. Philippe VI declared Edward's fiefs in France south of the Loire forfeit and in 1338 sent his troops into Guienne (Aquitaine). The war was on.

Edward III dispatched raiding parties from England and Flanders to attack northern and northeastern France. In 1339 Edward III invaded northern France, but he withdrew before Philippe VI's much larger army. Having defeated the English forces on land, Philippe VI planned to turn the tables and invade England, ending Edward III's claim to the French throne. French admiral Hughes Quiéret began the assembly of 200 ships, including 4 Genoese galleys, off the Flemish coast.

Edward III meanwhile gathered some 200 ships at Harwich for another invasion of France. Learning of the assembly of the French invasion force, Edward III launched a preemptive attack. He commanded in person, with the cog *Thomas* as his flagship. Under the influence of a northeast wind, the English fleet sailed from Harwich on June 22 and arrived off the Flanders coast the next day. There it was joined by a northern force of 50 additional ships. Edward sent men and horses ashore to reconnoiter. The reconnaissance completed, he decided to attack the next day.

Sea battles of that day resembled those on land and were decided at close range, often by boarding. Ships were virtually movable fortresses with temporary wooden structures, known as castles, added at bow and stern of converted merchant ships to create a height advantage for bowmen or the opportunity to hurl down missiles on an opposing ship's decks. It has been claimed, but not proven, that some of the ships in the battle carried primitive cannon as well as catapults.

The battle occurred off Sluys on the Flemish coast. There Quiéret had divided his 200 ships into three divisions. He ordered the ships of each division chained side by side, with each ship having a small boat filled with stones triced up in the mast so that men in the tops could hurl missiles down on the English decks. The French were armed chiefly with swords and pikes and had little in the way of armor. Quiéret also had some crossbowmen. In effect, he planned to face the English with three large floating forts incapable of rapid movement. Estimates of the number of Frenchmen on the ships range from 25,000 to 40,000.

Edward III had many archers and men-at-arms, the latter well-armored. He placed the largest of his 250 ships in the van, and between every two ships filled with archers he positioned ships filled with men-at-arms. The smaller ships formed a second division with archers. The decisive weapon in this battle, as it would be on land, was the longbow, which could outrange the crossbow.

The French held a council of war, and the commander of the Genoese galleys, Barbavera, urged that they put to sea. He pointed out that if they failed to do so they would yield the advantages of wind, tide, and sun to the English. His advice was ignored.

The battle opened at about noon on June 24, 1340. The English first attacked only the front division of the French formation. The archers poured volley after volley of arrows into the French ships. Once they grappled a French ship, the English boarded it and cleared its decks in hand-to-hand fighting. The English then proceeded to the next ship, taking one after another under a protective hail of arrows.

Having secured the first division of French ships, including four English prizes captured earlier, the English moved on to the other two divisions. The action lasted into the night and reportedly the slaughter was great, with 400 men killed in one ship alone. Normans manning the third division were the last to surrender.

The French fleet was almost annihilated. The English sank or captured 166 of the 200 French ships. Estimates of the number of dead vary widely, but the French and their allies may have lost as many as 25,000 men, while the English lost 4,000. Quiéret was among those killed.

Edward III now claimed the title "Sovereign of the Narrow Seas." His letter to his son about the battle is the earliest extant English naval dispatch. Edward III next landed troops and laid siege to Tournai, but the French forced him to raise the siege and to conclude a truce that same year.

The Battle of Sluys was the most important naval engagement of the Hundred Years' War. It gave England command of the English Channel for a generation, making possible the invasion of France and the English land victories that followed. Without the Battle of Sluys, it is unlikely that the war between England and France would have lasted long.

References

Clowes, William Laird. *The Royal Navy: A History from the Earliest Times to the Present,* Vol. 1. London: Sampson Low, Martson, 1897.

Rodgers, William Ledyard. *Naval Warfare under Oars, 4th to 16th Centuries: A Study of Strategy, Tactics and Ship Design.* Annapolis, MD: Naval Institute Press, 1967.

Seward, Desmond. *The Hundred Years' War: The English in France, 1337–1453.* New York: Atheneum, 1978.

Sumption, Jonathan. *The Hundred Years' War: Trial by Battle.* Philadelphia: University of Pennsylvania Press, 1988.

Battle of Crécy

Date	August 26, 1346	
Location	near the village of Crécy-en-Ponthieu, south of Calais in northern France	
Opponents (* winner)	*English	French
Commander	King Edward III	King Philippe VI
Approx. # Troops	Around 11,000	30,000–60,000, including 12,000 heavy cavalry and 6,000 Genoese mercenary crossbowmen
Importance	First great English land victory of the Hundred Years' War; leads to the English capture of Calais the next year; had Edward been defeated it would have probably ended both his ambitions in France and the war	

Crécy was the key land battle of the Hundred Years' War (1337–1453) between France and England. The English naval victory at Sluys (Sluis, Ecluse) in 1340 gave King Edward III control of the English Channel and with it access to northern France. Edward did not immediately take advantage of this, however. During 1341–1346 a dynastic struggle occurred in Brittany in which both Edward and the

French king Philippe VI intervened. To raise money, Philippe introduced the gabelle (salt tax), which led to increased dissatisfaction with his rule. In 1345 Edward raised an expeditionary force, and with it he invaded Normandy in July 1346, intending to assist his allies in Flanders and Brittany.

Edward landed at La Hogue near Cherbourg in mid-June with perhaps 15,000 men, including a heavy cavalry force of 3,900 knights and men-at-arms and a large number of archers. Most were veterans of the Scottish wars. Edward's army in France was experienced, well trained, and well organized. It was probably the most effective military force for its size in all Europe.

The fleet returned to England, and Edward marched inland. The English took Caen on July 27 following heavy resistance. Edward ordered the entire population killed and the town burned. Although he later rescinded the order, perhaps 3,000 townsmen died over the three-day sack of Caen, which set the tone for much of the war.

Edward then moved northeast toward the Seine, pillaging as he went. For the next month Philippe chased Edward across northern France without bringing him to battle. Meanwhile, Philippe's son, Duke John of Normandy, moved north against the English from Gascony, while Philippe assembled another force near Paris. Edward thus achieved his aim of drawing pressure from Guyenne and Brittany.

Reaching the Seine at Rouen, Edward learned that the French had destroyed all accessible bridges over that river except one at Rouen, which was strongly defended. Increasingly worried that he might be cut off and forced to fight south of the Seine, Edward III moved his army rapidly along the riverbank southeast and upriver toward Paris, seeking a crossing point that would allow a retreat into Flanders if need be. At Poissy, only a few miles from Paris, the English found a repairable bridge and, on August 16, crossed over the Seine. Philippe and a sizable French force at St. Denis made no effort to intercept him.

Only after the English had crossed the Seine and were headed north did Philippe attempt to intercept them. Edward reached the Somme River on August 22, about a day ahead of the pursing Philippe, only to learn that the French had destroyed all the bridges over that river except those at heavily fortified cities. After vainly attacking both Hangest and Pont-Remy, Edward moved north along the western bank trying to find a crossing. On August 23 at Ouisemont the English destroyed to a man the French defenders and burned the town.

On the evening of August 24 the English camped at Acheux. Six miles distant, a large French force defended the bridge at Abbeville, but that night the English learned of a ford only 10 miles from the coast that could be crossed at low tide and was likely to be undefended. Breaking camp in the middle of the night, Edward moved to the ford, named Blanchetaque, only to discover that it was held by some 3,500 Frenchmen under an experienced French commander, Godemar du Foy.

His now desperate supply situation and the closeness of the French army led Edward to decide that he must attempt to cross there. Battle was joined at low tide at 8:00 a.m. on August 1. Edward sent some 100 knights and men across the ford under the cover of a hail of arrows from his longbowmen. The English gained the opposite bank and were able to establish a small beachhead. Edward then quickly fed in more men, and under heavy English longbow fire the French broke and fled toward Abbeville. By 9:30 a.m. the entire English army was across. So confident was Philippe that the English would not be able to cross the Somme that no effort had been made to clear the area on the east bank of resources, and the English were thus able to resupply, burning the towns of Noyelles-sur-Mer and Le Crotoy in the process. Philippe then pursued.

Finally, having resupplied and reached a position where he could withdraw into Flanders if need be, Edward decided to stand and fight. On August 25 he selected a defensive position near the village of Crécy-en-Ponthieu. High ground over-looked a gentle slope over which the French would have to advance. The English right was anchored by the Maye River. The left, just in front of the village of Wadi-court, was protected by a great wood 4 miles deep and 10 miles long.

Edward III commanded more than 11,000 men. He divided his forces into three separate entities, known as "battles." Each "battle" contained a solid mass of dis-mounted men-at-arms, perhaps six ranks deep and about 250 yards in length. Edward III positioned two of the "battles" side by side as the front line of his defense. His 16-year-old son Edward, Prince of Wales (later known as the Black Prince), had nominal command of the English right, although Earl Marshal Warwick held actual command. The earls Arundel and Northampton commanded the left "bat-tle." Several hundred yards behind these two, in the center, Edward III positioned the third "battle," a reserve under his personal command. Archers occupied the spaces between the "battles" and were echeloned forward in V formations pointing toward the enemy to deliver enfilading fire.

Edward also located a detachment of cavalry to the rear of each "battle" to coun-terattack if need be. He had his men dig holes on the slope as traps for the French cavalry. The king used a windmill located between his own position and his son's right "battle" as an observation post during the battle and directed his forces accordingly.

It has been suggested that Edward III may have had some gunpowder artillery at Crécy, but that is by no means certain. The year before he had ordered 100 *rib-aulds,* light guns mounted on carts. If these were employed in the battle, it was the first European land battle for gunpowder artillery. In any case, they did not influ-ence the battle's outcome.

The French brought to Crécy an army variously estimated at between 30,000 and 60,000 men, including 12,000 heavy cavalry of knights and men-at-arms, 6,000 Genoese mercenary crossbowmen, and a large number of poorly trained in-fantry. This French force, moving without a reconnaissance screen or any real order, arrived at Crécy at about 6:00 p.m. on August 26, 1346. Without bothering to explore the English position, Philippe then attempted to organize his men for battle. He positioned the Genoese, his only professional force, in a line in front. At this point a quick thunderstorm swept the field, rendering the ground slippery for the attackers.

The well-disciplined Genoese then moved across the valley toward the English position, with the disorganized French heavy cavalry in a great mass behind them. Halting about 150 yards from the English "battles," they loosed their bolts; most fell short. They reloaded and began to move forward again, only to encounter clouds of English arrows. The Genoese could fire their crossbows about one to two times a minute, while the English longbowmen could get off an arrow every five seconds. The English arrows completely shattered the Genoese, who were not able to close to a range where their crossbow bolts might have been effective.

The French knights behind the Genoese, impatient to join the fray, then rode forward up the slippery slope, over and around the crossbowmen, and encountered the same swarms of arrows. The shock of the French charge carried to the English lines, however, where there was some hand-to-hand combat. The English cavalry then charged, and the remaining French knights were driven back. Repeatedly the French knights regrouped and charged (the English claimed some 15–16 separate attacks throughout the night), and each time they were decimated by the arrows of the longbowmen. The English held their positions until dawn.

The French dead included some 1,500 knights and men-at-arms, between 10,000 and 20,000 crossbowmen and infantrymen, and thousands of horses. Philippe was among the many Frenchmen wounded. English losses were only about 200 dead and wounded.

Crécy made the English a military nation. Europe, which was unaware of the advances made by the English military system, was stunned at this infantry victory over a numerically superior force that included some of the finest cavalry in Europe. Crécy restored the infantry to first place. Since this battle, infantry have been the primary element of ground combat forces.

After several days of rest, Edward III headed for the English Channel port of Calais and a long siege there, beginning on September 4. Only in July 1347 did Philippe make a halfhearted attempt at its relief. Calais fell to Edward a month later, on August 4. It turned out to be the sole English territorial gain of the campaign, actually of the entire Hundred Years' War. Calais remained in English hands until 1558.

References

Burne, Alfred H. *The Crécy War.* 1955; reprint, Westport, CT: Greenwood, 1976.

Seward, Desmond. *The Hundred Years' War: The English in France, 1337–1453.* New York: Atheneum, 1978.

Sumption, Jonathan. *The Hundred Years' War: Trial by Battle.* Philadelphia: University of Pennsylvania Press, 1988.

Battle of Poitiers

Date	September 19, 1356	
Location	Near Poitiers, in western France	
Opponents (* winner)	*English, Aquitanians	French
Commander	Edward, the Black Prince	King John II
Approx. # Troops	8,000	As many as 35,000
Importance	Second of three devastating French defeats in the Hundred Years' War; King John is taken prisoner	

The Battle of Poitiers was an important English victory on land over the French during the Hundred Years' War (1337–1453). Following English king Edward III's capture of Calais in 1347, both sides entered into a truce (1347–1354) while they dealt with the ravages of the Black Death (bubonic plague). After failing to reach a permanent peace, Edward crossed the English Channel in 1355 to lead devastating raids through northern France. In 1356 he sent his second son, John of Gaunt (the Duke of Lancaster), and some 6,000 men to raid into Normandy from Brittany and Anjou and meet up with a somewhat larger force under Edward, Prince of Wales (the Black Prince), that would at the same time raid north from Bordeaux, the English base in Guyenne in southwestern France.

The English did not seek battle with the far more numerous French army; their intent was simply to plunder and destroy. Edward III landed in France to strengthen the northern troops but was forced to return to England within a few days because the Scots had taken Berwick. John was unable to cross the Loire and effect a juncture with his brother's force.

The Black Prince had set out from Bergerac on August 4. Most of his men were from Aquitaine except for a number of English longbowmen. He reached Tours on September 3. There he learned that French king John II (John the Good) and as many as 35,000 men had crossed the Loire at Blois on September 8. The Black Prince had only about 8,000 men and ordered a rapid withdrawal down the road to Bordeaux, but the English were slowed by their loot. The French succeeded in cutting off the raiders and reaching Poitiers first. In the late afternoon of September 17 the English advance guard ran into the French rear at La Chabotrie. The prince did not want to fight, but he realized that his exhausted men could go no further without having to abandon their plunder, and he cast about for a suitable position from which to fight, moving to the village of Maupertuis some seven miles southeast of Poitiers.

John II wanted to attack the English on the morning of September 18 but the papal envoy, Cardinal de Perigord, persuaded him to try negotiations. The Black Prince offered to return towns and castles captured during the raid along with all his prisoners, to promise not to do battle with the French king for seven years, and to pay a large sum of money, but John II demanded the unconditional surrender of the prince and 100 English knights.

Edward refused. He had selected an excellent defensive site facing north, and his men used the time spent in negotiations to improve their positions. His left flank was protected by a creek and marsh, and his open right flank ended in a wagon park. The 1,000-yard front of the English position was a vineyard ending in a hedge line at the crest, traversed only by sunken lanes. Edward distributed his archers to the flanks but also placed a few bowmen forward in the vineyard as skirmishers. He dismounted his men-at-arms and placed them behind the hedge with archers in three separate divisions, or "battles," of about 2,000 men each. His small cavalry reserve was on the exposed right flank.

John II's army greatly outnumbered his opponent. It included 8,000 mounted men-at-arms, 8,000 light cavalry, 4,500 professional mercenary infantry (many of them Genoese crossbowmen), and perhaps 15,000 untrained citizen militia. Rejecting advice to use his superior numbers to surround the English and starve them out or turn the English position, the king decided on a frontal assault. He organized his men into four "battles" of up to 10,000 men each. He hoped to advance his mounted men-at-arms through the hedgerow on the largest of the sunken roads and deal with the English longbowmen before the main attack. The men-at-arms in all three French "battles" were to march the mile to the English lines in full armor.

The resulting Battle of Poitiers on September 19, 1356, was a repeat of the August 1346 Battle of Crécy. Early that morning Edward moved his wagons and two of his "battles" across the creek, apparently in an effort to escape. John II had not completed his preparations but, on learning of this movement by the English, ordered the select 300 knights on horseback to advance and deal with the English archers. The longbowmen, however, decimated the knights; many of them were slain on the ground by English knights on foot under the Earl of Salisbury, who came out from behind the hedge. On being informed of what was happening, the Black Prince returned with the other two "battles."

Meanwhile, the footmen in the first French "battle" who had not fallen prey to arrows reached the hedge. Salisbury's men were soon hotly engaged, but Edward's other two "battles" came up in time to relieve them. Still, the majority of the French troops were not yet engaged.

The next French division, under the Dauphin Charles, Duc d'Orléans, moved forward to the hedge, where there was desperate fighting. The French almost broke through, but Edward committed everything except a final reserve of 400 men, and the line held. The remaining French reeled back. The English were now in desperate straits, and if the next French "battle" commanded by the Duc d'Orléans, the brother of the king, had advanced promptly to support its fellows or had struck the exposed English right flank, the French would have won a great victory. Instead, on seeing the repulse of their fellows, d'Orléans's "battle" withdrew from the field with them.

This produced a slight respite for the defenders to reorganize before the arrival of the last and largest French "battle" of some 6,000 men, led by John II in person.

The French were exhausted by the long march in full armor, but the English were also at the end of their tether. Fearing that his men could not withstand an attack by such a large force, the Black Prince ordered his cavalry and infantry, along with the archers who had used up their arrows, to charge the French. He also sent about 200 horsemen around to attack the French rear. Desperate fighting in the vineyard ensued in which John II wielded a great battle-ax.

The issue remained in doubt until the English cavalry struck the French rear. The French then fled, and the English were too exhausted to pursue. Thousands of John II's forces were taken prisoner, including the king, his 14-year-old son Philippe and two of Philippe's brothers, and a multitude of the French nobility, including 17 counts. As the chronicler Jean Froissart remarked, at Poitiers all the nobility of France were slain. The French suffered perhaps 2,500 dead and a like number of prisoners. The English may have sustained 1,000 killed and at least as many wounded.

Following the battle the Black Prince withdrew to Bordeaux with both his booty and prisoners. Vast fortunes were made over the ransoming of the French nobles. Meanwhile, there was chaos in France with the collapse of the central government. The next 10 years saw the English raiding the French countryside almost at will, as did bands of freebooters known as *routiers*. Unwilling to meet the English in open combat, those French who could do so sought refuge in castles and fortified cities. In 1358 the peasants, who had been unable to defend themselves against their many attackers, rose up against the nobles in a short-lived *jacquerie*.

In 1360 the Dauphin signed the Treaty of Brétigny, ransoming John II in return for 3 million gold crowns (raised by heavy taxes on the French peasantry), Guyenne in full sovereignty, and the Limousin, Poitou, the Angoumois, the Saintonge, Rouerque, Ponthieu, and many other areas. King Edward III now possessed an independent Guyenne but also Aquitaine, a third of the area of France. Edward set up the Black Prince at Bordeaux as the Duke of Aquitaine. John II was allowed to return home from England, but his three sons remained behind as hostages until the ransom was paid. When one son escaped, the good king returned of his own free will to take his place, dying in England in 1364.

Incredibly, the lessons of the Battle of Poitiers seem not to have taken; it is said that the French remembered everything but learned nothing. The battle was virtually replicated in form and effect in October 1415 at Agincourt.

References

Barber, Richard. *Edward Prince of Wales and Aquitaine*. London: Allen Lane, 1978.

Hewitt, H. J. *The Black Prince's Expedition of 1355–1357*. Manchester, UK: University of Manchester Press, 1958.

Seward, Desmond. *The Hundred Years' War: The English in France, 1337–1453*. New York: Atheneum, 1978.

Sumption, Jonathan. *The Hundred Years' War: Trial by Battle*. Philadelphia: University of Pennsylvania Press, 1988.

Battle of Kosovo

Date	June 15, 1389	
Location	Kosovo in the western Balkans	
Opponents (* winner)	*Ottomans	Serbs, Bosnians, Albanians, and Wallachians
Commander	Sultan Murad I	Prince Lazar Hrebeljanović
Approx. # Troops	27,000–40,000, some 8,000 of them cavalry	12,000–30,000
Importance	Serbia becomes a vassal state of the Ottoman Empire with Central Europe now open to Muslim expansion	

With the defeat of the Christian Crusaders in the Holy Land, the most powerful Muslim state, the Ottoman Empire, began a drive to capture Constantinople and push north into the Danube River Valley to secure the Balkans and capture Vienna. To accomplish these goals, Ottoman sultan Murad I would first have to conquer the independent kingdom of Serbia. Toward this end, he sought to take advantage of the endemic rivalries in the Balkans. The stakes were considerable. An Ottoman victory over the Serbs would bring Muslim power into the heart of Europe, while a victory by the Serbs and their allies over the Ottomans would perhaps inject new life into the tottering Byzantine Empire and even open the possibility of a renewal of the Crusades against Islam.

Murad made careful preparations for his offensive. These included securing peace treaties with Venice and Genoa that brought mercenary troops to his aid. In the spring of 1389, Murad I moved his army north from Philippoupolis (Plovdiv) to Ihtiman, then proceeded via Velbuẓd (Kyustendil) and Kratovo. Murad arrived with his troops at Priština on June 14. Meanwhile, Serbian prince Lazar Hrebeljanović gathered a coalition force of Serbs, Bosnians, Albanians, and Wallachians at Niš. On learning of Murad's movements, Lazar transferred his army to Kosovo, an important Balkan trade crossroads close to Priština.

Much of the information about the resulting Battle of Kosovo is speculative. Murad's army, including its mercenaries, probably numbered 27,000–40,000 men, with as many as 8,500 of them cavalry. Lazar's force was smaller, probably only 12,000–30,000 men, with the Serbs constituting the great majority. Lazar had only several thousand cavalry. Lazar commanded the bulk of the Serbia contingent, with the remainder headed by Serbian noblemen Vuk Branković and Vlatko Vuković. Murad's Ottoman and mercenary forces were also much better armed and equipped than were the Serbs and their allies.

Serbian forces were drawn up on a Kosovo field about 3 miles northwest of Priština. Lazar commanded the Serb center, Vuk commanded the right, and Vlatko commanded the left. The heavy Serb cavalry were positioned in front, with lighter cavalry equipped with bows on the flanks. Murad commanded the Ottoman center, with his son Bayezid in charge of the right wing and another son, Yakub, on the left. Some 1,000 archers were on the wings, while the Janissaries were in the center with Murad and his cavalry guard behind them.

Battle was joined on June 15, 1389, St. Vitus' Day (celebrated on June 28 according to the Gregorian calendar). It began when Murad's archers opened up on the Serbian front-rank cavalry, who then formed into a great wedge and charged the Ottoman line. Although the Serbs enjoyed some success on the Ottoman left, they were turned back on the center and right. Bayezid won the battle by directing a decisive counterattack following the initial Serbian charge. Another factor in the Ottoman victory was the departure of Vuk and his troops at a critical juncture in the fighting, prompted by either the desire to save some of the Serb forces or perhaps treason.

Murad, though well protected by Janissaries, was killed either during or after the battle reportedly by a Serb, Miloš Obilić. Accounts differ as to how this occurred. Obilić either posed as a traitor to gain audience to the sultan or pretended to be dead but then stabbed the sultan when he walked the battlefield. Murad's tomb can still be seen on the battlefield today.

Bayezid, who succeeded Murad as sultan, immediately summoned Yakub and ordered him strangled so that there would be no other claim to the succession. Taken prisoner, Prince Lazar was executed.

The Battle of Kosovo is regarded by Serbs as a mythic event in their history, a symbol of Serb nationalism and resistance to foreign rule. Although the battle brought a pause in the Turkish advance because Bayezid had to go to Constantinople to be crowned sultan, Serbian losses in the battle were catastrophic, and Serbia was not able to recover immediately. Although some Serbian resistance continued, many Serbian noblemen were forced to wed their daughters to Ottomans as well as pay tribute and supply soldiers to the Ottoman Army. For the next 70 years Serbia was a vassal state of the Ottomans.

References

Judah, Tim. *The Serbs: History, Myth, and the Destruction of Yugoslavia.* New Haven, CT: Yale University Press, 1997.

Malcolm, Noel. *Kosovo: A Short History.* New York: New York University Press, 1998.

Singleton, Frederick Bernard. *A Short History of the Yugoslav Peoples.* New York: Cambridge University Press, 1998.

Battle of Ankara

Date	July 20, 1402	
Location	Ankara (then known as Angora) in central Turkey	
Opponents (* winner)	*Turkic Mongols	Ottomans
Commander	Timur	Sultan Bayezid I
Approx. # Troops	140,000–200,000	85,000
Importance	Brings great devastation to Asia Minor and civil war within the Ottoman Empire	

The Battle of Ankara (then known as Angora) on July 20, 1402, matched two redoubtable commanders. Sultan Bayezid I led an Ottoman army against a force led by the Turkic Mongol leader Timur. Bayezid became sultan in 1389 after the assassination of his father Murad on the battlefield at Kosovo. Although impetuous and unpredictable as a statesman, Bayezid was a capable military commander with an excellent instinct for battle. The swift movement of his armies earned him the nickname "Yildirim" ("Lightning").

After massacring much of the nobility of Serbia in retaliation for his father's death, Bayezid agreed that Serbia might be an autonomous vassal state. He then turned his attention to Asia Minor, conquering territory that secured access to the Black Sea port of Sinop (Sinope) and made him master of most of Anatolia. Turning back to Europe, in 1391 he undertook the first great Ottoman siege of Constantinople (present-day Istanbul). He next had to deal with a large Crusader army led by King Sigismund of Hungary, who planned to drive the Turks from Europe. On September 25, 1396, in the Battle of Nicopolis (Nikopol), Bayezid defeated the Crusaders. He was preparing the coup de grâce against Constantinople when a new threat arose to the east.

Mongol leader Timur (1336–1405), known in the West as Tamerlane (Timur the Lame) for an injury he had suffered as a youth, had built a considerable empire. He belonged to a Mongol clan in Transoxiana (present-day Uzbekistan) that had adopted Islam as its religion and Turkish as its language. He claimed descent from Genghis Khan, and was certainly the most powerful central Asian ruler to follow him. Timur joined with his brother-in-law, Emir Husayn, to secure all Transoxiana during 1364–1370. With the assassination of Husayn in 1369, Timur assumed sole rule.

During 1370–1380 Timur secured Khwarizm and Jatah (present-day Tajikistan). He invaded and conquered eastern Persia, including Khorasan, during 1383–1385 and also defeated an invasion during 1385–1386 from Russia led by his former lieutenant Toktamish. Timur took the remainder of Persia, including the territory of present-day Armenia, Azerbaijan, and Mesopotamia, during 1386–1387. Toktamish invaded again and was again defeated in 1388 and 1389.

Timur invaded Russia in 1390 and crushed Toktamish but was forced to return to Persia to crush a revolt there in 1392. Timur then reconquered Armenia, Azerbaijan, Fars, and Iraq, and he took Mesopotamia and Georgia in 1395. After defeating yet another invasion by Toktamish in 1395, in retaliation Timur invaded and ravaged most of southern Russia and Ukraine, reaching Moscow in 1396. He next invaded India and defeated Mahmud Tughluk's army at Panipat on December 17, 1398, taking Delhi.

There had been tensions between the Mongol and Ottoman empires for some time, but there need not have been war had Bayezid not been imprudent. Timur's interest lay to the south in Mesopotamia and Egypt, but Bayezid's demand for tribute from an emir loyal to Timur was taken by the Mongol ruler as a personal insult and a reason for war.

Taking the field, Timur besieged and captured Sivas and then buried thousands of its Armenian Christian defenders alive in its moats. He then turned south. Invading Syria, he took Aleppo in October 1400. After sacking it, he took Damascus. Capturing Baghdad, he massacred its population. With his army in winter quarters in 1401, he finally turned his intentions to Anatolia.

Bayezid meanwhile had failed to counter the loss of Sivas. Increasing debauchery had taken its toll, and the sultan showed none of the military characteristics of his nickname. He had let pass the opportunity posed by Timur's campaign in Mesopotamia and had taken no steps to placate the Mongol leader. Only in the summer of 1402, when Timur again moved his army west to Sivas, did Bayezid stir. He broke off his blockade of Constantinople and marched his army southeast to the fortress of Angora, in central Anatolia.

Bayezid's army was a hardened and disciplined force of perhaps 85,000 men. It boasted a large number of elite Janissaries as well as other infantry and cavalry and included Serbian knights. Fully a quarter of the men, however, were recently conquered Tatars of questionable loyalty. The army was also spent by its long march, and there was discontent among the men because their pay was in arrears.

As Bayezid's generals contemplated strategy, scouts discovered that Timur's army had circled in behind the Ottomans and was now approaching from the rear. Timur probably commanded between 140,000 and 200,000 men, principally cavalry, and also had 32 war elephants. He took Bayezid's former base camp and made it his headquarters. He also built a reservoir and, on the day of the battle, diverted the principal water source for the area, Cubuk Creek, denying its use to the Ottoman army, which was now advancing from the east.

Battle was joined on a plain before the city of Angora. Timur's two grandsons commanded the vanguard of the army, while his sons Mirah Shah and Shah Rukh commanded the right and left wings, respectively. Timur commanded the center.

Bayezid planned a defensive battle. His left flank consisted of his best troops, commanded by his eldest son Suleiman; the right flank was composed of Serbs and

the most loyal European troops under his Serbian brother-in-law, Stephen Laza-
revotch. Bayezid's son Mehmed commanded the rear guard, while Bayezid took
up position in the center with the Janissaries. In making his dispositions, Bayezid
committed a major error by placing his Tatar cavalry in the front line to take the
brunt of the initial Mongol attack. No sooner had the battle begun than they deserted to Timur, and cavalry from the recently subjugated emirates followed suit.
This reduced the Ottoman army by a quarter and, for all practical purposes, decided the battle.

Bayezid ordered an attack by his left wing, covering it by an attack of his Anatolian cavalry. Although the horsemen fought with courage, they encountered
hailstorms of arrows as well as Greek fire (a form of naphtha) and were driven
back in confusion with the loss of some 15,000 men. Timur then went on the attack, easily defeating the Ottoman cavalry on the left wing. The Serbs on the right
fought heroically, and Bayezid ordered his remaining Janissaries to support them.
Although surrounded on a small hilltop, they held off several Mongol attacks until
nightfall, with Bayezid in the thick of the fight. After dark Bayezid ordered the
survivors to attempt to break free, but he was overtaken, unhorsed, and captured.
Subjected to great humiliation by Timur, he is supposed to have lost his mind and
died in March 1403.

The capture of Bayezid and destruction of his army (each side lost up to 40,000
men) brought considerable devastation to Asia Minor. Bayezid's conquests in Anatolia were restored to their former lords. Civil war broke out between Bayezid's
four sons. Timur went on to capture Smyrna (Izmir), and received tribute from the
sultan of Egypt and Byzantine emperor John I before returning to Samarkand in
1404. He was preparing an invasion of China (which had driven out the Mongols
in 1389), when he fell ill and died in January 1405.

References

Manz, Beatrice Forbes. *The Rise and Fall of Tamerlane.* Cambridge: Cambridge University
   Press, 1989.
Marozzi, Justin. *Tamerlane: Sword of Islam, Conqueror of the World.* New York: Da Capo,
   2006.
Nicolle, David. *The Age of Tamerlane.* London: Osprey, 1996.
———. *Armies of the Ottoman Turks, 1300–1774.* London: Osprey, 1992.
Sokol, Edward D. *Tamerlane.* Lawrence, KS: Coronado, 1977.

Battle of Agincourt

Date	October 25, 1415	
Location	Agincourt in northeastern France	
Opponents (* winner)	English	French
Commander	King Henry V	Various nobles
Approx. # Troops	6,000	30,000
Importance	Third great English land victory of the Hundred Years' War; significantly increases the influence of Duke John of Burgundy in French affairs	

In 1413 King Henry IV of England died and was followed on the throne by Henry V. The Hundred Years' War (1337–1453) continued, with English kings claiming the throne of France and its territory and the French kings seeking to expel the English. In prosecuting the war, Henry V concluded an alliance with Duke John of Burgundy, who promised to remain neutral and be Henry V's vassal in return for territorial gains at the expense of France. In April 1415 Henry V declared war on King Charles VI of France, assembled a force of 12,000 men at Southampton, and crossed the English Channel to land at the mouth of the Seine on August 10.

Beginning on August 13, Henry laid siege to the Channel port of Honfleur. Taking it on September 22, he expelled most of its French inhabitants, replacing them with Englishmen. Only the poorest Frenchmen were allowed to remain, and they had to take an oath of allegiance. The siege, disease, and garrison duties all depleted Henry V's army, leaving only about 6,000 men.

For whatever reason Henry V then decided to march overland from Honfleur to Calais, moving without baggage or artillery. His army departed on October 6, covering as much as 18 miles a day in difficult conditions caused by heavy rains. The English found one ford after another blocked by French troops, so Henry V took the army eastward, up the Somme, to locate a crossing. High water and the French prevented this until he reached Athies (10 miles west of Péronne), where the English found an undefended crossing.

At Rouen the French raised a force of some 30,000 men under Charles d'Albert, constable of France. This force almost intercepted the English before they could get across the Somme. Henry V's trail was not hard to find, marked as it was by burning French farmhouses. (Henry once remarked that war without fire was like "sausages without mustard.")

D'Albert got in front of the English and set up a blocking position on the main road to Calais near the Château of Agincourt, where Henry's troops met them on October 24. Henry's force faced an army many times his own in size. His men were short of supplies, and enraged local inhabitants were killing English foragers and stragglers. Shaken by the prospects, Henry V ordered his prisoners released and offered to return Honfleur and pay for any damages he had inflicted in return for

BATTLE OF AGINCOURT, OCTOBER 25, 1415

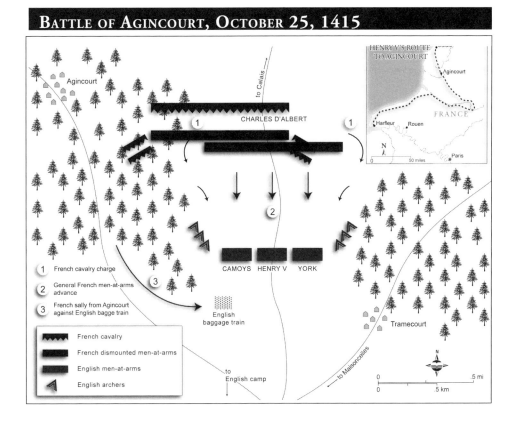

safe passage to Calais. The French, with a numerical advantage of up to five to one, were in no mood to make concessions. They demanded that Henry V renounce his claims in France to everything except Guyenne, which he refused to do.

The French nobles were eager to join battle and pressed d'Albert for an attack, but he resisted their demands that day. That night Henry V ordered absolute silence, which the French took as a sign of demoralization. Daybreak on October 25 found the English at one end of a defile slightly more than 1,000 yards wide and flanked by heavy woods. The road to Calais ran down its middle. Open fields on either side of the road had been recently plowed and were sodden from the heavy rains.

Drawing on English success in the battles of Crécy and Poitiers, Henry V drew up his 800 to 1,000 men-at-arms and 5,000 archers in three major groups, or "battles." The "battles," in one line, consisted of men-at-arms and pikemen, while the archers were located between the three "battles" and on the flanks, where they enfiladed forward about 100 yards or so to the woods on either side.

About a mile away d'Albert also deployed in three groups, but because of French numbers and the narrowness of the defile these were one behind the other. The first rank consisted of dismounted men and some crossbow men, along with perhaps 500 horsemen on the flanks; the second was the same without the horsemen; and the third consisted almost entirely of horsemen. Each commander hoped to fight a defensive battle, Henry in particular so that he might employ his archers.

Finally, in late morning when the French had failed to move, Henry staged a cautious advance of about a half mile and then halted, his men taking up the same formation as before, with the leading archers on the flanks only about 300 yards from the first French ranks. The bowmen then pounded sharpened stakes into the ground facing toward the enemy, their tips at breast height of a horse.

Henry's movement had the desired effect. D'Albert was no longer able to resist the demands of his fellow nobles to attack the English and ordered the advance. The mounted knights on either flank moved forward well ahead of the slow-moving and heavily armored men-at-arms. It was Crécy and Poitiers all over again, with the longbow decisive. A large number of horsemen, slowed by the soggy ground, were cut down by English arrows that caught them in enfilade. The remainder were halted at the English line.

The cavalry attack was defeated long before the first French men-at-arms, led in person by d'Albert, arrived. Their heavy body armor and the mud exhausted the French, but most reached the thin English line and, by sheer weight of numbers, drove it back. The English archers then fell on the closely packed French from the flanks, using swords, axes, and hatchets to cut them down. The unencumbered Englishmen had the advantage, as they could more easily move in the mud around their French opponents. Within minutes, almost all in the first French rank had been either killed or captured.

The second French rank then moved forward, but it lacked the confidence and cohesion of the first. Although losses were heavy, many of its number were able to retire to re-form for a new attack with the third "battle" of mounted knights. At this point Henry V learned that the French had attacked his baggage train, and he ordered the wholesale slaughter of the French prisoners, fearing that he would not be strong enough to meet attacks from both the front and the rear. The rear attack, however, turned out to be only a sally from the Château of Agincourt by a few men-at-arms and perhaps 600 French peasants. The English easily repulsed the final French attack, which was not pressed home. Henry V then led several hundred mounted men in a charge that dispersed what remained of the French army. The archers then ran forward, killing thousands of the Frenchmen lying on the field by stabbing them through gaps in their armor or bludgeoning them to death.

In less than four hours the English had defeated a force significantly larger than their own. At least 5,000 Frenchmen died in the battle, and another 1,500 were taken prisoner. Among those who perished were many prominent French nobles, including d'Albert. The Duke d'Orléans and Marshal Jean Bouciquan were among the captured. Henry V reported English losses as 13 men-at-arms and 100 footmen killed, but this figure is too low. English losses were probably 300 killed. Among the badly wounded was Henry V's brother, the Duke of Gloucester.

Henry V then marched to Calais, taking the prisoners who would be ransomed. The army reached Calais on October 29. In mid-November Henry V returned to England.

The loss of so many prominent French nobles in the Battle of Agincourt greatly increased Duke John of Burgundy's influence to the point of dictating French royal policy. Henry V returned to France in 1417 and went on to conquer Normandy by the end of 1419, with the exception of Mont St. Michel. In 1420 at Troyes he concluded peace with Charles VI, who agreed to the marriage of Henry to his daughter Catherine. The French king also disowned his son, the dauphin Charles, and acknowledged Henry as his heir. Over the next two years Henry consolidated his hold over northern France, but unfortunately for the English cause he died in 1422, leaving as heir to the thrones of England and France a son just nine months old.

References

Hibbert, Christopher. *Agincourt.* New York: Dorset, 1978.

Keegan, John. *The Face of Battle: A Study of Agincourt, Waterloo & the Somme.* New York: Vintage Books, 1977.

Seward, Desmond. *The Hundred Years' War: The English in France, 1337–1453.* New York: Atheneum, 1978.

Sumption, Jonathan. *The Hundred Years' War: Trial by Battle.* Philadelphia: University of Pennsylvania Press, 1988.

Siege of Orléans

Date	October 1428–May 1429	
Location	City of Orléans on the Loire River in north central France	
Opponents (* winner)	*French	English
Commander	Jean Dunois, comte de Longueville; Jeanne d'Arc	William de la Pole, Earl of Suffolk
Approx. # Troops	9,000	5,000
Importance	Jeanne d'Arc ends the English aura of military invincibility	

The relief of the siege of Orléans by a French army under Jeanne d'Arc (Joan of Arc) was the decisive event of the Hundred Years' War (1337–1453) between the French and the English. The course of the war had to that point constantly shifted. On October 25, 1415, King Henry V of England defeated the French in the Battle of Agincourt. Five years later French king Charles VI agreed to the Treaty of Troyes whereby his daughter Catherine was to marry Henry V. Charles VI also repudiated the dauphin, his son Charles, as illegitimate and acknowledged Henry as his heir. Henry V then campaigned successfully against French forces loyal to the dauphin until his untimely death in August 1422 reopened the matter of succession. The

English named Henry's nine-month-old son as king of France and England. Charles VI died that October, and many French supported his son Charles, the former dauphin, as the rightful king. Charles, however, was weak, degenerate, vacillating, and utterly incapable of leadership.

In these circumstances the regent for the young Henry VI, the Duke of Bedford, allied England with the powerful Duchy of Burgundy and on July 21, 1423, defeated the French at Cravant, establishing English rule over all of France north of the Loire River. On August 17, 1524, Bedford annihilated a French force at Verneuil. In the autumn of 1428 English-Burgundian forces launched an offensive to secure the crossing of the Loire River at Orléans to campaign in Armagnac, the heart of Charles's territory.

Orléans was a large city and one of the strongest fortresses in France. Three of its four sides were strongly walled and moated, and its southern side rested on the Loire. The city walls were well defended by numerous catapults and 71 large cannon, and stocks of food had been gathered. Jean Dunois, Comte de Longueville, commanded the city's garrison of about 2,400 soldiers and 3,000 armed citizens.

English troops under the Earl of Salisbury arrived at Orléans on October 12, 1428. Because he had only about 5,000 men, Salisbury was not able to invest Orléans completely. Nonetheless, on October 24 the English seized the fortified bridge across the Loire, although Salisbury was mortally wounded in the attack. In December William Pole, Earl of Suffolk, took over command of siege operations. The English constructed a number of small forts to protect the bridge as well as their encampments.

Although the French in Orléans mounted several forays and were able to secure limited supplies, by early 1429 the situation in the city was desperate, with the defenders close to starvation. Orléans was now the symbol of French resistance and nationalism. Charles was considering flight abroad, but the situation was not as bleak as it appeared. French peasants were rising against the English, and only a leader was lacking.

That person appeared in the young illiterate peasant girl, Jeanne d'Arc. She informed Charles that she had been sent by God to raise the siege of Orléans and to lead him to Reims to be crowned king of France. Charles allowed Jeanne, dressed in full armor, to lead (as *chef de guerre*) a relief army of up to 4,000 men and a convoy of supplies to Orléans. The Duc d'Alençon had actual command.

Jeanne's fame quickly spread far and wide, and her faith in her divine mission inspired the French. As the relief force approached Orléans, Jeanne sent a letter to Suffolk demanding surrender. Not surprisingly, he refused. Jeanne then demanded that the army circle around and approach the city from the north. The other leaders agreed; the French army was ferried to the north bank of the Loire and entered the city through a north gate on April 29.

Jeanne urged an attack on the English from the city, assuring the men of God's protection. On May 1 Jeanne awoke to learn that a French attack against the English at Fort St. Loup had begun without her and was not going well. She rode out in full armor and rallied the attackers, who were then victorious. All the English defenders were killed, while the French lost only two dead. Jeanne then insisted that the soldiers confess their sins and ban all prostitutes from the army and promised the men that they would be victorious in five days. Another appeal to the English to surrender met with derisive shouts.

On May 5 Jeanne led an attack out of the south gate of the city. The French avoided the bridge over the Loire, which the English had captured at the beginning of the siege. The French crossed through shallow water to an island in the middle of the river and from there used a boat bridge to gain the south bank. The French captured the English fort at St. Jean le Blanc and then moved against a large fort at Les Augustins, close to the bridge. The battle was costly to both sides, but Jeanne led a charge that left the French in possession of the fort.

The next day, May 6, Jeanne's troops assaulted Les Tournelles, the towers at the southern end of the bridge. Jeanne was hit by an arrow and carried from the field, but the wound was not major; by late afternoon she had rejoined the battle. On May 7 a French knight took Jeanne's banner to lead an attack on the towers. She tried to stop him, but the mere sight of the banner caused the French soldiers to follow it. Jeanne then joined the battle.

Using scaling ladders, the French assaulted the walls, with Jeanne in the thick of the fight. The 400–500 English defenders attempted to flee on the bridge, but it was soon on fire and collapsed. On May 8 the remaining English forces abandoned the siege and departed.

In his official pronouncements Charles took full credit for the victory, but the French people attributed it to Jeanne and flocked to join her. In successive battles, most notably at Patay on June 19, the French routed the English from their Loire strongholds. In July the French took Reims from the Burgundians, and there, on July 16, Charles was anointed king, with Jeanne in attendance in full armor and with banner in hand. The moral effect of this coronation was vast. Given the circumstances, few could doubt that Charles VII was the legitimate ruler of France.

Jeanne called for an immediate advance on Paris. Charles, however, wanted only to return to the Loire. Jeanne's attempt to capture Paris failed, and Charles signed a truce with the Duke of Burgundy. Charles ordered Jeanne to cease fighting and had her army disbanded. In May 1430 Jeanne was taken prisoner by the Burgundians. When Charles refused to ransom her, Duke Philip of Burgundy sold Jeanne to the English, who put her on trial at Rouen for heresy and sorcery and executed her in May 1431.

Although the Hundred Years' War continued for another two decades, the relief of the siege of Orléans was the turning point in the long war. Jeanne's death checked for a time the uprising of French nationality, but peace between France and Burgundy in 1435, Charles VII's effective advisers (he became known as "Charles the Well-Served"), and military reforms in France that provided for a standing army and infantry militia finally brought the expulsion of the English. The Hundred Years' War ended with the fall of Bordeaux to the French in 1453.

References

Gies, Frances. *Jean of Arc: The Legend and the Reality.* New York: Harper and Row, 1981.

Seward, Desmond. *The Hundred Years' War: The English in France, 1337–1453.* New York: Atheneum, 1978.

Sumption, Jonathan. *The Hundred Years' War: Trial by Battle.* Philadelphia: University of Pennsylvania Press, 1988.

Warner, Marina. *Joan of Arc: The Image of Female Heroism.* New York: Knopf, 1981.

Siege of Constantinople

Date	April 6–May 29, 1453	
Location	City of Constantinople (modern Istanbul, Turkey)	
Opponents (* winner)	*Ottomans	Byzantines
Commander	Sultan Mehmed II	Emperor Constantine XI
Approx. # Troops	100,000–200,000	10,000
Importance	Seminal event in European history; marks the end of the Byzantine Empire; Sultan Mehmed II makes Constantinople his capital, renaming it Istanbul	

The successful 1453 Ottoman Turk siege of the city of Constantinople marked the end of the Byzantine Empire. Throughout the course of the 14th century the Ottomans had expanded their power over Anatolia. In 1352 Ottoman forces crossed the Bosporus from Asia and established a foothold in Europe in Rumelia. From there the Ottomans moved into Thrace. Soon they controlled the land around Constantinople, although this great Christian city on the Bosporus, the capital of the once-great Byzantine Empire, remained free of their control.

Mehmed II (Muhammad II), who became sultan in 1451, made it his principal goal to take Constantinople. In 1452 he completed construction of the Rumili Hisar (Castle of Europe) at the eastern outlet of the Bosporus on the European shore, opposite the older Anadoli Hisar (Castle of Asia) in Anatolia. These two fortresses assured Mehmed control of the passage across the straits from Anatolia to Rumelia and gave him the ability to block shipping from the Black Sea to Constantinople. In addition, artillery at Rumili Hisar could bombard Constantinople. In June 1452 Mehmed's action brought war with Byzantine emperor Constantine XI.

In addition to a highly trained Janissary corps comprised of Christian boys taken as slaves, Mehmed could call on substantial mercenary and irregular troops. The force he took to Constantinople has been variously estimated at between 100,000 and 200,000 men. He also brought some 70 artillery pieces. Many of the Ottoman guns were cast by an experienced Hungarian cannon founder and renegade named

Mehmed II and his men entering Constantinople following their successful siege of the Byzantine capital. Mehmet's victory in 1453 marked the irrefutable end of the Byzantine Empire and significant progress in the western spread of Islam. Nineteenth-century engraving. (Ridpath, John Clark, *Ridpath's History of the World,* 1901)

Urban. They included a dozen large bombards and one bronze gun nearly 27 feet in length with a 2.5-foot-diameter barrel that fired a 1,300-pound projectile.

During the winter of 1452–1453 Mehmed ordered the assembly of some 125 naval vessels of various types. He was well aware that previous sieges of Constantinople had failed because they were from the land only. In the spring of 1453 his fleet sailed from Gallipoli into the Sea of Marmara. With a naval force five times that of the Byzantines, Mehmed was confident he had command of the sea and could block any relief attempt. At the same time, he began moving his vast land force from Thrace. The army arrived before the walls of Constantinople on April 2, 1453. Mehmed then sent messengers to offer the inhabitants freedom of life and property under Ottoman protection if they would surrender. These terms were rejected, and on April 6 Mehmed's heavy guns commenced fire.

Constantinople received limited aid from Venice and Genoa. To defend the city, Constantine had only 26 ships guarding the sea approaches and a small regular force of fewer than 10,000 men, 2,000 of whom were foreigners. The city's chief defense was its 14 miles of nearly impregnable walls, but this translated into 1 defender per 7.5 feet of wall. Actual command of the defense fell to the leader of the Genoese mercenaries and an expert in siege warfare, Giovanni Giustiniani. With news of the Ottoman approach, Constantine ordered the gates to the city closed, bridges over the moat demolished, and a great chain stretched across the mouth of the city harbor, known as the Golden Horn.

The Ottoman artillery bombardment of the western walls of the city continued for six weeks without letup, but each time there was a breach the defenders managed to fill it in and drive back the Ottoman infantry. Superior Byzantine seamanship and armaments enabled them to repulse attacks by the Ottoman fleet, but Mehmed had 70 galleys hauled overland to the Golden Horn on great greased rollers, bypassing the closed harbor entrance. When these were launched in the Golden Horn, the defenders knew that the battle was lost. Still, the Ottomans might have been repulsed had the major European powers made an effort to help defend the Christian city, but they did nothing.

By May food in Constantinople was in short supply, and the population was starving. Toward the end of that month the Ottomans managed to create a breach in the wall that the defenders could not completely block, and early on the morning of May 29 the Ottomans launched a great assault, accompanied by trumpets, drums, and war cries. Following human wave assaults, the Ottoman troops forced an entry. Although many of the defenders took refuge in the ships, Constantine refused to flee. He removed his insignia, plunged into battle with the oncoming Janissaries, and was promptly slain.

After a disciplined march into Constantinople, the conquerors broke ranks and for three days subjected the city to an orgy of slaughter and pillage, carrying off not only the contents of palaces and houses but also their attractive young inhabitants as well. Mehmed entered the city on horseback with a guard of Janissaries the evening it was taken and made his way to the great church of Hagia Sophia, which he ordered transformed into a mosque.

Regarded as a seminal event in the history of the West, the fall of Constantinople was a great psychological and strategic blow to the European powers. It ended the Byzantine Empire, which had been the last buffer between Europe and the Ottomans. Mehmed II, now known as Mehmed the Conqueror, renamed the city Istanbul and made it his capital. The city faced both Asia and Europe, and over the next several decades Mehmed directed from it the extension of Ottoman power to include Serbia, Greece, Albania, the Aegean, and even Otranto in southern Italy. Mehmed died in May 1481. Over the next two centuries his successors mounted repeated offensives to push Ottoman control west into the Mediterranean and north into Central Europe.

References

Browning, Robert. *Byzantine Empire.* New York: Scribner, 1980.

Gibbon, Edward. *The Decline and Fall of the Roman Empire, 1185–1453.* New York: Modern Library, 1983.

Kinross, Lord [John Patrick]. *The Ottoman Centuries: The Rise and Fall of the Turkish Empire.* New York: William Morrow, 1977.

Norwich. John Julius. *Byzantium: The Decline and Fall.* New York: Knopf, 1996.

Battle of Bosworth Field

Date	August 22, 1485	
Location	Leicestershire, England	
Opponents (* winner)	*Tudors	Yorkists
Commander	Henry Tudor, Earl of Richmond	King Richard III
Approx. # Troops	5,000	10,000
Importance	Last major battle of the War of the Roses; establishes the Tudor dynasty in England in place of the Plantagenet	

The Battle of Bosworth Field was the last significant combat in the Wars of the Roses (1455–1485), fought between the House of Lancaster and the House of York. The battle ended the Plantagenet dynasty in England and established the Tudors on the throne. On August 7, 1485, Henry Tudor, Earl of Richmond, landed at Milford Haven in Wales to lay claim to the English throne as heir in the Lancastrian line. Henry, who had earlier fled to France, took advantage of growing opposition in England to the rule of King Richard III, who had seized the English throne from 13-year-old King Edward V and was suspected of then causing the murder in the Tower of London of Edward and his younger brother Richard, Duke of York.

Henry had with him a small group of followers, including two seasoned soldiers—his uncle Jasper Tudor, 1st Earl of Pembroke (later 1st Duke of Bedford), and John de Vere, 13th Earl of Oxford—and some 1,800 French mercenaries but quickly gathered additional forces in Wales and western England. Shrewsbury rallied to him, and by August 20 and his arrival at Atherstone in Warwickshire, Henry had more than doubled his force.

Richard III marched from London northwest to meet Henry at Bosworth Field, 12 miles west of Leicester and 3 miles south of Market Bosworth, in the Midlands of central England. Thomas Stanley, 2nd Baron Stanley, husband of Margaret Buford and thus stepfather of Henry, had been in communication with Henry Tudor and refused to add his troops to those of Richard. Stanley and his brother, Sir William Stanley, did bring about 3,000 men to the battleground but refused appeals to join either side.

By the time the armies deployed on Bosworth Field, Henry had no more than 5,000 men, while Richard III some 10,000 men. Richard's superior numbers were offset, however, by the fact that many of his men were of dubious loyalty. Richard deployed his troops on the gently rising Ambion Hill, positioning them in three groups, or "battles," with his archers in front and cannon on the flanks.

John de Vere, Earl of Oxford, commanded Henry's forces. De Vere deployed his troops in two "battles." Sir William Stanley positioned his own men to the north, beyond the battle lines between the two sides, while Lord Thomas Stanley held his men off to the south.

De Vere attacked the Yorkish center, confident of treachery in its ranks. The Lancastrian charge was repulsed, but the Earl of Northumberland, commanding Richard's left wing, then refused Richard's order to advance. Simultaneously the Stanley brothers joined the battle on Henry's side, attacking the king's flank and rear.

Advised to quit the field, Richard refused. Seeing Henry's banner and declaring that he would remain king of England, Richard and a few followers charged, apparently hoping to kill Henry and reverse the battle. Richard slew Sir William Blandon, Henry's standard-bearer, with a single blow; unhorsed Sir John Cheney; and may actually have engaged Henry himself before being surrounded and killed by a sword cut to his head. Sir William Stanley picked up the king's golden crown and placed it upon Henry's head. The battle was over. In all the Lancastrians lost some 100 men. The accepted figure of 1,000 lost on the Yorkish side is probably exaggerated.

The Battle of Bosworth Field had immense political ramifications. The defeat of the Yorkists and the death of Richard III ended the Plantagenet dynasty that had ruled England since 1154. Henry, officially crowned five weeks later in Westminister Abbey as Henry VII, began the Tudor dynasty. Although Yorkish insurgencies occurred periodically during the next decade, Henry put all of them down. His marriage to Elizabeth of York also helped heal the divisions that caused the Wars of the Roses. During his 24-year reign Henry restored order in the kingdom, dramatically increased royal authority, built up the treasury, and laid the foundations for four centuries of English greatness.

References

Lander, J. R. *The Wars of the Roses.* New York: St. Martin's, 1990.

Ross, Charles. *The Wars of the Roses.* London: Thames and Hudson, 1976.

Rowse, A. L. *Bosworth Field and the Wars of the Roses.* New York: Macmillan, 1966.

Steward, Desmond. *The Wars of the Roses.* New York: Viking, 1995.

Weir, Alison. *The Wars of the Roses.* New York: Ballantine Books, 1995.

Siege of Granada

Date	1491–1492	
Location	Granada in southern Spain	
Opponents (* winner)	*Kingdoms of Aragon and Castile	Kingdom of Granada
Commander	King Ferdinand II of Aragon	Muhammad XI (known to the Spanish as Boabdil)
Approx. # Troops	Unknown	Unknown
Importance	Ends the last Muslim stronghold in Spain and marks the consolidation of Spain into one state	

The Arabs first raided southern Spain in 710. The next year Taraq, a freed Berber slave, mounted a true invasion across the Strait of Gibraltar, beginning the rapid Arab conquest of Spain. The Muslim expansion northward was halted in the Battle of Tours in France in 732, but the Moors (as the Spanish Muslims were known) ruled in Spain for the next seven and a half centuries. In the far north of Spain a few Christian fortresses held out, and in the late 11th century the Christian Spanish began the Reconquista (the long Christian effort to reconquer Spain) under Rodrigo Díaz de Bivar, known as El Cid (from the Arabic *al-sayyid,* or "chieftain"), who took Valencia in 1094. King Alfonso VIII of Castile was victorious at Navas de Tolosa in 1212.

From the middle of the 13th century the two sides faced one another in established positions, the Christian kingdoms in the north and the only remaining Moorish territory, the Kingdom of Granada, on the southern coast of Spain. At the end of the 15th century the marriage of Queen Isabella of Castile and Ferdinand II of Aragon united Christian Spain, and the Reconquista recommenced in earnest.

Muhammad XI, born Abu Abdullah and known to the Spanish as Boabdil, ruled the Kingdom of Granada from the famous Alhambra Palace in the beautiful fortified city of Granada. Under pressure from the powerful Christian kingdoms to the north, Muhammad had agreed to give over Granada to Ferdinand and Isabella if they could conquer Baza, Cádiz, and Almería. Thus, the siege of Granada was part of general operations throughout Granada.

By early 1488 the forces of Ferdinand and Isabella had conquered the western half of Granada. In June, Ferdinand advanced with his forces from his headquarters at Loja to Vera, which promptly surrendered. He then advanced on Almería, which, according to secret agreements, was also to surrender to him without a fight. This did not happen, and Ferdinand then withdrew with his forces. He recommenced operations in the spring of 1489 and laid siege to Baza with 13,000 cavalry and 40,000 infantry. With Baza resisting and Ferdinand's resources nearing exhaustion, Queen Isabella pawned her own jewels to enable the continuation of operations and joined her husband before the city, which capitulated on December

4, 1489. After taking Baza, Ferdinand and Isabella moved against Almería, which promptly surrendered. The monarchs then entered the city and received the fealty of its inhabitants. The same occurred at Cádiz. Ferdinand then sent emissaries to Muhammad to demand that he fulfill the agreement. The Moorish king replied that it was impossible for him to fulfill the pact's conditions immediately. However, Muhammad's true response became clear when his forces occupied the Christian fortress of Padul near Granada. He intended to fight.

In the spring of 1490 Ferdinand ordered all the trees cut down and crops destroyed in the fertile plain around the city of Granada in preparation for operations against the Moorish stronghold. Although Muhammad's cavalry carried out attacks on the Christian forces engaged in this activity and killed many of them, this did not prevent the operations from being completed. A belt of destruction now extended around the city of Granada. In reprisal, Muhammad's forces attacked and captured the Christian fortress of Alhendin, leading to a revolt of Moors in the surrounding area. Moorish forces also moved against other locations, especially the coastal city of Salobreña, to allow regular resupply from the Muslim Kingdom of Barbary in North Africa. The Christian garrison managed to hold out, however, and word that Ferdinand was arriving with a relief force caused the Muslim besiegers to withdraw to Granada.

In September, Ferdinand ordered destruction of the grain crop around Granada and then withdrew his forces to Córdoba. Muhammad then stirred up revolt against the Christian rulers in Almería, Baza, and Cádiz. Ferdinand then moved against Cádiz, his presence there restoring calm. In order to be certain of the security of his new territory, Ferdinand ordered all Moorish inhabitants of fortified cities to leave them and live in open cities or sell their property and relocate to Barbary.

In the spring of 1491 Ferdinand and Isabella finally began serious military operations against Granada. Ferdinand dispatched the Marquis of Villena with 3,000 cavalry and 10,000 infantry to destroy fortifications in the Lecrino Valley. Fearing that Villena might be ambushed, Ferdinand followed close behind with the rest of the army. Villena was successful, however, and Ferdinand then ordered the destruction of everything of value in the valley. Muhammad occupied the Tablate and Lanjaron passes, hoping to ambush Ferdinand's forces on their return. This failed, however, and Catholic forces drove the Moors from the passes. Ferdinand's entire army then assembled on the plain before Granada.

On April 26, 1491, Ferdinand opened the siege of Granada, establishing his headquarters in the nearby village of Atqa. Isabella remained in the field with her husband to observe events and inspire the troops. Granada was situated on two hills, with the Alhambra crowning one and the Alcazaba fortress the other. The Darro River ran between the two hills, and a long wall with numerous watchtowers and strong points surrounded the city. There were few major confrontations. One occurred in July, which the Spanish won, and the Moors attempted a number of small sorties, but all were beaten back.

By September the inhabitants of Granada were in desperate straits, the population of the city having swelled just prior to the siege. Realizing that relief from Muslim forces in North Africa would not be forthcoming and that there was no hope of reversing the situation, Muhammad entered secret negotiations with King Ferdinand. On November 25, 1491, Muhammad agreed to generous terms. The Muslims were to surrender all their artillery and fortresses but were able, for the time being, to continue practice of their religion, to keep their own language and customs, to be governed by their own laws, and to dispose of their property as they wished. They would also be exempt from royal taxation for a period of three years. Muhammad received the small territory of Alpujarras but would govern as a vassal of Castile. These terms were to go into effect in 60 days, but with opposition to Muhammad protesting this arrangement, the surrender was moved forward, and Ferdinand received the keys to the city from Muhammad's own hand on January 1, 1492.

The capitulation marked the end of the long Muslim rule in Spain and the consolidation of the Spanish kingdoms into one state. This long religious Crusade also resulted in Spanish nationalism being closely identified with the Catholic Church. Despite the terms granted in the capitulation of Granada, the militant Catholicism of Spain soon led to the persecution of both Muslims and Jews.

References

Fernández-Armesto, Felipe. *Ferdinand and Isabella.* New York: Taplinger, 1975.

Harvey, L. P. *Islamic Spain, 1250 to 1500.* Chicago: University of Chicago Press, 1990.

Hillgarth, J. N. *The Spanish Kingdoms, 1250–1516.* 2 vols. Oxford, UK: Clarendon, 1976–1978.

Melegari, Vezio. *The Great Military Sieges.* New York: Crowell, 1972.

Battle of Flodden Field

Date	September 9, 1513	
Location	County of Northumberland in northern England	
Opponents (* winner)	*England	Scotland
Commander	Thomas Howard, Earl of Surrey	King James IV
Approx. # Troops	25,000 (1,500 of them cavalry)	30,000
Importance	Largest battle in terms of numbers of men ever engaged between the two nations; turns back the Scottish invasion of England	

On August 11, 1513, following English king Henry VIII's invasion of France, King James IV of Scotland declared war on England and, on August 22, crossed the border with a large army. Aided by James's slow advance, Thomas Howard, Earl of Surrey, raised an English army to resist the invasion. The Scottish army included not only the king but most of the great nobles of the realm and numbered about 30,000 men. Most of the Scots were untrained infantry levies who were armed with the 18-foot pike. The Scots also had 18 artillery pieces, drawn by 400 oxen. Too heavy for field use, the artillery slowed the army's advance.

Surrey had perhaps 25,000 men. Except for some 1,500 cavalry all were infantry, armed with the longbow and with the bill (an English version of the continental halberd), an eight-foot weapon with an ax head and designed for slashing. Anxious that James not escape as he had during a previous invasion in 1497, Surrey issued a challenge to the Scottish king to do battle on September 9.

James accepted. He was confident of his superior numbers and heavy artillery, and many of his men had armor and carried heavy wooden shields to protect against the longbow. Notions of honor and chivalry may also have influenced his decision, as Surrey hoped. James replied that he would wait for the English until noon on that day.

James planned a defensive battle and drew up his forces in a long line on high ground in Northumberland known as Flodden Ridge. The Scottish artillery was dug in and well situated to cover the obvious English approach from the south. Surrey realized that any attack on this natural fortress would be suicide.

Surrey used his knowledge of the local terrain to great advantage. In a surprise move, he marched his forces rapidly around those of his adversary, crossed the Till River, and placed his men between the Scottish army and Scotland. This forced James to abandon his position and take up a new one to the north on Branxton Hill, near the village of Branxton (hence the alternate name for the battle).

The ensuing Battle of Flodden Field (Branxton Moor) was the last major battle in which the longbow played a significant part and one of the first in which gunpowder artillery was prominent. The English had 22 guns. They were lighter than those of the Scots, which made them far easier to manipulate and quicker to load; they were also of higher muzzle velocity and thus able to outrange the Scots' guns.

Surrey's tactics and generalship were excellent. The Scottish pike proved ill-suited to the Scots' fighting method, discipline, and the terrain. The highly effective harassing fire by the English artillery and longbowmen steadily wore down the Scots and forced them into a series of charges, which almost succeeded before they were broken up and beaten back by the English infantry and cavalry in a melee battle that lasted some three hours, from late afternoon until nightfall. First the English destroyed the Scottish flanks, and then they annihilated the center. The battle was extraordinarily hard-fought and bloody, but it ended in a complete English victory.

While English losses were on the order of 1,500 killed, the Scots sustained some 10,000 dead. Few prisoners were taken. Among the slain were King James IV (the last British monarch to die in battle) and most of his leading nobles. The king had fought bravely but had been both outmaneuvered and out-generaled. As a reward for his victory, Howard, Earl of Surrey, was raised to Duke of Norfolk. The Battle of Flodden Field was one of the most complete English victories over Scotland in the long history of wars between the two kingdoms and ended any serious Scottish threat to England for some time to come.

References

Elton, Geoffrey. *England under the Tudors.* New York: Routledge, 1991.

Guy, John. *Tudor England.* New York: Oxford University Press, 1990.

Knightly, Charles. *Flodden: The Anglo-Scottish War of 1513.* London: Almark Publishing, 1975.

Sadler, John. *Flodden, 1513: Scotland's Greatest Defeat.* London: Osprey, 2006.

Siege of Tenochtitlán

Date	May 26–August 13, 1521	
Location	Tenochtitlán (today Mexico City, Mexico)	
Opponents (* winner)	*Spanish and Tlaxcalan allies	Aztecs
Commander	Hernán Cortés	Emperor Cuauhtemoc
Approx. # Troops	Spanish: 184 arquebusiers, crossbowmen, and men-at-arms, with 86 horsemen, perhaps 700 infantry; Tlaxcalans: 50,000	Unknown
Importance	Spanish capture of the Aztec capital leads to their conquest of Mexico	

The siege and capture of the Aztec capital of Tenochtitlán was the most important event in the Spanish conquest of Mexico. The Aztecs, or people from Aztlan in the north (they were also known as the Mexica), came to dominate much of the region. Their society was highly developed, with a complex governmental structure and long-distance trade, but they had limited scientific knowledge and no modern weaponry.

In the mid-14th century the Aztecs established their capital in the city of Tenochtitlán (present-day Mexico City) on an island on the western side of Lake Texcoco connected to the shore by long causeways. The Aztecs worshiped Huitzilopochtli (the god of the sun and war) and other deities. Believing that daily human sacrifices were necessary to keep the sun healthy and shining, they built altars to Huitzilopochtli and the other gods in the form of great pyramids that dominated the city. On special days thousands of prisoners might be sacrificed. This practice did not endear the Aztecs to their conquered peoples and created ready allies for the Spanish. Ultimately Tenochtitlán came to be a large and wealthy city of approximately 60,000 buildings and 200,000 people, perhaps one-fifth of the total Aztec population. A million or so Aztecs ruled a subject population of perhaps 5 million.

Engraving depicting the capture of the Aztec capital of Tenochtitlán (present-day Mexico City) by Spanish conquistadores led by Hernán Cortés in 1521. (Wildside Press)

In 1519, 34-year-old Hernán Cortés landed on the west coast of Mexico from his base in Cuba under orders to establish a coastal trading post. Cortés, however, was determined to explore the mysterious land of the west, which was rumored to abound in gold. Cortés commanded a small force of 550 men with some 17 horses and 10 small cannon. In August he began his march to the interior, and during the next month he defeated the Tlaxcalan people in a series of battles and captured their capital of Tlaxcala. The Tlaxcalans then allied themselves with the Spanish.

In November 1519 Emperor Montezuma II received Cortés at Tenochtitlán with all possible honors. The Spanish, who were dazzled by the gold and wealth of the capital, soon made clear their intention to rule. Cortés was able to capitalize in part on the Aztec belief in a great white god, Quetzalcoatl, whose return had been proph-esied. With their horses, metal armor, and firearms, the Spanish could play the part.

Following the death of some Spanish soldiers on the coast near Veracruz, Cortés seized Montezuma and began to rule through him. This worked until Cortés sought to introduce Christianity. In the spring of 1520 Cortés departed Tenochtitlán to do battle with a rival Spanish force sent by his superior, Cuban governor Diego Ve-lázquez, to punish Cortés for disobeying orders. Cortés defeated that force and added the men he captured to his own forces.

On his return to Tenochtitlán, Cortés discovered that his lieutenant Pedro de Alvarado, whom he had left in charge, was under siege by the Aztecs. While Cortés was able to reestablish his authority, the situation in the city soon deteriorated, and warfare resumed. Montezuma was killed, but his brother Cuitlahuac had already been elected emperor by chiefs determined to fight the Spanish. Aztec numbers now prevailed over Spanish firepower, and on the night of June 30–July 1 (La Noche Triste as it was known to the Spanish, or "The Sad Night") Cortés and many of his followers were forced to fight their way out of the city. They lost most of the gold they had hoped to bring out along with 600 men and two-thirds of their 68 horses. The Aztecs harassed the Spanish in their retreat all the way to Tlaxcala.

Rather than pursue a guerrilla war, Emperor Cuitlahuac chose to fight a set-piece battle where the Aztec warriors came up against horse cavalry for the first time. At Otumba on July 7, the Spanish used their 28 horses to great advantage, driving against the conspicuously dressed Aztec leadership to win a victory in which thousands of Aztecs were killed.

Cortés then spent several months rebuilding his force. He sent ships to Jamaica to fetch replacement artillery and horses. At the same time Cortés had his men construct 13 small brigantines to approach Tenochtitlán across Lake Texcoco. Each vessel carried 25 Spanish soldiers and 12 native rowers.

Cortés was also aided by a surprise ally, for unwittingly the Spanish had brought smallpox to the New World. The natives had absolutely no resistance to the disease, which wiped out much of the population. Cuitlahuac was among those who perished. Cuauhtemoc, a son-in-law of Montezuma, succeeded Cuitlahuac as emperor.

In early 1521 Cortés was ready to move. The Spanish and their native allies began their approach to Tenochtitlán by taking control of towns around Lake Texcoco. By April this was complete. The Spanish had 184 harquebusiers, crossbowmen, and men-at-arms along with 86 horsemen, perhaps 700 infantry, and 18 artillery pieces. They were greatly aided by some 50,000 allied Tlaxcalans who opposed Aztec rule. Cortés divided his forces into three main groups under his lieutenants Alvarado, Gonzalo de Sandoval, and Cristóbal de Olid.

On May 26 forces under Sandoval and Alvarado destroyed the great aqueduct at Chapultepec, cutting off the water supply to Tenochtitlán. Five days later the Aztecs mounted an attack with hundreds of canoes across the lake. The Spaniards used cannon fire to destroy most of the canoes and win control of the lake. That same day Cortés launched an attack on Tenochtitlán. Some crossbowmen were able to land in the city, but they were soon driven out.

The fighting continued for 10 weeks, during which the Spaniards were able to view the sacrifice by the Aztecs atop the great pyramid of those the Aztecs had taken prisoner. At night the defenders made fresh breaks in the causeways providing access to the city, but the Spaniards and their allies were able to repair them. The Aztecs mounted human wave attacks, which the Tlaxcalans defeated at high cost. Finally, on August 13 Cortés launched an assault that brought victory the next day. Only a few Aztec survivors escaped in canoes. Reportedly, 150,000 people died in the city. One Spanish eyewitness said that it was impossible to walk in Tenochtitlán without stepping on corpses.

Following the capture of Tenochtitlán, Cortés set about completely dismantling Aztec society and replacing it with Spanish civilization. He was assisted in this by the continued ravages of smallpox that may have wiped out 90 percent of the native population. Within a generation both the Aztec language and religion had disappeared. Spain would be the dominant power in the region for the next 300 years.

References

Carrasco, David. *Montezuma's Mexico.* Niwot: University of Colorado Press, 1992.

Diaz del Castillo, Bernal. *The Discovery and Conquest of Mexico, 1517–1521.* Translated by A. P. Maudslay. New York: Harper, 1928.

White, Jon Manchip. *Cortés and the Downfall of the Aztec Empire.* London: Hamish Hamilton, 1971.

Siege of Rhodes

Date	July 28–December 21, 1522	
Location	Island of Rhodes in the Eastern Mediterranean Sea	
Opponents (* winner)	*Ottoman Empire	Knights of St. John and Genoese, Venetians and other mercenaries
Commander	Sultan Suleiman (Süleyman) I	Auguste de Villiers de L'Isle-Adam
Approx. # Troops	100,000	5,700
Importance	Removes the last serious threat to Ottoman naval power in the eastern Mediterranean and Aegean	

Rhodes is the largest of the Dodecanese islands in the eastern Mediterranean and lies about 10 miles from Anatolia. The Knights of St. John (Hospitallers) controlled Rhodes in the 16th century, the last Christian holding in the eastern Mediterranean. The Knights of St. John had been in possession of Rhodes since 1310, and over the years they fortified both its harbor and its high ground. The knights used the island, astride major Ottoman shipping lanes, to raid Muslim shipping throughout the eastern Mediterranean. This led Sultan Mehmed II (Mehmed the Conqueror) to mount an unsuccessful three-month siege of the island in 1480.

Continued raiding from Rhodes induced Ottoman sultan Suleiman I (Süleyman I) to plan a major effort against the island. In 1522 Suleiman assembled some 400 ships, 100,000 men, and siege artillery. On Rhodes the grand master of the Knights of St. John, Auguste de Villiers de L'Isle-Adam, commanded only about 5,700 men: 700 knights drawn from all over Christendom, 500 mercenaries from Crete, 500 Genoese, 50 Venetians, and 4,000 men-at-arms from other places. The knights did what they could to prepare for the attack. They closed off the entrance to the port with great chains, laid in supplies, and even demolished some buildings to create better fields of fire. Each of the principal defensive positions on the island was held by a particular language grouping.

The Ottoman host arrived off Rhodes on June 26 and anchored off Parambolino in the north, where the Ottoman troops landed uncontested. Among the artillery brought ashore were 40 bombards and 12 large basilisks. The Ottoman engineers took about a month to position their ordnance, opening fire on July 28. The Ottomans fired explosive shell, the first recorded use in battle in history. When this shelling failed to have the desired effect, at the end of August the Ottomans commenced mining operations. The defenders were well aware of this and dug countermines, setting off explosions against the Ottoman tunnels and venting them to disperse the blasts. Attempts to take the principal Christian stronghold, commanded by the grand master in person, were unsuccessful. The knights also launched a number of effective counterattacks.

Suleiman's forces had suffered heavily, and morale among them was low; Suleiman is said to have lost upwards of half his force. In recognition of both the tremendous costs of the siege and the heroic Christian defense, on December 10 he offered to discuss a Christian surrender on honorable terms. The onset of winter, their own precarious position, dwindling numbers and supplies, and unrest among the civilian population all prompted the knights to negotiate. On December 21 agreement was reached. Suleiman allowed the knights to depart the island with the full honors of war, their arms, their religious relics, and the treasury of the Order. Such civilians as wished to leave could also depart and take with them portable possessions.

The knights departed Rhodes on January 1, 1523. The siege had lasted 145 days. Suleiman had removed, at least temporarily, the last serious threat to Ottoman naval power in the eastern Mediterranean and Aegean. For five years the knights were homeless, but they eventually took up residence in Malta, from which they continued to harry Ottoman shipping. This induced Suleiman in 1565 to order military operations against that island, although these operations were unsuccessful.

References

Brockman, Eric. *The Two Sieges of Rhodes: The Knights of St. John at War, 1480–1522.* New York: Barnes and Noble, 1995.

Kinross, Lord [John Patrick]. *The Ottoman Centuries: The Rise and Fall of the Turkish Empire.* New York: William Morrow, 1977.

Prata, Nicholas C. *Angels in Iron.* Huntingdon Valley, PA: Arx Publishing, 1997.

Battle of Pavia

Date	February 24, 1525	
Location	Pavia in Lombardy, northern Italy	
Opponents (* winner)	*Spain, Holy Roman Empire	France
Commander	Viceroy of Naples Charles de Lannoy; Ferdinando Francisco d'Avalos, Marquis of Pescara	King François I
Approx. # Troops	20,000	Fewer than 20,000
Importance	François I is taken prisoner and forced to sign the Treaty of Madrid; the imperialists gain a temporary advantage in the long Valois-Habsburg Wars; marks the beginning of the decline of heavy cavalry and the predominance of infantry armed with handheld firearms	

The Battle of Pavia of February 24, 1525, ended the French siege of that northern Italian city. In 1515 King François I of France had invaded northern Italy and taken Milan. In 1521 François and Holy Roman Emperor (and King of Spain) Charles V began formal hostilities. François claimed Navarre and Naples, while Charles laid claim to Milan and Burgundy. Although some fighting occurred in northeastern France and north of the Pyrenees in Navarre, the chief battleground became northern Italy. Fighting began with French invasions of first Luxembourg and then Navarre, but in late November 1521, in a surprise attack, imperial forces captured Milan.

In April 1522 in the Battle of Bicocca near Milan, imperial troops under Italian condottiere Prosper Colonna defeated a larger French and Swiss force. The battle demonstrated the superiority of gunpowder small arms (the Spanish harquebus against attacking Swiss infantry). Bicocca brought the expulsion of the French from Lombardy. On September 28 François, at the head of 40,000 French troops, raised the imperial siege of Marseille and then pushed into northern Italy. The French retook Milan. Leaving a small force to garrison the city, François moved the bulk of his army to Pavia, 21 miles south, where they arrived on October 28, 1524. Some 5,000 German mercenaries along with 1,000 other mercenary troops and Italian levies defended the city.

Since no moat protected the city outside the walls, François immediately ordered artillery fire opened. The heavy French guns created a breach, but a following infantry attack encountered an interior moat full of water and came under heavy musket fire. François then decided to invest the city. Several weeks of work to divert the Ticino River from Pavia were wiped out by a sudden storm, so François decided to starve out the city. At the same time, however, he detached John Stuart, Duke of Albany, and a force of 15,000 men from his army to conquer Naples. This left him 26,000 men (2,000 of them cavalry) to invest Pavia.

Meanwhile, some 20,000 imperial troops of Charles de Bourbon and a force under Georg Frundsberg, a south German knight in imperial service, gathered at

Lodi before moving to Pavia on January 24. Viceroy of Naples Charles de Lannoy had nominal command, with the actual field command apparently exercised by the Spaniard Ferdinando Francisco d'Avalos, Marquis of Pescara. François detached part of his army to meet the imperial forces, digging defenses along the most likely route, while the bulk of his army continued the siege. During much of February the two armies faced one another across an unfordable stream and exchanged artillery fire. François further diminished the size of his army when he detached 6,000 Swiss to strengthen his lines of communication to Switzerland, which were being harassed by imperial forces. This left him with fewer than 20,000 men.

During the stormy night of February 23–24 under cover of an artillery bombardment and leaving only a small detachment behind to fool the French, the imperial forces disengaged and marched several miles to their right, crossed the brook, and turned the French left to attack the principal French camp, located in a large park at Mirabello north of Pavia. By dawn on February 24 the imperial forces had broken through the park wall and were drawn up in battle line about a mile north of the French camp.

To win time for his army to shift position and come up, François personally led a charge by his heavy cavalry against the imperial left flank. This caught the imperial forces by surprise and temporarily scattered their cavalry. Over the course of several hours the Spanish infantry used harquebus fire to halt first the French cavalry and then the infantry. With few harquebuses and crossbowmen, the French side was unable to silence the opponents' fire. To make matters worse, about a third of their forces, under Duke Charles d'Alençon, were never engaged, and some 8,000 Swiss defected.

François led dwindling cavalry charges until his horse was killed and he was badly wounded and taken prisoner. d'Alençon then led the remaining French forces in a retreat westward. The French sustained about 8,000 killed or wounded, including many prominent nobles. Most of the casualties were the result of Spanish harquebus fire. Among the hardest hit were 5,000 German mercenaries in French service who died without retreating when attacked by two squares of imperial pikemen (each square containing 6,000 pikes). Imperial troops killed or wounded came to only about 1,500 men. François remarked of the battle, "Tout est perdu, hors l'honneur" ("All is lost, except honor").

The Battle of Pavia gave the imperial side temporary advantage in the long Valois-Habsburg Wars (1494–1559). The battle also marked the beginning of the decline of heavy cavalry and the predominance of infantry armed with handheld firearms as decisive in warfare. François I, held prisoner in Madrid, was obliged to sign the Treaty of Madrid of January 14, 1526, by which he gave up all claims in Italy and surrendered Burgundy, Artois, and Flanders to Charles V.

References

Casali, Luigi, and M. Galandra. *La battaglia di Pavia: 24 Febbraio 1525*. Pavia: Luculano, 1984.

Giono, Jean. *The Battle of Pavia, 24 February 1525.* London: Peter Owen, 1965.

Knecht, R. J. *Renaissance Warrior and Patron: The Reign of Francis I.* Cambridge: Cambridge University Press, 1994.

Konstam, Angus. *Pavia, 1525: The Climax of the Italian Wars.* London: Osprey, 1996.

Battle of Panipat

Date	April 21, 1526	
Location	Panipat, Haryana district, 100 miles north of Delhi in northern India	
Opponents (* winner)	*Moghul Empire	Afghans
Commander	Babur	Sultan Ibrāhīm Lodi
Approx. # Troops	15,000	30,000–40,000
Importance	Babur takes Delhi, establishing himself there as sultan and head of the new Moghul Dynasty	

The Battle of Panipat near Delhi, India, established the Moghul dynasty. Moghul leader Zahir-ud-Din Muhammad Babur, better known as Babur, ruled in Kabul (in present-day Afghanistan) and sought to expand his territory. His father was Turkish and his mother a Mongol, and Babur claimed to be a direct descendent of Timur the Lame, known in the West as Tamurlane. Babur's goal was to reestablish the Indian empire of his ancestor. Babur's people were Muslims, known as Moghuls from the Arabic word for "Mongol."

In 1519 Babur raided into Punjab in northern India. This foray increased his desire to conquer Hindustan, then ruled by Sultan Ibrāhīm in Delhi. Babur was aided by the fact that Ibrāhīm's relatives disputed his right to rule, and several went to Kabul to request assistance from Babur in overthrowing him. A series of complicated alliances resulted, and in November 1525 Babur invaded the Punjab with perhaps 15,000 men.

That spring Babur marched through the Himalayan foothills until he reached the town of Panipat, about 100 miles north of Delhi. Learning that Sultan Ibrāhīm was moving against him with a much larger force, Babur established a defensive line anchored on the town of Panipat on its right and a gully on the left. Babur had his men scour the countryside for wagons. He then had them rope some 700 wagons together in a line, leaving gaps through which he could move his cavalry and infantry. Some gaps were covered by artillery, which was concentrated in the center with the guns chained together. Babur positioned musketeers armed with matchlocks and cavalry formations on each flank, and he had a small cavalry reserve behind the center of his line. Babur's possession of gunpowder weapons, which his opponents lacked, turned out to be a significant advantage.

Sultan Ibrāhīm was in no hurry. On April 12 he arrived from Delhi at the head of 30,000 to 40,000 men and with a number of elephants. He deployed his forces but made no move to attack. Knowing that he was heavily outnumbered, Babur hoped to fight a defensive battle, but the sultan refused to oblige him. Babur's troops were restive, and delay clearly favored his opponent. Arrow attacks and a few cavalry skirmishes did not elicit the desired response, so to provoke an assault, on April 19 Babur staged a cavalry raid by perhaps 5,000 men against Ibrāhīm's camp. The attackers withdrew the next morning in seeming confusion. This ruse had the desired effect. Ibrāhīm was lulled by the poor showing of the Moghul cavalry into ordering an attack on the morning of April 21.

Ibrāhīm's forces moved in echelon across the Moghul front to turn the Moghul right flank. This compressed the Hindustani forces in the vicinity of Panipat as they reorganized prior to launching an assault. Babur ordered his artillery, musketeers, and archers to open fire, which had a devastating effect on the packed Hindustani formation. Babur then launched cavalry forays from his flanks that circled behind the Hindustanis and attacked. Finally, Babur sent infantry and cavalry through gaps in his own line. In the ensuing melee, some 15,000–20,000 Hindustani troops were killed. The remainder managed to break free.

Babur sent his cavalry to pursue the fleeing remnants of the Hindustani force. He also dispatched his son, Humauyun, at the head of a cavalry formation to seize Ibrāhīm's treasury at Agra. Babur marched to Delhi, and at the end of April he established himself there as sultan and head of the new Moghul dynasty. The Moghuls ruled India until the British took control of the subcontinent in the 18th century.

References

Bābur. *The Babur-nama in English: Memoirs of Babur.* Translated by Annette Susannah Beveridge. London: Luxac, 1921.

Foltz, Richard C. *Mughal India and Central Asia.* Karachi: Oxford University Press, 1998.

Gascoigne, Bamber. *The Great Moghuls.* New York: Harper and Row, 1971.

Habib, Irfan, ed. *Akbar and His India.* Oxford: Oxford University Press, 1997.

Lane-Poole, Stanley. *Medieval India under Mohammedan Rule.* 1903 reprint, New York: Krause, 1970.

Battle of Mohács

Date	August 29, 1526	
Location	Mohács in southern Hungary	
Opponents (* winner)	*Ottoman Empire	Hungarians, Poles, and Germans
Commander	Sultan Süleyman (Suleiman) I	Pál Tomori, Archbishop of Kalocsa; King Louis II of Hungary and Bohemia
Approx. # Troops	100,000	25,000
Importance	Marks the beginning of the Ottoman domination of south-central Europe	

The Battle of Mohács between the Hungarians and the Ottomans marked the beginning of Ottoman domination of South-Central Europe. Mathias I (r. 1458–1490), one of Hungary's greatest kings, defeated the Ottomans in 1463. He then conquered Silesia and much of Bohemia. Mathias reformed the army, which he used to keep order, and defeated the Ottomans again in 1479. He then laid siege to Vienna and took it in 1485, adding Austria, Styria, and Carinthia to his domains. Mathias's vigorous rule and efforts to centralize power led to a reaction under his successors. There followed a period of decline in Hungary, where the nobles succeeded in disbanding the army. The Hungarians were then defeated by the forces of Holy Roman Emperor Maximilian and lost the Austrian lands.

Sensing weakness and having already taken Belgrade in 1521, Sultan Suleiman I (Süleyman I) invaded Hungary with a 100,000-man army in April 1526. Torrential rains and hailstorms delayed the Muslim advance, but the Ottomans finally crossed the Sava River on a bridge constructed by advance troops. Although most Hungarian forces had withdrawn, some remained in the fortress of Pétervárad (Peterwardein, present-day Petrovaradin in Serbia, near Novi Sad). Ibrahim Pasha captured that city, however, beheading 500 Hungarian nobles and selling the inhabitants into slavery.

Suleiman, expecting to engage the Hungarians, then crossed the Drava River on a pontoon bridge. However, internal rivalries and a lack of supplies prevented the Hungarians from concentrating their forces. Suleiman then proceeded with his army to the Plain of Mohács, where Louis II, king of Hungary and Bohemia, was waiting with 4,000 troops. Pál Tomori, archbishop of Kalocsa and a capable general, had actual field command. By the time of the battle additional forces joined including Poles and Germans, bringing the Hungarians' total strength to about 25,000 men. The new arrivals wanted to withdraw to allow time for additional reinforcements to come up under János Szapolyai from Transylvania and to force the Ottomans into longer lines of communication, but a number of Hungarian nobles demanded a fight on the Mohács, an open but uneven plain with some swampy marshes that leads down to the Danube River, so they could employ their cavalry to maximum advantage. Any advantage this might bring, however, was nullified by the far more numerous Ottoman cavalry.

Battle was joined on August 29, 1526, when the Hungarian cavalry attacked the center of the Ottoman line. Believing their cavalry successful, all the Hungarian forces then surged forward only to encounter the Janissaries, whom Suleiman had held back, and the Ottoman artillery, which was a key factor in the battle. The Ottomans surrounded the Hungarians and killed most of them, including much of the country's nobility. Reportedly, 14,000 on the Hungarian side died in the battle. The next day Suleiman ordered that all the prisoners taken be killed, resulting in the deaths of another 2,000. In the wild retreat that followed the battle, the wounded King Louis fell from his horse and, weighed down by his armor, drowned in the Csele River.

The battle had momentous consequences. On September 10 Suleiman entered Buda with his forces. There he slaughtered many of the inhabitants and burned the city before departing for home with more than 100,000 captives. One-quarter of Hungary had been utterly destroyed. Hungary was then partitioned between Austrian and Hungarian claimants to the throne. The Austrian claimant, Archduke (later emperor) Ferdinand I, took Buda. Suleiman could not allow this, and in 1529 he initiated another Ottoman invasion. In 1533, anxious to concentrate on Persia, Suleiman concluded peace with Ferdinand, producing a tripartite partition of the country. Ferdinand was left in possession of his former share, subject to annual tribute to the sultan; Transylvania and some adjacent counties went to John Sigismund (the son of King John [János Zapolya]) with the title of prince, who was then under the protection of the sultan; and the Ottomans annexed the rich Hungarian central plain. With some changes, this settlement lasted for the next 150 years.

References

Cook, M. A., ed. *A History of the Ottoman Empire to 1730.* New York: Cambridge University Press, 1976.

Hanák, Péter, ed. *The Corvina History of Hungary: From Earliest Times until the Present Day.* Translated by Zsuzsa Béres. Budapest: Corvina Books, 1988.

Junt, Metin, and Christine Woodhead, eds. *Suleyman the Magnificent and His Age: The Ottoman Empire in the Early Modern World.* New York: Longman, 1995.

Kinross, Lord [John Patrick]. *The Ottoman Centuries: The Rise and Fall of the Turkish Empire.* New York: William Morrow, 1977.

Siege of Vienna

Date	September 27–October 14, 1529	
Location	Vienna, Austria	
Opponents (* winner)	*Habsburg Empire	Ottoman Empire
Commander	Philip, Count Palatine of Austria	Sultan Süleyman (Suleiman) I
Approx. # Troops	2,000 cavalry, 22,000 infantry	120,000 men (?) in vicinity of Vienna
Importance	Marks the farthest extent of Ottoman power in central Europe and prevents a subsequent Ottoman invasion of Germany	

Bitter struggles between the major European powers in the 1520s presented the perfect opportunity for outside military intervention. The rivalry between King François I of France and Holy Roman Emperor Charles V divided much of Europe, allowing Ottoman sultan Suleiman I (Süleyman I) to open a campaign to restore his authority north of the Danube River and capture Vienna. Strategically located on the Danube, the city of Vienna was both the capital of the Habsburg Empire and a bastion of Germanic civilization and Christian Europe against the Slavs, the Magyars, and then the Ottomans.

In 1526 Ottoman forces had won a great but sanguinary victory at Mohács that gave them control of Hungary. Ottoman military forces were in fact as advanced as those of the West European powers, especially in heavy siege artillery and in heavy infantry. The Janissaries, formed of Christian children converted to Islam, were a particularly well-disciplined force.

In 1526 Suleiman took Buda. János Szapolyai (Zápolya) then claimed the Hungarian throne. Archduke Ferdinand of Austria (who was also king of Bohemia) contested this, and a rebellion broke out in Hungary, with Ferdinand ousting Szapolyai. This situation was unacceptable to Suleiman, and in the summer of 1529 he returned to Hungary at the head of a large army, determined to reverse the situation there and to take Vienna. During September 3–8 the Ottomans stormed Buda, massacred most of its defenders, and swept aside Ferdinand's advance posts. The Ottomans then moved along the river to the chief prize of Vienna.

As soon as Archduke Ferdinand learned of Suleiman's force he had called on his brother monarchs in Europe for assistance, but few responded with troops. Meanwhile, authorities in Vienna oversaw preparations to resist a Ottoman assault. They gathered in food, ammunition, and other stores; removed many of the women and children from the city to ease the strain on supplies; positioned the 72 pieces of artillery available to them; cleared fields of fire; and effected such interim repairs as were possible under the circumstances to the relatively low 250-year-old city walls. Philip, Count Palatine of Austria, had charge of the defense, ably assisted by Count

Nicholas zu Salm-Reifferscheidt and Field Marshal Wilhelm von Roggendorff. The defending troops numbered some 22,000 infantry and 2,000 cavalrymen.

Suleiman commanded a vast force. Counting the garrisons he had gathered en route, the Hungarian levies under King Szapolyai allied to him, and camp followers, Suleiman's force may have numbered as many as 350,000 people, although the actual Ottoman fighting force at Vienna was probably on the order of 120,000 men. The first Ottoman skirmishers arrived at Vienna on September 23, although the main army did not come up and surround the city until four days later, when the siege officially began. Some 400 ships of the Ottoman Navy meanwhile controlled the Danube.

The weather turned out to be a key factor aiding the defenders. It was a rainy autumn, and winter set in early. This delayed the Ottoman supply trains and prevented Suleiman from bringing up his heavy artillery. Although he had 300 guns immediately available, they were too small to make serious breaches in the city's walls.

Suleiman sent emissaries to demand the defenders' surrender. If they failed to do so, he promised that he would destroy the city so completely that nothing of it would remain. Receiving no reply, Suleiman began daily artillery fire against Vienna and commenced mining operations to blow holes in the walls and utilize his superior numbers of infantry. Made aware of Suleiman's plans by a deserter, the defenders commenced countermining, resulting in a number of underground battles. The defenders also made several sorties from the city to disrupt Ottoman siege operations but with little effect.

On October 12 the Ottomans managed to breach the wall with a mine, but the hole was not sufficiently large, and the defending pikemen were able to hold the Janissaries at bay, killing 1,200. That same night Suleiman met with his principal lieutenants and surveyed the situation. Supplies were insufficient to sustain his vast force. Suleiman's was basically a summer army, and winter was approaching.

Suleiman decided on one last attempt. On October 14 the Ottomans again exploded a mine under the city walls, but the section of wall fell outward, creating problems for the attackers. Despite hard fighting, the defenders again held.

On October 15 Vienna awoke to find that the sea of tents pitched before the city had disappeared. The Ottomans had struck camp, massacred their prisoners (except those young enough to qualify for the slave market), and departed. The harsh winter took a heavy toll of the army as it slowly withdrew southward to Istanbul, harassed also by Christian cavalry. The bells of Vienna peeled out in celebration amid salvos of gunfire.

Had Suleiman taken Vienna in 1529, he could have spent the winter there and then resumed campaigning in the spring in an invasion of Germany. It is by no means clear what France might have done in those circumstances. Suleiman returned to Austria in 1532, but a spirited imperial defense at Güns (Köszeg) and Emperor Charles V's success in assembling a substantial European force dissuaded him from further advance. Suleiman returned to Hungary in 1541, however, to recapture it from an invasion mounted by Ferdinand.

References

Bridge, Anthony. *Suleiman the Magnificent: Scourge of Heaven.* New York: Dorset, 1987.

Clot, Andre. *Suleiman the Magnificent.* London: Saqi Books, 1992.

Kinross, Lord [John Patrick]. *The Ottoman Centuries: The Rise and Fall of the Turkish Empire.* New York: William Morrow, 1977.

Battle of Cajamarca

Date	November 16, 1532	
Location	Cajamarca, Peru	
Opponents (* winner)	*Spain	Inca Empire
Commander	Francisco Pizarro	Emperor Atahualpa
Approx. # Troops	67 cavalry, some 100 infantry	6,000
Importance	Ends the Inca Empire and gives Spain control of Peru	

The Battle of Cajamarca on November 16, 1532, ended the Inca Empire and gave Spain control of Peru, then the wealthiest region of Latin America. Thanks to the voyage of Christopher Columbus in 1492 and the subsequent Treaty of Tordesillas (1494), Spain laid claim to most of the Americas. Over the next few decades expeditions led by conquistadores solidified Spanish control over much of Mesoamerica. Francisco Pizarro, leader of the expedition to Peru, was among soldiers in the expedition of Vasco Nuñez de Balboa to Panama in the 1520s.

Inspired by the success of Hernán Cortés against the Aztecs in Mexico and stories of fabulous wealth to the south of Panama, Pizarro joined with Diego de Almagro, Fernando Luque (vicar of Panama), and Pedrarias Dávila (governor of Panama). The four men entered into a contract with ship captain Bartolomé Ruiz to explore the Pacific coast of South America. During 1524–1528 they learned of an interior empire, reputed to possess vast amounts of gold.

His colleagues were unwilling to invest in a further venture, however, so Pizarro returned to Spain and put together a small expeditionary force that included his four brothers. The expedition arrived in Panama in December 1531. Consisting of 180 men and 30 horses, this force sailed down the west coast of South America, landing at Tumbes on the Peruvian coast in the spring of 1532. Here they were joined by 100 men and 50 horses under Hernando de Soto. Pizarro established the coastal settlement of San Miguel as his base.

Beyond the high Andes mountains to the east of San Miguel lay the Inca Empire, extending some 2,700 miles from present-day Ecuador to Santiago, Chile. The Inca, revered as both king and god, ruled this vast empire from the capital city of Cuzco. The Inca religion was based on worship of the sun.

The difficulties facing Pizarro and his small force were staggering, but the men began their expedition at a fortuitous time. A succession struggle had followed the death in 1527 of the great Inca Huayna Capac, who had conquered Ecuador. War broke out between his son and legitimate heir Huascar and Atahualpa, another son by a concubine. After a long civil war, Atahualpa triumphed in the spring of 1532. According to Spanish sources, Atahualpa was a bloodthirsty tyrant who ordered the execution of all of his father's reported 200 sons he could locate. Surprisingly, he spared Huascar but imprisoned him at Cuzco. Atahualpa also reportedly ordered the deaths of all members of Huascar's family he could find so that there would be no rival to the throne.

Pizarro's force departed San Miguel in September 1532 and began the ascent of the Andes. Atahualpa was aware of its progress and sent several deputations bearing gifts of welcome. Some of these presents were in gold, which only heightened Pizarro's hopes. On November 15 Pizarro's men descended a pass that overlooked the Inca city of Cajamarca. The Spanish found the city deserted but were impressed with its massive stone buildings that included several forts. Atahualpa was camped with some 6,000 warriors and royal attendants (some sources give a figure as great as 30,000–40,000 warriors) in tents near Cajamarca as Pizarro and his men occupied the city.

Pizarro sent some 45 horsemen under his brother Hernando and de Soto to ride into the Inca camp and meet with Atahualpa. Horses were unknown to the Incas and may have induced them to believe (as the Aztecs had) that the men mounted on them were emissaries from the gods. If that was the case, Athaualpa revealed no anxiety.

The Spanish emissaries invited Atahualpa to meet with Pizarro in Cajamarca. Atahualpa informed the Spaniards through an aide that they were then fasting but would visit the next day. Pizarro planned to make himself master of the situation by duplicating Cortés' tactic of seizing the ruler. Pizarro's men were concerned, however, for they were cut off from additional support. With only some 100 infantry and 67 cavalry, they were outnumbered at least 35 to 1.

Pizarro deployed his men in the large halls fronting the central square of the city. Not until the afternoon of November 16 did Atahualpa appear, borne on palanquin with 6,000 warriors and attendants (some sources say 10,000) marching the four miles from their camp to the city. With the Spanish in hiding and Cajamarca apparently deserted, Atahualpa and the procession halted about a half mile from the city; the Inca sent word to Pizarro that he would not visit that day. Knowing that the wait would severely test his men, Pizarro sent word that food and entertainments had been prepared. Perhaps other inducements were offered as well, but in any case the procession began again, passing between rows of warriors lining the road on either side.

On Atahualpa's arrival in the plaza of Cajamarca he was met by Father Vicente de Valverde, a Catholic priest who began telling the Inca about Christ and Spanish king Charles V. Growing impatient and realizing that the Dominican was asking him to concede both his divinity and authority, Atahualpa took the Bible from Valverde, opened it to look inside, and then threw it to the ground. Valverde snatched up the Bible and ran from the plaza.

As soon as Valverde was clear, Pizarro signaled to open fire on the square with two small cannon placed in a nearby fort. At the same time, Spanish cavalry issued from the buildings flanking the square. The Incas had come as emissaries and either were not armed or were armed only with slings and javelins under their clothing and therefore could not resist the Spaniards' heavy cavalry, firearms, and swords. The Incas were cut down to a man. Atahualpa was the only Inca taken alive. According to most sources Pizarro, mistakenly cut by one of his own men, was the only Spanish casualty. (Some sources state that five Spaniards were killed.) Surprisingly, the thousands of warriors outside the city made no effort to come to the rescue of the Inca.

Atahualpa's army instead began to melt away, especially those men impressed into it from the newly conquered territories. Atahualpa bargained with Pizarro for his release, offering to fill a room 17 by 22 feet and roughly 7 feet high with gold and to fill a second smaller room twice over with silver. Pizarro agreed, but at the same time he sent de Soto to Cuzco to meet with Huascar. On being informed of the Spanish victory at Cajamarca, Huascar said that he would treat with Pizarro and supply even more gold from his father's secret storehouses. Pizarro informed Atahualpa of this, and the Inca sent word through an attendant for his generals in the capital to kill Huascar, which they did.

Although the gold and silver were delivered as promised, Pizarro refused to release Atahualpa and instead brought him to trial on charges of having ordered the murder of his brother. Convicted and sentenced to be burned at the stake as a heathen, Atahualpa converted to Christianity to be executed by strangulation. Control of the area passed to Pizarro, who managed to suppress several rebellions. In 1538 a royal governor from Spain arrived in Peru. The gold and silver were stripped from the native people and shipped back to Spain. The Spanish also sought to eradicate Inca culture in favor of that of Spain and Catholicism. Peru did not achieve independence from Spain until 1821.

References

Davis, Paul K. *100 Decisive Battles: From Ancient Times to the Present.* Santa Barbara, CA: ABC-CLIO, 1999.

Innes, Hammond. *The Conquistadors.* New York: Knopf, 1969.

Means, Philip A. *The Fall of the Inca Empire and the Spanish Rule in Peru, 1530–1780.* New York: Gordian, 1971.

Prescott, William H. *The History of the Conquest of Peru.* 1847; reprint, New York: New American Library, 1961.

Richman, Irving Berdine. *Adventures of New Spain: The Spanish Conquerors.* New Haven, CT: Yale University Press, 1929.

Siege of Malta

Date	May 18–September 8, 1565	
Location	Island of Malta in the eastern Mediterranean Sea	
Opponents (* winner)	*Knights of St. John	Ottoman Empire
Commander	Jean Parisot la Valette	Piale Pasha (naval commander), Mustafa Pasha (land force commander)
Approx. # Troops	5,000	28,000
Importance	Ends Emperor Süleyman I's efforts to control the Mediterranean	

In 1522 following a six-month siege of Rhodes in the Dodecanese Islands, the Christian Knights of St. John of Jerusalem (Hospitallers) were forced to surrender to the Ottomans. Sustaining heavy casualties himself and impressed by the knights' valor, Ottoman emperor Suleiman I (Süleyman I) spared the defenders' lives, a decision he would have cause to regret. In 1530 Holy Roman Emperor Charles V gave the knights his possession of Malta. This island, strategically located in the narrows of the central Mediterranean, controlled east-west access and allowed the knights to raid to the east. At the same time, the Ottomans were conquering much of the North African coast and even raiding out into the Atlantic. Malta was the only barrier to Ottoman control of the entire Mediterranean.

Apparently Suleiman's influential daughter Mihrimah encouraged him to undertake the campaign on religious grounds. Suleiman's trusted military adviser and commander of his galleys, Dragut Torghoud, agreed. A competent artillerist, Dragut had taken Tripoli from the knights for the sultan and became its governor. There was popular support for an operation against Malta, particularly after the knights captured a large Ottoman merchant ship on its way from Venice to Istanbul.

Suleiman was then 70 years old and did not attempt to lead the expedition in person. He appointed Piale Pasha to command the naval force and his old general Mustafa Pasha to head land operations. Suleiman also sent along as advisers Dragut and Uluj Ali, insisting that his two commanders consult with them. The Ottoman naval force consisted of some 150 galleys, while the land force numbered 28,000 men, including 7,000 Janissaries.

About 5,000 men, most of them Spaniards, defended Malta. They were led by the grand master of the Knights of St. John, Jean Parisot la Valette. La Valette had been born in the same year as Suleiman and fought against him in the siege of Rhodes. La Valette combined effective military leadership with Christian fanaticism. Aware of Ottoman preparations, he sent out a call for assistance from all the knights in other countries, and a number responded. The people of Malta remembered what had happened at the hands of the Ottomans in 1551. The Ottomans had invaded with 10,000 men but then withdrew after only several days to move on to the neighboring island of Gozo. Its citadel surrendered after several days of bombardment, whereupon the Ottomans sacked Gozo and made slaves of virtually its entire population of 5,000 people. Now in 1565, the people of Malta were determined to resist the invaders. Galleys from Malta also ferried in supplies from Sicily.

Two main forts, St. Angelo and St. Michael, guarded the city of Malta. A brief raid by Dragut convinced the defenders to add a new fort, St. Elmo, to protect the entrance to the Grand Harbor and a parallel inlet, the Middle Harbor or Marsa Muscet, north of it. Just before the Ottomans arrived, the knights also placed a great chain across the Grand Harbor of the city of Malta.

The great Ottoman force appeared off Malta on May 18, 1565. The Ottomans were confident of an easy victory. The Ottoman naval and land commanders had decidedly different views on how to proceed, however. Ultimately Piale Pasha's views prevailed, and the Ottomans decided to first take the Marsa Muscet as a fleet anchorage. To accomplish this they would have to reduce Fort St. Elmo.

The Ottomans were well equipped with artillery, including three cannon especially cast for this undertaking. One gun reputedly weighed 40 tons and fired 200-pound round shot, and the other two guns weighed 20 tons each and fired 90-pound shot. After coming ashore, the Ottomans opened a bombardment of Fort St. Elmo, where the knights were heavily outnumbered. In heavy fighting the Ottomans captured the ravelin, or outer earthworks, but the knights used their own artillery to good advantage and repulsed successive attacks, inflicting heavy losses. Dragut then supervised erection of an additional siege works but was mortally wounded by rock splinter from a shell burst. He lived long enough to learn, in mid-June, that the Ottomans had taken the fort. Only nine knights were taken alive in the remains of the fortress.

Forts St. Angelo and St. Michael were the next Ottoman targets. Mustafa, with Rhodes as precedent, offered the remaining knights the chance to surrender, but La Vallette refused. The Ottomans attempted to destroy the boom but were met by Maltese swimmers, who were armed to the teeth and prevented the Ottomans from carrying out their design. For two months the Ottomans made land assaults on the Maltese forts without success. Both sides were now exhausted. Christian corsairs had taken a heavy toll of Ottoman supply ships, and the attackers were short of supplies. Many of their men were also sick with fever and dysentery.

In early September with the defenders down to as few as several hundred men and about to be overwhelmed, a relief force of some 10,000 Spaniards under Don Garcia de Toledo arrived from Syracuse and made landfall on the northern part of the island. This reinforcement, the threat of additional Spanish aid, low morale (some 24,000 Ottomans had been casualties thus far), and the approach of winter without a fleet anchorage all led the Ottomans to raise the siege on September 8 and return home. Little more than a quarter of the Ottoman force had survived. The defenders suffered more than 5,000 dead, including 240 knights. The rebuff at Malta ended Suleiman's efforts to control the Mediterranean.

References

Bradford, Ernie. *The Cruel Siege: Malta, 1565.* London: Wordsworth Editions, 1999.

Ellul, Joseph. *The Great Siege of Malta.* Siggiewi, Malta: Ellul, 1992.

Kinross, Lord [John Patrick]. *The Ottoman Centuries: The Rise and Fall of the Turkish Empire.* New York: William Morrow, 1977.

Prata, Nicholas C. *Angels in Iron.* Huntingdon Valley, PA: Arx Publishing, 1997.

Sire, H. J. A. *The Knights of Malta.* New Haven, CT: Yale University Press, 1996.

Battle of Lepanto

Date	October 7, 1571	
Location	Near Návpaktos (Lepanto) in the Gulf of Patras off Greece in the Mediterranean Sea	
Opponents (* winner)	*The Holy League (Spain, Venice, the Papacy, Malta, Genoa, Savoy)	Ottoman Empire
Commander	Don Juan of Austria	Ali Pasha
Approx. # Troops	Perhaps 41,000 men in some 237 ships	Perhaps 88,000 men in as many as 300 ships
Importance	Although important in tactical innovation (the galleass ship type and heavy cannon) and as a psychological lift for the Holy League, Lepanto settles nothing in the short run because of the collapse of the Christian alliance	

The Battle of Lepanto (present-day Návpaktos) was the largest galley engagement of the gunpowder era. It was also the first great fleet action decided by artillery. The naval battle pitted the Holy League of Spain, Venice, and the papacy against the Ottomans.

Early in 1570 Venice rejected an Ottoman demand that it surrender Cyprus. The Venetians decided to fight and appealed to Pope Pius V for aid. When the Ottomans invaded Cyprus, Pius persuaded King Philip II of Spain to join with him and Venice in a Holy League, ratified in May 1571.

The galley remained the principal ship type in the Mediterranean in the late 16th century. The galley of 1571 was little changed from that of the Battle of Salamis (480 BCE). Motive power was provided by lateen-rigged sails on two masts when wind permitted or by oars when the wind did not and in battle. The long, graceful shallow-draft galley was well suited to the more sheltered Mediterranean waters. Its striking power remained the ram, although cannon were also mounted in the bow and were trained by turning the vessel. Captains attempted to destroy their

Depiction of the Battle of Lepanto on October 7, 1571. The largest rowed galley engagement of the gunpowder era, it marked the beginning of the decline in Ottoman naval power in the Mediterranean. (Photos.com)

opponents with the ram and should that not prove successful by boarding and hand-to-hand combat.

A new ship type had also appeared in the galleass. Introduced by the Venetians, the galleass resembled the galley in appearance but was larger and more seaworthy and carried more men. An attempt at compromise between the galley and the sailing ships of Northern Europe, the galleass had three masts, with the fore and main square rigged. The galleass combined the freedom of movement of the galley with the seaworthiness and fighting power of the sailing warship, but as with most compromises, it was not a successful type, being sluggish and slow. Another ship type, smaller than the galley, was the Ottoman gaillot. Based on an older Byzantine design, it had 18–24 oars and shipped only about 100 men.

In the summer of 1570 Philip assembled squadrons of galleys from Naples and Sicily in addition to contracted Genoese galleys under Genoese admiral Giovanni Andrea Doria. These joined with Venetian and papal ships to relieve Cyprus. Philip hoped that Doria might also recover Tunis, where the Ottomans had ousted the ruler friendly to Spain. In mid-September the allied fleet, commanded by papal admiral Marcantonio Colonna, reached the Ottoman coast opposite Cyprus. Doria, however, believed that the season was too late to continue operations and withdrew his squadrons over the protests of his allies, bringing the campaign to an end.

The next September the allies assembled at Messina an armada of 207 galleys, 6 galleasses, and 24 great ships. In addition to their crews and rowers, the fleet shipped some 20,000 marine infantry. In early October the fleet learned of the surrender of Famagusta, which had taken place on August 1, 1571. This last Venetian stronghold on Cyprus had succumbed following a 10.5-month-long siege that cost the Ottomans perhaps 50,000 dead. Don Juan of Austria, Philip's half brother and supreme commander of the allied fleet, now decided to seek out and destroy the Ottoman fleet. At Corfu, Don Juan sent out reconnaissance vessels under Gil de Andrade, who located the Ottoman fleet at Lepanto.

Ali Pasha commanded the Ottoman fleet of nearly 300 galleys and smaller galliots. Including the 16,000 soldiers, the fleet carried perhaps 88,000 men. His fleet had screened Ottoman operations on Cyprus all summer. Ali had ravaged Venetian possessions in the Aegean and Ionian seas in late August and September and then raided the Adriatic before returning to Lepanto, where the Gulf of Corinth meets the Gulf of Patras.

Don Juan now brought his armada to the Gulf of Patras. The Ottomans decided to fight, and on Sunday, October 7, 1571, they emerged from their anchorage and formed an extended crescent-shaped line of three squadrons. The 40 smaller galliots backed the center of the Ottoman line. Although Ali's 300 ships were more than the Holy League could muster, they were also lighter and not as well protected, and they had nothing that could match the Venetian galleasses.

The allied armada rowed to close with the Ottomans. There were sharp divisions of loyalties within the fleet, and before sailing Don Juan had mixed his squadrons so that each ally had galleys. He also arrayed his armada into left, center, and right squadrons, backed by a rear guard of 30 galleys under Álvaro de Bazán, 1st Marquis of Santa Cruz. The center included most of the bigger galleys. Don Juan assigned the heavier and more powerful galleasses a more aggressive role in the battle, positioning them in pairs well in advance of each squadron. Another innovation was to remove the beaks from the galleys to allow their bow guns greater traverse. In taking these steps Don Juan assigned the primary role to the artillery, as opposed to muskets, pikes, slings, and swords. He also announced before the battle that all Christian slave oarsmen in the fleet would be pardoned and freed if the Ottomans were defeated.

The battle commenced near noon. The galleasses, which mounted more cannon (each had 10 heavy guns, 12 lighter guns, and small man-killers on the rail), used their heavier guns to engage the Ottoman ships and disrupt their advance. At first the Ottomans did not attempt to board but instead unleashed volleys of arrows. Once these were exhausted the battle degenerated into the customary melee, with attempts to board and hand-to-hand combat.

The disorganized Ottoman right under Mehmet Sirocco failed to turn the Holy League's inshore wing, commanded by the Venetian Agostino Barbarigo. The latter's line swung shoreward to trap the Ottomans against the beach. The bigger guns of Don Juan's center battered the Ottoman center as its ships closed to board. Don Juan personally led an attack on Ali Pasha's flagship, but before the two vessels could close Ali Pasha was shot and killed. Later his head was cut off and raised to the masthead for all to see.

The 90 galleys of the Ottoman left under Uluj Ali did not close with the Holy League right wing of 57 galleys under Doria but instead sailed wide in an effort to turn its flank. When Doria kept pace, Uluj Ali turned his wing abruptly and raced for the gap between Doria and the allied center under Don Juan. The two Venetian galleasses assigned to Doria were unable to reach their assigned station but did bombard the rear of the Ottoman center. The Ottomans then overwhelmed 3 galleys belonging to the knights of Malta and savaged 7 galleys of the Holy League vanguard under Juan de Cardona, who trailed Doria. But the Marquis of Santa Cruz detected Uluj Ali's maneuver in time and checked the Ottoman rush with his rear guard, until Don Juan and Doria could close to complete the allies' triumph. The battle was over by 4:00 p.m. Although both sides had invoked God, the battle proved that God tends to favor the side with more and larger guns.

Uluj Ali escaped with only 35 galleys, mostly Algerian, and many of these were later destroyed as unseaworthy. The Ottomans lost more than 200 galleys (117 were captured intact) and 20,000 people dead. Some 15,000 Christian galley slaves on the Ottoman ships were freed; most were Greeks who returned to their own country. The allies lost 10–15 ships sunk and perhaps 7,500 dead. Among the 15,000 allied wounded was Miguel de Cervantes, author of *Don Quixote*.

The battle was psychologically crucial for the Holy League, which the Ottomans had often defeated. Lepanto settled nothing in the short run, as the Christian alliance soon broke up. The Ottomans kept Cyprus and Tunis, but their navy never regained the same quality or prestige. Unhappy with Philip II's desire to use the Holy League against Tunis and Algiers, Venice made a separate peace with the Ottomans in 1573. Philip found himself under pressure to do the same. With revolt in the Low Countries and trouble with France and England, in 1578 he concluded a truce with the Ottoman sultan.

References

Beeching, Jack. *The Galleys at Lepanto.* New York: Scribner, 1983.

Braudel, Fernand. *The Mediterranean and the Mediterranean World in the Age of Philip II.* 2 vols. New York: Harper and Row, 1972.

Guilmartin, J. F. *Gunpowder and Galleys.* New York: Cambridge University Press, 1974.

Pierson, Peter. "Lepanto." *MHQ: Quarterly Journal of Military History* 9(2) (1997): 6–19.

Rodgers, William Ledyard. *Naval Warfare under Oars, 4th to 16th Centuries: A Study of Strategy, Tactics and Ship Design.* Annapolis, MD: Naval Institute Press, 1967.

Siege of Antwerp

Date	July 1584–August 17, 1585	
Location	City of Antwerp on the Scheldt River in the Netherlands	
Opponents (* winner)	*Spain	Dutch
Commander	Alessandro Farnese (future duke of Parma)	Philippe de Marnix, Lord of Sainte-Aldegonde
Approx. # Troops	60,000	20,000
Importance	One of the major military events of the Dutch Wars for Independence (1568–1648)	

The Spanish siege of the Dutch city of Antwerp was one of the major military events of the Dutch Wars of Independence (1568–1648). Antwerp, located on the Scheldt River that connected the city with the North Sea, had a population of about 100,000 people and was Northern Europe's most important economic center.

Fernando Álvarez de Toledo, Duke of Alva and Spanish commander in the Netherlands, combined skillful military operations with a reign of terror against the civilian population. In October 1576 mutinous Spanish troops who had not been paid captured and ravished Antwerp. This atrocity united the Netherlands against Spain in the Pacification of Ghent of November 1576. In 1578 Spanish king Philip II replaced Alva with Alessandro Farnese.

Farnese negotiated a peace settlement with the southern provinces of the Netherlands while continuing the war against the Protestant north. In 1582 he went on the offensive and the next year took both Diest and Westerlo, cutting communications between Antwerp and Brussels. In 1584 Farnese decided to take Antwerp, and Spanish forces captured a series of strategic positions that cut the city from the sea. For operations against Antwerp, Farnese had at his disposal some 60,000 men, while Philippe de Marnix, Lord of Sainte-Aldegonde and commander of the Antwerp garrison, had about 20,000 men. Antwerp's defenses were strong, however, leading Farnese to believe that it would be next to impossible to take the city by storm. He decided to starve it into submission.

To isolate Antwerp, Farnese built a series of strong points and a blockading pontoon bridge on the Scheldt that would cut seaborne supply. Completed in February 1585, the 800-yard bridge was an impressive engineering feat. Farnese is said to have designed it himself, while two Italian engineers, Giambattista Piatti and Properzio Boracci, supervised the construction. The bridge had a road running its entire length with parapets on either side to protect against musket fire. Thirty-two barges moored side by side in the Scheldt supported the center of the bridge, and each mounted two large cannon, one at bow and one at stern. The two wings of the bridge, each about 180 yards long, rested on pilings. Twenty galleys in the river constituted a mobile defense force, and two powerful forts with 10 cannon each guarded the ends of the bridge.

The Dutch were not idle. They employed an Italian engineer, Federico Giambelli (or Gianibelli), and a Fleming named den Bosche to develop the means to attack the bridge. Devices sent against the bridge included floating casks known as porcupines, which had sharp metal points on the outside and inflammables within. These and a raft filled with cannon powder to be ignited from the bank when it hit the bridge all failed. Den Bosche then came up with an armed craft filled with 1,000 men and mounting cannon, but Spanish artillery drove it ashore and destroyed it.

In the spring of 1585 Giambelli designed large flat-bottomed barges with reinforced sides. These were filled with explosives and covered with shrapnel, the charges to be set off by clockwork devices. On April 5 he sent four of these against the bridge. Only one worked, but its explosion blew out nearly 100 yards of the span. Eight hundred Spaniards died, and Farnese narrowly escaped death. The Dutch failed to exploit their temporary advantage, and the Spanish soon repaired the bridge and came up with a system whereby one or more of the pontoon barges could be moved to let any floating incendiary device pass through.

With starvation now taking hold in Antwerp, the Dutch attempted sorties from the city and relief expeditions, but Farnese's forces easily defeated these and launched their own attacks. Early in August the Spanish captured the city's citadel, whereupon Antwerp surrendered on August 17, 1585. The successful siege was the highpoint of Farnese's military career. The next year, on the death of his father who had held the title, he became Duke of Parma. The Dutch, who still controlled both banks of the Scheldt estuary, closed off the river to commerce. This led to Antwerp's decline and the exodus of more than half its population.

References

Melegari, Vezio. *The Great Military Sieges.* New York: Crowell, 1972.

Parker, Geoffrey. *The Dutch Revolt.* Rev. ed. London: Penguin Books, 1990.

Rady, Martyn. *From Revolt to Independence.* London: Hodder and Stoughton, 1990.

Spanish Armada

Date	July–August 1588	
Location	English Channel	
Opponents (* winner)	*England	Spain
Commander	Lord Howard of Effingham	Alonso Pérez de Guzmán, Duke of Medina Sidonia
Approx. # Troops	172 ships with 1,972 guns	124 ships with 1,124 guns
Importance	Prevents a Spanish invasion of England and marks the beginning of the end of Spanish greatness and the rise of England as a maritime power; considerable impact on naval warfare	

The defeat of the Spanish Armada was one of the most important events of early modern European history. King Philip II of Spain (r. 1556–1598) was a militant Catholic, determined not only to uphold the Catholic Church but also to lead a great Catholic counteroffensive. Into this vast effort he was prepared to pour the blood and treasure of his kingdoms. In the long struggle that ensued, Queen Elizabeth of England (r. 1558–1603) became the Protestant champion, supporting surreptitiously a revolt against Spain in the Netherlands led by William of Orange (called William the Silent). In 1585 when it appeared that Spanish troops in the Netherlands under the Duke of Parma might capture the port of Antwerp, Elizabeth intervened actively on the rebel side, dispatching 6,000 English troops to the Netherlands under the Earl of Leicester.

In addition to the religious issue and English support of the rebels in the Netherlands, there was a third cause of tension: the intrusion of English ships into the Spanish Empire in the New World. English privateers led by Sir Francis Drake were attacking Spanish shipping and selling slaves there in defiance of Spanish rule. In a sense, England and Spain were already at war to see which power would control the Atlantic Ocean.

For Philip, the decisive event was the execution of Mary, Queen of Scots, in February 1587. Mary was a Catholic and the former queen of France and Scotland, and there were a number of plots to overthrow Elizabeth and make her queen. With France distracted by religious civil war, Philip began planning his so-called Enterprise of England to punish England.

Philip secured papal sanction for his plans and ordered the collection of a fleet of the largest naval and maritime vessels. This force was intended as much for intimidation as outright invasion. Philip's strategy was to gain control of the English Channel and facilitate the passage of Parma's veteran Spanish army to England. A distinguished seaman, Álvaro de Bazán, 1st Marquis of Santa Cruz, had command of the Armada enterprise, but he died suddenly in February 1588 and was replaced by a reluctant Duke of Medina Sidonia, who had never held sea command before. Meanwhile, Parma cut a ship canal from Antwerp and Ghent to Bruges, assembled 28 warships at Dunkirk (Dunkerque), and built several hundred landing craft and barges to carry his men and horses across the Channel.

In the spring of 1587 Drake conducted a highly successful raid on the Spanish assembly port of Cádiz, "singeing the beard of the King of Spain" as he put it. He destroyed some Spanish ships and many supplies, including much of the Spanish stock of seasoned barrel staves. This condemned the Armada to suffer rotting provisions in unseasoned barrels.

In April 1588 the Spanish ships began to assemble. Delays led to refitting at the northern port of Carunna in June. The Armada of 124 ships, manned by 8,500 seamen and galley slaves and carrying 19,000 troops, finally set out on July 12. On July 20 the English sailed from Plymouth. The first engagement took place off

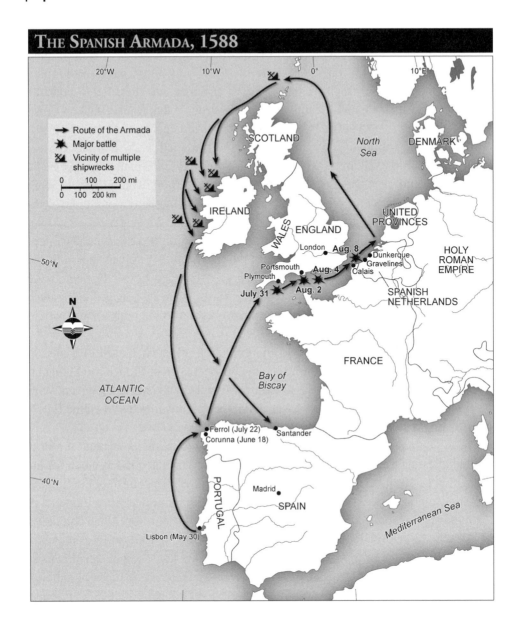

THE SPANISH ARMADA, 1588

Plymouth the next day, with the Spanish ships sweeping east up the Channel in a loose crescent-shaped formation.

Up until this point, battles at sea had been similar to those on land; the principal aim was to take enemy vessels by boarding. In the Armada fight, a new form of battle at sea emerged because of the long-range guns employed by the English. The English had 172 warships; 50 of these, only lightly armed, took little role in the battle. The English ships mounted a total of 1,972 guns, while the Spanish had 1,124. The Spanish outnumbered the English in short-range cannon (163 to 55) and medium-range perriers (326 to 43), but this was reversed in long-range culverins (635 for the Spanish to 1,874 for the English). While the Spanish hoped to fight in close, grapple, and board their opponents, the English planned to stand off and blast away at the Spanish ships beyond the range of the Spaniards' guns.

Admiral Lord Howard of Effingham had overall command of the English fleet; his key subordinates included Sir John Hawkins and Sir Francis Drake. The English early gained the weather gauge, establishing a position upwind and attacking the Spanish ships daily until the Armada anchored at the French port of Calais on July 27. Neither side had inflicted major damage on the other.

Parma sent word that he was under blockade by a Dutch fleet at Bruges under Justinus of Nassau. Then, before dawn on July 28 the English sent eight fire ships into the Calais anchorage, forcing the Armada ships to cut their cables and put to sea. Medina Sidonia intended that his ships reanchor once the fire ships had passed, but many of the Spanish vessels crashed together. Crews were unable to get at spare anchors, and the ships drifted northeastward along the coast. With the wind blowing out of the south-southwest, Medina Sidonia realized that his ships could not regain the harbor.

The Battle of Gravelines, off the Flanders coast, ensued with the English engaging individual Spanish ships unable to form a protective formation. The English maintained position to windward of the Spanish ships. The heeling hulls of the Armada ships were thus exposed to possible damage below the waterline. The English were forced to break off the fight, however, and returned to port to replenish stocks of ammunition. Through a week of fighting the Spanish had expended upwards of 100,000 rounds of shot, but no English ship was seriously damaged.

The famous Protestant Wind now swept the Spanish ships into the North Sea, leaving their captains no choice but to continue on around the British Isles and then sail down the western coast of Ireland en route back to Spain. The ships limped in singly during August through September. Sixty-three of the Spanish ships, or half of the total, were lost, of which the English sank or captured 15. A major Atlantic storm drove many weakened ships and their exhausted crews ashore, and 19 Spanish ships are known to have been wrecked on the Scottish and Irish coasts.

After 1588 nothing went right for Philip II. He continued his plans to conquer England and his efforts to defeat the Dutch rebels, and in the 1590s he even took on a new enemy in France. Philip died in 1598, having failed in his grand design. The Armada fight marked the beginning of the end of Spanish greatness and the rise of England and also had a pronounced influence on the conduct of naval warfare.

References

Anderson, David. *The Spanish Armada.* New York: Hempstead, 1988.

Fernández-Armesto, Felipe. *The Spanish Armada: The Experience of War in 1588.* London: Oxford University Press, 1988.

Lewis, Michael A. *Armada Guns: A Comparative Study of English and Spanish Armaments.* London: Allen and Unwin, 1961.

Martin, Colin, and Geoffrey Parker. *The Spanish Armada.* New York: Norton, 1988.

Mattingly, Garrett. *The Armada.* Boston: Houghton Mifflin, 1959.

Battle of Sekigahara

Date	October 21, 1600	
Location	Sekigahara, Gifu Prefecture, Japan	
Opponents (* winner)	*Eastern Army	Western Army
Commander	Tokugawa Ieyasu	Ishida Mitsunari
Approx. # Troops	70,000	80,000
Importance	Turning point in the Japanese Unification Wars (1550–1615)	

The Battle of Sekigahara was the turning point in the Japanese Unification Wars (1550–1615). During the Heian era (794–1192) the emperor ruled Japan from the city of Kyoto. In the 12th century, however, imperial rule was threatened by a new class of warriors known as the samurai, and in the 1180s war erupted between the two most powerful samurai clans. In the Battle of Dannoura (1185) the Minamoto clan was victorious. The emperor sought to buy off Minamoto-no-Yoritomi, leader of the victorious clan, by appointing him commander of the imperial army, in effect creating the position of shogun, with authority to call out the imperial army whenever he deemed it necessary. From this point on, because he controlled the army, the shogun was the real power in Japan. Minamoto soon established an alternate capital at Kamakura, and during the next century and a half Japan was under the shogunate.

Just below the emperor and shogun in importance were the barons known as the daimyo. In theory, these feudal lords owed allegiance to the emperor, but then two powerful daimyo led armies against one another in the Ōnin War (1467–1477). This led to a century-long civil war in Japan that ended only with the appearance of a highly effective military leader, Nobunaga Oda. As a commoner Nobunaga could not become shogun, but he established Yoshiaki Ashikaga in that position and ruled Japan through him. Nobunaga was assassinated in 1592, however, and was succeeded by another very capable military leader in Hideyoshi Toyatomi. Interested in projecting Japanese power beyond the home islands, Hideyoshi first had to unify Japan, which he did in 1590 by defeating the rival Hōjō clan.

Hideyoshi established his capital at Edo (later named Tokyo). Having secured his base and seeking to occupy the samurai, he mounted invasions of Korea during 1592–1593 and 1597–1598. Although initially successful, the invasions failed because of Chinese intervention. Hideyoshi died in 1598.

Toyatomi's death produced another civil war. Hideyoshi had created a council to rule until his son Hideyori, then only five years old, was old enough to exercise power. Tokugawa Ieyasu, a member of the Minamoto clan, was the most powerful daimyo and regent for the boy, but among his rivals was Mitsunari Ishida, who attempted but failed to assassinate Tokugawa in 1599. Mitsunari's supporters had control of young Hideyori, but Tokugawa held his mother prisoner. Eventually the diamyo declared their allegiance to one side or the other.

In 1600 when Tokugawa moved north to suppress a rebellion, Mitsunari attempted to gain control of Kyoto. However, his attempts to secure two key castles there met rebuff, and he withdrew southward. Tokugawa now commanded what came to be called the Eastern Army, while Mitsunari's forces were known as the Western Army. Tokugawa put together a force of about 105,000 men. He directly controlled some 30,000 men, while key allies led another 40,000. Tokugawa's son commanded another 35,000 men at Edo. Tokugawa ordered his son to follow the main body as he moved against Mitsunari to Sekigahara, a town located at the junction of the coastal and inland roads in a valley formed by four large hills. Mitsunari had a larger force, but Tokugawa, an adroit politician, had courted a number of the daimyo on Mitsunari's side, hoping that some would defect because Mitsunari was not of noble birth.

Samurai traditionally fought one another with swords, with pikemen and archers in support, but Oda had introduced Western firearms a quarter century earlier, and Tokugawa secured a supply of harquebuses (matchlock firearms). Mitsunari also had some firearms.

On October 20, 1600, Mitsunari's Western Army of some 80,000 men arrived at Sekigahara and utilized the cover of rain and fog to occupy strong positions in three of its four hills, flanked by two rivers. There Mitsunari and his men awaited the arrival of Tokugawa's Eastern Army. Hideaki Kobayakawa, a daimyo allied to Ishida, took up position with his men on Matsuo Hill, one of the three hills around the valley, just south of the Fuji River. Although they held a strong position, Mitsunari's men were tired from a long march, and much of their gunpowder was wet from the rain.

Tokugawa and his men followed but had the advantage that much of the storm had passed when they arrived on the battlefield early on the morning of October 21. Most of their gunpowder was dry. Both armies deployed; Tokugawa placed his allied forces in front and his own army in reserve. A wind scattered the fog at about 8:00 a.m., and the battle commenced with Tokugawa's army attacking. The fighting went on for three hours with no decision. At 11:00 a.m., however, Mitsunari signaled for Hideaki to attack and drive into Tokugawa's exposed left flank. Hideaki took no action despite several signals, which were clearly visible to the generals in both armies.

Both sides sensed a change in the battle. At 12:15 p.m. Hideaki decided to switch sides. His men charged from their hillside position, not north into Tokugawa's left flank but rather into the right flank and rear of Mitsunari's remaining forces, which now began to roll backward. Another of the daimyos also switched sides against

Mitsunari, and by 2:00 p.m. the battle was over. Mitsunari's army quickly disintegrated, suffering some 40,000 dead. Tokugawa's side sustained far fewer casualties, leaving him far more powerful.

The Battle of Sekigahara did not end the civil war, but it was the turning point. Fighting continued over the next 15 years, with Tokugawa defeating all daimyo opposed to him. Named shogun in 1603, Tokugawa moved the capital from Kyoto to Edo and became the virtual dictator of Japan. Except for a Christian peasant uprising during 1637–1638, Japan remained peaceful. The shogunate undertook no foreign adventures and instead turned inward. With peace, the samurai were no longer required and gradually lost their warrior skills. The Tokugawa shogunate lasted until the Meiji Restoration of 1867.

References

Bryant, Anthony. *Sekigahara, 1600.* London: Osprey, 1995.

Davis, Paul K. *100 Decisive Battles: From Ancient Times to the Present.* Santa Barbara, CA: ABC-CLIO, 1999.

Samson, George. *A History of Japan, 1334–1615.* Stanford, CA: Stanford University Press, 1961.

Turnbull, Stephen. *Battles of the Samurai.* New York: Arms and Armour, 1987.

———. *The Samurai: A Military History.* New York: Macmillan, 1977.

Siege of Breda

Date	August 28, 1624–June 5, 1625	
Location	The city of Breda in The Netherlands	
Opponents (* winner)	*Spain	Dutch
Commander	Ambrosio de Spinola	Justinius van Nassau
Approx. # Troops	60,000	9,000
Importance	Although the siege is one of the major military events of the Dutch Wars of Independence (1568–1648) and a Spanish victory, its heavy cost prevents the Spaniards from pursuing other operations	

The successful Spanish siege of the city of Breda in the Netherlands was one of the major military events of the Dutch Wars of Independence (1568–1648). In 1622 the struggle with the Dutch became part of the wider conflict of the Thirty Years' War (1618–1648). In July of that year Spanish general Ambrosio de Spinola laid siege to Bergen-op-Zoom, but a force of Dutch and German Protestants led by Prince Maurice of Nassau, stadtholder of Holland, raised the siege. Prominent officials in the Spanish court of King Philip IV, most notably the king's prime minister Gaspar Guzmán, Duke of Sanlucar and Count of Olivares, were jealous of Spinola's military successes and may have attempted to set him up for failure. In any case, they now persuaded Philip IV to order Spinola to lay siege to the fortified city of Breda, a Dutch stronghold in northern Brabant that many considered unassailable.

Spinola moved against Breda with some 60,000 men in his Army of Flanders. Prince Maurice had garrisoned Breda with about 9,000 troops, supported by artillery. The Dutch had also improved its defenses with moats, trenches, and revetments. Unlike previous Spanish sieges of Dutch towns except that of Jülich during 1621–1622, Spinola opted to starve out the city. While the siege lasted, the relief of the city was the focus of Dutch military efforts.

Spinola made his preparations carefully, mounting his artillery on raised platforms to secure maximum effectiveness. He ordered construction of barricades that blocked major egress points from Breda so that his troops could defeat any sorties. Spinola also held back most of his cavalry and infantry in a mobile reserve to meet anticipated Dutch relief operations.

The Dutch did attempt sorties from the city, and Prince Maurice of Nassau attempted to get supplies into the city. All met rebuff, including several efforts by Count Peter Ernst von Mansfeld, a German mercenary serving under Prince Maurice. At the same time, Maurice refused Spinola's efforts to draw him into a pitched battle.

The winter of 1624–1625 was severe, and both sides suffered, especially the Spanish in their field shelters. With the arrival of spring, the Dutch, reinforced by German troops, mounted several unsuccessful attempts to break the siege. Maurice died on April 23, 1625, and was succeeded as stadtholder of Holland by his younger brother Prince Frederick Henry, who continued to refuse a decisive battle with Spinola. Frederick Henry also continued efforts to relieve Breda, sending Mansfeld and 12,000 men on a fifth attempt to reach the city with supplies. On May 12, to distract the besiegers, 2,000 Dutch sortied from Breda against what they thought was a weak point in the line. Mansfeld approached the city from the opposite direction at the same time. Spinola beat back both, with heavy losses for the attackers.

Spinola had increased his artillery and was able to largely silence the guns of the fortress. He then brought up battering guns, effecting breaches in the walls. On June 5 with all hope of relief gone and with Spanish troops inside Breda, Governor Justinius van Nassau surrendered under favorable terms. The defenders were allowed to leave the city with their personal weapons, four artillery pieces, and such personal possessions as they could carry. Four thousand departed Breda, leaving behind 5,000 of their fellow soldiers dead along with 8,000 civilians dead of disease and hunger.

The Spanish success at Breda was actually a detriment to their overall plans. The city had little strategic value, and the siege had been costly in financial terms. Its heavy drain on troop resources also prevented the Spanish from pursuing other goals. Dutch forces finally retook Breda in 1637.

References

Geyl, Pieter. *The Netherlands in the Seventeenth Century: Part One, 1609–1648.* London: Ernest Bern, 1966.

Israel, Jonathan I. *The Dutch Republic and the Hispanic World, 1606–1661.* Oxford, UK: Clarendon, 1982.

Parker, Geoffrey. *The Dutch Revolt.* Rev. ed. London: Penguin Books, 1990.

Siege of La Rochelle

Date	August 1627–October 28, 1628	
Location	La Rochelle on the southwest Atlantic coast of France	
Opponents (* winner)	*French Army	Citizens of La Rochelle, supported by England
Commander	Armand Jean du Plessis, Cardinal de Richelieu	Jean Guiton; George Villiers, Duke of Buckingham
Approx. # Troops	Some 29,000	? City population of 27,000; 6,000 English troops
Importance	Richelieu amends the Edict of Nantes with the Huguenots losing the right to maintain fortified towns and military formations independent of the crown. The long siege also brings the creation of the French Navy	

The Protestant Reformation, especially the radical version preached by Frenchman John Calvin (né Jean Cauvin), who set himself up in Geneva, spread to France soon after it began. Calvinism was particularly appealing to the French middle class and nobles. As the nobles were often the chief source of opposition to the Crown, French kings naturally took alarm. In the 1550s the government of Henri II persecuted adherents of the new faith, who came to be called Huguenots, and burned a number of them at the stake. Despite this persecution, Calvinism continued to make inroads, especially in southwestern France.

During 1562–1598 France experienced a series of costly religious wars during which the Huguenots established a number of fortified cities, including La Rochelle on the southwestern Atlantic coast. The wars were settled when the Huguenot champion, Henri de Navarre, became king of France as Henri IV. Because the great majority of Frenchmen were still Catholic and because Henri IV wished to secure the Catholic stronghold of Paris, he converted to Catholicism ("Paris is well worth a mass," he is supposed to have said). To mollify his former coreligionists, he issued the Edict of Nantes in 1598 that granted religious toleration and full civil rights to the Huguenots. The edict also allowed them to fortify some 100 towns where the Huguenot faith was in the majority.

Unfortunately for France, Henri IV's reign was brief; he was stabbed to death in Paris by a religious fanatic in 1610. His son, Louis XIII (r. 1610–1643), was then only nine years old. Louis grew up to be weak and indecisive, but he had a capable chief minister in Armand Jean du Plessis, Cardinal de Richelieu, who was the virtual ruler of France during 1624–1642. This born administrator made raison d'état (reason of state) the dominant consideration in all his policies. Although he was a sincere Catholic, Richelieu never let religion get in the way of strengthening the state.

To Richelieu, the Huguenot-fortified towns formed a state within a state and were thus unacceptable. Alarmed by Richelieu's stance, the Huguenots rebelled under the leadership of the dukes de Rohan and Soubise. Richelieu responded by declaring the suppression of the rebellion his first priority in 1625. Protestant, rich, and looking toward England, La Rochelle relished its independence. The city itself lay at the end of a channel. Off it were two islands: the closest, Île de Ré, and the more distant Île d'Oléron. La Rochelle was the strongest of the Huguenot fortresses and the center of resistance to royal rule.

In 1626 La Rochelle had been forced to accept a royal commissioner, to agree not to arm its ships, and to accord full rights to Catholics. In March 1627 France formed an alliance with Spain that solidified its position. Six months later Richelieu's forces initiated a siege of the city and exchanged artillery fire with its Huguenot defenders. Because La Rochelle was a port it could receive aid by sea, and in June 1627 King Charles I of England sent 120 ships and 6,000 soldiers there under his favorite, George Villiers, Duke of Buckingham.

The English fleet arrived at Île de Ré on July 10. If the people of La Rochelle welcomed the troops, Buckingham was to place them under command of the Duc de Soubise, who arrived with him. If not, the men would return to England. Soubise went to La Rochelle to negotiate with its leaders, but they feared the consequences of welcoming English troops. Buckingham therefore ordered his men ashore to secure Fort St. Martin on Île de Ré, which was controlled by the royalists, as a base for future operations. His men, most of whom had been pressed, were poorly trained, and many refused to go ashore. Others bolted on the first gunfire with the royal garrison on the island. Buckingham was thus unable to take the fort; instead, he resorted to a blockade.

Richelieu was certain that if Buckingham took Fort St. Martin, his siege operation would fail. Richelieu therefore sent French ships to supply the fort, called up feudal levies, and sent about 20,000 men toward La Rochelle. The brother of the king, Gaston d'Orléans, had nominal command, but field command was held by the Duc d'Angoulême. As it worked out, Richelieu actually retained direction of affairs.

In August, Angoulême closed off the city from the land side, and the city fathers voted to call on Buckingham for arms and assistance. The royal garrison on the Île de Ré continued to hold out, although on October 1 its commander, Jean de St. Bonnet de Toiras, sent word that his men were almost out of food and that without relief he would have to surrender on the evening of October 8. Therefore, on the night of October 7 Richelieu sent a relief force of 47 vessels under an adventurer named Beaulieu-Persac. That night a battle took place off Île de Ré between the French and English warships. Although he was eventually forced to surrender, Beaulieu-Persac succeeded in distracting the English long enough for his 29 supply ships to beach themselves on the island.

A few days later King Louis XIII arrived in the vicinity of La Rochelle. Richelieu then personally led 9,000 reinforcements to the Île de Ré and Île d'Oléron from northern French mainland ports. Running short of supplies himself, in desperation Buckingham and 2,000 men launched a last attempt to storm Fort St. Martin on November 5. The English took the outer works but were then driven back and shortly thereafter came under heavy attack from the French relief force. On November 8 Buckingham sailed away with the half of his force that remained.

With Île de Ré secure, Richelieu could concentrate on La Rochelle. In November the French constructed a powerful siege line more than seven miles long with 11 forts and 18 redoubts. The French lacked the means to blockade the city completely from the sea, but after reading how Alexander the Great had built a great causeway to end the siege of Tyre, Richelieu ordered construction of a great stone dike at the end of the bay to close La Rochelle off from the sea. Jean de Thirot, architect to the king, and Clément Métezeau, the king's master builder, had charge of construction.

Work began in October and for all practical purposes was complete by January 1628, with the jetty and 56 ships chained together and armed to form a floating wall. In addition, Richelieu assembled 36 galleys and pinnaces in the roadstead to attack any expedition launched from La Rochelle to destroy the dike.

In March an English ship made it to La Rochelle with supplies and promised assistance from Charles I. The people of La Rochelle took heart and elected Jean Guiton as mayor. He infused new life in the defense. Moreover, in early May an English fleet under Lord Denbigh arrived. The English ships briefly bombarded the dike but without effect. Then, learning that a Spanish fleet was at sea, Denbigh sailed away on May 18. On September 28 a larger English fleet under Count Lindsey appeared off the dike, transporting 11 regiments and food for many months, but the troops were disaffected, and it departed without landing either men or supplies.

With this final disappointment and virtually no hope of resupply, on October 29 the La Rochelle garrison finally surrendered. During the siege, largely as the consequence of famine and disease, the population of the city went from 27,000 to only 5,000 people. Richelieu entered the city in triumph, and French troops immediately began the destruction of La Rochelle's walls and fortifications. Richelieu then amended the Edict of Nantes in the Peace of Alais, which formally ended the siege. The Huguenots lost the right to maintain fortified towns and military formations independent of the Crown. They did, however, retain full religious and civil rights until 1685, when King Louis XIV, much to the detriment of his kingdom, annulled the Edict of Nantes altogether.

One reason the siege had taken so long was that France did not have much of a navy. Richelieu may be regarded as the father of the French Navy, for he ordered construction of a force of 38 warships for the Atlantic and 10 for the Mediterranean.

References

Holt, Mack P. *The French Wars of Religion, 1562–1629.* Cambridge: Cambridge University Press, 1995.

O'Connell, D. P. *Richelieu.* New York: World Publishing, 1968.

Sutherland, N. M. *The Huguenot Struggle for Recognition.* New Haven, CT: Yale University Press, 1980.

Wood, James B. *The Army of the King: Warfare, Soldiers, and Society during the Wars of Religion in France, 1562–1676.* Cambridge: Cambridge University Press, 1996.

Battle of Breitenfeld

Date	September 17, 1631	
Location	Breitenfeld, 4 miles north of Leipzig in Saxony	
Opponents (* winner)	*Sweden and Saxony	Imperialists
Commander	King Gustavus Adolphus of Sweden; Lieutenant General Georg von Arnim (Saxon forces)	Johan Tserclaes, Count Tilly
Approx. # Troops	26,000 Swedes; 16,000 Saxons	36,000
Importance	The first major Protestant victory and decisive turning point of the Thirty Years' War, Breitenfeld reverses the military situation, giving the initiative to the Protestants and opening all Germany to Gustavus	

At the beginning of the 17th century, Germany was bitterly divided. The 300-plus states that constituted the Holy Roman Empire, most of them German, were held together only loosely by an elected emperor who endeavored both to impose his will and enforce religious conformity. The Protestant Reformation, which began in 1517 when Martin Luther publicized his Ninety-Five Theses at Wittenberg, had led to widespread warfare in Germany. Serious religious strife also wracked the Netherlands, France, Hungary, and the British Isles in the 16th century, but it had the most devastating and prolonged effects in Germany. The Knights' Revolt (1522) and the Peasants' Revolt (1524) in the German states were failures, but that of the higher orders of the Holy Roman Empire enjoyed considerable success. Many German princes embraced Lutheranism as a means of seizing lands belonging to the Roman Catholic Church and resisting the centralizing efforts of Holy Roman Emperor Charles V (r. 1519–1556).

Widespread fighting began in the German states in 1546 and did not end until the Peace of Augsburg of 1555. The Peace of Augsburg was a victory both for religious toleration and states' rights, the former because it permitted Lutheranism in addition to Catholicism and the latter because it allowed the government of any state to decide which faith its citizens would practice (cujus regio, ejus religio, or "whose region, his or her religion"). The so-called Ecclesiastical Reservation provided that if a Catholic spiritual prince (such as a bishop ruling a bishopric) became Protestant after 1552, his lands were to remain with the Catholic Church.

This compromise did not last. By the early 17th century Protestantism had made great advances. Militant Calvinism that preached the formation of a religious commonwealth was making serious inroads, and the Ecclesiastical Reservation had been repeatedly violated. At the same time, the Catholic Church had done much to reform itself. The formation of the Society of Jesus (Jesuits) and the accession of Holy Roman Emperor Rudolph II (r. 1576–1612), who was determined to restore the position of the Roman Catholic Church (and, not incidentally, his own authority), set up the clash. With the formation of the Protestant Union in 1608 and the Catholic League in 1609, Germany was divided into two hostile camps spoiling for a showdown.

In addition to being fought over religious and constitutional issues, the Thirty Years' War (1618–1648) was an international event. The leaders of France, the Dutch Republic, Spain, Sweden, and Denmark all had ambitions in Germany. There were also soldiers of fortune who fought at their convenience and endeavored to carve out territories of their own. The Thirty Years' War was extraordinarily complex; it was also the greatest of all European wars prior to the French Revolution (1789–1799).

Historians usually divide the Thirty Years' War into four phases: the Bohemian (1618–1625), the Danish (1625–1629), the Swedish (1630–1635), and the French or Franco-Swedish (1635–1648). The Catholic side, led by the Holy Roman emperor, emerged as the dominant force during the first two phases. The war began in May 1618 when Bohemians, fearful that they were about to lose their Protestant liberties and endeavoring to prevent Ferdinand, Duke of Styria, from being named Holy Roman emperor, hurled two imperial representatives from a castle window in Prague (they fell 50 feet to the ground but lived) and declared the emperor deposed. The Bohemian Diet subsequently elected the Calvinist Frederick of the palatinate as king (Frederick V). Meanwhile, the staunch Catholic Habsburg Ferdinand became emperor as Ferdinand II (r. 1619–1637).

Ferdinand II was determined to restore his authority in Prague. On November 8, 1620, in the Battle of White Mountain just west of Prague in fighting that lasted little more than an hour, the imperial forces under Johan Tserclaes, Count Tilly, defeated those of Frederick V (known thereafter as the Winter King) under Christian of Anhalt-Bernberg. Imperial troops conquered all Bohemia, which was re-Catholicized, and Tilly's troops and Spanish forces under the Marquis Ambrogio de Spinola overran the Palatinate.

This situation greatly alarmed the Protestant powers of England, the Dutch Republic, Sweden, and Denmark. They now entered into discussions. With King Gustavus Adolphus of Sweden busy with Russia and Poland, Danish king Christian IV became the Protestant champion. England, the Dutch Republic, and France all pledged financial support, and the fighting shifted from southern to northern Germany in 1625 when Denmark entered the fray.

To deal with the new Protestant threat, Emperor Ferdinand commissioned Albrecht Wenzel von Wallenstein, military governor of Prague, to raise a private army and come to Tilly's support. On April 25, 1626, Wallenstein defeated Protestant forces under Count Ernst von Mansfield at the Bridge of Dessau on the Elbe and then pursued him through Hungary. On August 27, 1626, in the Battle of Lutter am Barenberge in Brunswick, Tilly routed Christian IV. With Tilly wounded, Wallenstein led the subsequent imperial invasion and conquest of much of the Danish peninsula. In the Treaty of Lübeck in May 1629, Christian was forced to yield to the emperor a number of German bishoprics.

Meanwhile, in March 1629 Ferdinand II had issued the Edict of Restitution. This document was the high-water mark of the Catholic offensive. It demanded strict enforcement of the Peace of Augsburg (thus denying toleration to Calvinism and insisting on the return of extensive lands taken since 1552 to the Catholic Church). The preeminence of the Habsburgs now raised opposition, even from Catholic powers and Pope Urban VII. This found tangible expression when chief minister of France, Cardinal Richelieu, agreed to provide a subsidy of 1 million livres a year to Gustavus Adolphus to maintain a Swedish army of 40,000 men in Germany in support of the Protestant powers.

Gustavus was a gifted leader and an important military reformer. When he landed with his army in Pomerania in July 1630 he was only 35 years old, but he had already been king of Sweden for 16 years. He brought with him a well-equipped and well-trained military force honed in fighting against Russia, Poland, and Denmark. Gustavus was a deeply religious Protestant, and his army went into battle singing hymns, but he and Sweden, not Germany, stood to gain by his intervention.

Gustavus's first operations in Germany were directed at establishing a secure base of operations in Pomerania and other areas along the Baltic. Emperor Ferdiand had concentrated most of his forces in northern Italy, believing that the Swedes were little threat. Indeed, Count Tilly, the leader of the imperial forces in the north, took by storm and sacked the great Protestant city of Magdeburg on the Elbe in May 1631. Much of the city was subsequently destroyed in a sudden fire, and only about 5,000 of 30,000 people survived. This event shocked the heretofore reluctant Protestant princes and brought both Saxony and Brandenburg into alliance with Gustavus.

This enabled Gustavus to march south and seek a decisive battle with Tilly. When Duke Johann George of Saxony formally allied himself with Gustavus on September 11, Tilly with about 36,000 men began laying waste to Saxony. On

September 15 Tilly took Leipzig, which his men looted. At the same time, Swedish and Saxon forces (26,000 and 16,000, respectively) joined at Düben, some 25 miles north of the city. On the urging of his subordinate commander, Count Gottfried H. zu Pappenheim, Tilly abandoned Leipzig and took up position at Breitenfeld, 4 miles north.

The Battle of Breitenfeld (also known as the Battle of Leipzig) occurred on September 17, 1631. Tilly drew up his army with his infantry in the center and his cavalry on the wings. Tilly commanded the center and right, with Pappenheim in charge of the imperial left. The imperial artillery was massed in the center and center-right of the line.

Gustavus, on the other hand, had arranged his men not in the traditional Spanish-designed *tercio* (square) formation of massed pikemen with harquebusiers or musketeers on its corners but instead in smaller, more mobile formations where musketeers predominated, protected by pikemen. Gustavus's artillery was also lighter and more mobile than Tilly's heavier guns and throughout the battle exacted a heavy toll on the densely packed imperial formations. Saxon forces of infantry and cavalry, supported by artillery under Duke Johann George, held the left of the Protestant line opposite Tilly, while Swedish and other German infantry occupied the center. Swedish cavalry were on the right wing opposite Pappenheim. Additional Swedish cavalry were positioned in the center of the line, between and behind two lines of infantry.

The imperial artillery opened up as Gustavus's force was deploying. This continued until midday, when the impetuous Pappenheim, acting without orders, attacked with his cavalry in an attempt to turn the Swedish right flank. Gustavus wheeled his cavalry reserve, catching Pappenheim between his two cavalry forces. Gustavus was also able to reposition his lighter guns and open up with grapeshot against the imperial cavalry. These guns and the musketeers, outranging the pistol fire of Pappenheim's cavalry, forced an imperial withdrawal.

Tilly meanwhile advanced against the Saxons, whom he believed to be the weakest part of the Protestant force. After routing the Saxons, Tilly turned against Gustavus's now-exposed left flank. The more maneuverable Swedes countered and held against Tilly's attack. Gustavus then led his own cavalry, with the infantry closely following, against Tilly's left flank, retaking the artillery lost by the Saxons in their precipitous retreat as well as many of the heavy imperial guns. The quicker-firing and more mobile Swedish artillery combined with the captured imperial artillery to devastate the massed imperial formations.

Tilly's forces fled the field that evening after some seven hours of fighting. The Swedes pursued until nightfall and a stand by Pappenheim's reformed cavalry. Gustavus lost some 6,500 men killed or wounded, with most of these casualties occurring in the early artillery fire. The imperial forces lost some 13,000 (7,000 dead and 6,000 taken prisoner). Tilly, badly wounded, escaped.

The battle was the first major Protestant victory of the war. Gustavus's victory completely reversed the situation on the ground, giving the initiative to the Protestants and opening all Germany to him. Gustavus entered Leipzig the next day and then moved, without serious imperial opposition, to the Rhine.

References
Clark, G. N. *The Seventeenth Century.* Oxford, UK: Clarendon, 1950.

Dodge, Theodore Ayrault. *Gustavus Adolphus.* London: Greenhill Books, 1992.

Parker, Geoffrey. *The Thirty Years' War.* New York: Military Heritage Press, 1988.

Rabb, Theodore K. *The Thirty Years' War.* 2nd ed. Lanham, MD: University Press of America, 1981.

Wedgwood, C. V. *The Thirty Years' War.* London: Jonathan Cape, 1944.

Battle of Lützen

Date	November 16, 1632	
Location	Lützen	
Opponents (* winner)	*Swedes	Imperialists
Commander	King Gustavus Adolphus of Sweden; Bernard of Saxe-Weimar	Albrecht Wenzel von Wallenstein
Approx. # Troops	19,000	19,000
Importance	Although the Swedes are victorious and continue the war under Bernard of Saxe-Weimar, the Protestant cause has lost its greatest champion with the death of Gustavus. Germany is now apparently irretrievably divided and the war becomes a struggle for base material advantage	

The Battle of Breitenfeld north of Leipzig on September 17, 1631, was the decisive turning point in the Thirty Years' War (1618–1648). There the Protestant champion, Swedish king Gustavus Adolphus, achieved an overwhelming victory over the Catholic forces of Holy Roman Emperor Ferdinand II, led in the field by Johan Tserclaes, Count Tilly. Following Breitenfeld, Gustavus marched without serious opposition across Germany to the Rhine.

On December 22 Gustavus captured Mainz, where he wintered and rethought his plans. He had rescued the Protestant cause in Germany, but his rout of the imperial forces now led him to believe that he might reorganize the German states under his own control. To accomplish that, however, he would have to invade and conquer the Catholic strongholds of Bavaria and Austria. Gustavus could realistically contemplate such a step, for with his allies he now controlled 80,000 men. Faced with this imposing threat, Ferdinand II recalled his great captain, Albrecht

One of the great captains and military reformers in all history, Swedish king Gustav II Adolf, better known as Gustavus Adolphus, ruled Sweden during 1611–1632 and, as the Protestant champion, took his country into the Thirty Years' War. (Library of Congress)

Wenzel von Wallenstein. The two men had frequently quarreled, and the terms under which Wallenstein agreed to form a new army made him the virtual viceroy.

In early April 1632 Gustavus launched his campaign. Crossing the Danube at Donauwörth, he moved east into Bavaria to engage imperial forces under Tilly and Bavarian Duke Maximilian. Crossing the Lech River on a bridge of boats, Gustavus attacked Tilly's entrenched camp. In the Battle of the Lech of April 15–17, 1632, Gustavus was victorious. Tilly was mortally wounded, and Maximilian abandoned most of the artillery and baggage and withdrew. Gustavus then occupied Augsburg, Munich, and all of southern Bavaria.

On July 11 Wallenstein joined his forces to those of Maximilian at Schwabach. Wallenstein now commanded some 60,000 men. Gustavus, with only 20,000 men, sent for reinforcements that brought his strength up to 45,000.

During August 31–September 4, 1632, Gustavus repeatedly attacked Wallenstein's entrenched camp near the Alte Veste castle. Wallenstein had chosen well, for the terrain made it impossible for Gustavus to utilize his strength in cavalry and artillery. After suffering heavy casualties, Gustavus withdrew. Both armies then ravaged the vicinity around Nuremberg for provisions.

Beginning in September 1632 Wallenstein took the offensive, invading Saxony and threatening the Swedish line of communications. Wallenstein had about 30,000 men, and Gustavus had 20,000 men. Awaiting reinforcements, Gustavus entrenched at Naumburg while Wallenstein set up his headquarters in the town of Lützen, southwest of Leipzig. On November 14 after holding his army at battle stations for two weeks, Wallenstein made the worst mistake of his military career. Believing that Gustavus had gone into winter quarters, Wallenstein ordered his own forces to disperse, sending a large detachment of men under Count Gottfried H. zu Pappenheim to Halle.

The very next day, November 15, Wallenstein learned of Gustavus's approach. Immediately dispatching an appeal to Pappenheim to return, Wallenstein prepared to meet the Swedish attack. He threw up improvised defensive fortifications along a sunken road, with his right wing anchored on Lützen. That night both armies were drawn up in battle formation facing one another just east of Lützen.

The battle took place the next day. Each side had about 19,000 men. Gustavus positioned the bulk of his infantry in the center of the line, although the wings contained a mix of infantry and cavalry forces. Bernard of Saxe-Weimar commanded the Swedish left, while Gustavus was on the right.

The battle was prolonged, and both sides suffered heavy casualties. Fortunately for Wallenstein, heavy fog delayed the Swedish attack until about 11:00 a.m. Initially the Swedish right pushed back musketeers and cavalry under Count Heinrich Holk on the imperial left and threatened the artillery. Pappenheim's men then arrived, just in time to stabilize that flank. Wallenstein also ordered his men to set fire to Lützen; the smoke from the fires blew into the center of the Swedish line, blinding the men. Wallenstein further confused the Swedes by launching a cavalry attack there. Gustavus responded with a cavalry charge of his own, utilizing his left wing. Riding into an enemy formation, Gustavus was surrounded, shot three times, and killed. Bernard took command.

News of the king's death caused the Swedes to attack with a renewed fury that brought victory. That night Wallenstein decamped, with the imperial forces abandoning both their baggage and artillery, retreating to Leipzig, and then withdrawing entirely from Saxony into Bohemia. In the Battle of Lützen the Swedes suffered about 10,000 casualties, the imperial forces perhaps 12,000; Pappenheim was among those fatally wounded.

Although the Swedes had been victorious and they now carried on under Gustavus's able lieutenant, Count Axel Oxenstierna, the Protestant cause had lost its most notable champion. The war changed into a struggle for base material advantage. Germany was apparently irretrievably divided. In these circumstances, King Gustavus's chancellor, Axel Oxenstierna, renewed the alliance with France, which ultimately entered the war openly on the Protestant side.

References

Clark, G. N. *The Seventeenth Century.* Oxford, UK: Clarendon, 1950.

Dodge, Theodore Ayrault. *Gustavus Adolphus.* London: Greenhill Books, 1992.

Parker, Geoffrey. *The Thirty Years' War.* New York: Military Heritage Press, 1988.

Rabb, Theodore K. *The Thirty Years' War.* 2nd ed. Lanham, MD: University Press of America, 1981.

Roberts, Michael. *Gustavus Adolphus.* 2 vols. 2nd ed. New York: Longman, 1992.

Wedgwood, C. V. *The Thirty Years' War.* London: Jonathan Cape, 1944.

Battle of Nördlingen

Date	September 6, 1634	
Location	Nördlingen in Bavaria, southern Germany	
Opponents (* winner)	*Imperialists and Spain	Sweden and allied German states
Commander	King Ferdinand of Hungary; Cardinal *Infante* (Prince) Ferdinand of Spain	Count Gustav Horn (Swedes); Duke Bernard von Weimar (allied Germans)
Approx. # Troops	33,000	25,000
Importance	The battle almost wipes out the Swedish Army, reverses the Swedish victory at Breitenfeld, and leads to the recapture of southern Germany for Catholicism. In this situation France openly enters the war on the side of the Protestants.	

The Battle of Nördlingen on September 6, 1634, between Swedish and German forces and Imperial and Spanish forces was one of the major battles of the Thirty Years' War (1618–1648) in Germany. Following the death of King Gustavus Adolphus of Sweden in the Battle of Lützen on November 16, 1832, his chancellor Axel Oxenstierna ably continued the Swedish war effort. The divisions in Germany were more pronounced than ever, and the devastation of a decade and a half of civil war encouraged outside states to intervene and take what lands they could.

With the death of Gustavus, Albrecht Wenzel von Wallenstein became the dominant figure on the German scene. As Holy Roman Emperor Ferdinand II's preeminent field commander, it is unclear exactly what Wallenstein intended, but indications point to him favoring a peace plan that involved toleration of the Protestants. Believing that Ferdinand II and his Jesuit advisers would never accept such a scheme, Wallenstein opened secret negotiations with the Protestant military commanders Hans Georg von Arnim and Duke Bernard of Saxe-Weimar, in effect committing treason. His effort came to naught. Wallenstein, an unscrupulous man, made the mistake of not doubting the integrity of his own lieutenants. This proved his undoing. Secretly encouraged by the emperor, they murdered Wallenstein in Eger in Bohemia on February 24, 1634.

Meanwhile, the Swedes soldiered on. On September 6 at Nördlingen in western Bavaria some 25,000 Swedish and German forces under Gustav Horn and Duke Bernard met 35,000 Imperial and Spanish forces commanded by King Ferdinand of Hungary and his cousin Cardinal Infante (Prince) Ferdinand of Spain. The Protestant plan called for Horn to attack the Imperial right, while Bernard pinned the Imperial left and prevented it from reinforcing the right. Occupying an excellent defensive position, the Imperial and Spanish forces easily turned back the poorly coordinated Protestant attack. Imperial attacks on Bernard's forces then routed the

Protestant right and wheeled into the Swedes. More than 6,000 Swedes died, and only 11,000 men of the combined Protestant force escaped. The Catholic side sustained only 1,200 casualties.

Nördlingen almost wiped out the army created by Gustavus and, in effect, reversed the Swedish victory at Breitenfeld. Following the battle, King Ferdinand of Hungary, the son of Emperor Ferdinand II and himself the future Ferdinand III (r. 1637–1657), recaptured southern Germany for Catholicism. Although Swedish forces did take the offensive in northern Germany in 1637, the situation after Nördlingen appeared sufficiently dire that the chief minister of France, Cardinal Richelieu, brought his nation openly into the war. Following Nördlingen the war saw France and Sweden fighting Bavaria, Spain, and the emperor.

The French or Franco-Swedish period of the war began in 1635 when French forces invaded Germany. At first the fighting did not go well for France. Finally, on May 19, 1643, at Rocroi in the Ardennes region of northeastern France the 22-year-old French general Louis, Duc de Enghien, with 22,000 troops, won a brilliant victory over Spanish general Francisco de Melo's army of 27,000 men. Cavalry and massed artillery shattered the formerly invincible Spanish infantry. Spain lost 7,000 men killed and 8,000 captured in the battle. French casualties were only 4,000.

With all sides urging peace and Germany utterly exhausted, peace negotiations opened in 1644. The talks dragged on because the fighting itself continued. Not until 1648 was the Peace of Westphalia ending the long war concluded. France secured the Lorraine bishoprics of Metz, Toul, and Verdun as well as most of the province of Alsace. The Swedes received western Pomerania, including the city of Stettin. Bavaria was elevated in stature and secured the upper palatinate. Brandenburg gained eastern Pomerania and Magdeburg, important steps forward in the rise of what would become the Kingdom of Prussia. The United Provinces (Dutch Republic) and Swiss Confederation were both recognized as independent.

In terms of religion, the Peace of Westphalia reaffirmed the terms of the Peace of Augsburg of 1555 that allowed each state to determine the religion of its inhabitants but raised the number of faiths from two to three: Catholicism, Lutheranism, and Calvinism. In terms of church lands, those holding them on January 1, 1624, received possession, an arrangement that generally worked in the Protestants' favor.

Most important perhaps was the constitutional arrangement. The more than 300 German states were recognized as virtually sovereign, with each having the right to conduct its own diplomacy and make treaties with foreign powers. This arrangement was an open invitation to intervention in Germany by outside powers, particularly France, which with Sweden became a guarantor of the treaty. Thus, while much of the rest of Europe was being welded into strong centrally directed nation-states, Germany descended into chaos.

Germany had been devastated by the war. Cities were taken and sacked multiple times. Agriculture and crafts both fell into ruin. Pestilence and disease spread, and perhaps half the German population died of these and simple starvation. In consequence, it was the Atlantic peoples—the Dutch, the English, and the French—who now took the lead in world affairs. Only over time did new power complexes begin to form around Brandenburg-Prussia in the north and Austria in the south. In 1740 they began a 126-year-long struggle to see who would control Germany.

References

Clark, G. N. *The Seventeenth Century.* Oxford, UK: Clarendon, 1950.

Parker, Geoffrey. *The Thirty Years' War.* New York: Military Heritage Press, 1988.

Rabb, Theodore K. *The Thirty Years' War.* 2nd ed. Lanham, MD: University Press of America, 1981.

Wedgwood, C. V. *The Thirty Years' War.* London: Jonathan Cape, 1944.

Battle of Rocroi

Date	May 19, 1643	
Location	Rocroi in northeastern France	
Opponents (* winner)	*France	Spain
Commander	Louis II de Bourbon, Duc d'Enghien (later the Prince de Condé, known as Le Grand Condé)	Francesco de Melo
Approx. # Troops	6,000 cavalry; 17,000 infantry	8,000 cavalry, 19,000 infantry
Importance	Ends all chance for a further Spanish invasion of France from the Netherlands; it also marks the end of Spanish military greatness and the beginning of French hegemony in Europe	

With France having entered the Thirty Years' War (1618–1648), in May 1643 Spanish general Francesco de Melo led the 27,000-man Spanish Army of Flanders (8,000 cavalry and 19,000 infantry) from the Netherlands through the Ardennes toward Paris. The Spanish hoped to relieve pressure on Catalonia and in Franche-Comté. En route Melo laid siege to the French fortified town of Rocroi. The 22-year-old Louis II de Bourbon, Duc d'Enghien (later Prince de Condé, known as Le Grand Condé for his military prowess), commanded the French army of 23,000 men (6,000 cavalry and 17,000 infantry). He advanced to meet the Spanish along the Meuse River.

Learning that the Spanish were at Rocroi, Enghien hurried there and arrived on May 18. Receiving intelligence that 6,000 Spanish reinforcements were en route, Enghien decided on an attack against the advice of his older subordinate commanders. He ordered his army forward through the only available approach, a defile between woods and marshes that the Spanish had failed to block. That afternoon the French took up position on a ridge overlooking Rocroi. The Spanish army then formed up between the French and Rocroi, and both sides prepared to do battle the next day.

De Melo positioned his infantry in the center. The first ranks consisted of some 8,000 highly trained Spanish troops formed up in the traditional *tercios,* or squares. Mercenary infantry were behind them, and cavalry protected both flanks. The Spanish had 18 artillery pieces. The French were similarly arranged: infantry in the center, along with some artillery at the front, and cavalry on both flanks. The French had 14 guns.

The battle opened early on the morning of May 19 and took place on open farmland in front of Rocroi. The fighting began with Enghien leading a French cavalry attack on the Spanish left. After defeating the Spanish cavalry Enghien moved against the Spanish infantry, which was besting the French infantry. At the same time, though against Enghien's orders, the French cavalry on the left attacked the Spanish right and were repulsed. The Spanish mounted a counterattack but were halted by French reserves.

Enghien managed to get in behind the center of the Spanish infantry with his cavalry, smashing through to attack the Spanish right-flank cavalry that had engaged his reserve. When the Spanish cavalry scattered, it isolated the 18,000 Spanish infantry. The mercenaries promptly deserted. Long regarded as the finest in Europe, the veteran Spanish infantry held its formations and repulsed two French cavalry attacks. Enghien massed his artillery with guns captured from the Spanish, however, and systematically hammered the Spanish square formations.

Despite the artillery fire, the Spanish absorbed additional French cavalry attacks without breaking formation. Enghien then offered terms, and the Spanish accepted. When Enghien rode forward to take their surrender, however, some of the Spanish infantry apparently believed that this was the beginning of a French cavalry charge and opened fire on him. Angered by this seeming treachery, the French attacked the Spanish without quarter and with devastating result. The Spanish army was virtually destroyed.

Spanish casualties amounted to more than half their force. The Spanish lost some 8,000 men killed and another 7,000 taken prisoner. French losses totaled only 4,000. The Battle of Rocroi did not have any immediate impact on the outcome of the Thirty Years' War. Spain continued in the war, maintained its hold on the southern Netherlands, and had some success against the French in Catalonia and Italy, but the battle did end all chance of another Spanish invasion of France.

Indeed, with France in control of Alsace, Lorraine, and Trier and the Dutch controlling the English Channel, it was impossible for Spanish king Philip IV's government to resupply the Netherlands. The Dutch and the French were able to whittle away at the Netherlands. Spain lost Gravelines in 1644, Hulst in 1645, and Dunkirk (Dunkerque) in 1646.

Rocroi also led to the end the *tercio* formation. More important, though, the battle is usually regarded as marking the end of Spanish military greatness and the beginning of French hegemony in Europe.

References

Parker, Geoffrey. *The Thirty Years' War.* New York: Military Heritage Press, 1988.

Wedgwood, C. V. *The Thirty Years' War.* London: Jonathan Cape, 1944.

Battle of Shanhaiguan

Date	May 28, 1644	
Location	Shanhaiguan, Hebei Province, northeast China	
Opponents (* winner)	*Manzhu and Ming forces	Rebels
Commander	Dorgon (Manzhu commander); Wu Sangui (Ming army)	Li Zicheng
Approx. # Troops	60,000 Manzhus; 40,000 Mings	60,000
Importance	Brings establishment of the Qing Dynasty	

The Battle of Shanhaiguan (Shanhaikuan, or the Battle of Shanhai Pass) on May 28, 1644, pitted Manzhu (Manchu) and imperial Chinese troops against a force of rebel Chinese. It was the decisive event in the replacement of the Ming dynasty by that of the Qing (Ch'ing).

The Ming period (1368–1644) saw major military and administrative accomplishments and a great flowering in the arts, but by the 17th century the dynasty was under increasing pressure from the Japanese and the Dutch and from rebellions within China, especially by the Manzhu. Descended from the Mongols who had invaded China in the 12th century, the Manzhu in Manchuria had become tributaries to the Ming dynasty.

In 1616 Manzhu leader Nurhachi, after uniting the Jurchen (Nüzhen, Nü-chen) Mongolian tribes, proclaimed a new dynasty, the Later Jin (Chin), at his capital of Liaoyang. For the next decade he waged war against the Ming dynasty, capturing most of southern Manchuria and much of Mongolia. Nurhachi, known by his successors as Emperor Taizu (Ch'ing T'ai-tsu), died in 1626. He was succeeded by his son Huang Taiji (Hung Taiji, sometimes erroneously known in Western literature as Abahai). Huang Taiji ruled during 1626–1643. A highly effective administrator who was also respected for his military abilities, he was also determined to expand the empire.

Huang Taiji established a base in Korea and repeatedly raided into China. He also improved his army's weapons, adding significant numbers of gunpowder artillery to counter that of the Ming; his cavalry came to be regarded as the best in Asia. In 1634 the Manzhus conquered inner (southern) Mongolia and absorbed large numbers of the inhabitants into their forces.

At the same time, using the justification of nonpayment of tribute and the failure of the Koreans to contribute troops against the Ming, in 1636 Emperor Huang Taiji sent a large army into Korea and the next year compelled the Joseon dynasty to formally renounce the Ming dynasty. During 1636–1644 a series of expeditions established Manzhu control over the Amur River region. In 1636 at Mukden, Huang Taiji proclaimed the establishment of a new imperial dynasty, the Qing, which was merely a renaming of the Later Jin proclaimed by Nurhachi earlier. In 1643, however, Huang Taiji died, possibly at the hands of one of his officials. His five-year-old son Shunzhi (Shun-chih) became emperor (r. 1643–1661), although real authority was exercised by his uncle, Prince Dorgon, as regent.

Meanwhile, from 1635 the Ming dynasty had been further weakened by a number of internal rebellions. The greatest threat came from rebel chieftain Li Zicheng (Li Tzu-ch'eng). In 1640 Li seized control of Henan (Honan) and Shaanxi (Shensi) provinces south and southwest of Beijing, respectively. In 1644 Li moved against the imperial capital of Beijing. Ming emperor Chongzhen (Chu'ung-chen) then recalled two of his frontier armies, including the one at Shanhaiguan commanded by Wu Sangui (Wu San-kuei). Sources differ as to whether Wu refused to come to the aid of the emperor or his forces simply arrived too late; in any case, Li seized control of Beijing on April 25, 1644. Just before the rebel troops took Beijing, Emperor Chongzhen committed suicide.

Wu learned of Emperor Chongzhen's death while on his way to Beijing and evidently considered surrendering to Li, in part because the rebel had taken Wu's father hostage. Nevertheless, Wu returned to Shanhaiguan. After pillaging Beijing, on May 18 Li set out after Wu.

Wu meanwhile had decided that he would rather treat with the Manzhus than with Li, so he called on Prince Dorgon to assist him in overthrowing the rebel regime.

Li passed his army of some 100,000 men through Yongping (Yang-p'ing) and almost to Shanhaiguan. Accounts differ as to what happened next, but apparently on May 25, 1644, Wu appealed to Dorgon for immediate assistance. Dorgon promptly responded, arriving at the strategic Shanhai Pass at Shanhaiguan at the eastern end of the Great Wall on the next day with 100,000 men. Li may not have known the true strength of the forces against him until the actual battle on May 28. Had he known that he was confronted by a much larger and more experienced force, he probably would have refused battle. The allies were also aided by a large sandstorm that morning that masked their deployment. The Sino-Manzhu forces probably numbered 50,000 Manzhus and 40,000 Chinese. Wu may have been able to raise upwards of another 80,000 men in local Chinese militia, but there is no proof that they participated in the battle. Li probably commanded something on the order of 60,000 men.

The allies turned the battle when Wu's veterans attacked the rebel left. Sheer numbers told. Li's army then fled the field. The allies broke off the pursuit after a dozen miles. Li withdrew to Beijing but had neither the supplies nor the forces to resist a siege. He had himself hastily proclaimed as emperor on June 3 and then executed Wu's father. Li stripped Beijing bare of supply animals and anything of value and then withdrew the next day, leaving behind a city in flames.

Wu hoped to establish himself as viceroy in a continuation of the Ming dynasty, but Dorgon's force was simply too powerful. Wu bowed to the inevitable, agreeing to serve the Manzhus. Dorgon gave him the assignment of hunting down Li, which Wu accomplished in 1645, executing Li.

Dorgon moved the Manzhu capital to Beijing and there established the new dynasty of the Qing (1644–1911). The Manzhus adopted most of the Ming administrative system and culture, and the new dynasty became one of the greatest in Chinese history.

References

Hsu, Immanuel C. Y. *The Rise of Modern China.* New York: Oxford University Press, 1970.

Parsons, James Bunyan. *Peasant Rebellions of the Late Ming Dynasty.* Tucson: University of Arizona Press, 1970.

Battle of Marston Moor

Date	July 2, 1644	
Location	Near Long Marston, 7 miles west of York in northern England	
Opponents (* winner)	*Parliamentarians and Scottish Covenanters	Royalists
Commander	Fernando Fairfax, second Baron of Cameron; Alexander Leslie, Earl of Levin	Prince Rupert of the Rhine; William Cavendish, Earl of Newcastle
Approx. # Troops	22,000–27,000 (8,000 cavalry and remainder infantry)	7,000 cavalry; 11,000 infantry
Importance	The largest battle of the English Civil Wars, it gives the Parliamentarian side control of northern England	

The Battle of Marston Moor on July 2, 1644, was the crucial battle of the English Civil War (1642–1646). The war that began in 1642 between King Charles I (r. 1625–1649) and Parliament was a struggle between royal absolutism and parliamentary rule. The English Civil War was actually only one of a series of vicious, bloody conflicts in the mid-17th century that included fighting involving England, Scotland, and Ireland. Religion was an important factor in all of them. In the English Civil War the Parliamentary side rejected the high church Anglicanism of Charles I, the notion of religious authority associated with the monarch, and the Catholicism (or crypto-Catholicism) of certain of the king's circle. Charles I proved to be inflexible, devoid of common sense, and ultimately untrustworthy.

In January 1642 following a confrontation with Parliament, Charles I ordered the impeachment of five of its members, but the House of Commons refused to sanction their arrest. On January 4 Charles went to Parliament with a few hundred soldiers and attempted to seize the five men, but they had already fled. Charles left London on January 10, and the House of Commons, emboldened, passed bills excluding bishops from the House of Lords and giving command of the militia to Parliament. Charles, now at York, refused to sign the bills. The king was joined at York by 32 peers and 65 members of the House of Commons. Charles also had with him the great seal, required for the legality of documents.

An impasse between king and Parliament led the latter in July to appoint a committee of public safety and charge the Earl of Essex with raising an army of 4,000 cavalry and 20,000 infantry. On August 22 Charles raised the royal standard at Nottingham, and the military phase of the English Civil War began.

The king had the support of most of the aristocracy and the regions of northern and western England as well as Wales. Parliament's strength was in the southeast, especially the city of London. With financial support from the aristocrats, Charles was able to hire mercenary troops raised for the Thirty Years' War (1618–1648) on the continent. Parliament's control of the navy was a serious handicap to the Royalists, however, for it denied the king more substantial aid from the continent.

In the Battle of Edgehill on October 23, 1642, Prince Rupert, the son of the elector palatine and Elizabeth of England (daughter of King James I), distinguished himself as a commander of cavalry. Rupert went on to become the preeminent Royalist military commander. Oliver Cromwell led a Parliamentary force known as the Ironsides, who ultimately became the best troops of the war.

A series of raids and indecisive battles followed during which the Royalists registered major gains in western England. Parliamentary naval forces were able to relieve a number of their coastal strongholds, while the king's small fleet created after the Royalist capture of Bristol in 1643 remained too small to contest the Parliamentary side for control of the sea. Control of the English capital was a major goal on both sides in the war. Charles I marched on London but turned back at Brentford in mid-November when confronted by Parliamentary forces under Essex, a major blow to the Royalist cause for it ensured Parliamentary control of the wealthiest part of England.

On September 25, 1643, Parliament passed the Solemn League and Covenant by which the religions of England, Scotland, and Ireland were to be made as uniform as possible. Religion was to be reformed "according to the word of God, and the examples of the best reformed churches." All religious and military officials were required to sign the covenant. Nearly 2,000 priests refused and lost their livelihood as a result. The Scots now agreed to make common cause with the English, and a Scottish army crossed into England. Charles enlisted Irish Catholics, a step that allegedly proved his Catholic tendencies and angered many Protestant Englishmen.

On June 14, 1644, Charles I ordered Prince Rupert to raise the Parliamentary siege of York, in northern England. Learning of the approach of the Royalist army, on June 30 the Scots and Parliamentary forces broke off siege operations and marched to Long Marston to intercept Rupert.

The battle occurred some six miles west of York during a long evening on July 2, 1644. The Royalists occupied a strong position on high ground known as Marston Moor, just north of the road between the villages of Rockwith and Long Marston. They took up position behind a ditch north of the road and running parallel to it. The Scots and Parliamentary forces were south of the road. The battle line extended the full 1.5 miles between the two villages. On both sides cavalry held the flanks, with infantry in the center.

In terms of numbers of men engaged, it was the largest battle ever to be fought on English soil. Some 18,000 Royalists (7,000 cavalry and 11,000 infantry) opposed some 22,000–27,000 Parliamentary and Scottish forces (8,000 cavalry and the remainder infantry). Both sides possessed some artillery, although the 25 pieces for the allies far outnumbered those available to the Royalists. Prince Rupert and William Cavendish, Earl of Newcastle, were the principal Royalist commanders, while Fernando Fairfax, 2nd Baron of Cameron, along with Alexander Leslie, Earl of Levin, had charge of the allied force.

Newcastle was opposed to battle. He held that the allied army would eventually dissolve and that an engagement was unnecessary. Rupert was adamant that the letter from the king, which he never showed to Newcastle, was a command to immediately engage and defeat the enemy.

There was intermittent artillery fire as the lines formed during the afternoon. At about 7:00 p.m. a thunderstorm swept the area, and some 3,000 left-flank allied cavalry under Oliver Cromwell and David Leslie charged some 4,100 cavalry on the Royalist right. Lord Byron commanded Rupert's personal force of 2,600 cavalry, which was supported by a regiment of some 1,500 additional cavalry in reserve. Rupert had also positioned musketeers among the cavalry. Byron now charged forward to meet Cromwell head-on, in the process separating his cavalry from the musketeers and masking the fire of the latter. Byron's first line and part of the second were routed.

At the same time Scottish dragoons (mounted infantry) succeeded in clearing part of the ditch of Royalist musketeers, and the allied infantry went forward and captured the Royalist cannon. On the allied right (Royalist left), a charge by Sir Thomas Fairfax's 5,000 cavalry was in trouble from the beginning against Lord Goring's smaller number of Royalist cavalry supported by musketeers. Royalist musketeers in the ditch and on that ground unsuitable for a cavalry charge broke the Parliamentary attack on that flank.

Rupert rushed with his lifeguards to meet the threat from Cromwell's horse, and only a stand by the Scottish horse under Leslie saved Cromwell from defeat. Cromwell's forces then rallied and drove Rupert and his cavalry from the field. Resisting the impulse to drive on York and plunder it, Cromwell kept his men together to turn the tide of the infantry battle in the center of the line, which had thus far gone the Royalist way. Royalist infantry under Cavendish, their ammunition exhausted, were pinned against a hedgerow and slaughtered. Following the defeat of the Royalist infantry, Goring's cavalry scattered.

In the Battle of Marston Moor the Royalists lost some 3,000 to 4,000 men killed. Another 1,500 men were captured along with all the Royalist cannon. Only about 300 men on the allied forces were killed, although many more were wounded.

Marston Moor broke Royalist cohesion and, more important, gave the Parliamentary forces control of the north of England. York surrendered on July 16, and most of northern England was overrun thereafter. Charles I continued to hold much of Wales, western England, and the southern Midlands. After the Battle of Marston Moor, Charles I rejected advice to negotiate with Parliament; he again rejected negotiations in January 1645. Charles's sense of legitimacy proved the major stumbling block. Meanwhile, Parliamentary forces were reorganized as the New Model Army with a unified command structure: Sir Thomas Fairfax as commander in chief and Oliver Cromwell in command of the cavalry.

References

Bennett, Martyn. *The Civil Wars in Britain and Ireland, 1638–1651.* London: Blackwell, 1997.

Kenyon, John. *The Civil Wars of England.* London: Weidenfeld and Nicolson, 1989.

Newman, Peter. *The Battle of Marston Moor, 1644.* Chichester, UK: Anthony Bird, 1981.

Woolrych, Austin. *Battles of the English Civil War.* London: Batsford, 1961.

Young, Peter, and Richard Holmes. *The English Civil War.* London: Eyre Methuen, 1974.

Battle of Naseby

Date	June 14, 1645	
Location	Naseby, near Northampton in central England	
Opponents (* winner)	*Parliamentarians	Royalists
Commander	Sir Thomas Fairfax	King Charles I; Prince Rupert of the Rhine
Approx. # Troops	7,500 cavalry and dragoons, 5,500 infantry	3,300 cavalry; 4,100 infantry
Importance	This sweeping victory by the Parliamentarians brings about a general Royalist collapse	

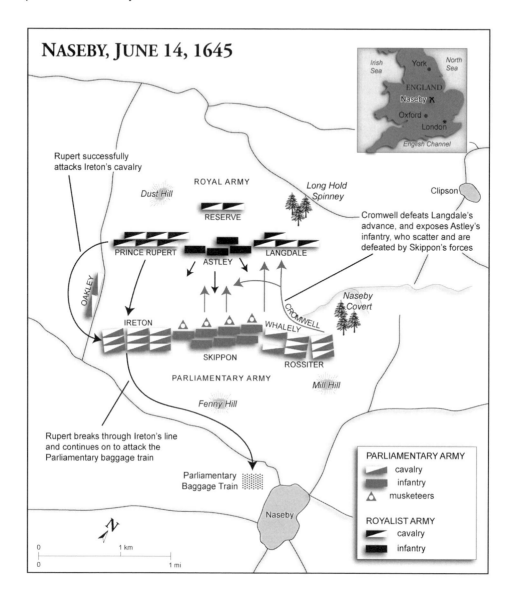

NASEBY, JUNE 14, 1645

Rupert successfully attacks Ireton's cavalry

ROYAL ARMY

Dust Hill

Long Hold Spinney

Clipson

RESERVE

Cromwell defeats Langdale's advance, and exposes Astley's infantry, who scatter and are defeated by Skippon's forces

PRINCE RUPERT

ASTLEY

LANGDALE

OAKLEY

IRETON

Naseby Covert

CROMWELL

WHALELY

SKIPPON

ROSSITER

PARLIAMENTARY ARMY

Mill Hill

Fenny Hill

Rupert breaks through Ireton's line and continues on to attack the Parliamentary baggage train

Parliamentary Baggage Train

Naseby

PARLIAMENTARY ARMY
- cavalry
- infantry
- △ musketeers

ROYALIST ARMY
- cavalry
- infantry

0   1 km
0   1 mi

Inset map: Irish Sea, York, North Sea, ENGLAND, Naseby ✗, Oxford ●, London, English Channel

The Battle of Naseby on June 14, 1645, was the last major battle of the first phase (1642–1646) of the English Civil War (1642–1646). It marked the first appearance of Parliament's New Model Army and led directly to the defeat and execution of King Charles I.

Although they were at a disadvantage when the English Civil War opened, the Parliamentary forces gradually secured the upper hand, and by 1645 Charles I was losing the war. The Royalists had been defeated at the Battle of Marston Moor (July 2, 1644) and lost northern England. This had been somewhat offset by Royalist successes in Scotland, however.

Parliament now reorganized its forces, placing them under the command of Sir Thomas Fairfax. Fairfax, aided by Oliver Cromwell, worked to instill discipline and train this force, which came to be known as the New Model Army. In June, Fairfax led the New Model Army to seek Royalist troops under Charles I. Fairfax commanded some 13,000 men, 7,500 of whom were either cavalry or dragoons (mounted infantry). Charles headed a far smaller force of perhaps 7,400 men, including 3,300 cavalry. Royalist leaders were divided about the wisdom of trying to engage the Parliamentarians, but confidence soared after a victory at Leicester on May 31, and those favoring battle had their way.

The two armies encountered one another near the village of Naseby, about 20 miles south of Leicester in Northamptonshire, on the morning of June 14. Underestimating Parliamentarian strength, the Royalists abandoned an excellent defensive position to seek out the enemy located on high ground just north of Naseby. On the Royalist side, Prince Rupert of the Rhine commanded the right wing of 1,600 cavalry and 200 musketeers. Infantry under Jacob, Lord Astley, held the center, and cavalry under Sir Marmaduke Langdale were on the Royalist left. Charles I was located with the Royalist reserve behind the center of the line with about 700 infantry and an unknown number of cavalry. The Parliamentary line consisted of 3,200 cavalry on the left under Henry Ireton and 3,500 on the right under Oliver Cromwell. Infantry held the Parliamentary center.

The battle began in midmorning with a Royalist advance. The cavalry under Prince Rupert drove back Ireton's cavalry and pursued it far from the battle, all the way to the baggage train. In the center the Royalist infantry commanded by Lord Astley initially enjoyed success but soon were hard-pressed, flanked by Cromwell's cavalry on their left and, because of the absence of Rupert's cavalry, also on their right. By the time Rupert realized his error and returned to the fray, it was too late: the Royalist center had given way. The king's reserve then fled, and with them went any hope of turning the tide.

Although the bulk of their cavalry managed to escaped, the Royalists suffered between 400 and 1,000 men killed as well as 4,500 taken prisoner, including most of the officers. The New Model Army lost only 200 men. Among the booty were important private papers written by Charles I. These became a useful propaganda tool for the Parliamentarians, for they revealed the king's plans to bring in French mercenaries and to grant religious concessions to English Catholics.

Naseby fostered a general sentiment among the Royalists that the war was indeed over. When news of the result arrived, Royalists at the fortress of Carlisle, which had resisted a Scottish siege since the previous October, immediately asked for terms. Indeed, a half dozen Royalist garrisons surrendered later in June, and a dozen more surrendered in July. Nearly two dozen others also surrendered by January 1646. By the end of 1645 Royalist forces controlled only Wales, southwestern England, and a few strongholds in the Midlands. The Parliamentary offensive continued, and finding it virtually impossible to challenge the Parliamentary forces, Charles I finally surrendered on May 5, 1646.

References

Ashley, Maurice. *The Battle of Naseby and the Fall of King Charles I.* Stroud, Gloucestershire, UK: Alan Sutton, 1992.

Kenyon, John. *The Civil Wars of England.* London: Weidenfeld and Nicolson, 1989.

Kishlansky, Mark A. *The Rise of the New Model Army.* Cambridge: Cambridge University Press, 1979.

Woolrych, Austin. *Battles of the English Civil War.* London: Batsford, 1961.

Young, Peter. *Naseby, 1645: The Campaign and the Battle.* London: Century, 1985.

Battle of Portland

Date	February 18–20, 1653	
Location	English Channel off Portland	
Opponents (* winner)	*English	Dutch
Commander	General-at-Sea Robert Blake	Admiral Maarten Harpertszoon Tromp
Approx. # Troops	80 ships	80 ships
Importance	A tactical draw but a strategic English victory, the battle effectively closes the English Channel to Dutch merchant shipping	

During the period 1652–1674 the Dutch and English fought three naval wars. The First (1652–1654), Second (1664–1667), and Third (1672–1674) Anglo-Dutch Wars resulted from maritime commercial competition between England and the United Provinces of the Netherlands. They were important not only because of the economic and political ramifications but also because they brought innovations in naval warfare. The line of battle formation came into prominence in this period, laying the foundation for the strategic and tactical doctrines inherent in modern naval warfare.

The Battle of Portland (also known as the Three Days' Battle) was an important naval engagement during the First Anglo-Dutch War. Following their defeat in the Battle of Dungeness on November 30, 1652, the English reviewed their tactics, which led to the March 1653 issuance of the first fighting instructions that called for line-ahead formations to make maximum use of the heavier broadside guns. The English also strengthened their fleet; at the beginning of 1653 they had 80 ships at Portsmouth under the joint command of generals-at-sea Robert Blake and Richard Deane. The English did not, however, have some of their largest ships available as a result of damage sustained in the Battle of Kentish Knock on September 28, 1652.

In early February 1653 Dutch admiral Maarten Harpertszoon Tromp assembled a fleet of 80 warships to escort 200 Dutch merchant ships returning to Holland. On learning that the English fleet was ready for sea Tromp hastened to pass up the English Channel, but on February 18 the English intercepted the Dutch ships. Despite the liability of his convoy, Tromp knew that his own fleet was approximately equal to that of the English, and he immediately attacked, leaving his convoy some four miles to windward and striking in three or four divisions before all the English ships were up. Admiral of the White George Monck was still five miles to leeward when the battle began.

The battle continued for three days, during which the fleets drifted to the northeast. In the running fight, some ships were captured more than once. In the first day of fighting Tromp was able to keep his convoy intact and moving up the Channel, but its presence undoubtedly hindered his conduct of the battle. Fighting resumed the next afternoon, during which the Dutch fleet, acting as a rear guard for the convoy and aided by light winds, managed to hold off the English. Dutch admiral Michiel Adrienszoon de Ruyter stymied repeated English attacks, but Tromp was running out of ammunition when darkness brought fighting to a close.

On February 20 the battle resumed near Beachy Head. The English at last penetrated the Dutch warship screen and attacked the merchantmen. Blake anchored for the night, expecting to resume the battle again on February 21, but Tromp got under way early and managed to bring the remainder of the convoy home. Still, Dutch losses in the Battle of Portland were heavy: 4 warships captured, 5 sunk, and 2 or 3 more burned. The English also captured between 30 and 50 of the merchantmen while losing only 1 or 2 ships, with 3 others disabled. The Battle of Portland was, in fact, a turning point in the war, for the Channel was now effectively closed to Dutch shipping.

References

Clowes, William Laird. *The Royal Navy: A History from the Earliest Times to the Present,* Vol. 2. London: Sampson Low, Marston, 1898.

Hainsworth, Roger, and Christine Churches. *The Anglo-Dutch Naval Wars, 1652–1674.* Phoenix Mill, Stroud, UK: Sutton, 1998.

Jones, J. R. *The Anglo-Dutch Wars of the Seventeenth Century.* New York: Longman, 1996.

Battle of the Dunes

Date	June 14, 1658	
Location	Along the English Channel near Dunkerque (Dunkirk), France	
Opponents (* winner)	*English, French	Spanish, English Jacobites
Commander	Marshal Henri de la Tour d'Auvergne, Vicomte de Turenne (French)	Don Juan of Austria; Louis de Bourbon, Prince de Condé
Approx. # Troops	9,000 cavalry, 6,000 infantry (includes 3,000 English troops)	6,000 cavalry, 8,000 infantry (includes 2,000 English Jacobites)
Importance	Brings the surrender of Dunkerque and ends all possibility of a Royalist invasion of England	

The Battle of the Dunes on June 14, 1658, saw a joint Anglo-French force defeat a Spanish army in the Netherlands, marking the decline of Spanish power and leading to peace between France and Spain. The battle also ended efforts by the claimant to the English throne, Charles II, to return to power on his own terms. In 1642 the English Civil War had begun, pitting the forces of Parliament against those of King Charles I. Following military victories by the Parliamentary forces led by Oliver Cromwell, in January 1649 Parliament voted for the execution of Charles I. His son continued the Royalist struggle against the Parliamentary forces but was defeated by Cromwell's New Model Army in the Battle of Worcester on September 3, 1651, and fled to France.

Charles II allied with Spain, long hostile to Protestant England, in an effort to help him recover his throne. He set about organizing a force in the Spanish Netherlands while also attempting to organize Royalist allies in England. Cromwell, now the dominant political and military figure in England, was kept well informed of these activities through his efficient intelligence service. He was thus able to stymie all of Charles II's attempts to secure a port in England through which he might land troops.

Relations between France and Spain meanwhile steadily deteriorated. Increased taxes and a concentration of royal power engineered by royal chief ministers cardinals Richelieu and Mazarin led to a civil war in France against the young Louis XIV. Known as the Fronde (1648–1652), it saw a leading French general and noble, Louis de Bourbon, Prince de Condé, defect to the Spaniards and Spanish troops invade France.

Mazarin was able to end the Fronde in 1653, but fighting between France and Spain continued, owing in large part to the French desire to annex the Spanish Netherlands. Condé, now leading the Spanish forces, dueled in the Spanish Netherlands during 1652–1657 with another capable general, Marshal Henri de la Tour d'Auvergne, Vicomte de Turenne, who commanded for France. Turenne refused to be drawn into battle under unfavorable circumstances, while Condé was often handicapped by Spanish suspicions regarding his loyalty. England was also at war with Spain in the New World, and in 1657 the two traditional enemies of France and England joined together against Spain. Cromwell and Mazarin concluded a treaty whereby the two nations would attack the English Channel towns of Gravelines, Dunkirk (Dunkerque), and Mardyck, with England to receive possession of Dunkirk.

In the autumn of 1657 Anglo-French forces captured the Flemish town of Mardyck, and then in May 1658 Turenne laid siege to Dunkirk,

The Battle of the Dunes, fought next to the English Channel on June 14, 1658. The French, assisted by the English, defeated the Spanish, also with an English (Jacobite) contingent. Painting by French artist Charles-Philippe Larivière (1798–1876). (Photos.com)

which was held by 3,000 Spanish troops. Turenne was joined by 3,000 English troops commanded by William Lockhart, bringing his ground strength up to about 9,000 cavalry and 12,000 infantry. The English fleet also blockaded the port.

To raise the siege of Dunkirk, Don Juan of Austria, viceroy of the Spanish Netherlands, put together at Ypres a 16,000-man relief force under himself and Condé. The force numbered 6,000 cavalry, 8,000 infantry, and 2,000 English Jacobites under Charles II's brother James, Duke of York. In early June 1658 this force advanced toward Dunkirk, and on June 13 it set up camp on the dunes northeast of the port, between the coast and pastureland inland.

Turenne took the initiative. Without waiting for the Spanish to attack him, he left some 6,000 men to maintain the siege and on the afternoon of June 13 advanced on the Spanish camp with 9,000 cavalry and 6,000 infantry. Some skirmishing occurred that evening, but the main battle occurred the next day.

Early on the morning of June 14 just before low tide, the French-English force deployed for the attack. The allies moved east in two lines with a reserve behind. Cavalry held the flanks, the left on the beach and the right in meadows south of the dunes. The allied force advanced slowly, giving the Spanish forces ample time to prepare, but this was deliberate on the part of Turenne, who had based his plans on the turn of the tide. The Spanish deployed their infantry on line, perpendicular to the shore, with the right flank on the beach and the left flank on a road and canal inland paralleling the shoreline and running to Dunkirk. Some cavalry were on the

Spanish left, but the bulk were in reserve. No Spanish cavalry were on the beach, which they feared might come under fire from the English fleet. James's contingent was on the center-right of the Spanish line, while the left contained a mix of Netherlanders, Germans, and Spanish. Don Juan commanded the Spanish right, and Condé commanded the left. Against Condé's advice, Don Juan had deployed so rapidly that he had not brought up his artillery. Turenne, on the other hand, had some of his siege artillery with him.

The battle began about 8:00 a.m., just before low tide, when the English infantry on the allied left charged the Spanish infantry. Cannon fire from the English ships supported the advance. The English boldly charged up a 150-foot dune and there broke the Spanish *tercio* (defensive square of pikemen supported by musketeers on the corners). Belatedly, Spanish reserve cavalry were sent forward and threatened the English, but they were in turn defeated by French cavalry under the Marquis Jacques de Castelneau.

In the center of the line the French infantry also advanced, while Condé's cavalry charge on the allied right (Spanish left) was nullified by the collapse of the Spanish center and right. Turenne then took full advantage of the arrival of low tide to concentrate his cavalry in an advance on the beach that enveloped the Spanish right wing.

The battle ended at noon in a complete allied victory. Turenne continued the pursuit until nightfall. Although the Spanish forces were in full retreat, one corps of 300 English Royalists held out. They surrendered on condition that they be allowed to rejoin Charles II at Ypres. From this unit Charles II later established the Royal Regiment of Guards, forerunner of the present-day Grenadier Guards. Allied losses were only about 400 men, most of them English, while the Spanish lost 1,000 dead and another 5,000 taken prisoner.

Dunkirk soon surrendered and was handed over to the English. It remained under English control until Charles II sold it to Louis XIV in 1662. On November 7, 1659, with Spain reeling and France united, the two powers concluded the Peace of the Pyrenees under which Spain ceded much of Flanders to France. Louis XIV married Maria Theresa, daughter of King Philip IV of Spain.

References

Ashley, Maurice. *Charles II: The Man and the Statesman.* New York: Praeger, 1971.

Gaunt, Peter. *Oliver Cromwell.* Oxford, UK: Blackwell, 1996.

Harris, R. W. *Clarendon and the English Revolution.* Stanford, CA: Stanford University Press, 1983.

Marichal, Paul, ed. *Mémoirs de Marsechal de Turenne.* Paris: Librairie Renouard, 1914.

Sells, A. Lytton. *The Memoirs of James II: His Campaigns as Duke of York, 1652–1660.* Bloomington: Indiana University Press, 1961.

Siege and Battle of Vienna

Date	July 14–September 12, 1683	
Location	Vienna, Austria	
Opponents (* winner)	*Austrians, Germans, Poles	Ottomans
Commander	Count Ernst Rüdiger von Starhemberg (commanding Vienna garrison); John III Sobieski, King of Poland (commanding the relief force)	Grand Vizier Ahmed Köprülü Pasha
Approx. # Troops	15,000 in the Vienna garrison; 70,000 in the relief force	As many as 150,000
Importance	Puts finis to Ottoman plans to conquer Europe and marks the beginning of the decline in Ottoman power	

The great 60-day siege of Vienna during July–September 1683 was the second effort by the Ottomans to take the capital city of the Habsburg Empire, their most powerful European rival. The siege captured the attention of all Europe as did no other event of the century, and in Catholic countries funds were raised as if for a Crusade.

While Ottoman power was not what it had been in the first siege of Vienna in 1529, Habsburg ruler and Holy Roman Emperor Leopold I was under attack from several sources. In the west King Louis XIV of France was endeavoring to add chunks of the Holy Roman Empire to his holdings. In Royal Hungary (the Habsburg portion of Hungary), Hungarians incited and financed by the French and the Ottomans rebelled. When the Habsburgs moved to put the insurgency down, the Hungarians appealed to the Ottomans for assistance. Sultan Mehmed IV responded by leading a large army up the Danube to take Vienna. Actual field command was in the hands of Grand Vizier Kara Mustafa Pasha. Mehmed IV called upon and was assisted by Transylvania, his vassal state. Louis XIV did not positively assist the Ottomans but at least declined to join the proposed Crusade against them.

With the addition of Transylvanian units, the Ottomans advanced up the Danube with perhaps 200,000 men. Ahmed detached part of his army to besiege Györ and then continued the advance toward Vienna. On July 7, 1683, the first Ottoman troops reached the gates of the city. On their approach, Emperor Leopold I and the court as well as about 60,000 inhabitants fled. Charles V, Duke of Lorraine, with an Austrian army of some 20,000 men also retired, to Linz. This left Vienna defended by a garrison of perhaps only 15,000 men commanded by Count Ernst Rüdiger von Starhemberg. The Viennese had ample time to prepare, and they demolished houses around the city walls and cleared away the debris to provide clear fields of fire for their artillery, which was both more numerous and more modern than that of the Ottomans. The Ottomans had only a few heavy pieces, sent up the Danube by barge.

On July 14 the main Ottoman force arrived at Vienna and encircled the city. Siege operations commenced on July 17. Starhemberg sought to keep the Ottomans off guard by frequent sorties, while the small imperial forces under Duke Charles tried to contain Ottoman raiding.

The vastly superior Ottoman numbers soon began to tell nonetheless. The Ottomans undertook mining operations and made a number of breaches in the city walls through which they launched assaults. The defenders contained the penetrations by throwing up makeshift fortifications, but by the beginning of September Starhemberg's force was down to about half of its original strength and running short of critical supplies.

At this point a Polish army arrived in present-day Wiener Neustadt, on the other side of a small mountain range from Vienna. The Polish army was under the personal command of King John III Sobieski, who was honoring a mutual defensive pact made in late March with Leopold I. Sobieski made the forced march of 220 miles from Warsaw in only 15 days. He now assumed command of an allied force of some 70,000 men: 30,000 Poles; 18,500 Austrian troops led by Duke Charles; 19,000 Bavarians, Swabians, and Franconians under Prince Georg Friedrich of Waldeck; and about 9,000 Saxons commanded by Elector John George III of Saxony. As the relief force approached Vienna, scouting reports spread terror among the allied troops, but Sobieski managed to keep them moving forward.

Sobieski's arrival surprised Grand Vizier Kara Mustafa, who nonetheless continued siege operations in an effort to take Vienna before battle could be joined. The Battle of Vienna began early on the morning of September 12, 1683, when at 4:00 a.m. the Ottomans attacked in an effort to interfere with the allied deployment. Fighting raged all day. The battle was decided by a surprise allied cavalry charge led by Sobieski in person from the hills near the city directly on Kara Mustafa's headquarters at about 5:00 p.m. The remainder of the Viennese garrison sallied to join in. During the fighting a cloud caused the crescent moon to fade from the sky, an omen that is said to have produced consternation among the Ottomans.

By nightfall the Ottomans had been defeated and were in full flight, although they found the time to execute thousands of Christian prisoners, including children, taken in their march against Vienna. Sobieski suspended the pursuit that night, fearing an ambush. The battle itself claimed some 2,000 killed and 2,500 wounded on the allied side. The Ottomans lost some 10,000 dead and 5,000 wounded as well as 5,000 prisoners taken along with all their cannon. Sobieski is said to have paraphrased Julius Caesar when he said, "Veni, vidi, Deus vicit" ("I came, I saw, God conquered").

Sobieski's victory was the last great military effort of the dying Kingdom of Poland. The next month Sobieski pursued the Ottomans into Hungary and inflicted a serious defeat on them before dysentery forced an end to the pursuit. The Polish contribution was not appreciated, as Sobieski noted with some bitterness. It certainly did not save Poland. Indeed, it strengthened the Habsburgs at the expense of Poland. In the late 18th century Austria took part in two partitions of Poland. The relief of Vienna in 1683 did put an end to the Ottoman dream of further European conquest.

References

Barker, Thomas M. *Double Eagle and Crescent: Vienna's Second Turkish Siege and Its Historical Setting.* Albany: State University of New York Press, 1967.

Hoskins, Janina. *Victory at Vienna: The Ottoman Siege of 1683, a Historical Essay and a Select Group of Readings.* Washington, DC: Library of Congress, 1983.

Kinross, Lord [John Patrick]. *The Ottoman Centuries: The Rise and Fall of the Turkish Empire.* New York: William Morrow, 1977.

Murphey, Rhoads. *Ottoman Warfare, 1500–1700.* New Brunswick, NJ: Rutgers University Press, 1999.

Stoye, John. *The Siege of Vienna.* New York: Holt, Rinehart, and Winston, 1965.

Battle of Blenheim

Date	August 13, 1704	
Location	Near Donauwörth in Bavaria, modern Germany	
Opponents (* winner)	*British, Austrians	French; Bavarians
Commander	John Churchill, First Earl (then Duke) of Marlborough; Prince Eugene of Savoy	Marshal Camille d'Hostun, Count de Tallard; Duke Maximilian of Bavaria
Approx. # Troops	52,000	56,000
Importance	Shatters French military prestige and reverses the tide of the war	

The Battle of Blenheim in southern Germany was an important military victory for English and Austrian forces against the French and Bavarians during the War of the Spanish Succession (1701–1714). It was also a personal triumph for John Churchill, 1st Duke of Marlborough.

Habsburg king Charles II of Spain was childless. At the behest of King Louis XIV, French diplomats worked hard to secure the inheritance for Louis's grandson, Philippe d'Anjou. On his death in November 1700, therefore, Charles left his considerable European and American possessions to Philippe on the proviso that they not be divided. European leaders had long dreaded the Spanish succession, and a partition of the inheritance might have averted a long and costly war, but Louis rejected any such arrangement. France aligned with Spain and its possessions would be a formidable power bloc.

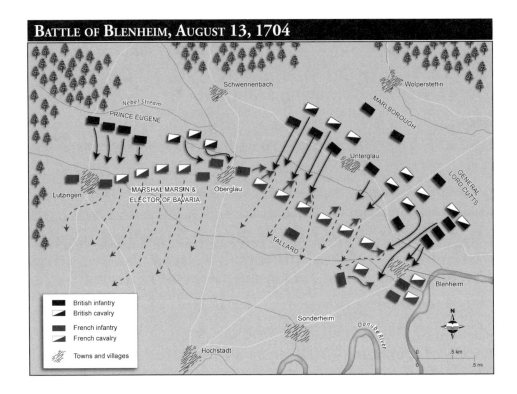

BATTLE OF BLENHEIM, AUGUST 13, 1704

Schwennenbach
Wolperstettin
MARLBOROUGH
Nebel Stream
PRINCE EUGENE
Unterglau
GENERAL LORD CUTTS
Lutzingen
MARSHAL MARSIN & ELECTOR OF BAVARIA
Oberglau
TALLARD
Blenheim
Sonderheim
Danube River
N
Hochstadt

British infantry
British cavalry
French infantry
French cavalry
Towns and villages

0   .5 km
0   .5 mi

The War of the Spanish Succession has sometimes been called "the first world war," for fighting occurred around the globe, including in North America and in India. King William III of Prussia took the lead in forming a coalition to block the French. England became a leading player in the coalition, allying itself with Austria, the Netherlands, Prussia, and most of the other German states. Fighting began in 1701. In May 1702 England declared war, and John Churchill, Earl of Marlborough, arrived in Holland as captain general of English and Dutch forces. Marlborough then waged a series of inconclusive maneuver campaigns. Hampered by Dutch caution, he nonetheless captured Venlo, Roermond, and Liège and was rewarded with the title of Duke of Marlborough.

Hoping to replace the Austrian Habsburg Leopold I as Holy Roman emperor, Duke Maximilian of Bavaria joined his country with France and Spain. Louis XIV then dispatched an army under Marshal Camille d'Hostun, Count de Tallard, to cooperate with the Bavarians in marching on Vienna. Leopold I recalled Austrian forces under Prince Eugene of Savoy from Italy to defend his capital. Marlborough meanwhile planned to drive deep into Germany, join forces with Eugene, and defeat the French and Bavarians before they could reach Vienna, thus forcing the French from Germany and forcing Bavaria from the war.

Leaving some 50,000 men to defend the Netherlands against a French army under Marshal François de Neufville, Duc du Villeroi, and without informing the Dutch government of his intentions, Marlborough struck south. Departing Holland in April with about 21,000 men (some 14,000 were English troops), he marched up the Rhine and Neckar rivers to reach Koblenz (Coblenz), Germany, in May. This was something of a military masterpiece, covering 250 miles in five weeks. Marlborough also tripled the size of his force by adding German mercenaries en route. Marlborough repeatedly feinted at an invasion west into France, forcing Villeroi to parallel his route.

Instead of proceeding up the Moselle River as the French expected, Marlborough then crossed the Rhine and made for the Danube. In a daring attack on July 2 Marlborough's troops took the fortified hill of Schellenberg, overlooking Donauwörth, and then the fortress of Donauwörth itself, allowing them to cross the Danube there.

During July and early August, French marshal Ferdinand de Marsin and Duke Maximilian of Bavaria moved forces to Augsburg to block any effort by Marlborough to advance on the Bavarian capital of Munich. The Bavarians refused battle until they could be reinforced, allowing Marlborough to devastate much of western Bavaria. At the end of July French reinforcements under Tallard reached Ulm, and shortly thereafter he joined Marsin and Maximilian south of the Danube. Meanwhile, Eugene duped Villeroi into believing that he would remain along the Rhine, but instead Eugene moved with about 20,000 men to link up with Marlborough. Villeroi decided to remain in the vicinity of Strasbourg in order to protect against a possible allied invasion of Alsace.

On August 10 the Bavarian-French forces crossed the Danube. Tallard, who commanded the joint force, planned to attack Eugene and force him back to the north. On learning of this Eugene sent a message to Marlborough urging that they join forces, which occurred on August 12.

At 2:00 a.m. on August 13 Marlborough and Eugene led their combined force of some 52,000 men and 60 guns some five miles from Donauwörth to the southeast to attack some 56,000 unprepared French and Bavarian forces (about equally divided) with 90 guns. Prince Eugene had command of the allied right that would face the Bavarians, while Marlborough commanded the allied left against the French. Marlborough had the larger force and was to make the major effort, while Eugene fixed the Bavarians (who outnumbered his own force 3 to 2) in place with an aggressive holding attack. The French and Bavarian forces were camped just across the Nebel River, a little tributary stream of the Danube. Tallard had not imagined that the allies might attack him.

Marlborough's columns, traveling over easy ground, arrived first, and at about 7:00 a.m. they opened artillery fire on the surprised French and Bavarians. The delay in Eugene's arrival allowed the French and Bavarians time to deploy. Tallard placed the bulk of his infantry on his flanks. The extreme right flank of the French infantry was at the village of Blenheim, on the banks of the Danube. The wide center of the allied French-Bavarian line was on a ridge overlooking the Nebel and was held mostly by supported French and Bavarian cavalry. It extended northwest about two miles to the village of Oberglau, while Marsin's Bavarians held the left flank of the line extending to the north.

Eugene's troops arrived at about noon, and at 12:30 p.m. they and Marlborough's men attacked simultaneously. Marlborough sent 10,000 infantry forward across the Nebel against Blenheim while Eugene attacked at Oberglau and northwest. The French repulsed the attack on Blenheim with heavy losses. Tallard then committed his reserves to the threatened flanks, enabling them to turn back a second attack by Marlborough on Blenheim, again with heavy losses for the attackers.

With 11,000 French now relatively isolated on the flank at Blenheim, Marlborough made his major effort in the center with his remaining infantry and cavalry. Crossing the Nebel, these forces came under a French cavalry attack and repulsed it. A second French attack by cavalry accompanied by infantry and artillery might have turned the tide, but Tallard failed to order it. Marlborough was also able to repulse a French cavalry attack against the right flank of his advancing troops, thanks to the timely intervention of Eugene's cavalry.

Marlborough's forces in the center of the line then reformed, and at 4:30 p.m. Marlborough ordered them forward. At 5:30 p.m. Marlborough's cavalry broke through the center of the French line, causing the Bavarian right to withdraw to the north on the remainder of the Bavarian army. Marlborough's infantry poured into the gap and, swinging left, cut off the French at Blenheim and pursued fleeing French troops, hundreds of whom drowned trying to cross the Danube. Tallard and two of his generals were among the many taken prisoner. After several attempts to break free failed, the French at Blenheim also surrendered. The unbeaten Bavarians, however, were able to retreat in good order from their numerically inferior foe.

The Battle of Blenheim resulted in allied losses of 4,500 killed and 7,500 wounded, while the French and Bavarians sustained 18,000 killed, wounded, or drowned and 13,000 taken prisoner. It was a superb example of seamless cooperation to achieve victory and a personal triumph for Marlborough, demonstrating his ability to both take risks and adjust to changing battlefield conditions. The battle shattered French prestige and reversed the military balance in the war. It cemented the Anglo-British-Austrian alliance against France, saved Vienna from attack, and removed Bavaria from the war. Duke Maximilian was forced to flee his country, which Austria then annexed.

References

Chandler, David G. *Marlborough as Military Commander.* London: Batsford, 1973.

Churchill, Winston S. *Marlborough: His Life and Times,* Vol. 2. London: Harrap, 1934.

Green, David. *Blenheim.* New York: Scribner, 1974.

Jones, J. R. *Marlborough.* New York: Cambridge University Press, 1993.

Verney, Peter. *The Battle of Blenheim.* London: Batsford, 1976.

Battle of Ramillies

Date	May 23, 1706	
Location	Ramillies, north of Namur in the Spanish Netherlands (today Belgium)	
Opponents (* winner)	*British, Dutch, Danes	French
Commander	John Churchill, First Duke of Marlborough	Marshal François de Neufville, Duc de Villeroi
Approx. # Troops	62,000	60,000
Importance	Allows the allies to overrun much of the Spanish Netherlands	

The Battle of Ramillies was an important allied victory against the French during the War of the Spanish Succession (1701–1714) and a personal triumph for the principal allied general, John Churchill, First Duke of Marlborough. Following the splendid allied victory at Blenheim in August 1704, a stalemate developed in the Spanish Netherlands (present-day Belgium), where Marlborough saw his desire for offensive operations frustrated by caution on the part of the Dutch. Operations along the Rhine and in northern Italy were inconclusive. This situation prevailed throughout 1705.

In May 1706 French marshal François de Neufville, Duc de Villeroi, believing that Marlborough intended to seize Namur in the province of Brabant in the Spanish Netherlands, moved there with about 60,000 men. Villeroi's army was intercepted north of Namur at Ramillies by Marlborough's allied force of about 62,000 British, Dutch, and Danish troops. The French took up position on high ground and partially entrenched, their center on Ramillies. The French position, however, was dangerously overextended.

The battle occurred on May 23, 1706. Marlborough feinted an attack on the French left. To meet this threat, Villeroi shifted his reserves and pulled some units from his right wing, whereupon Marlborough launched his main attack on that weakened sector. Although the French soldiers on the right flank fought well, the men were simply outnumbered and overwhelmed.

Sensing that the entire French line was near collapse, Marlborough ordered a general advance, aided by the aggressive action of the Danish cavalry. The French fled in disorder. Marlborough ordered a vigorous pursuit, and indeed his forces inflicted most of the casualties in this phase of the battle. The pursuit ended some 20 miles from Louvain. Total French casualties amounted to some 13,000 killed or wounded and 6,000 captured. Allied losses were only 1,066 dead and 3,633 wounded.

The Battle of Ramillies had significant consequences, allowing the allied forces to overrun the Spanish Netherlands. During June–October, Marlborough took a dozen important fortresses in the Netherlands and northeastern France, including Antwerp, Dunkirk (Dunkerque), Menin, Dendermonde, and Ath. The allies also captured an additional 14,000 prisoners. In August, King Louis XIV ordered Marshal Louis Josef, Duc de Vendôme, north from Italy to replace Villeroi and also put out tentative peace feelers.

References

Chandler, David G. *Marlborough as Military Commander.* London: Batsford, 1973.

Churchill, Winston S. *Marlborough: His Life and Times,* Vol. 2. London: Harrap, 1934.

Hugill, J. A. C. *No Peace without Spain.* Oxford, UK: Kensal, 1991.

Jones, J. R. *Marlborough.* New York: Cambridge University Press, 1993.

Battle of Poltava

Date	July 8, 1709	
Location	Poltava in eastern Ukraine	
Opponents (* winner)	*Russians	Swedes
Commander	Peter I, Tsar of Russia	Charles XII, King of Sweden
Approx. # Troops	40,000	20,000
Importance	Marks the turning point in the Great Northern War, the end of Sweden as a major military power, and the rise of Russia	

The Battle of Poltava on July 8, 1709 (N.S.; June 27, O.S.; June 28 by the transitional Swedish calendar) marked the end of Sweden as a major military power and the rise of Russia. In the 18th century small states could play a major role in European politics if they properly mobilized their resources. Field armies in this period were small—on the average only about 40,000 men—and a force of this size was within the reach of a small power. Sweden and Prussia are prime examples of this fact. Under its king, military innovator, and great captain Gustavus Adolphus, Sweden played a major role in the Thirty Years' War (1618–1648). Although Gustavus was killed in battle in 1632, at the peace Sweden secured western Pomerania and the former bishoprics of Bremen and Verden on the Baltic Sea.

A series of confused wars followed in which the rulers of Poland and Sweden each claimed the kingdom of the other, but Sweden went on to control most of the Baltic region. The final Swedish effort came under King Charles XII. Known as the "Alexander of the North" or the "Madman of the North," he became king in 1697, at age 15, on the death of his father. Russia, Poland, and Denmark then formed the Northern Union, an alliance that sought to take advantage of Charles's inexperience and end Sweden's domination of the southern Baltic.

Not waiting to be attacked, Charles invaded the weakest power arrayed against him: Denmark. This began the Great Northern War (1700–1721). After forcing the

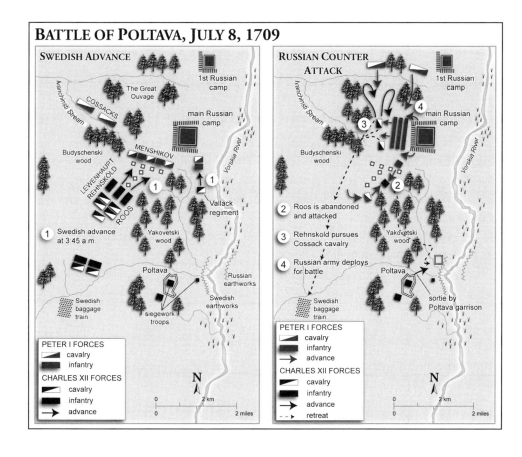

BATTLE OF POLTAVA, JULY 8, 1709

Danes to conclude peace in August, Charles XII turned his attention to Russia. He landed in Livonia with only 8,000 men to relieve the Russian siege of Riga but then learned that a force of 40,000 Russians was besieging Narva. Charles came on the Russians unawares at Narva in a snowstorm on November 30, 1700, and utterly defeated them. The Russians suffered 10,000 men killed or wounded—more than the strength of Charles's entire army—and the remainder were scattered. Russian czar Peter I thus learned a hard lesson about the need to modernize his military. Fortunately for Peter, Charles spent the next eight years campaigning in Poland, allowing Peter time to bring in Western military experts and reform his army.

In 1706 Charles managed to place his own candidate on the throne of Poland and forced that country to break its alliance with Russia. Rejecting peace overtures from Peter, Charles departed Saxony on August 22, 1707, and marched east. He entered Polish territory in mid-September. The Swedes waited for the Vistula River to freeze and crossed it on January 1, 1708. Charles invaded Russia from Poland with a well-equipped force of between 36,000 and 44,000 men, almost equally divided between infantry and cavalry. He hoped to ultimately capture Moscow. Charles secured Grodno at the end of January after Peter abandoned it but then halted near Minsk to await spring. The Swedish army then crossed the Berezina River at the end of June and defeated a larger Russian army at Holowczyn (Golovchin) on July 14. The Swedes reached the Dnieper River on July 19.

Peter had adopted scorched-earth tactics that denied the Swedes needed supplies. The Russians also attacked the increasingly long Swedish lines of communication. Charles therefore adopted a southern strategy, turning south and allying himself with the Cossacks of Ukraine under Hetman Ivan Mazeppa. Charles would then drive on Moscow from that direction. This plan collapsed when Mazeppa was ousted from power in October, and a Swedish relief corps of 11,000 men marching from Livonia under General Adam Loewenhaupt met defeat at Lesnaya (present-day Lyasnaya in Belarus) during October 9–10, 1708. Only 6,000 men of this force, including the wounded, were ultimately able to join Charles; 2,000 supply wagons and all their cannon had been lost.

Charles managed, with great difficulty, to hold his army together during the winter (November 1708–April 1709), but his army was reduced to only 20,000 men and 34 guns. With the spring thaw Charles advanced on Voronezh but stopped to besiege Poltava on the Vorskla River in Ukraine. The siege began on May 2. Peter put down a Cossack uprising along the Dnieper, convinced the leaders of the Ottoman Empire not to intervene, and ordered the Crimean Cossacks not to assist the Swedes. He then brought up a large force to relieve Poltava.

The fortress of Poltava proved more difficult to take than Charles had anticipated, and the Swedes were low on both food and gunpowder. Adding to Swedish difficulties, Charles was wounded in the foot and had to be carried about in a litter. Aware of the approach of Peter's relief force of 80,000 men and more than 100 guns, Charles should have ended the siege and withdrawn east into Poland. Instead, demonstrating both his aggressive nature and his disdain for the Russian soldier, he decided to stand and fight. Learning of Charles's wound, Peter resolved not to refuse battle. Indeed, to provoke Charles to attack, Peter ordered a fortified Russian camp constructed several miles north of Poltava. Its eastern flank rested on the Vorskla, and its southern flank was on a marsh and small stream.

Charles was equally ready for battle, and he attacked early on the morning of July 8, 1709. The initial Swedish assault was successful, but there was little coordination between the major elements of the army, and Peter was able to rally his forces to meet the final Swedish attack by 7,000 men, carried out against frightful odds. The Russians had 40,000 fresh troops and, with 102 guns, a crushing superiority in artillery. (Most of Charles's guns were still at Poltava.) The czar took personal command of an infantry division, riding among his men and shouting encouragement. Charles's wound prevented him from similarly rallying his men. The Swedes were cut down in large numbers by the Russian guns.

The battle was over by noon. It claimed some 3,000 Swedish dead and a like number captured. Russian losses were given as 1,345 killed and 3,290 wounded. Charles, removed from his litter, fled by horse with Ukrainian Cossack leader Ivan

Mazeppa and about 1,500 Cossacks and Swedes into Ottoman Moldavia. Loewen-haupt surrendered the remaining 12,000 Swedes at Perevolchina on July 30. Total Swedish losses were 9,234 killed or wounded and 18,794 taken prisoner.

The Battle of Poltava marked the turning point in the Great Northern War. Its immediate impact was to revive the coalition of powers against Sweden. Charles XII found refuge at Bendery in Ottoman Moldavia, and two years later he induced Turkey to enter the war against Russia. He returned to Sweden in 1714 and made a last effort against his many enemies but was killed in 1718. Three years later the Treaty of Nystad ended the Great Northern War and gave Russia control of the Baltic shore. It also granted Peter the warm water ports and "windows on the west" that he so desperately sought.

References

Anderson, M. S. *Peter the Great.* New York: Longman, 1996.

Cracroft, James E., ed. *Peter the Great Transforms Russia,* Lexington, MA: D. C. Heath, 1991.

Konstam, Angus. *Poltava 1709: Russia Comes of Age.* New York: Praeger, 2005.

Battle of Belgrade

Date	August 16, 1717	
Location	Belgrade, Serbia	
Opponents (* winner)	*Austrian Habsburgs	Ottomans
Commander	Prince Eugene of Savoy	Grand Vizier Damad Ali
Approx. # Troops	60,000	150,000
Importance	Eugene retakes Temesvár (Timişoara), the final Ottoman stronghold in Hungary; the Ottoman Empire is now on the defensive	

The Austrian defeat of the Ottomans in the Battle of Belgrade on August 16, 1717, led to the Ottoman cession of their portion of Hungary and much of Serbia. Otto-man military fortunes, in decline following the Ottoman rebuff before Vienna in 1683, revived in 1712 when the Ottomans defeated Russian czar Peter the Great's army on the Pruth River. With the large force mobilized against Russia still avail-able, Grand Vizier Damad Ali decided to wage war against Venice, a long-standing Ottoman enemy, that was then in decline and seemingly without allies.

In 1714 the Ottomans retook the Morea (southernmost Greece) from the Vene-tians; many Greeks welcomed the Ottomans as liberators, which made the task easier. Damad Ali miscalculated the reaction of Holy Roman Emperor Charles VI, however. Charles signed a defensive alliance with Venice to oppose the Ottomans. The Ottoman army then headed north, crossing the Sava River and moving up the south bank of the Danube to Peterwardein (present-day Novi Sad). The Habsburg leadership, awed by the size of the Ottoman force and Damad Ali's success in the Morea, was divided on the course to follow.

A number of Habsburg generals opposed a pitched battle and instead advocated a war of attrition. The brilliant Habsburg general Prince Eugene of Savoy carried the day, however. He respected the Ottoman soldiers for their bravery in assault but also recognized their weaknesses: antiquated weaponry, an inability to adjust to unforeseen tactics by the opposing side, and a tendency to panic in a reverse. Eugene urged an immediate offensive. The Austrians therefore marched to Peterwardein.

Damad Ali arrived there with 150,000 men to find Eugene with 60,000 Austrians drawn up to meet him. The battle occurred on August 5, 1716. The Janissaries (the Ottoman elite force) gained an immediate advantage in an attack on the Habsburg infantry in the center of the line. Eugene countered from the flanks, breaking the Ottoman formation with a heavy cavalry charge. Damad Ali galloped forward on horseback to try to rally his fleeing troops, but he was struck in the forehead by a bullet and mortally wounded. The Ottomans reportedly lost 6,000 men killed and a large number of wounded. The Austrians also secured all 140 Ottoman artillery pieces.

Following up his victory at Peterwardein, in August Eugene laid siege to Temesvár (Timişoara), the last remaining Ottoman stronghold in Hungary. The Ottomans had controlled it since the days of Suleiman the Magnificent. Temesvár surrendered after only five weeks. This was the prelude to the siege of Belgrade the next year, which Eugene undertook with some 70,000 men.

Held by some 30,000 soldiers, Belgrade was the strongest Ottoman post in the Balkans. As Eugene prepared his forces for an assault on Belgrade, an Ottoman army estimated at 200,000 men under the Grand Vizier Khahil Pasha arrived on the scene. Eugene was outnumbered more than 3 to 1, and his position seemed critical. Ottoman overconfidence, however, and their failure to launch an immediate attack worked to his advantage.

On August 16, 1717, while elements of his forces repelled a sortie by the Belgrade garrison, Eugene took the remainder and, in a daring move that caught the Ottomans by surprise, stormed their main lines. Eugene was wounded in the attack (his 13th and last battle wound) but remained on the field. The Austrians won through the boldness of his assault and the superb discipline of their infantry, which advanced with colors flying and drums beating despite Ottoman artillery fire. Holding their fire until they were but a short distance from the Ottoman lines, the Austrians launched a bayonet charge that broke up the Janissaries and produced victory. Ottoman casualties were estimated at 20,000 men, while the Austrians suffered only 2,000 casualties. Five days later, on August 21, Belgrade surrendered to the Austrians.

The Battle of Belgrade was a watershed. Following the Treaty of Kalowitz of 1699, the Ottomans were no longer a threat in terms of conquering the West. After the Battle of Belgrade they were firmly on the defensive, no longer expanding in Europe but merely seeking to retain conquered territory.

Over the next year Eugene and other Habsburg commanders continued offensive action, driving the Ottomans from much of Serbia, Wallachia, and the Banat. Eugene was reportedly preparing a campaign against Constantinople when the Ottomans sued for peace. On July 21, 1718, the two sides agreed to terms at the small village of Passarowitz, in Serbia. Austria gained Temesvár, the Banat, and Vojvodina, thus completing the liberation of Hungarian territory from Ottoman control begun in the Treaty of Karlowitz of 1699. Austria also secured Belgrade, most of Serbia, and a narrow strip of northern Bosnia south of the Sava River. The treaty made Austria a major Balkan power. Venice was forced to give up the entire Morea, retaining only Corfu and the Ionian Islands, and received some compensation in Albania and Dalmatia. However, the treaty marked the end of Venice as a power. Unfortunately for Austria, in renewed war with the Ottoman Empire during 1737–1739 most of the gains secured at Passarowitz were lost.

References

Henderson, Nicholas. *Prince Eugene of Savoy.* New York: Praeger, 1965.

Kinross, Lord [John Patrick]. *The Ottoman Centuries: The Rise and Fall of the Turkish Empire.* New York: William Morrow, 1977.

McKay, Derek. *Prince Eugene of Savoy.* London: Thames and Hudson, 1977.

Battle of Culloden

Date	April 16, 1746	
Location	Culloden Moor, 6 miles east of Inverness, Scotland	
Opponents (* winner)	*English, German mercenaries	Jacobite Scots, some French
Commander	William Augustus, Duke of Cumberland	Charles Edward Stuart; Lord George Murray
Approx. # Troops	5,000 English regulars and German mercenaries, and 4,000 Scottish loyalists	5,000 Highland Scots
Importance	The English ravage much of Scotland; Charles escapes to France but any hopes of reestablishing the Stuart dynasty are ended	

The Battle of Culloden Moor, six miles east of Inverness, Scotland, on April 16, 1746, brought to an end the last important English dynastic struggle and resulted in the devastation of much of Scotland by British government forces.

In 1688 Catholic king James II of England was ousted in the Glorious Revolution and replaced by his Protestant daughter Mary and her husband William of Orange, stadtholder of Holland. James fled to France, where he was recognized as king of England by French king Louis XIV. James died in 1701, and James Francis

Edward—usually known as James Edward or, to Jacobites, as James III—emerged as a pretender to the throne. He has gone down in English history as "The Old Pretender." Mary II had died in 1694, followed by her husband William III in 1702. The new English ruler was Mary's younger sister Anne (r. 1702–1714), the last Stuart monarch of England. The Union of England and Scotland was proclaimed during Anne's reign (1707), establishing the Kingdom of Great Britain.

Many Scots were unhappy with this arrangement, and in March 1708 James Edward landed in Scotland to lead a rebellion. Disappointed both by the lack of support among the Scots and the failure of the French to dispatch an expeditionary force (a French fleet did reach the Firth of Forth before it was scattered in a storm), James Edward returned to France. In 1714 Anne died without issue. Under provisions of the Act of Settlement of 1701, George, elector of Hanover, succeeded as ruler of Great Britain and Ireland.

During September 1715–February 1716 a Jacobite revolt occurred in Scotland. Known as "The Fifteen" (for 1715), it was led by John Erskine, Earl of Mar. Raising an army of some 4,000 men, he fought an inconclusive battle at Sheriffmuir on November 13 against loyal troops under John Campbell, Duke of Argyll. Meanwhile, other English forces under Major General Sir Charles Wills retook the town of Preston that had been seized by other rebels. This marked the end of the Jacobite uprising in England but not the end of the Scottish uprising.

The pretender James Edward sailed from Dunkirk (Dunkerque) and arrived at Peterhead in Scotland on December 22, just as the English were completing the task of crushing the rebellion. He started south but encountered an English force moving north and retreated to Montrose, where the rebellious Highlanders dispersed. James Edward returned to France on February 5, 1716. He died in 1766 and was followed as Jacobite pretender by his son Charles Edward Stuart, known as "The Young Pretender" or "Bonnie Prince Charlie."

Well before his father's death and against the recommendations of many of his advisers, the impetuous and imperious Charles Edward led a new rebellion in Scotland known as "The Forty-Five" (for 1745). Nearly alone, Charles arrived in the Hebrides Islands on August 4, 1745. During August and September he raised an army of some 2,000 men from the Highland clans. Commanded by Lord George Murray, the rebels marched on Edinburgh. On September 17 they took the Scottish capital, although General Joshua Guest and English troops held out in Edinburgh Castle.

On September 20 at Prestonpans, Murray and Charles defeated a British army of 3,000 men commanded by General Sir John Cope. Against the recommendations of many of his advisers, including Murray, in November Charles led his army, now grown to about 5,000 men, in an invasion of England. Charles hoped for an uprising by Stuart supporters there and for direct military assistance from France, but he was disappointed on both counts.

The rebels enjoyed some initial success, taking both Carlisle and Manchester. They reached Derby on December 4. Learning that two strong British armies were advancing against him and with a number of his supporters having deserted, however, two days later Murray extracted his forces and withdrew northward, closely pursued by forces under British commander William Augustus, Duke of Cumberland, the younger brother of England's King George II. With bad weather inhibiting the British pursuit, during January–February 1746 Charles laid siege to the city of Stirling. On January 17, 1746, in the Battle of Falkirk, Charles and Murray defeated a British army under General Henry Hawley that had previously retaken Edinburgh and then was attempting to raise the siege of Stirling.

Following careful preparations during the winter and spring months, on April 8, 1746, Cumberland, with a well-trained force of some 5,000 English regulars, German mercenaries, and 4,000 Scottish loyalists, advanced from Aberdeen on Inverness. There Charles had a force of some 5,000 men, almost all of them Highlanders but including some French. Charles and Murray hoped to surprise the English with a night march but found Cumberland and his army drawn up in formation and ready for battle at dawn on April 16 on Culloden Moor.

The rebels were at great disadvantage not only in terms of numbers of men but also in firepower, which decided the battle. The Scots were armed primarily with broadswords and shields, while the British were equipped with muskets. Each side had about a dozen cannon, but the Scottish artillerymen were poorly trained and possessed almost no powder and shot. The English had well-trained gunners and adequate quantities of both powder and shot.

The battle was a rout. It began at about 1:00 p.m. with the Scots firing what little shot they had at about 500 yards and to no effect. The British replied in kind, advancing their 3-pounders through gaps in the infantry. In contrast to those of the Scots, the British guns had significant effect, especially when they switched to grapeshot, against the standing Scots.

The Scots knew only the reckless charge accompanied by piercing battle cries, but by the time their first attack was launched they had already faced an hour of British cannonading. The infantry clash began with an unordered charge by the rebel center and right flank. Cumberland had his men drawn up in two ranks, and although the Scots pushed back the first rank, the second held firm and forced the attackers to withdraw. The rebels mounted three separate charges; all were repulsed by the well-disciplined English infantry. Since the Highlanders carried their sword in their right hand and their shield in their left hand, Cumberland had instructed his infantrymen to bayonet the Highlanders to their right instead of to their front, thus attacking the exposed side. After their third charge, the Highlanders broke and fled. Charles, urged by one of his advisers to charge with his men and "die like a king," refused. He took flight with the remnants of his force.

The infantry battle lasted only 40 minutes. The Highlanders lost about 1,250 men killed, 1,000 wounded, and 585 taken prisoner. The government side lost only 52 killed and 259 wounded. Cumberland ordered most of the prisoners summarily executed, for which he earned the sobriquet "The Butcher of Culloden." Over the next months Cumberland and his men hunted down fugitives of the battle, executing any they could find.

They also exacted a terrible revenge on Scotland. The English executed most of the leaders who had taken part in the rebellion and ravaged the land. They also carried out a kind of cultural warfare in Scotland against the Highland clans, making it a capital offense to speak Gaelic, wear tartans, or play bagpipes. Such policies created a long-standing enmity toward the English. Charles remained in hiding for five months until he escaped to France, disguised as a lady's maid, on September 20. Any realistic hope of reestablishing the Stuart dynasty was at an end.

References

Black, Jeremy. *Culloden and the '45.* New York: St. Martin's, 1990.

Preble, John. *Culloden.* New York: Atheneum, 1962.

Speck, W. A. *The Butcher: The Duke of Cumberland and the Suppression of the 45.* Oxford, UK: Blackwell, 1981.

Battle of Rossbach

Date	November 5, 1757	
Location	Rossbach, west of Leipzig in Saxony	
Opponents (* winner)	*Prussians	French, Austrians
Commander	Frederick II, King of Prussia	Charles de Rohan, Prince de Soubise (French forces); Prince Joseph Friedrich von Sachsen-Hildburghausen (Austrian/Imperial troops)
Approx. # Troops	22,000	41,000
Importance	A major embarrassment for the French, it ends the immediate threat to Prussia from the west and enables Frederick to shift his resources and meet the major Habsburg armies advancing from the south	

The Battle of Rossbach on November 5, 1757, was a brilliant victory for King Frederick II (Frederick the Great) and the Prussian Army over a combined French-Austrian force commanded by Charles de Rohan, Prince de Soubise, and Austrian-Imperial (Holy Roman Empire) forces under Prince Joseph Friedrich von Sachsen-Hildburghausen. In 1740 on Maria Theresa's accession to the Habsburg throne, Frederick had invaded Silesia and seized that rich province from Austria. This nearly doubled his population and also secured rich natural resources and industry. It also precipitated the War of the Austrian Succession (1740–1748) and brought in other major powers. France aided Prussia against its own traditional enemy of

Austria, and Britain sided with Austria. Despite Maria Theresa's best efforts, the war ended in 1748 with Prussia firmly in control of Silesia.

An uneasy peace followed. At the urging of Maria Theresa, Austrian foreign minister Count Wenzel Kaunitz pulled off the improbable. In the First Treaty of Versailles (May 1756) he achieved the "Diplomatic Revolution of the Eighteenth Century." France agreed to switch sides against its former ally of Prussia and join Austria. The coalition of powers that Kaunitz formed against Prussia ultimately included France, Russia, Sweden, and Saxony and was probably the most powerful of the 18th century. To maintain the balance of power on the continent, however, England now supported Prussia.

The ensuing struggle, known to history as the Third Silesian War (1756–1763) and that was part of the Seven

King Frederick II (the Great), victor in the Battle of Rossbach, was one of the most influential rulers in German history. He firmly established Prussia as one of the great powers of Europe. An enlightened despot, Frederick was also one of history's great captains and major military innovators. (Library of Congress)

Years' War of the same dates, ranks with the War of the Spanish Succession (1701–1714) as one of the greatest in Europe to that point. It was also fought all over the world, including North America, and might justifiably be called a world war. While it was the British who triumphed in the larger conflict, Prussia emerged from the war as a new European power. Ultimately Frederick II fielded an army of 200,000 men, although a third to a half of it was pressed men or mercenaries. Frederick accompanied his army in the field, conducting brilliant campaigns based on swift movement and surprise attacks. He was able to do this in part because his forces were operating on interior lines against allied forces who were often working at cross purposes.

Even with Silesia, Prussia had a population of only 6 million people. Any one of Prussia's three major enemies had 20 million or more. Prussia did have the great advantage of the best-trained and best-equipped army in Europe, although it was hardly the largest. Frederick's only hope of survival for his kingdom was to defeat his enemies piecemeal before they could concentrate against him. His best course of action was to strike through Saxony at Austria before it could fully mobilize against him. Whereas the War of the Austrian Succession was clearly an act of Prussian aggression, from the Prussian point of view the new war was justifiable from the standpoint of self-defense.

Frederick accordingly invaded Saxony on August 29, 1756, without declaration of war. He quickly occupied Dresden, drafted the Saxon forces into his own army, and imposed heavy financial demands on Saxony. It was a practice he would continue throughout the war.

Having secured Saxony, Frederick moved south to meet a Habsburg army of 50,000 men commanded by Marshal Maximilian Ulysses von Browne. In the Battle of Lobositz (Lovosice) on October 1, 1756, Frederick, with an equal force, defeated the Austrians; each side sustained about 3,000 casualties. Frederick then invaded Bohemia and on May 6, 1757, defeated the Austrians again in the Battle of Prague (Praha). Casualties this time were heavy: 13,400 Austrians and 14,300 Prussians.

Meanwhile, in the Second Treaty of Versailles of May 1757 France agreed to support Austria's effort to regain Silesia. King Louis XV promised to field an army of 105,000 men in the German states as well as finance 10,000 German mercenaries and provide Austria an annual subsidy of 12 million florins. In return France would receive the Austrian Netherlands (present-day Belgium), but this depended on Austria securing Silesia. France thus committed itself to a large-scale war with the promise of no gain whatsoever if Austria was not successful with Silesia.

Russia joined the coalition, as did most of the German states and Sweden, but Frederick now showed the qualities of military genius that would earn him the title "Frederick the Great."

A Russian army invaded East Prussia in August 1757, and on October 16 Russian forces briefly occupied and plundered Frederick's capital of Berlin. The allies operated cautiously, planning to draw the noose around Frederick and then pull it tight without risking separate military encounters.

As allied armies moved against Prussia from all directions, Frederick detached a small force for the relief of his capital while he accompanied an army into central Germany to deal with a combined Franco-Austrian force advancing east under Soubise and Saxe-Hildburghausen. Frederick commanded some 22,000 men, while the French and Austrians had perhaps 66,000. Frederick sought to trick his enemies into attacking on ground that would favor him. The two armies came together northeast of the village of Rossbach, west of Leipzig.

The battle occurred on November 5, 1757. The Franco-Austrian forces held high ground facing east. Soubise decided to envelop the Prussian left flank and sent three columns with some 41,000 men south to that end. Detecting this maneuver, Frederick feigned a withdrawal east while actually slipping the bulk of his army farther to his left, a move that was concealed from the allies by a line of hills. The fast-marching Prussian infantry were much better trained and more mobile than that of the allies. At the same time, Frederick sent 31 squadrons of Prussian cavalry under General Friedrich Wilhelm von Seydlitz wide to the east.

When the advancing allied columns swung north, they encountered heavy Prussian artillery fire and the repositioned Prussian infantry. Seydlitz's cavalry smashed into the right flank of the surprised allied infantry. In echelon (overlapping succession) formation, the Prussian infantry drove into the allied columns. Unable to re-form, the allied force was routed in less than an hour and a half. The Prussians suf-fered 169 killed and 379 wounded (including Seydlitz), while allied casualties came to some 10,000, half of them taken prisoner. The surviving allied forces joined in retreat the remaining 25,000-plus troops who had not been engaged in the battle.

Frederick II's victory was a tremendous boost to his cause and an embarrass-ment to the French. The Prussian victory at Rossbach removed the immediate threat to Prussia from the west. This enabled Frederick to quickly shift his re-sources and meet the major Habsburg armies advancing from the south. These forces came together one month later in the Battle of Leuthen.

References

Duffy, Christopher. *The Military Experience in the Age of Reason.* New York: Atheneum, 1988.

———. *The Military Life of Frederick the Great.* New York: Atheneum, 1986.

Reddaway, W. F. *Frederick the Great and the Rise of Prussia.* New York: Greenwood, 1969.

Ritter, Gerhard. *Frederick the Great: A Historical Profile.* Berkeley: University of Califor-nia Press, 1968.

Battle of Leuthen

Date	December 5, 1757	
Location	Leuthen in Prussian Silesia (today Poland)	
Opponents (* winner)	*Prussians	*Austrians
Commander	Frederick II, King of Prussia	Prince Charles Alexander of Lorraine
Approx. # Troops	33,000	65,000
Importance	Frederick's military masterpiece, it shatters the Austrian army	

The Battle of Leuthen, fought between the Prussians and Austrians on December 5, 1757, was one of the key battles of the Seven Years' War (1756–1763). In 1756 Austria, France, Russia, Sweden, and Saxony joined together against Prussia. King Frederick II of Prussia, not wishing to allow his enemies time to concentrate against him, invaded Saxony in late August 1756 and initiated the Third Silesian War (1756–1763), which was the catalyst for and a major part of the Seven Years' War.

After overrunning Saxony, Frederick next campaigned in Bohemia, defeating the Austrians in the May 6, 1757, Battle of Prague (Praha). Then, with large French forces having invaded his British ally's territory of Hanover, Frederick moved west. On November 5, 1757, in the Battle of Rossbach he defeated a combined French-Austrian force and secured his western flank for the time being.

Frederick immediately moved his army east to Silesia, where a strong Austrian force under Prince Charles Alexander of Lorraine had taken Schweidnitz and was moving on the Silesian capital of Breslau (the present-day Polish city of Wrocław in Lower Silesia). En route Frederick learned of the fall of Breslau (November 22). He drove his men forward, covering 170 miles in 12 days and joining up with surviving Prussian troops from the fighting at Breslau near Liegnitz (present-day Legnica). With about 33,000 men, Frederick then marched east to meet the Austrians.

Prince Charles commanded 65,000 men. Aware of Frederick's approach, Charles took up position facing west along a five-mile front in rolling country near the village of Leuthen. The bulk of Charles's forces were on his left wing that ended close to the Schwiednitz River; his right flank was anchored on a marsh.

Frederick II and his commanders were familiar with the area, as it was the site of Prussian military maneuvers. Outnumbered almost two to one, Frederick relied on a ruse. He moved toward the Austrian right wing in four columns; the two inner columns consisted of infantry, and the two outer columns consisted of cavalry. Frederick then took advantage of low hills to shift the two columns of infantry and one column of cavalry obliquely to the right. The left-most column of cavalry remained behind to demonstrate in front of the Austrian right.

Charles took the bait, shifting reserves from his left front to his right to meet the threatened Prussian attack. Frederick's three remaining columns meanwhile continued undetected across the Austrian front, overreaching the Austrian left wing. The main Prussian attack occurred in oblique formation, in two lines echeloned from the right. The Prussian fire increased as each successive battalion attacked. Highly mobile Prussian artillery supported the attack, directing their fire at the apex of the Austrian left flank. Prussian general Hans J. Von Ziethen charged into the disorganized Austrian cavalry on the left flank, forcing it back on the center of the line.

The Austrian army now wheeled toward the south to meet the Prussian attack. Charles attempted to form a new line while hurling his right-flank cavalry against the Prussians. The remaining Prussian cavalry defeated this thrust, and the Austrian infantry gave way in confusion. Nightfall ended the fighting and rendered impossible any Prussian pursuit. The bulk of the Austrian forces escaped across the Schwiednitz River to Breslau.

The Battle of Leuthen shattered Charles's army, which lost 6,750 killed or wounded and more than 12,000 captured. The Prussians also took 116 Austrian guns. Prussian losses were 6,150 killed or wounded. Frederick II retook Breslau five days later, capturing another 17,000 Austrians. Both armies then went into winter quarters, but only half of the Austrian army that had begun the campaign remained.

While Leuthen was one of the most decisive battles of the century and was Frederick's military masterpiece, much more fighting lay ahead. The French turned their efforts against Hanover, where they defeated a largely mercenary force commanded by Frederick's nephew, the Duke of Brunswick. Swedish forces meanwhile moved into Pomerania. The Russians and Austrians also made a major effort, leading one historian to refer to the war as a struggle of 90 million against 5 million. Frederick's position steadily deteriorated. The magnificently trained forces with which he had begun the war were gradually whittled away, replaced in large part by untrained levies expected to learn on the job.

On August 25, 1758, in one of the bloodiest battles of the 18th century, Frederick defeated an invading Russian army at Zorndorf, but on October 14 the Austrians were victorious over the Prussians at Hochkirch in Saxony. Frederick maneuvered ever smaller forces against his enemies, and on August 12, 1759, the Russians defeated Frederick at Kunersdorf, administering the worst setback of his military career. Two months later the Russians briefly took Berlin and burned the city.

By 1761 Frederick II was barely surviving. With little more initiative on the part of his enemies, he would have been defeated. He and Prussia were delivered by the so-called Miracle of the House of Brandenburg, when Czarina Elizabeth died suddenly on January 6, 1762. Elizabeth hated the Prussian king, but her successor, Peter III, was an unabashed admirer of Frederick and promptly recalled Russian troops from the war. This unhinged the coalition and isolated Empress Maria Theresa of Austria, who was forced to conclude peace with Prussia in the Treaty of Hubertusberg on February 15, 1763. The treaty restored the status quo ante bellum, and Maria Theresa reluctantly gave up all claims to Silesia. The net effect of the war was to raise Prussia to the status of one of the great powers of Europe despite a long and difficult recovery for the kingdom after the ravages of the long war.

References

Duffy, Christopher. *The Military Experience in the Age of Reason.* New York: Atheneum, 1988.

———. *The Military Life of Frederick the Great.* New York: Atheneum, 1986.

Reddaway, W. F. *Frederick the Great and the Rise of Prussia.* New York: Greenwood, 1969.

Ritter, Gerhard. *Frederick the Great: A Historical Profile.* Berkeley: University of California Press, 1968.

Battle of Plassey

Date	June 23, 1757	
Location	Plassey in Bengal, northeast India	
Opponents (* winner)	*British and Indians	Indians
Commander	Robert Clive	Sirāj-ud-Dawlah, the Nawab of Bengal
Approx. # Troops	1,100 British; 2,100 Indian sepoys	c. 60,000, including French artillerists
Importance	Turns the tide of war in favor of the British in their effort to control the subcontinent	

The Battle of Plassey in June 1757 marked the turning point in the long struggle between the British and French for control of India. Since they established trading stations on the Indian subcontinent in the 16th and 17th centuries, the European powers had all resorted to employing local men to help maintain their forts. The French Compagnie des Indes was the first to create wholly native Indian infantry units, however. Such native troops became known as sepoys.

In June 1756 Sirāj-ud-Dawlah, the nawab of Bengal, marched on Calcutta and captured it. The atrocities that followed, most notably the so-called Black Hole of Calcutta (a subterranean prison in which 146 British soldiers were allegedly imprisoned in one room 18 feet square with only a single window for ventilation, where a day later only 23 of the soldiers were alive), shocked the British into action. Historians now cast doubt on the numbers involved or even whether the Black Hole incident occurred at all. Certainly the British manipulated news of the event to discredit Sirāj-ud-Dawlah.

Lieutenant Colonel Robert Clive was sent to recapture Calcutta. With only 900 British troops and 1,500 sepoys, Clive retook the city on January 2, 1757. Following an inconclusive battle with Sirāj-ud-Dawlah, Clive signed a treaty with the nawab. The British were allowed to reoccupy Calcutta and were indemnified for their losses.

Clive was confident that the treaty was only temporary, and indeed Sirāj-ud-Dawlah soon opened negotiations with the French. Learning of this, Clive conducted secret negotiations with Sirāj-ud-Dawlah's uncle, Mir Jaffar, who assured Clive of his support in unseating the nawab. Sirāj-ud-Dawlah had insisted that the British and French not fight each other in India even though war had broken out between the two powers in Europe (the Seven Years' War of 1756–1763).

Clive now provoked a confrontation with Sirāj-ud-Dawlah, mounting an attack on a French settlement not far from the nawab's capital of Mursidabad. Sirāj-ud-Dawlah responded by assembling a Bengali force estimated to number as many as 35,000 infantry, 15,000 cavalry, and 10,000 militiamen. He also had 53 artillery pieces manned by French crews. Sirāj-ud-Dawlah then moved this large force toward Calcutta.

Clive had only 3,200 men (1,100 Europeans and 2,100 sepoys), as well as eight small cannon and two howitzers. Instead of remaining in the strong defensive position of Fort William, Clive took the offensive. Mir Jaffar assured him that when the battle began he would first withhold his troops, which constituted perhaps three-quarters of Sirāj-ud-Dawlah's force, and then turn them against the nawab.

On the evening of June 22, 1757, Clive set up camp in a mango grove south of Calcutta and north of the town of Pelasi, known to the English as Plassey. Clive anchored his western flank on the Bhagirathi-Hooghli River. Sirāj-ud-Dawlah's army took up position in a great semicircle facing west toward the British positions and the Bhagirathi-Hooghli. With his back against the river, Clive was almost surrounded.

The battle opened the next morning, June 23, when the French artillery opened up against the English. This fire was ineffective because Clive's men were positioned on the reverse slope of a hill next to the mango grove. Much of the morning was consumed in an artillery duel, but the British fire was far more effective because Sirāj-ud-Dawlah's troops were in the open. At noon a monsoon rain began. The French gunpowder became soaked and useless. Mir Mudin Khan, Sirāj-ud-Dawlah's field commander, assumed that the same had happened to the British powder and ordered an immediate attack. Clive, however, had covered his powder supply.

Sirāj-ud-Dawlah launched a large-scale cavalry attack on the British position. Clive's guns cut down large numbers of them and broke up the attack. Mir Mudin Khan was among those killed. Mir Jaffar withheld his 45,000 men, although he did not, as promised, turn them against Sirāj-ud-Dawlah. Sensing defeat, Sirāj-ud-Dawlah fled the scene with his 2,000-man bodyguard. Those of the nawab's troops who continued to fight were overwhelmed by British artillery fire, and by late afternoon the battle was over. Clive's casualties totaled 23 killed and 49 wounded. Sirāj-ud-Dawlah may have lost upwards of 1,000 men.

Sirāj-ud-Dawlah was captured a few days later and executed. Mir Jaffar replaced him as nawab and lavished considerable sums on Clive and his officers. London appointed Clive the governor of Bengal. He left India in 1760. Other battles between the French and British in India followed. The French sent reinforcements to their base of Pondicherry and later besieged Madras, but they failed to conquer it. The British, however, captured Pondicherry in 1763. By the terms of peace that ended the Seven Years' War in 1763, the French regained Pondicherry but were never again a major power on the Indian subcontinent.

References

Bruce-Jones, Mark. *Clive of India.* New York: St. Martin's, 1975.

Keay, John. *The Honourable Company.* New York: Macmillan, 1994.

Mason, Philip. *A Matter of Honour.* London: Jonathan Cape, 1974.

Robert, P. E. *History of British India.* London: Oxford University Press, 1952.

Battle of the Plains of Abraham

Date	September 13, 1759	
Location	City of Quebec, eastern New France (today Canada)	
Opponents (* winner)	*British	French
Commander	Major General James Wolfe	General Louis Joseph, Marquis de Montcalm
Approx. # Troops	4,500	4,500
Importance	Secures British predominance on the continent	

The Battle of the Plains of Abraham (Quebec) on September 13, 1759, was one of the most important military engagements in the history of North America, for it secured British predominance on the continent. In 1756 after fighting an undeclared war against the French in North America for two years (the French and Indian War, as the American colonists called it), Britain and France formally went to war. The ensuing conflict was known as the Seven Years' War (1756–1763) in Europe. Although both countries and their allies fought on the continent, the British government decided to make the main effort in America in a bid to win colonial mastery. The British therefore sent strong naval detachments and some 25,000 troops to North America.

The weight of the British commitment was not felt until 1758. That July the British captured the great French fort of Louisbourg that guarded Atlantic access to the St. Lawrence River. The next month British officers led a largely colonial force to capture Fort Frontenac on Lake Ontario. Its fall cut French communications westward and forced the French to abandon Fort Duquesne, which the British renamed Fort Pitt. Only at the recently constructed French Fort Ticonderoga on Lake Champlain did the British meet rebuff.

British prime minister William Pitt planned to deliver the decisive blow in 1759. In September 1758 he named Jeffery Amherst, who had commanded the successful expedition against Louisbourg, as major general and commander in North America, entrusting him with the seizure of Canada. With Louisbourg in their hands, the British could cut off French resupply. The British plan to take Quebec called for Amherst and 11,000 men, half of them colonials, to capture Ticonderoga and Crown Point on Lake Champlain, then advance down the water route to Montreal. After taking the city, they would move down the St. Lawrence to Quebec. An additional 9,000 troops under Major General James Wolfe, supported by naval forces under rear admirals Charles Saunders and Charles Holmes, would depart Louisbourg, enter the St. Lawrence, and take Quebec. Wolfe's men began disembarking on June 26 at Île d'Orléans and on the south bank of the St. Lawrence, some four miles east of the city.

Quebec stands on the northern shore of the St. Lawrence at the point where the river widens from three-quarters of a mile to nearly two miles across. Enclosed by walls, the Upper Town is situated at the top of steep bluffs overlooking the St. Lawrence River and the much smaller St. Charles River that flows into it. There were few possible means to assault the city by river. Below the town the St. Charles and Montmorency rivers presented formidable obstacles. West of Quebec farmland flattened into a plateau known as the Plains of Abraham, after early settler Abraham Martin. French general Louis Joseph, Marquis de Montcalm, commanded the French fortress at Quebec. He had 12,000 regular troops and militia assisted by some Indians to defend what appeared to be an impregnable fortress.

The eastern (downstream) approach to Quebec seemed the least formidable, and Wolfe first tried it. However, Montcalm had strongly fortified the riverbank for

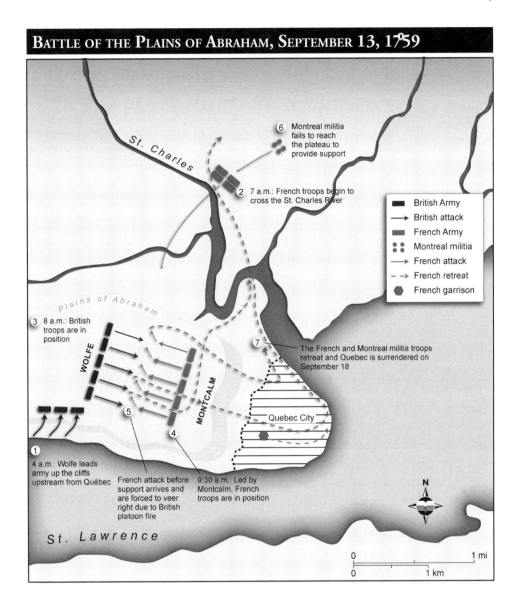

BATTLE OF THE PLAINS OF ABRAHAM, SEPTEMBER 13, 1759

6 Montreal militia fails to reach the plateau to provide support

2 7 a.m.: French troops begin to cross the St. Charles River

St. Charles

■ British Army
→ British attack
■ French Army
⋮ Montreal militia
→ French attack
- -→ French retreat
⬡ French garrison

Plains of Abraham

3 8 a.m.: British troops are in position

WOLFE

7 The French and Montreal militia troops retreat and Quebec is surrendered on September 18

MONTCALM

Quebec City

5

4

1 4 a.m.: Wolfe leads army up the cliffs upstream from Québec

French attack before support arrives and are forced to veer right due to British platoon fire

9:30 a.m.: Led by Montcalm, French troops are in position

N

St. Lawrence

0 ——— 1 mi
0 ——— 1 km

some distance. British efforts to draw the French troops out of Quebec and the entrenchments proved unsuccessful. The British cut off the city from Montreal, lobbed shells into Quebec, and raided nearby French settlements with a view toward demoralizing the Quebecois, but all of Wolfe's efforts to gain a foothold failed. To make matters worse, Wolfe was sick with a fever, and many of his men believed him to be dying. Saunders, fearing that his ships would be trapped in the winter ice in the St. Lawrence, threatened to depart. Wolfe realized that unless he could bring Montcalm to battle by the end of September, he would have to abandon the campaign.

Wolfe sought the advice of Captain Robert Stobo, who had been held prisoner in Quebec by the French and knew the city better than anyone in the British force.

Stobo informed Wolfe of a narrow footpath that angled up the steep cliffs just north of the city at Anse de Foulon. At the same time, the Royal Navy discovered that it could get some vessels through the supposedly impassable narrows upstream from Quebec.

Wolfe was determined to try this approach, and he secretly got his troops up this path during the night of September 12–13. French pickets assumed that the British boats were part of a French supply convoy due from Montreal. They had not been informed that the convoy was cancelled. Colonel William Howe's light infantry gained the top and captured the French positions overlooking the landing site. Wolfe and the main body of British troops then followed. By dawn Wolfe had some 4,500 men drawn up in line of battle facing east on the Plains of Abraham.

Montcalm carried out a personal reconnaissance of the British lines and decided to attack immediately with what forces he had before Wolfe could solidify his position and construct field fortifications. By midmorning on September 13, 1759, Montcalm had assembled a mixed force of French regulars and poorly trained colonial militia numbering about 4,500 men to face an equal number of well-trained British regulars. Montcalm had no artillery because his rival, French governor-general Pierre de Rigaud de Vaudreuil de Cavagnial, Marquis de Vaudreuil, insisted on retaining it for the defense of the city.

The battle began at about 10:00 a.m. when Montcalm's force attacked the British. The French militia fired too early, and there was little cohesion in the French force. The British showed excellent fire discipline, on the other hand, standing and firing in volleys when the French reached a range of 60 yards. When the French were at 40 yards, the British fired a devastating volley and moved forward. The French broke and fled back into Quebec. The entire battle had lasted little more than half an hour. Casualties were comparable—some 644 French to 658 for the British—but the French never recovered from the psychological shock of the defeat.

Both commanders were mortally wounded in the battle, but Wolfe at least had the satisfaction of knowing he had been victorious. French reinforcements under Count Louis Antoine de Bougainville came up from the west too late to affect the battle. De Vaudreuil decided to abandon Quebec and join up with Bougainville. The mayor of the city, Jean Baptise Nicholas Roche de Ramezay, entered into talks with the British in the hope that he might spin out negotiations until French reinforcements arrived, but he surrendered the city on September 18 to Wolfe's successor, Brigadier General George Townshend.

The loss of Quebec broke French resistance in Canada. The British victory was sealed by the Battle of Quiberon Bay on November 20, 1759, when Admiral Sir Edward Hawke's British ships defeated the French Brest Squadron, ensuring that the French would not be able to resupply their forces in America. The French did attempt to retake Quebec in April 1760 but failed. The French then withdrew to Montreal, where they held out until that September. On September 8, 1760, de Vaudreuil signed an instrument of surrender ceding all Canada to the British.

References

Anderson, Fred. *Crucible of War: The Seven Years' War and the Fate of Empire in British North America, 1754–1763.* New York: Knopf, 2000.

Hibbert, Christopher. *Wolfe at Quebec.* London: Longmans, Green, 1959.

La Pierre, Laurer L. *1759: The Battle for Canada.* Toronto: McClelland and Stewart, 1990.

Lloyd, Christopher. *The Capture of Quebec.* New York: Macmillian, 1959.

May, Robin, and Gerry Embleton. *Wolfe's Army.* London: Osprey, 1997.

Parkman, Francis. *Montcalm and Wolfe.* New York: Atheneum, 1984.

Battle of Lake Champlain

Date	October 11–13, 1776	
Location	Valcour Island, Lake Champlain, New York	
Opponents (* winner)	*British	Americans
Commander	Lieutenant Thomas Pringle	Brigadier General Benedict Arnold
Approx. # Troops	25 warships with a combined gun throw weight of 1,300 lbs	15 warships: 2 schooners, 1 sloop, 4 galleys, and 8 gondolas, with a combined gun throw weight of 703 lbs
Importance	Although a tactical American defeat, it is a strategic American victory, for Arnold has imposed delay on the British, who now call off their fall invasion from Canada	

Control of Lake Champlain was vital for the Americans in supplying their efforts to conquer Canada during the American Revolutionary War (1775–1783). It was also crucial to British plans to separate New England from the other rebellious colonies. Both sides had used row galleys and other small craft on the lake during the 1775–1776 American winter campaign. Even after the American retreat from Canada, the Continental Congress ordered Major General Philip Schuyler to hold northern New York and authorized him to build "gallies and armed vessels" to secure lakes Champlain and George. Continental Army brigadier general Benedict Arnold had charge of construction, and neighboring colonies sent materials and shipwrights.

Arnold preferred row galleys and hoped to meet the British with eight, each armed with two heavy 24-pounders and two 18-pounders. Only four were completed in time to take part in the battle, however. They were more than 72 feet in length with two masts and a lateen rig. Crew complement was 80 men. Most mounted two 12- or 18-pounders in the bow, two 12-pounders (along with possibly two 2-pounders) in the stern, and four 6-pounders in broadside. All carried smaller man-killing weapons known as swivels on their rails. As with all Lake Champlain squadron vessels, precise armament cannot be verified.

In 1935 one of the gondolas, the *Philadelphia,* was raised. It was an open boat 53 feet 4 inches in length. (The *Philadelphia,* today displayed in the Smithsonian Institution, is touted as the oldest U.S. Navy [actually army] warship in existence.) It had a single mast with a square course and topsail but was basically a rowing boat propelled by its 45-man crew. The gondolas each carried three guns: one at the bow on a slide mount and one on either side to fire over the rails. They also mounted swivels.

The British had both larger vessels and more guns on Lake Champlain. What they did not have was time. Winter would bring their operations to a halt because their invasion route on the lake would freeze over. By early October, Major General Sir Guy Carleton's fleet was ready to move.

The resulting engagements between the British and Americans began at Valcour Island, about 50 miles north of Fort Ticonderoga, on October 11, 1776. Arnold's 800 men had 15 warships: 2 schooners, 1 sloop, 4 galleys, and 8 gondolas, with a combined throw weight of 703 pounds. He positioned his vessels in a crescent shape at the island so that the British would have to tack into position to engage his anchored vessels.

Commander of the British squadron Lieutenant Thomas Pringle had some 25 warships, many of them mounting heavier guns than those available to Arnold. Pringle's smaller vessels alone were nearly a match for the Americans. The British warships were served by 667 trained Royal Navy seamen with 1,000 soldiers; their guns had a combined throw weight of 1,300 pounds.

On October 11 Pringle's vessels pounded the Americans for six hours. The Americans lost 1 schooner and 1 gondola, and 3 other vessels were badly damaged. They had also used up most of their ammunition. During the night Arnold's remaining 13 vessels slipped past the British in an effort to reach Fort Ticonderoga. The wind changed from the south though, and the Americans had to resort to their sweeps.

For a day the Americans kept ahead, but the British caught up with them, and a second engagement was fought on October 13 north of Crown Point. One American galley struck to the British, and Arnold then beached and set afire another galley and four gondolas. Although most of their vessels were either captured or sunk, the Americans lost only about 80 men. The others escaped ashore and got to Crown Point on foot, just ahead of pursuing Indians.

Although a tactical defeat for the Americans, the two small battles on Lake Champlain were also a strategic victory. They ended any possibility of a linkup in 1776 between Carleton's forces and those of Major General William Howe in New York. Carleton thought it too late in the year to begin a land campaign and withdrew. If the British had taken Ticonderoga and held it through the winter, mounting their 1777 campaign would have been easier and might have been a success. Instead, the 1777 British thrust southward ended in an American victory at Saratoga, the turning point of the war.

References

Allen, Gardner W. *A Naval History of the American Revolution,* Vol. 1. Cambridge, MA: Houghton Mifflin, 1913.

Chapelle, Howard I. *The History of the American Sailing Navy: The Ships and Their Development.* New York: Norton, 1949.

Nelson, James L. *Benedict Arnold's Navy: The Ragtag Fleet That Lost the Battle of Lake Champlan but Won the American Revolution.* New York: McGraw-Hill, 2006.

Battle of Trenton

Date	December 26, 1776	
Location	Trenton, New Jersey, on the Delaware River (eastern United States)	
Opponents (* winner)	*Americans	Hessian mercenaries
Commander	General George Washington	Colonel Johann Rall
Approx. # Troops	2,400	1,600
Importance	Restores confidence in Washington's leadership and in the possibility of ultimate American victory in the war	

Continental Army commander General George Washington's first military campaign ended in disaster. In July 1776 British commander in chief Major General William Howe and 32,000 British troops (the largest expeditionary force in British history until the 20th century) landed in New York and proceeded to drive Washington's troops from Long Island and Manhattan. Washington suffered one defeat after another; often his men simply broke and ran. Washington then left an isolated garrison at Fort Washington on the Manhattan side of the Hudson River. In mid-November, supported by ships in the Hudson, British forces cut off the garrison and captured it along with 3,000 prisoners, 100 cannon, and a huge quantity of munitions. The same thing almost happened a few days later to the colonials at Fort Lee, across the Hudson in New Jersey.

Washington fled to the interior. Howe pursued in dilatory fashion, ignoring the Hudson to go after the Continental Army. Washington got away, his army safely behind the Delaware River. On December 13, 1776, British forces caught up with Major General Charles Lee, who had rejected Washington's orders to join him. The British captured him and some of his 4,000 men near Morristown, New Jersey. The British then went into winter quarters, their forces covered by a line of outposts. The most important was located at Trenton, New Jersey, and was held by Colonel Johann Rall's Hessian mercenaries. What was left of Washington's force was deployed across the Delaware River from Trenton.

Washington's position was critical. Smallpox ravaged his force, and half of his 10,000 men were sick. To make matters worse, enlistments for most would expire in a few days, at the end of the year. Washington decided to risk everything and mount a surprise attack on Trenton. Everything depended on getting the men across the icy Delaware at night to achieve surprise. Crossings by 5,500 men, horses, and artillery were to occur at three separate locations, with the forces converging on Trenton. If circumstances allowed, they could then advance on the British posts at Princeton and New Brunswick.

The attempt was planned for Christmas night, December 25. The crossing was to start at 5:00 p.m., with the attack at Trenton scheduled for 5:00 a.m. the next morning, but weather conditions were terrible, and the troops were slow to reach their assembly areas. As a consequence, the men began loading an hour later than planned. Shallow-draft wooden Durham boats, 40–60 feet long by 8 feet wide, transported the men across the river. Perfect craft for such an operation, the Durham boats had a keel and a bow at each end. Four men, two to a side, used setting poles to push off the bottom and move the boats, which also had a mast and two sails. Horses and artillery went across the river in ferries.

All did not go smoothly, as a storm swept through. Of the three crossings, only the major one at McKonkey's Ferry under Washington with 2,400 men occurred in time for the planned attack. That force was divided into two corps under major generals John Sullivan and Nathanael Greene. Colonel Henry Knox commanded 18 pieces of artillery. Conditions were horrible. The men had to contend not only with the dark but also with wind, rain, sleet, snow, and chunks of ice in the Delaware. The password for the operation, "Liberty or Death," reflected its desperate nature.

Washington had planned for the crossing to be complete by midnight, but the last man was not across until after 3:00 a.m., and it was nearly 4:00 a.m. before the army formed and began to move. Washington's men were poorly clad for such an operation; some actually had no shoes and wrapped their feet in rags. The men thus marched the nine miles to Trenton.

Washington was determined that the attack would succeed. When Sullivan sent a message to him that the storm had wet the muskets, making them unfit for service, Washington replied, "Tell General Sullivan to use the bayonet. I am resolved to take Trenton." Washington's will, more than anything, kept the men going. On nearing Trenton, Washington split his force into the two corps to follow two different roads for a converging attack on the British outpost.

The attack began at 8:00 a.m., with the two columns opening fire within 8 minutes of one another. The battle lasted some 90 minutes. The Hessian garrison consisted of three regiments, 50 Hessian Jägers, and 20 light dragoons—about 1,600 men in all—along with six 3-pounder guns. Continental Army forces soon drove the Hessians back. Artillery played a major role, and here Washington enjoyed a 6 to 1 advantage, with his guns deployed to fire down the streets of the town. The battle itself was a confused melee of men fighting in small groups or singly. Rall rallied his men, intending a bayonet charge down Queen Street, but was soon mortally wounded, and the Hessians were cut down by individual Americans with muskets and rifles and by artillery fire.

The Hessians lost 22 troops killed and 92 wounded; 948 were captured. The remaining Hessians would have also been taken had the other columns gotten into position in time. The Continentals also secured a considerable quantity of arms and booty. The Americans lost only 2 men, both frozen to death, and 5 wounded. With little food or rest for 36 hours, Washington's men needed relief, and he was thus forced to suspend operations. On December 27 the Continentals were back across the Delaware.

Washington followed up Trenton by an attack against Princeton. Recrossing the Delaware on January 2, 1777, he routed 1,700 crack British troops at Princeton under Lieutenant Colonel Charles Mawhood. These two small Continental victories changed the entire campaign. Washington called Trenton "A glorious day for our country," while British minister for the colonies Lord George Germain exclaimed, "All our hopes were blasted by the unhappy affair at Trenton." Trenton helped end the Continentals' fear of the Hessian troops. More importantly, the two battles of Trenton and Princeton added immensely to Washington's prestige, which was at a low point a month before, establishing his reputation as a general and a leader of men. The battles also restored Continental morale, which had been at its lowest point since the start of the war. In two weeks Washington had snatched victory out of the jaws of death and fanned the dying embers of American independence into flame again.

References

Fischer, David Hackett. *Washington's Crossing.* New York: Oxford University Press, 2004.

Ketchum, Richard M. *The Winter Soldiers: The Battles for Trenton and Princeton.* New York: Anchor Books, 1975.

McPhillips, Martin. *The Battle of Trenton.* Parsippany, NJ: Silver Burdett, 1984.

Ward, Christopher. *The War of the Revolution,* Vol. 1. New York: Macmillan, 1952.

Battles of Saratoga

Date	September 19, October 7, 1777	
Location	Saratoga in upper New York State (eastern United States)	
Opponents (* winner)	*Americans	British
Commander	Major General Horatio Gates	Lieutenant General John Burgoyne
Approx. # Troops	6,000 (1st), 11,500 (2nd)	7,000 (1st), 6,617 (2nd)
Importance	The surrender of an entire British army convinces France to enter the war openly on the American side, making the American Revolutionary War a worldwide conflict	

Two battles fought at Saratoga, New York, in September and October 1777 marked a turning point in the American Revolutionary War (1775–1783). The Saratoga Campaign originated with British major general John Burgoyne. He had returned to England early in 1777 and presented to King George III and Secretary of State for the Colonies Lord George Germain a plan to split off New England, the font of the rebellion, from the remainder of the colonies and thus snuff out the revolt. Burgoyne envisioned a three-pronged campaign. The major thrust would drive from Canada down the Lake Champlain–Hudson Valley corridor, while a secondary effort pushed eastward from Lake Erie up the Mohawk Valley. The two forces were to meet at Albany and join the third prong, a British drive up the Hudson from New York City.

There were two principal problems with Burgoyne's plan. First, it took little account of logistics, and second, it depended heavily on simultaneous execution. It was further hampered by the fact that while he was approving Burgoyne's plan, Germain also approved a different plan submitted by Major General William Howe. Howe proposed to move south from New York against Philadelphia. He believed that Continental Army commander General George Washington would have to commit the bulk of his army to defend the capital and that the rebel army might thus be destroyed.

Germain made no effort to reconcile these two plans. Neither did he order the two commanders to cooperate. Neither Howe nor Burgoyne made any effort to coordinate with the other, although Howe did inform British commander in Canada Major General Sir Guy Carleton of his intentions. Howe promised to position a corps in the lower Hudson River area to maintain communications through the Highlands, which might then "act in favor of the northern army." Later this force went up the Hudson to a point above Hyde Park. Although Burgoyne saw this letter, it did not affect his planning.

Burgoyne and the main British force assembled at Saint Jean, south of Montreal. Lieutenant Colonel Barry St. Leger led the secondary effort at Lachine. St. Leger had only 875 British, Loyalist, and Hessian troops, assisted by 1,000 Iroquois Indians under Joseph Brant. This force struck from Oswego into the Mohawk Valley, but the Indian massacre of civilians produced a widespread mobilization of militia, supported by units of the Continental Army under Major General Benedict Arnold. Although St. Leger's force campaigned on the Mohawk during July 25–August 25, much of this time was spent in a fruitless siege of Fort Stanwix (Fort Schuyler, present-day Rome, New York), and they never joined Burgoyne.

Howe meanwhile left about one-third of his army under Major General Sir Henry Clinton to garrison New York and put to sea with some 16,000 men, sailing to the head of the Chesapeake Bay to approach Philadelphia from the south. Washington shifted his army to central New Jersey so he could act in either direction. As Burgoyne moved deeper into upper New York from Canada, however, Washington

Painting by John Trumbull depicting British Lieutenant General John Burgoyne surrendering to Continental Army Major General Horatio Gates at Saratoga on October 17, 1777. The American victory here marked a major turning point of the American Revolutionary War, because it induced France to enter the war openly on the American side. (National Archives)

detached some of his best troops and most capable commanders to reinforce that front. The opportunity to cut off and destroy a British army away from Royal Navy support was simply too tempting. Once Howe's intent was clear, Washington had ample time to move south and protect Philadelphia. The Continental Army met defeat in the Battle of Brandywine Creek on September 11, 1777, but managed to withdraw in good order. By the end of September Howe had seized Philadelphia, but it was a hollow victory, devoid of military significance.

Burgoyne now faced a difficult decision. After capturing Fort Ticonderoga in early July, he had advanced slowly. By early August he knew that Howe would not be reinforcing him and that St. Leger had been blocked. He also knew that winter would freeze over his Lake Champlain supply line, and communications to Canada were threatened by colonial actions against Fort Ticonderoga. Then, on August 16, Burgoyne suffered a disaster in the Battle of Bennington. He had detached a sizable force of Hessian mercenaries to secure provisions, and the American militia cut off and surrounded them at Bennington (in present-day Vermont). The British lost 207 killed and 696 captured versus American casualties of only 30 killed or wounded. The Americans also secured supplies and weapons.

Burgoyne had only 30 days of provisions for his 7,000 men, some 2,000 women, and a number of children who accompanied the troops. Local supplies were practically nonexistent due to the work of Major General Philip Schuyler, commander of the Northern Department and the unsung hero of the campaign. Burgoyne's long supply lines and Schuyler's skillfully planned retreat (after he had destroyed the countryside) were the keys to the campaign. Schuyler's continued withdrawals and aloof manner made him unpopular with his men, however. With Major General Horatio Gates also intriguing against him, Congress relieved Schuyler of command on August 19 and replaced him with Gates, who subsequently quarreled with Arnold.

The Indians in Burgoyne's service also helped to create hostility against the British. This included the scalping of a white woman, ironically the fiancée of a British officer. Gates played this up with great success. Burgoyne did not understand this and indeed inflamed the situation by threatening Indian reprisals against resisting Americans, which served to bring out militia in large numbers. Later, anticipating disaster, the Indians melted away, a serious loss for the British in gathering intelligence on American dispositions.

Burgoyne's advance, impeded at every turn by the Americans and slowed by the need to construct dozens of bridges and causeways across swamps and creeks, now was only a mile a day. On September 13–14 the British crossed to the west side of the Hudson River on a bridge of rafts. The troops at last reached Saratoga, only a few miles from their goal of Albany, but found their way blocked in a series of battles for control of the main Albany road. Collectively known as the Battles of Saratoga, these were the Battle of Freeman's Farm, or First Saratoga, and the Battle of Bemis Heights, or Second Saratoga.

The Battle of Freeman's Farm occurred on the afternoon of September 19. Some 6,000 Americans, their right flank anchored on the Hudson River, had established a fortified position of redoubts and breastworks on Bemis Heights, south of a 15-acre clearing known as Freeman's Farm. Burgoyne opened the battle when he ordered three regiments to attack across the clearing and dislodge the Americans from Bemis Heights. The British attack went poorly. Brigadier General Daniel Morgan and Arnold halted the advance, with Morgan's riflemen inflicting heavy casualties on the British, especially officers. Fortunately for Burgoyne, Gates refused to leave his entrenchments to support Arnold and Morgan. Hessian forces turned the American right flank, and that night the British encamped in the field, but they had failed to dislodge the Americans on Bemis Heights, the object of their attack. The British had also sustained some 600 casualties to only 300 for the Americans.

The Americans were now reinforced, and by the time of the second battle Gates had some 11,500 men to only 6,617 for Burgoyne. At a council of war on October 5, Burgoyne's officers pressed him to retreat while there was still an opportunity, but he steadfastly refused and ordered a full-scale attack to turn the American flank. This prompted the second battle on October 7. Gates committed Morgan's riflemen on the British right flank. Brigadier General Ebenezer Learned's brigade was in the center, and Brigadier General Enoch Poor's brigade was on the left. Gates's refusal to commit his entire force mitigated the British defeat, but Arnold, who had quarreled with Gates and had been removed from command, disregarded orders and charged onto the field to lead a general American assault that took two British redoubts. The Americans sustained only about 130 casualties to 600 for the British.

On October 8 Burgoyne ordered a general retreat, only to find that the Americans had blocked that possibility. On October 17, aware that Clinton would be unable to relieve him, Burgoyne formally surrendered his army of 5,895 officers and men. Gates granted the British paroles on condition that they not serve again in America, an action that Congress subsequently disallowed. Burgoyne was eventually cleared of any misconduct, but it was the end of his military career.

The British lost not only at Saratoga but also at Ticonderoga and the Highlands as well. All they had to show for the year's campaigning was the occupation of Philadelphia. The war now became a major issue in British politics. More important, the Battles of Saratoga caused France to openly enter the war. On December 4 Benjamin Franklin, in Paris as an ambassador for the colonists, received the news of Burgoyne's surrender; two days later King Louis XVI approved an alliance with the United States. A treaty was signed on February 6, 1778, and on March 11 Great Britain and France were at war.

For two years, France had been actively assisting the rebels with substantial quantities of military supplies, but the actual entry of France into the war was a threat to every part of the British Empire. The war then became largely a problem of sea power, accentuated when in 1779 Spain declared war on England, followed by Holland in 1780. Participation of French Army regiments in concert with the French Navy made possible the defeat of the British Army in America.

References

Black, Jeremy. *War for America: The Fight for Independence, 1775–1783.* Stroud, Gloucestershire, UK: Alan Sutton, 1991.

Ketchum, Richard M. *Saratoga: Turning Point of America's Revolutionary War.* New York: Henry Holt, 1997.

Lunt, James. *John Burgoyne of Saratoga.* New York: Harcourt, Brace, Jovanovich, 1975.

Ward, Christopher. *The War of the Revolution,* Vol. 2. New York: Macmillan, 1952.

Battle of the Chesapeake

Date	September 5, 1781	
Location	Chesapeake Bay off the Virginia coast (United States)	
Opponents (* winner)	*French	British
Commander	Admiral François Joseph Comte de Grasse	Rear Admiral Thomas Graves
Approx. # Troops	24 ships of the line	19 ships of the line
Importance	Tactically a draw, it is a French strategic victory for it makes possible the subsequent American/French land victory at Yorktown	

This key battle of the American Revolutionary War (1775–1783), also known as the Battle of the Capes, made possible the land victory of the Continental and French armies at Yorktown, Virginia, and is regarded as one of the most important naval battles in history. French admiral François Joseph Comte de Grasse, with a powerful fleet of 28 ships of the line, had been campaigning in the West Indies. Indeed, after France's entrance into the war in 1778, both Britain and France had deployed major fleet units to the West Indies to try to secure the lucrative sugar trade of the other. De Grasse, however, planned to bring his fleet north during hurricane season and would then be free to act to support Continental Army and French Army land operations in North America. Washington hoped to retake New York, but de Grasse decided to sail instead to Chesapeake Bay. Washington immediately saw the possibilities of bagging the sizable British force under the command of Lieutenant General Charles, Earl Cornwallis, at the port of Yorktown on the Chesapeake Bay.

On August 27 British rear admiral Samuel Hood, with 14 ships of the line, stood into Chesapeake Bay on his way north from the West Indies. With no sign of de Grasse, Hood sailed to New York. There he joined Rear Admiral Thomas Graves with 5 ships of the line. Graves also had heard nothing of de Grasse but informed Hood that French admiral Jacques Comte de Barras, with 8 ships of the line and 18 transports, had sailed from Rhode Island the day before. Hood assumed, correctly, that Barras was sailing south, probably for the Chesapeake. Graves and Hood, with 19 ships of the line, set out to intercept Barras on August 31.

De Grasse had arrived in the Chesapeake with 28 ships of the line, 4 frigates, and 3,000 land troops under Major General Claude-Ann, Marquis de Saint-Simon, on August 30. Disembarking the troops, de Grasse then ordered the transports and boats up the bay to ferry Washington's forces south. Graves arrived in the Chesapeake several days later but ahead of Barras.

On September 5 a French frigate signaled the British approach. Instead of swooping down on the unprepared French ships, Graves, hampered by an inadequate signaling system and unwilling to risk a general action against a superior enemy (28 ships of the line to 19), formed his ships into line ahead and waited for de Grasse to come out.

De Grasse, shorthanded with 90 of his officers and 1,500 sailors on ferrying duties up the bay but aware of his poor position, immediately set out with 24 ships of the line to meet the English. Hood and his officers had not had time to assimilate Graves's signals. Two signals were simultaneously flown: close action and line ahead at half a cable. Thus, while the British van bore down on the French, the British center and rear followed the van instead of closing. The vans engaged at 3:45 p.m., but the rest of both fleets remained out of action.

At 4:27 p.m. the line ahead signal was hauled down, yet it was not until 5:20 p.m. that Hood attempted to close with the French. But the French avoided close engagement. The battle ended at sunset. The British sustained 336 casualties, the French 221. No ships were lost on either side.

On the morning of September 6 there was only a slight wind, and Graves chose to repair his squadron's masts and rigging. On September 7 and 8 the French bore to windward and refused to engage. Then Graves learned that Barras had slipped into the bay with his eight ships of the line and transports. This persuaded Graves to hold a council of war with his captains, bringing the decision to gather additional ships.

The Battle of the Chesapeake doomed Cornwallis. Cut off from reinforcement, he surrendered his army, representing one-third of British Army strength in North America, on October 19. The defeat brought down the British government and led London to seek peace. Thus, a tactically inconclusive naval battle ranks as one of the most significant strategic victories in world history.

References

Larrabee, Harold A. *Decision at the Chesapeake.* London: William Kimber, 1965.

Syrett, David. *The Royal Navy in American Waters, 1775–1783.* Aldershot, UK: Scolar Press, 1989.

Tilley, John A. *The British Navy and the American Revolution.* Columbia: University of South Carolina Press, 1987.

Siege of Yorktown

Date	September 28–October 19, 1781	
Location	Yorktown, Virginia on the Chesapeake Bay (eastern United States)	
Opponents (* winner)	*Americans and French	British
Commander	General George Washington (Americans); Lieutenant General Jean Baptiste Donatien de Vimeur, Comte de Rochambeau (French)	Lieutenant General Charles, Earl Cornwallis
Approx. # Troops	9,000 Americans; 7,500 French	8,000
Importance	Brings the collapse of Lord North's cabinet and ushers in a new government pledged to negotiate an end to the war	

The Battle of Yorktown in Virginia was the last great battle of the American Revolutionary War (1775–1783). By 1781 the war was in stalemate. In 1778 the British had shifted the emphasis to the south, securing Savannah and Charleston as well as most of Georgia and South Carolina. The British commander in the south, Lieutenant General Charles, Earl Cornwallis, had waged an aggressive campaign, but after sustaining heavy casualties in defeating Continental Army forces led by Major General Nathanael Greene in the Battle of Guilford Court House in March 1781, Cornwallis decided to march the majority of his forces north into Virginia.

Continental Army commander General George Washington meanwhile hoped for a combined American and French assault on British-occupied New York. Toward that end he had positioned his main forces at White Plains. These numbered four infantry regiments, a battalion of artillery, and the Duc de Lauzun's 4,000-man French Legion under commander of the King's Forces in America Lieutenant General Jean Baptiste Donatien de Vimeur, Comte de Rochambeau.

In May 1781 French admiral Jacques Comte de Barras arrived with a small squadron at Newport, Rhode Island, bringing news that Admiral François Joseph, Comte de Grasse, was on his way from France with a powerful fleet. The war at sea was being fought between the British and French fleets chiefly in the West Indies, as both sides sought to deprive the other of the valuable sugar trade. Washington learned, however, that de Grasse would bring the fleet north during the hurricane season.

In the meantime Washington sent 1,200 men under Major General Marquis de Lafayette to trap British forces under the turncoat Brigadier General Benedict Arnold that had been operating along the James River in Virginia. Cornwallis arrived in Virginia just at this time. He now commanded about 7,000 men, approximately a quarter of British armed strength in North America. Cornwallis tried but failed to take Lafayette's much smaller force and then withdrew to the small tobacco port of Yorktown, on the York River just off Chesapeake Bay. Lafayette followed.

On August 14 Washington learned that de Grasse would not be coming to New York but instead would sail to the Chesapeake Bay, arriving there later the same month and remaining until the end of October. Washington immediately saw the possibilities. If de Grasse could hold the bay while Washington came down from the land side, they might bag Cornwallis at Yorktown.

Washington ordered Lafayette to contain Cornwallis and on August 21 sent 2,000 American and 4,000 French soldiers south, leaving only 2,000 men under Brigadier General William Heath to watch British forces at New York under British commander in chief in North America lieutenant general Sir Henry Clinton. Not until early September did Clinton realize what had happened. Although Clinton promised Cornwallis a diversion, he did little to help his subordinate.

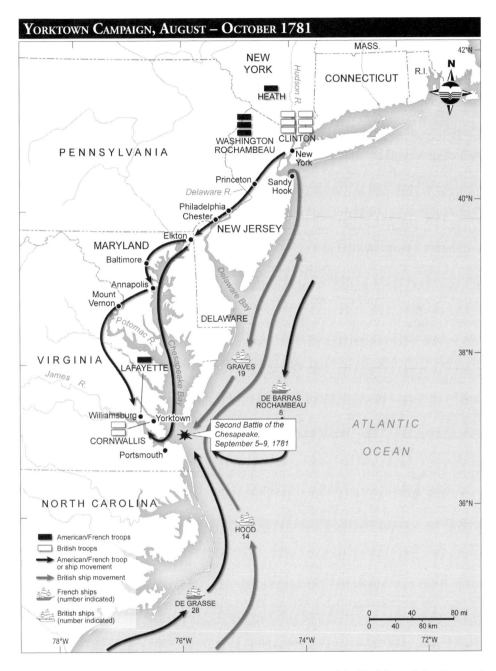

YORKTOWN CAMPAIGN, AUGUST – OCTOBER 1781

Legend:
- American/French troops
- British troops
- American/French troop or ship movement
- British ship movement
- French ships (number indicated)
- British ships (number indicated)

On August 30 de Grasse arrived in the Chesapeake with 28 ships of the line and 3,000 land troops. He immediately disembarked the troops under the command of Marquis de Saint-Simon and sent his transports and boats up the bay. During September 14–26 Washington and Rochambeau's troops were transported down Chesapeake Bay from Head of Elk (present-day Elkton), Baltimore, and Annapolis, Maryland, to land near Williamsburg, where they concentrated.

Barras meanwhile sailed south from Newport with 8 ships of the line convoying 18 transports also carrying siege guns. British rear admiral Thomas Graves with 19 ships of the line set out to intercept Barras on August 31. On September 5 a scout frigate in de Grasse's fleet signaled the approach of the British. Although short-handed, de Grasse stood out with 24 ships of the line to meet them. The French had a numerical advantage of 24 ships of the line to only 19 for the British. The resulting Battle of the Chesapeake (also known as the Battle of the Capes) ended in a tactical draw with damage and casualties but no ships lost on either side. Strategically, however, it was one of the most important naval battles in world history, for it left the French still in control of the bay. During the battle, Barras's ships arrived. Now facing even longer odds, Graves returned to New York to gather more ships, leaving Cornwallis, for the time being at least, to his own fate.

Marching from Williamsburg, Washington's combined American and French army arrived at Yorktown on September 28. Washington had some 9,000 American troops (3,000 were militia who played no role in the battle) and 7,500 French troops. He also had French field and siege artillery and the services of French engineers, who now directed a siege of Yorktown with European-style zigzag trenches and parallels dug toward the British defenses.

On October 9 the Americans and French began a bombardment. Two days later the allies began construction of a second siege line, this one only 400 yards from the British line. On the night of October 14 the allies stormed two key British redoubts. The French took No. 9 and the Americans seized No. 10, completing the second siege line. The allies were thus able to establish new firing positions that compromised the British defensive line. On October 16 the allies repulsed a desperate British counterattack. Too late, Cornwallis attempted to escape across the York River to Gloucester Point, which Washington had largely neglected. The plan was thwarted by a severe storm.

Now running low on food, on the morning of October 17 Cornwallis asked for terms, seeking parole for his men. Washington insisted that they surrender as prisoners of war, and Cornwallis agreed. On October 19 the formal surrender occurred: 8,077 British surrendered (840 seamen, 80 camp followers, and 7,157 soldiers). During the siege the British lost 156 killed and 326 wounded; the allies lost 75 killed and 199 wounded (two-thirds of them French). Clinton arrived with a powerful fleet and 7,000 land troops a week later. De Grasse had already departed for the West Indies.

The battle was in fact an amazing bit of luck. The British had lost control of the American seaboard for one brief period, and as a result they lost the war. The consequences of the British defeat at Yorktown were momentous. A terrific shock in England, it brought down the British Government of Lord North, a hard-liner, and ushered in a British policy of cutting its losses immediately, to the point of granting concessions to America, including independence, to separate it from its French ally.

References

Davis, Burke. *The Campaign That Won America: The Story of Yorktown.* New York: Dial, 1970.

Lumpkin, Henry. *From Savannah to Yorktown: The American Revolution in the South.* Columbia: University of South Carolina Press, 1981.

Morrissey, Brenden. *Yorktown, 1781: The World Turned Upside Down.* London: Osprey, 1997.

Battle of the Saints

Date	April 12, 1782	
Location	Off Îles des Saintes archipelago between Dominica and Guadeloupe in the West Indies	
Opponents (* winner)	*British	French
Commander	Admiral Sir George Rodney	Admiral François Joseph-Paul, Comte de Grasse
Approx. # Troops	36 ships of the line	30 ships of the line
Importance	The last major naval battle in the Caribbean of the American Revolutionary War, the British victory comes too late to affect the war's outcome but permits the British to retain all their West Indian islands in the resulting Treaty of Paris	

The Battle of the Saints (known to the French as the Battle of the Saintes) was the greatest British naval victory of the American Revolutionary War (1775–1783). The battle took its name from the Îles des Saintes, a small archipelago between Dominica and Guadeloupe in the West Indies. The battle was fought between a French fleet commanded by Admiral François Joseph-Paul, Comte de Grasse, and a British fleet under Admiral Sir George Rodney. The Caribbean sugar islands were vital to both sides for the revenues from their sugar production, and the presence of substantial French and British naval forces in the West Indies shows the much more important role of that area, rather than North America, in naval considerations.

On April 8, 1782, de Grasse sailed from Martinique with 35 ships of the line, 6 frigates, and 150 unarmed ships for an invasion of Jamaica. Rear Admiral Sir Samuel Hood, Rodney's second-in-command, immediately sailed from St. Lucia with 36 ships of the line and accompanying frigates. On the morning of April 9 the British caught up with the French off Dominica. De Grasse ordered his 2 50-gun ships to escort the convoy to safety at Guadeloupe and trusted in the superior sailing qualities of his ships to escape and rejoin his convoy. An indecisive engagement ensued when Hood's van of 8 ships separated from the rest of the fleet, whereupon de Grasse ordered 15 French ships under Marquis de Vaudreuil to attack. The French withdrew when the remainder of the British ships closed. One French ship was forced into Guadeloupe for repairs. Although some were badly damaged, none of Rodney's ships had to depart.

After making repairs that night, Rodney continued the pursuit. It looked as if de Grasse would escape when, on April 11, two of the French ships separated from the rest and dropped behind. With Rodney closing and hoping to cut the two ships off, de Grasse dropped back to protect them. That night one of the two French ships, the *Zélé,* rammed the French flagship, the *Ville de Paris* (110 guns), said to be the finest ship then afloat. The *Zélé* lost its foremast and bowsprit, and de Grasse ordered the frigate *Astrée* to take it in tow and head for Guadeloupe.

The British pursuers had been carrying a press of sail, and at dawn on April 12 Rodney could see both French ships making for Guadeloupe as well as the main body of the French fleet beyond. The two fleets were now between Dominica and the Saints. Rodney had 36 ships of the line to only 30 for de Grasse.

The battle opened with the two fleets in parallel lines exchanging broadsides. When the wind suddenly shifted, however, the French formation began to break apart, and the ships bunched up. Here superior British seamanship came into play, as Rodney quickly ordered his flagship *Formidable* through a gap in the French line. Five other British ships promptly followed, raking the French ships on either side as they did so. The *Duke* also pierced the French line in another place as did the *Formidable,* followed by other ships. The French formation was shattered and cut into three separate divisions. In the melee that followed the British inflicted serious damage on a number of French ships.

When the wind picked up again, de Grasse sought to escape westward with the British in pursuit. Three crippled French ships were quickly taken, and late that afternoon the British captured two additional French warships, including the *Ville de Paris* with de Grasse himself, the first time a French commander in chief had been captured at sea. At 6:45 p.m. Rodney signaled an end to the pursuit. The remainder of the French fleet, now under de Vaudreuil, managed to escape to Cape François.

Hood was appalled and criticized Rodney for his failure to continue the chase and finish off the French. Hood claimed that had he been in command, 20 ships would have been captured rather than 5. Rodney acknowledged he had been cautious, but many of his ships had been badly cut up aloft and were short of ammunition. The British spent the next four days repairing damage. On April 17 Hood took 4 additional French ships: the 2 64-gun ships badly damaged in the April 9 engagement, 1 frigate (32 guns), and 1 sloop (18 guns).

Following the battle, survivors on the captured French *César* (74 guns) broke into the spirit stores, and someone upset a candle. The ship caught fire and then exploded, killing 400 Frenchmen and 60 members of the British prize crew. Total

French casualties in the battle were more than 3,000; the British lost 243 dead and another 816 wounded.

The important British victory in the Battle of the Saints, the last major naval battle of the war in the Caribbean, came too late to affect the outcome of the war but was sufficient for the British to retain all their West Indian islands in the resulting Treaty of Paris and to place Hood and Rodney in the ranks of British naval heroes.

References

Clowes, William Laird. *The Royal Navy: A History from the Earliest Times to the Present,* Vol. 3. London: Sampson Low, Marston, 1898.

James, William M. *The British Navy in Adversity: A Study of the War of American Independence.* London: Longmans, Green, 1926.

Mahan, Alfred Thayer. *The Major Operations of the Navies in the War of American Independence.* Boston: Little, Brown, 1913.

Battle of Hanoi

Date	January 30, 1789	
Location	Hanoi in northern Vietnam	
Opponents (* winner)	*Vietnamese	Chinese
Commander	Emperor Quang Trung (Nguyen Hue)	Sun Shiyi
Approx. # Troops	Unknown	Unknown
Importance	One of the greatest victories in Vietnamese history, it expels the Chinese from Vietnam	

The Battle of Hanoi (Ngoc Hoi–Dong Da) of January 30, 1789, was fought between Vietnamese nationalists and the Chinese. Marking the end of the 1771–1789 Tay Son Rebellion, it is regarded as one of the greatest military victories in Vietnamese history. What might be called the First Tet Offensive, the Vietnamese offensive in 1789 was proof that this holiday was not always peacefully observed by warring Vietnamese and should have served as ample warning to the Americans and South Vietnamese authorities that the communist forces might strike during Tet in 1968.

In a brilliant campaign fought between May and July 1786, Nguyen Hue, the military genius of the three Tay Son brothers, defeated the Trinh lords in northern Vietnam and brought Emperor Le Chieu Thong under his control. After his victory Nguyen Hue returned to consolidate his authority in the south. Nguyen Hue's lieutenant in the north turned traitor, however, and in collusion with the emperor attempted to fortify the region against Nguyen Hue's return. Before Nguyen Hue could arrive with his army, Emperor Le Chieu Thong lost his nerve and fled to China. Once again, Nguyen Hue returned to the south.

Le Chieu Thong knew that the only hope of reclaiming his throne was Chinese assistance. Sun Shiyi, the Qing governor of territory bordering Vietnam, saw military intervention as an opportunity to assert Chinese influence in an area weakened by civil war. The Qing emperor agreed, and in November 1788 Sun Shiyi, assisted by General Xu Shiheng, led an expeditionary force of up to 200,000 men in an invasion of northern Vietnam. Faced with overwhelming Chinese strength, Nguyen Hue's generals sent ships with provisions south to Thanh Hoa while the troops retired overland.

The Qing forces took the capital of Hanoi in late December 1788 after a campaign of less than two months, but events worked to undermine their authority. The Chinese treated Vietnam as captured territory and forced Le Chieu Thong to issue pronouncements in the name of the Chinese emperor. Many Vietnamese resented reprisals against imperial officials who had earlier rallied to the Tay Son. Typhoons and disastrous harvests also led many northerners to believe that the emperor had lost the Mandate of Heaven.

On December 22, 1788, after learning of the Chinese invasion, Nguyen Hue proclaimed himself emperor of Vietnam with the throne name of Quang Trung. He then raised an army. To widen his appeal, he played to Vietnamese nationalism, stressing the long history of Chinese efforts to subjugate Vietnam. The key to his military success was careful planning. In the course of a 40-day campaign, Quang Trung devoted 35 days to preparations and only 5 to battle.

Quang Trung first ordered his soldiers to celebrate the Tet holiday early. He then sent a delegation to Sun Shiyi with a request that the Qing withdraw from Vietnam. Sun tore up the appeal and put the chief of the delegation to death, boasting that he would soon take Quang Trung.

Quang Trung ordered the main military effort to be made against the principal Qing line, where he concentrated his elite troops and the elephants that transported his heavy artillery. At the same time, he sent a part of his fleet north as a feint against the capital to prevent the Chinese from concentrating their reserves on the main front. His plan to attack on the eve of Tet was a brilliant stroke, catching the Chinese off guard celebrating the lunar new year. Quang Trung also profited from Chinese errors. Confident in his superior numbers, Sun Shiyi relaxed discipline.

Quang Trung's offensive, once launched, went forward both day and night (especially the latter) for five days. Each attack was mounted rapidly to prevent the Qing from bringing up reserves. Tay Son forces covered nearly 50 miles and took six forts defending access to the capital, a rate of 10 miles and more than one fort a day. The attackers were motivated by a desire to free their country from foreign domination. Indeed, tens of thousands of civilians joined the Tay Son army as it moved north.

At dawn on the fifth day of Tet (January 30, 1789), Tay Son forces approached the fort of Ngoc Hoi, at Dong Da in the southern part of Hanoi, and came under heavy enemy fire. Elite commandos assaulted the fortress in groups of 20, protected under wooden shields covered by straw soaked in water. Quang Trung exhorted his troops from atop an elephant. Following intense fighting, the Tay Son emerged victorious; large numbers of Chinese, including general officers, died in the attack.

Sun Shiyi learned of the disaster that same night. With fires clearly visible in the distance, he fled north across the Red River, not bothering to put on his armor or saddle his horse. Qing horsemen and infantry soon joined the flight, but the bridge they used was overburdened and collapsed. According to Vietnamese accounts thousands drowned, and the Red River was filled with bodies. Le Chieu Thong also fled and found refuge in China, ending the 300-year-old Le dynasty.

True to his word, on the afternoon of the seventh day of the new year Quang Trung entered Hanoi. His generals continued to pursue the Chinese to the frontier. Mobility and concentration of force, rather than numbers, were the keys to the Tay Son victory. Quang Trung's triumph is still celebrated in Vietnam as one of the nation's greatest military achievements. The Vietnamese celebrate the Ngoc Hoi–Dong Da victory every year by a festival in Hanoi on the fifth day of the first lunar month.

Quang Trung became one of Vietnam's greatest kings. Unfortunately, his reign was short. He died in the spring of 1792, so he did not have the "dozen years" that he believed were necessary to build a strong kingdom. His son was only six years old in 1792, and Quang Trung's brothers also died in the early 1790s. Within a decade, the surviving Nguyen lord, Nguyen Anh, had come to power, and the Nguyen dynasty was dominant throughout Vietnam.

References

Buttinger, Joseph. *The Smaller Dragon: A Political History of Vietnam.* London: Atlantic, 1958.

Déveria, G. *Histoire des Relations de la Chine avec L'Annam-Vietnam du XVIe au XIXe Siècle.* Paris: Ernest Leroux, 1880.

Le Thanh Khoi. *Histoire de Viet Nam des origines à 1858.* Paris: Sudestasie, 1981.

Truong Buu Lam. *Resistance, Rebellion, and Revolution: Popular Movements in Vietnamese History.* Singapore: Institute of Southeast Asian Studies, 1984.

Viet Chung. "Recent Findings on the Tay Son Insurgency." *Vietnamese Studies* 81 (1985): 30–62.

Battle of Valmy

Date	September 20, 1792	
Location	Between Sainte-Menehould and Valmy in northeastern France	
Opponents (* winner)	*French	Prussians, Austrians, Hessians, and French émigres
Commander	Generals François Estienne Kellermann and Charles François du Perrier Dumouriez	Karl Wilhelm, Duke of Brunswick
Approx. # Troops	54,000	30,000–34,000
Importance	Heralded as the first victory by a modern citizen army, it is indecisive tactically but a strategic French victory that ends any allied hopes of crushing the French Revolution in 1792	

The Battle of Valmy on September 20, 1792, was an important battle in the War of the First Coalition (1792–1798) during the French Revolution (1789–1799). In July 1792 an Austro-Prussian force assembled at Coblenz in the Rhineland with the aim of marching on Paris, rescuing King Louis XVI, and ending the revolution. Karl Wilhelm Ferdinand, Duke of Brunswick, accompanied in the field by Prussian king Frederick William II, commanded the allied force of some 84,000 men: 42,000 Prussians, 29,000 Austrians, 5,000 Hessians, and 8,000 French émigrés. Brunswick planned a movement whereby the main force would be protected on its flanks by two Austrian corps. He planned to move west between the two principal French defending armies: the Armée du Nord (Army of the North) under General Charles François du Perrier Dumouriez, and the Armée de Centre (Army of the Center) commanded by General François Estienne Kellermann. Once the invaders had taken the poorly provisioned French border fortresses, they could move to Châlons, and from there the way would be open to Paris.

Brunswick put his army in motion at the end of July and proceeded at a leisurely pace. On August 19 the allies crossed the French frontier. Longwy fell on August 23, and Verdun fell on September 2. Brunswick's forces then moved into the thickly wooded Argonne, terrain that favored the defender. Torrential rains played havoc with Brunswick's lines of communication, and dysentery claimed many men.

The government in Paris ordered Dumouriez to move south and block Brunswick. On September 1 Dumouriez led the majority of his troops from Sedan to take up position in the passes of the Argonne. Although Dumouriez's men fought well and bought valuable time, Brunswick managed to secure a lightly defended pass at Croix-aux-Bois, turning the French position. Dumouriez then withdrew to Sainte-Manehould and Valmy, where he could threaten Brunswick's flank. Kellermann joined him at Valmy, south of the Bionne River, on September 19. The French generals had planned to withdraw farther west, but the appearance of Brunswick's army from the north cut off that route.

While Brunswick was now closer to Paris than were Dumouriez and Kellermann, Brunswick needed to end the French threat to his supply lines but had only about 30,000–34,000 men to accomplish this. Kellermann commanded the first French line of some 36,000 men, drawn up along a ridge just west of Valmy. His troops consisted of an equal mix of trained prewar soldiers and untrained but enthusiastic volunteers. Dumouriez's exhausted force of 18,000 men formed a second line east of Valmy. Early morning fog on September 20 soon dissipated, and once Brunswick had identified the French positions, he prepared to attack. He had 54 artillery pieces, and Kellermann had only 36. Brunswick was confident of victory, for his troops were also far better trained.

The Battle of Valmy was more a cannonade than anything else. It began on the morning of September 20 when Frederick William II ordered the Prussian guns to bombard the French positions prior to an infantry assault. The French artillery, well handled by cannoneers of the pre–French Revolution army, replied. The distance of some 2,500 yards between the two sides and soft ground from recent heavy rains meant that the exchange did little damage to either side. The Prussians had expected the green French troops to break and run at the first volley and were amazed when they did not.

The Prussian infantry then began to advance. Perhaps Brunswick hoped that the French would bolt; when they failed to do so, he halted his troops after about 200 yards. One French battalion after another took up the cry of "*Vive la nation!*" Brunswick ordered a second advance at about 2:00 p.m., but his men got no farther than about 650 yards from the French. Brunswick then ordered a halt, followed by a retirement. At 4:00 p.m. Brunswick summoned a council of war and announced, "We do not fight here."

Losses in the battle were slight: the Prussians lost 164 men, the French about 300. Brunswick had never been enthusiastic about the offensive and wanted only to secure positions east of the Argonne in preparation for a major campaign the next spring. The king had insisted on the movement farther west. Brunswick now used the rebuff as an excuse to withdraw. The Prussian forces lingered in the area for 10 days, but on the night of September 30–October 1 they broke camp, recrossing the French border on October 23.

The Battle of Valmy ended any allied hopes of crushing the French Revolution in 1792. The government in Paris now authorized Dumouriez to invade the Austrian Netherlands, and on November 6 his forces defeated the Austrians at Jemappes. The Battle of Valmy was also important for marking the end of the age of dynastic armies and the arrival of the new age of patriotic national armies. Poet Johann Wolfgang von Goethe, present that day, understood this. When some Prussian officers asked him what he thought of the battle, he reportedly replied, "From this place, and from this day forth, commences a new era in the world's history, and you can all say that you were present at its birth."

References

Bertaud, Jean Paul. *Valmy: La Démocratie en Armes.* Paris: Julliard, 1970.

Creasy, Edward S. *The Fifteen Decisive Battles of the World: From Marathon to Waterloo.* New York: Heritage, 1969.

Davis, Paul K. *100 Decisive Battles: From Ancient Times to the Present.* Santa Barbara, CA: ABC-CLIO, 1999.

Fuller, J. F. C. *A Military History of the Western World,* Vol. 2. New York: Funk and Wagnalls, 1995.

Lynn, John. "Valmy." *MHQ: Quarterly Journal of Military History* 5(1) (Autumn 1992): 88–96.

British Capture of Toulon

Date	August 27, 1793	
Location	Port city of Toulon, France on the Mediterranean	
Opponents (* winner)	British, Spaniards	French
Commander	Vice Admiral Lord Alexander Hood (British); Admiral Don Juan de Langara (Spanish)	Rear Admiral Jean Honoré, Comte de Trogoff de Kerlessy
Approx. # Troops	21 ships of the line (British); 17 ships of the line (Spanish)	17 ships of the line ready for sea (4 others refitting and 9 repairing)
Importance	Britain and Spain seize almost half of the capital ships in the French Navy and occupy its principal Mediterranean base	

This major British naval action took place during the French Revolution (1789–1799). Fighting had begun the year before between revolutionary France and Austria and Prussia. The revolutionaries tried and executed King Louis XVI in January 1793, and Britain entered the fray against France in April.

The French Navy was not in the best condition at the start of hostilities. Revolutionary activities over the previous three and a half years had all but wrecked both the army and the navy. Virtually all senior professional officers were nobles, and most of these had either fled France or had been purged. Merchant captains were pressed into service as substitutes, but much more than with the army, enthusiasm was no substitute for the long years of training required to operate warships at sea, let alone fight.

In 1792 the crews were mutinous and poorly trained. Naval yards and shore facilities, having been starved of resources, were in poor repair. While the French possessed some 76 ships of the line at the start of hostilities, fewer than half could be manned and put to sea. The British Royal Navy could send to sea 125 ships of the line, although seamen were in short supply. Spain added another 56 ships of the line, and their crews were indifferently trained. The Dutch contributed 49 ships of the line, but these were somewhat lighter than most ships of the line in other navies.

Admiral Lord Richard Howe commanded the British Atlantic Fleet, while Vice Admiral Lord Alexander Hood commanded in the Mediterranean. In the summer of 1793 Hood had 21 ships of the line, including the 100-rates *Victory* and *Britannia*. Opposing him at Toulon, French rear admiral Jean Honoré, Comte de Trogoff de Kerlessy, had 58 warships, nearly half the French Navy. Seventeen of these were ships of the line ready for sea, including the giant 120-gun *Commerce de Marseille*. Trogoff had another 4 ships of the line being refitted and 9 being repaired.

In July, Toulon overthrew its Jacobin government and declared for the monarchy. When Paris dispatched troops, Toulon's counterrevolutionary leaders invited Hood to defend them. Accompanied by a Spanish squadron of 17 ships of the line under Admiral Don Juan de Langara, Hood arrived off Toulon in mid-August. Many of the French crews were willing to fight, but a great many simply deserted. On August 27 Hood's ships sailed into the port, and Spanish and other allied troops went ashore. The British disarmed the French ships and put 5,000 captured French seamen on board four disarmed and unserviceable 74-gun ships of the line to sail under passport to French Atlantic ports.

In September, French Republican forces arrived and invested the port from the land side. The Republican troops did little until December, however, when young artillery captain Napoleon Bonaparte convinced his superiors to use land artillery to force the British from the port. On December 17 French troops took the heights, and on the night of December 18–19 the British and Spanish sailed away, lifting off the allied land force and some French royalists.

Captain Sir Sidney Smith meanwhile volunteered to burn the dockyard and those French ships that could not be gotten off. His improvised effort was only partially successful. Although his men were able to fire some smaller storehouses, the large magazine escaped destruction. In all, 19 French ships (11 of them ships of the line), including those under construction, were destroyed. The Spanish took off 3 small French warships, and the British secured 15 French warships, including 3 ships of the line.

Few of the ships captured were of value. The *Commerce de Marseille*, which became the largest ship of the Royal Navy, was too weak structurally for fleet service and became first a storeship and then a prison hulk. The French recovered largely intact at least 16 warships, including 13 ships of the line. Later these formed the nucleus of the fleet that carried Napoleon's expedition to Egypt.

This operation at Toulon, in addition to signaling the beginning of the meteoric rise of young Napoleon Bonaparte, marked the end of Spanish participation in the naval war on the British side. Following the Toulon fiasco the French had only their Atlantic fleet, and it was in poor repair.

References

Crook, Malcom. *Toulon in War and Revolution: From the Ancient Regime to the Restoration, 1750–1820.* Manchester, UK: Manchester University Press, 1991.

Gardiner, Robert, ed. *Fleet Battle and Blockade: The French Revolutionary War, 1793–1797.* London: Chatham, 1996.

Battle of Fallen Timbers

Date	August 20, 1794	
Location	Just south of present-day Toledo, Ohio (United States of America)	
Opponents (* winner)	*Legion of the United States; Kentucky militia; allied Native Americans	Coalition of Native Americans; a few Canadian volunteers
Commander	Major General Anthony Wayne	Blue Jacket
Approx. # Troops	3,800 (2,000 Legion of United States, 1,600 Kentucky militia, 200 allied Native Americans)	1,000 Native Americans; 60 Canadian militiamen
Importance	Breaks the power of the Native Americans in the eastern region of the Old Northwest, restores the prestige of the army, and leads to Wayne being known as the father of the U.S. Army	

The Battle of Fallen Timbers, fought just south of present-day Toledo, Ohio, between the United States and Native Americans secured control of much of Ohio from the Native Americans. In the 1783 Treaty of Paris that ended the American Revolutionary War (1775–1783), the British government acknowledged U.S. claims west of the Appalachians and made no effort to protect Native American lands in the Ohio Valley. Incursions by American settlers there led to serious problems because the Native American leaders refused to acknowledge U.S. authority north of the Ohio River. Although during 1784–1789 the government persuaded some chiefs to relinquish lands in southern and eastern Ohio, most Native Americans refused to acknowledge these treaties.

Encouraged by the British, leaders of the Miami and Shawnee tribes insisted that the Americans fall back to the Ohio River. When the settlers refused, the Miamis attacked them, prompting Northwest Territory governor Arthur St. Clair to send U.S. troops and militia against the Native Americans along the Maumee River. Brigadier General Josiah Harmar led an expedition in October 1790, the first for the U.S. Army. Setting out with 1,300 men, including 320 regulars and Pennsylvania and Kentucky militiamen, Harmar divided his poorly trained force into three separate columns. Near present-day Fort Wayne, Indiana, the Miamis and Shawnees, led by Miami chief Little Turtle, defeated Harmar in detail, with the U.S. troops sustaining 300 casualties.

In the autumn of 1791 St. Clair, now commissioned a major general, led a second expedition of the entire 600-man regular army, along with 1,500 militia. On November 3 the men camped along the upper Wabash River at present-day Fort Recovery, Ohio. The next morning Little Turtle and his warriors caught them by surprise and administered the worst defeat ever by Native Americans on the British or Americans, inflicting some 800 casualties. Native American losses were reported as 21 killed and 40 wounded.

President George Washington did not attempt to conceal these twin disasters from the American people, and in December 1792 Congress voted to establish the 5,000-man Legion of the United States, commanded by a major general and consisting of four sublegions of 1,250 men, with each sublegion led by brigadier generals. Washington appointed retired general Anthony ("Mad Anthony") Wayne to command the legion.

Wayne set up a training camp 25 miles from Pittsburgh at a site he named Legionville and put the men through rigorous training. In May 1793 he moved the legion to Cincinnati and then a few miles north to a new camp, Hobson's Choice. In early October, Wayne moved north with 2,000 regulars to Fort Jefferson, the end of his defensive line. When Kentucky mounted militia arrived, Wayne moved a few miles farther north and set up a new camp, naming it Fort Greeneville (now Greenville, Ohio) in honor of his American Revolutionary War commander, Major General Nathanael Greene.

In December 1793 Wayne sent a detachment to the site of St. Clair's defeat on the Wabash. On Christmas Day the Americans reoccupied the battlefield and constructed Fort Recovery on high ground overlooking the Wabash. Aided by friendly Native Americans, the soldiers recovered most of St. Clair's cannon, which the Native Americans had buried nearby. These were incorporated into Fort Recovery, which was manned by an infantry company and detachment of artillerists.

Wayne's campaign timetable was delayed because of unreliable civilian contractors, Native American attacks on his supply trains, the removal of some of his men elsewhere, and a cease-fire that led him to believe that peace might be in the offing. But Little Turtle, Shawnee war chief Blue Jacket, and other chiefs rejected peace negotiations, in part because of a speech by British governor-general in Canada Sir Guy Carleton, who predicted war between Britain and the United States and pledged British support for the Native Americans. In February 1794 Carleton ordered construction of Fort Miami on the Maumee River to mount cannon larger than those that Wayne might be able to bring against it, further delaying Wayne's advance.

On June 29, 1794, Little Turtle struck at Fort Recovery, Wayne's staging point for the invasion. A supply train had just arrived there and was bivouacked outside the walls when 2,000 warriors attacked. Although a number of soldiers were killed, the Native Americans were beaten back with heavy casualties, and two days later they withdrew. Never again were the Native Americans able to assemble that many warriors. The repulse also prompted some of the smaller tribes to quit the coalition and led to the eclipse of Little Turtle, who was replaced as principal war leader by the less effective Blue Jacket.

Wayne now had 2,000 men. In mid-July some 1,600 Kentucky militia under Brigadier General Charles Scott began to arrive. Wayne also could count on 100 Native Americans, mostly Choctaws and Chickasaws, from Tennessee. On July 28 Wayne departed Fort Greeneville for Fort Recovery. Washington warned that a third straight defeat "would be inexpressibly ruinous to the reputation of the government."

The Native Americans were concentrated at Miami Town, the objective of previous offensives, and the rapids of the Maumee River around Fort Miami. A 100-mile road along the Maumee River Valley connected the two. Wayne intended to build a fortification at midpoint on the road, allowing him to strike in either direction and forcing the Native Americans to defend both possible objectives. By August 3 he had established this position, Fort Adams, and had also built a second fortified position, Fort Defiance, at the confluence of the Auglaize and Maumee rivers. Wayne then sent the chiefs a final peace offer. Little Turtle urged its acceptance, pointing out the strength of the force opposing them and expressing doubts about British support. Blue Jacket and British agents wanted war, which a majority of the chiefs approved.

Wayne decided to move to Fort Miami. After a difficult crossing of the Maumee River, on August 15 Wayne's men were still 10 miles away. Sensing a fight, Wayne detached unnecessary elements from his column to construct a possible fallback position, Fort Deposit, manned by Captain Zebulon Pike and 200 men. On August 20 Wayne again put his column in motion, anticipating battle that day with either the Native Americans or the British. Indeed, more than 1,000 braves and some 60 Canadian militiamen were lying in wait for the Americans, hoping to ambush them from the natural defenses of what had been a forest before it had been uprooted by a tornado and transformed into a chaos of twisted branches and broken tree trunks.

Blue Jacket had expected Wayne to arrive on August 19. In preparation for battle, the Native Americans began a strict fast on August 18 and then continued it the next day. When the Americans did not arrive, many of the Native Americans, hungry and exhausted, departed for Fort Miami.

Wayne marched in formation ready to meet an attack from any quarter. His infantry were in two wings: Brigadier General James Wilkinson commanded the right, and Colonel John Hamtramck commanded the left. A mounted brigade of Kentuckians protected the left flank, while legion horsemen covered the right. Additional Kentucky horsemen protected the rear and served as a reserve. Well to the front, Major William Price led a battalion to trigger the Native American attack and allow Wayne time to deploy the main body.

When the Native Americans did open fire, Price's men fell back into Wilkinson's line. Wayne rallied his men and sent them to defeat the ambush with an infantry frontal attack driven home with the bayonet. At the same time, the horsemen closed on the flanks. The Native Americans were routed, fleeing toward Fort Miami. The killing went on right up to the gates of the fort while the British looked on. Wayne's losses were 33 men killed and 100 wounded (11 of them mortally wounded), while Native American losses were in the hundreds.

Although Wayne disregarded Fort Miami, he destroyed the Native American communities and the British storehouses in its vicinity. The soldiers then marched to Miami Town. They occupied it without opposition on September 17 and razed it. They then built a fort on the site of Harmar's 1790 defeat, naming it Fort Wayne.

The Battle of Fallen Timbers broke forever the power of the Native Americans in the eastern region of the northwest. The victory did a great deal to restore U.S. military prestige, and Wayne is justifiably known as the father of the U.S. Army. The battle also led the British to evacuate their garrisons below the Great Lakes. When Wayne revealed that the British had agreed to withdraw their forts and recognize the boundary set in the 1783 Treaty of Paris, chiefs representing 12 tribes signed the Treaty of Greeneville. The treaty set a definite boundary in the Northwest Territory, forcing the American Indians to give up once and for all most of the present state of Ohio and part of Native Americana. Increased settler movement into the Ohio Territory, the ensuing Native American resentment, and the Native American turn to the British helped set the stage for the War of 1812 in the North American west.

References

Millett, Allan R. "Caesar and the Conquest of the Northwest Territory: The Wayne Campaign, 1792–95." *Timeline: A Publication of the Ohio Historical Society* 14 (1997): 2–21.

Nelson, Paul D. *Anthony Wayne: Soldier of the Early Republic.* Bloomington: Indiana University Press, 1985.

Nelson, Paul D. "Anthony Wayne's Indian War in the Old Northwest, 1792–1795." *Northwest Ohio Quarterly* 56 (1984): 115–140.

Palmer, Dave R. *1794: America, Its Army, and the Birth of the Nation.* Novato, CA: Presidio, 1994.

Sword, Wiley. *President Washington's Indian War: The Struggle for the Old Northwest, 1790–1795.* Norman: University of Oklahoma Press, 1985.

Tebbel, John W. *The Battle of Fallen Timbers, August 20, 1794.* New York: Franklin Watts, 1972.

Battle of Rivoli

Date	January 14, 1797	
Location	Rivoli, about 8 miles west of Turin in Piedmont (northern Italy)	
Opponents (* winner)	*French	Austrians
Commander	General Napoleon Bonaparte	General Count Josef Alvinci
Approx. # Troops	10,000–20,000	12,000–28,000
Importance	The most important battle of Bonaparte's Italian campaign, it marks an important step forward in his career	

The Battle of Rivoli on January 14, 1797, between the French and the Austrians occurred during the War of the First Coalition (1792–1797). Rivoli was the last and most important battle of Napoleon Bonaparte's Italian campaign and a significant step forward in his career.

In January 1797 Napoleon's forces were besieging Mantua. While Général de Brigade Philibert Sérurier maintained the siege with 8,500 men, other French forces were to the north and east of the city to intercept any Austrian attempt to raise the siege. Napoleon positioned Général de Division Barthelemi-Catherine Joubert to the north with 10,000 men, Général de Division Andrea Masséna at Verona with 10,000 men, and Général de Division Pierre François Charles Augereau at Adige with another 10,000 men. Another 4,000 French troops were scattered in garrisons at Brescia, Peschiera, and other locations at the south end of Lake Garda. The major French forces were thus as much as 70 miles apart.

Napoleon was off at Bologna with Général de Division Jean Lannes and 3,000 troops when he learned, on January 10, that Austrian general Count Josef Alvinci was on the move with a sizable force. The next day Napoleon was at Roverbella, where he learned of skirmishing between Austrian and French forces in the area between Legnago and Badia. Believing that this was Alvinci advancing from Trieste, on January 12 Napoleon ordered both Masséna and Augereau to shift to meet an attack from the east. He also ordered the garrisons at the south end of Lake Garda to join them.

The next day, January 13, Napoleon learned of his mistake when Joubert reported that Alvinci was instead pushing south from the Tyrol with substantial forces and had forced him to retreat southward to the vicinity of Rivoli. Napoleon immediately ordered Masséna and Augereau to make haste to Rovoli where Napoleon also moved, joining Joubert there at 2:00 a.m. on January 14.

Napoleon ordered Joubert to position his troops on the Trombalora Heights, just north of Rivoli. The French were in position and ready to meet the Austrians by dawn. Napoleon hoped to hold off Alvinci until the arrival of reinforcements and was aided by Alvinci's tendency to carefully position all his forces prior to any at-

French general Napoleon Bonaparte (on horseback, center) at the Battle of Rivoli, Italy, on January 14, 1797. Bonaparte's victory here marked an important advance in his military career. Painting by French artist Henri Felix Philippoteaux (1815–1884). (Chaiba Media)

tack. While the Austrian general had a total force of some 42,000 men, he arrived at Rivoli with only 12,000, having sent the remainder to circle the French position and take it from the rear.

Napoleon did not wait either for his reinforcements or for the Austrians to concentrate. He attacked at dawn the three Austrian divisions to his front, driving into gaps between them. The battle was going badly for the French, with the Austrians having opened a gap in their position, when at about 10:00 a.m. Masséna arrived on the battlefield with some 6,000 troops and took up position on the French right. Supported by French cavalry, these troops then attacked and broke into the Austrian rear.

Alvinci's detachments sent to surround the French were also defeated, whereupon the Austrian forces withdrew northward. Général de Brigade Joachim Murat and 600 cavalry crossed Lake Garda in gunboats and pressed the fleeing Austrians into the next day, adding substantially to the French prisoner count. The Austrians suffered some 14,000 casualties, while the French suffered only 5,000 casualties.

Following the battle, Archduke Charles, Austria's best field commander and the same age as Napoleon (27), replaced Alvinci. After a siege of two weeks, the French took Mantua on February 2. Napoleon then drove on Vienna, forcing the Austrian government to sign an armistice on April 18 at Leoben that led to a peace treaty on October 17 at Campo Formio. This ended the War of the First Coalition, since only Britain remained at war against France. In the treaty, France received Belgium, the Cisalpine Republic (with its capital at Milan), and part of Venetia and the former Venetian (Ionian) islands. Austria also confirmed the French possession of the left bank of the Rhine and secured much of the mainland of Venetia and Dalmatia. The war and the treaty were a personal triumph for Napoleon Bonaparte, who returned to Paris in December having firmly established his military reputation.

References

Chandler, David G. *The Campaigns of Napoleon.* New York: Macmillan, 1966.

Connelly, Owen. *Blundering to Glory: Napoleon's Military Campaigns.* Rev. ed. Wilmington, DE: Scholarly Resources, 1999.

Ferrero, Guglielmo. *The Gamble: Bonaparte in Italy, 1796–1797.* London: Walker, 1961.

Rothenberg, Gunther E. *Napoleon's Great Adversaries: The Archduke Charles and the Austrian Army, 1792–1814.* Bloomington: Indiana University Press, 1982.

Battle of Cape St. Vincent

Date	February 14, 1797	
Location	In the Atlantic Ocean, off Cape St. Vincent, southwestern Portugal	
Opponents (* winner)	*British	Spanish
Commander	Admiral Sir John Jervis	Teniente General José de Córdoba y Ramos
Approx. # Troops	15 ships of the line	27 ships of the line
Importance	It ends a possible invasion threat to Britain, has important impact on naval tactics, and marks the rise of Horatio Nelson.	

The Battle of Cape St. Vincent was a key naval battle in the Wars of the French Revolution between a British fleet under Admiral Sir John Jervis and a Spanish fleet under Teniente General (Lieutenant General) José de Córdoba y Ramos. In August 1796 Spain joined France in war against Britain. As Spain prepared to assist France in an invasion of England, in December Admiral Jervis collected the Mediterranean fleet at Gibraltar and concentrated its activities off the Atlantic coasts of Spain and Portugal. The French gathered their ships at Brest.

On February 1, 1797, Córdoba departed Cartagena, in the Mediterranean, with 27 ships of the line, 12 frigates, 1 brigantine, and some smaller craft, and sailed past Gibraltar into the Atlantic. He planned to put in at Cádiz, take on supplies, and then sail for Brest to rendezvous with the French and Dutch fleets for the invasion of England. Jervis, with 15 ships of the line, 5 frigates, 1 brig, and 1 cutter, was sailing off Portugal to prevent such a concentration. Had an easterly gale not driven the Spanish ships well to the west, Córdoba might have gained Cádiz, and Jervis would have been reduced to a blockade.

Informed of the presence of the Spanish ships by his scouting forces, Jervis sailed south and came on the Spanish off Cape St. Vincent early on the morning of February 14. The Spanish ships were moving in two divisions, one division of 18 ships and the other division of 9 ships. Jervis formed his own ships into a single-line formation to drive them between Córdoba's divisions. The Spanish crews were not well trained, and Córdoba knew that he could not hope to unite his two divisions. Instead, he brought his westerly division onto a northerly heading, intent on escaping astern of the British. Jervis responded by ordering his ships to tack in succession, reverse course, and engage the Spanish rear.

In an hour of fighting only a small number of the ships were engaged, and it looked as if Córdoba might bring most of his ships astern of the British and escape. Jervis then gave his famous signal Number 41: "The ships to take suitable station for their mutual support and to engage the enemy as arriving up with them in succession." This abandoned the traditional line of battle formation designed to take advantage of the broadsides firepower. Under it, a fleet would sail in line-ahead formation with the ships blasting away at close range at their opposites in the enemy line. Jervis's signal freed each ship to act on its own to form a new line of battle as quickly as possible.

Captain Horatio Nelson in the *Captain* (74 guns), third from the end in the British line, anticipated Jervis's command. Participating in his first fleet engagement, Nelson may or may not have seen the signal but had already acted and turned the tide of battle. He broke from the line and stood on the opposite tack into the path of the advancing Spanish line. Captain Cuthbert Collingwood in the *Excellent,* the last ship in line, followed his friend's ship.

Almost at once the *Captain* fell in with the 130-gun four-decker *Santísima Trinidad,* the largest warship in the world. Three other Spanish warships also joined in, including two 112-gun ships and one 80-gun ship. Soon Nelson's ship was a near wreck. Nelson's action forced the Spanish ships to alter course, and this allowed the remainder of Jervis's ships to close and join the fight.

In the ensuing melee battle the British took four Spanish ships, two of which fell to Nelson. The 80-gun *San Nicolás* and 112-gun *San Josef* collided, and Nelson ordered his ship to ram the *San Nicolás.* The three ships were soon locked together by spars and rigging. Nelson, with sword drawn, led a party of marines and sailors armed with pistols, pikes, and cutlasses to the *San Nicolás* and then crossed from the *San Nicolás* to the *San Josef.* This exploit, unique in the history of the Royal Navy, became celebrated in the fleet as "Nelson's patent bridge for boarding first rates."

Although the remaining Spanish ships escaped to Cádiz the next day, the Battle of Cape St. Vincent ended the possible invasion threat to Britain. The victory raised morale in Britain and convinced many that their nation could triumph against great odds. The battle depressed the Spanish, making it less likely that they would be willing to take on the Royal Navy again, and also showed the superiority of the melee battle over line of battle, at least for a more aggressive force with superior seamanship. Finally, the battle marked the rise of Horatio Nelson.

References

Clowes, William Laird. *The Royal Navy: A History from the Earliest Times to 1900,* Vol. 4. London: Sampson Low, Marston, 1899.

Gardiner, Robert, ed. *Fleet Battle and Blockade: The French Revolutionary War, 1793–1797*. London: Chatham, 1996.

Lloyd, Christopher. *St. Vincent and Camperdown.* New York: Macmillan, 1963.

Hough, Richard. *Nelson: A Biography.* London: Park Lane, 1980.

Tunstall, Brian. *Naval Warfare in the Age of Sail: The Evolution of Fighting Tactics, 1650–1815.* Edited by Nicholas Tracy. London: Conway Maritime, 1990.

White, Colin. *1797: Nelson's Year of Destiny.* Stroud, UK: Sutton, 1998.

Battle of the Nile

Date	August 1, 1798	
Location	Aboukir Bay, Egypt	
Opponents (* winner)	*British	French
Commander	Rear Admiral Horatio Nelson	Vice Admiral François Brueys d'Aigalliers
Approx. # Troops	13 ships of the line	13 ships of the line
Importance	The destruction of the French fleet cuts off General Napoleon Bonaparte's army in Egypt and ends his dream of establishing a Middle Eastern empire	

In 1798 the French mounted a major expedition under General Napoleon Bonaparte to capture Egypt and threaten India. This French force sailed on May 19. It numbered some 35,000 men in 400 transports, accompanied by 13 ships of the line and a number of smaller frigates. En route to Egypt the French took Malta, ruled by the Knights of St. John, and its sizable treasury. London dispatched a small fleet under Rear Admiral Horatio Nelson to seek out the French invasion force that had sailed east from Toulon to a then-unknown destination. In pursuit, Nelson actually passed close by the French ships on the night of June 22–23 without realizing it. He guessed Napoleon's objective to be Alexandria. With all sails set, Nelson's ships arrived there on June 28, but not seeing the French there he departed. Slower than the British because of their transports and supply ships, the French ships dropped anchor in Alexandria on July 1. Believing that the French might have made for Sicily, Nelson sailed for that island, only to learn that he had been correct in his original surmise.

Finally, at Aboukir Bay, Egypt, on August 1, 1798, Nelson and his 13 74-gun ships of the line caught up with the French fleet commanded by Vice Admiral François Brueys d'Aigalliers. Although the two sides were equal in number, many of the French ships were larger than those of the English. The English had 13 ships of the line of 74 guns each, 1 ship of 50 guns, and 1 sloop. The French had 13 ships of the line: 1 of 120 guns, 3 of 80 guns each, and 9 of 74 guns. They also had 4 frigates of 36–40 guns each, 2 brigs, 3 bomb vessels, and several gunboats. The French crews, however, had been decimated by disease, and they were short of water and supplies. Some of the French ships were also weakly armed, so the French battle line was considerably less formidable than it appeared.

The French were also unprepared for battle. Brueys, who flew his flag in the 120-gun *Orient,* thought his position secure. His 13 ships of the line were anchored in a single line, protected by shoals, gunboats, and shore batteries, but part of his crews were ashore. He had not ordered cables strung between the ships to prevent penetration by opposing vessels, nor did the French ships have springs attached to their anchor cables to prevent an opposing vessel from engaging them stern to stern. Also, the nearest French land batteries were three miles distant and thus quite unable to provide additional firepower to the fleet.

On seeing the French ships, Nelson ordered the general signal "Prepare for Battle" hoisted. As the British ships closed on the French, over dinner Nelson announced to his officers, "Before this time tomorrow, I shall have gained a Peerage or Westminster Abbey." He had foreseen the situation and already explained to his captains what he expected. No new orders were needed, and the attack occurred that same afternoon. The resulting Battle of Aboukir Bay, which the British remember as the Battle of the Nile, was a disaster for the French.

The French ships were anchored to allow them to swing with the current. Noting that if there was room for a French ship to swing there was sufficient space for a British ship to maneuver and guessing that the French ships were unprepared to fight on their port sides, Nelson sent his leading ships in from that direction. The risk was revealed when the first British ship, the *Culloden,* grounded. Three of Nelson's ships of the line led by the *Goliath* managed to get in between the French battle line and the shore, however, where they anchored. Nelson, in the *Vanguard,* took the remainder of his force down the outside of the French line.

Brueys's ships were now under attack from two sides. Such fighting was difficult in the best of circumstances, but it was made more so for the French because their ships were shorthanded. Systematically moving down the line, the British doubled up on one French ship after another.

The battle continued well into the night. The *Orient,* which was being painted when the British arrived, caught fire. The flames finally reached the magazine, whereupon the *Orient* went up in a great explosion that rocked the coast for miles. The flagship took down with it most of Napoleon's treasury, some £600,000 in gold and diamonds alone.

By dawn only two French ships of the line remained; the rest had been burned, sunk, or captured. One that did get away carried Admiral Pierre Charles Villeneuve, Nelson's opponent at the later Battle of Trafalgar; the other took Admiral Denis Decrès, subsequently Napoleon's minister of marine. Admiral Brueys was among those killed. More important from a strategic standpoint than the loss of the French ships, Napoleon's army was now cut off in Egypt. The British victory also led to the formation of a new coalition against France that included Russia, Austria, some of the Italian states, and the Ottoman Empire. Napoleon was in effect the prisoner of his conquest.

British sea power had ended Napoleon's dreams of a Middle Eastern empire. In 1799 he abandoned his army in Egypt, returning to France in a frigate in early October. The next month Napoleon took power as first consul in a coup d'état.

References

Foreman, Laura. *Napoleon's Lost Fleet: Bonaparte, Nelson, and the Battle of the Nile.* New York: Discovery Books, 1999.

Gardiner, Robert, ed. *Nelson against Napoleon: From the Nile to Copenhagen, 1798–1801.* London: Chatham, 1997.

Lavery, Brian. *Nelson and the Nile: The Naval War against Bonaparte, 1798.* London: Chatham, 1998.

Tracy, Nicholas. *Nelson's Battles: The Art of Victory in the Age of Sail.* Annapolis, MD: Naval Institute Press, 1996.

Battle of Hohenlinden

Date	December 3, 1800	
Location	Hohenlinden in Bavaria (southern Germany)	
Opponents (* winner)	*French	Austrians
Commander	General Jean-Viktor Moreau	Archduke Johann (John)
Approx. # Troops	50,000	62,300
Importance	Ends the War of the Second Coalition against France	

The brilliant French victory at the Battle of Hohenlinden, in Bavaria, ended the War of the Second Coalition (1798–1800) against France. England, which had remained at war with France since 1793, at the end of 1798 signed a treaty with Russia to initiate the War of the Second Coalition (1798–1800). The allies included Russia, Austria, the Ottoman Empire, and Naples. Their plan called for an Anglo-Russian force to expel the French from the Netherlands, while Austrian forces under Archduke Charles forced the French from Germany and Switzerland, and Russian-Austrian forces drove them from Italy.

At first events went according to allied plan. Austro-Russian forces defeated the French in Italy, and Anglo-Russian forces campaigned in the Netherlands. Reversals and rivalries among the coalition members soon brought its collapse, however. The Austrians abandoned Russian general Alexander Korsakov's forces in Switzerland in September 1799 when Vienna ordered forces under Archduke Charles to the Rhineland instead. Général de Division Victor-André Masséna defeated Korsakov at Zurich, obliging Russian forces under Alexander Suvorov to retreat over the Alps. Suvorov's army was decimated in the process. In October the British were obliged to evacuate Holland, and Russia withdrew from the war.

Napoleon Bonaparte now returned from Egypt to France. In a November 1799 coup d'état, he became first consul, effectively assuming full power. Napoleon then took the field against Austria, crossing the Alps and campaigning in Italy. On June 14, 1800, at Marengo, Napoleon lost a battle to the Austrians, having detached a corps under Général de Division Louis Desaix to find them. Fortunately, Desaix marched his men to the sound of the guns and, on his arrival, informed Napoleon that there was still time in the day to win another battle. Desaix attacked, and although he fell mortally wounded, he won the day for Napoleon. Peace negotiations dragged on, however, until Général de Division Jean-Viktor Moreau's victory over Austrian forces under Archduke Johann (John) at Hohenlinden in Bavaria on December 3, 1800.

At the beginning of December Moreau commanded some 50,000 men, while Archduke Charles commanded 64,000 men. Moreau's forces, which were moving west, were dispersed over a 30-mile front. Moreau assumed that he held the initiative and was surprised when he came under Austrian attack. Johann's chief of staff, Colonel Franz Weyrother, had convinced the archduke to go on the offensive. Overwhelming Austrian numbers forced French Général de Division Michel Ney and his 10,000 men into a fighting withdrawal from Ampfling on December 1. The Battle of Ampfling, however, cost the Austrians 3,070 casualties (1,077 prisoners) to only 1,707 (697 taken prisoner) for the French.

These figures should have given Johann pause, but he believed that the French were in full retreat and ordered his forces, advancing west on parallel axes, to continue toward München (Munich) and concentrate near Hohenlinden. Johann expected that if Moreau were to give battle, the decisive encounter would occur the next day near Haag, about eight miles east of Hohenlinden.

Austrian patrols discovered that the French had departed, however, as the archduke pushed his principal column of some 22,000 men under General Johann Kollowrat down the only hard-surface road, which ran through the Forest of Hohenlinden. Weyrother sent three other columns paralleling the main column: one just to the north under General Maximilien Baillet with 11,000 men; another farther north, just south of the Isen River, under General Michael Kienmayer with 16,000 men; and one to the south under General Johann Riesch with 13,300 men. Moreau had 32,000 men in his main body with two divisions to the south, one of 10,000 men under Général de Division Antoine Decaen and another of 8,400 men under Général de Division Charles Richepence.

The Battle of Hohenlinden opened at about 7:00 a.m. on December 3 when Kollowrat's main body, with the archduke and his staff, came under fire from French troops concealed in the forest on either side. Moreau was able to concentrate the bulk of his forces against the main Austrian body, while Johann was unable to bring his together in timely fashion. The Austrians pushed forward, and Ney and Général de Division Emmanuel de Grouchy to his right deserve much credit for the success of their two outnumbered divisions in repelling the main Austrian attack.

On the night of December 2 Moreau, aware of the broad outline of the Austrian plan, had ordered both Richepance and Decaen to flank the Austrian left. Their attack late on the morning of December 3 with 18,000 men caught the Austrians by surprise and caused the Austrian left to hesitate. Moreau, judging that the sudden collapse of Austrian momentum was the result of the flanking attack, ordered Grouchy and the rest of his forces to shift to the offensive. Under attack from the flank and the front, the more numerous Austrians withdrew in disorder. The limited road net and topography had both worked against an Austrian concentration of force.

The Austrians sustained some 13,500 casualties (1,750 taken prisoner) and lost 26 guns. The French probably lost 3,000 men and 1 gun. It was the greatest casualty ratio of any major battle of the Napoleonic Wars. Moreau's victory made possible the conclusion of peace with the Austrians in the Treaty of Lunéville, in effect ending the War of the Second Coalition. Under the peace terms France secured the Rhineland, this time including all Austrian territory there. All fortresses on the right bank of the Rhine were to be demolished, opening the way for the French there. France also won recognition of its puppet Swiss (Helvetic), Dutch (Batavian), and Italian (Ligurian and Italian) republics. Napoleon came to terms with Czar Paul of Russia. The British also concluded peace, recognizing the French gains on the continent and securing in return Ceylon and Trinidad. For the first time in 10 years, Europe was at peace. Unfortunately for France and Europe, Napoleon used peace as he did war to further his own interests, especially in Italy, leading to resumption of war with Britain in May 1803 and a new coalition, the Third Coalition, against him in 1805.

References

Arnold, James R. *Marengo and Hohenlinden: Napoleon's Rise to Power.* Lexington, VA: James R. Arnold, 1999.

Chandler, David G. *The Campaigns of Napoleon.* New York: Macmillan, 1966.

Connelly, Owen. *Blundering to Glory: Napoleon's Military Campaigns.* Rev. ed. Wilmington, DE: Scholarly Resources, 1999.

Rothenberg, Gunther E. *Napoleon's Great Adversaries: The Archduke Charles and the Austrian Army, 1792–1814.* Bloomington: Indiana University Press, 1982.

First Battle of Copenhagen

Date	April 2, 1801	
Location	Copenhagen, Denmark	
Opponents (* winner)	*British	Danes
Commander	Admiral Sir Hyde Parker; Vice Admiral Horatio Nelson commands the forces in the battle	Commodore Johan Fischer
Approx. # Troops	10 ships of the line, 1 54-gun ship, 1 50-gun ship, and 7 bomb vessels	7 ships of the line and 11 other warships, armed hulks, and floating batteries; plus shore batteries
Importance	Ends any threat to Britain from the Danish Navy, but is celebrated in Denmark for the bravery of the Danish participants	

Trade with the Baltic had long been important to Britain and included grain imports. The Royal Navy also relied on the Baltic for timber and naval supplies, especially flax, which was used in the production of both sails and rope. Thus, in 1800 when Czar Paul of Russia abandoned war against France and moved to create a pro-French Armed Neutrality of the North, the British government was greatly alarmed. London regarded the matter as sufficiently important to warrant military action.

The immediate problem arose with Denmark and its claimed right to convoy its merchant shipping through the British blockade without being subject to search. On July 25, 1800, a small British squadron brought a Danish convoy escorted by the frigate *Freya* into port to search it for contraband. Pressured by the presence of a British squadron off Copenhagen, the Danes agreed to allow their convoys to be searched. Although both the British and Danish governments declared themselves satisfied, the event pushed Denmark closer to Russia.

In December 1800 after the British seizure of Malta (to which Czar Paul had pretensions), Russia embargoed all British ships and signed a naval convention with Sweden that allowed noncontraband goods, including timber and flax, to pass to France. In February 1801 after Napoleon had forced Austria to sue for peace in the Treaty of Lunéville, Russia expanded the Armed Neutrality to include Prussia and Denmark, whereupon the British government decided on a show of force and, if necessary, a preemptive strike to break up the league.

Admiral Sir Hyde Parker received command of the Baltic expedition. Vice Admiral Horatio Nelson, recently returned from the Mediterranean, was made second-in-command. Denmark embargoed British shipping in March, and its forces occupied both Hamburg and Lübeck. The only question for the British was whether to descend on Denmark or move up the Baltic and attack the Russian fleet at Reval

(Tallinn) while the remainder of Russian ships were icebound at Kronstadt. This would have been the boldest, most certain course, but the cautious Parker rejected it.

Parker sailed from Yarmouth on March 12 with 53 ships, 20 of them ships of the line, and nearly two regiments of ground troops. The British had sent a diplomatic mission ahead, so the Danes had time to prepare. Even on his arrival, Parker delayed for a week. Nelson asked to lead an assault on Copenhagen, and on April 1 Parker agreed, giving him 30 ships, including 10 smaller ships of the line, 1 54-gun ship, 1 50-gun ship, and 7 bomb vessels. Parker would remain well offshore with eight ships of the line, including the 98-gun *London* and *St. George.*

At dawn on April 2, taking advantage of a favorable southerly wind, Nelson's ships weighed anchor to attack. Noting that the Danish line was strongest in the north, close to a large land battery, Nelson decided on an attack from the south, which began at 9:30 a.m. Danish commodore Johan Fischer commanded 18 warships, armed hulks, and floating batteries moored north and south paralleling the shore over about a mile and a half, all supported by several shore batteries.

From the start, things went badly for the British. Lacking adequate charts or pilots, one ship of the line grounded before the action began. Two other ships of the line grounded on the other side of the channel at extreme range. The other nine capital ships then closed to relatively long range of about a cable length (240 yards) and engaged the Danish ships and shore batteries. Subsequently the British learned that they might have improved their gunnery effectiveness by bringing their vessels in much closer and even doubled the Danish ships, as in the Battle of the Nile (1798).

Clearly Nelson underestimated the Danish defenders, who fought with great gallantry and effectiveness. The result was a long, slow slugfest, but after three hours of combat that included even Nelson's frigates, superior British gunnery began to tell.

At this point Parker, about four miles away with his larger ships of the line and slow to close, signaled a recall to all ships. Nelson ignored the order; it would have turned victory into disaster, for the only way Nelson's ships could withdraw was up the channel and across the undefeated northern Danish defenses (indeed, two British ships of the line grounded there after the cease-fire). An angry Nelson reportedly turned to his flag captain and remarked, "You know, Foley, I have only one eye, and I have a right to be blind sometimes." Placing the telescope to that blind eye, he remarked, "I really do not see the signal." Nelson's captains copied their commander and refused to disengage.

By 1:30 p.m., although several British ships were flying distress signals, Nelson had disabled a dozen Danish ships, including Fischer's flagship, and overwhelmed the southern shore defenses of Copenhagen. Nelson was then in position to bring up his bomb vessels to shell the city. The Danes agreed to a cease-fire an hour later. Human casualties were heavy and approximately equal. Of Nelson's battles, only the Battle of Trafalgar (1805) was fought at greater human cost. The Battle of Copenhagen was Nelson's most difficult battle and where he came closest to defeat, but it stands as one of his three most remarkable victories at sea, along with the Battle of the Nile and the Battle of Trafalgar. The Battle of Copenhagen had also been unnecessary.

Nelson negotiated directly with Crown Prince Frederick, and on April 9, faced with a British threat to bombard Copenhagen, the Danes agreed to a truce of 14 weeks. Denmark agreed to take no action under the Treaty of Armed Neutrality and also granted the British the right to secure water, food, and supplies from shore. Nelson had demanded 16 weeks, sufficient time for the British fleet to deal with the Russians. Nelson understood from the start that Russia was the real enemy. He had wanted to descend on the Russians at Tallinn, leaving only a squadron to keep the Danes in check. Had this course of action been followed, the British would have discovered that Czar Paul had been assassinated on March 24. His successor, Alexander I, had changed policies. The Armed Neutrality broke up, and by June 1801 British trade in the Baltic was again moving without threat of hindrance.

References

Clowes, William Laird. *The Royal Navy: A History from the Earliest Times to 1900,* Vol. 4. London: Sampson Low, Marston, 1900.

Gardiner, Robert, ed. *Nelson against Napoleon: From the Nile to Copenhagen, 1798–1801.* London: Chatham, 1997.

Pope, Dudley. *The Great Gamble.* London: Weidenfeld and Nicolson, 1972.

Tracy, Nicholas. *Nelson's Battles: The Art of Victory in the Age of Sail.* Annapolis, MD: Naval Institute Press, 1996.

Battle of Trafalgar

Date	October 21, 1805	
Location	Western Mediterranean, off the coast of Spain	
Opponents (* winner)	*British	French
Commander	Vice Admiral Horatio Viscount Nelson	Vice Admiral Pierre, Comte de Villeneuve
Approx. # Troops	27 ships of the line (2,148 guns)	33 ships of the line (18 French and 15 Spanish) (2,568 guns)
Importance	Prevents the combined fleet from intervening in the Mediterranean operations and shatters the French Navy for decades to come	

The Battle of Trafalgar was one of history's most important naval engagements. On May 16, 1803, after a scant 14 months of peace, fighting resumed between Britain and France. French first consul Napoleon Bonaparte collected along the northern French coast a large number of small craft and a sizable number of men in what he called the Army of England for an invasion attempt. How serious he was is by no means clear, but in early October 1804 British captain Sidney Smith led a raid of fire ships against the mouth of the Rhine, destroying a number of vessels in the purported invasion fleet. British naval units also kept French warships from concentrating elsewhere for an attempt at attacking across the English Channel.

In 1805 Napoleon, now emperor, ordered another invasion effort. This was based on a deception that he hoped would cause the British to leave the Channel unprotected. Admiral Pierre Charles Villeneuve's fleet at Toulon and allied Spanish ships under Admiral Federico Carlos de Gravina were to sail to the West Indies. At the same time, Admiral Honoré Ganteaume and his 21 ships were to break out from Brest and release Spanish ships at El Ferrol in northwestern Spain. French hopes rested on British warships pursuing west. The French fleets would unite at Martinique under Ganteaume, elude their pursuers, and make for the Channel. Napoleon assumed that he would then have available 60–70 ships of the line and at least a dozen frigates to provide a brief period of naval mastery sufficient to convoy a host of small vessels ferrying an invading army across the Channel to England.

British vice admiral Horatio Nelson had been carrying out a loose blockade of Toulon in the hope of enticing out his opponent. On March 30 Villeneuve indeed escaped Toulon and sailed west into the Atlantic, where he reached Cádiz and linked up with Admiral de Gravina. Their combined 20 ships of the line, 8 frigates, and some smaller vessels then sailed for the West Indies with Nelson's 10 ships in pursuit. Napoleon's orders were for Villeneuve to wait at Martinique no longer than 35 days. If Ganteaume was unable to break free of Brest, Villeneuve was to proceed to El Ferrol and then on to Brest to release Spanish and French ships for the invasion attempt.

After inconclusive maneuvering, on June 8 Villeneuve panicked on the news that Nelson was in pursuit and departed Martinique for Europe. Nelson followed and returned to Gibraltar on July 20. Two days later Admiral Sir Robert Calder, with 15 ships of the line and 2 frigates, clashed with Villeneuve's combined fleet off Cape Finisterre. The Spanish ships bore the brunt of the attack, and the British took 2 of them as prizes along with 1,200 seamen as prisoners. Poor visibility allowed the remainder of the combined fleet to escape, but 5 other Spanish vessels, including a frigate, were so badly damaged that they had to go into dry dock for repairs. Three British ships lost masts. Calder had won a nominal victory, but it was by no means decisive.

Villeneuve meanwhile proceeded to El Ferrol and then, on August 13, sailed south to Cádiz, where he was reinforced with Spanish ships. The British soon had this combined naval force under blockade. British prime minister William Pitt insisted that Nelson, then in England, take over command from Vice Admiral Lord Cuthbert Collingwood.

Arriving on station, Nelson rejected Collingwood's cautious close blockade in favor of a loose arrangement that kept his fleet out of sight of Cádiz. Nelson used

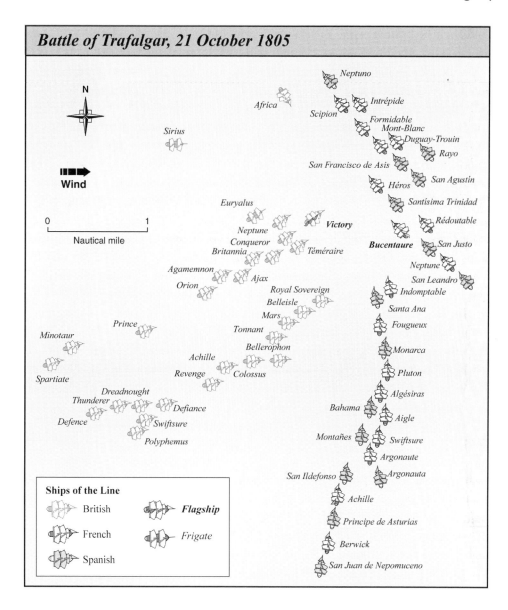

Battle of Trafalgar, 21 October 1805

N

Wind

0   1

Nautical mile

Neptuno

Africa

Intrépide

Scipion

Formidable
Mont-Blanc
Duguay-Trouin

Rayo

San Francisco de Asis

Héros   San Agustín

Santísima Trinidad

Euryalus

Neptune

Conqueror

Britannia

Victory

Téméraire

Rédoutable

Bucentaure   San Justo

Neptune

Agamemnon

Orion   Ajax

Royal Sovereign

Belleisle

Mars

San Leandro
Indomptable

Santa Ana

Prince

Tonnant

Fougueux

Minotaur

Bellerophon

Monarca

Achille

Revenge   Colossus

Pluton

Spartiate

Algésiras

Dreadnought

Thunderer

Defence

Defiance

Swiftsure

Polyphemus

Bahama

Aigle

Montañes

Swiftsure

Argonaute

San Ildefonso

Argonauta

Achille

Principe de Asturias

Berwick

San Juan de Nepomuceno

Ships of the Line

British   *Flagship*

French   *Frigate*

Spanish

Sirius

a line of frigates to signal the main body of the fleet over the horizon, some 50 miles out. He hoped that this would entice out the French and Spanish. A loose blockade was risky because his enemies might get away. Nelson, however, preferred it to no action at all.

Nelson had no way of getting the French and Spanish to oblige him, however. Napoleon arranged that. In mid-September he ordered the combined fleet to the Mediterranean to support French operations in southern Italy, a recipe for disaster. Villeneuve was well aware that his ships were not ready to do battle. Many of the Spanish crews were untrained, a large number of his own men were sick, and he could not be certain what British force was lurking offshore. His Spanish colleagues also urged him not to sail on because of approaching bad weather.

On the plus side, the wind was to the south, and Villeneuve was aware that Nelson had recently detached some of his ships to escort a convoy through the straits. Nelson also had committed the serious error of allowing Calder to sail home to a board of inquiry over Cape Finisterre in a ship of the line rather than a smaller vessel. Yet Villeneuve risked everything in the final analysis because he was stung by Napoleon's charges of cowardice and the news that he was about to be replaced as commander of the combined fleet. Indeed, Napoleon had dispatched Vice Admiral François Étienne Rosily-Mesros to Cádiz to succeed Villeneuve, whereupon Villeneuve was to return to Paris to explain his conduct.

On October 19 the French and Spanish ships began exiting Cádiz; in all 33 allied ships of the line (18 French and 15 Spanish) straggled out over that day and the next. His lookout frigates soon informed Nelson, off Cape Spartel. Nelson called his captains to a council of war and explained his daring plan. Outnumbered by his opponents, who also boasted the 2 largest ships, Nelson intended to attack in two or three columns to cut off some 20 or so ships in the allied van from the remainder. With the French and Spanish ships running before the wind, the others would find it difficult to tack back and rejoin the action. By the time they could come up, Nelson hoped to have the battle decided. This extraordinarily bold plan promised either great success or disaster.

When Nelson's ships appeared and approached the Franco-Spanish fleet, Villeneuve realized the size of his opponent's force and ordered the combined fleet to turn back toward Cádiz, a decision that astonished his flag captain. The five-mile-long irregular allied line became even more ragged; in places ships of the line bunched up and even came abreast. Nelson's 27 ships, in two divisions, did not hesitate and drove directly into the center of the opposing line, cutting it in two.

In numbers of guns, the British had only 2,148 to 2,568 for the allies. The French and Spanish also had some 30,000 men to slightly more than 17,000 for the British. But Nelson's ships were far superior in terms of gunnery training and seamanship. These factors and superior leadership more than compensated for any deficiencies in numbers.

In the resulting five-hour battle on October 21, 1805, the British took 19 allied ships. Another, the *Achille,* blew up. No English ship was lost, but human casualties were heavy, and Nelson was among them. His flag in the *Victory* had been easily visible to ships in the van of the combined fleet, and the flagship became a principal target for Spanish-French gun crews and sharpshooters. Pacing the deck in full uniform, early in the battle Nelson fell mortally wounded from a musket ball fired by a sharpshooter in the *Rédoutable.* Carried below, he learned of the great victory before he died.

The British seamen did not have long to mourn their beloved leader or to savor their victory. A great storm came up, and despite valiant efforts, most of the prizes were lost in the fierce tempest. Crewmen who had just fought each other now fought just as desperately to save their ships and themselves. Only four of the prizes were saved, a cruel disappointment to seamen who had hoped to profit from hard-earned prize money.

No British ships were lost, but of the original 19 prizes, excluding the 4 taken to Gibraltar, Collingwood ordered 4 scuttled, including the giant Spanish ship of the line *Santísima Trinidad.* Two others escaped to Cádiz. The remainder either sank in the storm or were dashed on the rocks, with heavy personnel losses. Although 13 ships of the combined fleet made it back to Cádiz, 3 of these soon broke up on the rocks. As a consequence of the Battle of Trafalgar, the Royal Navy had thus reduced its opponents by 23 capital ships.

Napoleon, who had just won a great victory over a Habsburg army at Ulm, dismissed the Battle of Trafalgar in one sentence: "Some ships have been lost in a gale following an unwisely undertaken engagement." In truth, the Battle of Trafalgar shattered the French Navy for decades to come. Trafalgar also marked the completion of the shift from the formalist school of fleet tactics to the melee school. Nelson's tactics, combined with a new signaling system, saw sailing ship warfare at its peak. Trafalgar was quite possibly the most important naval victory in British history and raised Nelson to the status of the greatest of Britain's military heroes. It also established Britain as mistress of the seas, not seriously challenged until the end of the 19th century.

More immediately, the battle confined Napoleon to the land. To get at the British thereafter, he resorted to a war against their trade from the land side by denying British goods entry into all parts of Europe. This led to the Continental System, which alienated many Europeans, and to the overextension of French military commitments.

References

Howarth, David. *Trafalgar: The Nelson Touch.* New York: Atheneum, 1969.

Pope, Dudley. *Decision at Trafalgar.* Philadelphia: Lippincott, 1960.

Schom, Alan. *Trafalgar: Countdown to Battle, 1803–1805.* New York: Oxford University Press, 1990.

Tunstall, Brian. *Naval Warfare in the Age of Sail: The Evolution of Fighting Tactics, 1650–1815.* Edited by Nicholas Tracy. London: Conway Maritime, 1990.

Battle of Austerlitz

Date	December 2, 1805	
Location	Austerlitz in Moravia	
Opponents (* winner)	*French	Austrians, Russians
Commander	Emperor Napoleon I	Tsar Alexander I of Russia; General Mikhail Kutuzov; Holy Roman Emperor Francis II of Austria
Approx. # Troops	70,000	86,000 (71,000 Russians; 15,000 Austrians)
Importance	Napoleon Bonaparte's greatest victory, it shatters the Third Coalition	

The December 1805 Battle of Austerlitz was Napoleon Bonaparte's greatest military victory. Leading the best troops he ever commanded, Napoleon smashed the combined Austrian and Russian armies.

In March 1802 France and Britain had concluded peace at Amiens, but it was little more than a truce. Although its terms were generous to France, Napoleon gave the peace no chance of survival. He used the respite to advance his own interests in Italy, in the German states, and in Haiti. In these circumstances, Britain declared war again in May 1803. Napoleon made extensive preparations to invade Britain, an operation that would require at least brief French naval mastery of the English Channel.

Britain put together a new coalition against France. Austria was alarmed over Napoleon's machinations in Italy, especially when he established the Kingdom of Italy with himself as its ruler, and in November 1804 Austria and Russia agreed that they would oppose Napoleon's designs there. In April 1805 Britain and Russia came to agreement, with the British providing subsidies. The three powers agreed that they would oppose France with 280,000 Russian and Austrian soldiers in southern Germany by October 1805. Despite pressure from both Holy Roman Emperor Francis II of Austria and Czar Alexander II of Russia, Prussian king Frederick William III refused to join the coalition. Napoleon had promised him Hanover if he remained neutral.

News of the allied plans reached Napoleon in August. He immediately shelved his preparations to invade Britain, broke up his military camp at Boulogne, and moved his forces against Austria before the allies could concentrate against him. As a result of both Austrian bungling and Napoleon's ability to scramble, the French emperor came on the Austrians unawares and won a brilliant victory over Austrian general Karl Mack von Leiberich at Ulm on October 17. Mack was surrounded and was forced to surrender his entire army of 27,000 men.

Napoleon's reformed army employed traditional battalions, regiments, and divisions, but for the first time Napoleon now combined divisions to form corps. Each corps possessed its own light and heavy infantry in addition to artillery and cavalry formations. It was also very well trained and was led by capable generals.

It made no difference in events on land that Napoleon suffered a decisive defeat at sea in the Battle of Trafalgar on October 21, four days after the Battle of Ulm. Napoleon shrugged off the defeat as his forces continued a rapid movement on separate axes east toward Vienna with the aim of driving Austria from the coalition before Russian forces could join. With the military situation on land rapidly changing in Napoleon's favor, Frederick William III, who had agreed in early November to join Russia and Austria against France within four weeks with 180,000 men, now refused to honor his pledge.

Napoleon took Vienna on November 12. The problem remained, however, of preventing a juncture of the numerically superior allied forces against him. Napoleon dispatched some 55,000 men to prevent 80,000 Austrians from crossing the Alps and joining the Russians. He also detached 20,000 troops at Vienna and other forces to intimidate the Prussians, who showed signs of wavering. Napoleon then advanced into Moravia with his remaining men. As his supply lines lengthened, his position became less satisfactory. Finally, he encountered Russian and some Austrian forces in late November at Olmütz near the Polish-Russian border.

Even though Napoleon was outnumbered, he was confident. He baited his opponents into battle by withdrawing from seemingly advantageous high ground before them. Carefully concealing his own numbers, Napoleon extended his right flank to invite an allied attack there, certain he could turn the tide of battle. Russian czar Alexander II, who had taken personal command of the Russian forces, overruled his senior commander, General Mikhail Kutuzov, and ordered the allied troops forward to attack Napoleon's right wing and cut the French off from Vienna. By all reports, Alexander had been impressed with his troops as they marched in review and was overeager for battle. Had the czar waited, the allies might have obliged Napoleon to advance farther, dangerously extending his lines of communication and making him even more vulnerable to being cut off and annihilated, or to withdraw. Prussia might also have joined the allied coalition.

In the Battle of Austerlitz, the allies deployed some 86,000 men (71,000 Russians and 15,000 Austrians), while the French had 70,000 men. Emperor Francis II was also present, and the resulting battle is thus sometimes known as the Battle of the Three Emperors. It occurred west of the small village of Austerlitz. The battle opened at 7:00 a.m., when half of Alexander's troops moved against the French right. The advance came to a halt as a consequence of the icy Goldbach, a stream between the two lines, and the timely arrival of 6,000 French reinforcements under Marshal Louis Nicolas Davout, whom Napoleon had ordered up from Vienna. By 9:00 a.m. a third of the allied force was engaged against the French right wing, with other forces moving across the French front to join them.

Napoleon now sprang his trap on the French left (allied right). Between 10:00 and 11:00 a.m., Marshal Nicolas Jean de Dieu Soult's corps retook the high ground of the Pratzen Heights abandoned earlier, cutting off the allied left. The corps then turned to the right to roll up the Russians who had attacked the French right and become mired in marshy ground. At the same time, on the French left Marshal Jean Lannes moved his corps east along the Olmütz highway, while another French corps under Marshal Jean Baptiste Bernadotte drove into the gap created by Soult and pushed on directly for Austerlitz, cutting off the Russian left under Prince Pyotr I. Bagration, which, despite valiant resistance, was shattered. Davout's forces also advanced.

By nightfall the allied army had ceased to exist as a fighting force, although many of the allied soldiers managed to escape the French trap. Napoleon's losses were some 2,000 killed and 7,000 wounded, while the Russians and Austrians lost 12,000 killed or wounded and another 15,000 taken prisoner. Napoleon later caused the 180 allied guns taken that day to be melted down to form the column to the Grand Armée that still stands in the Place Vendôme in Paris. The czar refused to make peace and simply removed his forces back to Russia. On learning of the battle, British prime minister William Pitt remarked, "Roll up the map of Europe; it will not be needed these next ten years."

Nowhere was Napoleon's military genius better illustrated than in this battle. Napoleon's skill in battle was not matched by his political and diplomatic sensibility, however. Foreign Minister Maurice de Talleyrand-Périgord urged Napoleon to conclude a generous peace with Austria and win its friendship. Talleyrand saw that if France was to have lasting peace, it would have to be content with hegemony over Europe rather than conquering all of it. Napoleon simply ignored the advice. His ambition drove all, and in the end the cost to France would be no territorial gains and hundreds of thousands of dead. In a sense, the Battle of Austerlitz was too great a victory. The defeated had been humiliated, and Napoleon was more convinced than ever that he could not be beaten. His reach began to exceed his grasp.

References

Chandler, David G. *The Campaigns of Napoleon.* New York: Macmillan, 1966.

Connelly, Owen. *Blundering to Glory: Napoleon's Military Campaigns.* Rev. ed. Wilmington, DE: Scholarly Resources, 1999.

Duffy, Christopher. *Austerlitz.* London: Archon, 1977.

Horne, Alistair. *How Far from Austerlitz? Napoleon, 1805–1815.* New York: St. Martin's, 1997.

Manceron, Claude. *Austerlitz: The Story of a Battle.* Translated by George Unwin. New York: Unwin, 1968.

Parker, Harold. *Three Napoleonic Battles.* Durham, NC: Duke University Press, 1983.

Battles of Jena and Auerstädt

Date	October 14, 1806	
Location	Jena and Auerstädt, in Thuringia (central Germany)	
Opponents (* winner)	*French	Prussians
Commander	Emperor Napoleon I (Jena); Marshal Louis-Nicolas Davout (Auerstädt)	Friedrich Ludwig Prince Hohenlohe (Jena); Frederick William III, King of Prussia; Karl Wilhelm Ferdinand, Duke of Brunswick (Auerstädt)
Approx. # Troops	90,000 (Jena); 27,000 (Auerstädt)	38,000 (Jena); 63,000 (Auerstädt)
Importance	The twin French victories totally demoralize the Prussian Army and help bring about the military collapse of Prussia	

The twin Battles of Jena and Auerstädt during the Napoleonic Wars on October 14, 1806, saw the French defeat two Prussian armies. On December 2, 1805, in the War of the Third Coalition (1803–1806), Napoleon Bonaparte smashed Russian and Austrian forces in the Battle of Austerlitz. Prussia, which had been about to join the coalition against France, now came to terms with the victor. Under the Treaty of Schönbrunn of December 15, 1805, Prussia received Hanover while yielding Cleves, on the left bank of the Rhine, as well as Ansbach and Neuchâtel. As a result, Austria was forced to sign with France the December 26 Treaty of Pressburg. France gained Piedmont, Parma, and Piacenza, and Austria yielded territory to Napoleon's Kingdom of Italy and recognized Napoleon as its ruler. Bavaria, Baden, and Württemberg also received Austrian territory.

Prussia now found itself at war with England, which shared a monarch with Hanover. The Royal Navy took hundreds of Prussia's merchant vessels and ruined its overseas trade. Many prominent Prussians now called for a repudiation of the French alliance and one with Russia instead. Indeed, secret negotiations between Prussia and Russia brought agreement that Prussia would not aid France against Russia. In return, Russia guaranteed Prussia's possessions.

Napoleon had meanwhile engaged in peace feelers with Britain, in the course of which he offered to return Hanover. Napoleon planned to compensate Prussia elsewhere, but news of the negotiations was sufficient to cause Frederick William III to issue an ultimatum to Napoleon demanding that France withdraw entirely from Germany and allow Prussia to reorganize northern Germany into a confederation under its leadership. Napoleon rejected the ultimatum, and the War of the Fourth Coalition (1806–1807) was on.

Prussia was in the worst possible situation, facing France without formal allies. (Negotiations with Russia were still in progress.) Worse, the Prussian Army was in terrible shape, and its commanders were for the most part old and incompetent. Command of Prussian field forces went to Karl Wilhelm Ferdinand, Duke of Brunswick. In late September 1806 the Prussian forces set out, expecting to meet the French in the Weimar-Jena-Erfurt region. Frederick William III accompanied the army in the field, and no decision was taken without the king and Brunswick spending hours discussing it, a fact that was well known in the army and that hardly inspired confidence.

The Prussian Army was advancing on two axes, and as in the 1805 Battle of Ulm (October 14, 1805), the French came upon their adversary unawares. At Jena, Friedrich Ludwig Prince Hohenlohe, with 38,000 Prussians, encountered Napoleon at the head of 90,000 Frenchmen. Fifteen miles north at Auerstädt, it was Brunswick and the king with 63,000 men against Maréchal de France Louis-Nicolas Davout and 27,000 Frenchmen.

Hohenlohe was defeated at Jena because he camped on a plain without bothering to secure the surrounding high ground and because of superior French numbers, although in the actual battle there were only 40,000 French troops engaged against 36,000 Prussians under Hohenlohe and 13,000 Prussian troops under Rüchel, who arrived on the field late and attempted to attack through the remnants of Hohenlohe's force. The French suffered 5,000 casualties, and the Prussians suffered 11,000 casualties as well as another 15,000 taken prisoner. The French also captured 112 Prussian guns.

At Auerstädt, Brunswick outnumbered the French almost three to one. Davout had only a single corps. He soon came under attack by troops led by the aggressive 64-year-old General Gebbard Leberecht von Blücher von Wahlstadt. The French held, however, and Blücher withdrew. The Prussians then mounted a four-division frontal attack against only two French divisions, but the Duke of Brunswick was mortally wounded, and the other Prussian generals were not privy to his battle plans. The king could not make up his mind whether to command himself or appoint someone else, and in the end he did neither. As a result, substantial portions of the Prussian forces were not committed to battle, and although the Prussians almost turned the French left flank, in the end they failed. At 1:00 p.m., after more than six hours of fighting, the Prussian troops broke. Davout's infantry and cavalry pursued the fleeing Prussians for several hours.

Davout achieved a complete victory but at the cost of 8,000 French casualties. The Prussians lost 12,000 men killed or wounded and 3,000 taken prisoner as well as 115 guns. Napoleon at first disbelieved that Davout had defeated 64,000 men. "Your marshal . . . saw double today," he told the messenger.

In the wild retreat following the twin French victories the two Prussian forces merged, which only heightened the confusion and panic. This single day totally demoralized the Prussian military, virtually ending resistance to the French. The fortress of Magdeburg, with 22,000 men and a million pounds of gunpowder, surrendered after a dozen shots at a French force of barely 11,000. On October 25 Hohenlohe surrendered 12,000 men at Prenzlau to a French force smaller than his own. Only in Silesia was there any substantial resistance to the French west of the Vistula River.

Napoleon now moved swiftly to Berlin. In that city on November 21, 1806, he issued a decree inaugurating the Continental System, closing the continent of Europe to British goods. In December, Napoleon signed a treaty with Saxony that raised it to a kingdom and enlarged its territory at the expense of Prussia.

Prussia now made peace with England, renouncing Hanover in exchange for subsidies. King Frederick William III also signed an agreement with Russia in April 1807 by which both powers promised not to lay down their arms until the French had been driven from Germany. Napoleon continued the campaign against what remained of the Prussian Army and against the Russians. He won bloody victories over the latter at Eylau on February 7–8, 1807, and Friedland on June 14, 1807, leading Czar Alexander II to abandon his ally and sign a peace agreement with Napoleon at Tilsit that July.

Tilsit was the high point of Napoleon's role. Russia entered into alliance with France and joined the Continental System. Prussia lost most of its territory, retaining only Brandenburg, Pomerania, western Prussia (excluding Danzig), and Silesia. Now little more than a buffer between France and Russia, Prussia also had to pay a heavy indemnity and maintain 150,000 occupying French troops. In these dire circumstances, however, Prussian leaders worked to reform the army toward the day when they might be able to secure revenge against France.

References

Chandler, David G. *Jena 1806: Napoleon Destroys Prussia.* London: Osprey, 1993.

Hourtoulle, F. G. *Jena-Auerstadt: The Triumph of the Eagle.* Paris: Histoire and Collections, 1998.

Maude, F. N. *The Jena Campaign, 1806.* London: Greenhill, 1998.

Sieges of Zaragoza

Date	June 15–August 17, 1808; December 20, 1808–February 20, 1809	
Location	Zaragoza (Saragossa) in Aragon, some 200 miles north of Madrid in Spain	
Opponents (* winner)	*French	Spanish
Commander	General Jean Antoine Verdier; Marshal Jean Lannes	General Don José Robolledo Palafox y Melzi
Approx. # Troops	c. 32,000	c. 40,000, including civilian volunteers
Importance	Although the French eventually take the city, the siege becomes a symbol of Spanish bravery and defiance of the French	

Following the conclusion of peace between France and Russia at Tilsit in July 1807, Emperor Napoleon of France turned his attention to Great Britain. The Battle of Trafalgar (October 1805) had established Britain as mistress of the seas. To get at the British thereafter, Napoleon resorted to a war against British trade, denying British goods entry into all parts of Europe. This Continental System alienated many Europeans and forced Napoleon to overextend his forces. To prevent British goods from entering the Iberian Peninsula, for instance, in 1807 Napoleon sent French troops into Portugal. The next year he sent them into Spain, where he had forced King Ferdinand VII to abdicate. Napoleon installed his brother Joseph on the Spanish throne, but riots broke out in Madrid on May 2, 1808, and spread throughout the country. Napoleon had not anticipated this Spanish nationalist reaction.

One of the principal centers of resistance was the city of Zaragoza (Saragossa). The chief city of Aragon, Zaragoza is about 200 miles northeast of Madrid on the Ebro River. In 1808 it had a population of about 60,000 people. General Don José Robolledo Palafox y Melzi had charge of the defense. He had only 300 royal dragoons, and only a third of these had horses, but Palafox recruited volunteers, called up retired and half-pay officers, and organized the city defenses as best he could, to include establishment of a munitions factory. Although he had artillery, few of his men were trained in its use.

The first fighting for Zaragoza took place on June 8 at Tudela, where a French force of 5,000 infantry, 1,000 cavalry, and two artillery batteries under the command of General François Joseph Lefèbvre-Desnouettes clashed with some 6,000 Spanish levies and armed peasants who tried to bar the way to Zaragoza. The French soon scattered them. A second and last effort to block the French approach occurred shortly thereafter at Alagon, where Palafox led 650 men and four guns against the French. He was wounded, and his force was defeated.

On June 15, 1808, Lefèbvre and his troops arrived at Zaragoza and commenced military operations against the city. Situated on a plain, Zaragoza was protected by the Ebro to the north. Its buildings were sturdy and tightly packed—ideal for defensive purposes—and the city was surrounded by a 12-foot-high stone wall. Palafox commanded about 10,000 men.

Lefèbvre assumed that a determined attack would soon carry the city. He directed his artillery against the west walls, while his infantry and some cavalry attacked the Santa Engracia gate to the south. Several French attacks encountered ferocious Spanish resistance, the attackers sustaining 700 casualties. Lefèbvre then decided to await reinforcements. Learning that a force of 4,000 Spaniards was en route to the city, Lefèbvre feigned an attack on Zaragoza but slipped away with most of his men, surprising and destroying the Spanish relief column.

On June 29 an additional French division with siege guns arrived at Zaragoza under General Jean Antoine Verdier, who took overall command of operations.

Verdier ordered his men to drive 300 Spanish defenders from Mount Torrero, a dominating hill south of the city where the French then placed their siege guns. From that position at midnight on June 30, 46 French guns opened fire on Zaragoza. Following a 12-hour bombardment, Verdier ordered his infantry forward.

Desperate fighting ensued, during which Augustina Saragossa, a heroine of the siege, made her appearance. Immortalized by British poet Lord Byron, who was her lover, Saragossa carried food to a gun crew and then took the place of a member of the gun crew, reportedly firing the gun herself and shouting that she would not leave the gun while she was still alive. At the same time a young boy seized a banner from a wounded standard-bearer and waved it. These actions helped rally the defenders, who were able to drive out those French troops who had gotten inside the city. The attackers sustained 500 casualties.

Verdier now decided to conduct a conventional siege. With only 13,000 men, however, he was unable to seal off access to the city and the Spanish continued to receive both supplies and reinforcements. Gradually the French pushed their lines forward and continued their bombardment. On August 4 the French made another breach in the walls. That afternoon 3,000 French troops attacked, entered the city, and took about half of it. The fighting was desperate, with no quarter given by either side. Verdier demanded that Palafox surrender, but the latter replied, "*Guerra a chillo*" ("War to the knife"). Desperate fighting raged over the next days, with priests and monks fighting alongside the people.

On the morning of August 14 Verdier withdrew his troops from the part of the city the French had captured; on August 17 he broke off the siege entirely. Verdier had learned that on July 19, 1808, a French army of 20,000 men commanded by General Pierre Dupont was surrounded at Baylen by some 32,000 Spanish troops and levies and was forced to surrender, the first capitulation of a Napoleonic army anywhere in Europe. The news of Baylen, his inability to seal off the city, and word that additional Spanish reinforcements were en route to Zaragoza all caused Verdier to end siege operations.

Napoleon then took personal command in Spain, and on December 20, 1808, the French returned to Zaragoza and again placed it under siege. This time the Spanish were ready. Palafox had managed to substantially improve the city defenses, which were now manned by 34,000 regular Spanish troops supported by 10,000 armed peasants. He also had 160 artillery pieces. Marshal Bon Adrien de Moncey led the French, reinforced by troops under Marshal Edouard Mortier. Moncey commanded 38,000 infantry, 3,000 sappers and gunners, 3,500 cavalry, and 144 guns.

Again concentrating on Mount Torrero, the French captured it on December 20, driving its 6,000 defenders into the city and capturing seven Spanish guns. Moncey called on Palaox to surrender, but the latter replied, "Spanish blood covers us with honor and you with shame." French siege operations began in earnest on December 23.

On January 2 General Jean Androche Junot arrived at Zaragoza to replace Moncey and with orders to detach Mortier and 10,000 men to keep upon the road to Madrid. The French defeated a series of small Spanish sorties directed at spiking the French guns, which now were concentrated against the southeast walls of the city at close range. By January 26 the French had made several breaches in the walls, and the next day infantry assaults penetrated the Spanish defenses.

Learning that 20,000 Aragonese were marching to relieve Zaragoza, Napoleon sent reinforcements to the city and entrusted command of operations to Marshal Jean Lannes, who ordered Mortier to move against the Spanish relief column, which the French surprised and scattered at Nuestra Señora de Magallón.

Inside Zaragoza, bitter house-to-house fighting raged and continued without letup for the next three weeks. With much of the city reduced to rubble and his main equipment factory destroyed by a mine, Palafox announced that he would surrender, which occurred on February 20, 1809. Zaragoza was by then a smoking ruin, with about a third of the city destroyed. The siege had claimed 54,000 Spanish lives, and only 8,000 of the Spanish garrison were still alive. Some 10,000 French had perished, 4,000 killed in action and 6,000 dead of disease.

Although the French triumphed at Zaragoza, the city's defenders had again distinguished themselves. Zaragoza's defiance became a symbol of defiance and a standard for other Spanish cities resisting the invader. Napoleon was never able to solve the problem of Spanish nationalism. The "Spanish Ulcer," as Napoleon styled his effort to control Spain, continued to sap French manpower and encourage resistance elsewhere. The widespread small military operations against the French, known as the guerrilla (little war), gave its name to the modern term "guerrilla warfare." The war was also the subject of great art: Francisco Goya's *Les Desastres de la Guerrar* (The Disasters of War), 80 aquatint etchings depicting the horrors of warfare.

References

Gates, David. *The Spanish Ulcer: A History of the Peninsular War.* New York: Norton, 1986.

Humble, Richard. *Napoleon's Peninsular Marshals: A Reassessment.* New York: Taplinger Publishing, 1974.

Rudorff, Raymond. *War to the Death: The Siege of Saragossa, 1808–1809.* London: Hamish Hamilton, 1974.

Battle of Tippecanoe

Date	November 7, 1811	
Location	Near Prophetstown (modern Battle Ground, Indiana, United States)	
Opponents (* winner)	*American forces	Native Americans of Tecumseh's Confederation
Commander	William Henry Harrison, Governor of the Indiana Territory	Tenskwatawa (the Prophet)
Approx. # Troops	970 (350 men of the 4th Infantry Regiment, 484 Indiana militia, 123 Kentucky volunteers, and 13 Native American guides	500–700
Importance	Leads Native Americans of the Old Northwest to side with the British in the War of 1812; at the same time, it fuels demands among U.S. citizens—who believe the British are encouraging the Native Americans—for war with Britain	

The Battle of Tippecanoe on November 7, 1811, fought between U.S. Army regulars and militiamen on the one hand and Native Americans on the other, had a major influence on the War of 1812. Many Americans, especially in Kentucky and Ohio, believed that British agents were goading the Indians to revolt. In fact, the settlers were doing that themselves. For the most part, the Native Americans had been living up to their treaty obligations while settlers routinely violated them, and the Native Americans found redress from settler juries impossible. The Indians were also angry that William Henry Harrison, superintendent of the Northwest Indians and governor of the Indiana territory, had used various methods, often questionable, to secure the cession of some 48 million acres of land from the Indians between 1795 and 1809.

Two Shawnee brothers, Tecumseh and Tenskwatawa, stoked Indian opposition. They claimed that land was held in common and that no chief had the right to cede it. Tenskwatawa, the medicine man known as the Prophet, called on Native Americans to reject the white man's ways. Tecumseh traveled widely to establish a confederation to resist further incursions. He had his work cut out for him. The Indians had only 4,000 warriors in the territory bordered by the Great Lakes, the Mississippi River, and the Ohio River against some 100,000 white men of fighting age.

Tensions increased especially after September 1809 when Harrison was able to get a number of Potawatomi, Miami, and Delaware chiefs to cede a large amount of land to the United States. This action also fueled Tecumseh's efforts to build his confederation. In the summers of 1810 and 1811 Tecumseh met with Harrison at

U.S. Army regulars and militiamen led by William Henry Harrison clash with Native American warriors from Prophetstown in the Battle of Tippecanoe on November 7, 1811. (Library of Congress)

Vincennes in Indian territory, warning Harrison not to purchase additional land without general Native American approval. The 1811 meeting was tense, as both sides arrived there with substantial forces. Tecumseh informed Harrison that his confederation merely emulated that of the United States and also that he was seeking to expand it by securing the support of southern Native Americans.

Alarmed by Tecumseh's success and fearing an expansion of the confederacy, Harrison decided in late September to take advantage of Tecumseh's absence to strike against the center of Indian resistance at Prophetstown. Harrison moved slowly north from Vincennes with a force of 970 men, including 350 soldiers of Colonel John Byrd's 4th Infantry Regiment, 484 Indiana militia, 123 Kentucky volunteers, and 13 guides. En route Harrison established a camp on high ground in a bend of the Wabash River (present-day Terre Haute, Indiana), completing this position, known as Fort Harrison, on October 27. He then moved to the mouth of the Vermillion River, where he erected a blockhouse. On November 6 the men arrived in the vicinity of Prophetstown, which Harrison had already resolved to destroy.

That same day, Tenskwatawa sent emissaries to Harrison to inform him that he was prepared to meet the next day and discuss Harrison's demands. Against the advice of his commanders, Harrison decided to bivouac and meet the Prophet. The campsite was about two miles west of Prophetstown on a tree-covered knoll bordered by Burnet's Creek to the northwest and wet prairie to the southeast. Concerned about the possibility of an Indian attack, the men went to sleep that night with their weapons loaded and bayonets fixed. Harrison instructed that in case of attack, they would immediately form a line of battle in front of their tents. Harrison positioned his mounted forces in the center of the camp as a mobile reserve. Although no breastworks were erected, Harrison did put out a guard force of 108 men.

That night at Prophetstown, egged on by two supposed British agents and informed by a captured wagon driver that Harrison had no artillery and indeed intended to attack the town, the Indians worked themselves into a fury. At 4:00 a.m. on November 7, assured by the Prophet that the American gunpowder had already turned to sand and that the bullets would soon become soft mud, some 550 to 700 Chippewas, Hurons, Kickapoos, Ottawas, Mucos, Piankeshaws, Potawatamis, Shawnees, and Wyandots and possibly some Winnebagos surrounded Harrison's sleeping camp. An American sentinel raised the alarm before he was shot dead.

As they struggled to form a line, many of Harrison's men were silhouetted before their campfires and became easy targets. Harrison's white horse had broken free during the night, and he located a black horse, riding about the camp on it to rally his men. He was fortunate, for the Indians were looking for the white horse and killed the officer riding it. The Indians employed the rare tactic, for them, of rushing forward in a group to fire and then withdrawing while another group did the same.

When it became light, Harrison sent mounted troops against the Indian flanks and soon had the attackers in full retreat. The Americans suffered 62 killed and 126 wounded, a casualty rate of more than 20 percent. Native American casualties were about the same. On a report that Tecumseh was close by with a fresh force, Harrison ordered his men to entrench, but a reconnaissance the next day revealed that the Indians had abandoned Prophetstown, whereupon Harrison's men marched in. There they found new equipment provided by the British. After seizing food and other useful supplies, the men put the town to the torch. Harrison then withdrew the 150 miles to Vincennes, a difficult passage for the wounded traveling in wagons.

Tecumseh returned from his southern mission to find Prophetstown destroyed. Harrison's victory over the Indians in the Battle of Tippecanoe, while it helped elect him president of the United States along with his vice presidential candidate John Tyler in 1840 ("Tippecanoe and Tyler Too"), in the short run had important negative repercussions for the United States. The Battle of Tippecanoe drove the Indians of the Old Northwest to fury and into an irrevocable alliance with the British, who decided that they must now aid the Indians. The battle also served to convince the Americans on the frontier that they could never be safe as long as the British retained influence among the Native Americans and thus fueled demand for war with Britain.

For these reasons, the Battle of Tippecanoe is sometimes referred to as the first battle of the War of 1812. In that conflict, Tecumseh proved to be a brilliant leader of guerrillas. The Native Americans played a decisive role in the defeat of U.S. forces invading Upper Canada in 1812 and 1813, ensuring that it would remain part of Canada. Tecumseh was killed in the Battle of the Thames in October 1813 and the Native Americans, abandoned by the British, were the war's principal losers.

References

Cleaves, Freeman. *Old Tippecanoe: William Henry Harrison and His Time.* New York: Scribner, 1939.

Edmunds, R. David. *The Shawnee Prophet.* Lincoln: University of Nebraska Press, 1983.

Gilpin, Alec R. *The War of 1812 in the Old Northwest.* East Lansing: Michigan State University Press, 1958.

Mahon, John K. *The War of 1812.* Gainesville: University of Florida Press, 1972.

Battle of Borodino

Date	September 7, 1812	
Location	Borodino, some 70 miles west of Moscow, Russia	
Opponents (* winner)	*French and allied armies	Russians
Commander	Emperor Napoleon I	General Mikhail Kutuzov
Approx. # Troops	130,000 men in the *Grande Armée*	120,000
Importance	Although it opens the way for them to occupy Moscow, this is a hollow victory for the French as the Russian Army escapes largely intact	

In 1811 Napoleon Bonaparte controlled most of Europe, but this appearance was deceiving, for the peoples of the continent were increasingly restive under French rule. Although Napoleon's troops were actively engaged only in Spain, four years of fighting there had failed to quell the nationalist opposition. Napoleon's Continental System, designed to weaken Britain economically by denying its goods to the continent, was working poorly and creating additional nationalist opposition.

Russia's Baltic ports were among the greatest leaks in the Continental System, but Napoleon was caught by surprise when, on the last day of 1810, Czar Alexander I repudiated both the Continental System and the alliance with France dating from the 1807 Treaty of Tilsit. Alexander I had been under increasing pressure to take this step. The Russian nobility had opposed the end of a lucrative trade with England and Napoleon's creation of a new Polish state (the Grand Duchy of Warsaw). They also feared the Westernization that French influence would bring.

Napoleon's answer was to punish the czar with an invasion. Those in the know opposed this step. French ambassador to Russia General Jacques Alexandre Law,

Marquis de Lauriston, had repeatedly told Napoleon that Alexander I would never start a war and that the break was solely due to French policies in Poland and Eastern Europe that violated the Treaty of Tilsit of 1807. He also warned Napoleon that any French invasion would be met with a lengthy Russian retreat and scorched-earth policies. Lauriston's predecessor in St. Petersburg, General Arnand de Caulaincourt, Duke of Vicenza, who accompanied Napoleon on the campaign, was equally opposed to war. For his mistaken decisions regarding Russia, Napoleon had only himself to blame.

All during 1811, Napoleon prepared. A great logistician who paid close attention to detail, Napoleon in this case made assumptions that would prove his undoing. He believed that he could dictate circumstances. He anticipated a short campaign with one or two decisive Russian defeats, after which the czar would see reason. Following Russian concessions, the alliance would be restored.

Although Napoleon assembled a vast quantity of supplies for what would be his largest invasion force, he assumed that his troops could in part live off the land, and he underestimated the problems of weather, straggling, sickness, losses of horses, and, above all, the vast distances. In the end it all came down to supplies, which were clearly insufficient. By June 1812 Napoleon's goal of supplies sufficient for 400,000 men for 50 days had shrunk to only 25 days.

In eastern Germany, Napoleon concentrated some 650,000 troops, the largest army under one command to that point in history. A third of the men came from France, and another third came from allied German states (including 30,000 from Austria and Prussia). The remainder came from throughout Europe, including Poles, Spaniards, and Portuguese. A vast heterogenous force, once La Grande Armée de la Russie (Grande Armée) was set in motion it would be difficult to control.

The campaign began in June 1812 when Napoleon led an estimated 450,000 men into Russia. The army carried only three weeks of supplies. From the beginning, everything went wrong. Napoleon expected to fight a decisive battle close to the border, but the badly outnumbered 150,000-man Russian Army had no recourse but to withdraw. Also, even in summer it was virtually impossible to feed the numbers of the Grande Armée in Russia.

On June 24 Napoleon's troops crossed the Niemen River unopposed. On June 28 they occupied the city of Vilna (Vilnius), and on August 17 they were in Smolensk. Taking the latter cost Napoleon about 12,000 men. Much of the city was destroyed in a fire set by the withdrawing Russians.

Napoleon's plan was to winter at Smolensk and organize his conquests, but his advance had gone smoother than expected, and more time remained in the campaigning season. He now made what would prove to be the fatal error of continuing on to Moscow. His army had already been reduced by about 100,000 men because of the need to protect his lines of communication and because of straggling, desertion, and disease.

On August 20 Alexander I appointed General Mikhail Kutuzov to command the Russian Army, replacing General Prince Mikhail Barclay de Tolly, who had been much criticized for the retreat. Alexander I appointed Kutuzov only with great reluctance, for the gulf between the two men was deep following the czar's decision, over Kutuzov's objections, that brought Russian defeat in the Battle of Austerlitz in 1805. Kutuzov had borne the blame for the czar's decision. Kutuzov was then 67 years old, bloated, and dissolute. He was also unflappable and cunning. Kutuzov had urged withdrawal and a scorched-earth policy to defeat the invaders. Ordered by the czar to stand and fight, Kutuzov planned to fight a defensive battle behind well-fortified positions at Borodino, the last natural defense before Moscow. A defensive battle would play to the stolid nature of the Russian soldiers.

Kutuzov's lines were some four miles in length, and he deployed 640 guns. Napoleon had only 587 guns, but they were superior to those of the Russians and better handled. However, for the first time in his career Napoleon, who relied primarily on mobility, would be forced to attack a well-entrenched enemy force. Because Napoleon had lost so many men during the march, the two armies were approximately equal in size: 130,000 in the Grande Armée to about 120,000 Russians.

Maréshal d'Empire Louis-Nicolas Davout, impressed with the strength of the Russian position, urged Napoleon to turn it in an attack around the Russian southern flank. Napoleon, fearing that the Russians would simply slip away, rejected this in favor of a frontal attack to destroy the Russian Army. The emperor planned for massed French artillery fire to destroy the Russian redoubts, which would then be taken by infantry assault. On September 6, with both armies in place, their commanders sought to inspire their troops. Napoleon had just received a painting of his son and had propped it on a chair for viewing by the men. Kutuzov rode among his soldiers with an icon of the Holy Virgin of Smolensk.

At 6:00 a.m. on September 7 the French artillery opened up, beginning the battle. The artillery fire failed to destroy the Russian redoubts or artillery. Successive French ground assaults against the Russian positions overlooking the battlefield gained ground only slowly and at heavy human cost in the face of determined resistance and savage counterattacks. In late afternoon the attackers at last forced the Russians from their redoubts, only to see them re-forming to the rear. It was one of Napoleon's principles to throw in his reserves at the decisive moment of battle. Maréchals de Empire Joachim Murat and Michel Ney now urged him in person to do so, but here, so far from home, the emperor was reluctant to commit the Imperial Guard, the last unbloodied formation and his personal reserve. The battle thus ended without decisive result.

That night both armies encamped on the battlefield, and the next day Kutuzov withdrew his army toward Moscow, enabling Napoleon to claim victory. The Battle of Borodino claimed 28,000–31,000 casualties in the Grande Armée (47 generals) and upwards of 45,000 in the Russian Army. Napoleon trumpeted a great victory, minimizing his own losses while exaggerating those of the Russians. He and his men knew better. The victory was hollow; the Russian Army was still largely intact.

On September 14, 82 days and 650 miles after crossing the Niemen, the Grande Armée, now only 100,000 men, entered Moscow. Most of the wealthy had already fled the city. A great fire soon engulfed Moscow, set by the retreating Russians. The French managed to save the Kremlin, where Napoleon set up his headquarters and waited for overtures of peace from Alexander I. The czar, however, refused to treat with Napoleon. Ignoring Caulaincourt's warnings of the approach of winter, Napoleon tarried five weeks in Moscow. Not until the first snows, on October 19, did Napoleon order the withdrawal.

It is said that Russia has two generals: General Distance and General Winter. When the snows came, there was nothing for the horses to eat. The Grande Armée, weighed down with loot, withdrew over the same route that had been picked clean before. For more than a century the retreat remained the last word in military horror. Terrible cold weather set in, with temperatures of 30 to 40 degrees below zero. Men froze and starved, equipment was abandoned, and the Russian Army attacked again and again. The Russians planned a trap at the Beresina River, destroying its bridges. During November 26–28 the French got across, thanks to the ability of Ney and the bravery of French engineers working under fire from two Russian armies, but 25,000 men perished there in one of the most horrible episodes of the retreat. The Russian pursuit did not stop until the remnants of the Grande Armée had recrossed the Niemen. Of some 490,000 men who had entered Russia in June, only 50,000–100,000 escaped. Another 100,000 were prisoners. More than 100,000 had died in battle and skirmishes, and an equal number had died of cold, disease, or famine. The Grande Armée was no more.

Napoleon left the army, barely escaping the Russians, and returned to Paris on December 18 to raise new forces. He could not replace the trained officers and noncommissioned officers, the cavalry horses, or the artillery lost in Russia. Napoleon had failed in his bid to conquer all Europe. The question now was whether Europe could conquer Napoleon.

References

Caulaincourt, Armand de. *With Napoleon in Russia: Memoirs of General de Caulaincourt, Duke of Vicenza.* New York: William Morrow, 1935.

Duffy, Christopher. *Borodino: Napoleon against Russia, 1812.* New York: Scribner, 1973.

Elting, John R. *Swords around a Throne: Napoleon's Grande Armée.* New York: Free Press, 1988.

Fezensac, Montesquieu. *The Russian Campaign, 1812.* Translated by Lee B. Kennett. Athens: University of Georgia Press, 1970.

Palmer, Alan. *Napoleon in Russia: The 1812 Campaign.* New York: Simon and Schuster, 1967.

Battle of Lake Erie

Date	September 10, 1813	
Location	Lake Erie, one of the five Great Lakes of North America bordered by the United States and Canada	
Opponents (* winner)	*Americans	British
Commander	Master Commandant Oliver H. Perry	Commander Robert H. Barclay
Approx. # Troops	9 warships mounting a total of 54 guns	6 ships with 64 guns
Importance	Perry's ships can now transport U.S. ground forces across Lake Erie, supply them, and make possible the defeat of the British and their allied Native American forces west of Niagara.	

At the beginning of the War of 1812, the U.S. Navy won a series of single-ship engagements that shocked the Royal Navy and the British public. By 1813, however, the Royal Navy had reinforced its naval presence off the United States, especially in frigates and ships of the line (of which the Americans had none) and imposed a blockade of the U.S. coastline. During the remainder of the war, from 1813 to the end of 1815, few American warships got to sea.

At the same time, however, naval history was being written on the Great Lakes. During the winter of 1812–1813 a naval builders' war took place along the shores of the Great Lakes, especially Lake Ontario and Lake Erie. As had been revealed early in the fighting, control of the lakes would be essential to either side in any cross-border invasion.

Both sides were therefore looking for a showdown battle, which occurred on September 10, 1813. On Lake Erie, U.S. Navy master commandant Oliver H. Perry commanded nine warships of 54 guns with a broadside weight of 936 pounds and 450 men. Royal Navy commander Robert H. Barclay commanded a squadron of six ships with 64 guns and a broadside weight of 496 pounds, manned by 565 men. Perry flew his flag in the brig *Lawrence* (20 guns). His second-in-command, Lieutenant Jesse D. Elliott, commanded the other American brig, the *Niagara* (20 guns). The other ships in Perry's squadron were the brig *Caledonia* (3 guns), the schooner *Somers* (2 guns), the sloop *Trippe* (1 gun), and the gunboats *Tigress, Porcupine, Scorpion,* and *Ariel* (each mounting 1 to 4 guns). Barclay flew his flag in the corvette *Detroit* (21 guns). The other ships in his squadron were the corvette *Queen Charlotte* (17 guns), the schooner *Lady Prevost* (13 guns), the brig *General Hunter* (10 guns), the sloop *Little Belt* (3 guns), and the schooner *Chippaway* (2 guns). Not only at a disadvantage in the number of ships and their total throw weight of shot, Barclay also had in his squadron guns of many calibers and types that required different charges and shot.

On September 10 the two squadrons approached on roughly parallel axes. Barclay hoped to stand off at some distance and use his long guns to batter the American ships, which were armed principally with short-range cannonades. Light winds initially worked against the Americans, but Perry was able to take advantage of a shift to secure the weather gauge and close. He wanted the *Lawrence* to engage the *Detroit* and the *Niagara* to battle the *Queen Charlotte* while his smaller ships engaged their British counterparts.

In the heavy fighting that followed, Elliott's *Niagara,* armed principally with cannonades, failed to close. This allowed the three largest British ships to concentrate on the *Lawrence,* which was badly damaged. Perry failed to signal Elliott to close, and Elliott remained in his battle position behind the *Caledonia* rather than come forward. After some two and a half hours of fighting, with few men on the *Lawrence* still able to fight, Elliott brought the *Niagara* forward, and Perry transferred his flag to that brig. Sending Elliott in a boat to direct the trailing gunboats, Perry brought the undamaged *Niagara* into the fight.

Perry successfully rallied his forces, and under a terrible pounding from the American broadsides the British ships surrendered one by one. The Americans lost 27 killed and 96 wounded, the majority of them on the *Lawrence,* which had taken a horrible beating. British personnel losses were 41 killed and 94 wounded, with Barclay among the latter. Perry reported laconically to North West Army commander Major General William Henry Harrison, "We have met the enemy and they are ours: Two Ships, two Brigs, one Schooner and one Sloop."

The Battle of Lake Erie marked a rare time in history that an entire British squadron surrendered. Perry's ships then transported U.S. ground forces across Lake Erie, kept them supplied, and made possible the defeat of the British and their allied Native American forces there. The subsequent Battle of the Thames on October 5, 1813, broke British power west of Niagara and resulted in the death of Tecumseh. The British were also forced to evacuate Detroit. The Battle of Lake Erie also ignited a prolonged and bitter controversy between Elliott and Perry over their roles in the battle that split much of the naval officer corps for years to come.

References

Dillon, Richard. *We Have Met the Enemy: Oliver Hazard Perry, Wilderness Commodore.* New York: McGraw-Hill, 1978.

Friedman, Lawrence J., and David Curtis Skaggs. "Jesse Duncan Elliott and the Battle of Lake Erie: The Issue of Mental Stability." *Journal of the Early Republic* 10 (Winter 1990): 493–516.

Skaggs, David Curtis. "The Battle of Lake Erie." In *Great American Naval Battles,* edited by Jack Sweetman, 64–84. Annapolis, MD: Naval Institute Press, 1998.

———. *Oliver Hazard Perry: Honor, Courage, and Patriotism in the Early U.S. Navy.* Annapolis, MD: Naval Institute Press, 2006.

Skaggs, David Curtis, and Gerard T. Altoff. *A Signal Victory: The Lake Erie Campaign, 1812–1813.* Annapolis, MD: Naval Institute Press, 1997.

Battle of Leipzig

Date	October 16–19, 1813	
Location	Leipzig in Saxony (eastern Germany)	
Opponents (* winner)	*Allied coalition of Russians, Austrians, Prussians, Swedes	French
Commander	Prince Karl Philip zu Schwarzenberg	Emperor Napoleon I
Approx. # Troops	410,000	195,000
Importance	The largest battle of the Napoleonic Wars, it forces Napoleon to quit Germany	

The Battle of Leipzig, also known as the Battle of the Nations for the large number of national armies participating in it, was the most important battle of the German War of Liberation of 1813 and one of the most important battles of the Napoleonic Wars. In 1813 following the defeat of Napoleon's army in Russia, the anti-Napoleonic forces at last coalesced. That March under heavy Russian pressure, Prussian king Frederick William III declared war on France, initiating what became known as the War of German Liberation. There was keen determination in Prussia to exact revenge for the humiliation visited by Napoleon, but enthusiasm for armed struggle that would bring the eviction of the French found enthusiastic response throughout the German states.

Russian general Mikhail Kutuzov, hero of the Borodino Campaign of 1812, headed the allied forces. General Gebhard Leberecht von Blücher, 70 years old, commanded the Prussian forces. Britain remained at war with Napoleon, so the coalition included Russia, Britain, and Prussia. Sweden, heavily influenced by heir apparent Crown Prince Karl Johan (Charles John, former French marshal Jean Baptiste Bernadotte), also joined. Sweden received a subsidy from Britain as well as a pledge of support for a union of Norway and Sweden. For the time being, Austria, nominally allied with France, remained neutral.

With substantial resources tied down in Spain, Napoleon was at a disadvantage. He arrived in the German theater of war at the end of April. Although the emperor could replace the men lost in Russia (many of the replacements came from the new class of 17-year-old conscripts, known to the veterans as the "Marie Louises"), he was short of equipment and artillery. Many of the new recruits did not receive muskets for the first time until they got to Germany. Above all, Napoleon lacked replacements for the trained noncommissioned officers, officers, and cavalry horses lost in the Russian campaign. To minimize his army's exposure and purchase time to rebuild, Napoleon might have stood on the defensive, but he followed his standard strategy of deciding the campaign with a bold advance to achieve decisive victory in one stroke.

The natural meeting point of the opposing armies was in Saxony, and the important battles of the campaign all occurred there. On May 2 at Lützen and on May 20–21 at Bautzen, Napoleon won important victories over the Russian and Prussian forces but was slow to concentrate, and his enemies were able to withdraw in good order. Also, Napoleon's casualties of 40,000 men were as great at those of his adversaries. After Lützen, however, Saxony came out on the French side.

On June 2 the allies asked for a suspension of hostilities to talk, and two days later an armistice was signed at Poischwitz, extending hostilities to July 20 (and later to August 16). Both sides saw this as an opportunity to rest, reorganize, and resupply their forces and as a chance to woo Austria. Austrian foreign minister Prince Klemens Wenzel Nepomuk Lothar von Metternich had suggested the armistice as a first step to a general European peace conference. On June 26 he met with Napoleon in the Marcolini Palace in Dresden. Metternich proposed a settlement that would include the restoration of Prussia's 1806 boundaries, the return of Illyria to Austria, the dissolution of the Grand Duchy of Warsaw, and an end to the French protectorate over the Confederation of the Rhine. In return, France could have the natural frontier of the Rhine River and the Alps along with Holland, Westphalia in Germany, and Italy. Napoleon rejected these terms. The furthest he was prepared to go was to return Illyria to Austria, and this only to keep it neutral. If Napoleon had been capable of concession, he might have unhinged the coalition against him and kept Austria neutral, but he claimed that Austria would never go to war against him. A peace congress held at Prague during July 5–August 11 was also a failure, and the struggle was renewed.

This time, however, the odds against Napoleon were greater, for Austria declared war against France on August 12, adding 150,000 men to the allied side. This put their strength at some 515,000 men against only 370,000 for Napoleon. Supreme command of the allied armies went to Prince Karl Philip zu Schwarzenberg, Kutuzov having died in April. Near Dresden during August 26–27 Napoleon, outnumbered 2 to 1, attacked, turned the allied left flank, and won a brilliant victory, his last on German soil. The French sustained 10,000 casualties, while the allies sustained 38,000 casualties.

By October 15 Napoleon's forces were being driven toward Leipzig, where during October 16–19 the largest battle of the Napoleonic Wars now occurred. On October 16 Napoleon commanded some 177,000 men and 700 guns; the allies had more than 200,000 men under Schwarzenberg in the south and 54,000 under Blücher in the northwest. On October 18 Napoleon had increased his numbers to 195,000 men and 734 guns, but the allies had added Swedish troops under Bernadotte and Russians under Beningsen for a total of 410,000 men and 1,335 guns. These numbers heavily influenced the battle's outcome. In terms of sheer numbers, the battle was probably the largest in history until the 20th century.

The first day of battle went to Napoleon, but the tide shifted with the arrival of 70,000 Russians on the night of October 17 and 85,000 Swedes early the next morning. Napoleon made a tentative attempt, without result, to negotiate with the allies on October 17. The decisive point came on the third day, October 18. Napoleon drew his army into a tight circle around Lepizig and secured his escape routes over the Elster and Luppe rivers. In "a miles-wide pant of pain," the allies opened a general attack on the length of the French lines. The French lines held, despite the fact that a contingent of Saxon troops defected to the allies. Napoleon was nonetheless forced to withdraw, beginning after dark.

The retreat continued into the next day, when the allied forces stormed Leipzig. The French rear guards held, and all seemed to be going well until a French corporal prematurely blew the bridge over the Luppe River, trapping four corps commanded by marshals Jacques Macdonald and Józef Antoni Prince Poniatowski and generals Jacques Lauriston and Jean Louis Ebénézer Reynier. Their men fought desperately but were driven into the river. Macdonald swam to safety, but Poniatowski, wounded several times, drowned. Lauriston and Reynier were taken prisoner. Napoleon sustained some 68,000 casualties (30,000 taken prisoner). He also lost 325 guns and 500 wagons. The allies lost about 54,000 men.

The Battle of Leipzig finished Napoleon in Germany. He now withdrew his forces behind the Rhine. The liberation of Germany was complete, and the allies were in position to invade France from the northeast as the Duke of Wellington and British forces invaded in the southwest from Spain. Napoleon's refusal to agree to continued but diminished allied peace offers led to his military defeat and abdication in April 1814.

References

Chandler, David G. *The Campaigns of Napoleon.* New York: Macmillan, 1966.

Connelly, Owen. *Blundering to Glory: Napoleon's Military Campaigns.* Rev. ed. Wilmington, DE: Scholarly Resources, 1999.

Elting, John R. *Swords around a Throne: Napoleon's Grande Armée.* New York: Free Press, 1988.

Nafziger, George. *Napoleon at Leipzig: The Battle of the Nations, 1813.* Chicago: Emperor's Press, 1996.

Smith, Digby. *1813, Leipzig: Napoleon and the Battle of the Nations.* London: Greenhill Books, 2001.

Battles of Lake Champlain and Plattsburgh

Date	September 11, 1814	
Location	Plattsburgh and Lake Champlain in upper New York State, United States	
Opponents (* winner)	*Americans	British
Commander	Master Commandant Thomas Macdonough (naval force); Brigadier General Alexander Macomb (land force)	Captain George Downie (naval force); Lieutenant General Sir George Prevost (land force)
Approx. # Troops	4 ships and 10 gunboats; 3,000 men (land force)	4 ships and 12 galleys (naval force); 11,000 men (land force)
Importance	Having suffered rebuff in his land assault and defeat in the naval engagement, Prevost withdraws his army back into Canada	

The September 11, 1814, Battle of Lake Champlain and concurrent fighting on land at Plattsburgh, New York, proved decisive in the War of 1812. Following the defeat of Napoleon in April 1814, Britain was able to send additional land and naval forces to North America. With these assets in place, the British planned to invade the United States successively from three points—Niagara, Lake Champlain, and New Orleans—as well as to raid simultaneously into the Chesapeake Bay. On the Niagara front, however, the Americans went on the offensive before the British forces could mount their attack. In July, U.S. troops captured Fort Erie and won important land victories in the Battle of Chippewa and the Battle of Lundy's Lane.

By mid-August, governor-general of Canada Lieutenant General Sir George Prevost assembled some 11,000 British regulars near Montreal to invade the United States by the classic route of Lake Champlain and the Hudson River. His immediate objective was the town of Plattsburgh, New York, and the U.S. naval base on Lake Champlain. Prospects appeared bleak for the United States, particularly as Secretary of War John Armstrong had ordered the commander of U.S. forces in the Lake Champlain area, Major General George Izard, to move most of his men from Plattsburgh to the Niagara frontier.

The British land force then began to move down the western shore of Lake Champlain. Following skirmishes along Beekmantown Road, the British reached Plattsburgh on September 6, 1814. Despite its importance, the town was defended by only a single brigade of regulars under Brigadier General Alexander Macomb along with about 800 New York and Vermont militia, at most 3,000 men.

Prevost proved to be an inept commander. He failed to secure a ford across the Saranac River to his front and then, much to the consternation of his senior officers, suspended land operations pending the arrival of the supporting British naval squadron on Lake Champlain, commanded by Captain George Downie. Prevost was resolved to gain control of the lake before continuing his advance. Downie, however, had taken command of the squadron only on September 2 and was determined not to hazard it until his most powerful ship, the *Confiance,* was fully prepared and all its guns mounted.

Prevost's land force remained inactive for nearly five days awaiting Downie's arrival, and Macomb used the delay to strengthen his defensive position, which consisted of three wooden forts and two blockhouses along the south bank of the Saranac River where it entered Lake Champlain. Although his forces were outnumbered almost 4 to 1, on the night of September 9 Macomb mounted a spoiling attack across the Saranac, with 50 men attacking a British rocket battery. The raid was successful, and the American force returned to its lines intact. Prevost nevertheless remained quiescent until the morning of September 11, when the British flotilla at last sailed into Plattsburgh Bay.

Immediately on Downie's arrival, Prevost ordered two brigades to begin the land attack. As the British flotilla engaged the U.S. Navy squadron under Master Commandant Thomas Macdonough, Major General Thomas Brisbane's brigade of 3,500 men attacked American troops in front of Plattsburgh to fix the defenders in place, while a second British brigade of 3,500 men under Major General Frederick Robinson searched for a ford on the Saranac in order to turn the American left flank. Prevost held a third brigade under Major General Manly Powers in reserve, ready to exploit any opportunity.

Unfortunately for the British, Robinson was late beginning his movement and lost additional time by marching down the wrong road. Brisbane also had difficulty in the face of determined resistance. Just as the British troops were registering progress against the outnumbered Americans, however, at 10:30 a.m. they received orders from Prevost to cease operations and withdraw immediately. Prevost took this decision in view of what had happened on the lake.

Downie's squadron of four ships—the frigate *Confiance* (39 guns), the brig *Linnet* (16 guns), the sloop *Chubb* (11 guns), and the sloop *Finch* (11 guns)—and 12 galleys mounting a total of 17 guns had rounded Cumberland Head and stood in to engage the American flotilla. The American force numbered 4 ships—the frigate *Saratoga* (26 guns), the brig *Eagle* (20 guns), the schooner *Ticonderoga* (17 guns), and the sloop *Preble* (7 guns)—and 10 gunboats mounting a total of 16 guns. The two sides were closely matched in firepower as well. Macdonough had a great advantage in that his ships were carefully positioned. In the week he had to prepare he had placed his ships in line, setting out anchors so that they might easily be swung in either direction to utilize their guns to maximum advantage as the situation dictated. Because the American vessels were anchored, their crews could concentrate on working the guns. The British crews, on the other hand, were forced to work the sails and guns of their ships at the same time.

The naval battle involving a total of about 1,800 men lasted 2 hours and 20 minutes. The two largest ships, the American *Saratoga* and the British *Confiance,* inflicted significant damage on each other. Downie was killed, and with heavy personnel losses the *Confiance* struck to the Americans. Three other British vessels also surrendered. Three British galleys were sunk, and the remainder withdrew. But with all of his own galleys in sinking shape, Macdonough was unable to pursue the British vessels.

Macdonough had won a classic victory. He reported to Secretary of the Navy William Jones that "The Almighty has been pleased to Grant us a Signal Victory on Lake Champlain in the Capture of one Frigate, one Brig, and two sloops of war of the enemy." American casualties were 47 dead and 58 wounded; British casualties totaled 57 dead and at least 100 wounded.

The casualties in the fighting on land and water were relatively insignificant—British losses in the land battle totaled perhaps 250 men, while American losses were only about 150 men—but the battle had immense consequences. Deprived of his naval support and well aware of what had happened to a British invading army in 1777 in this same region under Lieutenant General John Burgoyne during the American Revolutionary War (1775–1783), Prevost ordered a general withdrawal. This ended all danger of a British invasion from the north during the remainder of the war. Macomb's troops were astonished at the British departure. For his stand, Macomb received a gold medal and promotion to major general. Prevost was recalled to England to face an official inquiry.

News of the victory also influenced the Ghent Peace Conference. Coupled with the American victories on the Niagara front and at Baltimore, Maryland, the Battle of Lake Champlain contributed greatly to the British decision to end the war status quo ante bellum, without territorial concessions.

References

Everest, Allan S. *The War of 1812 in the Champlain Valley.* Syracuse, NY: Syracuse University Press, 1981.

Fitz-Enz, David G. *Plattsburg, the Final Invasion: The Decisive Battle of the War of 1812.* New York: Cooper Square, 2001.

Mahon, John K. *The War of 1812.* Gainesville: University of Florida Press, 1972.

Skaggs, David Curtis. *Thomas Macdonough: Master of Command in the Early U.S. Navy.* Annapolis, MD: Naval Institute Press, 2003.

Stanley, George F. G. *War of 1812: Land Operations.* Ottawa: National Museums of Canada and Macmillan, 1983.

Battle of Waterloo

Date	June 18, 1815	
Location	Village of Waterloo in southern Belgium	
Opponents (* winner)	*British, Dutch, and Prussians	French
Commander	Arthur Wellesley, Duke of Wellington (British); Field Marshal Prince Gebhard Leberecht von Blücher von Wahlstadt (Prussians)	Emperor Napoleon I
Approx. # Troops	68,000, later 140,000	72,000
Importance	Brings to an end the 100 Days	

The Battle of Waterloo on June 18, 1815, ended the Napoleonic Wars. On April 13, 1814, Napoleon had been pressed by his marshals to sign the Treaty of Fontainebleau, by which he abdicated the throne of France and received Elba as a sovereign principality along with an annual subsidy of 2 million francs. The squabbling of the major powers at the Congress of Vienna, disaffection in France over the return of the Bourbon king Louis XVIII, the excesses of the Ultras (royalist supporters), and Napoleon's endless ambition all led him to escape Elba and return to France in the adventure known as the Hundred Days. Napoleon claimed that he was formally absolved from upholding the Treaty of Fontainebleau when the Bourbon government failed to pay the promised subsidy.

Napoleon arrived by ship at Fréjus, France, on March 1, 1815. Troops sent to arrest him instead rallied to their former emperor, with the most important defection being that of their commander, Marshal Michel Ney, who had promised to return to Paris with Napoleon in an iron cage. On March 20 Napoleon returned to Paris and, despite general apathy among most of the French population, put together a field force of about 125,000 men. The allies had some 400,000 men in the theater of operations but could expand that to 700,000. Napoleon's only hope was thus to attack and defeat the allies in detail before they could concentrate against him.

He set out for the northwestern French frontier with the aim of defeating first the British and Dutch forces under Field Marshal Sir Arthur Wellesley, Earl of Wellington, and then Prussian troops under Field Marshal Prince Gebhard Leberecht von Blücher von Wahlstadt before having to face the Austrians and Russians under Prince Karl Philip zu Schwarzenberg on the eastern frontier. Napoleon left Paris on June 11, secretly concentrating his forces near Charleroi in Belgium and hoping to strike before his opponents realized he had left Paris. On June 15 Napoleon seized Charleroi. Blücher reacted by assembling his forces 10 miles north of Charleroi, while Wellington began his own slower concentration 15 miles to the west. The key point was Quatre Bras, a small crossroads town that linked the two allied armies.

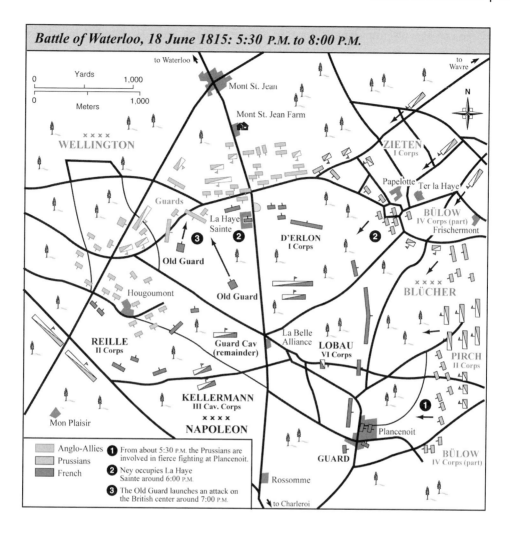

Battle of Waterloo, 18 June 1815: 5:30 P.M. to 8:00 P.M.

On June 16 Napoleon ordered Ney and 24,000 men of the French left wing to take Quatre Bras while he himself led about 71,000 men of the French center and right against 84,000 Prussians under Blücher at Ligny. Napoleon defeated Blücher but expected Ney to fall on the Prussian right flank and complete the French victory. Ney, however, had been slow to move and was held up at Quatre Bras until afternoon by forces under the Prince of Orange, one of Wellington's subordinate commanders. Wellington and British reinforcements then came up, achieved numerical superiority, and threw Ney back. Marshal Jean Baptiste Drouet, Comte d'Erlon, because of confusing orders from Ney, marched his corps of 20,000 men back and forth between the two French armies and was unable to aid either. Blücher was thus able to withdraw from Ligny toward Wavre in good order. In the two battles combined, the allies had lost about 21,400 men, while the French lost some 16,400 men.

Belatedly, on the morning of June 17 Napoleon made what turned out to be a fatal error, detaching Marshal Emmanuel de Grouchy and 33,000 men of the

French right wing to pursue Blücher and the Prussians. Napoleon and Grouchy assumed that the Prussians would retreat back on their base of Namur. Napoleon turned with the main body to assist Ney, planning to drive toward Brussels along the Charleroi road.

Wellington meanwhile was withdrawing north and concentrating at the small village of Waterloo, north of Quatre Bras on the Charleroi-Brussels road. Wellington appealed to Blücher to send him at least one corps; Blücher promised to come to his assistance with two corps or more. Wellington later called this "the decision of the century."

Napoleon joined Ney at Quatre Bras and, on the afternoon of June 17, set out after Wellington. Steady rain, quagmires of mud, and the superb hit-and-run tactics of British horse artillery under Lieutenant General Henry Paget, Lord Uxbridge, delayed the French arrival at the village of Waterloo until midnight. Both sides were arrayed along ridge lines about a mile apart. Wellington planned to fight a defensive battle until Blücher and the Prussians could arrive. Wellington made his dispositions carefully, confident in his men, and the superb well-trained veterans of the Peninsular War infused the Anglo-Dutch army with confidence. Still, Wellington knew that allied victory depended on whether the Prussians could arrive in time.

Napoleon was certain that the Prussians would not come to the aid of Wellington. He therefore overruled his staff and did not recall Grouchy. This meant that Napoleon had just 72,000 troops at Waterloo against 68,000 British and Dutch. Had he recalled Grouchy, Napoleon would have had more than 100,000 men on the field of battle. If Blücher had been able to join Wellington, however, the allies would have had an overwhelming advantage of nearly 140,000 men.

Heavy rains had made the battlefield soggy. Napoleon had expected to open the battle at 6:00 a.m., but on the advice of his artillery commander, who wanted firmer ground for movement of the guns, Napoleon delayed the attack. Battle was not joined until near noon, and it was after 1:00 p.m. when the grand battery of 80 French guns opened up. The first French infantry attack did not occur until about 1:45. Had the ground been firmer, Napoleon might well have destroyed Wellington's forces and reached Brussels that evening.

The battlefield at Waterloo measured only about three square miles. Napoleon was confident that massed artillery fire, followed by a frontal infantry assault, would carry the day. Wellington, however, positioned the bulk of his forces on the reverse slope of a ridge, protected from direct French artillery fire. The French infantry attack was launched against the center of the allied line. The English hollow squares withstood repeated French infantry attacks. Napoleon's younger brother Jérôme, moreover, disobeyed orders to only occupy the approaches to the château of Hougoumont, wasting an entire division in repeated unsuccessful charges against the building's thick walls. The French infantry and cavalry attacks were not coordinated, and Ney, whose courage was unquestioned, led his troops into battle piecemeal.

Despite savage fighting, British and Dutch forces managed to hold long enough to allow Blücher's Prussians to join them and save the day. Grouchy meanwhile was held up by the Prussian rear guard at Wavre and chose to continue his attack there rather than march to the sound of the guns at Waterloo, plainly audible less than 14 miles distant. The retreat of the Imperial Guard—the first time this had occurred—signaled the end of the battle. When word went out that the Imperial Guard had retreated before massed British musket fire there were cries of "*Sauve qui peut!*" ("Save yourselves!"), and the retreat became a rout. Casualties were 26,000 French (with 9,000 more captured), 15,000 for the British-Dutch forces, and 7,000 for the Prussians.

Napoleon fled the field, his escape purchased with the lives of two regiments of his Old Guard. He first went to Paris, where he found that Joseph Fouché had seized power in the name of the recently deposed Bourbons. Napoleon could have continued the fight, but he knew that all was lost. On June 22 he abdicated in favor of his son by Marie Louise of Austria and then went to Rochefort, where on July 15 he surrendered to the British and went aboard the British ship of the line *Bellerophon*. The British sent him to the small remote island of St. Helena in the windswept South Atlantic.

The Battle of Waterloo is regarded as one of the most important battles in world history, but it is significant only in that it marked the end of Napoleon's rule. What if the battle had gone the other way? Given the general lassitude of the French people and the determination of the allies to defeat him, it seems certain that Napoleon would have been beaten in another subsequent battle of the nations.

Napoleon's Hundred Days were costly for France. In the Second Treaty of Paris of November 20, 1815, France lost additional territory (being restricted to the borders of 1790 rather than 1792 under the First Treaty of Paris) and had to pay an indemnity of 700 million francs, support an allied army of occupation until the indemnity was paid, and return all captured artworks.

References

Hamilton-Williams, David. *Waterloo: New Perspectives.* London: Arms and Armour, 1993.

Hofschroer, Peter. *1815, the Waterloo Campaign: The German Victory, from Waterloo to the Fall of Napoleon.* Harrisburg, PA: Stackpole Books, 1999.

Howarth, David. *Waterloo: A Near Run Thing.* Conshohocken, PA: Combined Books, 1997.

Sibourne, William. *History of the Waterloo Campaign.* London: Greenhill Books, 1990.

Battle of Ayacucho

Date	December 9, 1824	
Location	Plain of Ayacucho, southern Peru	
Opponents (* winner)	*Patriots	Royalists (Spanish)
Commander	General Antonio José de Sucre	Viceroy José de La Serna y Hirojosa
Approx. # Troops	5,780	9,300
Importance	Brings a Spanish military withdrawal from Peru	

The Battle of Ayacucho in Peru occurred between the Royalists (Spanish) and Patriots during the South American Wars of Independence (1808–1829). Also known as the Battle of the Generals, it was fought on December 9, 1824, on the high plain in southern Peru and ended in victory for the forces seeking independence from Spain.

Although other Spanish colonies in America had already been granted independence, Spain sought to hold Peru because of its considerable mineral wealth and the largely apolitical attitude of its people. In 1823, however, revolution and upheaval in Spain created widespread dissension among the Spanish forces in Peru. In 1824 Patriot leader Simón Bolívar and General Antonio José de Sucre took advantage of this and opened a military offensive, hoping to retake Lima from the Royalists.

On August 6 their Patriot army of some 9,000 men met and defeated at Jurin, some 100 miles northeast of Lima, a Royalist army of equal size under General José Canterac. Only about 2,000 men on each side were engaged in a cavalry fight. No shots were fired; the battle was decided solely by sabers. Following this battle, the Spanish withdrew into the highlands southeast of Lima. While Bolívar organized a new government in Lima, Sucre continued the campaign against the Royalists.

After prolonged maneuvering during the autumn of 1824, the two sides came together in battle on the Plain of Ayacucho, 186 miles southeast of Lima. In the Quechua language Ayacucho means "dead corner," referring to a slaughter of natives there by the Spanish early in their conquest of Peru. Spanish Viceroy José de La Serna y Hirojosa commanded the Royalist force of some 9,300 men and seven guns. Sucre had 5,780 men and two guns. Both sides had some cavalry.

In the maneuvering before the battle, La Serna managed to position his force north of Sucre's army, hoping to cut the Patriots off from the sea and additional forces that Bolívar was raising in Lima. La Serna tried to employ his superior numbers to advantage by encircling his opponent, but Sucre avoided this, taking up an excellent defensive position on the plain. La Serna then planned to pin the enemy flanks while finishing off the Patriots with a drive into the center of their line. Sucre planned to allow La Serna to attack, hoping that he would be able to first contain the attack and then exploit it with a reserve of three battalions of infantry and five cavalry squadrons.

The battle opened early on the morning of December 9. The Royalist left wing advanced first against the Patriot right wing commanded by General José Maria

Córdoba. This attack failed, as did another Royalist assault on the Patriot center. Córdoba then counterattacked, driving back the Royalist left and opening a break in the Royalist lines that allowed Sucre to introduce his infantry and cavalry reserves to seal the victory. The entire battle had lasted less than an hour and a half.

Despite being outnumbered, Sucre had won a complete victory. The Royalists lost 1,400 dead and 700 wounded, while the Patriots sustained 309 dead and 607 wounded. Particularly grievous for the Royalist cause was the large number of senior officers—including 15 generals, 16 colonels, and 68 lieutenant colonels—among the 2,500 Royalists taken prisoner. For this reason the engagement is sometimes called the Battle of the Generals. La Serna, who had received a half dozen wounds, was among those captured.

Under the terms of capitulation, La Serna agreed to withdraw all Spanish forces from Peru. Sucre then moved into upper Peru. In August 1825 he declared the province of Chuquisaca independent and renamed it Bolivia, in Bolívar's honor. Although fighting by small isolated Spanish units continued thereafter, the Battle of Ayacucho marked the effective end of the South American Wars of Independence.

References

Anna, Timothy E. *The Fall of the Royal Government in Peru*. Lincoln: University of Nebraska Press, 1979.

Archer, C., ed. *The Wars of Independence in Spanish America*. Wilmington, DE: Scholarly Resources, 2000.

Lynch, John. *The Spanish-American Revolutions*. New York: Norton, 1986.

Prago, Albert. *The Revolutions in Spanish America*. New York: Macmillan, 1970.

Sherwell, Guillermo. *Antonio José de Sucre*. Washington, DC: Byron S. Adams, 1924.

Battle of Navarino Bay

Date	October 20, 1827	
Location	Navarino Bay, west coast of the Peloponnese, Greece	
Opponents (* winner)	*Allied British, French, Russian naval squadrons	Ottoman and Egyptian naval squadrons
Commander	Vice Admiral Sir Edward Codrington (British); Admiral Henry Gauthier de Rigny (French); Admiral Count L. Heidin (Heyden)	Ibrahim Pasha
Approx. # Troops	11 ships of the line and 15 other warships	3 ships of the line and 62 or 63 other warships
Importance	The most important engagement of the Greek War for Independence, it removes any barrier to the Russian Black Sea Fleet and the next year Russia declares war on Turkey.	

The Battle of Navarino Bay on October 20, 1827, was the most important engagement of the Greek War for Independence (1822–1832). With Ottoman and Egyptian forces fully in control of Greece, representatives of the French, British, and Russian governments concluded the Treaty of London. It called on the Ottomans to agree to an armistice and for the Egyptians to withdraw. Should the Ottomans reject an armistice, the three allied powers would come to the aid of the Greeks with their naval forces. In the meantime, the British made a strong but ultimately unsuccessful diplomatic effort to get Egyptian ruler Mohammed Ali to remove his forces from Greece.

On August 16 the European powers sent a note to the Sublime Porte demanding an armistice. When the Ottomans rejected it on August 29, the British, French, and Russian governments issued orders to their naval commanders in the Mediterranean to cut off waterborne Ottoman and Egyptian resupply to Greece. In late August 1827, despite warnings from the European governments not to do so, Ali sent a large squadron with reinforcements to Navarino Bay (Pylos) on the west coast of the Peloponnese. On September 8 it arrived and joined Ottoman ships already there. On September 12 a British squadron under Vice Admiral Sir Edward Codrington arrived off the bay. The French and Russian governments also had dispatched squadrons to Greece.

On September 25 Codrington and French admiral Henry Gauthier de Rigny met with Ibrahim Pasha, the Egyptian commander in Greece, to discuss a mediation arrangement already accepted by the Greeks. Ibrahim agreed to an armistice while awaiting instructions from the sultan. Leaving a frigate at Navarino Bay to watch the Egyptian and Ottoman ships there, Codrington then withdrew to the British-controlled Ionian island of Zante (Zakynthos).

Ibrahim learned that while he was expected to observe a cease-fire, Greek naval units under British mercenary commanders (Admiral Lord Cochrane had charge of the Greek Navy) were continuing operations in the Gulf of Corinth, at Epirus, and at the port of Patras. Then during September 29–30, a Greek steamer warship, the *Karteria,* sank nine Ottoman ships off Salona (Split) in Dalmatia. Codrington sent messages to warn these British officers, who were not under his command, to desist from such operations; this had little effect. Ibrahim duly protested and, when nothing changed, decided to act.

On October 1 Ibrahim ordered ships from Navarino Bay to assist the Ottoman garrison at Patras. Codrington's squadron intercepted these ships at the entrance to the Gulf of Calydon and forced them to return to Navarino. On the night of October 3–4 Ibrahim personally led another relief effort. Although they managed to avoid detection by the British picket ship at Navarino Bay in the darkness, a strong lee wind prevented his forces from entering the Gulf of Calydon. He was forced to anchor off Papas and wait for the storm to end. This allowed Codrington time to come up with his squadron, and firing warning shots, he forced Ibrahim to return to Navarino Bay.

Ibrahim continued land operations, which included the wholesale burning of Greek villages and fields. The fires were clearly visible from the allied ships. A British landing party reported that the Greek population of Messenia was close to starvation. On October 13 Codrington was joined off Navarino Bay by the French squadron under de Rigny and a Russian squadron under Admiral Count L. Heidin (Heyden). Both of these commanders were inferior in rank to Codrington, who also had the most ships, and they agreed to serve under his command.

On October 20, 1827, following futile attempts to contact Ibrahim Pasha, Codrington consulted with the other allied commanders and made the decision to enter Navarino Bay with the combined British, French, and Russian squadrons. The allies had 11 ships of the line and 15 other warships. Codrington flew his flag in the ship of the line *Asia* (84 guns). He also had 2 74-gun ships of the line, 4 frigates, and 4 brigs. French admiral de Rigny had 4 74-gun ships of the line, 1 frigate, and 2 schooners. Admiral Count Heidin's Russian squadron consisted of 4 74-gun ships of the line and 4 frigates. The Egyptians and Ottomans had 65 or 66 warships in Navarino harbor: 3 Ottoman ships of the line (2 of 84 guns each and 1 of 76 guns), 4 Egyptian frigates of 64 guns each, 15 Ottoman frigates of 48 guns each, 18 Ottoman and 8 Egyptian corvettes of 14 to 18 guns each, 4 Ottoman and 8 Egyptian brigs of 19 guns each, and 5–6 Egyptian fire brigs. There were also some Ottoman transports and smaller craft.

Around noon on October 20 the allied ships sailed in two lines into Navarino Bay. The British and French formed one line, and the Russians formed the other. The Ottomans demanded that Codrington withdraw, but the British admiral replied that he was there to give orders, not receive them. He threatened that if any shots were fired at the allied ships, he would destroy the Egyptian-Ottoman fleet.

The Egyptian-Ottoman ships were lying at anchor in a long crescent-shape formation with their flanks protected by shore batteries. At 2:00 p.m. the allied ships began filing into the bay. They then took up position inside the crescent. The British ships faced the center of the Egyptian-Ottoman line, while the French were on the Ottoman left and the Russians were on the Ottoman right. The shore batteries at Fort Navarino made no effort to contest the allied movement. Still, Codrington's plan appeared highly dangerous, for it invited the Ottomans to surround the allied ships, which with the prevailing wind out of the southwest risked being trapped. The plan simply revealed the complete confidence of the allies in their tactical superiority.

Codrington dispatched the frigate *Dartmouth* to an Ottoman ship in position to command the entrance of the bay with an order that it move. The captain of the *Dartmouth* sent a dispatch boat to the Ottoman ship, which then opened musket fire on it, killing an officer and several seamen. Firing immediately became general, with shore batteries also opening up on the allied ships.

The ensuing four-hour engagement, essentially a series of individual gun duels by floating batteries at close range without an overall plan, was really more of a slaughter than a battle. Three-quarters of the ships in the Egyptian-Ottoman fleet were either destroyed by allied fire or set alight by their own crews to prevent their capture. Only one, the *Sultane,* surrendered. Allied personnel losses were 177 killed and 469 wounded; estimates of the Ottoman and Egyptian killed or wounded were in excess of 4,000 men.

News of the allied victory was received with great popular enthusiasm in virtually all of Europe. The Porte, furious at what had happened, demanded reparations. Recalled to Britain, Codrington was subsequently acquitted on a charge of disobeying orders.

The Battle of Navarino Bay removed any impediment to the Russian Black Sea Fleet, and in April 1828 Russia declared war on Turkey. That August Egypt withdrew from hostilities, virtually ending the war. In the May 1832 Treaty of London, Greece secured its independence. The Battle of Navarino Bay, which made all this possible, is also noteworthy as the last major engagement between ships of the line in the age of fighting sail.

References

Anderson, R. C. *Naval Wars in the Levant, 1559–1853.* Liverpool: University Press of Liverpool, 1952.

James, William M. *The Naval History of Great Britain,* Vol. 6. London: Richard Bentley, 1859.

Ortzen, Len. *Guns at Sea: The World's Great Naval Battles.* London: Cox and Wyman, 1976.

Battle of Mexico City

Date	September 13–14, 1847	
Location	Mexico City, central Mexico	
Opponents (* winner)	*United States	Mexico
Commander	Major General Winfield Scott	General Antonio López de Santa Anna, President of Mexico
Approx. # Troops	7,180	15,000
Importance	Scott's capture of the Mexican capital leads to peace negotiations that end the war	

The Battle of Mexico City on September 13–14, 1847, between U.S. and Mexican forces caused Mexico to sue for peace and led to major territorial gains for the United States. U.S. president James K. Polk's insistence on acquiring upper California was the cause of the Mexican-American War (1846–1848). The excuse for the war came in U.S. claims regarding the southern boundary of Texas.

Polk, who took office in March 1845, was a staunch proponent of Manifest Destiny and sought U.S. expansion west to the Pacific Ocean and south to at least the

CAPTURE OF MEXICO CITY, SEPTEMBER 14, 1847

- ➡ U.S. troop movement
- ➡ Mexican troop movement
- ⌇⌇⌇ Mexican redoubts/fortifications
- ⑂ U.S. batteries
- ⑂ Mexican batteries
- ✖ U.S. troops
- ✖ Mexican troops

SANTA ANNA

WORTH

Santo Thoms

WORTH   San Cosmo Gate

Alameda

Cathedral

Palace

Mexico City

ditch   Paseo   Citadel

Santa Anna abandons Mexico City, September 14

Belen Gate

San Antonio Gate

Molino del Rey: *Defenses stormed by Marines, September 8*

ANDREWS

TISDALE

Nino Perdido Gate

QUITMAN

MCINTOSH

WRIGHT

SMITH

SHIELDS

Chapultepec: *Lines breached by U.S. forces, September 13*

MEXICO

JOHNSON

Tacubaya

QUITMAN

SCOTT

0   1/2   1 mi
0   1/2   1 km

Rio Grande. For Polk, the goal was to secure California. This rich Mexican province had a population of only 6,000 white men and seemed ready for the taking. Polk feared that if the United States did not act, Britain or France might acquire California. Polk tried on several occasions to purchase California, but the Mexican government refused. When Polk's efforts to stir up revolution in California failed, he baited Mexico into war over Texas.

U.S. settlers in the Mexican province of Texas had revolted in 1836 and gained their independence. The Republic of Texas was then admitted to the United States in February 1845. That July, Polk ordered U.S. Army units under Major General Zachary Taylor to the Nueces River, the southwestern border of Texas, supposedly to protect it from Mexican attack. In January 1846 after receiving word that the Mexican government refused to receive his emissary, Polk ordered Taylor to cross the Nueces River and occupy the left bank of the Rio Grande. This was in effect an act of war.

On April 25 a Mexican force crossed the Rio Grande and engaged in a cavalry skirmish with a troop of U.S. dragoons, inflicting several casualties. Polk immediately sent a message to Congress proclaiming that "Mexico has passed the boundary of the United States, has invaded our territory and shed American blood upon the American soil." Congress responded with a declaration of war on May 13. On June 15 Polk negotiated a resolution of the Oregon Boundary dispute with Britain, thus covering his northern flank.

Both Mexico and the United States were confident of victory. The United States had 17 million people while Mexico had only 7 million, but the Mexican regular army was a large European-type establishment of 32,000 men. Polk had permitted Mexican general Antonio López de Santa Anna, deposed after the loss of Texas, to return to Mexico from exile in Havana on the pledge that he would conclude the treaty that Polk sought. In September 1846 Santa Anna became president, and he was determined to fight.

The U.S. regular army numbered only 8,000 men. Congress authorized 50,000 volunteers and an increase in the size of the regular army to 15,000 men and eventually to 32,000. Mexico had virtually no navy, however, while the United States had 70 vessels. Control of the seas would be a key factor, enabling the United States to conduct offensive operations far from its home bases.

There were three major theaters of war: California, northern Mexico, and central Mexico. Fighting in California consisted of small-scale engagements, and by the end of 1846 U.S. forces were firmly in control there. Taylor crossed the Rio Grande into northern Mexico in late May 1846 and then during September 21–23 secured the major city of Monterrey. Taylor's grandstanding alarmed Polk, however, who saw in him a potential political rival. Polk therefore turned to Major General Winfield Scott. Scott now drew off much of Taylor's force, leaving him only 5,000 men, many of them untrained volunteers.

Learning of this situation, Santa Anna hurried north from Mexico City. Taylor received much-needed reinforcements from Brigadier General John E. Wood but was still badly outnumbered in the February 22–23, 1847, Battle of Buena Vista. Taylor nonetheless defeated Santa Anna, who then withdrew south to meet Scott.

Scott planned to win the war by marching on Mexico City from Veracruz, the capital's port. The U.S. Navy made this possible when on March 9, 1847, it landed Scott's entire army of 12,000 men along with their artillery, horses, and supplies near Veracruz. The city surrendered on March 27. At the same time, Mexico City was undergoing another revolution. As recent scholarship makes clear, internal Mexican discord greatly assisted the U.S. military effort throughout.

Scott's subsequent campaign was brilliant. He was forced to proceed with little more than half the number of men he had requested and was constantly hampered by jealous subordinates. He was often forced to live off the land and make do with captured ammunition. Scott's orchestration of the 260-mile-march from Veracruz to Mexico City ranks him among the greatest American military commanders. Scott wisely insisted on amicable relations with the Mexicans, requiring his men to pay for horses and food. This helped secure the army's rear areas during the march.

During April 17–18, 1847, Scott turned a strong Mexican blocking position at Cerro Gordo. Reaching and taking Puebla, he rested his army there for several months, replenishing it with volunteers to replace those whose enlistments had expired. The army was brought up to 11,000 men, but 30,000 Mexican troops still opposed them. With his supply lines now under constant harassment from the Mexican Army, Scott cut free of his base to advance on Mexico City, living off the land.

On August 20 the Americans fought a major battle at the Churubusco River, the last natural barrier to Mexico City. The Americans lost more than 1,000 men killed or wounded, while the Mexicans lost perhaps 7,000 men, including those captured. The well-handled American artillery was a major factor in the outcome, as it was in many other battles during the war. On August 23 Scott granted the Mexicans an armistice in the hope that this would bring reflection and meaningful peace negotiations, but Mexican officials balked at Polk's terms, and Santa Anna renewed the fight. On September 8 U.S. forces won the Battle of Molino del Rey in a bloody assault on an entrenched Mexican position. U.S. losses were about 800 men, while the Mexicans suffered 2,700 casualties.

Scott now had 7,180 men for the final assault on the Mexican capital against perhaps 15,000 Mexican defenders. Swinging in to attack Mexico City from the southwest, on September 13 U.S. forces stormed the last obstacle, the fortified castle of Chapultepec, site of the Mexican Military Academy. Nearly 100 cadets, some as young as 13, heroically defended it. Many of them died there, known ever after as Los Niños Héroes (The Boy Heroes). Scott's troops pushed on. Finally they were inside the city and setting up their artillery. Although Santa Anna's troops still outnumbered Scott's 2 to 1, Mexican government officials pleaded with Santa Anna to surrender and spare the city. Santa Anna and his men departed that night. Just before dawn on September 14, Mexico City surrendered.

Santa Anna abdicated, but months passed before any Mexican government was willing to negotiate. Polk insisted that the war resume, but Scott ignored the order. Finally, on February 2, 1848, U.S. negotiator Nicholas Trist concluded the Treaty of Guadalupe Hidalgo. Mexico ceded Texas with the Rio Grande boundary, New Mexico (including Arizona, Colorado, Utah, and Nevada), and upper California (including San Diego) to the United States. The U.S. government assumed $3 million in unpaid private U.S. claims against Mexico and paid Mexico an additional $15 million. For a relatively small cost (13,271 deaths, but only 1,721 were killed in battle or died of wounds), the United States greatly expanded its continental area. The debate over the territorial gains so intensified debate over slavery, however, that it hastened the coming of the American Civil War.

References

Bauer, Jack. *The Mexican War, 1846–1848.* New York: Macmillan, 1974.

Eisenhower, John S. D. *So Far from God: The U.S. War with Mexico, 1846–1848.* New York: Random House, 1989.

Singletary, Otis. *The Mexican War.* Chicago: University of Chicago Press, 1960.

Battle of Nanjing

Date	March 20, 1853	
Location	Nanjing (Nanking), on the lower Yangzi River in east central China	
Opponents (* winner)	*Taipings	Manzhus
Commander	Hong Xiuquan (Hung Hsiu-ch'üan)	Lu Jianying
Approx. # Troops	Up to 500,000	40,000–60,000 men, plus assistance from the city population of some 750,000
Importance	The Taipings make Nanjing their capital and proclaim a new dynasty, the Taiping Tianguo (The Heavenly Kingdom of Great Peace)	

The Battle of Nanjing (Nanking) in Jiangsu (Kiangsu) Province in March 1853 ended in the first great military victory for the Taiping (T'ai-p'ing) Rebellion in China, which began in 1851. The rebellion occurred because of agrarian unrest under the emperors Daoguang (Tao-kuang; r. 1821–1850) and Xianfeng (Hsien-feng; r. 1851–1861) caused by heavy taxation, natural disasters, and absentee landlordism. Hong Xiuquan (Hung Hsiu-ch'üan), a mystic from Guangdong (Kwang-tung) Province, led the revolt.

Hong claimed that the Manzhus (Manchus) had lost the Mandate of Heaven following the defeat of Chinese forces by Britain in the Opium War of 1840–1842. Hong vowed to destroy all forms of evil, including Manzhu rule. A self-proclaimed Christian, he emphasized the Ten Commandments and borrowed certain Protestant doctrines but rejected the Trinity. In the Taiping religious hierarchy, God was first, Jesus Christ was second, and Hong was third with authority to regulate all earthly affairs. One interesting aspect of Taiping ideology was their equal treatment of women, who could even be soldiers. The Taipings prohibited gambling and the consumption of alcohol and opium. Since the latter was a major element of Western trade with China, this stance eventually led to Western support of the Imperial government's efforts to overthrow the Taiping regime.

In January 1851 Hong assumed the title of "Heavenly King" and proclaimed a revolt against the Manzhus. The revolt began in Guangxi (Kwangsi) Province and extended into Hubei (Hupei) and Hunan provinces. Soon the Taipings had a well-trained army of 50,000 men and women. Later it grew to upwards of a half million. Its strengths were high morale, strict discipline (the troops had to obey a set of 62 rules), and religious conformity. The Taipings also had effective military commanders, especially Yang Hsiuqing (Hsiu-ch'ing), who led rebel military forces against the Imperial Army in the Yangzi (Yangtze) River Valley. In late December

1852 Taiping forces laid siege to the city of Wuchang in Hubei, taking it on January 12, 1853, after a 20-day siege. The Taipings now controlled the upper Yangzi River and its trade, cutting off the interior from the coast.

The Taipings then made their most serious strategic error. Instead of heading for Beijing (Peking), which they might have taken easily, they moved down the Yangzi to Nanjing. This cost them their best chance of taking the imperial capital and overthrowing the Manzhus. The Taiping leadership apparently took this decision because of reports that a large imperial force protected the capital.

In early February 1853 some 500,000 Taipings departed Wuchang, crossed the Yangzi, and burned their floating bridges behind them to delay an advancing imperial force. While part of the army moved by land on the north side of the river, the majority moved downriver in some 20,000 requisitioned river craft toward Nanjing. The Taipings easily took Jiujiang (Kiukiang) in western Jiangxi Province and Anqing (Anking), the capital of Anhui (Anhwei) Province. After reprovisioning from storehouses there, they continued on to Nanjing, the capital of Jiangsu Province.

The Taipings arrived before Nanjing on March 6, 1853. Prior to their arrival, the city population had swelled to three-quarters of a million people. Although ill-prepared, the defenders managed to hold the Taipings at bay for 13 days. On March 19 the Taipings employed hundreds of horses carrying effigies of soldiers bearing torches before the west wall. Expecting an attack from that quarter, defending soldiers crowded onto the wall. Too late they realized that it was a ruse to draw as many of them there as possible; two great explosions from Taiping mines then breached the wall. Although a third mine exploded late, killing many of the attacking troops, the Taipings secured access to the city.

News of the death of Lu Jianying (Chien-ying), the imperial commander in Nanjing, demoralized the defenders, and many fled. On March 20 the Taipings assaulted the Inner City, defended by 40,000 Manzhu troops. The Taipings took the city in costly human wave assaults, massacring some 30,000 of the defenders who had refused to surrender. The Taipings may have been aided in their success against Nanjing by spies. Reportedly they had sent some 3,000 of their number into the city disguised as Buddhist monks.

The rebels made Nanjing their capital and there proclaimed a new dynasty, the Taiping Tianguo (T'ien-kuo; Heavenly Kingdom of Great Peace). Hong was the ruler. Although their promise of reform had been a major factor in Taiping success, their subsequent failure to carry it out doomed their regime.

The rapid collapse of imperial authority encouraged widespread unrest throughout China. During 1853–1868 Nian (Nien) rebels organized bandit bands to ravage Anhwei, northern Jiangsu, and Shandong (Shantung) provinces. There was also a Muslim government at Dali (Tali) in Yunnan (1855–1873), and the Miao tribe in Guizhou (Kweichow) were successful for an even longer period in their revolt against the central government (1855–1881).

The central government was handicapped by having to fight a two-front war against internal revolts but also against inroads in China by the Western powers led by Britain. In the First Opium War (1839–1842) against Britain, China had been forced to cede Hong King. The Second Opium War began in 1856 due to hostilities with Britain in the Arrow War (1856–1858) that expanded to include the French in 1860. Foreign forces took Beijing and sacked (and later burned) the old Summer Palace. Forced to sue for peace, the imperial government surrendered Kowloon opposite Hong Kong to the British as well as special rights to the French. The Russians also took advantage of China's weakness to seize the left bank of the Amur River and the Maritime Provinces, establishing the port of Vladivostok. Western citizens residing in China, including those from the United States, also secured extraterritoriality from Chinese civil and criminal law.

With the wars against the European powers temporarily over in 1860, Imperial Viceroy Zeng Guofan (Tseng Kuo-fan) and Li Hongzhang (Hung-chang) worked to reform and revitalize the imperial government and subdue the Taiping regime to the south.

The Taiping regime had become increasingly repressive, and in 1860 wealthy Shanghai merchants financed an army under the command of Frederick Townsend Ward, an American merchant marine officer and soldier of fortune from Salem, Massachusetts. Ward led this force, which came to be known as the Ever Victorious Army, in a series of successful military campaigns. In 1861 he became a brigadier general in the Imperial Army. Over a four-month span, Ward and his army, assisted by British and French forces returning from their operations at Beijing, won 11 victories and cleared an area about 20 miles around Shanghai. However, on August 20, 1862, Ward was mortally wounded while leading an assault on the walled city of Cexi (Tzehsi) in Zhejiang (Chejiang).

In 1863 at the request of the Chinese imperial government, the British government assigned Captain Charles G. Gordon (thereafter known as "Chinese Gordon") of the Royal Engineers to succeed Ward. Gordon led the Ever Victorious Army south along the Grand Canal, taking Suzhou (Souchow) in Jiangsu Province on December 4. He then laid siege to the Taiping capital of Nanjing. Disgusted by the imperial government's execution of prisoners who had surrendered to him, Gordon gave up command of the army. Chinese imperial forces under Viceroy Zeng, however, ended the rebellion when they breached the Nanjing city walls on July 19, 1864. A few isolated Taiping detachments continued to resist, the last being destroyed in February 1866.

The Taiping Rebellion was the most destructive war of the entire 19th century. Most estimates place the number of dead from the rebellion directly or indirectly at 20 million people. This was not the end of fighting in China either. Suppression of the regional revolts extended into 1881, and China also fought an undeclared war with France during 1883–1885.

References

Elleman, Bruce A. *Modern Chinese Warfare, 1785–1989.* New York: Routledge, 2001.

Lindley, Augustus. *Ti-Peng Tien-kwoh: The History of the Ti-Ping Revolution.* New York: Praeger, 1970.

The Taiping Revolution. Peking: Foreign Languages Press, 1976.

Teng Ssu-Yü. *New Light on the History of the Taiping Rebellion.* New York: Russell and Russell, 1966.

Battle of Sinop

Date	November 30, 1853	
Location	Port of Sinope (Sinope) on the western coast of Anatolia (Turkey)	
Opponents (* winner)	*Russians	Ottomans
Commander	Admiral Paul S. Nakhimov	Vice Admiral Osman Pasha
Approx. # Troops	7 ships of the line, several smaller warships	7 frigates, 2 corvettes, several transports
Importance	It brings widespread support in Western Europe for the Ottoman Empire against Russia; it also demonstrates the superiority of explosive shell over solid shot against wooden ships, leading to the development of ironclad warships	

The Battle of Sinop (Sinope) was an important naval battle during the war between Russia and Turkey that grew into the Crimean War (1854–1856). The designs of Russian czar Nicholas I (r. 1825–1855) upon the Ottoman Empire led, in July 1853, to Russian occupation of the Ottoman Danubian principalities of Moldavia and Wallachia (later joined as Romania). The Ottomans declared war on Russia on October 4. Russian warships based at Sevastopol were active in the Black Sea from the beginning of the war, but there was little naval action apart from the Russian capture of an Egyptian frigate. That situation changed in November 1853.

Late that month, Ottoman vice admiral Osman Pasha was en route north along the western Black Sea coast with seven sailing frigates, two corvettes, and several transports to resupply Ottoman land forces. Osman flew his flag in the 60-gun *Avni Illah.* Caught by a storm in the Black Sea, he took his ships into the Ottoman port of Sinop. The largest Ottoman ship guns were only 24-pounders, but the anchorage was protected by 84 guns, some of them possibly landed from the ships.

A Russian naval force under Admiral Paul S. Nakhimov now arrived at Sinop. Nakhimov had three ships of the line and several smaller craft, but he secured from Sevastopol four 120-gun 3-deckers: the *Grossfürst Constantin, Tri Sviatitla, Paris,* and *Zvolf Apostel.* Their main armament comprised new 68-pounder shell guns.

A thick mist on the morning of November 30 masked the approach of the Russian ships into the harbor. The Ottomans barely had time to clear for action before battle was joined at 10:00 a.m. Within half an hour the *Grossfürst Constantin* had sunk an Ottoman frigate and silenced the Ottoman shore batteries. The battle raged until 4:00 p.m. Only one Ottoman vessel, the paddle steamer *Taif,* managed to escape; the rest were sunk. The Russians admitted to 37 dead; the Ottomans lost upwards of 3,000.

Although the Ottomans had been badly outgunned at Sinop, the inequity of the losses conclusively demonstrated the superiority of shell over shot against wooden vessels. The *Imperitritza Marie* had been struck by 84 cannon balls without major damage, but the Ottoman fleet had been destroyed. The battle heightened world interest in the construction of ironclad warships for protection against shell.

The Battle of Sinop also produced a wellspring of support in Britain and France for the Ottoman Empire. The British press labeled this legitimate act of war "a foul outrage" and a "massacre." In early January 1854 French and British warships entered the Black Sea, and in March both nations agreed to protect the Ottoman Empire's coasts and shipping against Russian attack. That same month, a strong Russian land force invaded the Ottoman territory of Bulgaria.

References

Barker, A. J. *The War against Russia, 1854–1856.* New York: Holt, Rinehart and Winston, 1970.

Lambert, Andrew, ed. *Steam, Steel and Shellfire: The Steam Warship, 1815–1905.* Annapolis, MD: Naval Institute Press, 1993.

Battle of Inkerman

Date	November 5, 1854	
Location	Southwestern Crimea, Ukraine	
Opponents (* winner)	*British, French	Russians
Commander	Fitzroy James Henry Somerset, Lord Raglan (British); General François Certain Canrobert (French)	Prince Aleksandr Sergeyevich Menshikov
Approx. # Troops	15,700 (7,500 British, 8,200 French)	35,000
Importance	The Russian failure to break the Allied ring means that the siege of Sevastopol will continue, but the battle does prevent an allied attack on Sevastopol before the onset of winter	

The Battle of Inkerman on November 5, 1854, was the largest and most deadly land engagement of the Crimean War (1854–1856). Fighting between the Ottoman

Empire and Russia began in October 1853 as the Russians sought to dismember the Ottoman Empire. The British and French governments were much alarmed at the designs of Czar Nicholas I (r. 1825–1855) on Ottoman territory and especially by the possibility that Russia might gain control of the straits and naval access to the Mediterranean.

In January 1854 on the suggestion of French emperor Napoleon III, French and British warships entered the Black Sea to protect the Ottoman coasts against a Russian naval attack. Russia responded by breaking off diplomatic relations with Britain and France, which then demanded that Russia evacuate the Ottoman Danubian principalities of Moldavia and Wallachia (later joined as Romania) that it had occupied the previous July. After Russian troops crossed the Danube, Britain and France declared war against Russia on March 28, 1854, beginning what became known as the Crimean War.

Austria mobilized its own forces, but on Vienna's threat to intervene, the Russians evacuated the principalities in August. The Ottomans had also forced the Russians to lift their siege of Silistria (in present-day Romania) and retire across the Danube. It appeared as if the war was a draw, but British public opinion sought a decisive victory, and the French government was bent on winning prestige. As the Russian fleet was still a threat, the British-French expeditionary force was diverted to the Crimea. The objectives were the capture of the great Russian naval base of Sevastopol (Sebastopol) and the destruction of the Russian Black Sea Fleet.

On September 13, 1854, allied troops began landing on an open beach on the Crimean Peninsula about 30 miles north of Sevastopol. Bad weather delayed the debarkation, which the Russians under Prince Aleksandr Sergeyevich Menshikov did not contest. Fitzroy James Henry Somerset, Lord Raglan, commanded the British forces, while General Armand-Jacques Leroy de Saint-Arnaud had charge of the French forces. On September 19 the allied expeditionary force of about 51,000 British, French, and Ottoman infantry along with 1,000 British cavalry and 128 guns began moving south toward Sevastopol. The allied fleet kept pace with them offshore. On September 20 the allies ran into 34,000 Russians under Menshikov on the bank of the Alma River. In the resulting Battle of the Alma River the allies were victorious. The allies (mostly British) suffered about 3,000 casualties, and the Russians suffered perhaps 5,700 casualties.

The Russians had not completed all of their land defenses, and a quick assault on Sevastopol might have been successful had Raglan not rejected that approach in favor of a siege, which began on October 8. Meanwhile, General Saint-Arnaud died of cholera and was succeeded by General François Certain Canrobert. On October 17 the allies first subjected Sevastopol to artillery shelling but lacked sufficient numbers of heavy guns to accomplish much. The Russians had sunk ships in the harbor entrance, preventing a naval assault. If Sevastopol was to be taken, it would have to be from the north by land.

On October 25 the allies won another battle, this one at Balaclava, a small seaport only eight miles from Sevastopol. Menshikov initiated the battle in an attempt to place his forces between the British base at Balaclava and the siege lines farther south. The Russians took some Ottoman guns, but an attempt by their cavalry to exploit the situation was defeated by the British Heavy Cavalry Brigade and men of the 93rd Highlanders (the "thin red line"). The battle also saw the tragic but heroic charge of the Light Cavalry Brigade. Through the stupidity of its commander Brigadier General James Thomas Brudenell, Lord Cardigan, the Light Brigade attacked Russian artillery at the end of a narrow mile-long valley ("the Valley of Death," in the words of Alfred Lord Tennyson). During the 20-minute ride the brigade lost 247 men and 497 horses. French general Pierre F. J. Bosquet remarked, "It is magnificent, but it is not war."

On November 5 Menshikov again attempted to cut the lines connecting the besiegers with their base areas. Beginning at dawn, enveloped in a heavy fog that ensured a lack of control on both sides, Menshikov's 35,000 Russians with more than 100 guns attacked British forces numbering perhaps 7,500 men and 38 guns on Inkerman Ridge under the temporary commander of the 2nd Division, Major General John L. Pennefather. The British Guards regiments bore the brunt of the Russian attack, which was poorly coordinated. Lieutenant Gerneral F. I. Soimonov, with 19,000 men and 38 guns, was to join with Lieutenant General P. I. Pavlov, with 16,000 men and 96 guns, for a simultaneous attack, but Pavlov was delayed crossing the Tchernaya River by repairs to the Tractir Bridge and changes in orders. Thus, the two Russian forces struck consecutively rather than simultaneously.

The battle raged all day, and much of the fighting was hand to hand. Meanwhile, some 20,000 Russians under Prince Mikhail Gorchakov were demonstrating against the French to hold them in place, but Gorchakov's lack of aggressiveness led General Bosquet to conclude that his attack was a feint. Bosquet dispatched 8,200 men (chiefly Zouaves) and 18 guns that afternoon to assist the hard-pressed British. The arrival of the French reinforcements brought a Russian withdrawal.

In the Battle of Inkerman the Russians suffered 10,729 killed (including Soimonov), wounded, or taken prisoner. British losses were 635 killed and 1,938 wounded, while the French sustained 175 killed and 1,625 wounded. Both sides then settled in for the winter. The Russian failure to break the allied ring around Sevastopol ensured that the siege would continue, but the battle also prevented an allied attack on Sevastopol before the onset of winter. Russian colonel Frank Todleben meanwhile supervised a substantial strengthening of the Sevastopol defenses. The allies, who had expected a short campaign, were without adequate tents or supplies. Even medicine was in short supply. The French were better prepared, but the British in particular passed a horrible winter with heavy losses from disease, especially cholera.

References

Barker, A. J. *The War against Russia, 1854–1856.* New York: Holt, Rinehart and Winston, 1970.

Barthorp, Michael. *Heroes of the Crimea: The Battles of Balaclava and Inkerman.* London: Blandford, 1992.

Edgerton, Robert B. *Death of Glory: The Legacy of the Crimean War.* Boulder, CO: Westview, 1999.

Mercer, Patrick. *"Give Them a Volley and Charge!": The Battle of Inkerman, 1854.* Staplehurst, UK: Spellmount, 1998.

Siege of Sevastopol

Date	October 17, 1855–September 9, 1856	
Location	Port city of Sevastopol, southwest Crimea, Ukraine	
Opponents (* winner)	*British, French, Ottomans; Piedmontese	Russians
Commander	General Sir James Simpson (British); General Aimable Jean Jacques Pélissier (French)	Prince Mikhail Gorchakov; Admiral Pavel Nakhimov
Approx. # Troops	160,000 men	43,000 men
Importance	The central event of the Crimean War, it brings peace negotiations and the end of the war	

The siege of the great Russian naval base of Sevastopol (Sebastopol) on the Crimean Peninsula was the primary allied military objective and military event of the Crimean War (1854–1856). Beginning on September 13, 1854, French, British, and Ottoman troops landed on the Crimean Peninsula and then moved south just north of Sevastopol. In their advance south the allies won battles on the Alma River on September 20, at Balaclava on October 25, and at Inkerman on November 5.

Although the Russians were defeated in all three battles, they did purchase time for military engineer Colonel Francis E. I. Todleben to improve Sevastopol's defenses. Because the Russians had blocked the mouth of the harbor with sunken ships, the allied fleets were unable to approach the port from the south. The allies might still have taken Sevastopol by land assault in mid-October, but British commander Fitzroy James Henry Somerset, Lord Raglan, rejected such an approach in favor of a siege.

The allies opened their first bombardment of Sevastopol from the northern (land) side on October 17. Because they lacked sufficient numbers of heavy guns, the initial shelling accomplished little. The allies settled in for the winter after the Battle of Inkerman. Unprepared for a long campaign and winter conditions, the

British forces were particularly hard hit, lacking even tents. The British lost large numbers of men to the cold and disease. Cholera was a major killer. The French were somewhat better prepared than the British, although cholera also claimed French commander Marshal Armand-Jacques Leroy de Saint-Arnaud. General François Certain Canrobert succeeded him. The Russians also suffered, sustaining numerous casualties, although Todleben actually improved the defenses in the midst of the allied shelling. Reports of the horrible conditions by British war correspondents (notably William Howard Russell of the *London Times*) led to the fall of the British government under Prime Minister George H. Gordon, Lord Aberdeen. One of the important changes that came out of this was improved medical facilities, including the sending out of nurses under Florence Nightingale.

In January 1856 the Kingdom of Sardinia (Sardinia-Piedmont) entered the war. Its government dispatched 10,000 men under General Alfonso Ferrero di La Marmora. Additional allied forces also arrived; ultimately the allies deployed more than 160,000 men and 500 heavy guns to operations against Sevastopol. In early 1855 the allies also improved the logistical net connecting the siege lines to their coastal bases. In an effort to disrupt this work, on February 17 new Russian commander Prince Mikhail Gorchakov mounted an attack on the allies at Eupatoria (Yevpatoriya), but the Ottomans met and drove this back.

The allies steadily pushed their siege lines closer to Sevastopol. On April 8 the allies opened a furious 10-day bombardment that destroyed a large section of the Russian defenses and killed some 6,000 Russian soldiers positioned to resist an assault. Angered by squabbling between the field commanders and their home governments, French commander General Canrobert resigned. General Aimable Jean Jacques Pélissier replaced him.

On May 24 the allies captured Kerch and cleared the Sea of Azov, cutting Russian communications from Sevastopol to the northeast. On June 7 the allies mounted a major assault on Sevastopol, taking part of the Russian outer defenses at a cost of 6,900 allied and 8,500 Russians casualties. The allies resumed their assault on the two Russian strong points of the Malakoff and the Redan during June 17–18. The attack was poorly coordinated, and both the French assault on the Malakoff and that of the British on the Redan failed. The attackers lost 4,000 men, and the defenders lost 5,400 men. Raglan died 10 days later and was succeeded by General Sir James Simpson.

The allies now subjected Sevastopol to constant shelling. Russian casualties amounted to some 350 a day, slowly draining the defenders' strength. With time running out, the Russians mounted one last effort to sever the allied lines to Sevastopol. On August 16 Gorchakov sent two corps against 32,000 French and Sardinian troops. The Battle of the Takir Ridge, fought on high ground above the Chernaya River, ended in a Russian defeat. The battle claimed 8,200 Russian (3,200 dead) and 1,700 allied casualties.

Following an intense four-day bombardment, on September 8 the French carried out perhaps the only well-planned and effectively executed assault of the war against the Malakoff. No signal was given; the attack was launched at midnight by the synchronization of watches alone. In fierce hand-to-hand combat, the French secured the Malakoff by nightfall. The Russians turned back a British assault on the Redan, but the French now directed their fire on the Redan, producing a Russian withdrawal from it with heavy losses. Gorchakov began blowing up the remaining Russian fortifications that night and evacuated Sevastopol on September 9. The final assault on the Russian fortress had claimed more than 10,000 allied casualties. Russian losses were perhaps 13,000.

Although fighting also took place in the Balkans and on the Black Sea, the siege of Sevastopol was the central event of the Crimean War. With Sweden threatening intervention and Austria presenting Russia with an ultimatum, on February 1 the Russians agreed to preliminary peace conditions. Each side lost about a quarter million men to battle and disease.

The Congress of Paris occurred during February 25–March 30, 1856. Although French emperor Napoleon III had hoped that the conferees would discuss all pressing European matters, including Italy and Poland, Britain sided with Austria in pushing a return to the status quo ante bellum. Their interest was solely in checking Russian expansionism and propping up the Ottoman Empire.

Under the terms of the Treaty of Paris therefore, the great powers upheld the territorial integrity of the Ottoman Empire. Russia was forced to cede the mouth of the Danube River and a strip of Bessarabia and also agreed to return Kars, taken during the war. Moldavia and Wallachia were placed under joint custody of the major powers. Elections in the principalities occurred in 1862, and in 1878 they achieved their independence as the Kingdom of Romania. Russia had to agree to the neutralization of the Black Sea. In the Declaration of Paris the major powers also adopted new rules of international law regarding naval warfare. These made privateering illegal, stipulated that neutral flags protected enemy goods except for contraband, provided that neutral goods other than contraband were protected from capture, and stipulated that a blockade must be effective in order to be binding under international law.

References

Barker, A. J. *The War against Russia, 1854–1856.* New York: Holt, Rinehart and Winston, 1970.

Edgerton, Robert B. *Death of Glory: The Legacy of the Crimean War.* Boulder, CO: Westview, 1999.

Battle of Kinburn

Date	October 17, 1855	
Location	Kinburn Forts, estuary at the mouth of the Dnieper and Bug rivers, Russia	
Opponents (* winner)	*French	Russians
Commander	Unknown	Unknown
Approx. # Troops	3 ironclad floating batteries	5 forts with 81 guns
Importance	Demonstrates the superiority of ironclad warships over those of wood	

The Battle of Kinburn during the Crimean War (1854–1856) demonstrated the success of ironclad warships. In the Battle of Sinop (Sinope), on November 30, 1853, a Russian squadron destroyed an Ottoman fleet at anchor largely through the use of shells as opposed to solid shot. This led to renewed interest in iron as armor for wooden vessels. After Britain and France had entered the war, French emperor Napoleon III proposed a system of iron protection for ships, and British chief naval engineer Thomas Lloyd demonstrated that four inches of iron could protect against powerful shot.

On October 17, 1855, three French armored floating batteries, the *Dévastation, Lave,* and *Tonnante,* took part in an attack on Russia's Kinburn Forts in an estuary at the mouth of the Dnieper and Bug rivers. Protected by 4-inch iron plate backed by 17 inches of wood, each of the floating batteries mounted 16 50-pounder guns and 2 12-pounders. They were each powered by a 225-horsepower steam engine, capable of propelling the vessel at four knots.

The Kinburn forts, three of which were of stone and two of sand, housed in all 81 guns and mortars. From a range of between 900 and 1,200 yards in an engagement lasting from 9:30 a.m. until noon, the French armored floating batteries fired 3,177 shot and shell and reduced the Russian forts to rubble. Although repeatedly hulled, the batteries were largely impervious to the Russian fire. The *Dévastation* took 67 hits, and the *Tonnante* took 66 hits. Two men were killed and 24 wounded, but these casualties resulted from two shots that had entered gun ports and another shot that had passed through an imperfect main hatch. The vessels' armor was only dented.

At noon allied ships of the line shelled what was left of the forts from a range of 1,600 yards, and in less than 90 minutes the Russians surrendered. Undoubtedly the success of the batteries was magnified because they were the emperor's special project, but many observers concluded that the Battle of Kinburn proved the effectiveness of wrought iron and marked the end of the old ships of the line.

References

Baxter, James Phinney. *The Introduction of the Ironclad Warship.* New York: Archon Books, 1968.

Darrieus, Henri, and Jean Quéguiner. *Historique de la Marine française (1815–1918).* Saint-Malo, France: éditions l'Ancre de la Marine, 1997.

Padfield, Peter. *Guns at Sea.* New York: St. Martin's, 1974.

Tucker, Spencer C. *Handbook of 19th Century Naval Warfare.* Annapolis, MD: Naval Institute Press, 2000.

Battle of Solferino

Date	June 24, 1859	
Location	Village of Solferino, south of Lake Garda, in Lombardy, northern Italy	
Opponents (* winner)	*French; Piedmontese	Austrians
Commander	Napoleon III, Emperor of France; Victor Emmanuel II, King of Sardinia; General Marie E. P. M. de MacMahon	Franz Joseph I, Austrian Emperor; General Ludwig von Benedek
Approx. # Troops	160,000	160,000
Importance	One of the bloodiest battles of the 19th century, it is an important step in the unification of Italy; it also leads to the establishment of the International Red Cross	

One of the bloodiest battles of the 19th century, the Battle of Solferino on June 24, 1859, marked an important step forward in the unification of Italy. The Italian War of 1859 pitting the Second French Empire and the Kingdom of Sardinia (Sardinia-Piedmont) against the Habsburg Empire resulted from the adroit diplomatic maneuvering of Premier Count Camillo Benso di Cavour, who was intent on unifying Italy under the Sardinian Crown. French emperor Napoleon III accepted the role assigned to him by Cavour because of his own interest in Italian affairs (as a youth he had participated in the Italian revolutions of 1830), his desire to supplant Austrian interest in Italy with that of France, and the lure of simple territorial aggrandizement.

In July 1858 Napoleon III and Cavour met at Plombières in southeastern France and worked out the so-called Pact of Plombières. Cavour would work to create a war with Austria in which the Habsburg monarchy appeared to be the aggressor. France would then join Sardinia to end Habsburg control over northern Italy. France would supply 200,000 troops, Sardinia would supply 100,000 troops, and the two would fight until Italy was freed "from sea to sea." Sardinia was to receive Lombardy, Venetia, Parma, Modena, and Romagna, establishing a new Kingdom of Upper Italy. Sardinia would in turn cede Nice and Savoy to France. Napoleon III's cousin Prince Jerome Bonaparte, who had married the daughter of Sardinian king Victor Emmanuel II, would receive Tuscany, Umbria, and the Marches as king of central Italy. The pope would retain the area around Rome known as the Patrimony.

The Kingdom of Naples would be left intact. These four Italian kingdoms would then be formed into a loose confederation under the presidency of the pope.

In March 1859 Cavour mobilized the Sardinian Army, but his efforts to bait the Habsburgs into war appeared not to be working, and on April 19 he ordered the army demobilized. Had there been a telegraph connection between Turin and Vienna, there would have been no war. But unaware of Cavour's action, on April 23 the Habsburg government dispatched an ultimatum to Turin demanding the demobilization. This made Austria appear to be the aggressor. Sardinia's rejection of the ultimatum then brought the war, which both sides in fact desired.

Habsburg troops were in position to strike quickly and indeed invaded Piedmont on April 29, but Austrian commander General Franz Gyulai proved incompetent. The advance was slow, allowing French forces time to come to Sardinia's assistance. On May 30 Sardinia won a victory over Habsburg forces at Palestro. Franco-Sardinian forces led by Napoleon III then invaded Lombardy.

On June 4 the French and Sardinians met the Habsburg forces at Magenta. Due to confusion in orders, Sardinian forces remained quiescent, and the French fought the Austrians alone. The elan of 54,000 French soldiers led them to prevail against 58,000 Austrians. French losses amounted to 5,000 killed or wounded and 600 missing; Austrian casualties came to 5,700 killed or wounded and 4,500 missing.

Following Magenta, Gyulai withdrew his forces into the so-called Quadrilateral, the fortified cities of Magenta, Pershiera, Verona, and Legnago. On June 8 Napoleon III and Victor Emmanuel II entered Milan in triumph. Emperor of Austria Franz Joseph dismissed Gyulai and advanced with forces under General Ludwig von Benedek in an effort to reconquer Lombardy. The sides were of approximately equal strength: about 160,000 men each, the largest number of combatants in any European battle since Leipzig in 1813. As at Magenta, the two armies blundered into a fight without much central direction from their commanders.

On June 24 the advance guards stumbled on each other in the village of Solferino, south of Lake Garda in Lombardy. General Marie E. P. M. de MacMahon commanded the French forces. Napoleon III, Victor Emmanuel II, and Franz Joseph were all present. Fighting began at 4:00 a.m., and much of it was hand to hand. As at Magenta, the battle was decided not by generalship but by the fighting spirit of the French soldiers. Fighting ended at about 8:00 p.m. with the collapse of the Habsburg center. Their forces were able to withdraw, however, thanks to a hard-fought rear-guard effort led by Benedek. Casualties were heavy, with the French suffering nearly 12,000, the Sardinians 5,500, and the Austrians 22,000.

The Habsburg forces again withdrew in good order into the Quadrilateral. Dislodging them would have entailed many more French casualties. Napoleon III was deeply affected by the carnage of the battle and by his role in bringing it about. French military leaders were also unhappy with the level of Sardinian assistance in the Battle of Magenta, and French public opinion had turned against the war. The Prussians were mobilizing forces in northern Germany and appeared to be threat-

The Battle of Solferino, on June 24, 1859, in which troops from France and Sardinia-Piedmont defeated the Austrians. The outcome helped usher in the unification of Italy. Napoleon III and Victor Emmanuel II are shown mounted on the left. (Library of Congress)

ening France along the Rhine. Italian nationalists had seized control of Tuscany and demanded union with Sardinia. All of these factors now led the emperor to renege on his agreement with Cavour.

Napoleon III met with Franz Josef near Villafranca on July 11 and there concluded an armistice. Austria agreed to evacuate all Lombardy except the fortified towns of Peschiera and Mantua in the Quadrilateral. To save face, Austria turned over Lombardy to France, which then gave it to Sardinia. Austria retained Venetia.

The Battle of Solferino had another major effect. The suffering of the wounded there was all the more horrible because of totally inadequate ambulance services. Many of the wounded lay under a hot sun for three days until they were attended to, and a number were robbed of their possessions by local peasants. Swiss businessman Henri Dunant, who had traveled to Solferino to talk with Napoleon III, witnessed the battle and its aftermath. In 1862 he published a small book about his experiences. Titled *Un Souvenir de Solférino* (1862), it dealt principally with the efforts to tend to the wounded in the small town of Castilogne. Dunant suggested that each country form societies to care for those wounded in battle. This led to the formation, in Geneva, of the International Committee of the Red Cross.

In August 1864, 12 nations signed an internationally treaty commonly known as the Geneva Convention. The powers agreed to guarantee neutrality to medical personnel, to expedite medical supplies for their use, and to adopt an identifying emblem of a red cross on a white field.

The armistice of Villafranca, which was confirmed in the subsequent Treaty of Zurich of November 10, 1859, did not end the movement for Italian unification. Most

Italians were outraged by it. Cavour sought to continue the war, but the king wisely rejected this. Believing that he had been betrayed, Cavour berated Victor Emmanuel II and then resigned. Cavour soon returned to office to oversee the remaining territorial acquisitions that rounded out the unification of Italy. Parma, Modena, and Tuscany as well as the Romagna voted to join Sardinia. This violated the terms of the Treaty of Villafranca, but Napoleon III agreed to these acquisitions on the condition that France receive Nice and Savoy. These terms were confirmed in the Treaty of Turin of March 1860. Sicily, Naples, the Marches, and Umbria were acquired in 1860 through the efforts of Italian nationalist Giuseppe Garibaldi, and on March 17, 1861, the Kingdom of Italy came into being. Cavour died just at his moment of triumph, but Italy added to its territory Venice in 1866 and Rome in 1870.

References

Beales, Derek. *The Risorgimento and the Unification of Italy.* New York: Barnes and Noble, 1971.

Blumberg, Arnold. *A Carefully Planned Accident: The Italian War of 1859.* Selinsgrove, PA: Susquehanna University Press, 1990.

Harder, Harry. *Italy in the Age of the Risorgimento, 1790–1870.* New York: Longman, 1983.

Battle of Hampton Roads

Date	March 9, 1862	
Location	Near the mouth of Hampton Roads, Virginia	
Opponents (* winner)	Union	Confederates
Commander	Lieutenant John Worden; later Lieutenant Samuel Greene	Lieutenant Catesby ap Roger Jones
Approx. # Troops	USS *Monitor*	CSS *Virginia*
Importance	This first battle between ironclads in history means that the Union Peninsula Campaign may continue; it also leads to a "Monitor" mania in the North	

The Battle of Hampton Roads during the American Civil War (1861–1865) was the first ever between two ironclad warships, the *Monitor* and the *Virginia*. The American Civil War began in April 1861 when, following sectional differences and the election of Republican Abraham Lincoln to the presidency in November 1860, the states of the Deep South seceded from the Union and formed the Confederate States of America. Their leaders believed that the North was bent on destroying slavery. Lincoln was determined to preserve the Union and, following some debate, decided to undertake the resupply of Fort Sumter in Charleston Harbor, still in Union control although in a Confederate state (South Carolina). Lincoln informed Confederate president Jefferson Davis of the expedition beforehand. Davis then authorized the shelling of Fort Sumter, which surrendered. The war was on.

Southerners were confident that they would prevail despite great Northern advantages in population size and manufacturing resources. Southerners believed that they could remain on the defensive and wear down the North, whereas for the North to win it would have to conquer the South. The U.S. Navy soon instituted a blockade of the Southern coasts, however, and in July 1861 the U.S. Army of the Potomac was sent from Washington, D.C., to secure the railhead of Manassas Junction, west of the capital, preparatory to an overland advance on Richmond.

On July 21, 1861, in the first major battle of the war, the Army of the Potomac met defeat in the First Battle of Bull Run, known to the Confederacy as First Manassas (the Union named battles after bodies of water, whereas the Confederacy designated them based on the closest settlement). The new Union commander, Major General George B. McClellan, then sought to take advantage of Union control of the sea to attack the Confederate capital of Richmond from the east on the peninsula formed by the York and James rivers. This so-called Peninsula Campaign set up a naval confrontation.

Union transports at Hampton Roads, Virginia, were threatened with destruction by the Confederate ironclad *Virginia* (built from the former Union *Merrimac*) commanded by Flag Officer Franklin Buchanan. The *Virginia* mounted 10 guns: six 9-inch Dahlgren smoothbores in broadsides and two 6.4-inch and two 7-inch Brooke rifles at bow and stern. On March 8, 1862, the *Virginia* steamed out from Norfolk on its maiden voyage. Most in the crew thought that it was a shakedown run, but Buchanan was determined to attack the Union warships protecting the transports.

Buchanan ordered a course set for the Union warships and used his ship's ram to sink the sailing sloop *Cumberland* (24 guns). He then attacked and burned the frigate *Congress* (50 guns). While maneuvering to escape, the Union flagship, the frigate *Minnesota* (40 guns), ran aground. With its pilots uncertain of the shoal water and Buchanan wounded, the *Virginia* retired at dusk. The crew was confident that they would complete their work of destruction the next day.

As the Confederates departed, the Union ironclad *Monitor* put into the roads. Commanded by Lieutenant John Worden, it was far more maneuverable than the Confederate opponent but was only a fraction of the *Virginia*'s size. The *Monitor* mounted only two 11-inch guns. Hastily completed, it had nearly sunk the day before while under tow south, and there were serious doubts that the ship would prove a worthy opponent for the *Virginia*.

The next morning, March 9, the *Virginia,* now commanded by Lieutenant Catesby ap Roger Jones, steamed out to attack the *Minnesota.* The *Monitor* then appeared in front of the grounded flagship. The battle occurred from about 8:00 a.m. until noon. It was fought at very close range, and both warships were constantly in motion. The *Virginia* rammed the more nimble *Monitor,* but since the Confederate ironclad had lost its ram in the *Cumberland* the day before, this did little damage. The *Monitor*'s gunners meanwhile tried to cripple their antagonist's vulnerable propeller and rudder.

The *Monitor*'s guns could fire only once every seven or eight minutes, but its rotating turret meant that they were a target only when they were about to fire. Almost all of its shots registered, and the *Virginia* sustained damage. Although the *Virginia* fired more shots, most went high and did little damage. Worden was temporarily blinded by the direct hit of a shell that struck the pilot house, however. In the resultant confusion the *Monitor* drifted away from the battle, and when the new commander, Lieutenant Samuel Greene, brought the ship back into position he saw the *Virginia* departing. Jones interpreted the *Monitor*'s actions as meaning that the Confederates had won, and with his own ship having been damaged he returned to Norfolk for repairs.

Tactically the battle was a draw, but the *Virginia* had been hit 50 times and was leaking. The *Monitor* had sustained only 21 hits and was virtually undamaged. The battle between the two ironclads was not renewed, but in merely surviving the *Monitor* ensured the safety of the Union transports and supply ships and thus McClellan's operation. The engagement also led to so-called Monitor Mania in the North. In effect, the battle marked a new era in naval warfare. It also sparked a frantic effort by both sides to manufacture larger-caliber guns capable of penetrating the new iron armor.

References

DeKay, James Tertius. *Monitor.* New York: Walker, 1997.

Holzer, Harold, and Tim Mulligan. *The Battle of Hampton Roads: New Perspectives on the USS MONITOR and CSS VIRGINIA.* New York: Fordham University Press, 2006.

Smith, Gene A. *Iron and Heavy Guns: Duel between the Monitor and Merrimac.* Abilene, Texas: McWhiney Foundation Press, 1998.

Battle of Antietam

Date	September 17, 1862	
Location	Sharpsburg, along Antietam Creek, northwest Maryland (United States)	
Opponents (* winner)	*Union	Confederates
Commander	Major General George B. McClellan	General Robert E. Lee
Approx. # Troops	87,000	41,000
Importance	Halts Lee's invasion of the North, weakens the prospects of Confederate recognition abroad, and gives President Lincoln the opportunity to issue the Preliminary Emancipation Proclamation	

The Battle of Antietam Creek, also known as the Battle of Sharpsburg, on September 17, 1862, was one of the most important military engagements of the American

Civil War. It is known by these two names because the North named its battles after the nearest body of water, in this case, Antietam Creek, and the South chose the nearest telegraph station, or Sharpsburg.

Following the March 1862 duel between USS *Monitor* and CSS *Virginia,* Union Army major general George B. McClellan's Army of the Potomac began a glacial advance up the peninsula formed by the York and James rivers toward the Confederate capital of Richmond. Confederate commander General Joseph E. Johnston was badly wounded during the fighting, and General Robert E. Lee took command of the Army of Northern Virginia and forced McClellan's withdrawal. Lee was determined to strike at Union forces before they could reunite and drive south against Richmond, and during August 29–30, 1862, Confederate major generals Thomas J. Jackson and James Longstreet surprised and defeated Union major general John Pope's new Army of Virginia in the Second Battle of Bull Run (First Manassas to the Confederates).

Pope withdrew to the defenses of Washington, and Lincoln reluctantly replaced him with McClellan, for on September 4 Lee and his Army of Northern Virginia had begun an invasion of the North. Lee hoped to cut key rail lines west and isolate Washington, with Harrisburg, Pennsylvania, as his probable objective. Southern leaders believed that a significant land victory might bring British and French diplomatic recognition of the Confederacy.

Lee's army crossed the Potomac River and moved east of the Blue Ridge Mountains. Arriving at Frederick, Maryland, on September 7, Lee divided his army into five separate parts, three of which were to converge on and take the major Union arsenal at Harpers Ferry. Overestimating Lee's strength, McClellan proceeded with his customary caution; in reality, his forces outnumbered Lee's two to one.

McClellan also fumbled away an incredible intelligence advantage. Near Frederick some of his soldiers discovered a copy of Lee's orders, wrapped around three cigars and verified by a Union officer who identified the handwriting of Lee's adjutant. McClellan now knew the entire disposition of Lee's forces. Despite this, McClellan moved with the same glacial speed that had earned him the nickname "Virginia Creeper" during the Peninsula Campaign. He delayed a full 18 hours before putting his army in motion and pushing through the Blue Ridge passes. On September 14 in small intense engagements in the Battle of South Mountain and the Battle of Crampton's Gap, Confederate forces held off the Union advance.

Lee's army was then split in three main bodies over 20 miles. Although initially inclined to retreat on learning of McClellan's moves, Lee decided to stand and fight. He ordered his remaining forces to join him as soon as possible and positioned his three available divisions along a low ridge extending about four miles north to south, just east of Sharpsburg and west of Antietam Creek. Hilly terrain enabled Lee to mask his inferior resources. The resultant battle was fragmented, in large part because of the terrain.

On the afternoon of September 15 the major part of the Army of the Potomac was within easy striking distance of Lee, who had only 18,000 men available. Had McClellan attacked then, Lee would have been routed. But Lee predicted that McClellan would not move that day or the next. Indeed, McClellan wanted first to rest his troops and then spent the entire day of September 16 placing his artillery and infantry and inspecting the line.

While McClellan dallied, Jackson's corps arrived from Harpers Ferry, giving Lee 30,000 men and leaving absent only three of his nine divisions. Even with Jackson's corps, Lee would be outnumbered 41,000 to 87,000. McClellan said after the battle that he thought Lee had 120,000 men. This is hard to believe, for McClellan planned a double envelopment to hit Lee's flank and then smash the Confederate center.

Lee was in position to observe and command throughout the battle. McClellan remained more than a mile to the rear, unable to observe the battle in progress and with little idea of what was going on. McClellan also failed to take advantage of his superior numbers. He withheld an entire corps (20,000 men failed to see battle) and employed a piecemeal, rather than a simultaneous, form of attack. Each Union corps was committed by successive oral orders from headquarters without informing the other corps commanders and without instructions for mutual support. This process was compounded, as corps commanders sent their own divisions to the attack in piecemeal fashion. In sharp contrast, Lee gave great latitude to his subordinate commanders. McClellan also failed to employ his cavalry to cut Confederate lines of communication and prevent Confederate reinforcements from moving to the battlefield from the south. Even a delay of an hour or two might have changed the battle, because Lee's remaining divisions arrived on the battlefield at the critical juncture, about 10:30 a.m. on September 17, with the Union attack already in progress.

The Battle of Antietam opened early on the morning of September 17 with an attack by Major General Joseph Hooker's 12,000-man I Corps against the Confederate left held by Jackson's corps. Hooker's men drove the Confederates back into the West Woods. Lee called up Brigadier General John Bell Hood's Texas Brigade, which repulsed the Union attack. Amid the smoke and ground fog, the battle lines were only 50 or even 30 yards apart. Units were destroyed as soon as they began to fight. The 1st Texas Regiment of Hood's Brigade lost more than 82 percent of its men killed or wounded in 20 minutes, the highest loss percentage of any regiment North or South in the war. Successive Union attacks on the Confederate left by Major General Joseph Mansfield's XII Corps and Brigadier General Edwin Sumner's II Corps also met rebuff.

Meanwhile, at the Confederate center a crisis developed as some 3,000 Confederates under Major General Daniel H. Hill fought to hold the Sunken Road, which came to be known as "Bloody Lane." Union major general William B. Franklin's VI Corps mounted three separate assaults there, all of which failed. Then two

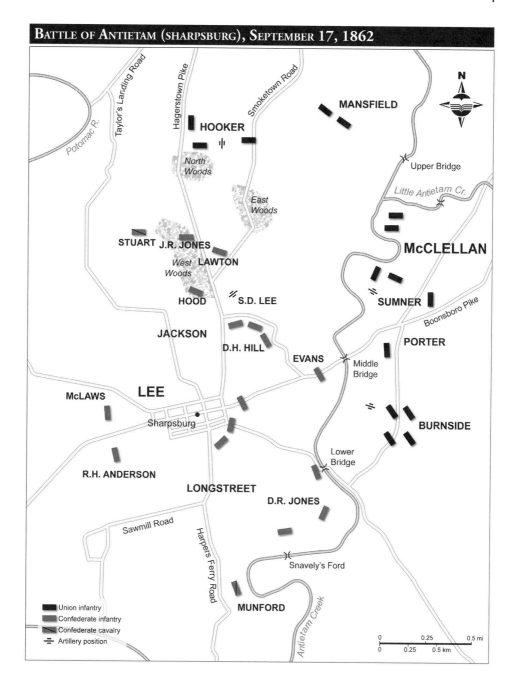

BATTLE OF ANTIETAM (SHARPSBURG), SEPTEMBER 17, 1862

Union regiments were able to enfilade the Confederate position on the Sunken Road, forcing the Confederates to fall back and opening a gap between the Confederate center and left. Confederate troops under Hill managed to plug the hole in time. Lee then ordered Jackson to counterattack the Union right, a move that was not successful. McClellan failed to take advantage of the situation and commit his reserve, however.

On the Union left, Major General Ambrose Burnside's IX Corps spent the morning trying to capture a bridge over Antietam Creek. Union forces finally crossed the creek via fords, but the Confederates withdrew to higher ground. By the time Burnside was ready to renew the attack, the last division of Lee's army, commanded by Major General Ambrose P. Hill, had arrived. Despite being exhausted from their forced march, they defeated the Union assault. The Battle of Antietam was over.

Union casualties amounted to 2,108 dead, 9,540 wounded, and 753 missing (15 percent). Confederate losses were 1,546 dead, 7,752 wounded, and 1,018 missing (26 percent). It was the bloodiest single day of fighting during the entire war. Lee waited a day and then pulled back into Virginia. McClellan failed to pursue. Lincoln was furious and soon removed McClellan from command. McClellan might have destroyed Lee on September 17 or the day after, but in the words of one historian of the battle, he was "so fearful of losing that he would not risk winning."

This inconclusive battle nevertheless had important results. Lee's defeat weakened Confederate hopes of securing recognition from Britain and France. Never again was the Confederacy as close to winning recognition abroad. The battle also helped ensure that the Democrats did not win control of the House of Representatives in the November elections. A 1 percent shift in the vote would have brought Democratic control and trouble for Lincoln. The Union victory also allowed Lincoln the opportunity on September 22, 1862, to issue the Preliminary Emancipation Proclamation, which as of January 1, 1863, freed all slaves in areas still in rebellion against the United States. This document transformed a war to preserve the Union into a struggle for human freedom.

References

Gallagher, Gary W., ed. *Antietam: Essays on the 1862 Maryland Campaign.* Chapel Hill: University of North Carolina Press, 1999.

McPherson, James M. *Crossroads of Freedom: Antietam.* New York: Oxford University Press, 2002.

Murfin, James V. *The Gleam of Bayonets: The Battle of Antietam and Robert E. Lee's Maryland Campaign, September 1862.* Baton Rouge: Louisiana State University Press, 2004.

Priest, John M. *Antietam: The Soldier's Battle.* New York: Oxford University Press, 1994.

Sears, Stephen W. *Landscape Turned Red: The Battle of Antietam.* New York: Ticknor and Fields, 1983.

Battle of Chancellorsville

Date	May 2–4, 1863	
Location	Chancellorsville and Fredericksburg in Spotsylvania County, northeastern Virginia (United States)	
Opponents (* winner)	*Confederates	Union
Commander	General Robert E. Lee	Major General Joseph Hooker
Approx. # Troops	Fewer than 61,000	134,000
Importance	Lee's most brilliant victory, it turns back the Union drive south toward Richmond	

The Battle of Chancellorsville in Virginia during the American Civil War (1861–1865) was Confederate general Robert E. Lee's most brilliant victory. The previous December at Fredericksburg, Virginia, on the Rappahannock River, Lee had won his most one-sided victory of the war when Union major general Ambrose Burnside's Army of the Potomac had attacked Lee's prepared positions on Marye's Heights. Burnside's force of 113,000 Union troops had been shattered by 75,000 Confederates. Union losses were nearly 11,000 men against Confederate casualties of only 4,600. With morale in the Army of the Potomac at a nadir, on January 25, 1863, U.S. president Abraham Lincoln replaced Burnside with one of his most outspoken critics, Major General Joseph Hooker. The aggressive and boastful Hooker, who had long sought the position, retrained the army and built its esprit de corps.

Lee meanwhile kept his forces in position below the Rappahannock. With Lincoln urging an advance on Richmond, Hooker planned to cross the Rappahannock River to the west of Fredericksburg and assault Lee's left and rear at Chancellorsville. Hooker had 134,000 men, while Lee had fewer than 61,000. Hooker sought to utilize his superior numbers in a double envelopment, with the eastern pincer under Major General John Sedgwick to demonstrate against Lee at Fredericksburg.

Hooker began his march westward on April 27; two days later the army was across the Rappahannock. On April 30 Hooker's troops entered the Wilderness, an area of thick woods and underbrush 10 miles west of Fredericksburg. By that evening 75,000 Union troops occupied areas to Lee's rear, while Sedgwick with 40,000 men threatened the Confederates at Fredericksburg. In the midst of this offensive, Hooker suddenly halted his advance to consolidate and see what Lee would do, thereby forfeiting the initiative. Hooker also erred in sending 10,000 Union cavalry under Major General George Stoneman in a wide sweep south below Fredericksburg to destroy Confederate supply depots. This uncovered the Union right wing and denied Hooker vital intelligence regarding Lee's intentions.

Lee responded with a daring maneuver. Learning from his cavalry commander, Major General J. E. B. Stuart, that Hooker's right flank was "in the air," Lee planned a double envelopment of a double envelopment. It was a military masterpiece in which a small force attempted to surround a much larger one. Lee would demonstrate in front of the Union line with about 17,000 men to hold Hooker in place while, in a daring gamble, Lieutenant General Thomas J. "Stonewall" Jackson with 28,000 men would march around the Union right flank. Success rested on Hooker's failure to exploit the Confederate separation or determine Jackson's intentions.

Jackson set off on May 2, with the march taking most of the day. His force was detected disengaging, but this was taken to mean that Lee was about to withdraw. Hooker ordered Union major general Daniel Sickles, commander of III Corps, to attack. His halfhearted advance further weakened the Union line, while Major General Oliver O. Howard, whose XI Corps occupied the far Union right flank, failed to make any defensive preparations despite Hooker's instructions that he do so.

When Jackson's blow came at about 5:30 p.m., it was a complete surprise and enfiladed the Union line. Union troops reeled back in confusion. Darkness, increasing Union resistance, and the loss of Confederate unit cohesion in the woods all prevented a Union catastrophe. That evening Jackson was unintentionally shot by his own men in front of his own lines while reconnoitering in the woods. On May 3 Stuart, replacing Jackson, resumed the Confederate attack, further constricting Hooker's lines.

Meanwhile, a second part to the battle, sometimes known as the Second Battle of Fredericksburg, was unfolding. On the night of May 2 Hooker ordered Sedgwick to attack. Sedgwick, despite having four times Major General Jubal A. Early's 10,000 men, believed that he was outnumbered and had not moved from the Fredericksburg heights. On May 3, however, Sedgwick advanced with 25,000 men from Fredericksburg, broke through Confederate positions, and advanced against Early at Salem Church.

Lee now feinted again. Leaving just a small force against Hooker, Lee turned east to deal with the new threat. Hooker's force vastly outnumbered Lee's but did not move. Sedgwick, surrounded on three sides and unaided, was forced to retire back across the Rappahannock during the night of May 4. On May 5 Hooker withdrew his army back across the Rappahannock. The battle was over.

Although Chancellorsville was Lee's military masterpiece, it also might have been the South's costliest victory. Union casualties were far higher than those for the Confederates—17,197 to 12,764—but the Union losses amounted to 13 percent of effectives, while the Confederate casualties amounted to 21 percent and would be much more difficult for the Confederates to replace. Particularly grievous was the loss of Jackson. He died on May 10 of complications from his wound. The Army of Northern Virginia was never quite the same without him, and Lee sorely missed Jackson in the Battle of Gettysburg two months later.

References

Furguson, Ernest B. *Chancellorsville, 1863: The Souls of the Brave.* New York: Knopf, 1992.

Sears, Stephen W. *Chancellorsville.* Boston: Houghton Mifflin, 1996.

Sutherland, Daniel E. *Fredericksburg & Chancellorsville: The Dare Mark Campaign.* Lincoln: University of Nebraska Press, 1998.

Battle of Gettysburg

Date	July 1–3, 1863	
Location	Gettysburg in southern Pennsylvania (United States)	
Opponents (* winner)	*Union	Confederates
Commander	Major General George Gordon Meade	General Robert E. Lee
Approx. # Troops	85,000	70,000
Importance	Rebuffs Lee's second invasion of the North and is the turning point of the war in the East	

Following his brilliant victory at Chancellorsville in May 1863, commander of the Confederate Army of Northern Virginia General Robert E. Lee fended off suggestions that part of his army be sent west to reinforce Vicksburg. Believing Vicksburg to be lost, Lee presented Confederate president Jefferson Davis with a plan to invade Pennsylvania. Far from an effort to take pressure off Vicksburg or to support a Southern peace offensive, it was instead a spoiling attack designed to delay an expected new offensive by Major General Joseph Hooker's Army of the Potomac and secure the rich resources of Pennsylvania. The Army of the Potomac had an edge in manpower of about 85,000–90,000 to 70,000 and in artillery pieces of 372 to 274, but these numbers were closer than they had been or would be again.

On June 3 Lee's army began moving west from around Fredericksburg, Virginia. Hooker moved on a parallel route north of the Rappahannock River, keeping his own forces between Lee and Washington, D.C. Lee then headed north through the Shenandoah Valley, crossing the Potomac River through Maryland and into Pennsylvania. Lee planned to take Harrisonburg and cut Union communications to the west. He would then be in position to threaten Baltimore and Washington and hoped thereby to force Hooker to attack him.

By the end of June, Lee's three corps—under lieutenant generals Richard Ewell, A. P. Hill, and James Longstreet—were widely scattered in southern Pennsylvania. Because there had been no word from his cavalry commander Major General J. E. B. Stuart, who was to screen the Confederate right flank in the march north, Lee assumed that the Union army was not a threat. But Stuart had become separated from the main Confederate force and circled behind the Union troops moving north. On the evening of June 28, with his own forces dangerously dispersed, Lee learned that Hooker's army was massing near Frederick, Maryland. Union forces

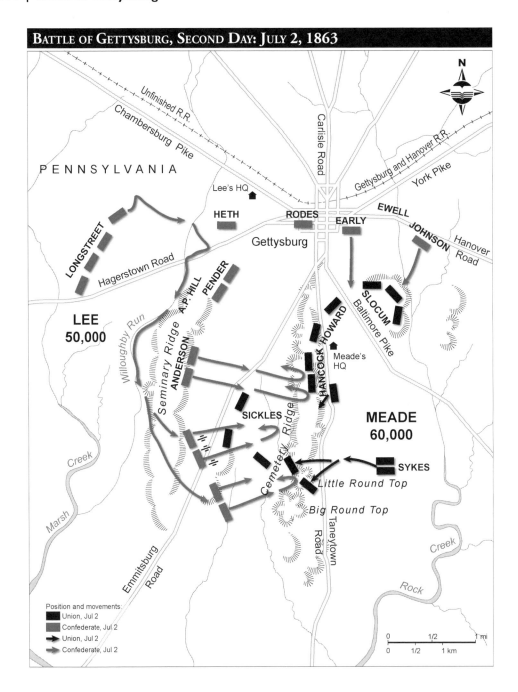

BATTLE OF GETTYSBURG, SECOND DAY: JULY 2, 1863

PENNSYLVANIA

Unfinished R.R.

Chambersburg Pike

Carlisle Road

Gettysburg and Hanover R.R.

York Pike

Lee's HQ

LONGSTREET

HETH

RODES

EARLY

EWELL

JOHNSON

Hanover Road

Gettysburg

Hagerstown Road

A.P. HILL

PENDER

SLOCUM

Baltimore Pike

LEE
50,000

Willoughby Run

Seminary Ridge

ANDERSON

HOWARD

HANCOCK

Meade's HQ

Creek

SICKLES

Cemetery Ridge

MEADE
60,000

SYKES

Little Round Top

Marsh

Big Round Top

Taneytown Road

Creek

Emmitsburg Road

Rock

Position and movements:
Union, Jul 2
Confederate, Jul 2
Union, Jul 2
Confederate, Jul 2

0   1/2   1 mi
0   1/2   1 km

were closer to portions of Lee's army than these were to each other. If Lee did not concentrate at once, he ran the risk of having his army destroyed in detail.

The Confederates assembled at Gettysburg, a little town of 2,400 people but a major road hub. The Army of Northern Virginia came in from the northwest, and the Army of the Potomac came in from the south. As of June 28 the Union forces had a new commander, Major General George Gordon Meade. At Chancellorsville in early May Hooker had hesitated, allowing Lee, with half his own numbers, to win. Lincoln and his advisers doubted that Hooker could stand up to Lee. Meade, one of Hooker's corps commanders, was regarded as stolid and unflappable.

Preliminary contact between the two forces occurred near Gettysburg on June 29. Union cavalry under Brigadier General John Buford entered Gettysburg and sighted A. P. Hill's Confederate infantry west of the town. Buford sent word to Major General Joseph Reynolds, commander of the Union I Corps, and attempted to hold Gettysburg as both sides rushed resources forward.

The Battle of Gettysburg lasted three days. The first day, July 1, was a Confederate victory. Reynolds reached the town in midmorning and moved his infantry forward to replace Buford's cavalry but was killed while placing his units. In early afternoon Major General Oliver O. Howard's Union XI Corps reached the field, but in the fierce fighting that followed the Confederates drove the Union troops back through Gettysburg into strong positions on Cemetery Hill and Culp's Hill.

The first day's battle had been costly for the Union; two-thirds of the 18,000 Union troops engaged were casualties. Reynolds and Buford had purchased sufficient time, however, for the resultant Union defensive line, which came to be known from its shape as the Fishhook, was Meade's greatest single advantage in the battle. The Fishhook was anchored on the right by Culp's Hill and then ran westward to Cemetery Hill and south along Cemetery Ridge to the two Round Tops. Union cavalry screened the flanks. The Confederates meanwhile occupied Seminary Ridge, a long partially wooded rise to the west that paralleled Cemetery Ridge.

The second day of battle, July 2, revealed the advantage of the Fishhook, as Meade, operating from interior lines, could more easily shift about troops and supplies than could Lee. Longstreet, commanding I Corps, urged Lee to secure the Round Tops at the south of the Union defensive line and then swing around behind the Union forces, threatening Baltimore and Washington to draw Meade from his defensive positions. Lee, however, decided on a two-pronged attack on the Union flanks.

These attacks were not simultaneous, enabling Meade to contain both. Longstreet's march to avoid Union observation posts took much of the afternoon. Nonetheless, his two-division attack against Major General Daniel Sickles's III Corps on the Union left was successful. Sickles had abandoned Cemetery Ridge and moved in advance of the rest of the Union line, forming a salient where he was completely unsupported. Locations here became famous from the fighting: the Peach Orchard, the Wheatfield, and the Devil's Den. Meade shifted forces south, and although Sickles's men were driven back to Cemetery Ridge, they held there. The Confederates also failed to take Little Round Top, thanks to Colonel Joshua Chamberlain's badly outnumbered 20th Maine Regiment, which arrived there just in time. Had the Confederates been successful here, Longstreet could have enfiladed the entire Union line.

The fighting then shifted to the Union center. Although Hill attacked with insufficient numbers, one Confederate brigade briefly secured a foothold on Cemetery Ridge. To the north at twilight two Confederate brigades were pushed back from Cemetery Hill, and Ewell's attack on Culp's Hill was also rebuffed. The second day ended in a draw.

Although Longstreet expressed opposition, Lee now planned a massive attack from Seminary Ridge against the center of the Union line, held by Major General Winfield Scott Hancock's II Corps. At the same time, the Confederate cavalry under Stuart, which had arrived only the day before, would sweep around the Union line from the north.

At about 1:00 p.m. on July 3 the Confederates began a massive artillery barrage with some 160 guns from Seminary Ridge. More than 100 Union guns on Cemetery Ridge replied in a two-hour cannonade. Then the guns fell silent, and the Confederates began an attack over a mile of open ground in ranks a mile wide, battle flags flying as if on parade. There were three divisions in the charge that day, with Major General George Pickett's division in the center. The two other divisions faded away and streamed back toward the Confederate lines, leaving Pickett's alone and exposed to enfilading Union fire. Only a few hundred Confederates reached the Union line, and they were halted there. Out of 12,000–13,500 men, Pickett lost 8,000–10,000 that day.

Lee then shortened his line. He remained in place along Seminary Ridge the next day hoping that Meade would attack him, but the Union commander refused to take the bait. The Confederate cavalry meanwhile was defeated five miles east of the battlefield by Union cavalry. Finally, on the night of July 4 Lee decamped, taking advantage of darkness and heavy rain to mask his withdrawal. Lee proceeded down the Cumberland Valley and back into Virginia with captured booty and 6,000 Union prisoners.

In the battle itself, Meade lost some 23,000 men. Lee's losses might have been as high as 28,000 men. Although the South trumpeted a victory, cooler heads could see that the battle was a Confederate defeat. The Union victory at Gettysburg, coupled with the simultaneous success at Vicksburg, Mississippi, decisively tipped the military-diplomatic balance in favor of the North.

References

Coddington, Edwin B. *The Gettysburg Campaign: A Study in Command.* New York: Scribner, 1984.

Hess, Earl J. *Pickett's Charge: The Last Attack at Gettysburg.* Chapel Hill: University of North Carolina Press, 2001.

Pfanz, Harry W. *Gettysburg: Culp's Hill and Cemetery Hill.* Chapel Hill: University of North Carolina Press, 1993.

———. *Gettysburg: The Second Day.* Chapel Hill: University of North Carolina Press, 1987.

Woodworth, Steven E. *Beneath a Northern Sky: A Short History of the Gettysburg Campaign.* Wilmington, DE: Scholarly Resources, 2003.

Siege of Vicksburg

Date	May 22–July 4, 1863	
Location	Vicksburg, Mississippi, on the Mississippi River (United States)	
Opponents (* winner)	*Union	Confederate
Commander	Major General Ulysses S. Grant	Lieutenant General John C. Pemberton
Approx. # Troops	77,000	33,000
Importance	Gives the Union control of the Mississippi River	

The struggle for the city of Vicksburg on the Mississippi River was one of the most important battles of the American Civil War (1861–1865). Control of the Mississippi was vital for the Union. By controlling the river, the Union could cut off the Trans-Mississippi West from the rest of the Confederacy and bind the Midwest to the Union cause by securing the movement of its goods to the Gulf of Mexico. The Union assault against Confederate positions on the mighty river began in early 1862. While Flag Officer Andrew Hull Foote's Western Flotilla moved down the Mississippi and tested its northern defenses, Flag Officer David G. Farragut's West Coast Gulf Blockading Squadron would attempt to take New Orleans and move up river from the south.

The northern Union flotilla worked in combination with U.S. Army forces ashore to capture a series of Confederate strongholds: Island No. 10 on April 8, Fort Pillow on June 4, and Memphis on June 6. On April 24 Farragut's ships ran past the Confederate forts at the river's mouth, and Union troops occupied New Orleans on May 1. The Union now controlled the entire length of the Mississippi except the fortified town of Vicksburg, located in a bend of the river.

Confederate lieutenant general John C. Pemberton commanded the city's defenses. Attempts at naval assault failed in May and June 1862, and in late summer and autumn the Confederates reinforced Vicksburg from the east and added a bastion downstream at Port Hudson, Louisiana, giving the South control of the intervening length of river.

In October 1862 Major General Ulysses S. Grant took command of the Army of the Tennessee. Operating from Memphis, he attempted but failed to take the city in the First Vicksburg Overland Campaign, which lasted through late December 1862. Vicksburg was strongly fortified and protected by the natural defenses of its high bluffs facing the river and swamps to the north. The city was most vulnerable from the south and east, but these were remote from Grant's supply base at Memphis to the north.

In January 1863 Grant encamped his Army of the Tennessee on the Louisiana side of the river, above Vicksburg, and began a series of unsuccessful efforts to get around the city, assisted by Rear Admiral David Dixon Porter's flotilla via various creeks and bayous. Then on March 29, 1863, Grant crossed the Mississippi above Vicksburg and marched down the Louisiana side of the river to a point south of the city where Porter's ships, which ran past the Vicksburg batteries on the night of April 16–17, ferried him across the river on April 30. In effect Grant now planned to attack Vicksburg from the rear.

Defying instructions from Washington, Grant abandoned his base at Grand Gulf and marched northeast with 20,000 men, carrying supplies in wagons and partially living off the land. Grant believed that any delay would give the Confederates time to reinforce and fortify. He therefore employed a daring cavalry raid to keep Pemberton confused as to his movements. Grant quickly took Jackson, Mississippi, held by only 6,000 Confederates. The Union troops destroyed everything of military value. Abandoned by Grant, the town was soon reinforced by the Confederates but was no longer available as a logistical center for Vicksburg to the west.

Confederate theater commander General Joseph E. Johnston ordered Pemberton to advance from Vicksburg and cut Grant's tenuous supply line. Grant learned of this plan through a spy and countered Pemberton's move. The two armies collided at Champion's Hill on May 16. Grant commanded 32,000 men, and Pemberton had 25,000 men. Although the battle was hard fought, Grant was victorious. Union casualties amounted to some 2,500 men, while the Confederates sustained 4,000 losses. Pemberton was forced back into the Vicksburg perimeter. Johnston had warned Pemberton not to get shut up in Vicksburg and to abandon the city if necessary, but Pemberton thought he knew better.

Outnumbered at the outset of the campaign, Grant had marched 200 miles in less than three weeks, had won five battles, and ended by shutting up the opposing army in a fortress. Grant then made two futile and poorly planned assaults against Vicksburg on May 19 and 22 before he settled down to a prolonged siege. Union siege guns and guns on the Union ships in the river kept the city and the Confederate lines under constant bombardment. At night Union soldiers advanced their trenches ever closer to the Confederate lines. The strain on the inhabitants of Vicksburg was immense. Food was in short supply, and starvation soon set in; people subsisted on whatever they could find. To escape the bombardment, they dug caves in the hard clay hillsides.

Two days' march to the east at Jackson, Johnston hovered with some 31,000 men raised specifically to lift the siege. Grant, reinforced, countered with a heavily manned line of eastward-facing defenses. Johnston, despite the urging of Confederate authorities, never attempted to test these or to relieve the garrison.

After six weeks, at 10:00 a.m. on July 4 Pemberton surrendered Vicksburg and 29,495 men. Union casualties of the Vicksburg campaign from October 1862 to July 1863 amounted to around 9,000 men. Confederate casualties were 10,000, not counting prisoners. Port Hudson, the remaining Confederate stronghold on the Mississippi, consequently surrendered on July 9. The entire Mississippi was under Union control, and the Confederacy was split north to south.

The capture of Vicksburg greatly benefitted the Union. Coming at the same time as the great Union victory at Gettysburg, the capture of Vicksburg lifted Northern morale and depressed that of the South. The Trans-Mississippi West was cut off from the rest of the Confederacy. Midwestern farmers could now use the Mississippi for their goods, and this brought that region solidly behind the Union war effort.

References

Arnold, James R. *Grant Wins the War: Decision at Vicksburg.* New York: Wiley, 1997.

Ballard, Michael B. *Pemberton: A Biography.* Jackson: University Press of Mississippi, 1991.

Bearss, Edwin C. *The Vicksburg Campaign.* 3 vols. Dayton, OH: Morningside, 1995.

Winschel, Terrence J. *Vicksburg: Fall of the Confederate Gibraltar.* Abilene, TX: McWhiney Foundation Press, 1999.

———, ed. *Triumph and Defeat: The Vicksburg Campaign.* Campbell, CA: Savas, 1998.

Battle of Mobile Bay

Date	August 5, 1864	
Location	Mobile Bay Alabama (United States)	
Opponents (* winner)	*Union	Confederates
Commander	Rear Admiral David G. Farragut	Rear Admiral Franklin Buchanan
Approx. # Troops	18 ships, including 4 ironclad monitors	4 ships: one ironclad and 3 gunboats
Importance	The bloodiest naval battle of the Civil War, it closes the last major Confederate port on the Gulf Coast	

The Battle of Mobile Bay was the bloodiest engagement on water of the American Civil War. Mobile Bay and the port of Mobile, Alabama, were vital to the Confederate war effort. Alabama was an important center for Southern iron manufacturing, including heavy guns and rolled iron plate. Mobile was one of the few deepwater ports available to the Confederacy in 1864 and was an important transshipment point for goods carried by blockade runners. After taking New Orleans in early 1862, U.S. Navy rear admiral David G. Farragut wanted to proceed against Mobile with his Gulf Coast Squadron, but he was forced to operate on the Mississippi, principally against Vicksburg. This delay allowed the Confederates time to strengthen Mobile's defenses.

After several further delays occasioned by a lack of Union troops to operate with the navy, early on the morning of August 5, 1864, Farragut led 18 ships, including 4 ironclad monitors, against Mobile Bay. Shortly after 6:00 a.m. the Union ships crossed the bar into the bay. Four monitors formed a column to the right of another column of wooden ships to mask them from the heavy guns of Fort

Morgan guarding the entrance to the bay. Farragut ordered his 7 smallest wooden ships lashed to the port side of the larger wooden screw steamers for additional protection.

Shortly before 7:00 a.m. the lead Union ironclad, the *Tecumseh,* opened fire at Fort Morgan, and the engagement became general. Rear Admiral Franklin Buchanan, commanding the Confederate squadron in the bay, moved to attack the advancing Union ships. He had the powerful ironclad ram *Tennessee* (flagship), supported by three gunboats.

The captain of the *Tecumseh* made right for the *Tennessee,* but there was a great explosion when the *Tecumseh* struck a mine. It went down in only half a minute, stopping the Union fleet in front of the guns of Fort Morgan. Lashed in the rigging of his flagship, the sloop *Hartford,* Farragut saw the sloop *Brooklyn* in front of him slow and then reverse engines. The Union ships now began to bunch up as Fort Morgan continued to fire.

This was the decisive point in the battle, and Farragut chose to take the risk of additional mines with his own ship, calling out, "I shall lead." The *Hartford* got up speed, and as it passed by the *Brooklyn,* Farragut shouted, "What's the trouble?" "Torpedoes" (mines) was the reply. "Damn the torpedoes," Farragut yelled out. He then ordered his ship to get up speed, and finally he called to the captain of the gunboat lashed to the side of the *Hartford,* "Go ahead, Jouett, full speed!" Farragut's words have passed into history in shortened version as "Damn the torpedoes; full speed ahead."

Although men below decks on the *Hartford* could hear primers going off beneath them, none of the remaining Confederate mines exploded. Some Union warships were damaged by Confederate shore fire, but all passed safely into the bay and beyond the range of the fort's guns.

Buchanan saw Farragut's pennant flying from the *Hartford* and ordered the *Tennessee* to attack. The gunboats also joined in. The *Tennessee* did not have sufficient speed up to ram, however, and passed by the Union flagship, firing at the remaining pairs of Union ships and inflicting some damage and casualties. Farragut ordered his smaller vessels cut free to attack the Confederate gunboats, which then hauled off and steamed up the bay. Of the three Confederate gunboats, the *Selma* surrendered, the *Gaines* was hit several times below the waterline and sank, and the *Morgan* escaped to the protection of Fort Morgan and later to Mobile.

The *Tennessee* also gained the protection of Fort Morgan, where Buchanan considered his next move. Rather than wait to be attacked, at 9:00 a.m. he brought his flagship back alone against the entire Union squadron. The Confederate artillerymen at Fort Morgan cheered the ram on in what seemed to be a suicide mission. The *Tennessee* with 6 guns faced 157 Union guns. Buchanan hoped to inflict what damage he could, return to Fort Morgan, and there ground the *Tennessee* as a stationary battery. He did not want to see a repeat of what had happened to the *Virginia* in the James River: the *Virginia* had been scuttled without a fight.

After ineffectual attempts on both sides to ram, the *Tennessee* was surrounded and pummelled by the Union guns. The *Tennessee* was holed only once. Union shot nonetheless jammed the Confderate ironclad's port shutters and cut its exposed steering chains. With his ship dead in the water, his ammunition nearly expended, and suffering from a wound, Buchanan finally surrendered.

Union troops under Major General Edward Canby landed. Confederate Fort Gaines surrendered on August 8; however, the commander at Fort Morgan refused to follow suit. Two weeks of bombardment followed in which the *Tennessee,* now recommissioned as a U.S. Navy ship, participated. Fort Morgan finally surrendered on August 23. Mobile, 30 miles from the Gulf of Mexico, was not taken until April 1865, which occurred in a joint army-navy operation.

Farragut's capture of Mobile Bay cost the Union side 145 killed and 170 wounded. Many of his wooden ships were heavily damaged, but only one was lost, a supply vessel hit by fire from Fort Morgan as it attempted to follow the fleet into the bay. The Confederates lost 12 killed and 20 wounded, and the crews of the *Tennessee* and *Selma* were captured. For all practical purposes, the Battle of Mobile Bay ended blockade running in the Gulf of Mexico. The battle also helped to ensure the reelection of U.S. president Abraham Lincoln.

References

Duffy, James P. *Lincoln's Admiral: The Civil War Campaigns of David Farragut.* New York: Wiley, 1997.

Friend, Jack. *West Wind, Flood Tide: The Battle of Mobile Bay.* Annapolis, MD: Naval Institute Press, 2004.

Hearn, Chester G. *Mobile Bay and the Mobile Campaign: The Last Great Battle of the Civil War.* Jefferson, NC: McFarland, 1993.

Symonds, Craig. *Confederate Admiral: The Life and Wars of Franklin Buchanan.* Annapolis, MD: Naval Institute Press, 1999.

Walter, Francis X. *The Naval Battle of Mobile Bay, August 5, 1864.* Birmingham, AL: Prester Meridian, 1993.

Battle of Königgrätz

Date	July 3, 1866	
Location	Near Sadowa (today Sadová) in Bohemia (today the Czech Republic)	
Opponents (* winner)	*Prussians	Austrians, Saxons
Commander	General Count Helmuth von Moltke (Moltke the Elder)	General Ludwig von Benedek
Approx. # Troops	221,000	206,000 (184,000 Austrians, 22,000 Saxons)
Importance	Ends the 120-year-long struggle between Prussia and Austria over which power will dominate Germany	

The Battle of Königgrätz (also known as the Battle of Sadowa, the German spelling of the Czech town of Sadová) was the culminating military event in the 1866 Austro-Prussian War and in the 120-year struggle to see which power would dominate the German states. It was also the largest European land battle before World War I.

In September 1862 Otto von Bismarck became minister-president (premier) of Prussia. Bismarck favored confrontation with Austria and supported the efforts of Minister of War Albrecht von Roon and chief of the Prussian General Staff General Helmuth von Moltke to strengthen the Prussian Army, whose weaknesses were readily apparent in its 1859 mobilization against France. In 1864 the new army proved highly effective in fighting between the German Confederation and Denmark, a conflict that Bismarck had created. The war ended with a Confederation victory and Danish cession of the two duchies of Schleswig and Holstein. Prussia administered Schleswig and Austria Holstein.

During 1865–1866 Bismarck engineered a new war, this one with Austria. He first secured the neutrality of Russia and France. The Russians, already in competition with the Austrians in the Balkans, were also bitter over Austria's role in the Crimean War. At the same time, Russian leaders were grateful to Bismarck for having closed Prussia's borders with Poland during the latter's 1863 uprising against Russian rule, which greatly assisted the Russians in crushing the revolt. Bismarck met with French emperor Napoleon III at Biarritz in October 1865 and promised compensation along the Rhine in return for French neutrality. Napoleon III was so eager for the war that he worked to secure Italy as a Prussian ally while at the same time assuring Austria that he was endeavoring to keep Italy neutral. Italian leaders hoped to gain Venetia.

Having isolated Austria, Bismarck then goaded it into war, demanding the abolition of the German Confederation. The states of the German Confederation joined Austria in voting for war against Prussia on June 14, 1866. The conflict thus pitted the other German states and Austria against Prussia and Italy. Bismarck was determined that the war would be of short duration. Indeed, it was a 19th-century blitzkrieg, lasting just seven weeks.

The scattered forces of the German Confederation were not able to concentrate, leaving the war basically a struggle between Prussia and Austria. The Prussians also utilized their new railroad net with great effectiveness to move both troops and supplies. The Austrians moreover fumbled away opportunities.

In northern Germany, within two weeks of the declaration of war Prussian West Army commander General Eduard Vogel von Falkenstein defeated the Hanoverians and ended any threat from that direction. He then turned his forces south, but the decision was already at hand. Moltke had three armies deployed against Austria along 250 miles of border. He planned to move all three, on parallel axes, south into Bohemia.

In the west the Army of the Elbe under General Karl Herwarth von Bittenfeld was to advance through central Saxony. The First Army under Prince Frederick

Karl would move from Görlitz in eastern Saxony, while in the east the Second Army under Crown Prince Frederick Wilhelm would cross directly into Bohemia. Moltke planned to concentrate the three near Gitschin (Jičin) before moving on Ölmütz (Olomouc), where intelligence reports indicated that the Austrians intended their own concentration.

The initial Prussian advance went well, brushing aside Austrian and Saxon troops at Münchengrätz on June 27 and at Gitschin on June 29. With Austrian North Army commander General Ludwig von Benedek slow to move, however, Moltke—who was in touch with his three subordinate commanders by telegraph—ordered the Army of the Elbe to swing wide to the south and then attack north to carry out a double envelopment. The two sides were almost exactly matched in terms of numbers. Moltke commanded about 221,000 men and 702 guns, while Benedek commanded about 206,000 men (184,000 Austrians and 22,000 Saxons) and 650 guns. The Prussians had a significant advantage in infantry firepower. Their Dreyse breech-loading Needle Gun rifle could be fired up to six times as fast as the Austrian Lorenz muzzle loader and with greater range and accuracy.

Benedek's great chance came when the Prussian armies separated. Per Moltke's orders the Army of the Elbe swung wide, and there was also a wide gap between the First Army and the Second Army. Benedek had already concentrated his own force and thus could not deploy it as rapidly as the three smaller Prussian component armies moved. Forced to stand and fight, he positioned his army facing west along a 10-mile front from Josefstadt south to Königgrätz and above the village of Sadowa.

Moltke planned to concentrate his own forces not before the battle but during it. The Prussian Elbe Army and First Army attacked in a pouring rain at dawn on July 3. A communications breakdown briefly threatened disaster. The Second Army had not received Moltke's attack order and remained stationary. The attackers also crowded into too narrow a front, providing ideal targets for the Austrian artillery. They were saved only by foolish Austrian bayonet counterattacks. By 11:00 a.m., however, the Prussian attack had clearly been blunted.

In the meantime, a courier reached the Second Army to deliver Moltke's attack order. Moving along muddy roads, the Second Army came up, falling on the Austrian northern lines at about 1:30 p.m. and entirely reversing the situation. Benedek ordered a retreat, covered by his artillery. Prussia sustained approximately 9,000 casualties (1,900 killed, 6,800 wounded, and 275 missing), while Austrian-Saxon losses were approximately 44,100 men (5,735 killed, 8,440 wounded, some 22,000 taken prisoner, and 7,925 missing). Austria also lost 116 guns. Moltke did not pursue. Although not routed, the Austrians were decisively defeated, and the North Army's losses were such that the government had no choice but to agree to an armistice on July 22.

Bismarck, who had to use all his influence on King Wilhelm I for war, now had to work to prevent the king from imposing harsh peace terms on Austria. Already thinking about the need to isolate France, Bismarck handed easy terms to Austria. In the Treaty of Prague of August 23, 1866, Austria ceded Holstein to Prussia and allowed Prussia to reorganize Germany north of the Main River into the North German Confederation under its leadership. Prussia went on to annex Hanover, Hesse-Casel, Nassau, and Frankfurt. In all, Prussia secured 25,000 square miles of territory with a population of 5 million people.

The Italians meanwhile met defeat on land in the Second Battle of Custozza on June 24 and on the seas in the Battle of Lissa on July 20. Nonetheless, Italy was on the winning side and had substantially aided Prussia merely in diverting Austrian troops south. Italy now acquired Venetia. Napoleon III had expected a long war in which he would be able to step in and secure a settlement on his own terms, but Königgrätz ended this possibility, and he was unable to influence events. The ruin of Napoleon's German and Italian policies seemed complete.

References

Craig, Gordon A. *The Battle of Königgrätz: Prussia's Victory over Austria, 1866.* Westport, CT: Greenwood, 1975.

Rothenberg, Gunther E. *The Army of Francis Joseph.* West Lafayette, IN: Purdue University Press, 1976.

Wawro, Geoffrey. *The Austro-Prussian War: Austria's War with Prussia and Italy in 1866.* New York: Cambridge University Press, 1996.

Battle of Lissa

Date	July 20, 1866	
Location	Off the island of Lissa in the Adriatic Sea	
Opponents (* winner)	*Austrians	Italians
Commander	Rear Admiral Wilhelm von Tegetthoff	Admiral Count Carlo Pellion di Persano
Approx. # Troops	27 ships with 532 guns	31 ships with 645 guns
Importance	The first naval battle between ocean-going ironclad fleets	

The Battle of Lissa was the key naval battle of the 1866 Austro-Prussian War and the first battle between oceangoing ironclad fleets. The war pitted Austria and virtually all of the smaller German states against Prussia and Italy. Fighting between Italy and Austria occurred at sea in the Adriatic. Rear Admiral Wilhelm von Tegetthoff commanded the Austrian Fleet. A strong believer in the ram, the energetic 38-year-old Tegetthoff preferred it to naval gunfire even though not one of his warships had a true ram bow. Instead they had hastily fitted joined-armor bow plates. Italy had built up its navy before the war, adding ironclads acquired from Britain and the United States. At King Victor Emmanuel II's insistence, Admiral Count Carlo Pellion di Persano commanded the fleet.

On July 15 Persano took 29 of his ships to sea but not to Pola, where the Austrians were located. He sought an easy victory at Lissa, an Austrian-held Adriatic island whose fort mounted 88 guns. For two days the Italian fleet bombarded Lissa with little effect, and the Austrian shore batteries badly damaged the 20-gun ironclad capital ship *Formidabile,* which suffered 60 casualties.

News of the Italian attack soon reached Pola, and on July 19 Tegetthoff set out with his fleet for the island, his flag in the ironclad *Erzherzog Ferdinand Maximilian.* He placed his ships in three wedge-shaped divisions. The flagship and six other ironclad frigates led. They were followed by seven large wooden ships headed by the screw ship of the line *Kaiser,* and seven wooden gunboats made up the third division. Small dispatch boats were in the intervals to relay messages.

All together, Tegetthoff had 27 ships. They displaced 57,300 tons, mounted 532 guns, and carried 7,870 men. Persano had 31 ships, 12 of them ironclads. They displaced 86,000 tons, mounted 645 guns, and carried 10,900 men. The Italians had the advantage in everything except leadership and discipline.

At dawn on July 20 in a rough sea with mist, lookouts aboard the Italian scout boat *Esploratore* spotted the approaching Austrians. The *Esplotatore* immediately warned Persano, who had no contingency plan and was landing troops on Lissa. By 10:00 a.m., however, the Italian ships, although somewhat scattered, were under way toward the approaching Austrians. Eleven of the Italian ironclads began to form up in column. The wooden ships held back and did not participate in the action. The ironclad *Formidabile,* damaged by the Austrian shore batteries, also did not participate. Without informing his captains, Persano transferred his flag to the iron-hulled *Affondatore* (meaning "sender to the bottom"), Italy's newest warship with two turrets and a pronounced bow ram.

At 10:30 a.m. Tegetthoff signaled his armored ships to charge the Italian ships and attempt to sink them. Considerable gun smoke led to confusion on both sides, and Tegetthoff's ironclad rams missed their targets. Their return charge damaged four of the Italian ships, however. Austrian gunfire also damaged the Italian broadside ironclad *Re d'Italia*'s exposed steering apparatus, and a shell set the central battery ironclad *Palestro* on fire and caused it to leave the line.

Tegetthoff then ordered his *Erzherzog Ferdinand Maximilian* to ram the *Re d'Italia.* The Austrian ship struck the Italian ship at a speed of about 11.5 knots and tore a gaping hole in its side, sending the *Re d'Italia* to the bottom in only five minutes. The sinking was actually a fluke; the *Re d'Italia* had been dead in the water and was thus vulnerable to the ram. Persano ordered the *Affondatore* to ram, but its efforts were largely ineffectual. The wooden *Kaiser* rammed the broadside ironclad *Re di Portogallo,* but the collision actually did more damage to the Austrian vessel, forcing it to retire.

At about 2:30 p.m. the blazing central-battery Italian ironclad *Palestro* suddenly blew up, with the loss of 204 officers and men. Persano then broke off the action. The Italians had lost two ships, and four others were badly damaged. They also had suffered 619 dead and 39 wounded. Later the *Affondatore* foundered in a squall off Ancona, largely as a result of damages sustained in the battle. Austrian losses were slight: several ships damaged, 38 men killed, and 138 wounded.

Tegetthoff had not only saved Lissa and denied Italy a bargaining chip at the peace conference but also had defeated a superior force. Vienna promoted him to vice admiral and later decreed that the Austrian Navy would always have a ship named after Tegetthoff. Lissa was the only major fleet encounter between ironclads in which the principal tactic was ramming. Even though only one ship was sunk by this method during the battle, for the next three decades the world's navies made the ram standard equipment in battleship construction.

Unfortunately for the Austrians, their victory in the Battle of Lissa went for naught. The Prussian triumph over Austria in the Battle of Königgrätz (Sadowa) in Bohemia on July 3, 1866, had decided the war.

References

Greene, Jack, and Alessandro Massignani. *Ironclads at War: The Origin and Development of the Armored Warship, 1854–1891.* Conshohocken, PA: Combined Publishing, 1998.

Hall, Richard. *The War at Sea in the Ironclad Age.* London: Cassell, 2000.

Sandler, Stanley. *The Emergence of the Modern Capital Ship.* Newark: University of Delaware Press, 1979.

Tucker, Spencer C. *Handbook of 19th Century Naval Warfare.* Annapolis, MD: Naval Institute Press, 2000.

Battle of Gravelotte–St. Privat

Date	August 18, 1870	
Location	Villages of Gravelotte and St. Privat in eastern France	
Opponents (* winner)	*Germans	French
Commander	Prince Friedrich Karl; General Karl Friedrich von Steinmetz	Marshal François Achille Bazaine; Marshal François Certain Canrobert
Approx. # Troops	188,000	112,000
Importance	The French inflict heavier casualties on the Germans but withdraw to the fortress of Metz, missing a chance to break free	

The Battle of Gravelotte–St. Privat was an important battle during the Franco-Prussian War (1870–1871). In 1866 Prussian minister-president Otto von Bismarck had engineered a war with Austria that ended with Prussia becoming the dominant power in northern Germany. Although Prussia dominated the new North German Confederation, Bismarck knew that he could not complete his plan of unifying Germany under Prussian leadership without first defeating France.

French emperor Napoleon III had been humiliated by the 1866 war. Promised compensation by Bismarck in return for French neutrality, Napoleon expected that the war would be of long duration and that France would then be able to impose a settlement. The war lasted only seven weeks, far too short for France to have any role in determining peace terms. When Napoleon pressed for compensation, Bismarck asked for it to be put in writing. When Napoleon complied, Bismarck reneged. Later he used the document to help secure defensive alliances with the southern German states of Baden, Bavaria, and Württemberg. Furious, French leaders were bent on revenge, yet the government did little to prepare the French Army for war.

In 1870 Bismarck attempted to present the French with a fait accompli by placing the German Catholic Prince Leopold of Hohenzollern-Sigmaringen on the throne of Spain. The French government learned of the secret plan, and Foreign Minister Duc Antoine de Gramont demanded, through French ambassador to Prussia Count Vincent Benedetti, that the candidacy be withdrawn. Prussian king Wilhelm I, at Ems and away from Bismarck in Berlin, agreed.

France thus achieved a mild diplomatic victory, but Gramont wanted more. He ordered Benedetti to secure a pledge for the future that no Prussian prince ever be a candidate for the throne of Spain. Wilhelm I politely but firmly rejected the request and communicated this information to Bismarck, who then edited the communication and released it to the press. This Ems Dispatch was so cleverly presented that it inflamed opinion in both countries and led to war. Most Europeans were not aware of Bismarck's hand in events and blamed France.

French government ministers had whipped up public opinion to the point that it was next to impossible to back down. Premier Émile Olivier encouraged the national illusions by saying that he "accepted war with a light heart." Among the French leadership, only Napoleon expressed doubts. Minister of War Edmond Leboeuf's assertion that the army was ready "down to the last gaiter button" was entirely misplaced.

On July 15, 1870, the French Corps Législatif (the elected branch of parliament) nonetheless voted war credits, with only 10 deputies dissenting. Prussia mobilized immediately. From this point there was no wavering on either side, and on July 19 the French government declared war. Prussia's treaties with the southern German states now came into force, so it was really a Franco-German war.

By the end of July, chief of the Prussian General Staff General Count Helmuth von Moltke had positioned three armies of some 380,000 in the Rhineland along the French frontier. From north to south, these were General Karl Friedrich von Steinmetz's First Army of 60,000 men, Prince Friedrich Karl's Second Army of 175,000 men, and Crown Prince Friedrich Wilhelm's Third Army of 145,000 men. Moltke held another 95,000 troops in reserve until he was certain that Austria would not intervene. King Wilhelm I had nominal command, but Moltke exercised actual command authority through the General Staff. The Prussians were fully prepared for the war, and their military intelligence and maps of France were both excellent.

The French mobilization was not complete by the time the war began. The French Army deployed some 224,000 men in eight corps. The army had élan, but its recent military experience was in North Africa. The French breech-loading Chassepot rifle was superior to the basic Prussian rifle, the Dreyse Needle Gun. The French also had a new weapon in the *mitrailleuse,* which formed about a fifth of the French artillery. Developed in great secrecy, it was a 37-barrel machine gun that could fire about 150 shots a minute and had a range of some 2,000 yards. A lot depended on how the *mitrailleuse* was deployed, and the French chose to use it as artillery at long range, where it was inaccurate and could be destroyed by the new Prussian Krupp artillery. French mobilization procedures, logistical arrangements, and military intelligence were all abysmal. There was no general staff in the Prussian sense of the term, and senior military leadership was inept and unimaginative.

At the end of July, Napoleon ordered a general advance. The emperor was not well, but he accompanied the army in the field. On August 2 a skirmish at Saarbrücken, just across the border, saw the French advancing from the fortress of Metz to scatter the few Prussian troops defending there, although the French failed to occupy the city. Moltke then attacked to the south, driving French forces back toward Strasbourg. Attempting to halt this offensive, on August 6 Marshal Patrice MacMahon sacrificed his cavalry in gallant but costly charges near the town of Fröschwiller (Wörth). MacMahon was forced to evacuate Alsace, and the road to Paris was now open to the Prussians.

To the north a second Prussian thrust enjoyed success at Spieheren, and Napoleon ordered Metz abandoned. The emperor's defeatism rapidly spread through the army. On August 12 Napoleon yielded field command to Marshal François Achille Bazaine to lead a reorganized Army of the Rhine. Napoleon departed for Châlons in order to raise a new army. Moltke sought to cut off the withdrawing French, but in the ensuing August 16 battles at Vionville, Merse-la-Tour, and Rezonville the French fought well. They lost 13,761 men to 15,780 for the Prussians, but Bazaine, having given up hope of breaking out, ordered the army to return to Metz.

On August 18 Moltke attacked Bazaine with his First Army and Second Army, hoping to destroy the French. The battle was fought between the villages of St. Privat la Montaigne and Gravolette, with the major point of combat the walled village of St. Privat. This battle differed from previous engagements in its size—more than 188,000 Germans with 732 guns fought 112,000 French with 520 guns—and in that both sides expected it.

At St. Privat, commander of the Second Army Friedrich Karl sent in the elite Prussian Guard against Marshal François Certain Canrobert's VI Corps. The attackers lost 8,000 men, and Canrobert's corps of 23,000 men held against some 100,000 Germans. Bazaine ignored Canrobert's pleas for reinforcement. Not until a Saxon corps arrived to the north and threatened to cut off his force was Canrobert obliged to order a withdrawal back toward Metz.

Meanwhile, on the French right two German corps battled their way east of Gravolette, only to become trapped in a ravine. The German attempt to disengage resulted in a panicked withdrawal. The French counterattack was checked only by effective German artillery fire and Moltke's personal intervention with reinforcements. Although the French withdrew, the next morning there was little sense of victory among the Germans. They had lost some 20,163 men; the French lost 12,273 men.

The tragedy of St. Privat–Gravolette for the French was that had Bazaine made a concerted effort there, he would most likely have achieved a victory and broken free. As it was, on August 19 the French were back at Metz, where the Germans promptly sealed them in. The separation of their two field armies proved a disaster for France.

References

Howard, Michael. *The Franco-Prussian War.* New York: Routledge, 2001.

Wawro, Geoffrey. *The Franco-Prussian War: The German Conquest of France in 1870–1871.* New York: Cambridge University Press, 2003.

Battle of Sedan

Date	September 1–2, 1870	
Location	Sedan on the Meuse River, northeastern France	
Opponents (* winner)	*Germans	French
Commander	General Count Helmuth von Moltke (Moltke the Elder)	Marshal Patrice MacMahon; Napoleon III, Emperor of France
Approx. # Troops	250,000	85,000
Importance	Brings an end to the Second Empire and opens the way for the Germans to lay siege to Paris	

The Battle of Sedan in northeastern France during September 1–2, 1870, was the most important engagement of the Franco-Prussian War (1870–1871). The battle there between German and French forces brought an end to the Second Empire in France and for all practical purposes decided the outcome of the war.

Following the Battle of Gravelotte–St. Privat on August 18, 1870, French marshal François Achille Bazaine withdrew his Army of the Rhine into the fortress of Metz on the Moselle River. German forces under chief of the Prussian General Staff General Count Helmuth von Moltke surrounded Metz, in effect rendering Bazaine's force hors de combat but also tying down a large number of Prussian forces.

Metz normally had a garrison of 20,000 men and a civilian population of around 70,000. It simply did not have facilities for an army of 140,000 men and its 12,000 wounded. Over the next two weeks Bazaine made only two efforts to break out, on August 26 and 31. Both were timid affairs, with the pessimistic Bazaine ordering a withdrawal as soon as Prussian resistance stiffened. French emperor Napoleon III refused to adopt the one plan that might have saved France: a delaying action back on the city of Paris while additional forces were being gathered. (This plan worked in World War I, although in 1870, unlike in 1914, France fought alone.) Fearing the political effects of a retreat, the emperor accompanied the 120,000-man French Army of Châlons, commanded by Marshal Patrice MacMahon, in an attempt to relieve Metz. MacMahon departed Châlons on August 21.

Leaving a holding force at Metz, Moltke turned the bulk of his forces against MacMahon. On August 30 the two forces collided at Beaumont. MacMahon withdrew toward Sedan, pursued by Crown Prince Friedrich Wilhelm's Third Army and Crown Prince Albert of Saxony's Army of the Meuse. At Sedan, a fortified city on the Meuse River some 120 miles northeast of Paris and close to the Belgian border, Moltke assembled 250,000 Prussians and Bavarians along with some 500 artillery pieces. Although the French had established their positions on high ground, the Germans held still higher ground dominating the city and its environs.

The battle opened at dawn on September 1 with a German artillery bombardment of the French positions, shelling some 85,000 French troops packed into an area of less than two square miles. The more modern breech-loading rifled Prussian guns easily outranged the French artillery. Steadily the Prussians tightened their grip. Napoleon, ill from kidney stones, seemed at peace and wedded to his fate. Heedless of danger, he rode his horse about to encourage the men and perhaps gain a martyrdom that might secure the throne for his son. The French marines did make a fine defensive stand in the outlying village of Bazeilles before having to yield that place.

MacMahon was wounded early in the battle and thus escaped onus for the result. His successor, General Auguste Ducrot, immediately ordered a breakout. Before this could be attempted, however, Ducrot was met by General Emmanuel de Wimpffen, who had just arrived under appointment from Paris. Wimpffen took command, countermanded Ducrot's order, and insisted that Bazeilles be retaken.

That afternoon the Germans turned back desperate French cavalry charges by the Chasseurs d'Afrique at Floing, a mile north of Sedan. Informed of events and with French casualties steadily mounting, Napoleon took the initiative. Although Wimpffen objected, Napoleon insisted on opening surrender talks. A truce was arranged that evening.

Talks continued into the night, but the next morning, September 2, Napoleon insisted that Wimpffen sign the surrender document. The emperor was among the 83,000 French soldiers taken prisoner. Napoleon was escorted to Prussian king Wilhelm I and Chancellor Otto von Bismarck, both present with Moltke to observe the battle.

The Germans secured substantial supplies, 419 guns, 6,000 horses, and more than 1,000 wagons. Prior to the surrender, the Prussians had captured another

21,000 French troups. French killed or wounded in the battle ran to 17,000 men. Prussian and Bavarian losses were about 9,000 men killed, wounded, or missing. The way to Paris was now completely open, and on September 19 the Germans began a siege of the French capital, where a new republican government had taken control.

References

Horne, Alistair. *The Fall of Paris: The Siege and the Commune, 1870–1871.* New York: Doubleday, 1965.

Howard, Michael. *The Franco-Prussian War.* New York: Routledge, 2001.

Wawro, Geoffrey. *The Franco-Prussian War: The German Conquest of France in 1870–1871.* New York: Cambridge University Press, 2003.

Siege of Paris

Date	September 19, 1870–January 28, 1871	
Location	City of Paris, France	
Opponents (* winner)	*Germans	French
Commander	General Count Helmuth von Moltke (Moltke the Eloer)	General Jules Trochu
Approx. # Troops	250,000	120,000 soldiers and marine infantry, 80,000 *gardes mobiles,* and 300,000 *gardes nationales*
Importance	The culminating act of the war, it leads to an armistice and French national elections to decide the issue of war or peace	

The siege of Paris was the culminating act of the Franco-Prussian War (1870–1871). On September 2, 1870, the French Army of Châlons surrendered to the Prussians and Bavarians at Sedan. The Germans took prisoner 83,000 men and 419 guns. Among the prisoners was French emperor Napoleon III who, following several months in Germany, went into unlamented exile in England.

The emperor, but not the empire, survived the disaster of Sedan. When news of the defeat reached Paris, there was an immediate explosion of popular outrage. On September 4 crowds converged on the Corps Legislatif, and a new republican government, the third in French history, was proclaimed. Full of the myth of the Battle of Valmy in 1792, many Frenchmen believed, even as the German armies advanced unopposed on Paris, that a great national effort might yet bring victory. Dynamic young Léon Gambetta, the chief figure in the new government, took the posts of minister of war and minister of the interior and set about organizing the national defense. On September 6 Foreign Minister Jules Favre announced that the government would not yield an inch of French soil.

On September 19 troops of the Prussian Third Army and the Army of the Meuse reached the outskirts of Paris. Several forts guarded the city, which was also ringed by a bastioned enceinte, but little had been done to prepare for a prolonged siege. General Jules Trochu, military governor of Paris and now also president of the new Third Republic, manned the forts defending the city with 120,000 men (including veterans, reservists, and 20,000 marine infantry), 80,000 *gardes mobiles* (untrained recruits under 30), and 300,000 *gardes nationales* (untrained recruits between the ages of 30 and 50).

The Prussians set up their headquarters at the château of Versailles outside the city. Prussian Army chief of staff Count Helmuth von Moltke had no intention of trying to take Paris by storm. He ringed the city with two belts of German troops, cut off food supplies into Paris, and waited for hunger to do its work. By September 23 Paris was completely surrounded. Eventually the only way out was by balloon.

On October 7 in order to organize other forces for the relief of Paris, Gambetta made the hazardous trip out. The winds blew him and a friend almost to Belgium before they descended and were able to make their way on foot to southeastern France. Trochu made three attempts to break the siege in November, December, and January. All were unsuccessful, although the strongest attempt on November 29–30 by 140,000 men and 400 guns destroyed a Bavarian corps and almost broke free before it was turned back.

Gambetta had reason to hope, for French marshal François Achille Bazaine and his Army of the Rhine, although shut up by the Germans at Metz, were nonetheless tying down more than that number of the enemy. The siege of Paris required another 250,000 German troops, and additional forces were necessary to maintain lines of communication back to Germany, which were now under harassment from irregular French forces (francs-tireurs).

Gambetta's hopes were dashed, however, when Bazaine surrendered his Army of the Rhine (133,000 men) at Metz on October 27. Bazaine rejected a Prussian offer of the honors of war and inexplicably refused to order the destruction of his arms. The Prussians thus gained 600 French guns in working order. More important, this released the Prussian First Army and Second Army for operations elsewhere. (In 1873 Bazaine was tried and sentenced to death by a military court, a sentence commuted to 20 years in prison. He subsequently escaped to Spain.)

Whatever chance Gambetta had of liberating Paris now depended on securing time to train new provincial French armies from the south. Mistakenly believing that Paris could not hold out long, Gambetta in November and December committed these forces to battle before they were fully ready. Heavy fighting occurred at Orléans during December 2–4. Gambetta's Army of the Loire was soon cut in two, and he was forced to withdraw to the southwest to Bordeaux.

Paris was now alone in its hunger, cold, and disease. As is usually the case in such circumstances, the wealthy fared far better than the poor. A black market was soon flourishing, and all manner of animals, including those from the zoo as well as common dogs, cats, and even rats, were sold for gold. Plague reached alarming proportions. On January 5 at Bismarck's insistence, the Prussians began shelling the city in the assumption that this would demoralize the civilian population and force a capitulation. It did not. Several hundred Parisians died, however, before the Prussians, who came under considerable international pressure, broke it off. The siege ended only after shortages of food, medicine, and fuel had worked their effect.

On January 26, 1871, the government in the city opened negotiations. Two days later, over Gambetta's objections and with an estimated eight days of food remaining for the city, French foreign minister Favre agreed to an armistice. All Parisian forts were given up, and the city was required to pay a tribute of 200 million francs. There would be a three-week armistice all over France except at Belfort, which—in a glorious chapter of French arms—still held out. The armistice was to allow the country to decide whether the war would continue.

On February 8, with the Germans occupying much of France, Frenchmen went to the polls to decide the issue of war or peace. Except for Republican Paris and the northeast, the country voted overwhelmingly for monarchist candidates and for peace. French politician Adolphe Thiers, one of the few members of the Corps Legislatif who had refused to vote for the war, now was charged with negotiating its end. He tried to get Bismarck to accept overseas territorial compensation, including Indochina, but to no avail. Bismarck blamed the French for prolonging the war and for the harsh peace he imposed.

The preliminary peace signed at Versailles was confirmed in the Treaty of Frankfurt on May 10. The Prussians took Alsace (except Belfort) and much of Lorraine and were allowed a triumphal parade through Paris. France agreed to an indemnity of 5 billion francs, more than twice the actual cost of the war, and German troops would occupy northeastern France until it was paid off.

The effects of the war and the peace treaty that ended it were momentous. A France of 36 million people now faced a united Germany of 41 million people, for on January 18, 1871, Bismarck proclaimed at Versailles the establishment of the German Empire. German unification was thus at last achieved but on Bismarck's terms and under a constitutional arrangement that left Prussia dominant and the bulk of the powers in the hands of the king of Prussia, now also emperor of the Germans.

Taking Alsace and Lorraine may have been a mistake. Alsace had been French since 1648, and Lorraine had been French since 1766. Both were thoroughly French. The indemnity fueled Germany's industrial expansion after the war, but if Bismarck had hoped that the payments would allow Germany to meddle further in French affairs, he was mistaken. In an outpouring of nationalist sentiment, Frenchmen oversubscribed bond issues and paid the indemnity off well ahead of schedule. Most important, the Prussian diktat made cooperation between Germany and

France next to impossible, for Frenchmen were determined to recover the two lost provinces and to secure revenge. Bismarck later boasted that he had been responsible for three wars. This is undoubtedly correct, but it is also true that the treaty he imposed on France sowed the seeds that sprouted World War I, which in turn gave rise to World War II.

References

Horne, Alistair. *The Fall of Paris: The Siege and the Commune, 1870–1871.* New York: Doubleday, 1965.

Howard, Michael. *The Franco-Prussian War.* New York: Routledge, 2001.

Wawro, Geoffrey. *The Franco-Prussian War: The German Conquest of France in 1870–1871.* New York: Cambridge University Press, 2003.

Siege of Pleven

Date	July 19–December 10, 1877	
Location	Pleven (Plevna) in northern Bulgaria	
Opponents (* winner)	*Russians, Romanians, Bulgarians	Ottomans
Commander	Grand Duke Nicholas; Prince Charles of Romania	Ghāzī Osmān Pasha
Approx. # Troops	150,000, including 120,000 Russians plus Romanians and Bulgarian volunteers	Probably more than 50,000
Importance	Regarded as the birthright of modern Bulgaria, the battle opens the way for the Russians to move south against Constantinople (Istanbul), but their stand here wins considerable sympathy in Western Europe for the Ottomans	

In the early 1870s Ottoman power was in decline, but the empire still controlled most of the Balkan Peninsula. In the south Greece was independent, while to the north Romania, Serbia, and Montenegro enjoyed the status of autonomous principalities. In 1875 and 1876 uprisings occurred in Herzegovina, Bosnia, and Macedonia. Then in mid-1876 the Bulgarians also rose, only to be slaughtered by the Ottomans. Serbia and Montenegro then declared war on the Ottoman Empire. Russia, defeated in the Crimean War of 1854–1856 by a coalition that included the Ottomans, sought to recoup its prestige in the Balkans and secure a warm-water port on the Mediterranean. As a result, concerns mounted that fighting in the Balkans might lead to a general European war.

While the major European powers discussed intervention, the Ottomans, led by Ghāzī Osmān Pasha, were winning the war. By the autumn of 1876 it was clear that they would soon capture Belgrade, the capital of Serbia. That October Russia demanded an armistice, which the Ottomans accepted. A conference at Constantinople in December soon disbanded without tangible result, and in March 1877 Serbia made peace with the Ottoman Empire. Sentiment in Russia was then so strong for intervention that despite warnings of bankruptcy from his minister of finance, Czar Alexander II declared war on the Ottomans in April 1877, beginning the Russo-Turkish War of 1877–1878.

Because the Ottomans controlled the Black Sea with ironclad warships, a Russian land invasion proved necessary. In the last week of April 1877 two Russian armies invaded: one in Caucasia, advancing on Kars, Ardahan, and Erzurum, and the other in the Balkans. Romania was essential to a Russian drive down the eastern part of the Balkan Peninsula, and following agreement between Prince Charles of Romania and Alexander II, Russian troops crossed the Prut (Pruth) River into Moldavia. The Ottomans responded by shelling Romanian forts at the mouth of the Danube, whereupon on May 21 Romania declared both war on the Ottoman Empire and its independence. Serbia reentered the war in December. Bulgarian irregular forces fought with Russia, and Montenegro remained at war, as it had been since June 1876. Romanian support was vital to the Russian effort in terms of both geographical position and manpower in the ensuing campaign.

Russian forces under nominal command of Grand Duke Nicholas, brother of the czar, crossed the Danube River on June 26 and took Svistov (Stistova) and Nikopol (Nicopolis) on the river before advancing to Pleven (Plevna, Plevne), about 25 miles south of Nikopol. The Bulgarians acclaimed the Russians as liberators. Russian general Nikolai P. de Krüdener, who had actual command, established his headquarters at Tirnovo and sent forces across the Balkan Mountains into Thrace, then back toward Shipka Pass through the mountains to defeat the Ottomans. Russian troops, assisted by Bulgarian partisans, also raided in the Maritza Valley, seemingly threatening Adrianopole.

The military situation changed when Sultan Abdul Aziz appointed two competent generals: Mehemed Ali, named Ottoman commander in Europe, and Ghāzī Osmān Pasha. Mehemed Ali defeated the Russians in the south, driving them back to the Balkan Mountains with heavy losses. To the north the main Russian armies encountered a formidable obstacle in Ottoman forces sent to the Danube under Osmān Pasha. Soon he had entrenched his men at Pleven. Ottoman engineers created in the rocky valley there a formidable fortress of earthworks with redoubts, trenches, and gun emplacements. The 10-mile Ottoman defensive perimeter was lightly held, with reserves in a secure central location from which they could rush to any threatened point.

Superior numbers led the Russians to underestimate their adversary. Failing to adequately reconnoiter the Ottoman positions, on July 19, 1877, the Russians assaulted the strongest portion of the line and, to their surprise, were repulsed with 3,000 casualties. The battle demonstrated the superiority of machine weapons in the defense, as the Ottomans were equipped with modern breech-loading rifles imported from the United States. They also had light mobile artillery. On July 30 Russian forces again attacked and again were repulsed.

Over the next six weeks Osmān Pasha worked to improve his defenses, while the Russians demanded that Prince Charles of Romania furnish additional manpower. Charles agreed on the condition that he receive command of the joint Romanian-Russian force. Confident of victory, the allies then planned an attack from three sides with 110,000 infantry and 10,000 cavalry. On September 6, 150 Russian guns began a preparatory bombardment. The Ottoman earthworks suffered little damage, and there were relatively few personnel casualties. Wet weather also worked to the advantage of the defenders.

The infantry attack began on schedule on September 11. With Alexander II in attendance, at 1:00 p.m. the artillery fire ceased, and the infantry began their assault. The attackers took a number of Ottoman redoubts, and for several days it appeared that the allies would be victorious. But on the third day the Ottomans successfully counterattacked. The allies suffered 21,000 casualties for their efforts.

Russian war minister Dimitri Aleksevich Miliutin now recalled brilliant engineer General Franz Eduard Ivanovich Todleben, who had directed the defense of Sevastopol during the Crimean War. Todleben advised that Pleven be encircled and its garrison starved into submission. Osmān Pasha, having twice defeated a force double his own in size, would have preferred a withdrawal while it was still possible, but the battle had captured the attention of Europe and created a positive image of Ottomans as heroic and tenacious fighters. Sultan Abdul Hamid therefore ordered him to hold out and promised to send a relief force.

The Russians committed 120,000 men and 5,000 guns to the siege. They also placed Todleben in charge of siege operations. Other Russian forces under General Ossip Gourko ravaged the countryside, preventing Ottoman supply columns from reaching Pleven from the south. The Russians also easily defeated and turned back the sultan's poorly trained relief force.

Winter closed in, and the Ottoman defenders at Pleven, short of ammunition, were soon reduced to starvation. Osmān Pasha knew that his only hope was a surprise breakout. On the night of December 9–10 the Ottomans threw bridges across the Vid River to the west and then advanced on the Russian outposts. The Ottomans carried the first Russian trenches, and the fighting was hand to hand. At this point, Osmān Pasha was wounded and his horse shot from beneath him.

Rumors of Osmān Pasha's death led to panic among the Ottoman troops, who broke and fled. Osmān Pasha surrendered Pleven and its 43,338 defenders on December 10. Although the Russians treated Osmān Pasha well, thousands of Ottoman prisoners perished in the snows on their trek to captivity, and Bulgarians butchered many seriously wounded Ottoman prisoners left behind in military hospitals. Some 34,000 allied troops perished in the siege. With the Russians threatening Constantinople itself, in February 1878 the Ottomans sued for peace.

Russia imposed harsh terms in the Treaty of San Stefano on March 3, 1878, leaving the Ottoman Empire only a small strip of territory on the European side of the straits. Romania, Serbia, and Montenegro were enlarged, but the major territorial change was the creation of a new large autonomous Bulgaria, including most of Macedonia from the Aegean Sea to Albania. This would make Bulgaria the largest of the Balkan states, although the assumption was that it would be dominated by Russia. The Battle of Pleven is therefore regarded by Bulgarians as marking the birth of their nation. The treaty did not last, however. Britain and Austria-Hungary threatened war if the treaty was not revised, and Russia agreed to an international conference that met in Berlin in June and July 1878.

Under the terms of the Treaty of Berlin, Bulgaria was divided into three parts. Bulgaria proper (the northern section) became an autonomous principality subject to tribute to the sultan; eastern Rumelia, the southeastern part, received a measure of autonomy; and the rest of Bulgaria was restored to the sultan. Romania, Serbia, and Montenegro all became independent, and Greece received Thessaly. Russia received from Romania the small strip of Bessarabia lost in 1856 and territory around Batum, Ardahan, and Kars that it had conquered in the Caucasus, while Romania had to be content with part of the Dobrudja. Austria-Hungary secured the right to occupy and administer, though not annex, Bosnia and Herzegovina.

The region continued to smolder, however. During 1912–1913 there were two Balkan wars, both of which threatened to become wider conflicts. Then in June 1914 the assassination of Austrian archduke Franz Ferdinand led to a third Balkan war that this time became World War I. The military lesson of the siege of Pleven—that modern machine weapons gave superiority to the defense—was soon to be relearned.

References

Herbert, Frederick William von. *The Defense of Plevna, 1877*. Ankara, Turkey: Ministry of Culture, 1990.

Kinross, Lord [John Patrick]. *The Ottoman Centuries: The Rise and Fall of the Turkish Empire*. New York: William Morrow, 1977.

Sumner, B. H. *Russia and the Balkans, 1870–1880*. Oxford: Oxford University Press, 1937.

Battle of Tel el Kebir

Date	September 13, 1882	
Location	Tel el-Kebir, northern Egypt	
Opponents (* winner)	*British	Egyptians
Commander	Lieutenant General Sir Garnet Wolseley	Colonel Ahmed Arabi
Approx. # Troops	24,000	22,000–25,000
Importance	Their victory gives the British control of Egypt	

The Battle of Tel el Kebir between British and Egyptian forces on September 13, 1882, gave Britain control of Egypt. Egypt had long been a part of the Ottoman

Empire. Its location gave the Ottomans ready access to the Middle East and Africa. For at least a century though, Ottoman power had been in steady decline. The event that brought British forces to Egypt, however, was the completion of the Suez Canal.

In the 1860s French entrepreneur Ferdinand de Lesseps formed a company that realized what had long been advocated: construction of a sea-level canal connecting the eastern Mediterranean with the Red Sea across Egyptian territory. It opened in 1869, and de Lesseps became a French national hero. The canal quickly altered the trade routes of the world.

Because of the difficulty of securing sufficient funds for the project, however, de Lesseps had enlisted the support of the ruler of Egypt, Khedive Ismail Pasha, who had eventually subscribed to 44 percent of the shares of the company. Once the canal was constructed and in successful operation, it soon became obvious that it was an important link in the British Empire's lifeline east to India. In the 1870s fully two-thirds of the tonnage passing through the canal was British. Therefore, Great Britain could not be indifferent to its control.

Consequently, when in 1875 the khedive found himself in financial difficulties, British prime minister Benjamin Disraeli, without waiting for the consent of Parliament, boldly purchased his shares for Great Britain (176,602 of the outstanding 400,000 shares) at a cost of £4 million. By this coup he at once secured for London an influential position on the canal's board of directors.

In 1878 at the Congress of Berlin, Disraeli not only helped to halt Russia's advance into the Balkans but also strengthened Britain's own position in respect to the Suez Canal. In return for the promise of British support against Russia, the Ottoman sultan ceded to Great Britain the island of Cyprus, strategically located in the eastern Mediterranean north of Egypt.

During the following years Great Britain's ability to control and protect the Suez Canal was further increased as the result of developments in Egypt. The khedive's spending was on such an extravagant scale that the government was forced to declare bankruptcy in 1876. Ismail was then forced to accept British and French financial advisers but rebelled at this, and the Ottoman sultan in 1879 removed him and replaced him as khedive with Tewfik, Ismail's son. From 1879 Egypt was subjected to the "dual control" of France and Great Britain.

A nationalist movement soon developed in Egypt that was led by Egyptian Army officers, who were displeased with Tewfik and angered by the growing number of foreigners in the Egyptian government. In February 1881 Egyptian officers led by Colonel Ahmed Arabi staged a revolt that overthrew Tewfik under the slogan of "Egypt for the Egyptians." The presence of the allied ships off Alexandria led to disorders in Alexandria, where some 50 foreigners were murdered by an Egyptian mob on June 11, 1882.

British Mediterranean Fleet commander Vice Admiral Sir Beauchamp Seymour had eight ironclads and five gun vessels at his disposal, a force that he believed was sufficient for restoring order. On July 11, 1882, he bombarded the

Egyptian forts defending the port of Alexandria. It was the only occasion when the ironclad battleships of the mid-Victorian British Royal Navy went into action. The forts fought back, and Seymour was forced to concentrate on one of them at a time. After a bombardment of more than 10 hours, the Egyptian defenders were forced from the city. British landing parties went ashore the next day, only to discover Arabi still defiant and Egyptian forces regrouping in the surrounding countryside. Seymour landed naval brigades to hold the city until additional troops could be brought to Egypt.

London sent some 24,000 men under Lieutenant General Sir Garnet Wolseley, who let it be known that he intended to land at Aboukir Bay but then proceeded instead to land at Ismailia, at the mouth of the Suez Canal, on August 20, 1882. Although Arabi had some 60,000 men, he was forced to disperse them to defend different possible British axes of advance. Arabi established a defensive position manned by about 22,000 to 25,000 men equidistant between Cairo and the Suez Canal along a rail line connecting the two. British advance forces drove the Egyptians back into a strong defensive position some four miles in length along a ridge line at Tel el Kebir. The terrain in front of the ridge line was flat, with excellent fields of fire for Arabi's 60 artillery pieces. In front of their defensive line the Egyptians had dug a long trench some six feet wide and four feet deep.

Wolseley was impressed with the Egyptian defensive preparations and spent four days planning his attack. Discovering that the Egyptians did not man their advanced posts at night, Wolseley decided to position his forces then. The British advance began on the night of September 12–13; Wolseley allowed the men five hours to cover the 5.5 miles to the Egyptian lines. By dawn, the British were in position only 300 yards from the Egyptian lines with the sun at their backs. Wolsley had in line, from right to left, the 1st Division of English and Irish troops and the 2nd Division of Scottish Highlanders. He positioned his cavalry on both flanks. In all, Wolseley had 17,400 men.

When the Egyptians discovered the British troops they immediately opened fire, and the battle began. The two infantry divisions assaulted and managed to break the Egyptian lines, but the flanking cavalry enveloped the Egyptian lines and turned what had been an orderly Egyptian retreat into a rout. The battle was over in about two hours, although British forces pursued the Egyptians the 50 miles to Cairo. Arabi lost some 2,000 men killed and 500 wounded. The British captured all the Egyptian artillery. British casualties were 58 killed, 379 wounded, and 22 missing.

British cavalry entered Cairo on September 15, almost without opposition. Arabi surrendered, and the revolt quickly collapsed. He was subsequently tried and condemned to death but was spared and exiled to Ceylon. Although Gladstone's government formally notified other powers that the British Army would be withdrawn "as soon as the state of the country, and the organization of the proper means for the maintenance of the Khedive's authority, will admit of it," British troops remained in Egypt. The real ruler of the country was the British consul-general and high commissioner Lord Cromer, who in effect ruled Egypt for the next 23 years. British imperialists soon considered the Nile Valley part of the British Empire. The last British troops did not leave Egypt until June 1956.

References

Barthorp, Michael. *War on the Nile: Britain, Egypt, and the Sudan, 1882–1898.* Poole, UK: Blandford, 1984.

Farwell, Bryon. *Queen Victoria's Little Wars.* New York: Harper and Row, 1985.

White, Colin. "The Bombardment of Alexandria." *Mariner's Mirror* 66 (1980): 31–49.

Battle of the Yellow Sea

Date	September 17, 1894	
Location	Yellow Sea off the Yalu River in far northwestern Korea	
Opponents (* winner)	*Japanese	Chinese
Commander	Admiral Ito Yuko	Admiral Ding Ruchang (Ting Ju-ch'ang)
Approx. # Troops	14 ships: 4 heavy cruisers, 4 light cruisers, 6 torpedo boats	12 ships: 2 battleships, 4 light cruisers, 6 torpedo boats
Importance	Insures that Japan can supply its forces in Korea at will; the battle also reveals the vulnerability of unarmored wooden ships to modern steel warships	

Unlike the leaders of China, the Japanese recognized the need for their nation to Westernize, at least to the point of acquiring advanced Western military technology. This process was intended to prevent Japan from falling under the control of a Western power or powers, but by the closing decade of the 19th century Japanese leaders were ready to embark upon their own program of imperial expansion. They were especially interested in securing Korea, a tributary kingdom of China across the narrow Tsushima Strait from Japan. As a result of Japanese interference in Korean affairs, war between China and Japan began in 1894. When the showdown came the Japanese military was modern, while that of China was largely antiquated.

On July 20 Japan seized control of the Korean government. Five days later Japanese admiral Kozo Tsuboi attacked a Chinese convoy bringing reinforcements to Korea, sinking one transport and severely damaging its naval escorts. At the same time fighting began on land, and on August 1 both sides declared war. Both sides now rushed reinforcements to Korea by sea, although neither attempted to interfere with the other's resupply effort.

Chinese admiral Ding Ruchang (Ting Ju-ch'ang) had two newer ironclad battleships: the *Ding Yuen* (*Ting Yuen*) and *Zhen Yuen* (*Chen Yuen*). He also had four light cruisers and six torpedo boats. These escorted six transports carrying 4,500 men

Japanese woodblock print depicting the Japanese victory over the Chinese in the Battle of the Yellow Sea on September 17, 1894, during the Sino-Japanese War. Its victory in the war marked the rise of Japan as a major military power. (Library of Congress)

and 80 guns to the Yalu River. Simultaneously, Admiral Ito Yuko disembarked Japanese troops some 100 miles farther down the Korean coast, after which he sailed north to locate Ting's squadron.

At about 10:00 a.m. on September 17, 1894, Ito's larger force came upon Ding's ships between the mouth of the Yalu River and Haiyang Island. Ito had four heavy cruisers, four light cruisers, and six torpedo boats. Despite Ding's advantage in having the heaviest and longest-range guns in the battle (the 4 12-inch guns on each of his two battleships), Ito had the benefit of newer and faster ships and enjoyed a considerable advantage in his many 4.5-inch and 6-inch quick-firing guns, the most effective naval guns of the period. Japanese gunnery and ship handling were superior to those of the Chinese, and Japanese shells soon riddled the unprotected Chinese ships, setting their exposed wooden areas ablaze.

The Chinese lost three of their cruisers and two of their sloops. A number of Ito's ships had been hit, but only one was seriously damaged, and none were sunk. Ito feared the two larger Chinese battleships and did not press his attack. During the night the remaining Chinese vessels escaped to Lüshunkou (Lüshun Port, formerly Port Arthur).

The Battle of the Yellow Sea, also known as the Battle of the Yalu River, demonstrated that unarmored wooden ships were no match for the new steel warships. In March 1895 the Japanese took both Lüshunkou and Weihaiwei (Wei-hai-wei), fortified harbors guarding access to Beijing (Peking). China then sued for peace and, in the Treaty of Shimonoseki, ceded to Japan the island of Taiwan (Formosa) and the Liadong (Liaotung) Peninsula in southern Manchuria. China was also forced to pay an indemnity of $150 million and recognize Korea as an independent kingdom, a step toward Korea's absorption by Japan. The Japanese acquisition of a foothold on the Asian mainland was particularly distasteful to Russian leaders. Pressured by Russia, France, and Germany, Japan was forced to return the Liadong Peninsula to China. Russia's subsequent lease of the peninsula led directly to the Russo-Japanese War of 1904–1905.

References

Busch, Noel F. *The Emperor's Sword: Japan vs. Russia in the Battle of Tsushima.* New York: Funk and Wagnalls, 1969.

Evans, David C., and Mark R. Peattie. *Kaigun: Strategy, Tactics, and Technology in the Imperial Japanese Navy, 1887–1941.* Annapolis, MD: Naval Institute Press, 1997.

Inouye Jukichi. *The Japan-China War: The Naval Battle of Haiyang.* Yokahoma, Japan: Kelly and Walsh, 1895.

Battle of Manila Bay

Date	May 1, 1898	
Location	Manila Bay, off Manila on the island of Luzon in the Philippines	
Opponents (* winner)	*Americans	Spanish
Commander	Commodore George Dewey	Rear Admiral Patricio Montojo y Pasarón
Approx. # Troops	4 protected cruisers, 2 gunboats, and a revenue cutter	2 large cruisers, 5 small cruisers; shore batteries
Importance	The United States may now safely bring land forces to the Philippines, leading to the acquisition of those islands from Spain	

The Battle of Manila Bay was the decisive naval engagement of the Spanish-American War. Commodore George Dewey's U.S. Asiatic Squadron was located at the British port of Hong Kong when Dewey was informed on April 23, 1898, by British acting governor Major General Wilsone Black that war had been declared. Black then issued a proclamation of British neutrality and ordered Dewey's ships to leave Hong Kong's territorial waters by noon the next day.

Dewey repaired to Mirs Bay, an anchorage in Chinese waters, where he received a cablegram from Washington ordering him to the Philippines. The message instructed him to "commence operations at once, particularly against the Spanish fleet. You must capture vessels or destroy. Use utmost endeavors."

Dewey's squadron consisted of the protected cruisers *Olympia* (flagship; main battery of 4 8-inch and 10 5-inch guns), *Baltimore* (6 8-inch and 6 6-inch guns), *Boston* (2 8-inch and 6 6-inch guns), and *Raleigh* (1 6-inch and 10 5-inch guns);

the gunboats *Concord* (6 6-inch guns) and *Petrel* (4 6-inch guns); and the *McCulloch,* a revenue cutter that had been pressed into service. Dewey left behind the old paddle wheeler *Monocacy,* but two colliers also accompanied the squadron. Dewey was concerned about his ammunition supply, for when the squadron departed for the Philippines, the ship magazines were only about 60 percent of capacity.

An hour before the squadron sailed, former U.S. consul to the Philippines Oscar Williams briefed Dewey and his commanders on board the *Olympia.* Williams confirmed that the American squadron was superior to that of the Spanish, which would most likely be found in Subic Bay, 30 miles from Manila.

That same afternoon, April 27, the American ships departed Chinese waters. They made landfall at Cape Bolineau, Luzon, at daybreak on April 30. Dewey detached the *Boston* and *Concord,* later reinforced by the *Baltimore,* to make a quick reconnaissance of Subic Bay. The Americans soon determined that the Spanish squadron was not in evidence. Reportedly, Dewey was pleased at the news and remarked, "Now we have them."

Dewey then ordered his ships to steam to Manila Bay, which the squadron entered on the night of April 30. Dewey chose to ignore the threat of mines and the fortifications guarding the entrance to the bay. He selected Boca Grande channel, and the ships steamed in single file with as few lights as possible. Not until the squadron had passed El Fraile rock did the Spanish discover the American presence. Both sides then exchanged a few shots but without damage. The American ships were now into the bay. Detaching his two supply ships and the *McCulloch,* Dewey proceeded ahead, although he did not intend to engage the Spanish until dawn.

The Spanish had some 40 naval vessels in and around Manila, but most were small gunboats. Spanish rear admiral Patricio Montojo y Pasarón's squadron consisted of six ships: the two large cruisers *Reina Cristina* and *Castilla* of about 3,000 tons each, the latter of wood (the main battery of the *Reina Cristina* consisted of six 4.7-inch guns, while the *Castilla* mounted four 5.9-inch and two 5.7-inch guns) and five small cruisers (the *Don Juan de Austria, Don Antonio de Ulloa, Isla de Cuba, Marqués del Duro,* and *Isla de Luzon*). Each of the small cruisers was less than 1,200 tons, and none had more than four 4.7-inch guns in its main battery. Other ships were undergoing repairs. The Spanish warships were greatly inferior in armament to the ships in the American squadron. The American ships also had better-trained crews.

Montojo originally had his ships at Subic Bay during April 26–29, but its defenses were unready. The promised shore batteries were not yet in place, and the harbor entrance had not been mined. The water there was also 40 feet deep. Pessimistic about his chances and reportedly deciding that if his ships were to be sunk he would prefer it to occur in shallower water, Montojo returned to Manila Bay. His captains concurred in the decision.

To help offset his weakness in firepower, Montojo anchored his ships in Caña-cao Bay just south of Manila off the fortified naval yard of Cavite so that they might be supported by land batteries. There the water was only 25 feet deep, and if the ships were sunk or had to be scuttled, the Spanish crews would stand a better chance of escape. Believing that the Americans did not pose an immediate threat, Montojo went ashore for the night. He was alerted to the American presence by the sound of the exchange of gunfire as Dewey's ships entered the bay.

Early on the morning of May 1, only a week after the declaration of war, Dewey's ships steamed toward Manila, with the *Olympia* leading followed by the *Baltimore, Raleigh, Petral, Concord,* and *Boston.* Off Manila a little after 5:00 a.m., the Spanish shore batteries opened up with wildly inaccurate fire that inflicted no damage. The *Boston* and *Concord* returned fire. Dewey then turned his ships toward the Spanish squadron. As the American ships advanced in a single line, two Spanish mines exploded at some distance away from the *Olympia* and without effect. Closing to about 5,000 yards of the Spanish line, at 5:40 a.m. Dewey turned to his flag captain, Charles Gridley of the *Olympia,* and said, "You may fire when you are ready, Gridley."

The ships of the American squadron now closed to about 3,000 yards and turned west, running back and forth along the Spanish line and pounding it with their fire. The 150-pound shells fired by the 8-inch guns on the U.S. cruisers exacted the most damage. The Spanish ships and shore batteries responded but failed to inflict significant damage. Dewey then called a halt to assess damage and the status of ammunition stocks; at the same time he ordered breakfast served to the crews.

At 11:16 a.m. the U.S. ships stood in again to complete their work. In little more than an hour they sank the remaining Spanish vessels firing at them and secured the surrender of the naval station at Cavite. Dewey sent a message to the Spanish commander at Manila that if the shore batteries did not cease fire, he would shell the city and destroy it. Shortly thereafter, the city's guns fell silent.

The Spanish lost 167 dead and 214 wounded, all but 10 aboard the ships. The Americans later salvaged and pressed into service three of the Spanish ships. The Americans had no men killed and only 8 wounded. Rarely was a victory more cheaply obtained.

Dewey took Cavite and blockaded the city of Manila while awaiting troops to take it. On June 30 Major General Wesley Merritt arrived with 10,000 men. On August 13 the troops, assisted by naval gunfire from Dewey's squadron and Filipino guerrillas under Emilio Aguinaldo, attacked Manila. The city surrendered after a short nominal defense. In only 10 weeks the United States had secured an empire from Spain, and it was control of the ocean that enabled this. The Philippines had been secured as a bargaining chip to persuade Spain to conclude peace, but in the final agreement the United States decided to keep the islands. This decision led to a war with Filipino nationalists who wanted independence and set up the future confrontation between the United States and Japan.

References

Conroy, Robert. *The Battle of Manila Bay: The Spanish-American War in the Philippines.* New York: Macmillan, 1968.

Freidel, Frank. *The Splendid Little War.* Boston: Little, Brown, 1958.

Spector, Ronald H. *Admiral of the New Empire: The Life and Career of George Dewey.* Baton Rouge: Louisiana State University Press, 1974.

Trask, David F. *The War with Spain.* New York: Macmillan, 1981.

Battle of Omdurman

Date	September 2, 1898	
Location	Near Khartoum in central Sudan	
Opponents (* winner)	*British and Egyptians	Sudanese Dervishes
Commander	Major General Sir Herbert Kitchener	Khalifa Abdullah
Approx. # Troops	8,000 British, 17,000 Egyptians	35,000–50,000
Importance	Brings Anglo-Egyptian control of the Sudan	

In the September 2, 1898, Battle of Omdurman, British, Egyptian, and Sudanese forces defeated nationalists in the Sudan, leading to the establishment of the Anglo-Egyptian Sudan. The battle also illustrated the technological advantage of European military establishments over their brave but primitively armed opponents in the wars of imperialism that preceded World War I.

Concern over the security of the Suez Canal, Britain's lifeline to India, led the British government to send naval and land forces to Egypt in 1882. Following the Battle of Tel el Kebir on September 13, 1882, the British established their control over all Egypt. Although the khedive was still nominal ruler, the real power in the country rested with the British consul-general and high commissioner, and British imperialists soon considered the Nile Valley part of the British Empire.

From Egypt, the British were soon drawn into difficulties in the vast, poor, and hostile Sudan. Egypt had long sought to establish its control over the Upper Nile region but aroused strong opposition through actions against the slave trade and heavy taxes. In 1883 a prophet, Muhammad Ahmad ibn as-Sayyid Abd Allah, the son of a Nile boatbuilder, arose in the Sudan, calling himself the Mahdi. Soon he had thousands of warrior followers, known as Dervishes.

The Egyptian government decided to intervene to put down the uprising. Former Indian Army officer General William Hicks marched 8,500 Egyptian Army troops into the desert, only to be annihilated on November 3 at El Obeid by Sudanese forces under command of Abu Anja, one of the Mahdi's best generals. The Mahdi's reputation soared after this victory, and the entire Sudan was in revolt.

The Egyptians then sought assistance from the British government. The Egyptians still held the Nile and the city of Khartoum, at the confluence of the Blue and White Niles, but Prime Minister William Gladstone decided that the Sudan must be evacuated. To accomplish this, he sent out Major General Charles Gordon.

Gordon's nickname was "Chinese," earned for his command of the Chinese Imperial Army that put down the Taiping Rebellion in the 1860s. He had once been governor of the Sudan for the Egyptians and had taken an aggressive stance against the slave trade there. Deeply religious and eccentric, Gordon was the worst possible choice for a mission involving capitulation. He completely ignored Gladstone's original instructions and convinced the Egyptian ministry to reestablish British control in the Sudan. Gordon then proceeded up the Nile to Khartoum, where he dallied and got besieged by the Mahdists. Gladstone was furious; only after five months had passed did his government respond to public pressure and send relief forces under General Garnet Wolseley.

Wolseley's own trip up the Nile was as slow as that of Gordon. As his relief expedition neared Khartoum and after a siege lasting 317 days, on January 26, 1885, the Dervishes swept over Gordon's defenses, stormed the palace, and massacred the entire garrison, presenting Gordon's severed head to the Mahdi. On June 21, 1885, the Mahdi died. His successor, Kalifa Abdullah, and his Dervish followers completed the conquest of the Sudan, with the British this time evacuating.

Not until 1896 did the British government decide to reconquer the Sudan, part of a plan to provide a defense in depth for the Suez Canal fueled by French and Italian interest in the Sudan. Under orders from London, Egyptian army commander in chief (*sirdar*) major general (only a colonel in the British Army) Horatio Herbert Kitchener marched forces south from Egypt. Kitchener commanded six brigades of infantry. He had only four British battalions, and most of his 25,000-man force consisted of Egyptians and Sudanese. Kitchener also had some 20 Maxim guns, artillery, and river gunboats. He had a considerable supply train of camels and horses and built a rail line as he proceeded southward.

The methodical Kitchener captured Dongola on September 21, 1896, and Abu Hamed on August 7, 1897. He then defeated Mahdist forces under Osman Dinga and Khalifa Abdullah in the Battle of the Atbara River on April 7, 1898. On September 1, 1898, Kitchener arrived outside Omdurman, across the Nile from Khartoum, to face the main Mahdist army. Among those present on the British side was 23-year-old soldier and reporter Winston Churchill.

After some preliminary skirmishing, on the morning of September 2 some 35,000–50,000 Sudanese tribesmen under Abdullah attacked the British lines. The Mahdists had perhaps 15,000 rifles, with the remainder of their men armed only with spears and swords. There was no real sense of how the troops should be deployed; riflemen were merely mixed in with the spearmen and swordsmen. The riflemen were to provide cover for the others to close with the enemy and fight hand to hand in true warrior fashion. The Mahdist riflemen also fired from the hip, standing or running, rather than from the shoulder; they considered firing from the prone position to be cowardly.

In a series of charges against the British position the Mahdists were simply annihilated, although disaster was narrowly averted that afternoon when Kitchener, who thought that the fight was over and was anxious to avoid a street battle for Omdurman, tried to place his forces between the Mahdists and the capital. As they moved, Kitchener's infantry encountered a fresh force that had not participated in the earlier fighting. Fortunately for Kitchener, this attack came in separate waves. General Hector MacDonald's Sudanese brigade managed to hold the Mahdists off, and the 21st Lancers charged and defeated another force that suddenly appeared on the British right flank. After the battle it was learned that the men of the Sudanese brigade were down to an average of only two rounds apiece.

During the Battle of Omdurman the British had used their magazine rifles and Maxim guns to kill perhaps 10,000 Dervishes and wound as many more, with 5,000 taken prisoner. The cost to the British side was 48 dead and 434 wounded. Kitchener, surveying the battlefield from horseback, is said to have announced (in considerable understatement) that the enemy had been given "a good dusting." The battle led Hilaire Belloc to have the character Blood proclaim in *The Modern Traveller:*

"Whatever happens we have got
The Maxim Gun, and they have not."

The Battle of Omdurman also gave Britain control of the Sudan for all practical purposes, and made Kitchener a British national hero.

References
Barthorp, Michael. *War on the Nile: Britain, Egypt, and the Sudan, 1882–1898.* Poole, UK: Blandford, 1984.

Harrington, Peter, and Frederick A. Sharf. *Omdurman, 1898: The Eye-Witnesses Speak.* London: Greenhill Books, 1898.

Spiers, Edward M., ed. *Sudan: The Reconquest Reappraised.* London: Frank Cass, 1998.

Vandervort, Bruce. *Wars of Imperial Conquest in Africa, 1830–1914.* London: UCL Press, 1998.

Siege of Beijing

Date	June 20–August 14, 1900	
Location	Beijing (Peking) in northeastern China	
Opponents (* winner)	*Eight-Nation Alliance of Austria-Hungary, France, Germany, Great Britain, Italy, The Netherlands, Spain, and the United States	Society of Harmonious Fists (Boxers); Chinese Imperial Army
Commander	Sir Claude MacDonald	Dong Fuxiang (Tuan Fu-hsiang), General Rong Lu (Jung-lu)
Approx. # Troops	364 troops in the Beijing legations and 125 civilian volunteers; relief force of 17,000 men (total force 55,000)	Total force 50,000–100,000 Boxers; 70,000 Imperial troops
Importance	Brings the end of the Boxer Uprising (Rebellion)	

In the 19th century China suffered a series of catastrophic defeats at the hands of the Western powers and Japan. During the so-called Opium War of 1840–1842 the British defeated Chinese imperial forces. Britain had initiated the war when Chinese authorities sought to halt imports of opium from India. China was forced to cede Hong Kong to Britain and to open treaty ports in Guangzhou (Canton) in Kwangtung Province, Xiamen (Hsian-men) in Fujian (Fukien) Province, Fuzhou (Foochow) in Fujian Province, Ningbo (Ningpo) in Zhejiang (Chekiang) Province, and Shanghai in Jiangsu (Kiangsu) Province. Other countries, including the United States, demanded and received similar commercial concessions.

The Chinese soon found themselves second-class citizens in their own land. Foreigners enjoyed special privileges, including the right of extraterritoriality whereby Europeans accused of crimes against Chinese could be tried in European courts. Chinese culture was also under attack from foreign Christian missionaries.

These circumstances gave rise to Chinese nationalist societies, which the imperial government of Empress Cixi (Tz'u-hsi) encouraged. Among them was the Society of Harmonious Fists, dubbed the "Boxers" by Westerners because of its martial arts exercises. This movement, which formed in Shandong and southern Chihli (now Hebei Province), soon spread to the capital, encouraged by the antiforeign Manzhu (Manchu) clique at court.

With the Boxers came increasing violence against foreigners in China, and members of the foreign diplomatic corps in Beijing demanded that the imperial government take action. The empress promised to act but nevertheless allowed the Boxers to carry out antiforeign demonstrations in Beijing (Peking). Alarmed, the diplomats then requested that crewmen be sent to Beijing from their national naval vessels stationed at Dagu (Taku). These detachments arrived in the Chinese capital at the end of May and in early June 1900, although a larger allied contingent from Tianjin was forced to turn back. Troops of the Chinese Imperial Army under General Rong Lu (Jung-lu) also arrived at Beijing.

On June 19 Cixi demanded that the foreign legations relocate to Tianjin. The diplomatic corps requested additional time and adequate military escort. The next day, however, German minister Baron von Kettler was killed in Beijing by Boxers, and the foreign legations found themselves under siege. That same day the Chinese government declared war on the foreign governments for the Western seizure of the Dagu forts on June 17.

All the legations were located in the same area of Beijing, within the so-called Tatar City section. The ministers of Austria-Hungary, Belgium, France, Germany, Great Britain, the Netherlands, Spain, and the United States met and decided to abandon the legations belonging to Belgian and Netherlands, which were deemed too difficult to defend, and to withdraw into a quadrilateral formed by the remainder. All the women and children were collected at the large British legation, which was less exposed to attack. Defenders occupied portions of the Great Wall, which ran nearby, to observe Chinese troop movements.

Another gathering point for foreigners, isolated from the legations, was Beidang (Pei-Tang), the residence and cathedral of the Catholic archbishop of Beijing. It was defended by French sailors and some Italians. A number of European men living in Beijing as well as some Chinese assisted in the defense at Beidang and the legations. The defenders dug trenches and constructed barricades. They included only 364 foreign troops: 72 Russians, 61 British marines, 51 Italians, 50 U.S. sailors, 45 French, 31 Italians, 30 Austrians, and 24 Japanese. They had only small arms, one machine gun, and several small artillery pieces.

On the afternoon of June 20, with the deadline for the diplomats' departure past, a force that ultimately reached some 18,000 regular Chinese troops surrounded the legation quadrilateral. These regular forces opened fire on the legations, in effect making common cause with the Boxers, who were led by Dong Fuxiang (Tuan Fu-hsiang). The Chinese attacks, most of which were carried out by the Boxers, were only halfhearted, however. Then in mid-July a truce was arranged, and the empress sent in several wagons of food to the besieged, who were by then fast running out of provisions.

On August 9 the regular Chinese forces departed, leaving the siege to the Boxers, a sign that an allied relief column from Tianjin (taken by the allies in July) was on the way. Dong's troops tried to stop the foreign force from reaching Beijing during the night of August 11–12 but were rebuffed. The relieving troops were in two columns: 7,000 Japanese in the first column and 10,000 British, French, German, Italian, Russian, and U.S. troops (the first time since the American Revolutionary War that American troops had participated in an allied operation) in the second column. Russian artillery battered down the heavy gate of the Chinese City sector of Beijing and entered on the night of August 13–14. Early on the morning of August 14 the British made contact with the legations. On August 15 the imperial court fled to Sian (Xi'an) in Shaanxi (Shensi) Province, where in December it accepted allied demands.

Elsewhere, Chinese killed at least 231 foreigners, mostly missionaries, in Shanxi (Shansi). Russians at Blagovestchensk drove thousands of Chinese to their deaths in the Amur River in response to Chinese artillery fire from across that waterway. The Russians also seized southern Manchuria. German troops, who had arrived late at Beijing but were encouraged by Kaiser Wilhelm II to take reprisals, mounted three dozen punitive missions.

Repercussions for China were severe. Under the terms of the Boxer Protocol of September 1901, the imperial government was forced to apologize, punish 96 officials, allow a larger legation quarter, raze all forts, and make payment from customs collections to the foreign governments of more than 450 million taels with interest (in gold, some $740 million). Chinese leaders now realized the absolute necessity of carrying out reforms in education, the economy, and the military.

References

Bodin, Lynn E. *The Boxer Rebellion.* London: Osprey, 1996.

Esherick, Joseph W. *Origins of the Boxer Rebellion.* Berkeley: University of California Press, 1987.

Elleman, Bruce A. *Modern Chinese Warfare, 1785–1989.* New York: Routledge, 2001.

Fleming, Peter. *The Siege at Peking: The Boxer Rebellion.* New York: Dorsey, 1990.

Gernet, Jacques. *A History of Chinese Civilization.* New York: Cambridge University Press, 1994.

Martin, Christopher. *The Boxer Rebellion.* London: Aberlard-Schuman, 1968.

O'Connor, Richard. *The Boxer Rebellion.* London: Robert Hale, 1974.

Siege of Port Arthur

Date	February 8, 1904–January 2, 1905	
Location	tip of the Liaodong (Liaotung) Peninsula in southern Manchuria	
Opponents (* winner)	*Japanese	Russians
Commander	General Nogi Maresuke	Lieutenant General Baron Anatoli M. Stoessel
Approx. # Troops	80,000	40,000
Importance	A major psychological blow to the Russians, it also permits the Japanese easier supply of their land forces in Manchuria	

Port Arthur (present-day Lüshunkou, China) was the site of both an important naval battle and a siege during the Russo-Japanese War (1904–1905). Japan was victorious in its 1894–1895 war with China, and in the Treaty of Shimonoseki the Japanese forced the Chinese to cede the island of Taiwan (Formosa) and the Liao-dong (Liaotung) Peninsula in southern Manchuria, pay a heavy indemnity, and recognize Korea as an independent kingdom, in effect under Japanese control.

Russia strongly opposed Japan's acquisition of territory on the Asiatic mainland. Japan's acquisition of Korea gave it control over both sides of the Tsushima Strait, the southern outlet of the Sea of Japan, upon which the Russian Pacific port of Vladivostok was located. Moreover, Japanese control of Port Arthur and the Liaodong Peninsula would prevent Russia from obtaining a warm-water port in that region.

Assisted by France and Germany, Russia forced Japan to renounce its claim to the Liaodung Peninsula. Russia then concluded a treaty of friendship with China and secured the right to build the Chinese Eastern Railway across Manchuria to Vladivostok, a much more direct route than the circuitous Trans-Siberian Railway. In 1898 Russia also secured a 25-year lease on about 500 square miles of territory— including part of the land surrendered by Japan in 1895—at the end of the Liaodong Peninsula and the right to construct a branch rail line to connect it with the Chinese Eastern Railway at Harbin. The Japanese were furious at this development.

The Russians subsequently improved the harbor of Dalny (Dairen) for commercial use and began construction on a powerful fortress and a naval base at Port Arthur as well. Russia now had a warm-water outlet for its Trans-Siberian Railway. It also appeared that Manchuria would invariably come under Russian control.

In January 1902 Japan secured an alliance with Britain. The terms of the alliance provided for the "independence" of China and Korea but recognized Japan's special interests in the latter. The terms also provided that if either power became involved in war with a third power, the other would remain neutral. If another power or powers should join the war, however, the allied power was committed to joining the conflict. Japan then attempted to reach an agreement with Russia in 1903. St. Petersburg delayed making a definite reply, however, and Tokyo broke off diplomatic relations. The Japanese believed with considerable justification that Russia was seeking to postpone a war until it was ready. Czar Nicholas II and his advisers were certain that Japan would never dare to initiate hostilities, but the Japanese decided not to wait.

For Japan, the necessary prerequisite to a land war in Manchuria was control of the seas. Aside from a few warships at Chemulpo (Inchon), Korea, the Russians had at Vladivostok 4 first-class cruisers and 17 torpedo boats. Their most powerful ships—7 battleships and 4 cruisers—were at Port Arthur. The Japanese cut the telegraph cable between Port Arthur and Korea early on February 7, 1904. Thus, the Russians did not know of the earlier Japanese attack on Chemulpo without declaration of war.

At 11:50 p.m. local time on February 8 Japanese Combined Fleet commander Admiral Tōgō Heihachirō launched an attack against Port Arthur, sending in his destroyers in a surprise torpedo attack. The Russian squadron had just returned to Port Arthur after a period at sea and was outside the harbor. The Russian battleships *Retvizan* and *Tsarevitch* and the cruiser *Pallada* were all hit and badly damaged. The *Pallada* grounded near the harbor; both battleships attempted to make it to the dockyards but grounded in the channel.

Near noon the next day Tōgō brought up six battleships, five armored cruisers, and four protected cruisers to shell the Russian ships, shore batteries, and town from long range. The Russian ships, now anchored next to the forts, and the shore batteries replied. Only one Russian ship, the cruiser *Novik,* ventured out and fired a torpedo in the direction of the Japanese ships. Most of the Japanese vessels were hit by Russian shells, and Tōgō reluctantly ordered his ships to withdraw after about an hour.

Four Russian ships were damaged in the exchange, but all eventually returned to duty, as did the three ships badly damaged in the torpedo attack. The Japanese had suffered considerable damage to four battleships and a cruiser, among others. The Japanese sustained 132 casualties, and the Russians sustained 150 casualties. There were no pangs of conscience in Tokyo over the surprise attack, and only on February 10 did Japan formally declare war on Russia.

Frustrated at their inability to destroy the Russian naval forces at Port Arthur in their initial attack and to safeguard the lines of communication to Korea, the Japanese adopted attrition tactics at Port Arthur. On March 8, however, Russian vice admiral S. Ossipovitch Makarov took command there and initiated a series of sorties to harass the Japanese cruisers while avoiding contact with Tōgō's battleships. Both sides also laid mines, but Makarov was killed and the battleship *Petropavlovsk* was lost when he ran it over a known Japanese minefield. In all, the Russians lost one battleship and the Japanese lost two battleships to mines off Port Arthur.

The Japanese brought Port Arthur under siege from the land as well. Lieutenant General Baron Anatoli M. Stoessel commanded the Russian Port Arthur garrison of 40,000 men and more than 500 guns. During May 5–19, 1904, the Japanese Second Army, commanded by General Oku Yasukata, landed at Pitzuwu, 40 miles northeast of Port Arthur. The Japanese moved south but were halted at the Port Arthur outpost of Nanshan Hill. This key terrain feature guarded the entrance of the Liaodong Gulf and was held by 3,000 Russians.

On May 25, however, the Japanese flanked the Russian left by wading through the surf and in heavy fighting forced the garrison to withdraw. Japanese casualties were 4,500 of 30,000 men engaged, while the Russians lost 1,500 men. The capture of Nanshan Hill uncovered the port of Dairen, which became a Japanese base. Port Arthur was now cut off from the land side.

Japanese general Nogi Maresuke (who had captured Port Arthur from the Chinese in 1894) now concentrated his Third Army at Dalny. While the Second Army moved north to counter a Russian offensive, the Third Army took over the investment of Port Arthur. Three defensive lines, some of them incomplete, protected Port Arthur from the north. Stoessel, however, had insufficient food stocks for a protracted siege.

The Japanese steadily built their strength to more than 80,000 men and some 474 guns. On June 23, with his damaged ships repaired, Admiral Vilgelm Vitgeft, Makarov's successor, sortied. Tōgō, with only four battleships and a reduced cruiser force, prepared to meet the Russians, but Vitgeft returned to Port Arthur. His second attempt resulted in the August 10 Japanese victory in the Battle of the Yellow Sea in which Vitgeft was killed. Only one Russian cruiser was sunk in the battle; most of the ships made it back to Port Arthur.

The land fighting continued. On August 7–8 the Japanese attacked the hills constituting the Russian outer defenses and were victorious in hard fighting. Three weeks later, during August 19–24, the Japanese struck again. Much of the fighting was at night, with Russian searchlights and flares illuminating the attackers and machine guns exacting a frightful toll. The Japanese lost 15,000 men. Russian losses were only 3,000 men.

Nogi now called for heavy siege guns and resorted to systematic siege operations, sapping closer to the Russian positions. His third assault of September 15–30 was partially successful but failed to take its chief objective of 203 Meter Hill, the key point in the Russian defenses. In October 1904 the Japanese began shelling Port Arthur with 500-pound projectiles from 19 10.9-inch (28-centimeter) howitzers. During October 30–November 1 the Japanese mounted their fourth assault, concentrating on 203 Meter Hill, but they were again defeated with heavy losses. A fifth attack on November 26 was also repulsed at a cost of 12,000 Japanese casualties.

Finally, after an assault during November 27–December 5 that claimed 11,000 Japanese, the attackers at last took 203 Meter Hill. It overlooked the harbor only 4,000 yards away, and its fall sealed the fate of the Russian fleet. The day after taking 203 Meter Hill, the Japanese opened fire on the Russian ships in the harbor. Japanese land assaults continued against the remaining Russian forts as well; the last fell on January 1, 1905. Stoessel surrendered his 10,000 starving men the next day. The Japanese captured considerable stocks of arms and foodstuffs, a shocking testimony to Stoessel's mismanagement. Japanese losses in the siege were 59,000 killed, wounded, or missing and another 34,000 sick. The Russians suffered 31,000 casualties.

The Russian defeat at Port Arthur and in the battles at Mukden and Tsushima led to the Treaty of Portsmouth that transferred Port Arthur to Japan.

References

Connaughton, Richard Michael. *The War of the Rising Sun and the Tumbling Bear: A Military History of the Russo-Japanese War, 1904–1905.* London: Routledge, 1991.

Walder, David. *The Short Victorious War: The Russo-Japanese Conflict, 1904–5.* New York: Harper and Row, 1973.

Warner, Denis, and Peggy Warner. *The Tide at Sunrise: A History of the Russo-Japanese War, 1904–1905.* New York: Charterhouse, 1974.

Westwood, J. N. *A New Look at the Russo-Japanese War, 1904–1905.* Boulder, CO: Net-Library, 1999.

Battle of Mukden

Date	February 21–March 10, 1905	
Location	South of the city of Shenyang (formerly Mukden) in northeastern China	
Opponents (* winner)	*Japanese	Russians
Commander	General Oyama Iwao	General Alexsei Kuropatkin
Approx. # Troops	Up to 310,000	Up to 310,000
Importance	The largest land battle of the war, it leads to the Russian decision to seek peace and recognition of Japan as a major military power	

The Battle of Mukden (present-day Shenyang) was the last large battle of the Russo-Japanese War (1904–1905). The war resulted from a collision of Russian czar Nicholas II's efforts to control Manchuria and the determination of Japanese leaders to prevent this and further Japan's own expansion on the Asian mainland. Acquisition of Manchuria's rich natural resources particularly appealed to resources-starved Japan.

One of the provisions of the peace settlement imposed by Japan following its victory in the Sino-Japanese War (1894–1895) provided that China would surrender the Liaodong (Liaotung) Peninsula in southern Manchuria. Russian leaders desired the peninsula for themselves and therefore opposed the Japanese. Russia secured the support of France and Germany for its position. The governments of all three pressed the Japanese leaders, who could not contemplate war against a coalition of major European powers, to surrender the territory. Japan eventually gave up its claim to territory on the Asian mainland in return for an additional indemnity from China.

Russia then advanced its own position in China under the pretense of defending Chinese territorial integrity. In 1896 the two states concluded a treaty in which Russia agreed to aid China if it was attacked by a third power. Russia also secured economic concessions, including the right to build the Chinese Eastern Railway across Manchuria to Vladivostok. This railway, protected by Russian troops, would connect Russia's port in the Far East with inland Siberia and European Russia. In 1898 Russia also secured a lease of about 500 square miles of territory—including part of the land surrendered by Japan in 1895—at the end of the Liaodong Peninsula and the right to construct a branch line to connect this territory with the Chinese Eastern Railway at Harbin. Subsequently the Russians improved the harbor of Darien and constructed a powerful fortress and naval base at Port Arthur. Russia now had a warm-water port and an outlet for the Trans-Siberian Railway, and it appeared that Manchuria would pass under Russian control. Indeed, during the 1900 Boxer Rebellion, Russia sent troops into Manchuria apparently with a view to detaching it from China, and then failed to withdraw them.

In 1902 Japan concluded an alliance with Britain, which was also worried about Russian expansion in the Far East. The terms assured Japan that in the event of war between itself and Russia, Great Britain would remain neutral; the terms also stipulated that if any power assisted Russia in such a war, Great Britain would fight on the side of Japan.

In 1903 Japanese leaders offered the Russians a compromise. Japan would recognize Russian ascendancy in the greater part of Manchuria if Russia withdrew its troops from Manchuria, recognized Japan's right to intervene in Korea, and gave Japan the right to build a railroad from Korea into Manchuria that would connect with the Chinese Eastern Railway. When Russian leaders hesitated, Tokyo broke off diplomatic relations. Japanese statesmen believed that Russia was merely trying to postpone war until it had completed its strategic rail net in the region. The czar and his advisers anticipated a war, but they were certain that Japan would never begin it.

The Japanese, however, decided to strike before Russia was ready. On February 8, 1904, Japan launched surprise attacks on Russian warships at Chemulpo (Inchon) in Korea and at Port Arthur. Not until two days later did Japan formally declare war.

Although Russia was vastly superior to Japan in manpower and resources, it was handicapped at the outset by being unable to bring its full strength to bear. The conflict was distant from the Russian heartland, and troops and supplies sent to Manchuria still had to travel 5,000 miles over the single-track Trans-Siberian Railway. Although the Russian troops were probably not greatly inferior to the Japanese, the Russians lacked enthusiasm for the war. Russian tactics were both unimaginative and out of date, stressing massed infantry attacks that did not take into account the new machine weapons. Finally, Russian military leadership was sadly lacking. Inefficiency and corruption, which had undermined Russian armies in the past, were again present.

Japan was much better prepared for the war. It was geographically close to the theater of war and in position to place its forces in the field with a minimum of difficulty. Japan's military was well trained, well equipped, highly efficient, and ably led. Army morale was high, and the Japanese people loyally supported the war. Thanks to its attacks without declaration of war, Japan won control of the sea, which it held throughout the war. This was crucial for Japan's chances.

With the Russian fleet at Port Arthur severely crippled, Japan rushed troops into southern Manchuria. General Nogi Maresuke and his Third Army cut off Port

Arthur and drove back Russian efforts to relieve the fortress. That autumn, Japanese land forces under General Oyama Iwao engaged the main Russian forces under General Alexsei Kuropatkin. In the great Battle of Liaoyang during August 25–September 3, 1904, the Japanese lost 23,000 men against only 19,000 Russians. Kuropatkin repulsed three days of Japanese assaults, but believing that he had lost, he began a well-managed systematic withdrawal toward Mukden. During October 5–17 the two sides fought another battle at the Shao-Ho. Here the Russians lost some 40,000 men, while the Japanese 20,000 men.

On January 2, 1905, Port Arthur, blockaded by land and sea, surrendered, releasing the bulk of Nogi's Third Army for deployment north. During January 26–27 another land battle occurred at Sandepu (Heikoutai). The Russians, now reinforced to 300,000 men, took the offensive against Oyama's 220,000 Japanese. Kuropatkin was close to victory but failed to press his advantage; the battle ended in stalemate.

By the third week in February, Russian forces were drawn up along a 47-mile line south of Mukden, an important rail center in southeastern Manchuria. The Russians deployed three armies, and the Japanese deployed four. Estimates of strength vary widely, but the two sides appear to have been evenly matched in numbers, with each side fielding up to 310,000 men. The battle during February 21–March 10, 1905, saw the Japanese attacking the entrenched Russians.

Oyama's initial attacks came at the strongest point of the Russian line, against the First Army on the eastern flank. Kuropatkin sent in reserves, halting the attack. Oyama then sent Nogi's Third Army in a wide flanking maneuver across the Hun River in an attempt to turn the Russian right flank, held by the Russian Third Army under General Baron A. V. Kaulbars.

By the end of the first day's fighting the Japanese had driven the Russian right back so that it faced west, defending the rail line to the north instead of to the south. Russian reserves again blunted the Japanese attack. Attacks and counterattacks continued. Oyama then reinforced Nogi, and the Japanese again tried to outflank Kaulbars on the Russian right. In heavy fighting during March 6–8 the Russians were driven back to the point that Kuropatkin feared that his lines of communication north might be cut. On March 10 Kuropatkin withdrew his forces northward in orderly fashion on the cities of Tieling (Teih-ling) and Harbin. Casualty figures vary widely, but the Russians lost something on the order of 100,000 men and much equipment, while Japanese casualties may have totaled 70,000 men.

Kuropatkin's forces were still largely intact. Nonetheless, the heavy losses sustained at Mukden and in prior battles coupled with increasing domestic unrest in Russia gave the czar and his advisers pause. Russia's leaders made one more toss of the dice. They had already dispatched the Baltic Fleet in a voyage around the world to Vladivostok. On May 15 these ships encountered the Japanese in the Battle of Tsushima to decide whether Russia would continue the struggle.

References

Connaughton, R. M. *The War of the Rising Sun and the Tumbling Bear.* London: Routledge, 1991.

Walder, David. *The Short Victorious War: The Russo-Japanese Conflict, 1904–5.* New York: Harper and Row, 1973.

Warner, Denis, and Peggy Warner. *The Tide at Sunrise: A History of the Russo-Japanese War, 1904–1905.* New York: Charterhouse, 1974.

Yung, Louise. *Japan's Total Empire: Manchuria and the Collapse of Wartime Imperialism.* Berkeley: University of California Press, 1998.

Battle of Tsushima

Date	May 27, 1905	
Location	Straits of Tsushima	
Opponents (* winner)	*Japanese	Russians
Commander	Fleet Admiral Tōgō Heihachirō	Rear Admiral Zinovi Petrovitch Rozhdestvenski
Approx. # Troops	4 battleships, 8 cruisers, 21 destroyers, 60 torpedo boats	8 battleships, 8 cruisers, 9 destroyers, several smaller auxiliaries
Importance	Marks the end of Russia as a major Pacific power for a half century; it is also the only major decisive fleet action for steel battleships	

The Battle of Tsushima was the principal naval battle of the Russo-Japanese War (1904–1905) and one of the decisive fleet engagements in history. In the summer of 1904 the Russian government decided on one last effort to win the war and sent the Baltic Fleet, renamed the 2nd Pacific Squadron, on a voyage around the world to the Far East. If the Russians could gain control of the sea, they could cut off Japanese forces in Manchuria and bombard Japanese coastal cities, forcing Japan from the war. On October 15 Rear Admiral Zinovi Petrovitch Rozhdestvenski's 36 warships set out on what would be a seven-month-long odyssey. The most powerful units were the four new 13,500 ton Borodino-class battleships: the *Borodino, Alexander III, Orel,* and *Kniaz Suvarov* (flagship).

The voyage went badly from the start. On October 21 off the Dogger Bank in the North Sea, jittery Russian crews opened fire on their own cruiser, the *Aurora,* and the British Hull fishing fleet, mistaking them for Japanese torpedo boats and sinking several trawlers. This incident almost brought war with Britain.

After the fleet rounded Portugal, some ships proceeded eastward through the Mediterranean Sea and the Suez Canal, while the main detachment continued

BATTLE OF TSUSHIMA STRAIT, MAY 27–28, 1905

GROZNY

ULLUNG ISLAND

IZUMRUD

DMITIRI DONSHOI

LIANCOURT ROCKS

BIEDOVY
(Surrenders)

MAIN FLEET
Dawn May 28

Surrender
10:30 AM
MAY 28

0   50 mi
0   50 km

N

RUISTRY   SVETLANA

K O R E A

CRUISERS
Dawn May 28

USHAKOV

Sea of
Japan

Masan

Pusan

ALMUZ

BRAVY

SISSOI VELIKL

NAVARIN

NAKHINOV

VLADIMIR MONOMAKH

Takeshiki

ENQUIST

HONSHU

12:00

OKINOSHIMA

Shimonoseki

TSUSHIMA

Western Channel

4:45 AM
May 29

IKISHIMA

Eastern Channel

KYUSHU

Sasebo

Korea Strait

Nagasaki

⊗	Sunk Russian ship
●	Russian ship
→	Russian main body
—	Isolated Russian ships
····	Japanese squadron
◉	Naval base
✴	Main battle site

south around Africa. With the British (a Japanese ally) refusing to supply coal, the Russians were forced to secure it from German colliers. The lack of coaling stations led Rozhdestvenski to order the ships to take on whatever they could, placing it in every possible space and precluding training and gunnery practice.

Reunited at Madagascar, on March 16 the fleet started across the Indian Ocean, refueling five times at sea; this was an unprecedented feat. Rozhdestvenski hoped to get to Vladivostok without battle, but the fleet made one last stop to take on supplies and coal at Cam Ranh Bay in French Indochina. The Russian ships then slowly made their way north through the South China Sea and up the Chinese coast.

Rozhdestvenski sent most of his auxiliary vessels to anchor at the mouth of the Yangtse River, and he timed his advance through the Tsushima Straits to be at night. He also sent two cruisers toward the east coast of Japan in an attempt to persuade the Japanese that the entire fleet would follow.

At sea for eight months and halfway around the world from their Baltic bases, the Russians would meet fleet admiral Tōgō Heihachirō's modern, efficient, battle-tested Japanese fleet in its home waters. Tōgō gambled that Rozhdestvenski would choose the most direct route to Vladivstok, by means of the Tsushima Straits, and planned a trap there. The Japanese also had cut off Vladivosotok by sowing 715 mines at the entrance to Peter the Great Bay.

On the night of May 26–27 Japanese picket ships sighted the Russian fleet in the straits. Tōgō's ships immediately left their bases, dumping coal as they went to increase their speed. Tōgō relied on radio messages to keep informed of the location of the Russians. (Tsushima was the first naval battle in which the radio was used in action.) The total Russian fleet consisted of eight battleships, eight cruisers, nine destroyers, and several smaller vessels. The firepower of the two fleets was slightly to the Russian advantage, but this was offset by the fact that the Japanese crews were far superior to the Russians in gunnery.

Tōgō had 4 battleships, 8 cruisers, 21 destroyers, and 60 torpedo boats. Many factors favored Tōgō. His ships had been recently overhauled and repaired. The Japanese ships also possessed the important advantage of superior speed; they were, on the average, about 50 percent faster than the Russian vessels, even the newest of which were fouled from the long voyage. Tōgō's men were fresh, eager, and battle-tested and were sailing in their own waters and led by highly skilled officers.

On the afternoon of May 27, trailed by Japanese cruisers, the 2nd Pacific Squadron sailed past Tsushima Island. When the Russian ships came out of some fog at 1:19 p.m., Tōgō in the battleship *Mikasa* to the northeast at last sighted his prey. The Russian ships were steaming in two columns. Rozhdestvenski had his flag in the *Suvarov,* the lead ship in the starboard column.

The Russians assumed that Tōgō would turn south and bridge the gap, allowing his battleships to fire on the weaker Russian divisions, but this would have left the Russian ships headed toward Vladivostok, with the Japanese moving in the opposite direction. Instead, Tōgō made a daring move, ordering his cruisers to make a

270-degree turn to the northeast to cut the Russians off from Vladivostok. This brought the Japanese ships onto a course parallel to that of the Russians; with their superior speed they would turn east and cross the Russian "T" at leisure.

This maneuver carried grave risks, because during the long turn Tōgō exposed his whole line of ships to the full broadsides fire of the Russian fleet. Seconds after the *Mikasa* began its turn, the *Suvarov* opened fire at a range of about 6,400 yards. Other Russian ships followed suit. As the fleets formed into two converging lines, each blasted away at the other. Rozhdestvenski altered course slightly to port, reducing the range, but the Russian fire rapidly deteriorated as the range closed. The Russians scored few direct hits.

Russian fire damaged three Japanese ships, hit many others, and forced a cruiser out of the battle line. But soon the *Suvarov* was on fire, and another battleship, the *Oslyabya,* was holed in its side. The Japanese concentrated their fire on these two crippled battleships, and their superior gunnery gradually told.

By nightfall the Japanese victory was nearly complete. Wounded in the battle, Rozhdestvenski yielded command to Rear Admiral Nicholas Nebogatov. That night Tōgō sent his destroyers and torpedo boats to finish off those Russian vessels that were not already sunk or that had escaped. Isolated fighting continued throughout the night, but by the next day the Japanese had sunk, captured, or disabled eight Russian battleships.

Of 12 Russian ships in the battle line, 8 were sunk, including 3 of the new battleships; the other 4 had been captured. Of the cruisers, 4 were sunk, 1 was scuttled, 3 limped into Manila and were interned, and 1 made it to Vladivostok. Of the destroyers, 4 were sunk, 1 was captured, 1 was interned at Shanghai, and 2 reached Vladivostok. Three special service ships were sunk, 1 was interned at Shanghai, and 1 escaped to Madagascar. Tōgō lost only 3 torpedo boats. Although other ships suffered damage, all remained serviceable. The Russians lost 4,830 men killed or drowned and just under 7,000 taken prisoner. Japanese personnel losses were 110 killed and 590 wounded.

In just one day Russia ceased to be a major Pacific power. Fifty years would pass before it regained status at sea. The battle confirmed Japan as the premier military power of the Far East and also led the Japanese to believe that wars could be turned by one big battle. Ironically, the Battle of Tsushima was also the only major decisive fleet action in the history of the steel battleship. Only the gun had counted. In the future, underwater or aerial weapons would often exercise the dominant influence at sea.

Tōgō's victory at Tsushima forced the Russian decision to sue for peace. Although Russia might have raised new armies to continue the war, popular discontent and revolutionary outbreaks threatened the government's very survival.

At U.S. president Theodore Roosevelt's invitation, a peace conference opened at Portsmouth, New Hampshire. By terms of the Treaty of Portsmouth of September 5, 1905, Russia's lease of the Liaodong (Liaotung) Peninsula, its railway from Port

Arthur north to Changchun, and its mining rights in southern Manchuria were all transferred to Japan, converting southern Manchuria into a Japanese sphere of influence. Russia recognized Japan's preponderant interest in Korea and its right to control and protect the Korean government. In addition, Russia surrendered to Japan the southern half of Sakhalin Island, which Japan had occupied during the war.

The treaty, favorable as it was to Japan, was not popular there. The Japanese government had not obtained the indemnity it had sought, but the Japanese people did not know that the country was close to running out of financial resources to continue the war.

References

Busch, Noel F. *The Emperor's Sword: Japan vs. Russia in the Battle of Tsushima.* New York: Funk and Wagnalls, 1969.

Grove, Eric. *Big Fleet Actions: Tsushima, Jutland, Philippine Sea.* London: Arms and Armour, 1995.

Hough, Richard. *The Fleet That Had to Die.* New York: Viking, 1958.

Westwood, J. N. *Witnesses of Tsushima.* Tokyo: Sophin University, 1970.

Siege of Liège

Date	August 5–16, 1914	
Location	City of Liège, east central Belgium	
Opponents (* winner)	*Germans	Belgians
Commander	General der Infanterie Otto von Emmich	General Gérard Mathieu Leman
Approx. # Troops	60,000	25,000
Importance	Belgian resistance here and elsewhere delays the German military timetable by only a few days, but this is crucial given the tight time requirements of the German strategic plan	

The Belgian city of Liège is located on the Meuse River and is the gateway to Belgium for any force invading from Germany. The city dominates the narrow gap between the so-called Limburg Appendix to the north and the Ardennes Forest to the south, guarding access to the rich Brabant Plain. The Meuse itself is also a formidable barrier; it is some 200 yards wide at Liège, with steep banks and boggy lowlands.

At the beginning of the 20th century, German Army chief of staff Generaloberst Alfred von Schlieffen recognized that if a general European war occurred, Germany would have to fight both France and Russia. Because France had the more powerful military, Schlieffen planned to concentrate the bulk of German military resources against that country to defeat it quickly and then turn against the Russian

Army, which would be slower to mobilize. In Schlieffen's view, the best way to defeat France quickly was a broad-front invasion from Belgium, and the key was the reduction of Liège.

In the crisis that followed the assassination of Austrian archduke Franz Ferdinand in Sarajevo by Serbian terrorists on June 28, 1914, Russia mobilized its military in support of Serbia in the hope of bluffing down Austria-Hungary. This triggered the German war plan and that country's declarations of war against Russia on August 1 and France on August 3. Consequently, Liège became the first major German military objective in the war.

The city of Liège was ringed by 12 forts, 6 large and 6 smaller forts, located on high ground and divided equally between each bank of the river. The forts were four to five miles from the center of Liège and two to three miles from each other. Built in the 1880s at the insistence of King Leopold II and under the supervision of military architect Henri Brialmont, the forts (and those built at the same time at Namur) were sufficiently strong to resist shells from any weapon of the time. They had extensive underground chambers and were capped with massive concrete crowns. They were also surrounded by wide and deep dry moats defended by earthen breastworks.

The dozen forts contained a total of 400 artillery pieces, the largest being 210-millimeter (mm) howitzers. These large guns were mounted in rotating, disappearing cupola turrets. Between the forts Belgian general Gérard Mathieu Leman's 3rd Infantry Division manned field fortifications. Three regiments garrisoned the forts themselves, the largest of which each held 400 men. In all, the Belgians had some 25,000 troops at Liège. They hoped to hold the Germans as long as possible in the area before and between the forts and then withdraw toward other forces forming on the Gette River, 30 miles to the west.

The Germans planned to knock out the forts and capture Liège within three days. Chief of the German General Staff generaloberst Helmuth von Moltke ("Moltke the Younger") hoped to defeat France in only 39 days, so he could tolerate no delay here. The Germans hoped to accomplish this while their First Army and Second Army were still completing their concentration. These two armies would then pass on either side of Liège on their way to France. For the reduction of Liège the Germans allocated 60,000 German troops from Generaloberst Karl von Bülow's Second Army, consisting of the 2nd and 4th Infantry divisions (a total of six infantry brigades) and the 9th Cavalry Division. General der Infanterie Otto von Emmich commanded this attacking force, designated the Army of the Meuse. Generalmajor Erich Ludendorff, the staff officer who had developed the German plan, accompanied the attackers as liaison between Emmich and Bülow.

The Germans advanced cautiously. Although the Belgians blew the main bridges over the Meuse, the attackers crossed north of the city at Visé, arriving in the wooded hills near the forts on August 4. They encountered unexpectedly strong Belgian resistance. During the night of August 5 Emmich's troops attacked but sustained heavy losses for little or no progress. That same night German Army zeppelin *LZ.6* dropped converted artillery shells rigged as bombs on Liège. It was the first strategic bombing raid in history, but it was also ineffective.

Gradually the weight of German numbers and superior firepower told, and the Belgian 3rd Division began to withdraw. Some of the defenders fell back on the resisting forts; most retired to the riverbanks and the city itself. Crossing the Meuse at Visé and Lixhe to the north of Liège, the Germans moved between forts Barchon and Pontisse, surrounding them.

After two days of fierce fighting, on August 6 Liège itself came under fire, and conditions for civilians in the city became increasingly difficult. At 7:30 a.m. on the 6th Leman ordered his 3rd Division to withdraw on the Gette. The last troops departed the nearly surrounded city the next day. At 6:00 a.m. on August 7 the German 14th Brigade entered Liège with the help of a Belgian traitor. The Germans soon reached the Belgian headquarters, but Leman had escaped to Fort Loncin. Although Liège itself had surrendered, the forts kept up constant artillery fire on the roads that would have to be taken by the Second Army. The Germans therefore could not continue their advance without first taking the forts.

On August 8 after four bloody and frustrating days of infantry assaults against the forts, German heavy artillery, brought up expressly for that purpose, opened up. Fort Brachon came under fire from heavy 305-mm (12-inch) Skoda siege howitzers and surrendered at 4:30 p.m. that same day. The Germans then moved the heavy howitzers into position to fire on Fort d'Evegnée. They opened fire on it the evening of August 10, and the fort surrendered the next morning. From August 12 even heavier, although less mobile, guns became available in German 420-mm (16.5-inch) Krupp "Big Bertha" howitzers. Fort Pontisse was the first victim of their 1,700-pound shells. One after another, the forts were destroyed by the German heavy weapons.

Conditions inside the forts were appalling: ventilation was soon inadequate, shells destroyed plumbing and released sewer gases, water was scarce, and concussions from the huge explosions took a heavy toll on the defenders. Three-quarters of the garrison at Pontisse died before the wounded officer left in command surrendered it on August 13. That same day Embourg and Chaudfontaine fell. At the latter fort, hundreds of defenders died when a German shell struck its magazine.

The remaining forts fell one after the other. Leman commanded at Fort Loncin until August 15, when its magazine exploded, wounding all the defenders. The Germans carried Leman unconscious from the debris. The two remaining forts of Hollogne and Flemalle surrendered on August 16. On August 17 the Second Army implemented the next stage of the German war plan.

The siege of Liège marked the rise of Ludendorff. He had taken a leading role in the siege and secured the surrender of the city. By 1916 Ludendorff was the first quartermaster general of the German Army, its de facto chief of staff with a major say over military operations. The fall of Liège also convinced many observers that forts could not withstand concerted attack. This led French Army commander General Joseph J. C. Joffre to remove artillery from the Verdun fortress complex and send it elsewhere, with unfortunate consequences for the French in February 1916. Finally, Belgian resistance at Liège and throughout the country may have delayed the German timetable by only a few days, but this was crucial given the tight time requirements of the Schlieffen Plan. Widespread German atrocities in Belgium also provided the Allied side with both an example and a cause.

References

Gliddon, Gerard. *1914*. Stroud, Gloustershire, UK: Sutton, 1997.

Hilditch, A. Neville. *The Stand of Liège*. London: Oxford University Press, 1915.

Tuchman, Barbara W. *The Guns of August*. New York: Macmillan, 1962.

Battle of Tannenberg

Date	August 26–31, 1914	
Location	Tannenberg, East Prussia (modern Poland)	
Opponents (* winner)	*Germans (Eighth Army)	Russians (Second Army)
Commander	Generaloberst Paul von Beckendorff und von Hindenburg	General Aleksandr V. Samsonov
Approx. # Troops	165,000	205,000
Importance	It and the Battle of the Masurian Lakes help the Germans survive the early months of the war on the Eastern Front and are a tremendous psychological blow to the Russians, casting serious doubts as to their military capabilities.	

The Battle of Tannenberg in East Prussia at the beginning of World War I (1914–1918) revealed serious Russian military shortcomings, above all in leadership. French and Russian prewar military planning was based on the presumption that Germany would deploy the vast bulk of its military strength west against France. Both powers agreed that Russia would have to strike hard and fast to divert some German strength east. In joint staff talks, the two powers agreed that each would launch a massive offensive against Germany, with Russia launching its offensive on the 15th day following the start of mobilization.

While some speculate that the ensuing rapid Russian offensive actions were evidence of self-sacrifice, they actually reflected common sense. An immediate Russian invasion of East Prussia nonetheless carried substantial risk. Even though the Russian Army outnumbered German forces in East Prussia by almost three to one and that historic province seemed vulnerable to invasion from both the east and the south, the Russians were sharply lacking in logistical support.

General Yakov Zhilinsky, commander of the Russian Northwest Front Group, had at his disposal two large armies: the First Army, commanded by General Pavel K. Rennenkampf, and the Second Army, led by General Aleksandr V. Samsonov. Both men had undistinguished records. Worse, they hated one another. Each of the two armies contained five corps totaling some 300,000 men, but many of the men did not have rifles or even boots. The Russians were also hindered by poor maps, and they had exceptionally limited communications capability.

The Masurian Lakes presented a formidable geographical barrier, and the Russian strategic plan called for Rennenkampf's army to move west north of the lakes, while Samsonov's army struck west south of that barrier. The two armies would then link up in the vicinity of Allenstein, wipe out the German forces caught between them, and drive on Berlin. For the plan to succeed, the two armies would have to keep pace, but because of the lakes they would be unable to support one another or even maintain contact.

The German strategic plan presumed a slow Russian mobilization, delayed further by the poorly developed Polish road and rail net. The German Eighth Army in East Prussia consisted largely of garrison troops and reserve units and totaled only 13 divisions. Its commander, Generaloberst Maximilian von Prittwitz und Gaffron, was incompetent. Fortunately for the Germans, his deputy chief of staff, Colonel Max Hoffmann, was an officer of great ability. It was he who formulated the plan for the German victory at Tannenberg.

Prittwitz's orders called for him to defend East Prussia in the unlikely event of a Russian attack. If that proved impossible, he was to retreat to the Vistula, where a permanent defensive line would be held until help arrived from the West. Thus, the German Oberste Heeresleitung (High Command, or OHL) was willing to cede, temporarily, much of East Prussia.

Germany declared war on Russia on August 1, and at dawn on August 17 Rennenkampf's First Army (6.5 infantry and 5 cavalry divisions) began crossing the East Prussian border on a 35-mile front. Its objective was the fortified city of Königsberg to the west. Two days later Samsonov's Second Army also crossed the frontier. It was to make its way around the Masurian Lakes toward Danzig.

The first fighting occurred on the afternoon of August 17 just inside the East Prussian frontier when units of the German I Corps under General der Infanterie Hermann von François blocked the Russian advance. François deliberately disobeyed Prittwitz's instructions to retire to Gumbinnen, where the Germans had established a preliminary defensive line. Instead, he rashly attacked three advancing Russian corps at Stallupönen. This inconclusive battle worked to the German advantage, for it heightened Rennenkampf's innate caution.

The Germans enjoyed a significant advantage in intelligence collection. Not only did they receive information via aircraft reconnaissance, but they were also able to intercept Russian radio communications. The poor training and illiteracy of

Russian radio operators precluded mastering codes, and there was insufficient wire. As a result, Russian Army communications were broadcast by radio in the clear. The Germans knew the orders from Stavka (the Russian high command) as soon as the Russian field commanders knew them.

On August 19 Rennenkampf halted to allow Samsonov to catch up. At the same time there was growing dissension at German headquarters between Prittwitz, who was showing signs of panic, and Hoffmann, who recognized Russia's weaknesses. Prittwitz finally gave way and authorized an attack against Rennenkampf, which took place on August 20 at Gumbinnen. Despite initial German success, the Russians held.

Prittwitz now learned of Samsonov's advance to the south. Conflicting intelligence reports led Prittwitz to believe that a third Russian army had invaded, and sensing disaster, he ordered a retreat to the Vistula. He also informed OHL at Koblenz that he might not be able to hold even that line.

Hoffmann, however, understood that Rennenkampf's army was in disarray and posed no threat. Hoffmann conceived a plan to turn the entire German force against Samsonov that would take advantage of German interior lines and superior railroad net. This plan, to which Prittwitz consented, became known as the Tannenberg Maneuver, a classic example of mass, surprise, and economy of force. Hoffmann would send the bulk of German forces opposing Rennenkampf south to encircle and destroy Samsonov's army before Rennenkampf became aware of what was happening. If successful against the Russian Second Army, German forces could then reconcentrate in the Insterburg Gap and destroy the First Army.

Unaware of Prittwitz's change of heart, chief of the German General Staff Generaloberst Helmuth von Moltke sacked him. The Eighth Army's new commander was 68-year-old Generaloberst Paul von Beckendorff und von Hindenburg, a Prussian Junker recalled from retirement. Generalmajor Erich Ludendorff, celebrated for his role in the capture of the Belgian fortress city of Liège, became his chief of staff. Hindenburg and Ludendorff drew up a plan nearly identical to that already devised by Hoffmann. Ultimately three German corps—I Corps under François, XVII Corps under General August von Mackensen, and I Reserve under Generalleutant Otto von Below—comprising the bulk of German forces in East Prussia moved south by train to join XX Corps under General der Artillerie Friedrich Scholtz, which was already in position near the southern border.

The plan was extraordinarily daring, for it left only a single cavalry division in the north to keep watch on Rennenkampf. The two Russian armies greatly outnumbered the German Eighth Army, and had Rennenkampf moved his army west and then south, there would have been nothing to prevent him from taking the Eighth Army from the rear. But Rennenkampf sat in place. The Germans named the resultant August 26–31 engagement the Battle of Tannenberg, after one of the towns in the area. This was to "reverse" a 1410 defeat of the Teutonic Knights at the hands of Polish and Ukrainian forces.

Zhilinsky was unaware of German intentions. He blithely assumed that Rennenkampf and Samsonov were coordinating their movements when in fact the two had lost contact. Zhilinsky urged Samsonov to drive to the Vistula and close the pincers around the Germans, but Samsonov replied that his troops had no rations and were near exhaustion. Samsonov also assumed that Rennenkampf protected his northern flank.

The opposing forces came into contact on August 23. The Eighth Army had some 165,000 men and the Second Army some 205,000 men, but the Second Army was dangerously spread out over a 60-mile front with its two wings separated from its center. The main German attack opened on August 26 when Mackensen's and Below's corps struck the exposed Russian northern flank. François's corps then struck from the south. By August 28 the Germans had turned both Russian flanks, dooming the Second Army.

Moltke, apprehensive about the battle's outcome, offered reinforcements from the Western Front. Ludendorff protested that they were not needed and pointed out that in any case they would arrive too late. Moltke insisted, and on August 25 he withdrew five divisions from the critical German right wing in Belgium and sent them east by rail, inadvertently helping to save France.

Rennenkampf was oblivious to what was transpiring to his south. Zhilinsky, now suspecting the worst, repeatedly urged him to attack the Germans from the north, but to no avail. Rennenkampf continued to inch forward, unaware that only a light cavalry screen opposed him.

On August 29 Samsonov ordered his two central corps to retreat through the woods to the Russian frontier, but it was too late. Only one 15-mile corridor along the Omulev River remained open. German artillery wiped out three Russian corps in the center. On the afternoon of August 30 a despondent Samsonov committed suicide. Exhausted and starving, his men surrendered by the thousands. On the night of August 30–31 some Russian units that had been without food or water for several days tried to break out. Illuminated by searchlights, they were cut down by German machine gun and artillery fire.

The Battle of Tannenberg was a Russian disaster. The Russian Army sustained 122,000 casualties, including some 90,000 taken prisoner. The Russians also lost 500 guns. German losses were between 10,000 and 15,000 men.

The German Eighth Army, now significantly reinforced by Moltke's Western Front additions, then wheeled north to engage the First Army. Although the Russians still held a numerical advantage, this was offset by the psychological lift that the Germans gained from Tannenberg and their knowledge of Russian plans through radio intercepts. Rennenkampf dug in, taking advantage of natural obstacles. What is known as the First Battle of the Masurian Lakes opened on September 7, and the fighting became general two days later. Rennenkampf managed to disengage under cover of a two-division counterattack, preventing an envelopment, and on September 13 his forces regained the Russian border. The Russians lost another 100,000 men killed or wounded, however, along with 45,000 taken prisoner and 150 guns. German casualties were around 70,000 men. Zhilinsky was sacked, but Rennenkampf retained his command.

The Russians could replace the men lost in these twin defeats, but it would be a long time before they would come up with trained officers and noncommissioned officers. Concurrent Russian and Serbian victories against Austro-Hungarian forces in Galicia and Serbia disguised the immediate impact of the Battle of Tannenberg, although Allied confidence in Russia was badly shaken. On the German side there was renewed confidence in victory and in generals Hindenburg and Ludendorff to achieve it.

References

Asprey, Robert B. *The German High Command at War: Hindenburg and Ludendorff Conduct World War I.* New York: William Morrow, 1991.

Herwig, Holger H. *The First World War: Germany and Austria-Hungary, 1914–1918.* New York: St. Martin's, 1997.

Showalter, Dennis. *Tannenberg: Clash of Empires.* Hamden, CT: Archon, 1991.

Stone, Norman. *The Eastern Front, 1914–1917.* New York: Scribner, 1975.

Sweetman, John. *Tannenberg, 1914.* London: Cassell, 2002.

First Battle of the Marne

Date	September 5–12, 1914	
Location	Marne River, east and northeast of the city of Paris, France	
Opponents (* winner)	*French and British	Germans
Commander	General Joseph J. C. Joffre (French); Field Marshal Sir John French (British)	Generalobersts Karl von Bülow; Alexander von Kluck; and Albrecht, Duke of Württemberg
Approx. # Troops	About 1 million men	More than 1 million men
Importance	Upsets the German strategic plan and denies them the quick victory they sought on the Western Front, which they probably need to win the war	

In August 1914 when Germany declared war on Russia, Germany immediately faced the dilemma of fighting a two-front war, for Russia was allied with France. German military strategists had long known of that military pact and decided to meet the strategic dilemma by concentrating the bulk of their army first against France. Only after the defeat of France, which the Germans expected to achieve quickly, would the army be redirected against Russia. Russia's plan to complete a strategic rail that would enable it to concentrate its resources more quickly against

Germany was one factor that brought war in 1914, although the actual German declaration of war was driven by the Russian decision to mobilize its forces against Austria-Hungary. If Russia was allowed time to mobilize, this would nullify the entire German war plan. Germany declared war against Russia on August 1, 1914, and against France on August 3.

The broad outlines of the German war plan are usually attributed to Generaloberst Alfred von Schlieffen, chief of the German General Staff during 1891–1906. Schlieffen's offensive scheme was probably doomed in any case, but his successor, Generaloberst Helmuth von Moltke ("Moltke the Younger") made two modifications that proved fatal. Schlieffen had an overwhelming concentration on the right wing of German forces that would invade first Belgium and then France. These German armies were to secure the English Channel ports and then sweep around Paris and drive French forces back against German Lorraine.

With French plans to invade Alsace and Lorraine in the event of war an open secret, Moltke assigned new army units that came on line in the years before the war to the left wing in order to strengthen that sector. This meant that when war came, the weight of German forces would not be 59 divisions for the right wing north of Metz and 9 for the left wing but rather 55 divisions on the right and 23 on the left. This adjustment was sufficient to repel the French forces invading Lorraine in August 1914, but the French units could then be redeployed against the main German armies to the north.

Moltke's second mistake was to misread the threat posed by Russia, which was faster to mount an offensive than anticipated. While the campaign against France was in progress, Moltke detached five divisions (some 80,000 men) from the right wing and sent them east. These troops were in transit at the time of the Battle of Tannenberg.

The heavily defended French frontier with Lorraine posed a formidable obstacle for an attacker, and the quickest way for the Germans to get at France was through neutral Belgium. The Belgian government rejected German demands for transit across its territory, forcing Germany to subdue that little country by force of arms, an act that brought previously neutral Great Britain into the war. Subduing Belgium upset the German timetable, but two weeks later they launched their invasion of France.

The British government meanwhile dispatched five divisions, virtually all of its regular army, to France. The small British Expeditionary Force (BEF), commanded by Field Marshal Sir John French, bought valuable time for the Western Allies to mobilize their resources, but everywhere the Allies were driven back. While to the north French Army units retreated in good order, French general Joseph J. C. Joffre saw his offensive into Lorraine repulsed by two German armies. He then put together a new army—the Sixth Army, commanded by General Michel Maunoury— to guard the capital while he regrouped his remaining forces. Although the Germans seemed to be enjoying great success in their advance, they were exhausted from the 300-mile march, and the French could rely on their excellent railroad net to bring up men and supplies.

By September 4 five German armies pressed along a line that sagged below the Marne River east and northeast of the French capital of Paris. These forces were, however, thinned by men left behind in Belgium or siphoned off to the Eastern Front, and along the Marne the Allies actually enjoyed a slight numerical advantage.

German First Army commander Generaloberst Alexander von Kluck meanwhile had taken a momentous decision. Believing his forces too weak to swing west and south of Paris as provided in the original plan, he ordered his army to swing east of the French capital to roll up the flank of the retreating French Fifth Army. The speed of his advance moved him ahead of Generaloberst Karl von Bülow's Second Army and exposed Kluck's right flank to the French Sixth Army and the Paris garrison.

Aerial reconnaissance identified the exposed German flank. Military governor of Paris General Joseph Gallieni, who had charge of defense of the capital, won approval from Joffre for an attack by the Sixth Army, then under his control, north of the Marne. Joffre personally went to Field Marshal French's headquarters and there secured British support. Kluck, believing that the French and British were still in retreat and as yet unaware of the French Sixth Army's presence, continued to press his advance and disregarded an order from Moltke to protect Bülow's right flank, which he knew would halt his advance for two days.

On the afternoon of September 5, the Sixth Army's advance guard clashed with part of Kluck's First Army on the Ourcq River north of Meaux. The resulting contest was one of history's most decisive battles. Ranging from Belfort to north of Paris, the engagement involved more than 2 million men on the two sides. That night Joffre ordered all the Allied left-wing armies to turn and launch full-scale attacks on the Germans. His order, read to the men at first light on September 6, is as follows:

> Now, as the battle is joined on which the safety of the country depends, everyone must be reminded that this is no longer the time for looking back. Every effort must be made to attack and throw back the enemy. A unit which finds it impossible to advance must, regardless of cost, hold its ground and be killed on the spot rather than fall back. In the present circumstances, no failure will be tolerated. (Tuchman, *The Guns of August,* 434)

Kluck, with his army split facing south on the Marne River and west on the Ourcq, now became aware of his grave situation. He ordered the rest of his army north to the Ourcq and turned to deal with the Sixth Army. In fighting during September 7–9, Kluck forced the French onto the defensive. With General Michel Maunoury's

Sixth Army fighting desperately to hold, Gallieni commandeered some 600 Parisian taxicabs to transport 6,000 men to the front. Although the actual impact of these reinforcements does not match the postevent mythology, it did symbolize the linkage between Paris and the battle only 30 miles away.

When Kluck maneuvered on September 7 to meet Maunoury's threat, a gap of some 30 miles opened between his army and that of Bülow. Into this gap moved 20,000 men of the BEF, along with elements of General Franchet d'Esperey's French Fifth Army. The next day Moltke, at German headquarters in Luxembourg, sent a trusted staff officer, Lieutenant Colonel Richard Hentsch, to visit commanders in the field and assess the situation. Moltke instructed Hentsch that if he discovered that the BEF had crossed the Marne and was moving into the gap between the First Army and the Second Army, he was to order Bülow back to the Aisne River. Hentsch had sweeping powers to make whatever adjustments seemed appropriate.

It is a compliment to the German staff system that so junior an officer could have such authority. On September 9 after Hentsch had reviewed the situation with a deeply pessimistic Bülow and other commanders, Hentsch concurred with Bülow's decision to order the Second Army to withdraw to the Aisne. Kluck's position was thus untenable, and he too had to withdraw to the Aisne. By September 9 the Germans had fallen back all along the front. The battle ended three days later.

German losses in the First Battle of the Marne are unknown, but the allies captured at least 15,000 prisoners and 36 guns. The British sustained 1,700 killed, and the French around 80,000 killed. Probably about a quarter of those engaged— roughly 250,000 men on each side—were casualties.

The tragedy of the Marne, from the French point of view, was that Joffre was unable to exploit his victory. The Germans retreated in good order; French troops were always too few and too late. Nevertheless, what the French soon called the "Miracle of the Marne" upset the German plans and denied Germany the quick victory it needed to win the war.

References

Barnett, Correlli. *The Swordbearers: Supreme Command in the First World War.* Bloomington: Indiana University Press, 1963.

Blond, Georges. *The Marne.* Translated by H. Eaton Hart. 1966; reprint, London: Prion Books, 2002.

David, Daniel. *The 1914 Campaign.* New York: Military Press, 1987.

Strachan, Hew. *The First World War,* Vol. 1, *To Arms.* New York: Oxford University Press, 2001.

Tuchman, Barbara W. *The Guns of August.* New York: Macmillan, 1962.

Dardanelles Campaign

Date	February 19–March 22, 1915	
Location	Dardanelles, Turkey	
Opponents (* winner)	*Ottomans	British, French
Commander	General Otto Liman von Sanders	Vice Admiral Sackville Carden; Rear Admiral John de Robeck
Approx. # Troops	Unknown; some 100 shore guns	1 super dreadnought, 1 battle cruiser, 16 old battleships (4 of them French), 20 destroyers (6 French), and 35 minesweeping trawlers and a seaplane carrier
Importance	With their failure to force the Dardanelles with ships alone, the British and French embark on a land campaign	

The Dardanelles Campaign during World War I (1914–1918) was an Allied effort to open the straits connecting the Black Sea with the Mediterranean and drive the Ottoman Empire from the war. One of the war's most controversial operations, it was also one of its great missed opportunities.

The Ottoman Empire's entry into the war on the side of the Central powers severed French and British access to the Black Sea and greatly increased the difficulty of sending military supplies to Russia. It also denied Russia a means of exporting goods to the West, thus exacerbating that country's financial difficulties.

Reopening the Dardanelles was not initially a priority for the Allies; their attention was fixed on the campaign in France. Stalemate there, however, led to increased interest in a flanking movement elsewhere. First Lord of the Admiralty Winston Churchill was also anxious to employ British sea power.

At the end of December 1914 Lieutenant Colonel Maurice Hankey, secretary of the War Council in London, submitted a plan for a Dardanelles campaign. He argued that Britain should use its navy and three corps of troops to attack the Ottoman Empire. Churchill embraced the plan and became its avatar. First Sea Lord John Fisher was persuaded to go along as was secretary of state for war Field Marshal Horatio Kitchener, 1st Earl Kitchener of Khartoum, moved by a Russian plea for a diversionary attack to relieve Ottoman pressure in the Caucasus.

With Kitchener opposed to drawing troops from France, after much debate the War Council decided on a purely naval operation. The council assumed that once the fleet had reached Constantinople, its threat of naval bombardment would drive the Turks from the war. Fisher and the admirals of the War Staff Group saw what Churchill did not see: the need for a properly mounted combined-arms operation. Churchill also did not appreciate the vulnerability of ship-to-shore fire.

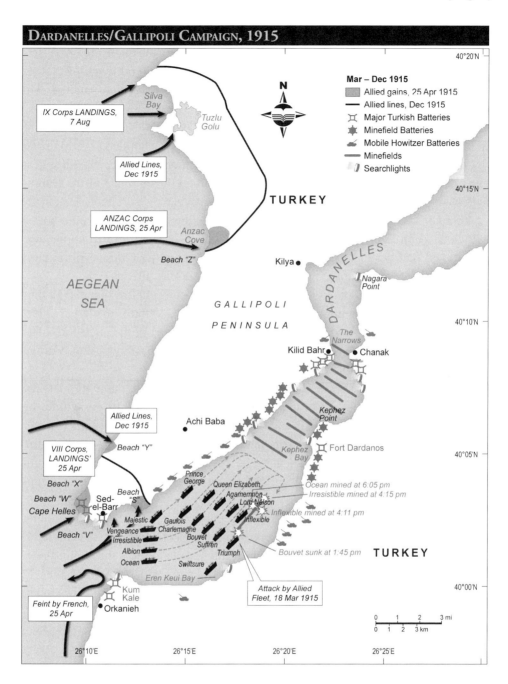

DARDANELLES/GALLIPOLI CAMPAIGN, 1915

Mar – Dec 1915
- Allied gains, 25 Apr 1915
- Allied lines, Dec 1915
- Major Turkish Batteries
- Minefield Batteries
- Mobile Howitzer Batteries
- Minefields
- Searchlights

40°20'N
40°15'N
40°10'N
40°05'N
40°00'N

TURKEY

Silva Bay
IX Corps LANDINGS, 7 Aug
Tuzlu Golu
Allied Lines, Dec 1915
ANZAC Corps LANDINGS, 25 Apr
Anzac Cove
Beach "Z"
Kilya
Nagara Point
DARDANELLES

AEGEAN SEA

GALLIPOLI PENINSULA

The Narrows
Kilid Bahr • Chanak
Kephez Point

Allied Lines, Dec 1915
Achi Baba
Beach "Y"
Kephez Bay
Fort Dardanos
VIII Corps, LANDINGS, 25 Apr
Beach "X"
Beach "S"
Beach "W"
Sed-el-Barr
Cape Helles
Beach "V"
Prince George
Queen Elizabeth
Agamemnon
Lord Nelson
Ocean mined at 6:05 pm
Irresistible mined at 4:15 pm
Inflexible *mined at 4:11 pm*
Majestic
Gaulois
Vengeance
Charlemagne
Irresistible
Bouvet
Albion
Suffren
Ocean
Triumph
Swiftsure
Bouvet sunk at 1:45 pm
TURKEY
Eren Keui Bay
Attack by Allied Fleet, 18 Mar 1915
Feint by French, 25 Apr
Kum Kale
Orkanieh

0 1 2 3 mi
0 1 2 3 km

26°10'E 26°15'E 26°20'E 26°25'E

Vice Admiral Sackville Carden, commander of the blockading squadron off the Dardanelles, had charge of the operation. Carden was less than enthusiastic and requested a considerable force, including battle cruisers to deal with the powerful German battle cruiser *Goeben* that had escaped to Constantinople at the beginning of the war. France also agreed to send a squadron commanded by Vice Admiral Émile Paul Guépratte.

Carden's force was the strongest ever assembled in the Mediterranean. It consisted of the superdreadnought *Queen Elizabeth* (flagship), the battle cruiser *Inflexible,* 16 old battleships (4 of them French), and 20 destroyers (6 French). A flotilla of 35 minesweeping trawlers and a seaplane carrier were also dispatched, and cruisers and submarines were available if needed.

The Ottomans had some 100 guns defending the Dardanelles, 72 of which were in fixed emplacements in 11 different forts. The Germans supplied several dozen 5.9-inch (15-centimeter) howitzers and some other modern pieces. The heaviest guns, along with searchlights and minefields, guarded the entrance of the Dardanelles. The defenders were, however, short of shells.

Although Carden came to believe that a naval bombardment alone would not be sufficient to force the Dardanelles, the War Council ordered him to commence operations. Bad weather delayed bombardment of the outer Ottoman forts until February 19. The weather then closed in, forcing a six-day interruption.

The bombardment recommenced on February 25. Naval gunfire silenced all four outer Ottoman forts, and minesweepers began clearing a path for the larger ships. Demolition parties also went ashore to complete destruction of the outer forts. The fleet then sailed into the straits and began bombarding the inner forts. Carden hoped to be off Constantinople in two weeks.

Carden's optimism proved unfounded. Although the forts could be hit, damage was not that great. In any case, the mobile Turkish howitzers, firing behind the crests of the hills, were not easily accessible to the flat trajectory high-velocity naval guns, and they scored a growing number of hits on Allied vessels. This fire did not bother the battleships, but it did affect minesweeping operations. Until troops could be landed to destroy the mobile howitzers, their fire prevented sweeping the minefields.

On March 3 Admiral Sir John de Robeck reported that the operation would not succeed unless troops were landed to control the shores of the straits, but Churchill had assured the War Council that the navy would be able to force the straits alone. He had even failed to send out the Royal Naval Division, which was available.

Captain Roger Keyes, Carden's chief of staff, took charge of the minesweeping, which went forward day and night. Churchill meanwhile kept up pressure on Carden, urging speed before the Germans sent submarines. Despite his near-total lack of losses, Carden was fearful of taking responsibility for the destruction of any ships. On March 16 his health broke, and de Robeck assumed command of the grand assault planned for two days later.

The naval effort to force the narrows began on schedule on March 18, when the Allied battleships bombarded the land batteries in the narrows. Three ships (two British and one French) sustained damage, but most shore batteries were hit hard. Then disaster struck. The French battleship *Bouvet* took a hit in one of its magazines and blew up, sinking with the loss of 640 men. Allied shelling of land batteries continued throughout the afternoon, and de Robeck ordered his minesweepers forward, but they fled after coming under fire. Then the British battle cruiser *Inflexible* struck a mine and withdrew from action. A few minutes later the battleship *Irresistible* also was disabled by a mine. De Robeck then ordered a withdrawal for the night but instructed Keyes to stay in the straits with the destroyers and organize a tow for the *Irresistible* with the help of two other battleships, the *Ocean* and *Swiftsure.*

Instead of concentrating on the salvage operation, the *Ocean* shelled shore installations. It was then torn by an internal explosion, its steering disabled. Keyes ordered the *Swiftsure* to retire with the crew of the *Ocean.* He then secured permission to sink the *Irresistible* by torpedo and determine if the *Ocean* could be salvaged. As Keyes returned, there was a great explosion. No trace of the two battleships was found. Later, it was learned that all three battleships had run into a new and very small minefield, which Allied seaplane patrols had failed to detect.

Keyes and other senior officers believed that one more determined push by the fleet would be decisive. In fact, the Ottoman shore batteries had used up half of their supply of ammunition in that one day and were down to their last armor-piercing shells. They were also virtually out of mines.

A great storm now blew up, damaging some British and French ships. Still, preparations for renewal of the offensive went forward, and a message from the Admiralty ordered de Robeck to renew the assault. On March 20 de Robeck had 62 vessels ready as minesweepers and said that the offensive would be renewed in a few days. Two days later, however, after meeting with newly arrived land force commander British Army general Sir Ian Hamilton, de Robeck changed his mind. In an acrimonious session, the War Council decided to let the views of its commanders on the spot prevail.

The attempt to force the Dardanelles with warships alone cost the British and French 700 lives, three battleships sunk and two crippled, and damage to other ships. The naval offensive was not renewed. The campaign now shifted to land operations on the Gallipoli Peninsula, and naval activities from this point consisted of gunfire support and resupply.

References

Churchill, Winston S. *The World Crisis,* Vol. 2. New York: Scribner, 1923.

James, Robert Rhodes. *Gallipoli: The History of a Noble Blunder.* New York: Macmillan, 1965.

Moorehead, Alan. *Gallipoli.* New York: Harper and Row, 1956.

Gallipoli Campaign

Date	April 25, 1915–January 9, 1916	
Location	Gallipoli Peninsula, Turkey	
Opponents (* winner)	*Ottomans	British, French, Australians and New Zealanders, Indians
Commander	General Otto Liman von Sanders	General Sir Ian Hamilton
Approx. # Troops	500,000	400,000
Importance	The Dardanelles remain closed, the Ottoman Empire continues in the war, and the Allies are unable to secure easy access to Russia, which helps to bring about the military collapse of that country	

The Gallipoli Campaign was the unsuccessful Allied ground effort during World War I to secure the Turkish Straits and drive the Ottoman Empire from the war. Although the naval effort to force the Dardanelles during February–March 1915 had failed, much had been invested, and political pressure to continue the campaign meant the belated injection of land troops.

London had actually taken the decision to send out land forces even before the naval bombardment of March 18, 1915. While First Lord of the Admiralty Winston Churchill exhorted naval commander Vice Admiral Sackville Carden to greater action, first sea lord Admiral John Fisher and secretary of state for war Field Marshal Horatio Kitchener, 1st Earl Kitchener of Khartoum, came to the conclusion that troops would have to be landed on the Gallipoli Peninsula at the northern entrance to the Dardanelles. Rear Admiral John de Robeck, who replaced Carden as Allied commander on March 16, concluded, after meeting with ground force commander General Sir Ian Hamilton on March 22, that army support would be necessary before the naval assault could continue.

Kitchener arranged to send the untrained Australian and New Zealand Corps (ANZAC) of two divisions, then in Egypt. He also decided to send the crack British 29th Division and the Royal Navy divisions. The French also agreed to send a division. Kitchener appointed General Sir Ian Hamilton to command the force of 75,000 men. There was little preliminary planning for the troop landing on Gallipoli. Maps were few and inaccurate, and intelligence about Ottoman forces was virtually nonexistent. Hamilton also lost valuable time by deciding to concentrate his forces in Egypt.

Tipped off by the naval bombardment, the Ottomans prepared for Allied landings. Inspector general of the Ottoman Army German generaloberst Otto Liman von Sanders took charge of the defenses. He had available the Ottoman Fifth Army of six widely dispersed divisions. Hilly and rocky, the Gallipoli Peninsula was ideal defensive terrain, and Liman von Sanders organized strong positions in the hills immediately behind likely invasion beaches. He was ably assisted by Ottoman colonel Mustafa Kemal (later known as Atatürk).

An armada of 200 Allied ships gathered for the landings, which were supported by 18 battleships, 12 cruisers, 29 destroyers, 8 submarines, and a host of small craft. On April 25, 1915, Allied troops went ashore at five beaches around Cape Helles (the extremity of the peninsula) and on the southwest side of the peninsula to the north near Gaba Tepe, at a beach still called Anzac. Ottoman opposition was fierce, and Allied casualties were heavy; however, by nightfall the forces were established ashore. French troops landed on the Asiatic side of the straits at Kum Kale, where they met a larger Ottoman force. With advance impossible, on April 27 the French were evacuated and transferred to Helles.

The Allied troops were in two lodgements about 15 miles apart, controlling only small pieces of territory. The fighting took the form of trench warfare, with opposing lines often only a few yards apart. The Ottomans could easily detect any Allied moves to drive them from their almost impregnable positions. Ottoman artillery was ideally situated to shell the beaches.

Early in May the Allies sent out two additional divisions and a brigade from India. Although some ground was gained, stalemate soon followed. The British then supplied five additional divisions, monitors for shore bombardment, more naval aircraft, and armored landing barges, but Ottoman strength increased apace, to 16 divisions.

A new naval attack was abandoned in mid-May after the Ottomans sank the British battleship *Goliath.* Only submarines could make the passage through the narrows to interfere with Ottoman shipping, and 7 of 12 submarines sent (9 British and 3 French) were lost. One, the *E-14,* did get into the Sea of Marmara and sank a troopship with 6,000 men aboard, all of whom perished. The *E-11* also blew up an ammunition ship. German submarines were also active. The *U-21* torpedoed and sank the old British battleships *Triumph* and *Majestic.*

The Allies landed two of their new divisions at Suvla Bay, north of Anzac, on the night of August 6–7. Kemal, now a corps commander, helped limit the landing to little more than a toehold. The Allied plan called for reinforced units to break out and seize the high ground to the east of Suvla that dominated the landing areas. Although Liman von Sanders shifted his resources north to meet the Suvla Bay threat, Allied commanders wasted this opportunity.

At the end of August the French offered to send a whole army, and the British found two additional divisions for yet another invasion, planned for November. This was postponed when Bulgaria entered the war on the side of the Central powers. By the middle of September the French government concluded that there was no hope for the campaign. The British government persisted, unwilling to sacrifice a venture in which so much had been invested. Meanwhile, a storm of criticism appeared in the Australian and British press, based on reports by war correspondents about the incompetence of British land commanders.

In October 1915 Lieutenant General Sir Charles Monro replaced Hamilton. Pointing out the unsatisfactory nature of the Allied positions ashore and the impending winter, Monro pressed for evacuation. A blizzard at the end of November, the worst in recent memory, resulted in Allied casualties of 10 percent at Gallipoli. Kitchener went out to inspect the situation in person and also argued for evacuation. On December 7 London agreed.

Despite Monro's fears of up to 40 percent losses, Kitchener predicted that it would go smoothly. The Allies steadily withdrew supplies by night, and the evacuation was completed during the night of January 8–9, 1916. It was the largest operation of its kind prior to the extraction of the British Expeditionary Force from Dunkirk in 1940. Much to the astonishment of the Allied command, it was carried out with virtually no losses.

Accurate casualty totals for the entire 259-day campaign are not available. The official Ottoman figure of 86,692 killed and 164,617 ill or wounded is undoubtedly too low. A reasonable figure might be 300,000 casualties. Total Allied casualties were about 265,000, of whom some 46,000 died.

The Allied failure meant that the straits remained closed, the Ottoman Empire continued in the war, and easy access to Russia was cut off. The effect of this in bringing about the military collapse of Russia and the Bolshevik Revolution can only be guessed. At the time and for years afterward, Churchill received most of the criticism for the failure. In August 1916 the British appointed a commission to investigate the campaign. At the end of 1917 the commission concluded that the campaign had been a mistake. The Gallipoli Campaign failed because of faulty planning, poor leadership, and indecision.

Although the operation had failed, the Gallipoli landing was much studied in the years following the war. The operation utilized considerable experimentation in naval aviation and landing and resupply techniques, which proved influential in the development of U.S. Marine Corps amphibious doctrine in World War II.

References

Churchill, Winston S. *The World Crisis,* Vol. 2. New York: Scribner, 1923.

Great Britain, Dardanelles Commission. *The Final Report of the Dardanelles Commission.* London: HMSO, 1919.

Hamilton, General Sir Ian. *Gallipoli Diary.* New York: George H. Doran, 1920.

James, Robert Rhodes. *Gallipoli: The History of a Noble Blunder.* New York: Macmillan, 1965.

Moorehead, Alan. *Gallipoli.* New York: Harper and Row, 1956.

Second Battle of Ypres

Date	April 22–May 25, 1915	
Location	Ypres, Belgium	
Opponents (* winner)	*Germans	Canadians, French Colonials, French, Belgians, British
Commander	Generaloberst Albrecht, Duke of Württemberg	General Horace Smith-Dorrien
Approx. # Troops	100,000?	100,000?
Importance	The first use of poison gas on the Western Front and a wasted opportunity for the Germans	

The April–May 1915 Second Battle of Ypres on the Western Front in World War I saw the first widespread use of poison gas in warfare. Undeterred by previous failures, in the winter of 1914–1915 French Army commander General Joseph J. C. Joffre laid plans for a new offensive against the German Army. With the Germans concentrating against Russia in 1915, Joffre and commander of the Northern Army Group General Ferdinand Foch sought to exploit the numerical advantage of Allied forces in the West with a breakthrough in the Artois region.

Allied goals were the same as in late 1914: to capture Vimy Ridge, which commanded the Douai Plain, and then force a German withdrawal from northern France. To maximize the chance of success, Joffre convinced British Expeditionary Force (BEF) commander Field Marshal Sir John French to participate. Field Marshal French agreed to relieve two French corps in the Ypres salient and attack at Aubers Ridge in what would be the largest in a series of supporting assaults all along the front. Allied preparations were disrupted on April 22, 1915, however, by the first successful use of poison (chlorine) gas in the war. This event initiated the Second Battle of Ypres during April 22–May 25.

At the end of October 1914 the Germans had fired artillery shells containing an irritant gas in the Neuve Chapelle sector but without apparent effect. They first used tear gas, xylyl bromide (code-named "T-Stoff"), on the Eastern Front on January 31, 1915, firing some 18,000 gas shells against the Russians at Bolimov. It was not a success. The weather was so cold that the gas failed to vaporize; it froze and sank into the snow.

The Germans then decided to employ chlorine gas on the Western Front. Chemist Fritz Haber had charge of the new weapon. Haber was certain that it would be successful and urged his army superiors to exploit it. They remained skeptical. Hard-pressed by the shift of significant manpower to the Eastern Front, they regarded it largely as an experiment and refused to allocate reserves to Duke Albrecht of Württemberg's Fourth Army to exploit any breach that the chlorine gas might effect in the enemy line.

The ruins of St. Martin's Cathedral following the Second Battle of Ypres in 1915. The destruction of the cathedral was widely reported in the world's press and became a useful propaganda tool for the Allies. (National Archives)

Chief of the General Staff Generaloberst Erich von Falkenhayn's goals at Ypres were accordingly modest. He sought merely to reduce the salient and to mask the transfer of reinforcements to the Eastern Front for the Gorlice-Tarnow Offensive. Haber was also forced to release the gas from commercial metal cylinders and depend on the wind for dispersal, which delayed the attack.

The Allies received warnings of an impending German gas attack. In March the French took prisoners who described preparations for such an attack, and on April 13 a German deserter described to his French interrogators "tubes of asphyxiating gas," in batteries of 16, being placed every 40 yards or so along the front. This information was ignored, as was the deserter's crude respirator gas mask. Accurate reports also reached Second Army commander General Sir Horace Smith-Dorrien, but he neither issued a general warning nor ordered precautionary measures.

At about 5:30 p.m. on April 22, with the wind finally in the correct direction and following a brief German artillery bombardment, Allied pilots overhead and troops of the 45th Algerian Division and 87th Territorial Division holding a section of line in the salient around Ypres spotted an advancing greenish yellow cloud. The Germans had opened the valves of some 4,000 gas cylinders, releasing 168 tons of chlorine gas. At some points the opposing trenches were only about 100 yards apart. The cloud wiped out the two French divisions manning a four-mile section of front, killing or incapacitating the defenders or causing them to flee their positions.

German infantry advanced cautiously behind the cloud. On the right of the Allied front under attack, men of the 1st Canadian Division saw the cloud, but most of it passed by them, and the Canadians held their ground. On the left (northern) end of the Allied line, the gas dissipated somewhat, allowing Belgian and French troops to make a stand. German troops took 2,000 Allied prisoners and 51 guns. By the end of the day 15,000 Allied soldiers were casualties, 5,000 of them dead.

Fortunately for the Allies, the Germans lacked sufficient manpower to exploit the situation. Allied reserves rushed forward and, over the next several days, slowed the German advance and sealed the breach. A second German gas attack on April 24 was less successful. Canadian troops used handkerchiefs soaked in water or urine as crude respirators.

British counterattacks were not successful, and Smith-Dorrien sensibly suggested withdrawing to a more tenable line along the Yser Canal and Ypres ramparts. Field Marshal French took this as a lack of will and transferred responsibility for the Ypres sector to General Herbert Plumer. Smith-Dorrien was sacked and sent home to Britain, a loss for the BEF. Ironically, Field Marshal French allowed Plumer to pull back as Smith-Dorrien had urged, but three miles short of Ypres.

The Germans renewed their attack on May 8 and made some gains. Another attack on May 24 by four German divisions against three British divisions, preceded by gas over 4.5 miles of front, failed. The Second Battle of Ypres ended the next day. It was the most successful German offensive action in France during 1915. Casualties through May 25 amounted to some 60,000 British, 10,000 French, and 35,000 Germans. The downside for the Germans was that their use of poison gas provided an immense boost to Allied propaganda, helping to influence opinion against the Germans abroad, especially in the then-neutral United States.

The Allies thereafter developed their own poison gases; the British employed gas for the first time at Loos on September 25, 1915. Both sides also introduced gas masks, which by 1916 had become standard issue. The result was a stalemate of sorts. World War I poison gases incapacitated or wounded far more men than they killed. From the standpoint of the attacker, this was an advantage because wounded enemy soldiers neutralized additional men to transport the casualties to the rear. Wounded soldiers also increased the burden on enemy logistical and medical systems.

References

Cassar, George. *Beyond Courage: The Canadians at the Second Battle of Ypres.* Ottawa: Oberon, 1985.

Cook, Tim. *No Place to Run: The Canadian Corps and Gas Warfare in the First World War.* Vancouver: University of British Columbia Press, 1999.

Dancocks, Daniel G. *Welcome to Flanders Fields, the First Canadian Battle of the Great War: Ypres, 1915.* Toronto: McClelland and Stewart, 1988.

Haber, L. F. *The Poisonous Cloud: Chemical Warfare in the First World War.* New York: Oxford University Press, 1986.

Macdonald, Lyn. *1915: The Death of Innocence.* New York: Henry Holt, 1995.

Moore, William. *Gas Attack: Chemical Warfare, 1915 to the Present Day.* New York: Hippocrene Books, 1987.

Siege of Kut

Date	December 7, 1915–April 29, 1916	
Location	Kut-al-Amara, Mesopotamia (today Iraq)	
Opponents (* winner)	*Ottomans	Indians and British
Commander	Generalfeldmarschall Colmar von der Goltz	Major General Charles V. F. Townshend
Approx. # Troops	More than 13,000	13,000
Importance	Greatly raises both Ottoman morale and prestige in the Middle East	

The World War I Ottoman siege of Kut (Al Kūt, Kut-Al-Amara, Kut El Amara) in Mesopotamia ended in a major British military defeat. The great plain of Mesopotamia that comprises present-day Iraq is drained by the Tigris and Euphrates rivers, which in 1914 provided the region's chief avenues of communication. Military operations in the region were difficult especially in summer, when water had to be transported for both men and horses and temperatures could reach 120 degrees Fahrenheit for as long as 10 hours a day. Sunstroke, heatstroke, diarrhea, malaria, typhoid, yellow fever, and cholera all took their toll on both sides. The area was important to Britain, however, as its new capital ships were dependent on oil from the refinery at Abadan Island, at the head of the Persian Gulf. Baghdad, the largest city of the region, lay 415 miles upriver.

Prior to the Ottoman Empire's entry into the war, the British sent a reinforced brigade to the mouth of the Shatt al-Arab waterway to protect Abadan. After Britain declared war on the Ottomans and increased its strength to a division, in late November 1914 Indian Army forces moved upriver and took both Basra and Qurna. This also protected the Abadan refinery, which lay 50 miles south.

During the first half of 1915 additional British reinforcements arrived, commanded from Basra by Indian Army general Sir John E. Nixon. London favored a defensive strategy to protect the oil fields, but before Nixon had left India, the commander of the Indian Army, General Sir Beauchamp-Duff, counseled an advance on Baghdad up the Tigris. In May 1915 Nixon ordered Major General Charles V. F. Townshend to carry out a reconnaissance in force. At the head of an Indian division and a cavalry brigade and assisted by a small naval flotilla, on May 31 Townshend routed the Ottomans at Qurna. This easy victory gave the British a false impression of Ottoman military ability.

Townshend's amphibious force continued its advance and on June 3 took Amara (Al Amārah). Nixon now secured grudging approval from London to continue on to Kut, more than 100 miles farther upriver. Kut fell to the British during September 26–28, but the long march, weather, and low water in the Tigris prevented Townshend from pursuing the Ottomans, the bulk of whom escaped to the north.

Despite the fact that the British river supply line was now twice as long as that of the Ottomans (200 miles to Basra versus only 100 to Baghdad), London authorized Nixon to move against Baghdad if he was satisfied that he possessed sufficient strength for the task. London promised to supply two divisions from France, but only to assist with occupation duties. Nixon was not worried; he depreciated Ottoman ability and overestimated the capabilities of his own forces.

Townshend, however, opposed an advance on Baghdad without reinforcements and so informed Nixon, explaining the problems posed by the weather, lack of water, and supply shortages. Townshend required more than 200 tons of supplies a day but, partly from pillage, was receiving only 150 tons. Undeterred, Nixon ordered the offensive to proceed, and in late November Townshend dutifully began to move on Baghdad, supplied by riverboats and improvised camel and donkey transport.

The Ottomans benefitted from reinforcements, and during November 22–26, 1915, in the Battle of Ctesiphon, fought on the outskirts of Baghdad, they halted his advance. Townshend lost half the number of men as did Ottoman commander General Nur-al-Din (4,600 to 9,500), but unlike Townshend, Nur-al-Din continued to receive additional manpower. The Ottomans then forced the British to fall back.

On December 3 following an epic retreat, Townshend's exhausted troops arrived back at Kut. Townshend wired Nixon that he had one month's full rations for his British troops, two months' worth for the Indians, and plenty of ammunition. Nixon responded that he would make every effort to relieve Townshend and hoped to accomplish this within two months. Nixon ordered Townshend to send ahead his cavalry and as many vessels as possible. Townshend, however, informed Nixon that within two months he would be surrounded by six Ottoman divisions. Townshend believed that it would be best if he retreated to Ali Gharbi, but Nixon ordered him to stay where he was; at Kut he would be tying down superior numbers of Ottoman troops.

By December 7 the Ottomans had closed the ring around Kut, and the siege had begun. In January 1916 Nixon gave up his command, ostensibly for health reasons, and was succeeded by Lieutenant General Sir Percy Lake. That same month the two Indian divisions arrived from France. Under Major General Fenton J. Aylmer they tried to reach Kut but were halted by the Ottomans. The steamer *Julnar* tried to run the blockade but was taken by the Ottomans when it became trapped in wire stretched across the river by the besiegers. A few British aircraft dropped bags of flour to the besieged garrison, perhaps history's first effort at aerial resupply.

In March, Aylmer's successor, Major General George F. Gorringe, attempted a surprise attack on the south bank of the Tigris. The Ottoman Sixth Army, now led by German generalfeldmarschall Colmar von der Goltz, repulsed it. The relieving forces suffered some 23,000 casualties while trying to rescue the 13,000 trapped men. At the same time, the Russians mounted a halfhearted relief operation of their own from northwestern Persia, but it soon bogged down.

In Kut, food was in short supply. Townshend made an effort to ransom the garrison, offering the Ottomans £1 million and all the artillery in Kut in exchange for paroling the garrison. The Ottomans, however, insisted on unconditional surrender. After destroying as much equipment as possible, Townshend surrendered on April 29. The Ottomans took more than 2,700 British and 6,500 Indian troops prisoner. Although Townshend was treated well, nearly 5,000 of his men died of mistreatment and starvation before the end of the war. Their successful siege of Kut greatly raised both Ottoman morale and their prestige in the Middle East. A shocked British government now took over direction of the Mesopotamian front, to include reorganizing and greatly strengthening forces there.

References

Barker, A. J. *The Bastard War: The Mesopotamian Campaign of 1914–1918.* New York: Dial, 1967.

———. *Townshend of Kut: A Biography of Major-General Sir Charles Townshend K.C.B., D.S.O.* London: Cassell, 1967.

Braddon, Russel. *The Siege.* New York: Viking, 1970.

Erickson, Edward J. *Ordered to Die: A History of the Ottoman Army in the First World War.* Westport, CT: Greenwood, 2001.

Millar, Ronald William. *Death of an Army: The Siege of Kut, 1915–1916.* Boston: Houghton Mifflin, 1970.

Moberly, F. J. *The Campaign in Mesopotamia, 1914–1918.* 3 vols. Nashville, TN: Battery Press, 1997–1998.

Townshend, Sir Charles V. F. *My Campaign in Mesopotamia.* London: Thornton Butterworth, 1920.

Battle of Verdun

Date	February 21–July, 20, 1916	
Location	Verdun, Lorraine, eastern France	
Opponents (* winner)	*French	Germans
Commander	General Henri Philippe Pétain	Crown Prince Wilhelm
Approx. # Troops	450,000	500,000
Importance	The French do not break and the Germans are unable to mount another such attack in the west until the spring of 1918, but the battle also has serious negative effects on French army morale	

German Army chief of staff Generaloberst Erich von Falkenhayn planned a major offensive for early 1916. He well understood that the Central powers could not afford to remain on the defensive indefinitely. The Allies had superior resources, and the British naval blockade was creating shortages in Germany of both food and raw materials. Germany had to strike a decisive blow in 1916. Falkenhayn vetoed attacks on the Italian or Russian fronts, deciding that the offensive would be launched against France at Verdun. By the end of 1915 France had sustained 2 million casualties, half of them dead, and Falkenhayn hoped that a major offensive might drive France from the war. A German attack would at least forestall the planned Allied offensive.

Split by the Meuse River, Verdun lies 160 miles east of Paris. It had been a fortress as early as Gallic times, and following the 1871 loss of Alsace-Lorraine to Germany, Verdun became the cornerstone of a new French defensive system. The rapid reduction by the Germans of the Belgian fortresses of Liège and Namur in August 1914, however, suggested the ineffectiveness of fortifications, and in 1915 French Army commander General Joseph J. C. Joffre had siphoned off men and armament, especially heavy guns, from Verdun to other sectors.

In 1916 Verdun lay in the middle of a narrow salient projecting into German-controlled territory; its southern face was the countersalient of Saint-Mihiel. The French had few troops there. Not until the last week of January did Joffre begin to improve the defenses, the result of prodding by Lieutenant Colonel Émile Driant, a National Assembly deputy serving at Verdun who bypassed the chain of command to report the dire situation directly to his fellow parliamentarians. They in turn reported it to minister of war General Joseph Galliéni, who put pressure on Joffre.

The Verdun salient lent itself to a converging German attack and allowed concentrated artillery fire from three sides. Its woods and hills screened troops and artillery, which the Germans could easily bring up by rail. At the same time, the French would find it difficult to resupply and reinforce there. Only one road and a single rail line connected Verdun to the rest of France. The extreme narrowness of the salient would also make it difficult for the French to maneuver.

If the Germans could take Verdun, this would provide security for their rail communications south, which were less than 15 miles from the French lines. Falkenhayn also believed that this would severely impact French morale and threaten their entire right wing. Victory would significantly boost German morale, shaken by the start of rationing. At the very least, Falkenhayn hoped to hold a shortened front with fewer men.

Falkenhayn expected Operation GERICHT (JUDGMENT) to catch the French by surprise. He planned a narrow-front attack with massive artillery support. Falkenhayn believed that France would throw all remaining manpower into the defense of the fortress, and he planned to use massive artillery fire to bleed counterattacking French infantry to death in a battle of attrition (*Aufblutung*).

Falkenhayn entrusted the offensive to his Fifth Army, commanded by Crown Prince Wilhelm. By February 11 the Germans had assembled more than 850 guns

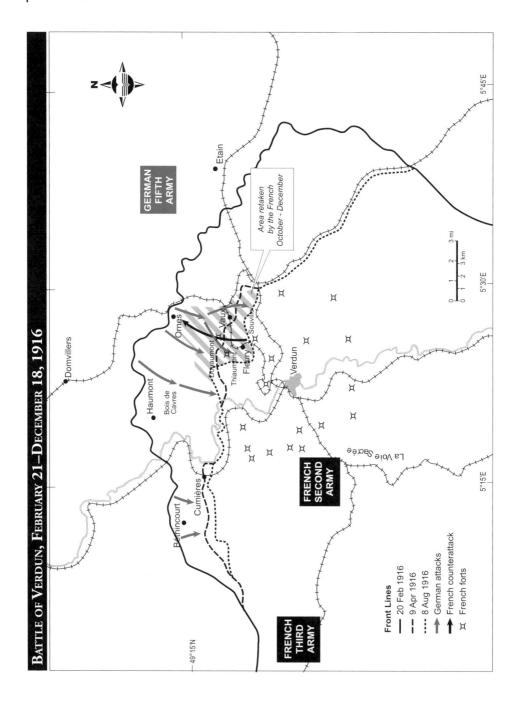

BATTLE OF VERDUN, FEBRUARY 21–DECEMBER 18, 1916

GERMAN FIFTH ARMY

FRENCH SECOND ARMY

FRENCH THIRD ARMY

Area retaken by the French October - December

Etain

Domvillers

Haumont

Bois de Cavres

Béthincourt

Cumières

Ornes

Douaumont

Thiaumont

Fleury

Vaux

Souville

Verdun

La Voie Sacrée

49°15'N

5°15'E

5°30'E

5°45'E

0 1 2 3 mi
0 1 2 3 km

Front Lines
— 20 Feb 1916
– – 9 Apr 1916
···· 8 Aug 1916
⬆ German attacks
⬆ French counterattack
¤ French forts

and 72 battalions of elite assault troops. Additional German artillery on the flanks brought the total up to more than 1,220 guns, all for an assault frontage of only eight miles. The French had only 270 guns and 34 battalions of infantry. Bad weather postponed the attack, originally scheduled for February 12. This enabled the French to detect the German increase in strength and bring up reinforcements, although Joffre still largely discounted the buildup's importance.

The preliminary German bombardment opened at 7:15 a.m. on February 21. The ensuing bombardment of more than 1 million shells was the heaviest to that point in the war. At about 4:00 p.m. the Germans launched their ground attack on a six-mile front between Brabant and Ornes. They employed a new weapon, the flamethrower.

The Germans easily took the outlying French defense zone. In order to reach the main French forts, they had to capture the Bois des Caures, a small wooded area held by Driant's 1,300 men. The French held for two critical days, although Driant was among those killed. By February 24 the defenders had lost half their manpower.

The Germans now faced Fort Douaumont. Located on high ground that commanded any approach, it was the linchpin of the Verdun defensive system. Reputedly impregnable, its interior vaults could house a whole battalion of infantry. On February 25 because of a command mixup, however, the fort was manned by just 57 men. That same day a handful of German soldiers took it without loss. It was almost fatal for the French, as Douaumont dominated the remaining French defensive positions.

That same night French general Henri Philippe Pétain took command at Verdun. Pétain set up his headquarters at Souilly, a village south of Verdun on the Bar-le-Duc road. He immediately rushed in reinforcements and developed an elastic defensive scheme. Pétain questioned the strategic value of Verdun and even suggested withdrawal, which President Raymond Poincaré rejected out of hand. As Falkenhayn expected, Verdun became a matter of national honor for the French, but the same calculus kept the Germans from breaking off their attacks.

The French faced a critical situation. The sole route into Verdun was a secondary road from Bar-le-Duc. Along what became known as La Voie Sacrée (The Sacred Way), 66 French divisions—three-quarters of the entire French Army—marched to the furnace fires. "*Ils ne passeront pas*" ("They shall not pass"), which probably did not originate with Pétain, became the French rallying cry. By rotating units in and out of the battle, Pétain frustrated the German plan to wear the French down. He also organized an effective supply system along the Sacred Way to sustain an eventual French force at Verdun of 450,000 men and 140,000 animals. Despite German artillery fire, a steady stream of trucks (as many as 6,000 a day, or 1 every 14 seconds in each direction around the clock) brought in supplies and carried out wounded.

Falkenhayn now expanded the battle by extending it to both banks of the Meuse River. Pétain, however, had anticipated this and reinforced there, with the result that the Germans gained little. Attacks and counterattacks raged throughout March, and casualties steadily mounted in savage fighting. On June 7 Fort Vaux, the smallest of the Verdun forts and the northeast bastion of its permanent fortifications, fell to the Germans, enabling them to assault the last ridges on the right bank of the Meuse before Verdun. They assigned 19 regiments to the attack in what would be the largest attack against Verdun.

The German assault began on June 23 after a two-day artillery preparation that included, for the first time, phosgene gas. Pétain doubted that the French could hold and recommended abandoning the eastern Meuse line, but with the British assault on the Somme imminent, Joffre refused. Although the Germans reached the superstructure of Fort Souville less than 2.5 miles from Verdun (the closest they ever came), by July 20 French counterattacks pushed them back.

The British Somme Offensive and the Russian Brusilov Offensive helped the French, and Falkhenhayn was forced to send three German divisions east to assist the Austro-Hungarians. In autumn the French took the offensive. Utilizing a creeping barrage (shifting fire forward 100 yards every four minutes, with the aim of suppressing German fire rather than destroying specific targets), the French retook Douaumont on October 24 and Vaux on November 2. Finally, in August 1917 the French recovered their frontline positions of February 1916.

The Germans had not bled France to death or even taken Verdun. They had captured a few square miles of territory but at a terrible price. Casualty estimates vary. The official French figure for losses for 10 months of 1916 is 377,231 men. The Germans lost roughly 337,000 men. Taking into account fighting at Verdun before and after the 1916 battle, the French estimate for the battlefield is 420,000 dead and 800,000 gassed or wounded. Historian Alistair Horne called Verdun "the 'worst' battle in history" (Horne, *The Price of Glory: Verdun, 1916*, 327).

The battle profoundly affected the Germans' military strategy. They were unable to mount another such attack in the West until the spring of 1918, after the collapse of Russia. The battle also discredited Falkenhayn. The outcome of the battle and the Romanian decision to enter the war at the end of August 1916, which Falkenhayn said would not occur, led to his replacement by Generalfeldmarschall Paul von Hindenburg as chief of staff and General der Infanterie Erich Ludendorff as his quartermaster general (actual chief of staff of the army). They believed that the solution to the war lay in the East and promptly shifted the major German effort to that front.

The Battle of Verdun was a victory of sorts for France, but it had deleterious effects on that nation as well. In December Joffre lost his post as commander of the French Army and was replaced by General Robert Nivelle. War weariness gripped the country and raised doubts about final victory. For France, Verdun symbolized heroism and fortitude but also great suffering. The battle influenced France for years thereafter. After Verdun, the French Army, perhaps even France, was not the same.

References

Hermanns, William. *The Holocaust: From a Survivor of Verdun.* New York: Harper and Row, 1972.

Horne, Alistair. *The Price of Glory: Verdun, 1916.* New York: Penguin, 1993.

Battle of the Somme

Date	July 1–November 19, 1916	
Location	Near the river Somme about 90 miles northeast of Paris	
Opponents (* winner)	*Germans	British, including Canadians, Australians, New Zealanders; French
Commander	Generaloberst Fritz von Below	Field Marshal Sir Douglas Haig, with General Sir Henry Rawlinson and Lieutenant General Sir Edmund Allenby (British); General Marie Fayolle (French)
Approx. # Troops	Up to 800,000 Germans (95 divisions)	Some 600,000 British, Canadians, Australians, New Zealanders; 200,000 French
Importance	The British relieve some of the German pressure on Verdun but fail to achieve the desired breakthrough and the battle severely saps both British and German manpower, affecting future operations on both sides; it also sees the first use of tanks in the war	

The Battle of the Somme was the second great land battle of 1916 on the Western Front and the bloodiest single battle of World War I (1914–1918). The battle was closely tied to the other great engagement of that year at Verdun. The British and French had planned to launch a major offensive in the autumn along the Somme River, but the German offensive at Verdun shifted the brunt of that attack to the British. The purpose of the attack also changed from a war-winning breakthrough to relieving German pressure on Verdun.

It is easy in hindsight to criticize both the location and the plan for the Somme attack. Commander of the British Expeditionary Force General Sir Douglas Haig wanted the offensive to occur in the Ypres sector but had yielded to French Army commander General Joseph J. C. Joffre's decision for the Somme, which was probably selected because it was the juncture between the two armies and would thus ensure maximum British cooperation. The offensive occurred along 20 miles of front north of the Somme, with General Sir Henry Rawlinson's British Fourth Army, formed only in January 1916, making the main effort. General Marie Fayolle's French Sixth Army carried out a supporting attack south of the Somme, while in the north two divisions of Lieutenant General Sir Edmund Allenby's British Third Army mounted a diversionary attack.

Haig hoped to break through the German lines and then insert Major General Sir Hubert Gough's reserve army of three British infantry and two Indian cavalry divisions to exploit the breach and swing to the northeast. Rawlinson favored a more modest bite-and-hold approach of lengthy bombardment, limited infantry advance to readjust the line, consolidation, and then destruction of counterattacks to inflict maximum casualties on the Germans. Clearly, British resources were inadequate for what Haig intended. In Haig's defense, Joffre urged that the offensive begin as soon as possible, and it was thus launched six weeks before Haig thought that his men would be ready. Haig also expected a larger French commitment and believed that Joffre deceived him on that score.

Opposing the British, German Second Army commander Generaloberst Fritz von Below had six divisions in the line, with five others in close reserve. Although the German High Command expected an Allied effort to relieve pressure on Verdun, German Army chief of staff Generaloberst Erich von Falkenhayn believed that it would come in Alsace. Below assumed that the attack would occur in his sector and planned accordingly. His defensive preparations included numerous deep bunkers, some of which were 40 feet underground and largely impervious to shell fire. The Germans constructed three and in some places four defensive lines to an average depth of five miles.

Haig committed 18 divisions to the attack, 11 of which were from the half-trained New Army under the command of minister of war Field Marshal Horatio Kitchener, 1st Earl Kitchener of Khartoum. Most of the men were volunteers who had joined in large groups, in some cases from whole neighborhoods, villages, associations or clubs. Such units were known as Pals Battalions. To compensate for the infantry's lack of training, the British planned a massive artillery preparation, which it was believed would eliminate the majority of the first-line German defenders. After the shelling, the British soldiers would leave their trenches and walk (not run) in linear formation across no-man's-land.

On June 24 the British commenced a bombardment with 1,537 guns. By the time the shelling lifted seven days later, the British had fired more than 1.6 million shells. A high number of duds and the fact that the British lacked a sufficient number of heavy guns to destroy the German defensive works lessened the overall effect, however. The shelling also failed to destroy the German barbed wire. British patrols reported that the wire was mostly intact or even jumbled into greater obstacles, news that headquarters refused to believe.

At 7:20 a.m. on July 1 the British detonated the first of three large and seven smaller mines dug under the German positions. The decision to blow this mine at

A British Mark I tank during the Battle of the Somme, 1916. The Mark I weighed 62,700 lbs and had a top speed of only 3.7 mph (half that over rough ground). Its two-wheeled trailing unit assisted with steering but was ineffective over rough ground. It could span a 10-foot trench but armor thickness was only 6–12mm. (Library of Congress)

7:20, a full 10 minutes before the assault, alerted the defenders, and their artillery immediately fired on every British trench in the area. At 7:28 the British blew the other mines, including two with 24 tons of explosives each, the largest mines yet detonated on the Western Front.

Exactly at 7:30 the British halted artillery fire to allow resighting of their guns. British artillery fire then shifted from the forward German positions, and almost 70,000 British troops in 84 battalions began to move across the 500–800 yards between the lines. Weighed down with 70-pound packs, the men had been assured that after such a bombardment nothing would be left of the enemy and that this would be an occupation rather than an assault.

As soon as the British shelling shifted, the German soldiers left their deep bunkers and set up machine guns in the newly created shell craters, slaughtering the advancing British. Because Haig wanted to keep the momentum going in order to break through all the German lines, the British reserves moved forward at the same time as the assault troops. Inevitably the attackers bunched up at the wire. Some units did not even get past their own wire before being mowed down. Others took their initial objectives but at a high cost.

Rawlinson continued to feed more troops into the battle, and by the end of the day he had committed 143 battalions. At the end of what would be the bloodiest single day in British military history, almost half of the assaulting troops were casualties, with a rate of 75 percent for officers. In all the British had sustained 57,470 casualties, 19,240 of them killed outright or mortally wounded. German losses for the day were only about 8,000 men.

Although almost none of the first day's objectives were secured, senior British commanders in the rear were slow to realize this. French forces on the British right, thanks in part to their heavier artillery, did make some gains, but theirs was not the main attack. Only the British XIII Corps had some success, taking Montauban and defeating a subsequent German counterattack.

Despite the lack of success Haig continued the offensive, in part because Joffre stressed the need to relieve pressure on Verdun. Haig also believed that sooner or later his forces would break through. He decided to concentrate on his right, where there had been some success. He reorganized his forces, establishing a new army on the left, later designated the Fifth Army under Gough and astride the Ancre River. French divisions were also brought up.

The next major British effort came in a daring night attack on July 13–14 with minimal losses. Attacking abreast, four British divisions took a 6,000-yard stretch of Bazentin Ridge, the forward slope of which was the Germans' second defensive line. The Germans quickly rushed up three reserve divisions. On July 20 the French and British mounted another attack with 17 divisions; the French took a German position between Maurepas and the north bank of the Somme. On July 23 the British attempted to extend their advances farther north along Bazentin Ridge, but the sole British success here came when two Australian divisions took Pozières.

The Germans continued to reinforce, and Falkenhayn reorganized Below's units south of the Somme into another army under General Max von Gallwitz. On September 4 the French committed General Joseph Micheler's Tenth Army to the battle, extending the fighting 12 miles south of the Somme. The Allies then continued the assault on both sides of that river north to the Ancre.

Haig launched another major assault on September 15, with 12 divisions, along a 10-mile front from Combles to the Ancre. The offensive bogged down in rain and mud. To the south French forces achieved some success, advancing 5 to 8 miles, but this had little influence on the main battle.

The most significant aspect of this attack was the first use of tanks. Only 59 tanks were in France when Haig made his decision, and of these only 49 reached the battlefield. Plagued by mechanical problems, only 9 surmounted all problems and pushed on ahead of the infantry. Although the tanks were far from impressive in their debut, Haig was sufficiently impressed to request 1,000 more.

Haig attacked again on September 25, this time north of the Ancre. Two days of heavy fighting produced only slight gains. By now rains had turned the shell-torn ground of the Somme battlefield into a sea of mud. Although Haig favored shutting the campaign down for the winter, Joffre insisted on maintaining the pressure, with fighting continuing on a lesser but still lethal scale. On November 13 the British won their last victory of the Somme campaign: a seven-division attack on either side of the Ancre. They advanced three-quarters of a mile and captured a fortified position at Beaumont-Hammel and 1,200 prisoners. On November 19 a blizzard hit, followed by more rain. The campaign was over.

Altogether the British had committed to the Somme Offensive a total of 55 divisions (including 4 Canadian divisions, 4 Australian divisions, and 1 New Zealand division), the French had committed 20 divisions, and the Germans had committed 95 divisions (German divisions tended to be slightly smaller than their French and British counterparts). The losses were even higher than those at Verdun. In five months of fighting British forces suffered nearly 420,000 casualties, and French forces suffered 195,000 casualties, all for an advance of at most 7 miles on a 20-mile front, none of this key terrain.

The British paid a heavy psychological cost that was felt for decades afterward. Although the Germans had fought the Allies to a standstill, the Germans also had paid a terrible price of up to 650,000 casualties, a loss they could not afford.

The Somme battles did help relieve pressure on Verdun. Tacticians on both sides advocating change were also now taken more seriously. The heavy losses, particularly among officers and noncommissioned officers, contributed to the German decision to pull back to the Hindenburg Line, a shorter and better-prepared position that could be held more easily with fewer troops. From that position the Germans perfected their doctrine of flexible defense in depth that would cause the Allies so much difficulty in 1917.

References

Cowley, Robert. "The Somme: The Last 140 Days." *MHQ: Quarterly Journal of Military History* 7(4) (Summer 1995): 74–87.

Macdonald, Lyn. *Somme.* London: Michael Joseph, 1983.

Middlebrook, Martin. *First Day on the Somme.* New York: Norton, 1972.

Travers, Tim. "The Somme: The Reason Why." *MHQ: Quarterly Journal of Military History* 7(4) (Summer 1995): 62–73.

Winter, Denis. *Haig's Command: A Reassessment.* New York: Viking, 1991.

Battle of Jutland

Date	May 31–June 1, 1916	
Location	North Sea off the coast of Denmark	
Opponents (* winner)	*British	Germans
Commander	Admiral Sir John Jellicoe	Grossadmiral Reinhard Scheer
Approx. # Troops	28 dreadnoughts, 9 battle cruisers, 34 cruisers, and 80 destroyers	16 dreadnoughts, 6 pre-dreadnoughts, 5 battle cruisers, 11 cruisers, and 63 destroyers
Importance	Although the British lose more ships than do the Germans, they also have more ready for combat after the battle than do their adversary; the blockade of Germany also continues as before and the Germans avoid again risking their capital ships in a showdown battle.	

While the great Battle of Verdun raged on land, the Battle of Jutland occurred at sea. Leaders in both the British Royal Navy and the German Imperial Navy anticipated a major battle, probably in the North Sea, that would decide the war and world mastery. Such an event almost came true on the afternoon of May 31, when the British Grand Fleet and the German High Seas Fleet met off the western coast of the Jutland Peninsula, near the outer entrance of the straits into the Baltic Sea known as the Skagerrak (as the battle is known even today in Germany). It was the largest naval engagement of the war and one of the largest in world history.

In January 1916 Grossadmiral Reinhard Scheer became commander of the German High Seas Fleet. Scheer favored using the fleet in carefully prepared surprise attacks that would reduce the size of the British Grand Fleet preparatory to an all-out encounter. In April 1916, for instance, Scheer ordered the shelling of the English coastal towns of Lowestoft and Yarmouth; during the operation the German fleet had allowed an inferior British force to get away. The Jutland operation was designed to be similar but much larger, in part because German naval leaders were under pressure to carry out a major action while the army was engaged in the great bloodletting of Verdun.

On May 30 Scheer took the High Seas Fleet out on a sweep of the North Sea. A scouting force of 40 fast vessels preceded the main German force beyond visual contact, at a range of about 40 miles. Commanded by Vizeadmiral Franz von Hipper, the fleet included 5 battle cruisers. Hipper's task was to lure a portion of the Grand Fleet back into the main body of the High Seas Fleet, where it might be destroyed.

The Germans, however, suffered from poor scouting. Unknown to them, the entire Grand Fleet, alerted by heavy German signals traffic, was at sea. British admiral Sir John Jellicoe commanded 28 dreadnoughts, 9 battle cruisers, 34 cruisers, and 80 destroyers against Scheer's 16 dreadnoughts, 6 predreadnoughts, 5

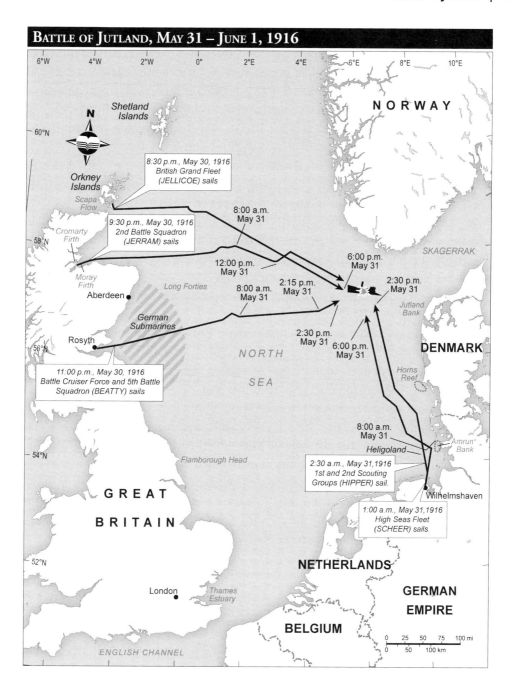

BATTLE OF JUTLAND, MAY 31 – JUNE 1, 1916

NORWAY

Shetland Islands

8:30 p.m., May 30, 1916
British Grand Fleet
(JELLICOE) sails

Orkney Islands

Scapa Flow

9:30 p.m., May 30, 1916
2nd Battle Squadron
(JERRAM) sails

Cromarty Firth

8:00 a.m. May 31

SKAGERRAK

Moray Firth

12:00 p.m. May 31

6:00 p.m. May 31

2:30 p.m. May 31

Aberdeen

Long Forties

8:00 a.m. May 31

2:15 p.m. May 31

Jutland Bank

German Submarines

2:30 p.m. May 31

6:00 p.m. May 31

DENMARK

Rosyth

NORTH SEA

11:00 p.m., May 30, 1916
Battle Cruiser Force and 5th Battle
Squadron (BEATTY) sails

Horns Reef

Amrun Bank

8:00 a.m. May 31

Flamborough Head

Heligoland

2:30 a.m., May 31,1916
1st and 2nd Scouting
Groups (HIPPER) sail.

Wilhelmshaven

GREAT BRITAIN

1:00 a.m., May 31,1916
High Seas Fleet
(SCHEER) sails.

NETHERLANDS

GERMAN EMPIRE

London

Thames Estuary

0 25 50 75 100 mi
0   50   100 km

BELGIUM

ENGLISH CHANNEL

battle cruisers, 11 cruisers, and 63 destroyers. As the German ships cruised north, a British scouting force, about 70 miles from the main body of the Grand Fleet, steamed to meet them. The scouting force consisted of 52 ships, including Vice Admiral David Beatty's 6 battle cruisers and Rear Admiral Hugh Evan-Thomas's squadron of 4 new fast, powerful dreadnoughts.

The two opposing scouting forces made contact at about 2:30 p.m. on May 31, about 100 miles off Jutland. Hipper then turned south to draw the British ships into Scheer's trap. Beatty did as Hipper hoped, turning on a parallel course and signaling Evan-Thomas to follow. At about 3:45 p.m. both sides opened fire at a range of about nine miles. Evan-Thomas's dreadnoughts, however, missed Beatty's signal and were slow to close; the result was a disaster for Beatty's battle cruisers.

Their inadequacies as ships of the line (at least in turret armor and magazine protection) were soon apparent. Beatty's flagship, the *Lion,* was badly damaged when it took a direct hit on one of its midships turrets. The *Lion* was saved only by quick flooding of the midships magazines. The *Indefatigable,* struck by three German shells, blew up and immediately sank. Only 2 members of the 1,000-man crew survived. Within 30 minutes another battle cruiser, the *Queen Mary,* also blew up. Beatty merely ordered his remaining ships to engage more closely. To this point, the Germans had suffered no losses.

Beatty now played the lure himself. Upon sighting the High Seas Fleet, he reversed course toward Jellicoe, drawing Scheer after him. This chase to the north continued for more than an hour, with the main British and German fleets, nearly 250 warships in all, closing at an aggregate speed of about 40 knots. At about 6:00 p.m. another British battle cruiser, the *Invincible,* was struck by a German shell. The *Invincible* blew up, and only six men survived.

At dusk, about 6:30 p.m., the Germans were proceeding north in line-ahead formation, confidently expecting soon to finish off the remainder of Beatty's ships. Then out of the smoke and mist Jellicoe's main body suddenly appeared in one long line on the horizon. The British opened fire and their shells began splashing among the leading German ships, hitting three. Jellicoe was in the most desirable position in naval warfare, having crossed the "T" of the German line and allowing all his turret guns to fire, whereas only the forward turret German guns could return fire.

Although the Germans enjoyed certain advantages in long-range gunnery and fire control, their ships were outclassed by the heavier guns of the more numerous British dreadnoughts. Before Jellicoe could complete deployment of his forces, however, at 6:35 p.m. Scheer ordered a difficult high-speed 180-degree turn. The German warships promptly disappeared back into the mist. Jellicoe, instead of pursuing, continued southward in an effort to cut the Germans off from their base.

Twenty minutes later Scheer executed another 180-degree turn in hopes of finding a better position, but British cruisers spotted his ships. Once again Jellicoe crossed the "T" of the German line. This time it appeared that the Germans might not escape, but Scheer reversed course yet again, ordering his destroyers to lay down a smokescreen and launch torpedoes.

There were then two ways to deal with torpedo attacks at sea. One was to turn directly into their path in order to present the smallest possible target. The other was to turn away and attempt to outrun them. Jellicoe chose the latter. This should have come as no surprise, as Jellicoe had twice told the Admiralty that he would order such a maneuver in torpedo attack, a policy approved by the Admiralty. The decision may have cost the British the opportunity for a decisive victory, but pressing the attack could also have brought disaster; as Churchill later put it, Jellicoe "was the only man on either side who could lose the war in an afternoon" (Churchill, *The World Crisis,* 2:106).

Scheer used nighttime to make good his retreat. Although there were numerous individual ship encounters, on June 1 the High Seas Fleet had returned to its bases. In this only major encounter of battle fleets during the war, the British lost 14 ships (3 battle cruisers, 3 cruisers, and 8 destroyers) to only 11 for the Germans (1 battleship, 1 predreadnought, 4 cruisers, and 5 destroyers). The disparity in tonnage losses was even greater: 111,980 for the British and 62,233 for the Germans.

The German claim of victory was false, though. Within 24 hours Jellicoe had 24 dreadnoughts available for action, whereas Scheer had only 10 (as opposed to 37 and 21, respectively, before the battle). The long-term effects also favored the British. Their blockade of Germany continued, and the Germans avoided again risking their capital ships in a showdown battle. Increasingly, the big ships rode at anchor as the German Imperial Navy concentrated on the submarine war.

References

Campbell, N. John M. *Jutland: An Analysis of the Fighting.* London: Conway Maritime, 1998.

Churchill, Winston S. *The World Crisis,* Vol. 2. New York: Scribner, 1923.

Corbett, Julian S., and Henry Newbolt. *Naval Operations: History of the Great War, Based on Official Documents,* Vol. 3. London: Longman, 1923.

Gordon, G. A. H. *The Rules of the Game: Jutland and British Naval Command.* Annapolis, MD: Naval Institute Press, 1996.

Marder, Arthur. *From Dreadnought to Scapa Flow: The Royal Navy in the Fisher Era, 1904–1919,* Vol. 3. London: Oxford University Press, 1967.

Brusilov Offensive

Date	June 4–September 1, 1916	
Location	vicinity of Lemberg, Kovel, and Lutsk, in Galicia, in present-day Ukraine	
Opponents (* winner)	*Russians	Austrians and Germans
Commander	General Aleksei Brusilov	Field Marshal Franz Conrad von Hötzendorf
Approx. # Troops	600,000	500,000
Importance	The greatest feat of Russian arms in World War I, it is perhaps the worst crisis for the Austro-Hungarian forces until the end of the war, but its high casualties contribute to Russian popular disillusionment with the war	

The Brusilov Offensive was the greatest feat of Russian arms of World War I (1914–1918). Both France, under heavy pressure by the Germans at Verdun, and Italy, being pressed by Austria-Hungarian forces in the Trentino, appealed to Russia for an offensive that would draw off some Central powers forces in the spring of 1916. On April 14 at a meeting presided over by Czar Nicholas II, army leaders debated renewing the offensive. Front commanders generals Aleksei Evert and Aleksei Kuropatkin argued that Russian forces were too weak. But General Aleksei Brusilov, who in March had replaced Nikolai Ivanov as commander of the Southwestern Front, and inspector general of artillery General Sergei Mikhailovich, thought otherwise. Brusilov, who had distinguished himself during the Carpathian retreat and was probably the best senior Russian general of the war, urged simultaneous attacks at several points.

Stavka (Russian high command) grudgingly accepted Brusilov's proposal and adopted a plan whereby he would stage an attack in the direction of Kowel (Kovel), with supporting attacks aimed at L'viv (Lwów, L'vov, Lemberg) in Galicia and Czernowitz in the Bukovina. Evert was to launch the main Russian drive toward Vilna, however, and all available resources were directed to the northern sectors of the front. The plan ran afoul of Stavka's inability to coordinate complex maneuvers and Evert's disdain for offensive operations.

Brusilov had to deal with innumerable problems, including lack of will in his subordinates and doubts from the top. Chief of staff General Mikhail Vasilievich Alekseev believed that Brusilov's plan was both too ambitious and too diffuse. Alekseev wanted a concentration of forces at one point for a massive breakthrough, but Brusilov clung to a simultaneous dispersed attack along the 300-mile front to make it impossible for the Austro-Hungarian Army to shift resources.

The Russians sapped their frontline trenches to within 75–100 yards of the Austrian lines. They dug tunnels under the enemy wire, stockpiled reserves of shells, and constructed huge dugouts to hold reserves. They also made accurate models of the Austrian defenses and trained in them. Brusilov used aerial photography to locate enemy guns, and his artillery and infantry worked closely together. Another tactical innovation was positioning the bulk of his guns no farther than 1.2 miles from the front.

Brusilov's four armies in the southwest (40 infantry and 15 cavalry divisions) faced an Austro-Hungarian army group of 49.5 divisions (38.5 infantry, 2 of them German, and 11 cavalry) strongly entrenched in three fortified belts. He held a manpower advantage of about 100,000 men (600,000 to 500,000) and 1,938 guns as opposed to 1,846, but only 168 of these were heavy guns, while his opponents had 545 heavy guns. Appeals from Stavka, prompted by further French and Italian pleading, caused Brusilov to advance the date of his attack forward to June 4 even though Evert said that he would not be ready to attack until June 14.

Brusilov was largely successful in achieving surprise. On June 4 the Russians began a massive and accurate barrage that silenced much of the Austro-Hungarian artillery. The next day Brusilov's infantry advanced. The Austrians had been hard hit in their frontline positions by accurate Russian fire, and three of Brusilov's four armies broke through. Within the first day, the two Russian flank armies advanced 10 miles. By June 6 Brusilov had taken 41,000 prisoners (including some Czech units that defected en masse) and 77 guns; by June 9 the total was more than 72,000 prisoners and 94 guns. The Austrian Fourth Army and the Seventh Army were routed.

On June 8 the Russians took Lutsk; Austrian archduke Frederick Joseph, enjoying a birthday lunch there, barely escaped capture. By June 23 Brusilov's troops had taken some 204,000 prisoners and 219 guns. Austria-Hungary seemed near collapse, but Brusilov could not immediately follow up on his victory. His own losses had been heavy, he had outrun his supply lines, and he had only one division in reserve. He could do no more. It now rested on Evert, with 1 million troops and two-thirds of the Russian artillery—a 3 to 1 superiority in men and guns over his opponents—to attack the Germans in the north.

This offensive was to have begun on June 14, but Evert repeatedly claimed shortages, and German maneuvers hindered his ability to proceed. Despite Brusilov's success, he put the attack off until the end of June and then again to July 3.

The Germans were not so hesitant. On June 8, during a meeting in Berlin, German Army chief of staff Generaloberst Erich von Falkenhayn insisted that Austro-Hungarian army chief of staff Field Marshal Franz Conrad von Hötzendorf transfer forces from the Italian front to the East. Utilizing the excellent German railroads, German commander in the east Generalfeldmarshall Paul von Hindenburg also sent reinforcements south. On June 16 German generaloberst Alexander von Linsingen's mixed Austro-German army group launched a counteroffensive southeast of Kowel, temporarily checking Brusilov but at the cost of 40,000 casualties during June 16–24.

On July 28 Brusilov, slowed by ammunition shortages, resumed the offensive. His third assault, between August 7 and September 20, brought the Russians into the Carpathian foothills. Between June 4 and August 12 his armies had taken nearly 379,000 prisoners and 496 guns. During the next month, however, the offensive bogged down, handicapped by the distances involved and supply problems. Linsingen managed to stabilize the front well east of Russia's final objectives of Lemberg and Kowel, eventually forcing Brusilov to abandon the Bukovina and Galicia.

Brusilov later contended that had Evert attacked on schedule, Austria-Hungary would have been driven from the war. This conclusion seems valid. Without German reinforcements, Austria-Hungary would certainly have been defeated. Even so, the Brusilov Offensive probably finished Austria-Hungary as a military power and contributed to Austrian emperor Karl's removal of Conrad from command in February 1917. The offensive may also have saved the Italian Army when Austrian units were transferred from the Trentino to the Russian front, although this has been questioned. The Brusilov Offensive also weakened the German attack at Verdun, brought Romania into the war on the Allied side, and helped bring about the fall of

Falkenhayn. Hindenburg became the supreme commander on the entire Eastern Front. German officers and troops were mixed into Austro-Hungarian units, and the Austro-Hungarians became totally dependent on Germany for support.

Although the greatest Russian feat of arms of the entire war occurred during the Brusilov Offensive, the offensive's cost had been high: as many as 1.412 million Russian casualties (212,000 of them taken prisoner) against some 750,000 Austro-Hungarian casualties (380,000 of them taken prisoner). More importantly, the Russian people saw the offensive as just another military failure, and this contributed to their revolution the next year.

References

Brusilov, A. A. *A Soldier's Note-Book.* 1930; reprint, Westport, CT: Greenwood, 1971.

Dowling, Timothy. *The Brusilov Offensive.* Bloomington: Indiana University Press, 2008.

Herwig, Holger H. *The First World War: Germany and Austria-Hungary, 1914–1918.* New York: St. Martin's, 1997.

Stone, Norman. *The Eastern Front, 1914–1917.* New York: Scribner, 1975.

Battle of Caporetto

Date	October 24–November 12, 1917	
Location	Northeastern Italy	
Opponents (* winner)	*Austro-Hungarians and Germans	Italians
Commander	Generalfeldmarschall Svetozar Boroević von Bojna (Austro-Hungarians); General der Infanterie Otto von Below (Germans)	General Luigi Capello; General Luigi Cadorna
Approx. # Troops	350,000	400,000
Importance	The collapse of their Second Army almost drives Italy from the war and leads to a search for scapegoats, but the nation recovers surprisingly quickly	

The Battle of Caporetto on the Italian front, also known as the Twelfth Battle of Isonzo, brought the near collapse of the Italian Army and its withdrawal to the Piave River. In the Eleventh Battle of the Isonzo River during August 18–September 15, 1917, Italian Army commander General Luigi Cadorna sent 52 divisions against the Austro-Hungarian lines in northern Italy. On the Italian left, General Luigi Capello's Second Army struck north of Gorizia, while the Duke of Aosta's Third Army attacked on the right between Gorizia and Trieste. Although Austrian field marshal Svetozar Boroević von Bojna's Fifth Army easily halted Aosta's thrust, Capello's army captured the strategically important Bainsizza Plateau before being forced to halt to reorganize. His forces near collapse, new Austro-Hungarian chief of staff General Artur Arz von Straussenburg appealed to the Germans for assistance.

Convinced that Austria-Hungary required assistance to remain in the war, German Army first quartermaster general General der Infanterie Erich Ludendorff took the lead in the creation of a new army, the Fourteenth Army, commanded by German General der Infanterie Otto von Below. Seven of its 15 divisions were German, as was most of its artillery. The Fourteenth Army would play a key role in a new offensive by 35 divisions (28 Austrian and 7 German) against 41 Italian divisions. Although Boroević von Bojna had overall command of the offensive, Below and his chief of staff, Generalleutnant Konrad Krafft von Delmensingen both planned and led it.

To offset their slight numerical disadvantage, the Central powers planned to use both surprise and new tactics successfully employed on the Eastern Front at Riga in September 1917. These included secretly massing fully briefed and highly trained assault forces at the last moment. Artillery would be brought up in secret, and registration would be performed by single guns firing over several days. The customary long preliminary bombardment was discarded in favor of short but intense barrages of mixed high-explosive, gas, and smoke shells to mask enemy strong points. The artillery plan was designed to cause maximum confusion and to disrupt enemy communications and artillery.

The short bombardment would be followed immediately by an attack spearheaded by the assault troops with large numbers of rapid-fire weapons. The attackers would bypass enemy strong points, leaving them to be taken by following forces. Supported by light artillery, the attackers would flow into enemy weak points, opening routes deep to the rear rather than attempting a broad advance. Such tactics were designed to isolate Italian frontline units, disrupt communications, and allow the attackers to reach rear areas before the enemy could deploy reserves. The Central powers also augmented their air assets on the Italian front. This gave them area aerial superiority, prevented Italian aerial intelligence gathering, and ensured secrecy, which was also aided by poor weather.

Despite these precautions, Cadorna knew that something was afoot, for deserters had warned of a major assault. Cadorna believed that the offensive would occur not in the rugged terrain of the Isonzo front but instead in the Trentino region. This seemed to be confirmed by an Austro-Hungarian diversionary attack in that sector on October 27. Consequently, Cadorna placed his reserves behind his Third Army rather than along the Isonzo. He did order a defense in depth along the entire line, with only light forces to hold forward positions, but Second Army commander Capello, who was ill, did not carry out the order. Worse, Capello's poorest troops were located in the area of greatest danger.

The Central powers plan called for Below's Fourteenth Army to lead the assault, supported by the Austro-Hungarian Tenth Army on its right and the Austrian Fifth

Army on its left. Overall the attackers were at a numerical disadvantage, but their strength at the point of attack was much greater. The Central powers also positioned 4,126 guns to support the offensive.

The October 24 barrage, which included gas and smoke shells, was intense, short, and deep. It opened at 2:00 a.m. on a 25-mile front and lasted only six hours. The infantry then moved forward. By the end of the first day, the Central powers had advanced up to 12 miles.

Gaps in the Italian lines torn by the attackers threatened the Italian Third Army's flanks to the south. In addition, the First Army and the Fourth Army to the west and north, respectively, might be turned if the attackers reached the Tagliamento. This river also guarded Cadorna's headquarters at Udine.

With the key Italian stronghold of Montemaggiore lost and his line fast disintegrating, Cadorna ordered a withdrawal to the Tagliamento. He intended to hold there until positions could be prepared along the Piave River. While probably correct under the circumstances, Cadorna's decision conceded to the Central powers a major tactical victory.

By the evening of October 31 the Italians were over the Tagliamento. They repulsed Central powers' efforts to cross until the night of November 2–3, when falling water levels allowed elements of an Austrian division to ford at Cornino. On November 4 Cadorna ordered all bridges on the Tagliamento destroyed and an Italian withdrawal behind the wide Piave, the bridges of which were destroyed on November 9. General Armando Diaz replaced Cadorna as Italy's supreme commander that same day.

With only 33 divisions, 3,986 guns, and six airfields left behind the Piave, the Italians faced 55 enemy divisions. But the attackers, worn down from their 50-mile advance, had outrun both their supply lines and artillery support. General Diaz had a much shorter front to defend and also had an excellent strategic position, with his troops entrenched behind a river line in the south and anchored on the Asiago Plateau and Monte Grappa in the north. Efforts during December 11–18 by the Central powers to force the Piave line and flank it by overwhelming the Italian Fourth Army at Monte Grappa failed, and on Christmas Day Boroević suspended the offensive.

In salvaging a situation that seemed lost, the Italians believed that they had reclaimed their honor. The arrival, in early November of 11 Allied divisions (5 British and 6 French), commanded by British general Sir Herbert Plumer, further bolstered morale. Still, the Italian Army had suffered grievously. It sustained 320,000 casualties (265,000 taken prisoner) and lost 3,152 guns, 1,732 mortars, 3,000 machine guns, 2,000 submachine guns, and more than 300,000 rifles. Austro-German losses in the battle were only about 20,000 men.

The Battle of Caporetto is the only battle fought in Italy during the war that has survived in popular memory. Although Italian historian Mario Caracciolo believes that Italy's allies played up the disaster to disguise their own poor performance in 1917, Italians themselves have kept the debate about Caporetto alive because it came as such a shock and triggered a search for scapegoats. Italian popular opinion attributed the debacle to defeatism, political corruption, and military incompetence. Some blamed workers from Turin who had been sent to the front as a punishment for spreading defeatist attitudes, while others held Cadorna and Capello responsible for depressing morale with their rigid personalities and their harsh discipline. The army did resort to summary execution to punish mutinous units and to make examples of those who fled during the retreat. Such action, however, reinforced a popular impression of chaos and panic in which incompetent and bloodthirsty generals punished the troops for the generals' own failures.

Surprisingly, the Italian Army soon recovered from Caporetto. By the summer of 1918 Diaz had 7,000 guns along the Piave, including 1,100 provided by France and Britain. With 50 Italian and 4 Allied divisions, he easily repulsed Boroević's last major offensive; in October the Italians virtually annihilated the Austrians in the Battle of Vittorio Veneto, on the first anniversary of the Battle of Caporetto. Another important result of the Battle of Caporetto was the Allied conference at Rapallo on November 5, 1917, which led to the creation of the Supreme War Council, the first real Allied effort to achieve unity of command.

References

Caracciolo, Mario. *L'Italia e i suoi Alleati nella Grande Guerra. Con Nuovi Documenti.* Milan: Mondadori, 1932.

Falls, Cyril. *Caporetto 1917.* London: Weidenfeld and Nicolson, 1971.

Kraff von Dellmensingen, Konrad. *Der Durchbruch am Isonzo.* 2 vols. Stalling: Oldenburg, 1926.

Morselli, Mario A. *Caporetto 1917: Victory or Defeat?* London: Frank Cass, 2001.

Seth, Ronald. *Caporetto: The Scapegoat Battle.* London: Macdonald, 1965.

Battle of Cambrai

Date	November 20–December 5, 1917	
Location	Vicinity of Cambrai, in northern France, some 35 miles south of Lille	
Opponents (* winner)	*Germans	British
Commander	General der Kavalrie Georg von der Marwitz	General Julian Byng
Approx. # Troops	20 divisions	19 infantry divisions, three tank brigades
Importance	The first combined arms offensive employing infantry and tanks, it returns the element of surprise on the Western Front and demonstrates the potential for future warfare; unfortunately for them, thanks to the heavy losses of the Somme the year before, the British lack the infantry reserves for a breakthrough	

The November–December 1917 Battle of Cambrai saw tanks come into their own on the battlefield. In the course of the Third Battle of Ypres (also known as the Battle of Passchendaele) during July–November 1917, the British Expeditionary Force (BEF) sustained heavy losses. Nonetheless, BEF commander Field Marshal Sir Douglas Haig persevered with offensive operations; within a few weeks he initiated the Battle of Cambrai. On the British side, the battle involved 19 divisions and three tank brigades of General Julian Byng's Third Army. Initially only six German divisions were engaged, all from General der Kavalrie Georg von der Marwitz's Second Army. During its course, however, the Germans committed a total of 20 divisions.

From their first use in September 1916 during the Somme Offensive, the British had deployed tanks in small packets. At Cambrai they had a Tank Corps of more than 400 tanks commanded by Brigadier General Hugh Elles. These included 376 of the latest Mark IV model, a slightly more powerful version of the 1916 Mark I. To the crews, the chief difference was that the Mark IV's enhanced use of 12-millimeter armor meant a far greater possibility of keeping out the new German armor-piercing bullets. For the first time tanks were the key element of the British plan, and this time they were used en masse.

Haig directed his main attack at German-held Cambrai, about 35 miles south of Lille. The area had firm, dry ground, which was essential for tank operations. It also had sufficient cover for the British to assemble a large attacking force in secrecy. Also, the German defensive line here was only thinly held. It consisted of a series of outposts in front of three well-constructed lines of the main Hindenburg Line and two secondary lines located about 1 and 4 miles farther back. A 13-mile tunnel, 35 feet below ground, allowed German reserves to wait in safety.

The chief of staff of the Tank Corps, Colonel J. F. C. Fuller, developed the initial attack plan. He saw it as the first in a series of tank raids that would lead to a decisive battle in 1918. Haig and Byng expanded the plan into a full-blown offensive designed to smash a six-mile gap in the German lines, capture Bourlon Ridge four miles west of Cambrai, and then launch five cavalry divisions through the gap between the Canal du Nord and the Canal de l'Escaut to disrupt the German rear. Haig's plan was clearly too ambitious for World War I conditions. Success depended on the British achieving complete surprise and securing Bourlon Ridge before the Germans could deploy their reserves.

The British employed low-flying aircraft to mask the noise of the arrival of tanks in their staging areas behind the front lines. The British also brought up 600 additional artillery pieces to provide supporting fire. These guns did not have the benefit of registration before the battle, however.

The assault by nine tank battalions (374 tanks) followed by five infantry divisions began at 6:20 a.m. on the dry but foggy morning of November 20. Instead of a long and counterproductive preliminary bombardment, 1,003 British guns laid

British tanks being readied for combat at a "tankdrome" near Cambrai. (Wallace, Duncan-Clark, and Plewman, *Canada in the Great War,* 1919)

down a short but intense barrage on the German front line. The British then shifted their artillery fire rearward to disrupt the movement of enemy reserves and to blind German direct-fire artillery with smoke.

Tanks led the attack, each transporting at its front a large fascine (a bundle of brushwood). They were closely followed by the infantry, advancing in small groups in open order rather than in the usual extended-line assault formation. The tanks worked in teams of three, with each having a precise task. The first tank would crush a gap in the wire; without crossing the German front trench, it would turn left to work down the near side of the trench, sweeping it with machine-gun fire. The second tank would drop its fascine in the trench, thereby enabling the tank to cross the trench (often as much as 13 feet wide) and then turn left to work down the far side. The third tank would then move to the support trench, drop its fascine to cross, and also turn left. With fascines, each team of tanks would be able to cross three trench obstacles. British infantry were to mop up survivors, secure captured German trenches against counterattack, and prepare for the next move forward.

On the first day the British attack went largely according to plan. Most German infantry simply fled. At Masnières the Germans blew up a bridge while a tank was crossing the canal there, forcing the infantry to fight without tank support and impeding progress. The chief obstacle was at Flesquières, however. There a British infantry division came under withering German fire, and more than a dozen British tanks were knocked out in succession by German guns firing from behind well-sited and well-camouflaged concrete bunkers. (One of the enduring myths of the Battle of Cambrai is that at Flesquières a single German defender knocked out up to 16 tanks with one field gun.) If the infantry had been able to operate with the tanks, the German artillery pieces might have been destroyed.

By nightfall of the first day the advancing British had penetrated the Hindenburg Line up to five miles. In Britain church bells pealed in celebration, but the revelry was premature. The Germans held at Bourlon Ridge, and German Sixth Army commander Generalfeldmarschall Prince Ruprecht of Bavaria rushed up reserves to plug the gap. Because of heavy losses they had sustained in the Third Battle of Ypres (also known as the Battle of Passchendaele), the British did not have sufficient infantry reserves to counter the German reinforcements.

The British also lacked tank reserves. Too many tanks had been committed in the first two waves, and many were either knocked out by German field guns or, more often, suffered mechanical breakdowns. In the first day 65 tanks were lost to enemy action, 71 broke down, and 43 got stuck. The great tank armada had disappeared.

When the British resumed their attack the next day, cooperative action between tanks and infantry was largely at an end, and the battle reverted to the typical World War I pattern. Although the British gained a foothold there, they never completely captured Bourlon Ridge. In the week that followed, virtually no more gains were made. Reinforced to 20 divisions, the Germans mounted a counterattack beginning on November 29. Utilizing new infiltration techniques, they also made effective use of ground-attack aircraft.

On December 3 Haig ordered a partial withdrawal. When the battle ended two days later, the Germans had not only recovered 75 percent of the territory lost on the first day but in the extreme south they had also made inroads into the original British positions. The British sustained about 44,000 casualties (9,000 of these taken prisoner). They also lost 166 guns and 300 tanks. German casualties totaled more than 41,000 men (11,000 taken prisoner) and 142 guns.

Although a failure from the British viewpoint, the Battle of Cambrai nonetheless restored surprise on the Western Front. It showed that tank and infiltration tactics could bring back battlefield fluidity. The battle demonstrated conclusively that for an attack to be successful, tanks, infantry, and artillery would all have to work together as combined-arms teams. This would be a hallmark of fighting on the Western Front in 1918.

References

Baumgartner, Richard. "Relentless Mechanized Assault." *Military History* 3(4) (February 1987): 34–41.

Cooper, Bryan. *The Ironclads of Cambrai: The First Great Tank Battle.* London: Cassell, 2002.

Smithers, A. J. *Cambrai: The First Great Tank Battle, 1917.* London: Leo Cooper, 1992.

Tucker, Spencer C. *Tanks: An Illustrated History of Their Impact.* Santa Barbara, CA: ABC-CLIO, 2004.

Ludendorff Offensive

Date	March 21–July 18, 1918	
Location	Northeastern France	
Opponents (* winner)	French, British, Americans, Belgians, etc.	*Germans
Commander	Marshal Ferdinand Foch	Generalfeldmarschall Paul von Beckendorff und von Hindenburg
Approx. # Troops (Overall strength)	3.9 million	2.9 million
Importance	The Germans register major gains in their last major bid to win World War I but lack the strength for a breakthrough	

At the beginning of 1918 during World War I (1914–1918) the Allies were in an unfavorable situation. On the seas their surface fleets were dominant and the German submarine threat had been contained, but on land, except for the Middle East, their offensives had failed. Italy was close to collapse, and Russia had been driven from the war. This was somewhat balanced by the entry of the United States, which was mobilizing its considerable resources to supply large quantities of finished goods, supplies, and foodstuffs. American forces were only slowly arriving in France, and they needed extensive training. U.S. troops were vital for the Entente, and in the winter of 1917–1918 a race to France began.

The Central powers were also reeling. The Allied naval blockade was slowly strangling Germany; Bulgaria, the Ottoman Empire, and even Austria-Hungary were wavering in their allegiance; and popular unrest was spreading. If Germany was to win the war, it would have to be in 1918, and Germany itself would bear the brunt of the effort.

Chief of the German General Staff Generalfeldmarschall Paul von Hindenburg and first quartermaster general of the German Army General der Infanterie Erich Ludendorff had concluded that the only way Germany could win the war was to drive Russia from the war and then shift forces to the West for an all-out offensive there before American forces could influence the outcome. An armistice with the new Bolshevik government of Russia went into effect in mid-December, and although a formal peace treaty was not signed until March 1918, the Germans immediately began shifting manpower to the Western Front. The Treaty of Brest Litovsk, by which Russia lost 1.3 million square miles of territory and a third of its population, provides an indication of what German terms in the West might have been. In May, Romania was forced to sign the equally harsh Treaty of Bucharest.

Hindenburg and Ludendorff sought nothing less than a victorious peace, a *Siegfrieden*. Still, Ludendorff committed a major error in not transferring more men.

He retained 1 million soldiers in the East. A large proportion of these were older men, but if half of this number had also been sent west they could have gone to quiet sectors of the front and released younger men for the forthcoming offensive. Ultimately more troops had to be sent West in any case so that by the end of the war the Germans had only 500,000 million men in the East. Had the additional forces been available in March 1918, this might have tipped the balance in favor of Germany in the war.

By the third week in March 1918 Ludendorff was ready to launch his offensive. This spring 1918 German drive is usually known as the Ludendorff Offensive. It envisioned a series of attacks to push the British Army back on the English Channel, isolating it from the French Army. Defeating the British, Ludendorff believed, would force France to give up.

The first German drive, code-named MICHAEL (after Germany's patron saint), was directed at the hinge where the British and French armies met and lasted from March 21 to April 5. Ludendorff amassed 207 divisions against only 173 Allied divisions (this included 4.5 U.S. divisions, which at 27,000 men each are here calculated at 9 divisions). The attack itself involved 74 German divisions supported by 6,473 guns and 730 aircraft. With only 34 infantry and 3 cavalry divisions defending this point of the line, at places the British were outnumbered 4 to 1. The defenders had 2,804 guns, 579 aircraft, and 217 tanks.

The Allies knew that the Germans would soon attack. The Allied Supreme War Council sought a 30-division reserve, but both French Army commander General Henri Philippe Pétain and British Expeditionary Force (BEF) commander Field Marshal Sir Douglas Haig objected. In the end, both commanders planned their own defensive battles.

The Germans utilized the infiltration tactics already proven against the Russians at Riga and the Italians at Caporetto. These employed elite *Stosstrüppen* (shock troops) formed into *Sturmbattallione* (assault battalions) moving in combined-arms platoons of about 50 men each and armed with machine weapons and supported by light direct-fire artillery and ground-attack aircraft. To deceive the Allies, all German commanders were led to believe that the attack would be made in their own sectors. Deceptive shelling in the Verdun sector also served to convince Pétain that the northern attack was a feint.

The Germans were aware that the bulk of British forces were employed on the vulnerable northern end of the line in Flanders. Two months earlier the British had extended their front, taking over some 28 miles of French trenches. Lieutenant General Sir Hubert Gough's Fifth Army troops discovered that the French had largely neglected that sector's defenses. Haig also underestimated the threat there.

Although the Allies had come to recognize the value of an elastic defense in depth, deployments were incomplete. In Gough's sector the forward defensive zone was too densely held. Haig had no reserves there but hoped that in a crisis

Pétain would send troops, although a January agreement called for him to send only six divisions within four days of any request.

The Germans opened MICHAEL, now dubbed the Kaiserschlacht (Emperor's Battle) and also known as the Second Battle of the Somme, at 4:40 a.m. on March 21. The German artillery preparation lasted only five hours but numbered 1.2 million shells, including gas and smoke. The 74 German divisions attacked along the 50-mile front from La Fère to Arras, held in the north by General Sir Julian Byng's Third Army of 14 divisions and in the south by Gough's Fifth Army of 12 infantry and 3 cavalry divisions.

The attackers easily drove back the Fifth Army. On the second day the British lost contact with the French to their right, and Gough ordered a retirement beyond the Somme. General der Infanterie Oskar von Hutier's Eighteenth Army had been successful as well, but to the north the Second Army and the Seventeenth Army encountered the better-prepared defenses of Byng's Third Army. Ludendorff still might have achieved decisive victory had he concentrated on taking the vital railroad junction of Amiens, but on March 23, believing that the British were beaten, he gave his three attacking armies divergent axes of advance.

Although the British continued to withdraw—Baupaume fell on March 24 and Albert on March 26—their lines did not break. The Germans had now outrun their supply lines, which had to traverse terrain torn up in the earlier fighting. This inhibited bringing up heavy artillery. The attackers also had sustained heavy casualties and lacked the reserves to exploit breakthroughs. They suffered as well from British aircraft attacks against their troops in the open.

MICHAEL did bring a change in Allied command structure. While not affecting that battle, it did have profound implications for the war's outcome. Allied leaders knew that one reason for the initial German success was lack of cooperation between the British and French. Believing that the major German attack would come in the Champagne area, Pétain had refused to send reinforcements to the BEF. MICHAEL was thus a great tactical success for Ludendorff. The German Army recaptured much of the ground it had abandoned in 1916 and created a 10-mile wide gap in the Allied lines. In these desperate circumstances, on March 26 the Allied leaders finally adopted a unified command structure, entrusting overall command on the Western Front to French general Ferdinand Foch. He now brought up reserves that halted the German drive.

With his offensive on the Somme stalled, Ludendorff prepared another attack. On March 25 he shifted the offensive emphasis back to the center and right, where his Second Army and Seventeenth Army had been held up. Code-named MARS, the new operation had Arras as its objective and began on March 28. Stronger British positions there held. At the end of the month Ludendorff shifted to take Amiens, but by now the German troops were exhausted. Clear weather allowed Allied aircraft to savage the attackers. On April 5 Ludendorff suspended the offensive.

The British had been driven back up to 40 miles. Haig unfairly made Gough the scapegoat and removed him from command. General Sir Henry Rawlinson replaced him, and on April 2 the Fifth Army was renamed the Fourth Army. To this point in the offensive, the British had suffered approximately 178,000 casualties (72,000 taken prisoner) and lost more than 1,100 guns, 200 tanks, and about 400 aircraft. The French, with 20 divisions engaged, sustained around 77,000 casualties (approximately 15,000 taken prisoner). The push had also been costly to the Germans, particularly to the elite Storm Troops. They had lost 239,000 men and now needed more men to hold a longer line.

The Allies fully realized their perilous situation. Within a month London had sent to the continent its military reserve of 355,000 men. Also by March 1918 some 325,000 U.S. troops were in France, and efforts were made to expedite their deployment.

After a brief pause to regroup, Ludendorff launched his second blow to the north in Flanders. A smaller version of the original plan, GEORGE, it was code-named GEORGETTE. The Fourth Army and the Sixth Army attacked just south of Ypres on both sides of the east-west–running Lys River, which gave its name to the battle during April 9–21. The two German armies had 2,208 artillery pieces; the British First Army opposing them only 511. Ludendorff also assembled 492 aircraft.

Ludendorff hoped that this second attack, on the British left wing, would break the BEF or at least cripple it sufficiently to allow him to shift back to the south and finish the job. His commitment of significant resources, however, meant that his forces would be vulnerable to an Allied counterattack. In addition, more than half of the assault troops were trench divisions rather than elite attack divisions.

The Sixth Army's attack fell in a sector near Neuve Chapelle held by the Portuguese 2nd Division, one of two fighting in France under British control since 1916. This division was of poor quality and had been held in the line longer than normal. The Portuguese broke immediately and left a six-mile gap in the line. The next day the German Fourth Army, attacking to the north, drove the British off Messines Ridge and forced them to evacuate Armentières, between the converging German thrusts.

On April 11 Haig issued a desperate order: "There is no other course open to us but to fight it out. Every position must be held to the last man: there must be no retirement. With our backs to the wall and believing in the justice of our cause, each one of us must fight on to the end."

Although the British were forced back 15 to 20 miles in places, their lines did not break. Three new divisions—two British and one Australian—also arrived. And on April 14 Foch became general-in-chief with more power to move French forces from a reluctant Pétain. By April 19 the French had taken over a nine-mile sector of front previously held by the Second Army. This came too late, however, to enable General Sir Herbert Plumer to hold, and Foch ordered Plumer to withdraw his Second Army from Passchendaele Ridge to a more secure line just east of Ypres.

On April 24 the Germans again struck toward Amiens from Villers Bretonneux. The battle was notable in that the Germans employed a dozen A7V tanks, six of which fought with three British Mark IVs in the first tank-to-tank battle in history. That night Rawlinson launched a counterattack and drove the Germans back.

Ludendorff was forced to regroup again, and on April 29 he called off the offensive. Allied losses in this battle were more than 146,000 men (two-thirds of them British) and at least 573 guns. German losses were perhaps 109,000 men.

By early May, Ludendorff had succeeded in replacing approximately 70 percent of his losses. He still had a numerical advantage over the Allies on the Western Front—206 divisions against 160—but he no longer had the fine troops of the start of the offensive. Moreover, as Ludendorff readied his third drive, U.S. Army divisions were at last in the Allied line.

Ludendorff's new attack, again aimed at the juncture between the British and French armies, was to be the final decisive blow against the British. Before that offensive could be launched, however, Ludendorff planned a diversionary attack against the French Army on the Chemin des Dames front. He believed that French reinforcements had twice saved the British (this was not how the British saw it), and these new attacks were designed to hold the French in place so that Ludendorff could return and finish off the British in Operation HAGEN.

Ludendorff's third drive, known as Operation BLÜCHER or the Third Battle of the Aisne, began on May 27 and lasted until June 3. The Germans secretly positioned the 30 divisions of General der Infanterie Hans von Boehn's Seventh Army in the Chemin des Dames sector, giving Crown Prince Wilhelm's Army Group a total of 41 divisions. The Germans relied heavily on artillery; their 5,263 guns faced only 1,422 British and French guns.

The Germans were also aided by the fact that commander of the Aisne sector French Sixth Army commander General Denis Auguste Duchêne ignored Pétain's call for an elastic defense. In order to retain the high ground of the Chemin des Dames, which had been won at such high cost, Duchêne placed most of his 16 divisions (including 5 British divisions) forward in trenches along the crest of the 25-mile front. An elastic defense would have had only outposts there, with the bulk of forces positioned behind the river. The British divisions had been sent to a quiet sector of the front to recuperate from the earlier offensives, and three of them were in the front line when the German blow fell.

The May 27 massive 160-minute battering-ram artillery preparation shattered the French defenders in their forward positions. The German Seventh Army easily broke through the French lines and secured the bridges over the Aisne and undefended terrain behind it to the Vesle River. Within two days the Seventh Army had taken Soissons and by the end of the month was in the Marne River Valley, the natural route to Paris some 50 miles away.

Ludendorff had not learned from his previous attacks, however. An opportunist rather than a strategist, he continued the assault too long, lulled by the surprising ease of the 40-mile advance toward Paris. The Germans had again outrun their supply lines, while the French had managed to withdraw in good order. The Allies, fighting on interior lines, were able to make excellent use of railroad lines to bring up supplies and reinforcements, including U.S. Army divisions. On May 28 the U.S. 1st Division recaptured Cantigny, and Americans also helped blunt the subsequent German advance at Château-Thierry and Belleau Wood.

The Germans had once again made a tremendous advance but had been unable to exploit it, and they occupied a deep salient that was difficult to supply and hold. In their three offensives they had sustained more than 600,000 casualties, and these could not be replaced. Ludendorff's next goal was to link the salient north along the Somme with the other to the south on the Marne and shorten the line. His fourth drive, known as GNEISENAU and mounted by Hutier's Eighteenth Army, began on June 9 on a 22-mile front between Montdidier and Noyon.

Foch anticipated Ludendorff's move. In any case, German preparations were more open, and deserters gave away its timing. This enabled the French to open counterbattery fire on the German artillery and infantry in their assault positions. Again the Germans made a spectacular gain on the first day (six miles) but assisted by the Americans, the French halted the German advance. On June 11 the French counterattacked, ending Hutier's drive.

Losses in the fighting during June 9–14 came to 35,000 French (15,000 taken prisoner) and 30,000 Germans. The month-long delay that followed proved invaluable for the Allies, who brought more U.S. troops into the line. Ludendorff now prepared for one additional offensive against the French, which led to the Second Battle of the Marne during July 15–18.

References

Gilbert, Martin. *The First World War: A Complete History*. New York: Henry Holt, 1994.

Herwig, Holger H. *The First World War: Germany and Austria-Hungary, 1914–1918*. New York: St. Martin's, 1997.

Holmes, Richard. *The Western Front*. London: BBC Books, 1999.

Ludendorff, Erich. *Ludendorff's Own Story: August 1914–November 1918*. 2 vols. New York: Harper, 1919.

Paschall, Rod. *The Defeat of Imperial Germany, 1917–1918*. Chapel Hill, NC: Algonquin Books, 1990.

Pitt, Barrie. *1918: The Last Act*. New York: Ballantine Books, 1963.

Zabecki, David T. *Steel Wind: Colonel Georg Bruchmüller and the Birth of Modern Artillery*. Bridgeport, CT: Praeger, 1994.

Second Battle of the Marne

Date	July 15–18, 1918	
Location	Marne River in northeast France	
Opponents (* winner)	*French, British, Americans	Germans
Commander	Field Marshal Ferdinand Foch	Generalleutenant Eric Ludendorff
Approx. # Troops	580,000	480,000
Importance	The Allies take and hold the initiative for the remainder of World War I	

The Second Battle of the Marne (Champagne-Marne Offensive) of July 15–18, 1918, turned the tide of battle on the Western Front and gave the Western Allies the initiative for the remainder of World War I (1914–1918). The battle followed the fourth of German Army first quartermaster general General der Infanterie Erich Ludendorff's Western Front drives of 1918. The official German name for the offensive was MARNESCHUTZ-REIMS, but the cover name by which the German troops knew it was FRIEDENSTRUM (PEACE OFFENSIVE), chosen to give German troops the impression that it would end the war.

Following the failure of Ludendorff's fourth offensive (GNEISENAU, the Noyon Offensive, during June 9–14, 1918), the German Army no longer was in position to win on the Western Front. Ludendorff could not, however, bring himself to abandon Operation HAGEN, his plan to drive the British Expeditionary Force (BEF) from the war. He believed that it would bring a general Allied collapse.

Before he could launch HAGEN, however, Ludendorff had to resolve two problems created by his earlier attacks. Operations BLÜCHER (the Chemin des Dames Offensive) and GNEISENAU had drawn off some Allied reserves to the south, but Allied forces in the north were still too powerful for HAGEN to be successful. Also, Ludendorff needed to develop some means to supply German forces in the huge salient caused by BLÜCHER and thus had no real alternative but to attack again in the same sector.

Ludendorff's overly ambitious plan involved a double envelopment by Crown Prince Wilhelm's Army Group east and west of the city of Reims. The goal was to take both the city and the vital railroad running from Paris to Nancy. General der Infanterie Hans von Boehn's Seventh Army would move up the Marne, while General der Kavallerie Karl von Einem's Third Army would strike south toward Châlons-sur-Marne. Ludendorff believed that this offensive would force the supreme Allied commander, General Ferdinand Foch, to pull his remaining reserves from Flanders and that within a few days of victory at Reims he could launch HAGEN and finish off the British. But there was no guarantee that the Germans would not continue up the Marne Valley to Paris, and the fear that now gripped the French capital was reminiscent of the summer of 1914. When the battle began, the sound of the explosions from the shells of the heavy guns could clearly be heard in the French capital, some 50 miles away.

General Henri Joseph Eugène Gouraud's French Fourth Army defended east of Reims, while the French Sixth Army under General Jean Marie Degoutte was positioned west of that city, almost to Château-Thierry on the Marne. In all, 48 German divisions faced 36 French divisions, while the advantage in artillery also lay with the Germans: 6,353 guns to only 3,080 for the Allies.

Ludendorff launched Operation MARNESCHUTZ-REIMS at dawn on July 15. It was the farthest south and east of all the great German drives of 1918. German deserters and prisoners betrayed most of the German plan, however, including its timing. The German artillery preparation began at 1:10 a.m. on July 15, but at midnight the French artillery began an enhanced program of harassing and interdicting fire. At 1:20 a.m. the French opened full counterpreparation artillery fire. The intensity caught the Germans by surprise, and the attack found the German infantry in its assembly areas, inflicting many casualties. At 4:50 a.m. the German infantry nevertheless began its attack behind a creeping barrage that included gas.

West of Reims, the French counterpreparation artillery fire separated the Seventh Army's infantry from their creeping barrage and disrupted the German bridging operation across the Marne. By nightfall on July 15 the Germans had managed to cross some six divisions to the south bank of the Marne, but hardly any artillery had gotten over the river. The bridgehead was then about 12 miles wide and 3 miles deep. The French artillery, working in conjunction with their aircraft, concentrated on the bridges in order to cut off the Germans on the south bank.

East of Reims, the German First Army and Third Army encountered heavier French artillery fire than anticipated but little French infantry resistance. At about 7:30 a.m. the German creeping barrage reached its maximum range and lifted. The attackers then found themselves facing a fully manned zone defense that hardly had been touched by the German artillery preparation or the creeping barrage.

The Germans had walked into a trap. Knowing the timing of the attack, the Fourth Army had abandoned its frontline positions except for light security forces. The massive German artillery preparation had mostly struck empty ground.

Operation MARNESCHUTZ-REIMS was already a failure by nightfall on July 15. The fighting dragged on, however. Ludendorff ordered the Third Army to halt its attack and ordered the Seventh Army, on the west flank, to consolidate its gains. On July 17 the Germans began bringing up artillery from the Seventh Army to support the First Army's attack on Reims.

The French now launched a surprise counterattack, however. Even as the battle for Reims had raged, Foch husbanded a reserve of 20 divisions—2 American and 18 French—along with 350 tanks. Early on July 18 he launched a counteroffensive with General Charles Mangin's Tenth Army and General Jean Degoutte's Sixth Army against the BLÜCHER salient on both sides of Château-Thierry, precisely the area the Germans had stripped of reinforcing artillery the day before.

The U.S. 1st and 2nd divisions spearheaded the Tenth Army's attack, which fell on the right side of the Reims salient, five miles south of German-held Soissons. Although casualties were heavy for the Allies (the 1st Division alone sustained 7,200 casualties that day, and the 2nd Division sustained nearly 5,000 casualties), the attack succeeded brilliantly. The 1st Division captured 3,800 prisoners and 70 guns from the seven German divisions it encountered, while the 2nd Division took 3,000 prisoners and 75 guns. In all, the Allies took 12,000 prisoners and 250 guns from 11 German divisions. The threat to Paris was now ended, and from this point on the Allies advanced and the Germans retreated. On July 20 Ludendorff called off his planned Flanders drive to concentrate on holding the area to the south, but he rejected sound advice that the army retire to the Hindenburg Line.

By August 3 the Germans had been pushed back to their original May 27 starting line for Operation BLÜCHER. Slightly more than two weeks of fighting cost the Allies 160,000 casualties, while costing the Germans 110,000 casualties and 600 irreplaceable guns. On August 8 the Allies launched their own Amiens Offensive to the north. They would hold the initiative for the remainder of the war.

References

Herwig, Holger H. *The First World War: Germany and Austria-Hungary, 1914–1918.* New York: St. Martin's, 1997.

Holmes, Richard. *The Western Front.* London: BBC Books, 1999.

Ludendorff, Erich. *Ludendorff's Own Story: August 1914–November 1918.* 2 vols. New York: Harper, 1919.

Paschall, Rod. *The Defeat of Imperial Germany, 1917–1918.* Chapel Hill, NC: Algonquin Books, 1990.

Pitt, Barrie. *1918: The Last Act.* New York: Ballantine Books, 1963.

Zabecki, David T. *Steel Wind: Colonel Georg Bruchmüller and the Birth of Modern Artillery.* Bridgeport, CT: Praeger, 1994.

Battle for Warsaw

Date	August 16–25, 1920	
Location	Near Warsaw, Poland	
Opponents (* winner)	*Poles	Russians
Commander	General Józef Piłsudski	General Mikhail N. Tukhachevsky
Approx. # Troops	180,000	200,000
Importance	Halts Russian expansion west and allows Poland to establish its borders.	

The Battle for Warsaw in 1920 was the most important engagement of the Russo-Polish War of 1920–1921. Poland had disappeared at the end of the 18th century, absorbed by Russia, Prussia, and Austria. During World War I (1914–1918) U.S. president Woodrow Wilson's call for a "free and independent Poland with access to the sea" became an Allied war aim, and after the war Poland reappeared as a legal entity. The matter of its future frontiers, especially those to the east, remained open, however.

Many in both Germany and Russia regarded Poland as a temporary state to be eradicated at the first opportunity. Poland's leaders opted to resolve their security problems through territorial expansion, which was justified in their eyes as recovering the borders before the partitions. Creation of the Polish Corridor, which provided Poland with access to the sea across East Prussia, and the existence of the free city of Danzig led to animosity with Germany, which was exacerbated by Poland's seizure of Upper Silesia. Eventually the League of Nations awarded the larger part of that province's population and territory to Germany but gave Poland the area with the greater economic resources. Poland's seizure of Vilna (Vilnius) caused bitter hostility with Lithuania. Poland also forcibly took eastern Galicia over the opposition of its majority Ukrainian population, and Poland's seizure of part of Teschen from Czechoslovakia embittered relations with that country.

There were also border disputes with Russia. A Paris Peace Conference commission at the end of 1919 set Poland's eastern borders along general ethnographic lines (the Curzon Line, named for Lord Curzon, the head of the commission), but Poland took advantage of the civil war in Russia to occupy areas of mixed Polish-Russian population in the undefined frontier area bordering Belorussia (present-day Belarus) and the Ukraine. The Poles refused to cooperate with the anti-Bolshevik White opposition, though. Had that occurred, the Bolsheviks might have been overthrown.

In 1920 when the Red (Bolshevik) armies at last triumphed over the Whites, the Bolshevik government turned its attention to the Poles. The government presented an ultimatum that would have meant a Russian protectorate. With General Józef Piłsudski as head of the new Polish state, there was no chance that Poland would accept the Russian terms. When the Russians massed military forces in the west, the Poles decided not to wait to be attacked but instead to seize the initiative.

Russian commander Mikhail N. Tukhachevsky's Western Front (army) was located north of the Pripet Marshes. Opposing it was a smaller Polish army under General Władysław E. Sikorski. South of the Pripet Marshes was Russian general Alexander I. Yegorov's Southwestern Front. Opposing it was a Polish force commanded by Piłsudski, the overall Polish commander. Each side fielded about 200,000 troops.

The campaign began on April 25, 1920, when Piłsudski launched an offensive that lasted until May 7. His force drove for Kiev, supported on its right flank by a mixed force of anti-Bolshevik Ukrainians under Simon Petlyura. Capturing Kiev on May 7, Piłsudski prepared to swing north behind the Pripet Marshes to hit Tukhachevsky in the rear, but this proved too ambitious for the forces and logistical support available.

Tukhachevsky's Western Front meanwhile pushed southwest, pinning back Piłsudski's left. At the same time, First Cavalry Army commander Semeyon M. Budeyonny of Yegorov's army drove northwest with a cavalry corps of some 16,000 men and 48 guns against Piłsudski's right flank. Budeyonny reached Zitomir, southwest of Kiev, almost taking Piłsudski's right wing. By June 13 the Polish left was also in full retreat, and Cossacks swept to the outskirts of Lwów (Lemberg; today L'viv in Ukraine). North of the Pripet Marshes, Tukhachevsky reached Vilna on July 14 and Grodno on July 19, while Budeyonny kept up pressure on the southern front. By July 25 the Polish forces lay in two groups, one around Lwów and the other near Warsaw, the fall of which appeared imminent. Indeed, Tukhachevsky expected to take the Polish capital on August 14.

France had a major interest in the existence of a strong Poland to guard against a resurgent Germany from the east, and late in July 1920 a French advisory team arrived in Warsaw. General Maxime Weygand, who had been chief of staff to Allied commander Marshal Ferdinand Foch at the close of World War I, headed the group. Piłsudski did not need advice, though. He had the great advantage of being able to read the ciphers used by the Russians to exchange messages.

Weygand advised a counterattack north of Warsaw, launched from behind the defensive line of the Vistula River. Piłsudski knew through radio intercepts, however, that the Russians had outrun their supply lines and were short of almost everything, including food. Thus, while the seemingly irresistible Russian right pushed forward, passing to the north of Warsaw, Piłsudski ordered a daring counterattack against Tukhachevsky's left. Signal intercepts had revealed that as the Russian weak point.

On the orders of Joseph Stalin, chief political officer of the Southwestern Front's Revolutionary Military Council, Budeyonny's army was moving to take L'viv rather than advancing to support Tukhachevsky's drive on Warsaw. Tukhachevsky desperately needed Budeyonny's assistance and pleaded with Red Army headquarters to provide reinforcements. Headquarters indeed ordered Budeyonny to join Tukhachevsky, but Stalin directed Budeyonny to ignore the order.

With his weight concentrated at Deblin 50 miles southeast of Warsaw, on August 16, 1920, Piłsudski opened the Battle of Warsaw by driving against the weakly held Russian Western Front's left along the Warsaw to Brest-Litovsk road. The Polish breakthrough was swift. Piłsudski ignored Russian elements to the south to swing northward and encircle the bulk of the Russian forces by linking with the Polish drive from the north under Sikorski.

Caught between the Polish pincers, Tukhachevsky's command disintegrated. Some 30,000 Russians made it across the frontier into East Prussia, there to be disarmed by the Germans. Before Tukhachevsky could rally his forces on August 25, the Poles had captured 66,000 prisoners, more than 230 guns, 1,000 machine guns, and 10,000 vehicles. Russian casualties totaled 150,000 men. The stunning Polish victory was one of the decisive battles of the 20th century, marking the first check to westward Bolshevik expansion.

The Russians lost another 100,000 men before agreeing on October 19, 1920, to an armistice. In the Treaty of Riga of March 18, 1921, the Russians accepted an eastern boundary for Poland that gave the Poles large areas of Belorussia and Ukraine, almost 52,000 square miles of territory east of the Curzon Line. Except for the territory that had become the new Republic of Lithuania, this corresponded roughly with Poland's border just before the final partition of 1795. Nonetheless, Poland's policies had resulted in borders that one Polish leader identified as 75 percent permanently menaced, 20 percent insecure, and only 5 percent safe.

References

Davies, Norman. *White Eagle, Red Star: The Polish-Soviet War, 1919–1920.* New York: St. Martin's, 1972.

Fiddick, Thomas C. *Russia's Retreat from Poland, 1920: From Permanent Revolution to Peaceful Coexistence.* New York: St. Martin's, 1990.

Zamoyski, Adam. *The Battle for the Marchlands.* New York: Columbia University Press, 1981.

Siege of the Alcázar

Date	July 20–September 28, 1936	
Location	City of Toledo, Spain	
Opponents (* winner)	*Nationalists	Republicans
Commander	Colonel José Moscardó Ituarte; General José Enrique Varela Iglesius	Candido Cabello
Approx. # Troops	Some 800 inside the fortress	8,000
Importance	One of the most dramatic episodes of the Spanish Civil War, but the Nationalist decision to send troops to relieve the siege may have prevented them from taking Madrid and ending the war early	

The siege of the Alcázar in Toledo, Spain, in 1936 was one of the most dramatic episodes of the Spanish Civil War (1936–1939). Fighting began on July 17, 1936, with a revolt of army regiments in Spanish Morocco and then Spain itself. The Republicans had just won a narrow victory in the national elections, and senior army commanders led traditionalist elements, known as the Nationalists, who were determined to prevent the Republicans from (purportedly) destroying the character and traditions of Spain. The central issue was whether the Catholic, agrarian, and centralized rule that had prevailed in Spain for centuries should continue or whether the nation would embrace the ideas accepted by much of the West, such as land reform, capitalism, civil rights, and the separation of church and state.

The rebels, who were forced to begin their revolt before all plans were in place, hoped to take Madrid at the outset. They believed that if the Spanish capital, then unfortified, could be captured promptly, the war might be ended. The Nationalist side failed to accomplish this, largely because of the Republican siege of the Alcázar of Toledo, a city about 75 miles south-southwest of the capital.

Alcázar is the Spanish term for a fortified castle, and the Toledo Alcázar had 10-foot walls. The Alcázar was also the home of the Spanish Military Academy, commanded in July 1936 by Colonel José Moscardó Ituarte. The fortress was situated on high ground that dominated both the city and the Tagus River.

On July 20 the Republican government in Madrid ordered Moscardó to send to the capital all the arms from the Alcázar. He refused, stating that he sided with rebels. The government immediately declared him a traitor and dispatched hastily organized militia there. Moscardó realized that he could not control all Toledo, so he ordered the local garrison of the Guardia Civil into the fortress with his regular troops. Long known for its metalwork and arms production, Toledo was home to an important arms factory, and the rebels removed its stocks to the fortress. They thus had some 1,000 rifles, 13 machine guns, a large quantity of ammunition, and a number of grenades. The government forces soon began the siege, but they lacked the modern heavy artillery necessary to breach the fortress walls.

There were some 1,500 people inside the Alcázar. Although figures differ, Moscardó probably commanded about 150 officers and noncommissioned officers assigned to the Spanish Military Academy, 650 members of the Guardia Civil, and 7 cadets (the others being on vacation). There were more than 500 women and children, all military dependents, inside as well. The colonel had also taken about 100 civilian hostages into the fortress, including the city's civil governor and his family.

On July 23 in what is perhaps the most celebrated incident of the Spanish Civil War, Candido Cabello, leader of the militia in Toledo, talked by telephone with Moscardó. Cabello allegedly told Moscardó that unless he surrendered the fortress within 10 minutes, he would shoot Moscardó's 17-year-old son Luis. As proof that he held Luis, Cabello put the boy on the phone. Moscardó told Luis that he should commend his soul to God, shout "Long live Spain," and prepare for a hero's death. Cabello then came back on the phone, and Moscardó told him that the Alcázar would never surrender. Luis Moscardó was indeed executed, although on August 23.

Moscardó meanwhile organized the defenses of the fortress. With electricity and water into the fortress shut off, the colonel ordered strict rationing of food and water; 124 horses and mules, destined to be the meat supply for the besieged, were placed in the safest part of the fortress. Only 6 of these animals (including 1 thoroughbred racehorse) were still alive at the end of the siege. A daring night raid from the fortress against a nearby storehouse yielded some 2,000 sacks of grain. This was then ground inside the fortress into flour. Crude lamps that burned animal grease provided illumination.

By early August some 8,000 government troops surrounded the fortress. The Republican side controlled both the Spanish Air Force and the Spanish Navy, and the aircraft carried out some 120 sorties against the Alcázar. Thirty-five people deserted the fortress during the siege, including 10 civil guardsmen.

On September 9 a brief cease-fire occurred when Moscardó agreed to meet with government envoy Major Vicente Rojo, but Moscardó rejected demands that he surrender with a promise of freedom for the civilians, with the defenders to be subject to court-martial. On September 11 in response to Moscardó's calls for a priest, Monsignor Vázquez Camarrasa was allowed into the fortress during a three-hour cease-fire. He granted a general absolution to the defenders.

The government then ordered mines to be dug under the two great fortress towers nearest the city. On September 17, to prevent civilian casualties, the government ordered the city evacuated and called in the foreign press to Toledo to witness the Alcázar's end. On the morning of September 18 the first mine went off, collapsing the tower on the southeast corner of the fortress and opening a breach in the wall. Desperate fighting ensued as government troops tried to storm the fortress.

Nationalist general José Enrique Varela Iglesius and a force of Moroccans bound for Madrid were only about 25 miles from Toledo at this time. General Francisco Franco y Bahamonde, who had become the Nationalists' leader, decided to divert them to Toledo. Franco understood that this might cost him Madrid, but he remarked that relieving the Toledo garrison was more important. Securing the arms factory there was probably the deciding factor. On September 23 Varela's forces set out; three days later they cut the road linking Toledo with Madrid.

On September 27 the Republicans exploded another mine, this one on the northeast side of the fortress. Varela's relief force arrived at sunset and entered the Alcázar, which was in flames. The next morning Moscardó handed over command of what was left of the fortress to Varela with the phrase "*Sin novedad*" ("Nothing to report"), which had been the rebel password during July 17–18. The Moroccan troops meanwhile massacred all the Republicans in Toledo they could find, including the wounded in San Juan Hospital.

The Alcázar had no strategic significance, but diverting their troops there may have cost the Nationalists the opportunity to take Madrid and end the war. The capital did not fall until March 1939, marking the end of the fighting. Perhaps 600,000 Spaniards died on both sides in the Spanish Civil War, and afterward another 100,000 were executed by the victorious Nationalists. Half a million more fled the country to France.

References

Eby, Cecil D. *The Siege of the Alcazar, Toledo: July to September 1936.* London: Bodley Head, 1966.

McNeill-Moss, Geoffrey. *The Siege of Alcazar: A History of the Siege of the Toledo Alcazar, 1936.* New York: Knopf, 1937.

Thomas, Hugh. *The Spanish Civil War.* New York: Harper and Brothers, 1961.

Guernica Bombing

Date	April 26, 1937	
Location	Guernica in Vizcaya, northern Spain	
Opponents (* winner)	*Nationalists (German and Italian air force units)	Republicans
Commander	Generalleutnant Hugo Sperrle, Colonel Baron Wolfram von Richthofen	Unknown
Approx. # Troops	German Heinkel He-111 bombers and He-51 fighters; Italian Savoia-Marchetti 79 bombers	Unknown
Importance	Not an experiment in the terror bombing of civilians, it is seen as such by much of the world along with false lessons as to the effectiveness of air attacks on civilian centers	

The April 1937 air attack by German and Italian bombers on the Basque city of Guernica during the Spanish Civil War (1936–1939) horrified the world and was one of the defining moments in the development of modern airpower. Guernica, the Basque province of Vizcaya in northern Spain, was considered by Basques as their cultural, spiritual, and historical capital.

Following their failure to take Madrid in early 1937, Nationalist generals Francisco Franco y Bahamonde and Emilio Mola launched a major offensive in northern Spain that severed the Basque country from Republican Madrid and Catalonia. The Nationalist goal was to secure coal reserves, iron production facilities, and ports used by the Republican government. The chief objective was the city of Bilbao, the center of what became known as the Iron Ring.

Franco therefore ordered an all-out drive on the Basque country in which the Nationalists would make full use of German and Italian aircraft and artillery, primarily the planes of the German Condor Legion. Certainly not volunteers as Berlin claimed, the Condor Legion numbered about 5,000 regular Luftwaffe personnel and more than 100 aircraft. Generalleutnant Hugo Sperrle commanded the legion, with Colonel Baron Wolfram von Richthofen as chief of staff.

On March 31, 1937, General Mola announced his intention "to raze all Vizcaya to the ground." Accordingly, on March 31, 1937, Condor Legion aircraft attacked the town of Durango, a rail and road junction east of Bilbao. The raid inflicted great damage and killed at least 137 people. Still, Nationalist forces on the ground found the going difficult. Sperrle and Richthofen were convinced that their Spanish allies were too cautious, and Richthofen worked out an agreement with Mola's chief of staff, Colonel Juan Vigón, to permit German and Italian aircraft to act independently of Nationalist control and attack Republican troop concentrations "without regard for the civilian population."

During the first three weeks of April, German and Italian aircraft supported Nationalist troops on the ground and regularly attacked Bilbao. By late April the Basques were feeling the pressure and began withdrawing toward Bilbao. Richthofen hoped to trap sizable Basque forces and toward that end ordered the destruction of the key Renteria Bridge, near Guernica. The Germans and Italians were coordinating their air operations in support of the Nationalists, and both committed bombers to this mission, although the bulk of the aircraft involved were German.

The raid began at 4:40 p.m. on April 26, a market day in Guernica, when a twin-engine German Heinkel He-111 medium bomber appeared over Guernica. There was no fire from the ground, as the town had no antiaircraft guns, and the aircraft's bombs fell not on the bridge but instead in Guernica itself. Twenty-five minutes later, three other He-111s appeared. Their bombs, released from several thousand feet, hit a candy factory near the bridge, turning it into an inferno that soon spread to the town. Bombs also struck the marketplace. Soon much of Guernica was on fire and obscured by smoke.

Five pairs of Heinkel He-51 fighters then arrived, passing back and forth and strafing civilians in the open. At 6:00 p.m. some 40 German trimotor Junkers Ju-52 bombers from Attack Bomber Squadron K/88 as well as several Italian Savoia-Marchetti 79s arrived, carrying a mix of high-explosive and incendiary bombs that were dropped from perhaps 12,000 feet. Because smoke and dust obscured the entire area, the pilots did not attempt to locate specific targets.

By the time the bombers departed, two-thirds of the buildings of Guernica had been leveled or were on fire. Fighter aircraft then again strafed the civilians trying to flee. Casualty figures from the attack remain in dispute. They range from 250 dead to as many as 1,654 dead and 889 wounded. The Renteria Bridge was unharmed.

The Germans were proud of what they had accomplished. Four days later Richthofen wrote in his diary: "Guernica, city of 5,000 inhabitants, literally leveled." He noted the success of the bomb mix and concluded, "Bomb craters are plainly to be seen—absolutely fabulous!" Clearly the Germans and Italians saw undefended Guernica as a legitimate target. Richthofen probably ordered the attack without consulting the Spaniards, including Franco.

Although the Germans saw the Spanish Civil War as a testing ground for military equipment and tactics, their raid on Guernica was not an experiment in the terror bombing of civilians. Much of the world perceived it as such, however, drawing false lessons from it as to the effectiveness of airpower in attacks on civilian centers. Guernica was a major story in the world's press, giving the Spanish Republican government a powerful propaganda weapon against the Nationalists. The attack even became the subject of one of the world's most famous paintings, Pablo Picasso's *Guernica*. In a gesture of protest, Picasso would not allow the painting to be displayed in Spain until the fall of the Nationalist government.

The Nationalist side and the German government claimed that there had been no attack and that the fires and destruction in Guernica had been arranged by the Republicans to discredit the Nationalists. This lie was repeated in print as late as 1979, four years after Franco's death. Anticipating an international investigation, as soon as Guernica was in Nationalist hands Sperrle sent men from the Condor Legion to clear out telltale dud bombs and bomb fragments.

References

Large, David Clay. "Guernica: Death in the Afternoon." *MHQ: Journal of Military History* 1(4) (Summer 1989): 8–17.

Maier, Klaus. *Guernica 26.4.1937: Die deutsche Intervention in Spanien und der "Fall Guernica."* Freiburg, Germany: Rombach, 1975.

Proctor, Raymond L. *Hitler's Luftwaffe in the Spanish Civil War.* Westport, CT: Greenwood, 1983.

Ries, Karl, and Hans Ring. *The Legion Condor: A History of the Luftwaffe in the Spanish Civil War, 1936–1939.* London: Schiffer, 1992.

Battle of Shanghai

Date	August 14–November 9, 1937	
Location	Shanghai, China	
Opponents (* winner)	*Japanese	Nationalist Chinese
Commander	Admiral Jasegawa Kiyoshi; General Matsui Iwane	General Zhang Fakui (Chang Fa-kuei); Generalissimo Jiang Jieshi (Chiang Kai-shek)
Approx. # Troops	200,000	500,000 to as many 700,000
Importance	The first major battle of the Sino-Japanese War of 1937–1945 (some would say the first important battle of World War II), it consumes the best Nationalist Chinese troops.	

The fight for Shanghai in Jiangsu (Kiangsu) Province during August–December 1937 between Japanese and Chinese Guomindang (GMD, Nationalist) troops was the first important battle of the Sino-Japanese War of 1937–1945. Some scholars contend that it was the first important battle of World War II (1939–1945).

Japanese leaders were determined to take advantage of European and U.S. weakness occasioned by the world economic depression to secure the natural resource of East Asia. On the night of September 18, 1931, Japanese staff officers of the elite Guandong (Kwantung) Army in southern Manchuria set off an explosion near the main line of the South Manchurian Railway near Mukden (Shenyang) in Liaoning Province. They subsequently blamed the act on nearby Chinese soldiers and used this as a pretext to seize control of Mukden and begin the conquest of all Manchuria. Tokyo, presented with a fait accompli by its own military, supported the action and refused demands of the League of Nations that it withdraw from the territory it had occupied. In February 1932 Japan proclaimed the alleged independence of Manchuria in the new state of Manzhouguo (Manchukuo).

Manzhouguo was larger than France and Germany combined, but in March 1932 Japanese troops added to it the province of Rehe (Jehol, the old province comprising parts of today's Inner Mongolia and Hebei [Hopeh] and Liaoning provinces). Early in April they also moved against Chinese forces south of the Great Wall to within a few miles of Beijing (Peking) and Tianjin (Tienstin) in in Hebei Province. In May Chinese forces evacuated Beijing, then under the authority of pro-Japanese Chinese leaders. These latter concluded a truce with Japan, which required Chinese troops to be withdrawn south and west of a line running roughly from Tianjin to Beijing. Japanese troops withdrew north of the Great Wall, creating a demilitarized zone administered by Chinese friendly to Japan.

Japan asserted its right to control China and continued to push its influence in the northern provinces. The Chinese government at Nanjing (Nanking) in Jiangsu, headed by Generalissimo Jiang Jieshi (Chiang Kai-shek), initially pursued a policy of appeasement. Jiang was more interested in pursuing his military campaign against the Chinese communists, but students and the Chinese military demanded action against the Japanese.

In the Sian (Xi'an) Incident of December 1936, a coup staged by two Nationalist generals forced Jiang to accept a United Front against Japan and helped focus Chinese Nationalist fervor against the Japanese. Japanese leaders found the rapid growth of anti-Japanese sentiments in China and the increasing military strength of the Nationalists disturbing and tried to establish a pro-Japanese regime in China's five northern provinces.

On the night of July 7, 1937, in the so-called Marco Polo Bridge Incident, an unexpected clash occurred west of Beijing between Japanese and Chinese troops near the historic Lugouqiao (Lu-kou-ch'iao) Marco Polo Bridge, a major railroad artery 10 miles from Beijing. Later that month after the Chinese government in Nanjing rejected Tokyo's ultimatum, Japanese troops invaded the coveted northern provinces. In a few days they had occupied both Tianjin and Beijing, and by the end of the year Japan had extended its control into all five Chinese provinces north of the Huang He (Huang Ho, Hwang Ho, Yellow River). In mid-December the Japanese installed a new government in Beijing.

Fighting was not confined to northern China, though; in August 1937 it engulfed the great port and commercial city of Shanghai. On August 7 Jiang ordered GMD forces to attack Japanese troops in their settlement there. Jiang hoped that urban warfare might negate Japanese superiority in heavy weapons. He also hoped that drawing attention to central China would allow his troops in the north time to reorganize.

On August 9 Chinese soldiers killed two Japanese marines in Shanghai. On August 11 Jiang ordered his troops to positions within the greater Shanghai area, carefully avoiding the foreign sections of the city. Jiang committed some of the best units of his army to Shanghai, including the German-trained 87th and 88th divisions. General Zhang Fakui (Chang Fa-kuei) commanded the GMD Eighth Army Group fighting in the city.

The Japanese rushed reinforcements to Shanghai, but when the battle began on August 13, some 80,000 Chinese troops faced only 12,000 Japanese. Heavy fighting continued for almost three months. On August 14 Chinese Air Force planes attacked Japanese warships moored in the harbor, but most of the bombs missed their targets and hit civilian areas in the city instead. Japanese warships in the Changjiang (Yangtze) and Huangpu rivers responded by shelling Nationalist positions at point-blank range. For a week the battle hung in the balance, and the Chinese almost drove the Japanese into the Huangpu (Whampoa) River.

From August 20, large numbers of Japanese reinforcements began arriving by sea. They landed on the banks of the Changjiang River and initiated a siege of Shanghai. Ultimately the Japanese committed a total of 15 divisions under General Matsui Iwane, commander of the Shanghai Expeditionary Force. Jiang ordered Shanghai's defenders to hold out, and for several weeks of bitter house-to-house fighting they did. The fighting was ferocious, and casualties were heavy. Between August and November 1937, 270,000 Chinese troops were killed or wounded in the Battle of Shanghai, along with many thousands of civilians, while the Japanese sustained some 40,000 casualties. Much of the city was devastated, although both sides left the foreign settlements largely undisturbed.

In early November a Japanese amphibious force landed at Hangzhou (Hangchow) Bay, some 50 miles south of Shanghai, outflanking the Chinese forces and threatening the city from the rear. In what swiftly became a disorganized rout, the Chinese forces evacuated Shanghai. Unfortunately for the Nationalists, the Battle of Shanghai consumed many of their best troops. Instead of withdrawing to newly built fortifications along the Shanghai-Nanjing (Nanking) railway line at Wuxi (Wu-hsi), the Nationalists fell back on their capital of Nanjing, which became the next Japanese target. Japanese forces swiftly advanced up the Changjiang, and in December they took Nanjing, where they committed wide-scale atrocities in what became known as the Rape of Nanjing.

References

Boyle, J. H. *China and Japan at War, 1937–1945: The Politics of Collaboration.* Stanford, CA: Stanford University Press, 1972.

Dorn, Frank. *The Sino-Japanese War, 1937–41: From Marco Polo Bridge to Pearl Harbor.* New York: Macmillan, 1974.

Eastman, Lloyd E. *Seeds of Destruction: Nationalist China in War and Revolution, 1937–1945.* Stanford, CA: Stanford University Press, 1984.

Fairbank, John K., and Albert Feuerwerker, eds. *The Cambridge History of China,* Vol. 13, *Republican China, 1912–1949, Part 2.* Cambridge: Cambridge University Press, 1986.

Morley, J. W., ed. *The China Quagmire: Japan's Expansion on the Asian Continent, 1933–1941.* New York: Columbia University Press, 1983.

Wilson, Dick. *When Tigers Fight: The Story of the Sino-Japanese War, 1937–1945*. New York: Viking, 1982.

Yeh Wen-hsin, ed. *Wartime Shanghai*. New York: Routledge, 1998.

Battle of the Ebro

Date	July 25–November 16, 1938	
Location	Ebro River in northern Spain	
Opponents (* winner)	*Nationalists	Republicans
Commander	General Fidel Dávila	Colonel Juan Modesto
Approx. # Troops	90,000	100,000
Importance	The last great military effort by the Republican side in the Spanish Civil War	

The Ebro Offensive, or Battle of the Ebro, fought during July 25–November 16, 1938, was the last great military effort by the Republican (Loyalist) forces in the Spanish Civil War (1936–1939). By 1938 the Republican cause was plainly faltering. The Nationalist (fascist) forces led by General Francisco Franco y Bahamonde had taken the Basque country—indeed virtually all of northern Spain—and now controlled two-thirds of the country. It appeared to most foreign observers that it was now only a matter of time before the Nationalists would triumph.

In these circumstances, premier of the Spanish Republic Juan Negrín approved a plan developed by Spanish Army chief of staff General Vicente Rojo Lluch to stake everything on a major counteroffensive from Catalonia to halt Nationalist forces advancing in Valencia. The Republicans (Loyalists) committed three army corps of some 100,000 men from their 400,000-man army to reestablish communications with Castile and draw the Nationalists away from Valencia. Critics have charged that it would have been better for the Republicans to have remained on the defensive in hopes of prolonging and widening the war.

On the night of July 24–25 Republican engineers constructed pontoon bridges across the Ebro, and early on the morning of July 25, 1938, their infantry attacked across the river. Colonel Juan Modesto had command of the attacking troops, while General Fidel Dávila had charge of the Nationalist defenders. The primary Republican objective was Gandesa, a key communications hub about a dozen miles behind the Ebro. Taking it was assigned to XV Corps. The Republican 11th Division was to advance toward the south. Facing XV Corps was the Nationalist 50th Division of the Moroccan Corps. The Nationalist plan was to hold their line with minimal forces and then bring up reserves to counter any attack.

The initial crossing of the Ebro went well and caught the Nationalists by surprise. Some frontline Nationalist units were wiped out. Among the first of the International Brigades units across the river was the Abraham Lincoln Brigade from the United States.

Although the attackers reached Gandesa by the end of the first day, they were not able to take it. On July 26 the Nationalists opened the floodgates of the Ebro at Tremp, impeding Republican resupply efforts. Fierce fighting raged during July 26–August 2 at Villalba, Cuatro Caminos, and Gandesa, but the Republicans enjoyed little success in these battles. During July 27–28 the Nationalist 74th Division arrived, while the Republican 16th Division joined the battle on July 29. Although the Loyalists seized some 500 square miles of territory and mounted major attacks during August 1–2, these failed. The Nationalists were able to replace their losses quickly, thanks to German and Italian assistance, while the Republicans could not do the same.

On August 3 the Republican side assumed the defensive. Nationalist airpower and artillery played key roles in the outcome, again thanks to the Germans and Italians. The Nationalist side enjoyed near-total air superiority, probably the difference in the war as a whole. Nationalist aircraft struck the Republican troops in the open and attacked supply columns. Also, the Republicans eschewed deep penetrations, which meant that their offensive bogged down as they were forced to clear pockets of Nationalist resistance.

The fighting degenerated into World War I–style encounters, with infantry charges against entrenched enemy positions. Once the Nationalists had contained the Republican advance, fighting raged over the Loyalist bridgehead, and it took the Nationalists more than three and a half months to push the Republican troops back across the Ebro.

Although the Battle of the Ebro had forced the Nationalists to halt their offensive into Valencia and jolted the Nationalist regime as had nothing else in the war, the cost had been high. Loyalist losses amounted to more than 30,000 dead, 20,000 wounded, and some 19,500 taken prisoner. The Nationalist side suffered 6,500 dead, 30,000 wounded, and 5,000 taken prisoner.

The failure of their summer offensive marked the beginning of the end for the Republican side and sped its defeat. The Ebro fighting was also the last big battle for the International Brigades on the Republican side; Premier Negrín withdrew them halfway through the battle. Of some 7,000 members of the International Brigades who fought in the offensive, three-quarters were casualties.

With the end of the battle on November 16, the Nationalists resumed their advance. They took Barcelona on January 26, 1939, and by the end of February both Britain and France had recognized the Nationalist government. Fascist troops entered Madrid on March 28, and Franco declared the war at an end on April 1, 1939.

References

Matthews, Herbert L. *Half of Spain Died: A Reappraisal of the Spanish Civil War.* New York: Scribner, 1973.

Thomas, Hugh. *The Spanish Civil War.* New York: Harper and Brothers, 1961.

Dunkirk Evacuation

Date	May 26–June 4, 1940	
Location	Vicinity of Dunkerque (Dunkirk), France on the English Channel	
Opponents (* winner)	*British	Germans
Commander	General Lord John Gort	Generaloberst Karl Rudolf Gerd von Rundstedt; Reichsmarshall Hermann Göring
Approx. # Troops	400,000	200,000
Importance	Although bereft of their equipment, nearly 365,000 men of the British Expeditionary Force escape back to Britain, allowing them to participate in its defense and in subsequent operations elsewhere	

The World War II evacuation of British and French forces from France was one of the largest military extractions in history. On September 1, 1939, German armies invaded Poland. Two days later Britain and France declared war on Germany, officially beginning World War II (1939–1945). Poland, invaded from the east by the Soviet Union on September 17, was overwhelmed in less than a month. In April 1940 German forces invaded Denmark and Norway.

The German invasion of France and the Low Countries, unleashed on May 10, 1940, also caught the Allies by surprise. British and French forces advanced into Belgium, but the British Expeditionary Force (BEF) was soon in danger of being cut off by a powerful German armored thrust through the Ardennes Forest, in large part because the Belgian government decided to surrender despite promises to its allies that it would not do so unilaterally. In a critical decision, with the battle for France in effect lost, BEF commander Lord John Gort rejected French demands for a push against the principal German invasion force to its south, choosing instead to withdraw northward. The BEF was able to consolidate at Dunkirk, however, in large part because German chancellor Adolf Hitler ordered a halt in the advance of his tanks for nearly three days.

Commander of the Luftwaffe Reichsmarshall Hermann Göring had asked Hitler that the destruction of the British ground forces be left to the Luftwaffe and its dive-bombers. Göring even requested that the German Panzer tanks be pulled back several miles to leave the area clear for the aircraft. The Luftwaffe had not received much credit for its brilliant efforts in Poland in September 1939 and the Western offensive, and Göring believed that it could destroy the BEF in France. Hitler concurred.

In late May 1940 the 250,000 men of the BEF were pinned against the English Channel in the vicinity of the port of Dunkirk (Dunkerque), facing annihilation or

Soldiers of the British Expeditionary Force (BEF) awaiting evacuation by ship on the beach at Dunkerque, France (May 1940). (Photos.com)

capture. At best, London hoped to rescue 20,000 men over a two-day period. In Operation DYNAMO, however, the British sent across the Channel virtually everything that could float, including civilian craft, to assist in the evacuation.

Royal Air Force (RAF) fighters were not available in sufficient numbers to provide adequate air cover, and the vessels involved took a horrible pounding from the Luftwaffe. Flying from bases in southern England, the RAF pilots did what they could and probably made the evacuation possible. British destroyers rescued the most men, but they were also the chief targets for Luftwaffe attacks. By the fourth day of the evacuation, 10 destroyers had been sunk or put out of action.

Such losses induced the Admiralty to make the difficult decision to remove all modern destroyers from the operation. The same reasoning limited the number of fighter aircraft available. Head of Fighter Command Air Marshal Hugh Dowding refused to sacrifice valuable aircraft in a battle already lost. He believed that the planes would be desperately needed for the defense of Britain, certain to be the next target.

From May 26 through June 4 the Royal Navy—assisted by civilian craft and some vessels from other nations—evacuated a total of 364,628 men from the vicinity of Dunkirk; 224,686 were members of the BEF. Before the evacuation was over the BEF had lost in France more than 68,000 men killed, captured, or wounded, including at least 2,000 during DYNAMO itself. RAF Fighter Command lost 106 aircraft and 80 pilots, and Bomber Command lost an additional 76 aircraft. Of 693 British vessels in the operation, 226 were sunk, including 6 destroyers; 19 other destroyers were put out of action. Other nations lost 17 of 168 vessels taking part. The BEF was forced to abandon in France virtually all its equipment but escaped largely intact as far as personnel were concerned.

In Britain the evacuation swept away the phoniness of the war, but the British also falsely believed that they had been betrayed. Many were oblivious to the fact that in May 1918 there had been 10 times the number of British divisions in France than in May 1940, that the British evacuation had left the French in the lurch, or that the French First Army had held the Germans from the beaches and allowed them to get away. The French troops contested every bit of ground, and ultimately between 30,000 and 40,000 of the First Army's 50,000 men were forced to surrender.

Britain now appeared to be in grave peril. The bulk of the 12 BEF divisions that had been in Europe returned to Britain, joining 15 other divisions (6 formed only in May), still only partially trained. In early June there was only 1 properly equipped and trained division to defend the British Isles. BEF equipment abandoned in France included 120,000 vehicles, 600 tanks, 1,000 field guns, 500 antiaircraft guns, 850 antitank guns, 8,000 Bren guns, 90,000 rifles, and 500,000 tons of stores and ammunition. The army had in Britain only about 500 artillery pieces and a like number of tanks, half of them light models. There was 1 battalion of 50 infantry tanks, with the remaining tanks scattered at training schools. The fleet was kept far to the north, away from the Luftwaffe.

In contrast, the German Army numbered 114 divisions and 2,000 tanks. If its forces could have landed in Britain in the weeks after the Dunkirk Evacuation, there would have been few means of stopping them. But Hitler and his military chiefs were caught off guard by the speed of the French defeat and had no plans for a follow-up invasion of Britain. Not until late July did the Germans begin planning for a descent on England, code-named SEALION (SEELÖWE), but the necessary precondition to that was German command of the air.

References

Divine, David. *The Nine Days of Dunkirk.* New York: Norton, 1959.

Gelb, Norman. *Dunkirk: The Complete Story of the First Step in the Defeat of Hitler.* New York: William Morrow, 1989.

Lord, Walter. *The Miracle of Dunkirk.* New York: Viking, 1982.

Battle of Britain

Date	July 10–October 31, 1940	
Location	Great Britain	
Opponents (* winner)	*British	Germans
Commander	Air Marshal Hugh Dowding	Reichsmarschall Hermann Göring
Approx. # Troops	700 fighter aircraft	1,260 bombers, 316 dive bombers, 1,089 fighter aircraft
Importance	This first major German defeat in the war leads to the shelving of plans to invade Britain and causes Adolf Hitler to shift his attention to an invasion of the Soviet Union	

The decision of the French government to surrender and end fighting on the battlefields of France on June 25, 1940, left Britain as Germany's only remaining major military opponent. Although the bulk of the 12 British divisions from Europe returned to Britain to join 15 other divisions forming, in early June there was only 1 properly equipped and trained division in the entire British Isles. The army had only about 500 artillery pieces and a like number of tanks. The fleet was kept far to the north, away from the Luftwaffe. If the Germans could have landed in Britain in the several weeks after Dunkirk, there would have been few means of stopping them.

The Germans had not expected France to fall so quickly, however, and German chancellor Adolf Hitler had no plans for a follow-up invasion of Britain. Not until late July did the Germans begin planning the invasion—Operation SEALION (SEELÖWE)—which would not be ready until at least mid-September. Any invasion of Britain would require not just massive naval logistical planning and assembly of resources but also control of the air.

Generalfeldmarschall Erhard Milch, the air inspector general, pleaded with Hitler to send Luftwaffe units to secure airfields in southern England and then rush in ground forces by air. Milch stated prophetically that if the British were left undisturbed for a month it would be too late, but Hitler rejected the advice. Even after the defeat of France in late June, Hitler postponed a decision, expecting that the British people would recognize the inevitable and agree to peace.

On June 3 the Royal Air Force (RAF) Fighter Command, which had lost more than 400 planes over France, had only 413 serviceable aircraft, 79 of them bombers. In Generalfeldmarschall Albert Kesselring's Luftflotte 2 and Generalfeldmarschall Hugo Sperrle's Luftflotte 3 alone, the Luftwaffe counted 1,480 bombers and dive-bombers and 980 fighters as well as 140 reconnaissance aircraft. Three additional Luftflotte were also available: Luftflotte 1 in Poland, Luftflotte 4 in Austria and the former Czechoslovakia, and Luftflotte 5 in Norway and Denmark. (Indeed, Luftflotte 5 did participate in the battle, striking the northeast coastal area

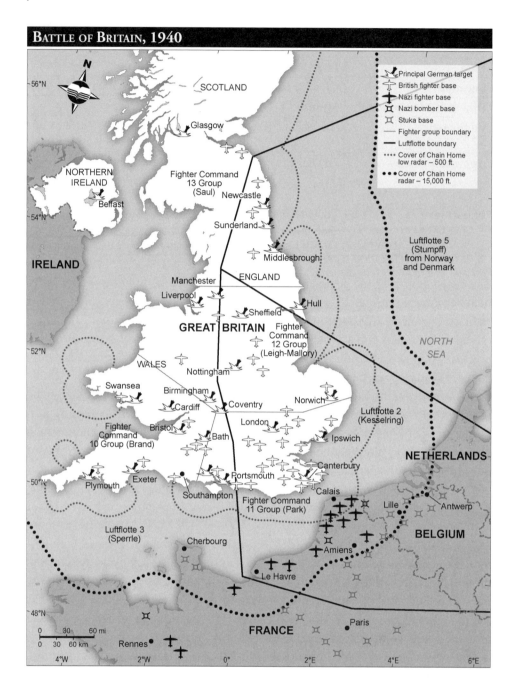

BATTLE OF BRITAIN, 1940

Legend:
- Principal German target
- British fighter base
- Nazi fighter base
- Nazi bomber base
- Stuka base
- Fighter group boundary
- Luftflotte boundary
- Cover of Chain Home low radar – 500 ft.
- Cover of Chain Home radar – 15,000 ft.

of Britain beginning on August 15.) Reichsmarschall Hermann Göring predicted a quick victory.

Official British dates for the Battle of Britain are July 10–October 31, 1940. The battle began with an attack on shipping in the English Channel. Until August 7, the Luftwaffe only conducted fighter sweeps along the Channel approaches and against land targets. The next phase, August 8–23, saw German attacks near the coast in southern England and bomber strikes against ground installations, radar stations, and aircraft factories. The final phase of the battle, August 24–October 31, saw attacks on London and other targets designed to affect civilian morale. The Germans failed, however, in their aim of driving the RAF from the skies.

There were many reasons for the German failure. Göring's lack of leadership was one. He intervened in the battle intermittently without ever understanding the true situation. The Germans also consistently overestimated their effectiveness. The early shift from attacks against shipping in the Channel approaches was a major blunder. The Germans then shifted their attention from radar masts and vector stations to airfields just as their attacks were rendering Fighter Command blind. Raids moved prematurely from airfields to London and also to industrial centers.

The British had in place an excellent early warning system of signals intelligence (Ultra), radar, and a ground observation corps. Ultra provided advance warning of some raids. Radar gave advance warning of the size and direction of the German bomber streams, allowing the smaller number of British fighters to scramble and intercept them. Coastal watchers armed with binoculars provided tallies of German aircraft and their types. Dummy British Q and K airfield sites also drew a number of German air strikes, exploding much German ordnance harmlessly.

One great disadvantage for the Germans in the Battle of Britain was the short range of their aircraft. Counting time to target and return, a German fighter pilot had, at best, 20 minutes over England. Consequently, many German planes crashed, out of fuel and short of their bases. Short fighter range also prevented German bombers from striking British airfields north of London.

Germany's crash building program before the war also meant that many of its aircraft over Britain in 1940 were obsolete. The chief problem confronting the Luftwaffe, however, was trying to make a tactical air force work at the strategic level. The German bombers were medium types, intended for ground support. They were only lightly protected with machine guns and thus required large numbers of fighters as escorts, but in 1940 only a third of German aircraft production was in fighters. With three or four fighters required for every bomber sent over Britain, this sharply limited the number of bombers that could be utilized.

The Germans had also put great emphasis on dive-bombers, but the JU-87 Stuka proved highly vulnerable to attacks by British Hurricane and Spitfire fighters, forcing withdrawal of the JU-87 Stuka, and with it went a third of the German bombers. The Luftwaffe was simply not ready for strategic bombing in 1940.

The British also were able to put thousands of damaged aircraft back on line. Of the British aircraft involved in the Battle of Britain, fully one-third were repaired machines. The number of aircraft available to Fighter Command continued to increase throughout the battle: 413 on June 3, 602 on June 30, and 675 on August 1.

Pilot replacement was even more important, and Fighter Command managed to keep replacements ahead of casualties and increases in aircraft. In this foreign pilots, including Poles and Czechs, played a vital role. Fighting over their home territory helped the RAF immensely as well, as any pilot forced to bail out might easily return to fight another day. Any German pilot who crashed or abandoned his aircraft, on the other hand, likely became a prisoner and was lost for the remainder of the war.

Finally, there was the German concentration on London. On the night of August 24–25, 10 German bombers became lost and dropped their bombs on London. British prime minister Winston Churchill immediately ordered a retaliatory air strike on Berlin. Only a third of the 81 British aircraft reached the German capital, but the incident led Hitler into a fatal mistake. He ordered the Luftwaffe to concentrate on London rather than on the vastly more important RAF airfields and production facilities. Chief of Fighter Command Air Marshal Hugh Dowding heralded the shift to bombing London on September 7 as a "supernatural intervention." The switch to the bombing of cities ended any chance that the Luftwaffe would obtain air superiority over southern England.

The Germans hoped that their concentration on London would bring up the remaining British fighters so that they might be destroyed. Dowding refused to be drawn into a fight for London or other forward areas, though. Instead he used his aircraft to cover vital sectors, particularly the airfields.

This decision was unpopular but decisive. Some 14,000 people died in London alone, but the city's productive activity continued. Far from breaking civilian morale as the airpower theorists had predicted, the bombing strengthened British resolve. The Battle of Britain provided the first proof that bombing, at least when used against civilians, had been overestimated.

Finally, on November 1, with the Luftwaffe taking prohibitive losses, the Germans went over to night bombing, what Londoners called the Blitz. As part of this, on the night of November 14–15 the Germans dropped 1 million pounds of bombs on Coventry, flattening the center of the city. At the height of the Blitz an average of 200 German planes came over London for 57 nights in a row. Heavy bombing continued into May 1941. Although it was savage and relentless, night area bombing had no strategic result. The German air offensive had failed.

The Battle of Britain was the first serious German military setback of the war. On October 12, 1940, the Germans officially shelved SEALION until the spring, when it was put off indefinitely. The chiefs of the German Army and the German Navy, never happy about the prospects of SEALION, were glad to suspend it. More surprising is Hitler's concurrence. He failed to recognize the need to continue the pressure on Britain. He might have continued air and submarine attacks against shipping, which might have brought starvation and eventual British collapse, but Hitler's attention was increasingly drawn eastward to the Soviet Union.

References

Churchill, Winston L. S. *The Second World War,* Vol. 2, *Their Finest Hour.* Boston: Houghton Mifflin, 1949.

Hough, Richard, and Denis Richards. *The Battle of Britain: The Greatest Air Battle of World War II.* New York: Norton, 1989.

Irving, David. *The Rise and Fall of the Luftwaffe: The Life and Death of Field Marshal Erhard Milch.* Boston: Little, Brown, 1974.

Parkinson, Roger. *Summer, 1940: The Battle of Britain.* New York: David McKay, 1977.

Terraine, John. *A Time for Courage: The Royal Air Force in the European War, 1939–1945.* New York: Macmillan, 1985.

Townsend, Peter. *Duel of Eagles.* London: Butler and Tanner, 1991.

Battle of Taranto

Date	November 11, 1940	
Location	Port of Taranto, Italy	
Opponents (* winner)	*British	Italians
Commander	Rear Admiral Lumley Lyster	Admiral Inigo Campioni
Approx. # Troops	21 Fairey Swordfish aircraft from the carrier *Illustrious*	More than 200 Antiaircraft guns, other defenses
Importance	At minimal cost to itself, the Royal Navy effectively alters the naval balance in the Mediterranean and demonstrates the effective role of naval aviation	

The attack on Taranto, Italy, by British forces on November 11, 1940, was the world's first major carrier strike battle. With France on the brink of defeat, Italian dictator Benito Mussolini had taken his country into the war on the side of Germany on June 10, 1940. Italy possessed a sizable navy, and the fortified harbor of Taranto was its principal base. Admiral Sir Andrew Cunningham, commander in chief of British naval forces in the Mediterranean, and Rear Admiral Sir Arthur Lumley St. George Lyster, commanding aircraft carriers in the Mediterranean, planned the operation. Code-named JUDGMENT, it was centered on two British carriers, the *Illustrious* and *Eagle.* The date for the operation was to be October 21, 1940, the anniversary of the Battle of Trafalgar and a night with a full moon. Thirty Fairey Swordfish aircraft were to make the attack. The Swordfish, a 10-year-old biplane, was nonetheless a reliable, sturdy torpedo platform and was especially effective in night operations.

A fire on the *Illustrious* that destroyed several aircraft forced postponement of the operation, however. Then the *Eagle* was found to have been more seriously damaged than originally thought by earlier near hits of Italian bombs. The attack was therefore put off to the next full moon, when it was conducted by the *Illustrious* alone. Twenty-one Swordfish fitted with extra fuel tanks took part, 11 armed with torpedoes and the remainder carrying bombs and flares. Their torpedoes were modified to negate the effects of porpoising, or skipping, in the harbor's shallow water.

At 10:30 p.m. on November 11 the *Illustrious,* commanded by Rear Admiral Lumley Lyster, began launching its aircraft some 170 miles from Taranto. All six of Italy's battleships were in the harbor, protected by barrage balloons, more than 200 antiaircraft guns, and torpedo nets, although the latter were far short of the number that the navy believed necessary. The British planes were launched in two waves an hour apart.

The first wave achieved complete surprise when it arrived at Taranto at 11:00 p.m. The pilots cut off their engines and glided to within a few hundred yards of their targets before releasing their torpedoes against the battleships, which were well illuminated by the flares and Italian antiaircraft tracers. The *Conte di Cavour* was the first battleship hit, followed by the *Littorio*. In the second attack at 11:50 p.m. the *Littorio* was struck again, and the *Duilio* was also hit.

The *Conte di Cavour* was the only battleship to sink, and it went down in shallow water. Italian tugs towed the other two damaged ships to shore. The *Conte di Cavour* later underwent repair, which was not completed, and the ship was never recommissioned. Repairs to the other two ships took up to six months. Two cruisers were also badly damaged, and two auxiliaries were sunk. Fifty-one Italian sailors died in the attack. The British lost two planes; the crew of one was captured by the Italians.

This single raid deprived Italy of its advantage and altered the naval balance of power in the Mediterranean for the duration of the war. The raid also underscored the effectiveness of naval aircraft, which affected the subsequent war in the Pacific. The Japanese found in the attack confirmation for their planned strike against Pearl Harbor, which occurred on December 7, 1941.

References

Lowry, Thomas P. *The Attack on Taranto: Blueprint for Pearl Harbor.* Mechanicsburg, PA: Stackpole Books, 1995.

Schofield, Brian B. *The Attack on Taranto.* London: Allan, 1973.

Smithers, A. J. *Taranto, 1940: "Prelude to Pearl Harbor."* Annapolis, MD: Naval Institute Press, 1995.

Battle of Crete

Date	May 20–31, 1941	
Location	Island of Crete in the eastern Mediterranean	
Opponents (* winner)	*Germans	British. Greeks, Australians, New Zealanders
Commander	Generalleutnant Kurt Student	Major General Bernard Freyberg
Approx. # Troops	40,000	29,000 Germans; 2,700 Italians
Importance	This first large-scale employment of airborne forces in history secures the Germans' southern flank for their invasion of the Soviet Union	

The Germans had employed small airborne forces with spectacular success in May 1940 in order to secure key bridges in their invasion of the Netherlands and Belgium. The assault on Belgium in particular provided a spectacular example of what the new tactics of vertical envelopment might accomplish when German paratroopers captured two key bridges over the Albert Canal as well as the formidable bastion of Fortress Eben Emael. German chancellor Adolf Hitler developed the plan, which his field commanders had greeted with considerable skepticism.

The Germans sent a force of just 78 men against Eben Emael with its 1,200-man garrison. Landing directly on top of the fort in gliders, the Germans employed 56 hollow-charge explosives to blow up its armored turrets and casemates. The tiny attacking force secured its objective in only 28 hours. The vital bridges at Veldwezelt and Vrownhoven were also taken by coup de main, all of which allowed the German ground forces to move forward.

The first large-scale invasion by airborne forces in history, however, occurred a year later on the island of Crete. Beginning in late 1940, Hitler acted in the Balkans to counter Soviet moves there and to shore up his southern flank before invading the Soviet Union. In November 1940 he forced Hungary and Romania to join the Axis and accept German troops. Bulgaria followed suit in March 1941, and in April the Germans conquered Yugoslavia.

German troops also came to the aid of the hard-pressed Italians in Greece. The Greeks had the bulk of their divisions fighting the Italians in Albania and had only three divisions and border forces in Macedonia, where the Germans attacked. The British Expeditionary Force (BEF) sent to Greece was unprepared to deal with German armor and the Luftwaffe, and during April 26–30 the BEF was precipitously evacuated from Greece. Many of the 43,000 British troops taken off were landed on Crete. British naval units were savaged by the Luftwaffe. The Royal Navy lost 26 vessels, including 2 destroyers, to German air attack, and many other ships were badly damaged.

In May 1941 the Germans invaded Crete. This operation, dubbed MERKUR (MERCURY), was conceived and planned by the head of German paratroopers, Generalleutnant Kurt Student. He saw it as the forerunner of other more ambitious airborne operations against the island of Malta or even Suez. Hitler saw it only as a cover for his planned invasion of the Soviet Union, to secure the German southern flank against British air assault and protect the vital Romanian oil fields at Ploesti. The invasion would be conducted by parachutists and mountain troops brought in by transport aircraft. British prime minister Winston Churchill's decision to try to hold Crete, unprepared and bereft of Royal Air Force (RAF) fighter support, ignored reality.

Major General Bernard Freyberg commanded British forces on Crete, with a corps centered on the 2nd New Zealand Division. Ultra intercepts provided Freyberg with advance knowledge of German intentions and identified the German drop zones and targeted airfields. Ironically, the intercepts actually also hampered

Freyberg's dispositions because they revealed that the Germans were sending a seaborne force as well. The latter turned out to be only a small-scale operation easily blunted at sea, but the threat led Freyberg to divert some of his scant resources from the three airfields to the coast, which probably cost him the battle. Freyberg also made a major blunder in not releasing stocks of weapons and not forming a Cretan home guard before the invasion.

MERKUR began on May 20. The Germans barely managed to secure one airfield, at Maleme. This was sufficient, for they were then able to bring in mountain troops by transport aircraft and expand the perimeter. The Luftwaffe was able to hit Crete and the Royal Navy units offshore with impunity. The British withdrew to the coast on May 28. Thus, in little more than a week of fighting, the British were forced into another evacuation. The few cutoff elements that remained were forced to surrender on May 31.

British and British Empire forces sustained 3,479 casualties (1,742 dead) and 11,835 prisoners. The Cretans also paid a heavy price. They fought the Germans with what little means they had and suffered savage reprisals both in the battle and during the subsequent occupation. The Germans sustained 6,700 casualties (3,300 dead) and 200 transport aircraft destroyed. Although there were concerns in the Luftwaffe that codes might have been broken, nothing was done.

Hitler was furious at the heavy German losses and removed Student from command during the battle. Never again did Hitler employ paratroops in airborne assault in significant number. From that point on Student's men were used mainly as elite infantry. Ironically, the Allies now embraced paratroop operations.

The Battle for Crete also demonstrated that warships without fighter support were defenseless against attacking aircraft. British admiral Andrew Cunningham's Mediterranean Command smashed the German amphibious operation of May 21–23 sent to reinforce the airborne troops on Crete, sinking a number of the small craft shuttling troops and killing several hundred Germans, but the Luftwaffe then mauled the Royal Navy ships, sinking three cruisers and six destroyers; six other ships, including two battleships and an aircraft carrier, were heavily damaged. More than 1,800 British sailors died. Churchill ignored this lesson, which would cost the Royal Navy two capital ships in the South China Sea in December 1941. Hitler's aggressive Balkan moves barred Soviet expansion in the region and secured protection against possible British air attack from the south. These goals accomplished, he was ready to move against the Soviet Union.

References

Kiriakopoulos, G. C. *The Nazi Occupation of Crete, 1941–1945.* Westport, CT: Praeger, 1995.

MacDonald, Cullum. *The Lost Battle: Crete 1941.* New York: Free Press, 1993.

Pack, S. W. C. *The Battle for Crete.* London: Ian Allan, 1973.

Thomas, David. *Nazi Victory: Crete 1941.* New York: Stein and Day, 1973.

Siege of Leningrad

Date	July 10, 1941–January 27, 1944	
Location	Leningrad (today St. Petersburg) in northern Russia	
Opponents (* winner)	*Soviets	Germans, Finns
Commander	Andrei Zhdanov; Marshal Kliment Voroshilov; General Kirill A. Meretskov; General Leonid A. Govorov	Generalfeldmarschall Wilhelm R. von Leeb
Approx. # Troops	250,000	350,000
Importance	One of the most costly sieges in history, it ties down large numbers of German troops who might have been employed more effectively elsewhere and serves as a symbol of Russian defiance and heroic sacrifice	

The siege of the city of Leningrad in the Soviet Union by the Germans in World War II (1939–1945) was the longest since biblical times and the most costly ever in terms of lives lost. The siege lasted from July 10, 1941, to January 27, 1944. Czar Peter the Great had founded the city, originally named St. Petersburg, on the Baltic at the beginning of the 18th century as Russia's window to the West. Renamed Petrograd during World War I (1914–1918), it became Leningrad following the 1924 death of Bolshevik leader Vladimir Lenin. Today it is St. Petersburg in the Russian Federation. In 1941 the city was a vibrant urban center of 3.2 million people. By March 1943 it had been reduced to a militarized fortress of only 700,000 inhabitants.

Germany invaded the Soviet Union on June 22, 1941. The capture of Leningrad—in German leader Adolf Hitler's words the "hotbed of Communism"—was one of the strategic goals of the campaign. Hitler assigned the task to Generalfeldmarschall Wilhelm R. von Leeb's Army Group North. Leeb was confident, believing that his troops would be supported by the Finns striking from the north. The Finns had reentered the war to regain the territory lost to the Soviets in the Winter War of 1939–1940. Indeed, Finnish forces soon were driving south both east and west of Lake Ladoga toward the Svir River and Leningrad.

On July 8 the German Fourth Panzer Army reached the old fortress of Schlüsselburg (now Shlisselburg), east of Leningrad, which guarded the point where the Neva River flows out of nearby Lake Ladoga. Taking Schlüsselburg would cut off Leningrad from the Soviet interior. The siege of the city, actually a blockade, officially began on July 10. Leeb's hopes for a quick victory were dashed, however, when the Finns merely reoccupied their former territory.

After gaining these lines in late September, the Finns did advance a slight distance into Soviet territory to about 26 miles from Leningrad, but only to shorten their front lines on the Karelian Isthmus. They steadfastly refused to take part in operations against Leningrad. This was a major factor in Leningrad's survival. Leeb's operations against the city were also severely handicapped when he lost much of his Fourth Panzer Army, which Hitler diverted to the drive on Moscow.

Hitler ordered Leningrad obliterated through artillery fire, air attack, and blockade; he specifically prohibited accepting surrender, were it offered. He intended not to take the city by storm but rather to starve it into submission. He was, he declared, "indifferent" to the plight of the civilians.

Leningraders were in difficult straits. Authorities in the city had done little to prepare for a blockade. Although Leningrad was believed to be a major German military objective, efforts to evacuate part of the population suffered from bureaucratic delays. Andrei Zhdanov, the Communist Party boss in Leningrad and second in the party hierarchy only to Joseph Stalin, and Marshal Kliment E. Voroshilov, appointed by Stalin to defend the city, were reluctant to order any measures that might be branded as defeatist. Only on July 11, 1941, therefore, had the Leningrad Party Committee ordered the civilian population to participate in the construction of tank traps and other defensive positions in front of the city. Between July and August nearly half the city population aged 16 to 55 was engaged in this effort, which proceeded under constant German artillery and air attacks. The city government also ordered the establishment of civilian combat units, men and women alike, but they were poorly trained and had virtually no weapons.

In normal circumstances, Leningrad was dependent on outside sources for its food, fuel, and raw materials for its factories. Now it had to find food for some 2.5 million civilians as well as the forces of the Leningrad front and the Red Banner Fleet in the Baltic. In mid-October, Hitler ordered Leeb to make a wide sweep of some 150 miles around Lake Ladoga to link up with the Finns on the Svir River. On November 8 the Germans took the vital rail center of Tikhvin, about halfway to the Svir. Soviet leader Stalin then shifted major reinforcements north, and in mid-December Hitler authorized a withdrawal. Soviet troops reoccupied Tikhvin on December 18.

Rations inside the city had been cut to a starvation level of 900 calories per day. The soldiers and sailors received priority in the allocation of food, and rationing authorities held the power of life and death. Rations were cut again and again, beyond the starvation level. People tried to survive any way they could, including by eating stray animals and glue from wallpaper. Hunger even led to instances of cannibalism. The hardships were not evenly shared, and communist officials ate relatively well throughout the siege.

Lake Ladoga was the only means of accessing the rest of the Soviet Union. In winter trucks were able to travel across the ice, and in summer some boats got through. This route was insufficient to overcome the fuel shortage, though. The temperature dropped to 30 degrees below zero, but there was still no heat, no light, and no public transportation. Surprisingly, a number of factories continued to function, producing weapons, munitions, and even some tanks. The Russians rebuilt the rail line from Tikhvin, but the Germans bombed and shelled it as well as the Lake Ladoga route.

In January 1942 Stalin ordered General Kirill A. Meretskov's Volkhov Front (army group) to strike the German lines from Lake Ladoga to Lake Ilmen. After punching a narrow gap in the German lines, however, the Soviet offensive faltered. When Stalin refused to allow a withdrawal, in June the Germans cut off the Soviet forces and restored their lines. Between January and July 1942 Soviet authorities managed to evacuate 850,000 people from Leningrad, including a large number of children.

Hitler's plans for the summer 1942 campaign called for the destruction of Leningrad and the occupation of the area between Lake Ladoga and the Baltic in order to free up the Finns for operations against Murmansk. In August, Meretskov carried out another attack against the eastern part of the German lines. Generalfeldmarschall Erich von Manstein, dispatched to Leningrad, replied with a counterattack in September. The Soviets nevertheless managed to lay both pipelines and electric cables under Lake Ladoga. The Germans responded with small E-boats, and the Italians operated some midget submarines in the lake.

In January 1943 Meretskov's forces and Red Army troops in Leningrad, which the Russians had managed to reinforce and were now commanded by General Leonid A. Govorov, struck the Germans from the north and east in Operation SPARK. The offensive was successful, with the two Russian armies meeting at Schlüsselburg on January 19, breaking the siege, and opening a 10-mile corridor. On February 7 a Russian train reached Leningrad through the corridor and across the Neva on track over the ice. Although this line came under constant German attack and had to be repaired daily, it operated continuously thereafter.

On January 14, 1944, Govorov and Meretskov, with a superiority of two to one in men and four to one in tanks and aircraft, again struck the German positions. Hitler refused to authorize a withdrawal, and the Soviets drove the Germans back in bitter fighting. On January 27, 1944, with the Leningrad-to-Moscow railroad line reopened, Stalin declared the so-called 900-day blockade at an end.

During the German siege, perhaps 1 million people in Leningrad—40 percent of the prewar population—died of hunger, with the majority perishing in the winter of 1941–1942. The entire city was within range of German artillery fire throughout the siege, and the bombing and shelling claimed many of the city's buildings and architectural and art treasures, including works from the Hermitage Museum. The travail of Leningrad became the chief subject of Soviet war literature. Like the bombings of Dresden and Hiroshima, the siege of Leningrad became a national and international symbol of the horrors of war.

References

Fadeyev, Aleksandr. *Leningrad in the Days of the Blockade.* Westport, CT: Greenwood, 1971.

Gure, Leon. *The Siege of Leningrad.* Stanford, CA: Stanford University Press, 1962.

Inber, Vera. *Leningrad Diary.* New York: St. Martin's, 1971.

Meretskov, K. A. *Serving the People.* Moscow: Progress Publishers, 1971.

Salisbury, Harrison E. *The 900 Days: The Siege of Leningrad.* New York: Harper and Row, 1969.

Skrjabina, Elena. *Siege and Survival: The Odyssey of a Leningrader.* Carbondale: Southern Illinois University Press, 1971.

Battle of Moscow

Date	September 30, 1941–April 1942	
Location	Area west of Moscow, Russia	
Opponents (* winner)	*Soviets	Germans
Commander	General Georgi Zhukov	Generalfeldmarschall Fedor von Bock
Approx. # Troops (Sept 30, 1940)	1,250,000	910,000
Importance	One of the most important battles of the Second World War, it saves the city of Moscow and marks the farthest eastward advance of German forces in the central part of the Eastern Front	

The struggle for Moscow was perhaps the most important battle on the Eastern Front during World War II (1939–1945). The German invasion of the Soviet Union (Operation BARBAROSSA) that began in June 1941 had three major objectives: Leningrad, Moscow, and Kiev. The first phase of the invasion went well for the Germans, with the unprepared Red Army driven back considerable distances on all three fronts.

Generalfeldmarschall Fedor von Bock's Army Group Center had the task of capturing Moscow. In July 1941 his forces took Minsk; three weeks later they reached Smolensk. With Bock only 225 miles from Moscow, German leader Adolf Hitler decided to divert some forces to Leningrad and Kiev, effectively bringing the advance on Moscow to a halt.

Following a period of reorganization and consolidation, the Germans launched the second phase of their invasion. This proved more difficult, as the farther the Germans advanced, the more Soviet defenses stiffened. The Soviets had mobilized and committed to battle an estimated 5 million additional men. Hitler and his generals had underestimated both the material resources of the Soviet Union and the conditions working against their lightning war (blitzkrieg), notably the vast distances of the Soviet Union, its primitive communications, and the adverse weather.

Hitler and his generals also disagreed on strategy. The generals considered Moscow the main objective, not only because it was a key communications and industrial center but also because they believed that Soviet leader Joseph Stalin would commit the bulk of his military assets to defend the capital city, thus offering the best chance of destroying the Red Army and ending the campaign. Hitler initially believed that taking Leningrad to the north and linking up with the Finns should have priority. In mid-August, however, Hitler focused on securing the resources of Ukraine and the Caucasus region, thus relegating both Leningrad and Moscow to secondary status. He reinforced Army Group South, stripping Panzer forces from the other two army groups.

The second phase of the German advance began with an assault on Kiev, which fell on September 19. The Germans took 650,000 prisoners. Autumn rain and mud then slowed the German drive in the south. Progress toward Leningrad also slowed, due partly to increased resistance but also because Hitler conceived the plan of simply encircling Leningrad and starving it into submission.

The encirclement and capture of Moscow now, finally, received highest priority. Panzer forces previously transferred to the other army groups were returned to Army Group Center, and operations in the new plan, Operation TYPHOON, began on September 30. Arrayed against the Red Army from north to south, Bock had the Ninth Army, the Third and Fourth Panzer groups, the Fourth Army, and the Second Panzer Group.

The Battle for Moscow divides into three phases: the first German offensive from September 30 to the end of October, the second German offensive during November 17–December 5, and the Russian counteroffensive from December 6 into the spring of 1942. Generaloberst Heinz Guderian's Second Panzer Group spearheaded the offensive. The Second Panzer Group took Orel on October 3 and then 17 days later captured 665,000 Soviet prisoners around Vyazma and Bryansk. On October 6 the Germans pierced the Rzhev-Vyazma defensive line and advanced toward the Mozhaisk Line, a series of improvised defensive fortifications thrown up by the Soviets during the summer.

Heavy snows and subzero temperatures came early. On the night of October 6–7, the first wet snow fell. Alternating rain and snow then fell almost continuously. On October 10 General Georgi Zhukov took command of Moscow's defense. Stalin had ordered reinforcements from the Far East to the Moscow front, and assisted by the weather, Soviet resistance stiffened. The Red Army contested the German advance every step of the way.

Still, the Germans bypassed the Mozhaisk Line on the south and captured Kaluga on October 12 and Kalinin (Tver) two days later. On October 15, with the Germans within 50 miles of the capital, the Soviet government and diplomatic community were ordered evacuated from Moscow to Kuibyshev on the Volga. Moscovites panicked, believing that they were being abandoned, but on October 15 the Soviet government announced that Stalin was in the Kremlin, where in fact he remained throughout the war. This word helped restore calm, but on October 18 the Soviets abandoned Mozhaisk following heavy fighting. On October 20 the State Defense Council declared Moscow in a state of siege in order to deal swiftly with any possible disorder.

Local Soviet counterattacks and the weather continued to slow the German advance. It was in this context that on November 7 the Soviet government held ceremonies commemorating the 24th anniversary of the Bolshevik Revolution in Moscow's Red Square and Stalin delivered his "Holy Russia" speech. He appealed both to the Russian Orthodox faith and to historic "Mother Russia" rather than calling for the defense of communism.

The German failure to capture Moscow in October buoyed Soviet morale and gave the Soviet High Command time to assemble additional reserves to the east. At the beginning of November, however, everything pointed to another all-out German attack.

The first major blow fell on November 16 in the Kalinin-Volokolamsk sector, and in two days the Germans entered Klin, north of Moscow, and Istr, only 15 miles west, the closest to Moscow the Germans were able to reach in force. To the south on December 3 Tula, connected to Moscow only by a narrow bottleneck, was encircled for a short time, but the Soviets counterattacked and reopened the roadway.

Temperatures were now well below freezing and remained there throughout one of the coldest Russian winters in decades. This worked to the Soviet advantage. The Germans were short of winter clothing, and frostbite casualties exceeded deaths. Also, much of the German equipment was inoperable in such conditions.

On December 6 Zhukov launched his winter counteroffensive along the Moscow front, from Kalinin in the north to Yelets in the south. His forces were strengthened by some 20 Soviet Far East divisions that had been transferred west after Soviet spies learned that Japanese leaders had opted to go to war against the United States instead of the Soviet Union.

The German Fourth Army and Ninth Army bore the brunt of the Soviet attack. To hasten their advance, the Soviets dropped forces behind the German lines, but these were encircled and eventually destroyed. Hitler dismissed many of his commanders, including Bock who was ill, and on December 19 assumed command of the army himself. By the end of January 1942 the German defense had stiffened, and the Red Army counteroffensive had ground to a halt. Fierce fighting continued in the Moscow area until the end of April 1942, by which point the German Army had been driven up to 160 miles from the Soviet capital.

The German failure to take Moscow in the winter of 1941–1942 was of great symbolic and military importance. The Battle of Moscow demonstrated Soviet determination to remain in the war, shattered the myth of an invincible German Army, and demonstrated Hitler's inability to conquer the Soviet Union as he had Western Europe. It remained to be seen, however, if Stalin could defeat Hitler.

References

Erickson, John. *The Road to Stalingrad: Stalin's War with Germany.* New York: Harper and Row, 1975.

Piekalkiewicz, Janusz. *Moscow: 1941, The Frozen Offensive.* Novato, CA: Presidio, 1981.

Salisbury, Harrison E. *The Unknown War.* New York: Bantam Books, 1978.

Werth, Alexander. *Russia at War, 1941–1945.* New York: Dutton, 1964.

Ziemke, Earl F., and Magna E. Bauer. *Moscow to Stalingrad: Decision in the East.* Washington, DC: U.S. Government Printing Office, 1987.

Pearl Harbor Attack

Date	December 7, 1941	
Location	Pearl Harbor, Oahu, Hawaiian Islands	
Opponents (* winner)	*Japanese	Americans
Commander	Vice Admiral Nagumo Chūichi	Admiral Husband E. Kimmel; Brigadier General Short
Approx. # Troops	Naval task force centered on 6 aircraft carriers carrying a total of 411 aircraft; 5 miniature submarines	8 battleships, 6 cruisers, other smaller warships; 325 aircraft
Importance	Allows Japan to establish its defensive ring but brings the United States into the war fully committed to the conflict	

The preemptive Japanese Navy attack on Pearl Harbor brought the United States into World War II (1939–1945). Supreme commander of the Japanese fleet Admiral Yamamoto Isoroku developed a plan to gain time for the Japanese to establish a defensive ring in the Southwest Pacific. The previous strategy was to carry out the southern conquests while the battle fleet waited in home waters for the arrival of the U.S. Pacific Fleet, which they hoped would be savaged by Japanese torpedo and air attacks on the long voyage to the Far East.

Yamamoto took advantage of the fact that in the summer of 1940 President Franklin Roosevelt had ordered the Pacific Fleet relocated from San Diego, California, to Pearl Harbor in the Hawaiian Islands. Yamamoto believed that the United States would need two to three years to recover from a blow at Pearl Harbor, giving the Japanese time to build up their defensive ring. He also hoped that the attack might cause the United States to lose heart and negotiate with Japan. As the Japanese gathered intelligence through their Honolulu consulate, their fleet, already possessing the world's finest naval air arm, went through intensive training.

The Japanese plan took advantage of the recently increased range of the Zero fighter. The British attack on the Italian fleet at Taranto on November 11, 1940, had shown that torpedo attacks by aircraft were possible in shallow waters. Japanese bombers also carried armor-piercing shells fitted with fins. Dropped vertically as bombs, no deck armor could withstand them.

The Japanese knew that Pacific Fleet commander Admiral Husband E. Kimmel brought the fleet back into Pearl Harbor on weekends, and the ships would not be

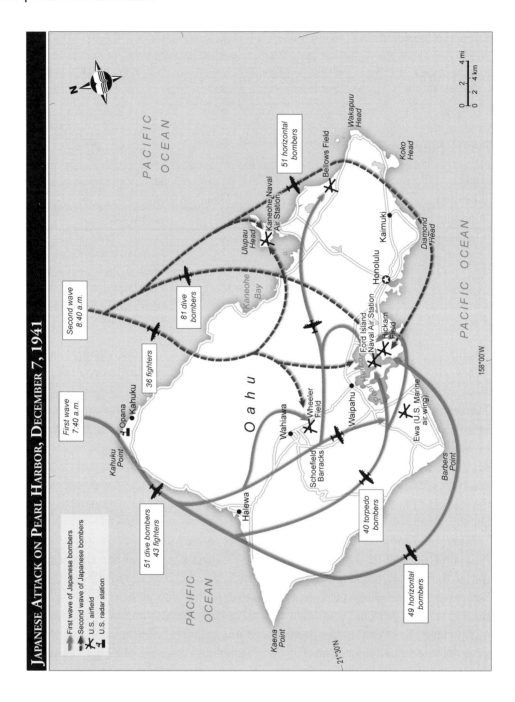

JAPANESE ATTACK ON PEARL HARBOR, DECEMBER 7, 1941

fully manned then. A Sunday was the natural choice for the attack, and after mid-December the weather was likely to be unfavorable for concurrent Japanese amphibious landings in Malaya and the Philippines. On the night of December 6–7 there would be no moonlight, aiding the surprise approach. The chief Japanese targets were the carriers, next the battleships, and then oil tanks, port facilities, and aircraft on the ground.

Vice Admiral Nagumo Chūichi commanded the Japanese task force. It was centered on six carriers with 411 aircraft, of which 360 were slated to be employed in two attack waves (350 actually took part, 183 in the first wave and 167 in the second). These numbered 129 high-level bombers, 103 dive-bombers, 40 torpedo-bombers, and 78 fighters. Escorting the strike force were two battleships, three cruisers, nine destroyers, three submarines, and eight tankers. The air strike was to coincide with an attack by midget submarines.

The submarines departed Japan on November 21, while the carrier strike force sortied on November 26. The Japanese arrived off the Hawaiian Islands undetected, and Nagumo ordered the aircraft launched some 275 miles north of Pearl Harbor between 6:00 and 7:16 a.m. (Hawaii time) on December 7. The Japanese submarines were detected, and U.S. destroyers sank one at 6:51 a.m. and another at 7:00 a.m. Radar warned of the approaching aircraft, but this was interpreted as B-17s coming from the mainland and was therefore ignored.

Of eight U.S. battleships at Pearl Harbor, the Japanese sank four and severely damaged the others. Damage to the infrastructure of Pearl Harbor was superficial. In two strikes the Japanese sank three destroyers and four smaller vessels and damaged three light cruisers and a seaplane tender. Some 188 American aircraft were destroyed, and 63 were badly damaged; most had been packed together to protect against ground sabotage. The Japanese lost only five midget submarines along with 29 planes destroyed and 70 damaged. U.S. casualties totaled 3,535 people killed or wounded; Japanese killed were fewer than 100.

Ultimately all U.S. battleships were refloated except the *Arizona,* and all of these except the *Oklahoma* saw subsequent service. The loss of U.S. life in the attack, while tragic, was not catastrophic for the subsequent U.S. war effort and certainly was far less than what it would have been had the fleet been caught at sea.

Thanks to the attack, the Japanese could carry out their operations in the Southwest Pacific without threat of U.S. naval interference. They also gained time to extend and build up their defensive ring. The main drawbacks were that the strike missed the chief target, the U.S. carriers, which were on ferrying duties. Had the Japanese mounted an additional strike and destroyed the oil tanks and facilities, the Pacific Fleet would have been forced to relocate to San Diego. Nagumo did not want to risk his own ships, however. He had achieved his objectives at virtually no cost and worried about the location of the U.S. carriers. The fleet would return home.

Although their attack had a historical parallel in their strike without declaration of war on the Russian fleet at Port Arthur in 1904, the Japanese had intended to keep within the bounds of legality. They planned to present a declaration of war to the U.S. government a half hour before the attack, but the declaration's extreme length and delays in decoding it at the Japanese embassy in Washington meant that it was not ready for delivery until a half hour after the attack.

The failure of the carefully scripted Japanese scenario secured the moral high ground for Washington on what President Franklin Roosevelt referred to as "a day that will live in infamy." This was the primary negative for Japan. Coming without declaration of war, the attack aroused such anger in the United States as to sweep away any isolationist sentiment and mobilize the entire nation behind the war effort.

For Americans the air strike on Pearl Harbor produced widespread criticism of the authorities and suspicion that factors beyond mere ineptitude were responsible for the disaster. These conspiracy theories have persisted, but there is no proof that Roosevelt knew about the Japanese plan or sought Pearl Harbor as a means of bringing the United States into the war.

References

Morison, Samuel Eliot. *History of United States Naval Operations in World War II*, Vol. 1, *The Rising Sun in the Pacific, 1931–April 1942*. Boston: Little, Brown, 1948.

Prange, Gordon W., with Donald M. Goldstein and Katherine V. Dillon. *At Dawn We Slept: The Untold Story of Pearl Harbor.* New York: McGraw-Hill, 1981.

———. *Pearl Harbor: The Verdict of History.* New York: McGraw-Hill, 1986.

Battle of Bataan

Date	January 7–April 9, 1942	
Location	Bataan Peninsula, Island of Luzon, the Philippines	
Opponents (* winner)	*Japanese	Americans, Filipinos
Commander	Lieutenant General Homma Masaharu	Major General Edward P. King
Approx. # Troops	75,000	12,500 U.S., 67,500 Filipinos
Importance	The largest surrender of American forces since the Revolutionary War, it is nonetheless a remarkable defense given the resources available and it upsets the Japanese military timetable	

The Bataan Peninsula on the Philippine island of Luzon is about 25 miles long and 20 miles wide and extends into Manila Bay. Bataan figured prominently in U.S. lieutenant general Douglas MacArthur's plan to defend the Philippines against possible Japanese attack. This called for U.S. and Philippine forces to withdraw onto that peninsula and hold there until the arrival of reinforcements from the United States.

Confident that he could defend Luzon at the beaches, MacArthur changed the plan. This included scrapping the prepositioning of supply depots on both Bataan and the island of Corregidor, at the tip of the peninsula, sufficient for 43,000 men on Bataan and 7,000 on Corregidor for 180 days. MacArthur had at his disposal 22,400 U.S. regulars (including 12,000 well-trained Philippine Scouts), 3,000 Philippine Constabulary, and 107,000 poorly trained and poorly equipped Philippine Army troops. He also planned to employ submarines and B-17 bombers against any Japanese invasion force. There were a large number of potential landing points, however, and a lot would depend on where the Japanese came ashore.

MacArthur kept most of his regulars back near Manila. The extensive Philippine coastline was covered only by the Philippine Army, which meant that the Japanese would encounter little resistance coming ashore. Much of Admiral Thomas C. Hart's already weak U.S. Asiatic Fleet was withdrawn, leaving only 4 destroyers, 28 submarines, and some torpedo boats. U.S. air assets in the islands were also woefully inadequate. MacArthur's air commander, Brigadier General Lewis Brereton, had 35 B-17s and 90 fighter aircraft, most of them modern P-40s, plus a dozen Philippine Army fighters.

News of the Japanese attack at Pearl Harbor reached Manila at 2:30 on the morning of December 8, 1941. Ground fog delayed an early morning Japanese strike by 500 Formosa-based aircraft against the Philippines, but this turned to Japan's advantage. On learning of the Pearl Harbor attack, Brereton sought MacArthur's approval for an immediate air strike on Japanese warships and shipping assembled at Takao Harbor, Formosa, for the invasion of the Philippines. MacArthur refused without explanation. He later held that his task was to defend the Philippines rather than initiate an attack.

U.S. bombers and fighters ordered into the air as a precaution therefore returned to base, and thus with few exceptions all U.S. aircraft in the Philippines were on the ground when, without advance warning, late on the morning of December 8 Japanese aircraft arrived over Clark Field. Japanese planes also struck Iba Field. By the end of the day, 17 of the 35 B-17s had been destroyed, along with 55 of 72 P-40s and many of the older fighters. Only 7 Japanese planes were shot down. Although the army and navy commanders at Pearl Harbor had been sacked for their shortcomings, MacArthur not only escaped censure but on December 22 was promoted to full general.

On December 8 the first Japanese troops came ashore on Bataan. Two days later they landed unopposed at Aparri on the north end of the big island of Luzon. The Philippine Army infantry broke and ran on the first appearance of the invaders. U.S. major general Jonathan Wainwright, commander of the North Luzon Force, had assumed that the landings would take place in the Lingayen Gulf, on the eastern side of the island, and he had the bulk of his forces there. The main body of 43,000 men of Lieutenant General Homma Masaharu's Fourteenth Army came ashore from 85 transports in the southern Lingayen Gulf only on December 22.

MacArthur now reverted to the original plan of withdrawing all his forces into the Bataan Peninsula. Aided by the fact that Japanese strength was half their own, the bulk of MacArthur's troops had withdrawn into the peninsula by the beginning of January 1942. Unfortunately for the defenders, many supply dumps, relocated when MacArthur altered his plans, were lost in the hasty retreat.

Japanese command of the air and the sea precluded resupply. The defenders immediately went on half-rations. MacArthur also had to feed some 67,500 Filipino troops and 12,500 U.S. troops, along with 26,000 civilians on Bataan and Corregidor, rather than the 43,000 of the original plan. Many of the defenders soon fell victim to malaria, malnutrition, and dysentery.

Despite the terrible conditions, MacArthur's forces put up a stout defense. Although the Japanese pierced the main defensive line in January, the Filipinos and Americans withdrew to a second defensive line about 15 miles from the tip of the peninsula and held there against strong Japanese assaults in late January and early February. Assisted by PT boat attacks and artillery fire from Corregidor, the defenders also defeated Japanese invasion attempts on the western coast of the peninsula behind the battle line. Homma then decided to await reinforcements from Japan.

Because the Pacific Fleet had been shattered in the Pearl Harbor attack, Washington deemed it impossible to attempt immediate relief of the islands. Rather than yield a tremendous propaganda advantage to the Japanese with the capture of the U.S. commander in the Far East, U.S. president Franklin D. Roosevelt ordered MacArthur out to Australia on February 22. MacArthur, who had been raised to full general on December 22 but was derisively referred to by many of the defenders as "Dugout Doug" for his failure to leave Malinta Tunnel on Corregidor (he visited Bataan but once), departed on March 11 and was later awarded the Medal of Honor.

Wainwright took up command of the Philippines, with Major General Edward P. King in charge of the defense of Bataan. Rations were now one-quarter of normal, which seriously affected the ability of the defenders to fight. Disease and sickness continued to extract a heavy toll. Reinforced, Homma attacked on April 3 and broke through. In two days the Japanese drove back the defenders some 10 miles, and on April 9 King had no option but to surrender. The fight for Bataan claimed the lives of some 20,000 Americans and Filipinos. Roughly 2,000 escaped to Corregidor. The Japanese took 76,000 prisoners, some 64,000 Filipino soldiers and 12,000 Americans.

The Japanese forced the weakened survivors to march 55–60 miles to prisoner-of-war camps. Most of the prisoners were sick and hungry, and there was little food. While the Japanese were unprepared for the large influx of prisoners, they also ignored the norms of warfare, even denying the prisoners water. Up to 650 Americans and 5,000–10,000 Filipinos died in the infamous Bataan Death March to Camp O'Donnell. Another 1,600 Americans and 16,000 prisoners perished in the first six or seven weeks of imprisonment.

The fight then shifted to Corregidor, separated from Bataan by only two miles. This short distance enabled the Japanese to bombard the island by artillery. They also attacked from the air. On May 5 the Japanese mounted a successful amphibious assault in which they employed tanks. The next day, his resources exhausted and with less than three days of water remaining, Wainwright ordered U.S. forces throughout the Philippines to surrender. Formal resistance ended on June 9, although some soldiers escaped into the jungle to continue the fight through guerrilla warfare.

What is remarkable about the Philippine campaign is not its result, which was a foregone conclusion, but rather the skill and determination of the American and Filipino defenders, who waged a spirited defense for six months. Tokyo had expected the conquest to take only two months, and General Homma was called home to Japan in disgrace. Perhaps the greatest surprise was the loyalty of the Filipinos to the United States. The Japanese expected Filipino forces to rally to them, but that did not happen. During the campaign and the long Japanese occupation that followed, the vast majority of the Filipino people remained loyal to the United States.

References

James, D. Clayton. *The Years of MacArthur,* Vol. 2, *1941–1945.* Boston: Houghton Mifflin, 1975.

Mallonée, Richard. *Battle for Bataan: An Eyewitness Account.* New York: I Books, 2003.

Morton, Louis. *United States Army in World War II: The War in the Pacific; Fall of the Philippines.* Washington, DC: Office of the Chief of Military History, United States Army, U.S. Government Printing Office, 1953.

Whitman, John W. *Bataan: Our Last Ditch: The Bataan Campaign, 1942.* New York: Hippocrene Books, 1990.

Battle of Singapore

Date	February 8–15, 1942	
Location	Singapore, Malaya (today Singapore)	
Opponents (* winner)	*Japanese	British, Australians
Commander	Lieutenant General Yamashita Tomoyuki	Lieutenant General Arthur E. Percival
Approx. # Troops	30,000	85,000
Importance	The greatest defeat in modern British military history, it opens the way for Japan to exploit the natural resources of South Asia. British prestige never recovers from this blow, which also signals the end of the colonial era in Asia	

Simultaneous with their attack on the U.S. Pacific Fleet at Pearl Harbor, on December 8, 1941, the Japanese struck Malaya from the air. Lieutenant General Yamashita Tomoyuki's Twenty-fifth Army then landed undetected at Kota Bharu and at Singora and Patani in northern Malaya. Yamashita's 60,000 men, supported by artillery and tanks, consolidated their positions and moved south, brushing aside the few British defenders and making their way toward their chief objective: Singapore.

The Japanese had to secure Singapore because it would pose a threat to their north-south supply lines to the vast natural resources (especially oil) of the Netherlands Indies. The Japanese also considered Singapore the key British defensive bastion guarding both the eastern approach to India and the northern approach to Australia. Throughout the campaign for Malaya and Singapore, Yamashita kept up the pressure and held the initiative. British commander Lieutenant General Arthur E. Percival had many more men—about 100,000—but he had anticipated Japanese attacks farther south and thus had the bulk of his defenders deployed there.

British forces were stretched thin, defending not only the British Isles but also the Mediterranean. Churchill also had to send supplies to the Soviet Union. There was a definite limit to what the British could do, and London expected Singapore to hold out until it could be relieved by naval units sent from Europe. Largely because Prime Minister Winston Churchill pressed for a show of strength, however, at the end of October 1941 the British Admiralty had ordered the new King George V–class battleship *Prince of Wales,* the old battle cruiser *Repulse,* the new aircraft carrier *Indomitable,* and four destroyers out to the Far East. The *Indomitable* ran aground near Jamaica and had to be left behind for repairs, but the remaining ships arrived at Singapore on December 2. They were entirely dependent for air cover on the few British land aircraft available.

On learning of the Japanese invasion of Malaya, British Eastern Fleet commander Admiral Tom Phillips immediately departed Singapore with Force Z, comprised of the two capital ships and several destroyers, to attack Japanese ships supporting the landings. Lacking reconnaissance aircraft, Phillips was unable to find the Japanese, however. Force Z was returning to Singapore when it was attacked on December 10 by at least 80 Japanese aircraft based in southern Indochina. Despite evasive tactics and antiaircraft fire, both ships were sunk by Japanese torpedo bombers. The Japanese lost only three aircraft. The British lost some 900 men killed, including Phillips; destroyers rescued the remainder.

Churchill later blamed Phillips for the disaster, claiming that he should not have attempted to intercept the Japanese invasion force. In fact, Churchill, Phillips, and the Admiralty had previously rejected the notion that battleships under way and firing antiaircraft guns could be sunk by air attack. The engagement demonstrated that battleships would need to have air cover of their own if they were to survive air attack. With the loss of the *Prince of Wales* and the *Repulse,* the Allies had no capital ships remaining in the Pacific except three U.S. aircraft carriers. The event also sealed the fate of Malaya and Singapore.

Singapore resembles a flattened diamond in shape; at its widest points it is some 27 miles east-west and 12 miles north-south. Singapore is joined to the Malay Peninsula to the north by a causeway just west of its northern apex. The colony's principal defenses were concentrated on the southern (seaward) side of the island. Three of the four British airfields were in the north and center and were highly vulnerable to land attack.

The great naval base of Singapore in the south, 20 years in the building and long touted for its supposed impregnability, now fell victim to British complacency and the failure to anticipate a northern overland attack. This "Gibraltar of Asia" had been built to withstand an attack from the sea rather than by land. Singapore boasted heavy coastal defense guns of up to the 15-inch type. Contrary to popular misconception, these did not just point toward the sea; most of the defending batteries were capable of 360-degree traverse.

The problem lay in their ammunition. Large quantities of armor-piercing shell for use against ships were available, but there was little in the way of high-explosive shell for employment against troops.

In the north, moreover, virtually nothing had been done to prepare for a Japanese attack. Areas of beach there lacked even barbed wire or trenches. The defenders of Singapore, many of them Australian and Indian units, were poorly trained and lacked both antiaircraft and antitank guns. Modern aircraft were especially in short supply. The Japanese completely dominated the skies.

In their assault on Singapore, Japanese forces were actually greatly outnumbered (30,000 to 85,000 men); their ammunition was low, they had no reserves, and many of the men were sick. Percival was nevertheless unable to take advantage of this situation. Certainly his defensive dispositions were faulty. Percival decided to defend the northern beaches, and the bulk of British forces were thus placed in unprepared forward defensive positions. British troops retreating from the mainland to Singapore made only an ineffectual effort to destroy the causeway.

Yamashita paused to make careful preparations. On the night of February 8 the Japanese launched their attack, crossing over to the island in collapsible boats and supported by artillery and air attacks. Unprepared for the speed and ferocity of the assault, many British officers ordered their men to withdraw prematurely, but there were no secondary positions or strong points north of the city on which to fall back. The Japanese also cut the water supply to Singapore Island, leaving the population there with only a few days' supply. Many of Percival's men actually deserted, including the engineers who were to destroy the naval dockyard.

Nonetheless, Yamashita and his staff were stunned by Percival's decision to surrender unconditionally on February 15. Percival did have the welfare of civilians to consider. For weeks, refugees had been pouring into the island from the Malay Peninsula. The Japanese took 70,000 prisoners and had only contempt for their captives who, they believed, had not shown proper martial spirit. Some of the British, including those already sick and wounded in Singapore's Alexandra Hospital, were simply massacred along with the medical staff. Others were imprisoned or shipped to various points in the Japanese Empire as slave labor for military construction projects. General Itagaki Seishiro explained sending British prisoners to

Korea as necessary "to stamp out the respect and admiration of the Korean people for Britain and America and establish a strong faith in Japanese victory."

Malaya and Singapore had fallen in only 70 days. In the entire campaign the British sustained 138,700 casualties, mostly captured; Japanese losses were trifling by comparison: only 9,824 men. The fall of Singapore opened the way for the Japanese to secure control of the natural resources of South Asia. British prestige in Asia never quite recovered from the shock. The Battle of Singapore signaled the end of the colonial era in Asia and is rightly considered Britain's greatest military defeat in its modern history.

References

Falk, Stanley L. *Seventy Days to Singapore*. New York: Putnam, 1975.

Harries, Meirion, and Susie Harries. *Soldiers of the Sun: The Rise and Fall of the Imperial Japanese Army*. New York: Random House, 1991.

Roskill, Stephen. *Churchill and the Admirals*. London: William Collins, 1977.

Battle of the Coral Sea

Date	May 7–8, 1942	
Location	Coral Sea, Pacific Ocean	
Opponents (* winner)	*Americans	Japanese
Commander	Rear Admiral Frank Fletcher	Vice Admiral Innoye Shigeyoshi; Rear Admiral Goto Aritomo; Vice Admiral Hara Chūichi
Approx. # Troops	Task force centered on carriers *Lexington* and *Yorktown* with 141 aircraft	Two task forces including the light carrier *Shoho* (30 aircraft), and the fleet carriers *Zuikaku* and *Shokaku* (124 aircraft total)
Importance	The first naval battle in history in which the opposing fleets do not come into visual contact of one another and which is fought by naval aviation, it turns back the Japanese invasion force headed to Port Moresby. Although losses are somewhat heavier for the Americans, they are able to return the carrier *Yorktown* to service in time for the Battle of Midway, while the two Japanese fleet carriers in the battle are not able to participate	

The World War II Battle of the Coral Sea was the first naval battle in which two opposing fleets engaged without actually coming into contact other than by naval aviation.

Following their string of early military successes, the Japanese were reluctant to go over to a defensive posture. They were spurred in this course by a series of U.S. carrier raids early in 1942. While inflicting little damage, these were a blow to Japanese pride and forced Japanese military leaders to shift resources.

The Japanese therefore decided to mount a major strike against Midway Island and then cut off the sea-lanes to Australia. They planned first to seize Tulagi as a seaplane base and then take Port Moresby, on the southern coast of New Guinea, bringing Queensland, Australia, within bomber range. Once that had been accomplished, Admiral Yamamoto Isoroku's Combined Fleet would occupy Midway. Following destruction of the U.S. Pacific Fleet reacting to the Midway attack, the Japanese planned to resume their southeastern advance to interdict the sea routes from the United States to Australia.

Vice Admiral Innoye Shigeyoshi at Rabaul in New Britain Island had overall command of the operation. He planned to seize Tulagi on May 3, 1942, and Port Moresby a week later. To prevent any U.S. interference with the landings, Innoye deployed two covering forces: a Close Covering Group centered on the light carrier *Shoho* (30 aircraft), four heavy cruisers, and a destroyer, all under Rear Admiral Goto Aritomo, and Vice Admiral Hara Chuichi's Carrier Division 5 of fleet carriers *Zuikaku* and *Shokaku* (124 aircraft total). They were escorted by Vice Admiral Takagi Takeo's two heavy cruisers and six destroyers. An additional 150 Japanese aircraft were available at Rabaul. The two naval covering forces sortied from Truk in the Carolines, 1,000 miles north of Rabaul, on April 30 and May 1, respectively.

U.S. code breaking uncovered the outline of the Japanese plan. To intercept the Japanese, Pacific Fleet commander Admiral Chester W. Nimitz sent from Pearl Harbor a task force under Rear Admiral Frank Fletcher centered on the carriers *Yorktown* and *Lexington,* with 141 aircraft between them. Royal Navy rear admiral J. G. Crace's small force of U.S. and Australian cruisers and destroyers joined him. Nimitz also ordered the carriers *Enterprise* and *Hornet,* returning from their raid on Tokyo, to the Coral Sea, but they arrived too late to participate in the action.

The first Japanese move went well, with troops going ashore at Tulagi on May 3. Warned of their approach, the small Australian garrison on the island was hastily extracted. The *Shoho* then steamed north to join the larger Japanese force at Rabaul bound for Port Moresby.

On May 4 aircraft from the *Yorktown* struck Tulagi, sinking a Japanese destroyer. The *Yorktown* then joined other Allied ships in the central Coral Sea. Meanwhile, the Japanese carrier group passed east of the Solomon Islands, entering the Coral Sea from that direction to take the U.S. carriers from the rear as they moved to intercept the Port Moresby invasion force. The U.S. force was entering the Coral Sea from the Solomons to the north en route to the Louisiade Islands and thence to Port Moresby. On May 5 and 6 the two carrier groups searched for one another without success, although at one stage they were only about 70 miles apart.

On May 7 Japanese reconnaissance aircraft reported sighting a carrier and a cruiser, whereupon Japanese aircraft launched an all-out bombing attack. They sank both ships, which turned out to be a tanker and an escorting destroyer. Hara then gambled on a night strike by 27 aircraft, but the Japanese attackers encountered U.S. F4F Wildcat fighters. Some of the Japanese pilots located the American carriers, but in the dark they assumed them to be friendly and tried to land on them. Only six Japanese planes returned to their carriers.

On May 7 Fletcher's aircraft were also led astray by a false report and expended their effort on the covering force for the Port Moresby invasion. The aircraft sank the light carrier *Shoho,* which went down in only 10 minutes. This had unforeseen consequences; with the loss of his air cover, Admiral Inouye ordered the invasion force to turn back.

On the morning of May 8 the two carrier forces at last came to blows. They were evenly matched. The Japanese had 121 aircraft, while the Americans had 122. The Japanese had four heavy cruisers and six destroyers, and the United States five heavy cruisers and seven destroyers. The U.S. ships were under a clear sky, however, while the Japanese ships had the advantage of cloud cover. As a result the carrier *Zuikaku* escaped detection. U.S. aircraft located and badly damaged the *Shokaku,* however.

Seventy Japanese aircraft attacked the American carriers; the *Lexington* was struck by two torpedoes and three bombs. Subsequent internal explosions forced its abandonment, and the U.S. destroyer *Phelps* later sank with its torpedoes. The *Yorktown* was damaged. Both sides then departed the Coral Sea, the Japanese in the mistaken belief that both U.S. carriers had been sunk.

The Americans lost 74 planes, and the Japanese lost more than 80. But the Americans lost a fleet carrier, while the Japanese lost only a light carrier. Even so, the Americans had prevented the Japanese from realizing their principal objective of capturing Port Moresby. The Americans were also able to sufficiently ready the *Yorktown* to allow it to fight in the next big battle, at Midway, whereas the *Shokaku* could not be readied in time for that second and decisive fight. The *Zuikaku,* which could have participated, was not able to take part in that battle simply because of a lack of trained pilots. Thus, while the Battle of the Coral Sea may have been a tactical Japanese victory, strategically it went to the Americans.

References

Dull, Paul S. *A Battle History of the Imperial Japanese Navy, 1941–1945.* Annapolis, MD: Naval Institute Press, 1978.

Hoyt, Edwin P. *Blue Skies and Blood: The Battle of the Coral Sea.* New York: S. Eriksson, 1975.

Lundstrom, John. *The First Team: Pacific Naval Air Combat from Pearl Harbor to Midway.* Annapolis, MD: Naval Institute Press, 1990.

Millot, Bernard. *The Battle of the Coral Sea.* Annapolis, MD: Naval Institute Press, 1974.

Morison, Samuel Eliot. *History of United States Naval Operation in World War II*, Vol. 4, *Coral Sea, Midway and Submarine Actions, May 1942–August 1942*. Boston: Little, Brown, 1949.

Battle of Midway

Date	June 3–6, 1942	
Location	West and north of Midway Island in the central Pacific Ocean	
Opponents (* winner)	*Americans	Japanese
Commander	Rear Admiral Frank Fletcher	Admiral Yamamoto Isoroku; Admiral Nagumo Chūichi
Approx. # Troops	27 ships (3 carriers) and 348 planes, including 115 land-based at Midway	86 ships (5 carriers) and 325 planes
Importance	Devastates the superb Japanese naval air arm and turns the tide of the war in the Pacific	

The Battle of Midway was the decisive World War II (1939–1945) naval engagement between the United States and Japan. With their amazing run of successes in the first months of the Pacific War, the Japanese were understandably reluctant to go on the defensive. Admiral Yamamoto Isoroku and his Combined Fleet Staff wanted to secure Midway Island, 1,100 miles west of Pearl Harbor. They hoped that this would draw out the U.S. Pacific Fleet so they could destroy it.

The half dozen U.S. carrier raids from February to May 1942, especially the April 18 raid on Tokyo, helped silence Yamamoto's critics and produce approval for his Midway plan. Under the revised plan, the Japanese would advance deeper into the Solomons and take Port Moresby, on the southern coast of New Guinea. Yamamoto's Combined Fleet would then occupy Midway Island, which Yamamoto saw as a stepping stone toward a possible Japanese invasion of Hawaii. In any case, Midway could be used for surveillance purposes. After the Midway operation and the destruction of the U.S. fleet, the Japanese would resume their southeastern advance to cut off Australia.

In the May 8, 1942, Battle of the Coral Sea, U.S. carriers caused the Japanese to call off the invasion of Port Moresby. Planning for the Midway attack nevertheless went forward. Yamamoto's plan was both comprehensive and complex. It involved an advanced submarine force to savage U.S. ships on their way to Midway; an invasion force under Vice Admiral Kondo Nobutake of 12 transports with 5,000 troops, supported by 4 heavy cruisers and a more distant covering force of 2 battleships, 1 light carrier, and 4 heavy cruisers; Admiral Nagumo Chuichi's First Carrier

Force of fleet carriers *Hiryu, Soryu, Kaga,* and *Akagi,* with 2 battleships, 2 heavy cruisers, and a destroyer screen; and the main battle fleet under Yamamoto of 3 battleships (including the giant *Yamato,* his flagship), a destroyer screen, and 1 light carrier. The total was 8 carriers, 11 battleships, 22 cruisers, 65 destroyers, 21 submarines, and more than 600 aircraft, some 200 ships representing almost the entire Japanese Navy.

For the Aleutians, Yamamoto allotted an invasion force of three escorted transports carrying 2,400 troops, with a support group of two heavy cruisers, two light carriers, and a covering force of four older battleships. Apart from its tie-in with Midway, this force was to enable the Japanese to occupy Attu and Kiska, thus blocking a supposed U.S. invasion route to Japan.

The battle would begin in the Aleutians, with air strikes on June 3, followed by landings on June 6. On June 4 Nagumo's carrier planes would attack the airfield at Midway. On June 6 cruisers would bombard Midway, and troops would be landed, covered by the battleships. The Japanese expected that there would be no U.S. ships in the Midway area until after the landings, and their hope was that the U.S. Pacific Fleet would hurry north to the Aleutians, enabling the Japanese to trap it between their two carrier forces.

Commander of U.S. forces in the Pacific Admiral Chester W. Nimitz could only deploy 76 ships; he had no battleships and only 2 carriers fit for action. By an astonishing effort the *Yorktown,* heavily damaged in the Battle of the Coral Sea, was readied in 2 days instead of the estimated 90 days. Nimitz did have the advantage of an accurate picture of the Japanese order of battle, and thanks to code breaking he was reasonably certain that Midway was the Japanese objective. By contrast, the Japanese had virtually no information on the Americans, but at this point in the war the Japanese tended to dismiss the Americans and exaggerate their own abilities.

Nimitz packed Midway with B-26 and B-17 bombers. He positioned the three U.S. carriers, with 233 planes, some 300 miles to the northeast. He hoped that the carriers would remain hidden from Japanese reconnaissance planes and counted on information on Japanese movements from Catalina aircraft based on Midway. He hoped to catch the Japanese by surprise, their carriers with planes on their decks.

Rear Admiral Raymond Spruance had tactical command of U.S. naval forces in the battle. The Japanese deployed 86 ships against 27 U.S. ships, and there were 325 Japanese planes against 348 (including 115 land-based aircraft) for the United States. Carrier strength was five for Japan and three for the United States.

On June 3, the day after the U.S. carriers were in position, American air reconnaissance detected the Japanese transports some 600 miles west of Midway. A gap in the search pattern flown by Japanese aircraft allowed the American carriers to remain undetected. In any case, the Japanese did not expect the U.S. Pacific Fleet to be at sea yet.

Early on June 4 Nagumo launched 108 aircraft against Midway, while a second wave of similar size was prepared to attack any warships sighted. The first wave did severe damage to Midway at little cost to itself, but the pilots reported the need for a second attack. Since his own carriers were being bombed by planes from Midway, Nagumo ordered the second wave of planes to change from torpedoes to bombs.

Shortly thereafter a group of American ships was spotted about 200 miles away, but the Japanese thought that it was only cruisers and destroyers. Then at 8:20 a.m. came a report identifying a carrier. Most of the Japanese torpedo-bombers were now equipped with bombs, and most fighters were on patrol. Nagumo also had to recover the first wave of aircraft from the strike at Midway.

The U.S. aircraft carrier *Yorktown*, shortly after it was struck by three Japanese bombs on June 4, 1942, during the Battle of Midway. (Naval Historical Center)

Nagumo accordingly ordered a change of course to the northeast. This helped him avoid the first wave of American dive-bombers. When three waves of U.S. torpedo-bombers attacked the Japanese carriers between 9:00 and 10:24 a.m., 47 of 51 were shot down by Japanese fighters or antiaircraft guns. The Japanese believed that they had won the battle.

Two minutes later, however, 37 American dive-bombers from the *Enterprise* swept down to attack the Japanese carriers, while the Japanese fighters that had been dealing with the torpedo-bombers were close to sea level. Soon the *Akagi* and the *Kaga* were flaming wrecks, with the torpedoes and fuel on their decks feeding the fires. The *Soryu* took three hits from the *Yorktown*'s dive-bombers that also arrived on the scene, and soon the *Soryu* was also abandoned.

The *Hiryu*, the only Japanese fleet carrier still intact, then sent its planes against the limping *Yorktown,* forcing the Americans to abandon it. Then 24 American dive-bombers, including 10 from the *Yorktown,* caught the *Hiryu,* which went down the next day. Yamamoto now suspended the attack on Midway, hoping to trap the Americans by drawing them westward. Spruance, however, refused to take the bait.

The Battle of Midway was a crushing defeat for Japan. The Americans lost the carrier *Yorktown* and about 150 aircraft, while the Japanese Imperial Navy lost four fleet carriers and some 330 aircraft, most of which went down with the carriers, and a heavy cruiser. The loss of the carriers and their well-trained aircrews and support personnel was particularly devastating. The subsequent Japanese defeat in the important Battle of Guadalcanal was principally due to a lack of naval airpower.

The Battle of Midway also provided the Americans a respite until, at the end of 1942, the new Essex-class fleet carriers began to come on line. In Nimitz's words,

"Midway was the most crucial battle of the Pacific War, the engagement that made everything else possible."

References

Dull, Paul S. *A Battle History of the Imperial Japanese Navy, 1941–1945.* Annapolis, MD: Naval Institute Press, 1978.

Fuchida, Mitsuo, and Masatake Okumiya. *Midway, the Battle That Doomed Japan: The Japanese Navy's Story.* Annapolis, MD: Naval Institute Press, 1955.

Kernan, Alvin. *The Unknown Battle of Midway.* New Haven, CT: Yale University Press, 2005.

Parshall, Jonathan, and Anthony Tully. *Shattered Sword: The Untold Story of the Battle of Midway.* Washington, DC: Potomac Books, 2005.

Prange, Gordon W., with Donald M. Goldstein and Katherine V. Dillon. *Miracle at Midway.* New York: McGraw-Hill, 1982.

Smith, Peter C. *Midway, Dauntless Victory: Fresh Perspectives on America; Seminal Navy Victory of 1942.* Barnsley, UK: Pen and Sword Maritime, 2007.

Battle of Guadalcanal

Date	August 7, 1942–February 1943	
Location	Guadalcanal Island, southwest Pacific	
Opponents (* winner)	*Americans	Japanese
Commander	Marine Major General Alexander A. Vandegrift; then Army Major General Alexander Patch	Lieutenant General Hyakutake Haruyoshi
Approx. # Troops	60,000	24,600
Importance	Halts the Japanese advance in the southwest Pacific; U.S. forces now take the offensive toward the Philippines	

During May–July 1942 the Japanese expanded their military presence in the central and lower Solomon Islands. Units of Lieutenant General Imamura Hotishi's Eighth Army from Rabaul landed on the island of Guadalcanal and on July 6 began construction of an airfield. On July 21 the Japanese also landed on the northwestern coast of Papua at Buna and then began an overland advance south to Port Moresby.

U.S. military leaders were also anxious to take the offensive following their June 1942 victory at Midway. Information that the Japanese were building an airfield on Guadalcanal prompted action, for this would place Japanese bombers within range of the advanced Allied base at Espiritu Santo. The United States therefore sent a task force of some 70 ships to Guadalcanal. An amphibious force under Rear Admiral Richmond K. Turner lifted Major General Alexander A. Vandegrift's 19,000-

man reinforced 1st Marine Division. Vice Admiral Frank J. Fletcher's three-carrier task force provided air support.

The stakes were high. Neither side could allow the other to establish a major base on Guadalcanal. The struggle was therefore a protracted and complex battle of attrition, with the period from August 1942 to February 1943 witnessing some of the most bitter fighting of the entire war in any theater. There were some 50 separate actions involving warships or aircraft, including 7 major naval battles and 10 land engagements.

On August 7, 1942, the marines went ashore at both Tulagi and Guadalcanal, surprising the small Japanese garrisons of 2,200 men on Guadalcanal and 1,500 on Tulagi. That same day the marines seized the airfield on Guadalcanal, which they renamed Henderson Field for a marine aviator killed in the Battle of Midway. Vandegrift recognized the importance of Henderson Field and immediately established a perimeter defense around it.

The lack of a harbor made U.S. supply difficult, as did Japanese air and naval attacks. Coast watchers on islands did, however, provide early warning of Japanese air and sea movements down the so-called Slot of the Solomons. American land-based airpower thus controlled the Slot during the day, but the Japanese initially controlled it at night. Their navy excelled at night fighting, as was seen early on in the Battle of Savo Island later that summer. The Japanese sent not their main fleet but instead small groups of ships.

Early on August 9 in the Battle of Savo Island, the Japanese nevertheless administered the worst defeat ever suffered by the U.S. Navy, sinking four Allied cruisers (three U.S. and one Australian) and a destroyer for no ship losses of their own. However, the Japanese failed to attack the amphibious force. Fletcher had already withdrawn his carriers, and following the battle Turner now withdrew his transports as well despite the fact that many had not been unloaded. This left the marines without adequate supplies and forced them to rely on captured rations and Japanese construction equipment to complete the airfield.

On August 21, the day the Japanese mounted a major attack on the field, the first U.S. aircraft landed at Henderson Field. From this point on the Japanese could not keep their ships in waters covered by the land-based U.S. aircraft, and they could not conduct an air campaign over the lower Solomons from as far away as Rabaul. U.S. air strength on Guadalcanal gradually increased to about 100 planes.

Both sides now reinforced. At night the so-called Tokyo Express of Japanese destroyers and light cruisers steamed down the Slot and into the sound to shell marine positions and to deliver supplies. The latter was an insufficient and haphazard effort that often took the form of drums filled with supplies pushed off the ships to drift to shore. The Japanese made a major mistake in failing to exploit the temporary departure of the U.S. Navy and rushing substantial reinforcements to Guadalcanal.

During August 24–25 another naval action, the Battle of the Eastern Solomons, occurred. In it the Japanese lost the light carrier *Ryujo* and 90 aircraft; the Americans had the carrier *Enterprise* damaged and lost three dozen aircraft. On August 31 a Japanese submarine torpedoed and severely damaged the carrier *Saratoga,* which was out of action for three months. The *Wasp,* the lone remaining U.S. carrier in the South Pacific, was badly damaged by torpedoes from a Japanese submarine on September 15, forcing its scuttling.

Actions ashore were marked by clashes between patrols. During September 12–14 the Japanese mounted strong attacks in an effort to seize U.S. positions on Lunga Ridge, overlooking Henderson Field from the south. The Japanese suffered 600 dead, while American casualties were 143 dead or wounded. Both sides continued building up their ground strength while naval and air battles raged over and off Guadalcanal.

During October 11–13 Japanese and U.S. covering forces collided in the Battle of Cape Esperance. The Japanese lost two ships, a cruiser, and a destroyer and had a cruiser heavily damaged. The United States lost a destroyer sunk and two cruisers damaged. The Americans upped their tally when U.S. aircraft from Henderson Field sank two more Japanese destroyers. Although not decisive, the Battle of Cape Esperance was the first U.S. night victory against the Japanese.

Vandegrift now had more than 23,000 men on the island, while Japanerse lieutenant general Hyakutake Haruyoshi also commanded about 23,000 men. During October 23–25 the Japanese launched strong but widely dispersed and uncoordinated land attacks against Henderson Field. The Japanese suffered 2,000 dead, while U.S. casualties were fewer than 300. Immediately after halting the Japanese offensive, Vandegrift began a six-week effort to expand the defensive perimeter to a point where the Japanese could not bring Henderson Field under artillery fire.

On October 26 in the Battle of the Santa Cruz Islands, U.S. strike aircraft badly damaged the light carrier *Zuiho* and the fleet carrier *Shokaku.* The U.S. carrier *Enterprise* was badly damaged, and the *Hornet* was sunk. However, the Japanese took such losses that they were unable to exploit the situation. The Japanese also lost 100 aircraft, about half as many as the Americans, who in 1942 produced more than five times as many aircraft than the Japanese and had a superior pilot replacement system.

During November 12–15 a series of intense sea fights took place off Guadalcanal. In the first, U.S. forces blocked Japanese efforts to land reinforcements. The Japanese also lost the battleship *Hiei* and two destroyers. The United States lost two cruisers and four destroyers. In the second, during November 13–14, the Americans sank six Japanese transports and a heavy cruiser. During November 14–15 the Americans lost two destroyers, but the Japanese lost the battleship *Kirishima* and a destroyer. They also had six transports sunk and had to beach another four. U.S. forces now had round-the-clock control of the waters around the island. On November 30 U.S. and Japanese naval forces again clashed. In the Battle of Tassafaronga the Japanese lost one destroyer, while the Americans had a cruiser sunk.

On December 8 Vandegrift turned command of the island over to U.S. Army major general Alexander Patch, who organized his forces into XIV Corps, including the 2nd Marine Division (replacing the veteran 1st Marine Division, which was withdrawn) and the army's 25th Infantry Division. At the beginning of January 1943 Patch commanded 58,000 men, while Japanese strength was less than 20,000. The Americans were now well fed and supplied, while the Japanese were losing men to sickness and starvation.

On January 10 Patch began an offensive to clear the island. In a two-week battle the Americans drove the Japanese from a heavily fortified line west of Henderson Field. The Japanese were forced from Tassafronga toward Cape Esperance, where a small U.S. force landed to prevent them from escaping by sea.

Tokyo had already decided to abandon Guadalcanal. The Japanese had invested 24,600 men (20,800 troops and 3,800 naval personnel) in the struggle. In daring night operations during February 1–7, 1943, their destroyers brought off 10,630 men (9,800 army and 830 navy). The United States had committed 60,000 men to the fight for the island; of these the marines lost 1,207, while army casualties came to 562. U.S. casualties were far greater in the naval contests for the island, where the navy and marines lost 4,911 and the Japanese at least 3,200. Counting land, sea, and air casualties, the struggle for Guadalcanal claimed 7,100 U.S. dead and permanently missing.

The Japanese also lost 1 aircraft carrier, 2 battleships, 3 heavy cruisers, 1 light cruiser, 14 destroyers, and 8 submarines. In the previous six months Japan also lost 140 transports. Twenty-nine destroyers were damaged or in need of repair; their absence contributed to the later destruction of Japanese aircraft carriers. Particularly serious from the Japanese point of view was the loss of 2,076 aircraft (1,094 to combat) and so many trained pilots. The Japanese advance had now been halted, and General Douglas MacArthur could begin the long and bloody return to the Philippine Islands.

References

Frank, Richard B. *Guadalcanal: The Definitive Account of the Landmark Battle.* New York: Random House, 1990.

Hammel, Eric. *Guadalcanal, Decision at Sea: The Naval Battle of Guadalcanal, November 13–15, 1942.* Pacifica, CA: Pacifica Press, 1988.

Takushiro Hatsutori. *Daitoa Senso Zenshi* [Complete History of the Greater East Asian War]. Tokyo: Hara Shobo, 1965.

Tregaskis, Richard. *Guadalcanal Diary.* New York: Random House, 1943.

Battle of Savo Island

Date	August 9, 1942	
Location	Savo Island, Solomon Sea, southwest Pacific	
Opponents (* winner)	*Japanese	Americans; Australians
Commander	Vice Admiral Mikawa Gunichi	British Rear Admiral Victor Crutchley
Approx. # Troops	5 heavy cruisers, 2 light cruisers, 1 destroyer	6 heavy cruisers, 2 light cruisers, 8 destroyers
Importance	Demonstrates superior Japanese night-fighting techniques; brings major changes in U.S. Navy training	

The Battle of Savo Island occurred off Guadalcanal between the Japanese and the Americans during the campaign for the Solomon Islands. The Japanese know it as the First Battle of the Solomon Sea. On August 7, 1942, U.S. marines landed on Tulagi and Guadalcanal. At Rabaul, Japanese vice admiral Mikawa Gunichi immediately made plans to reinforce the garrison on Guadalcanal and to attack Allied ships at the landing site. His troop reinforcement never reached the island; a U.S. submarine sank the single transport sent, the *Meiyo Maru,* the next day.

Mikawa's naval force consisted of five heavy cruisers (including the flagship *Chokai*), two light cruisers, and a destroyer. This force departed Rabaul on the evening of August 7. Mikawa planned to arrive off Guadalcanal in the early hours of August 9, destroy the Allied warships and transports there, and then retire before daylight. The plan was risky because of the chance of detection as the Japanese steamed down the so-called Slot of the central Solomons during daylight.

The Japanese had the advantage of concentration of force. They also possessed the superb Long Lance torpedo, and they were well trained in night-fighting techniques. The Americans and Australians were inexperienced at night fighting and were exhausted from having been at general quarters for nearly two days in association with the landings. U.S. air reconnaissance was inadequate, in part because of bad weather.

Rear Admiral Victor Crutchley, a British Royal Navy officer serving in the Australian Navy, commanded the screening forces, which he divided into three groups to guard approaches to the sound. A small force under Rear Admiral Norman Scott of two light cruisers and two destroyers would patrol between Tulagi and Guadalcanal. Six heavy cruisers and four destroyers divided defense of the two western approaches on either side of Savo Island. Two other destroyers with new centrimetric type SC search radars were set up as pickets to the west. Crutchley took command of the southern group consisting of three cruisers (including the flagship HMAS *Australia*) and two destroyers. The northern force consisted of three cruisers and two destroyers.

At about 6:10 p.m. on August 8 U.S. vice admiral Frank F. Fletcher began withdrawing his three-carrier task force, depriving the landing force of air cover. Two days of operations had reduced fighter strength by 21 percent, and he was also short of fuel; however, the chief reason for the withdrawal was that he had already lost the carriers *Lexington* and *Yorktown* and did not intend to lose another. Fletcher did not consult with the commander of the amphibious force, Rear Admiral Richmond K. Turner, beforehand. Although Turner had requested extra reconnaissance missions over the Slot on the afternoon of August 8, these were not carried out. Not informed of this, Turner mistakenly assumed that the Slot was under Allied observation throughout the day. Convinced that there would be no attack that night, Turner called a meeting aboard his flagship, the transport *McCawley.* Crutchley departed in the *Australia* for the meeting, turning over command to Captain Howard D. Bode of the cruiser *Chicago.*

Mikawa's task force, steaming at high speed in radio silence, escaped detection visually or by radar from the destroyer pickets, both of which were spotted by the Japanese. Mikawa ordered his one destroyer to protect his rear from the two American picket destroyers and then moved with the rest of his ships against the Allied southern force.

The battle began at 1:33 a.m. on August 9. Two torpedoes struck the Australian cruiser *Canberra.* Then, at a range of less than a mile, it was taken apart by Japanese gunfire. The *Chicago* was hit in the bow by a torpedo and by Japanese gunfire. Bode ordered the cruiser to steam west away from the transports it was supposed to protect, which had the effect of removing it from the battle. Mikawa's cruisers moved against the northern group of the western defenses. Pounded by gunfire, the cruiser *Astoria* was badly damaged and sank the next day. The cruiser *Quincy* was also hit and later sank, and the cruiser *Vincennes* was destroyed by gunfire and torpedoes.

Then at 2:40 a.m., before moving to attack the largely unprotected transports where he might have affected the campaign's strategic balance, Mikawa ordered his ships to return to Rabaul. The Japanese admiral feared a daylight air attack on his ships from Fletcher's carriers, which were then in fact steaming away from the battle. Later on August 9 Turner departed with his remaining warships and all his transports, leaving the marines ashore desperately short of supplies.

In only 32 minutes the Allies had lost four heavy cruisers and one destroyer. Three other Allied ships were heavily damaged; 1,270 men were dead, and another 709 were wounded. Mikawa's ships sustained only negligible damage, and Japanese casualties totaled only 35 killed and 57 wounded. On the Japanese return trip to Rabaul, however, a U.S. submarine sank the cruiser *Kako.*

The after-action investigation apportioned blame so evenly that nobody was punished, although Captain Bode later committed suicide. Admiral Chester W. Nimitz summed up the defeat succinctly when he attributed it to "lack of battle mindedness." Naval historian Samuel Eliot Morison called the battle "one of the worst defeats ever inflicted on the United States Navy" (Morison, *History of United States Naval Operations in World War II,* 5:17).

References

Lacouture, Captain John. "Disaster at Savo Island." *Naval History* 6(3) (Fall 1992): 11–15.

Loxton, Bruce. *The Shame of Savo.* Annapolis, MD: Naval Institute Press, 1997.

Morison, Samuel Eliot. *History of United States Naval Operations in World War II,* Vol. 5, *The Struggle for Guadalcanal, August 1942–February 1943.* Boston: Little, Brown, 1989.

Warner, Denis, and Peggy Warner. *Disaster in the Pacific: New Light on the Battle of Savo Island.* Annapolis, MD: Naval Institute Press, 1992.

Battle of Stalingrad

Date	August 24, 1942–January 31, 1943	
Location	Stalingrad (modern Volgograd), southwest Russia	
Opponents (* winner)	*Soviets	Germans, Romanians, Italians, Hungarians, Croatians
Commander	General Georgi Zhukov	Generalfeldmarschall Friedrich Paulus
Approx. # Troops	More than 1,000,000	1,000,000
Importance	The first encirclement and defeat of a large German army in the war	

During the winter of 1942–1943 the Germans suffered a major reversal on the Eastern Front at Stalingrad (present-day Volgograd). Hard-pressed for manpower, German chancellor Adolf Hitler secured 51 divisions from Italy, Hungary, Romania, Slovakia, and Spain. The second great German summer offensive opened on June 28, 1942. General der Infanterie Erich von Manstein, commander of Army Group South, had urged Hitler to concentrate in the center of the front. Manstein believed that Soviet leader Joseph Stalin would commit all available resources to defend Moscow, and this would offer the Germans the best chance to destroy the Red Army. It would also leave the Germans defending a more compact front.

Hitler disagreed. Following elimination of the salients created by the previous Soviet offensive during the winter of 1941–1942, he would divide his resources. He planned to take Leningrad in the north and link up with the Finns. The main effort, though, would be Operation BLAU (BLUE) to the south. He sent Generalfeldmarschall Fedor von Bock's Army Group South east from around Kursk to take Voronezh, which fell on July 6. Hitler then reorganized his southern forces into Army Group A and Army Group B. Generalfeldmarschall Siegmund List commanded the southern formation, Army Group A, while Generaloberst Maximilian von Weichs had charge of the northern formation, Army Group B.

Hitler's original plan was for groups A and B to cooperate to secure the Don and Donets valleys and to capture the cities of Rostov and Stalingrad. The two would then move southeast to take the Caucasus oil fields. On July 13, however, Hitler ordered a change of plans, demanding the simultaneous capture of Stalingrad and the Caucasus. This placed tremendous strain on already-inadequate German resources and meant that a gap would inevitably appear between the two German army groups, enabling most Soviet troops caught in the Don River bend to escape eastward. On July 23 Army Group A captured Rostov and then crossed the Don River, advanced deep into the Caucasus, and got to within 70 miles of the Caspian Sea.

Hitler now intervened again, slowing the movement of General Friedrich Paulus's Sixth Army of Army Group B toward Stalingrad when he detached Generaloberst Hermann Hoth's Fourth Panzer Army to join Army Group A in securing the Caucasus oil fields. The Germans could have taken Stalingrad in July had Hoth not been diverted south. Nonetheless, the Sixth Army reached the Volga north of the city on August 23.

Stalingrad, a major industrial center and key crossing point on the Volga, spread for some 20 miles along the high western bank of the river. Hitler originally intended to control the river by gunfire and destroy the city's arms factories (notably the Tractor, Red October, and Barricades works), but now he demanded a full occupation. Stalin meanwhile poured men and equipment in to defend Stalingrad. General Vasily Chuikov commanded the Sixty-second Army, on the west bank of the Volga.

Angered by the slow progress of the Sixth Army, on August 11 Hitler ordered Hoth's Fourth Army north from the Caucasus, leaving a badly depleted Army Group A holding a 500-mile front and stalling the southernmost drive. Hitler also ordered his sole strategic reserve in the area, Manstein's Eleventh Army, all the way north to Leningrad. These shifts of scant German resources over vast distances took a terrible toll on men and equipment and used up precious fuel. Hitler's military advisers at headquarters expressed alarm that Wehrmacht forces in the Soviet Union were stretched dangerously thin along a front of more than 2,000 miles. Between the two armies of Army Group B, a single division held a 240-mile gap. North of Stalingrad, Romanian forces protected the sole railroad bringing supplies to the Sixth Army.

From August 24 a costly battle of attrition raged over Stalingrad. Luftwaffe carpet bombing at the end of August killed some 40,000 people but also turned the city into defensive bastions of ruined buildings and rubble. Stalin refused to allow the evacuation of the civilian population, believing that their presence would force the defenders, especially local militia, to fight more tenaciously. The ruined city posed a formidable obstacle. Stalin ordered his namesake city held at all costs, and Soviet forces resisted doggedly. Chuikov meanwhile ordered his troops to keep within 50 yards of the Germans in order to make it as difficult as possible for German artillery and aviation to attack. On August 29 General Georgi Zhukov, recently appointed Soviet deputy supreme commander, arrived at Stalingrad to take overall charge of operations there.

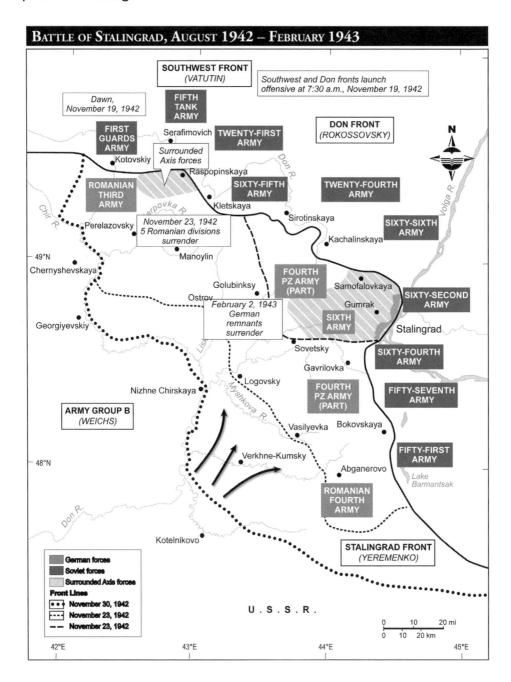

BATTLE OF STALINGRAD, AUGUST 1942 – FEBRUARY 1943

SOUTHWEST FRONT
(VATUTIN)

Southwest and Don fronts launch offensive at 7:30 a.m., November 19, 1942

Dawn, November 19, 1942

FIFTH TANK ARMY

FIRST GUARDS ARMY

Serafimovich

TWENTY-FIRST ARMY

DON FRONT
(ROKOSSOVSKY)

N

Kotovskiy

Surrounded Axis forces

Raspopinskaya

ROMANIAN THIRD ARMY

SIXTY-FIFTH ARMY

TWENTY-FOURTH ARMY

Kletskaya

Chir R.

Tsarpovka R.

Perelazovsky

November 23, 1942 5 Romanian divisions surrender

Sirotinskaya

Kachalinskaya

SIXTY-SIXTH ARMY

49°N

Chernyshevskaya

Manoylin

Golubinksy

FOURTH PZ ARMY (PART)

Samofalovkaya

SIXTY-SECOND ARMY

Ostrov

February 2, 1943 German remnants surrender

Gumrak

Georgiyevskiy

Lisa R.

SIXTH ARMY

Stalingrad

Sovetsky

SIXTY-FOURTH ARMY

Gavrilovka

Nizhne Chirskaya

Logovsky

Myshkova R.

FOURTH PZ ARMY (PART)

FIFTY-SEVENTH ARMY

ARMY GROUP B
(WEICHS)

Vasilyevka

Bokovskaya

48°N

Verkhne-Kumsky

Abganerovo

FIFTY-FIRST ARMY

Don R.

Lake Barmantsak

ROMANIAN FOURTH ARMY

Kotelnikovo

STALINGRAD FRONT
(YEREMENKO)

German forces
Soviet forces
Surrounded Axis forces
Front Lines
• • • November 30, 1942
- - - - November 23, 1942
– – November 23, 1942

U . S . S . R .

0   10   20 mi
0   10   20 km

42°E   43°E   44°E   45°E

Hitler became obsessed with Stalingrad and wore down his army in repeated attempts to capture it. Germany's strength lay in maneuver warfare, but Hitler compelled the Sixth Army to play to the Soviet strength of static defense. Taking Stalingrad was unnecessary from a military point of view; the 16th Panzer Division at Rynok already controlled the Volga with its guns, closing the river to north-south shipping. Hitler insisted that the city itself be physically taken. For a month the

Sixth Army did its best. The German troops pressed slowly forward, but casualties were enormous on both sides, and advances were measured in yards. The battle disintegrated into a block-by-block, house-by-house, and even room-by-room struggle for survival.

Paulus has been much blamed for refusing to disobey Hitler's order to stand firm and extract his army before it was too late. His (and Hitler's) greatest failing, though, lay in not anticipating a Soviet encirclement. Zhukov patiently assembled 1 million men in four fronts (army groups) for a deep double envelopment.

This movement, Operation URANUS, began on November 19. It was timed to coincide with the frosts that would make Soviet cross-country tank maneuvers possible against Axis infantry. For the northern pincer the Soviets assembled 3,500 guns and heavy mortars to blast a hole for three tank and two cavalry corps and a dozen infantry divisions. They encountered Romanian infantry divisions that fought bravely, but their 37-millimeter (mm) guns and light Skoda tanks were no match for Soviet T-34 tanks. The southern Soviet prong of two corps, one mechanized and the other cavalry, broke through on November 20 against two Romanian infantry divisions.

By November 23 the Soviets had sealed off the Sixth Army, driving some units of the Fourth Army into the pocket. Hitler now ordered Manstein from the Leningrad front and gave him a new formation, Army Group Don drawn from Army Group A, with instructions to rectify the situation. Hitler forbade withdrawal, convinced that the Sixth Army could be resupplied from the air. He was no doubt misled by Luftwaffe success the previous winter in dropping supplies by parachute to German troops cut off at Kholm and at Demyansk (which held out for 72 days). But at Stalingrad the Soviets enjoyed air superiority.

By November 20, the second day of URANUS, the Soviets committed as many as 1,414 combat aircraft to Stalingrad, while General Wolfram Freiherr von Richthofen's Luftflotte 4, flying in support of the Sixth Army, had only 732 aircraft, of which only 402 were operational. The Soviets used their air advantage to attack German Army positions and carry out bombing raids on the main Ju-52 transport base at Zverevo, where they destroyed a substantial number of German aircraft. Worsening weather also made flying a severe test, and much of the Luftwaffe's airlift capability was redeployed to resupply Axis troops in North Africa following the Allied landings there in early November.

A fair appraisal of air transport available, even in the best weather conditions, was that the Luftwaffe could bring in 10 percent of the Sixth Army's requirements, condemning the German forces in the pocket to slow starvation and death. Then on January 16 the Soviets took Pitomnik, the principal airfield within the Stalingrad pocket. Its loss was the death blow for the airlift operation. The last days saw supplies dropped only by parachute, and many of these fell into Soviet hands.

Hitler still would not authorize any attempt by the Sixth Army to break out; only a linkup of forces was permitted. None of the hard-won land was to be surrendered.

But it was simply impossible for the Sixth Army to accomplish both of these tasks. Paulus favored a breakout, but he was not prepared to gamble either his army or his career. Manstein's scratch force of three understrength Panzer divisions managed to get to within 35 miles of Sixth Army positions, and he urged a fait accompli to force Hitler's hand. Paulus replied with a pessimistic assessment of his army's ability to close the short distance to reach Manstein's relief force. There was insufficient fuel, the horses had mostly been eaten, and the operation would take weeks to prepare. The relieving forces would have to come closer. A linkup could succeed only if the Sixth Army pushed from the other side against the Soviets, but this could not be done without shrinking the Stalingrad pocket, which Hitler had expressly forbidden.

In mid-December the Volga froze, allowing the Soviets to cross vehicles over the ice. In the next seven weeks they sent 35,000 vehicles over the river along with 122-mm howitzers. By then seven Soviet armies surrounded the Sixth Army, and breakout was impossible. Even with the situation hopeless, Paulus, who had been promoted to generalfeldmarschall, refused to disobey Hitler and order a surrender. Paulus surrendered on January 31 (he claimed that he had been "taken by surprise"), but he refused to order his men to do the same. The last German units surrendered the next day, however.

Perhaps 294,000 Axis troops were trapped at Stalingrad, including Hiwis (Soviet auxiliaries working with the Germans) and Romanians. Of only 91,000 taken prisoner (including 22 generals) by the Soviets, fewer than 5,000 survived the war and Soviet captivity. The last Germans taken prisoner at Stalingrad were not released until 1955. Counting casualties in Allied units and the rescue attempts, Axis forces lost upwards of 500,000 men. The Stalingrad campaign may have cost the Soviets as many as 1.1 million casualties, more than 485,000 of them dead.

Historians have hotly debated the effect of the Battle of Stalingrad on the German war effort. The battle is sometimes referred to as the turning point in the European theater of war. The Battle of Stalingrad was both focused and dramatic, and it was the first encirclement and defeat of a large German army in the war. Militarily, though, the battle was not irredeemable and certainly did not finish off the Wehrmacht. By the end of the battle the German front lines had been largely rebuilt, and the Germans would go on the offensive again. The Battle of Stalingrad was far more important for its psychological rather than its military value. The Battle of Kursk, six months away, was the real turning point in the East, after which the Soviets kept the initiative.

References

Beevor, Antony. *Stalingrad: The Fateful Siege, 1942–1943.* New York: Viking, 1998.

Craig, William. *Enemy at the Gates: The Battle for Stalingrad.* New York: Dutton, 1973.

Hayward, Joel S. A. *Stopped at Stalingrad: The Luftwaffe and Hitler's Defeat in the East, 1942–1943.* Lawrence: University Press of Kansas, 1998.

Manstein, Erich von. *Lost Victories.* Edited and translated by Anthony G. Powell. Chicago: Henry Regnery, 1958.

Battle for El Alamein

Date	October 23–November 4, 1942	
Location	El Alamein in western Egypt	
Opponents (* winner)	*British, Australians	Germans, Italians
Commander	Lieutenant General Bernard Montgomery	Generalfeldmarschall Erwin Rommel
Approx. # Troops	195,000 men; 1,029 tanks	104,000 men (50,000 Germans, 54,000 Italians)
Importance	Obliges Axis forces to withdraw to the west into Tunisia, marking the beginning of the end for the Axis in North Africa	

British Eighth Army commander Lieutenant General Bernard Montgomery initiated the final contest for control of North Africa. By the autumn of 1942 there were signs that the war in North Africa was turning in favor of the British. Axis forces under Generalfeldmarschall Erwin Rommel failed to break through the British lines at Ruwiesat Ridge in July and at Alam el Halfa Ridge in September. Prime Minister Winston Churchill repeatedly pressed for an earlier attack, but Montgomery carefully gathered the resources he thought necessary for success and held off Churchill's demands. General Sir Alan Brooke, chief of the Imperial General Staff, and General Harold Alexander, British commander in chief in North Africa, managed to placate Churchill.

Montgomery set the operation, code-named LIGHTFOOT, to begin on the night of October 23–24 under a full moon. When LIGHTFOOT began, Montgomery had an overwhelming advantage of 195,000 men, 1,029 tanks (including 300 U.S.-built M-4s), 2,311 artillery pieces, and 750 aircraft. Opposing these, Rommel commanded 104,000 men (50,000 Germans and 54,000 Italians); 489 tanks; 1,219 guns, 80 of them 88-millimeter (mm); and 675 aircraft. Rommel had no confidence that his forces could hold against the anticipated British offensive.

The restricted front from the Mediterranean Sea to the Qattara Depression could not be turned. It was heavily fortified in depth, with the defenders relying on an estimated 450,000 mines. Montgomery hoped to catch the Axis defenders off guard with a feint to the south while the main thrust was delivered in the north, against the strength of the Axis line, by Lieutenant General Sir Oliver Leese's XXX Corps; indeed, elaborate British deceptions led the Germans to expect the major offensive to come in the south.

The Battle of El Alamein began under a full moon at 9:40 p.m. on October 23, when 1,000 British guns bombarded a six-mile sector of the German left flank near the Mediterranean. Twenty minutes later XXX Corps moved out, while Lieutenant General Sir Brian Horrocks's XIII Corps began the southern diversionary attack near the Qattara Depression to fix Axis forces there. Infantry of XXX Corps managed to clear two corridors in the German minefields, and Lieutenant General Herbert Lumsden's X Armored Corps then moved through them. The Italians, who held this sector, fought well, and a counterattack by the 15th Panzer Division nearly halted the British advance. Rommel, in Germany on sick leave when the attack began, hurried back to North Africa and on October 25 resumed command of Axis forces in the battle.

Montgomery soon halted the southern diversion and concentrated his effort along the coast. Over the next week both sides flung armored units into the main battle sector south of the coastal road and railroad. The Eighth Army enjoyed air superiority, and the German tanks, which came into the battle piecemeal, were steadily reduced in number. Rommel's lack of armor reserves and his chronic shortages of fuel and ammunition were influential in the battle's outcome. Rommel did manage to extricate his 164th Division, which had been pinned against the coast by the Australian 9th Division; on November 1 he withdrew to new positions three miles to the west.

The next day the New Zealand 2nd Division managed to clear a path through the minefields for the British tanks. Rommel mounted a Panzer counterattack, but by the end of the day he had only 35 tanks remaining. British tactical air and artillery fire neutralized the German 88-mm antitank guns. Hitler now held up the general westward withdrawal of Afrika Korps for two days with an order that Rommel hold in place.

British forces broke cleanly through the German lines, however, and Rommel disregarded Hitler's command, disengaged his forces, and withdrew to the west. The ever-cautious Montgomery delayed his pursuit for 24 hours.

Casualty figures for the battle vary. The British claimed to have inflicted 55,000 casualties, but the Axis forces probably sustained something on the order of 2,300 killed, 5,500 wounded, and 27,900 captured. Rommel also lost almost all his tanks and many of his artillery pieces. For the British Eighth Army, casualties were 4,600 killed and 9,300 wounded. Montgomery had 432 tanks destroyed or disabled. The Battle of El Alamein was one of the decisive engagements of the war. Churchill wrote of it that "Before Alamein we never had a victory. After Alamein we never had a defeat" (Churchill, *The Second World War,* 4:603).

Despite the outcome, military historians have criticized Montgomery for attacking the strength of the German line and for the high cost of the victory. Montgomery's assertion that everything went according to plan is simply not true. The chief negative for the Allies, however, came in the Eighth Army's leisurely pursuit of Axis forces after the battle. Despite Montgomery's plans to keep constant pressure on the Germans, during November 5–December 11 Rommel made good his escape. Rommel's forces repeatedly eluded Montgomery's lethargic encirclement attempts.

References

Carver, Michael. *El Alamein.* London: Batsford, 1962.

Churchill, Winston S. *The Second World War,* Vol. 4, *The Hinge of Fate.* Boston: Houghton Mifflin, 1950.

Greene, Jack, and Alessandro Massignani. *Rommel's North Africa Campaign, September 1940–November 1942.* Conshohocken, PA: Combined Publishing, 1999.

Guingand, Francis de. *Operation Victory.* London: Hodder and Stoughton, 1946.

Hamilton, Nigel. *Monty: The Battles of Field Marshal Bernard Montgomery.* New York: Random House, 1994.

Rommel, Erwin. *The Rommel Papers.* Edited by B. H. Liddell Hart. London: Collins, 1953.

Battle of Kursk

Date	July 5–13, 1943	
Location	Vicinity of Kursk in Ukraine	
Opponents (* winner)	*Soviets	Germans
Commander	General of the Army Konstanin Rokossovsky; General of the Army Nikolai F. Vatutin	Generalfeldmarschalls Erich von Manstein and Günther von Kulge
Approx. # Troops	1,300,000 men; 5,128 tanks	780,900 men; 2,928 tanks
Importance	The largest tank battle in history and the decisive turning point on the Eastern Front in the war	

The Battle of Kursk during World War II (1939–1945) marked the turning point in the war on the Eastern Front and saw the largest armor engagement in history. German leader Adolf Hitler now personally directed his nation's military operations. In the spring of 1943 he no longer had the resources for one short, victorious campaign on the Eastern Front. He therefore planned a series of attacks against the Red Army's positions, first in the south-central part of the front at the Kursk pocket and then in the north at Leningrad. Hitler expected these offensives to use up Soviet reserves and allow the Germans to hold the Eastern Front with fewer men.

Hitler planned to attack as soon as spring weather allowed solid ground suitable for the tanks, but with German positions north and south of the Kursk salient vulnerable to Soviet counterattack, he agreed to a delay to strengthen them and to add additional Tiger and new Panther tanks. German Army Group South commander Generalfeldmarschall Erich von Manstein disagreed with Hitler's approach, however. Manstein favored maintaining a flexible defense that would inflict maximum casualties on the Red Army and force a stalemate. This would mean only a spoiling attack and counterattack of a forthcoming Soviet spring offensive. It would also involve yielding some territory, at least temporarily. Hitler rejected this and insisted that the German Army retain all Soviet territory taken by force of arms. Manstein then planned a preemptive "blow of limited scope" before the Red Army could recover from its losses of the previous winter campaign, but Hitler recast Manstein's plan into an all-out offensive.

The German offensive, code-named Operation ZITADELLE (CITADEL), was to be a double envelopment against both shoulders of the Kursk salient. Generalfeldmarschall Günther von Kulge's Army Group Center would drive south against the salient from near Orel, while Manstein's Army Group South would strike north against the southern face of the Kursk bulge from near Belgorod. The two would then meet well to the east behind Kursk, cutting off the salient and destroying Soviet forces trapped in the pocket. Hitler sought a major victory that would restore German prestige and be "a signal to all the world."

ZITADELLE had been scheduled to begin in the first half of May, but Hitler delayed its start until June to strengthen the Panzer divisions with new tanks. A number of German generals disagreed with this decision, including new German Army chief of staff Generaloberst Kurt Zeitzler, who planned much of the operation. The two army group commanders involved, Kulge and Manstein, strongly opposed any delay, which they believed only gave the Soviets additional time to fortify.

In fact, Soviet leader Joseph Stalin's generals, above all Marshal Georgi Zhukov, persuaded him to allow the Germans to take the offensive while the Red Army worked on defenses in depth. The Red Orchestra (Rote Kapelle), the Soviet spy apparatus in Berlin, knew about the German plans, and the Soviets learned of the basic outline of ZITADELLE in April. Soviet preparations included frontline defensives 2 to 3 miles in depth and secondary and tertiary defenses extending up to 25 miles. The entire defensive belt was studded with bunkers and strong points, supported by massive amounts of heavy artillery and antitank guns. The Soviets also laid up to 1 million mines and brought up 5,128 tanks and self-propelled guns. More than 1 million troops were in position. Four Soviet armies held the northern shoulder, six held the south, and five were in reserve. Five additional Soviet armies north and south of the salient could be shifted there as a last resort.

Even with the delay, German resources were still inferior to those of the Soviets. The German forces sent against the north face of the salient consisted of the Ninth Army (four Panzer corps and one army corps) and the Second Army; Manstein's Army Group South consisted of the Fourth Panzer Army (three Panzer corps) and Army Detachment Kempf, commanded by Generaloberst Werner Kempf. Altogether the Germans had available 780,900 men and 2,928 tanks and assault guns.

ZITADELLE began on July 5 and lasted until July 17, but if the subsequent Soviet elimination of the Orel and Kharkov salients (beginning on July 10 and August 3, respectively) is considered, Kursk was actually the largest battle of World War II, lasting some 50 days. The battle ultimately involved nearly 3.5 million men, 12,000 aircraft, and more than 10,600 tanks.

In the north Generalfeldmarschall Walter Model's Ninth Army enjoyed initial success, reaching the second Soviet defensive belt at the end of the first day. On July 6 Soviet General of the Army Konstantin Rokossovsky, commander of Soviet forces in the north of the bulge, ordered up reserves, and on the third day the Ger-

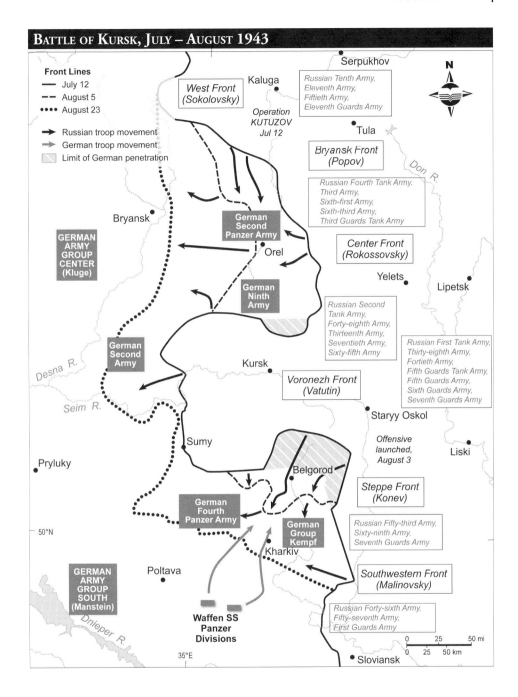

man drive stalled well short of the final Russian line. Subsequent German attempts to break through were unsuccessful, and the fighting settled down to slow-moving attrition warfare. This played to Soviet defensive strength and minimized the chief German asset of mobility.

To the south, Manstein's assaulting formations sustained heavy losses as they moved to their assembly areas in the predawn hours of July 5. Fully informed of the German plans, General of the Army Nikolai F. Vatutin, commander of the Boronezh front army that defended the southern face of the bulge, ordered a massive preemptive artillery bombardment that caught the German troops while they were deploying. Despite this setback, the German drive from the south enjoyed initial success. In only a few hours Manstein's troops broke through the first Soviet defensive belt, but they were temporarily halted by a great thunderstorm that impeded tank movement.

When the attack resumed, the Germans quickly realized the full extent of the Russian defensive preparations. Despite a heavy cost in men and equipment, Manstein's forces pushed ahead and by July 11 had covered 25 miles. The next day, July 12, the largest tank battle of the entire war occurred at Prokhorovka and involved some 1,200 tanks. The Soviets lost 400 tanks while the Germans lost 300, but the Soviets managed to hold. Soviet Air Force IL-2 Sturmovik aircraft proved invaluable; flying at very low altitude and firing rockets, they knocked out large numbers of the German Tigers.

At this point other events influenced the battle. On July 9 British and American forces invaded Sicily, bringing Benito Mussolini's regime in Italy to the brink of collapse. With the Soviets also threatening offensives north and south of Kursk, Hitler broke off the attack on July 13 to shift resources elsewhere, including reinforcing the Mediterranean. Manstein argued for continuation of the offensive. Confident of breaking through, he was prepared to commit his reserves, but Hitler refused.

ZITADELLE was over. During the two weeks of fighting the Soviets lost 177,847 men out of more than 1.9 million engaged and also lost 1,614 tanks; the Germans lost 49,822 of 780,900 men and an unknown number of their 2,928 tanks. The extended Battle of Kursk would cost the Soviets 863,303 of 2.5 million men engaged and 6,064 tanks out of 7,360. German losses in the extended battle are unknown.

Key factors in the battle's outcome included Soviet foreknowledge of German plans, Hitler's postponement of the operation, the German failure to understand the extent of Soviet defensive preparations, harassment of supply lines by Soviet partisans, and the superb Soviet T-34 tank. The Battle of Kursk proved to be the graveyard of the German Panzer armies, and its outcome left the Soviets with the military initiative on the Eastern Front.

References

Glantz, David M., and Jonathan M. House. *When Titans Clashed: How the Red Army Stopped Hitler.* Lawrence: University Press of Kansas, 1995.

Jukes, Geoffrey. *Kursk: The Clash of Armour.* New York: Ballantine Books, 1968.

Salisbury, Harrison E. *The Unknown War.* New York: Bantam Books, 1978.

Werth, Alexander. *Russia at War, 1941–1945.* New York: Dutton, 1964.

Regensburg-Schweinfurt Raids

Date	August 17, October 14, 1943	
Location	Scheweinfurt and Regensburg	
Opponents (* winner)	*Germans	Americans
Commander	Unknown	Major General Ira Eaker
Approx. # Troops	Unknown number of fighter aircraft and antiaircraft guns	376 B-17 bombers (1st raid); 291 B-17s (2nd raid)
Importance	The raids inflict damage, but this comes at prohibitive cost, leading to a crash program for mass production of a long-range fighter, the P-51 Mustang, which dramatically changes the air war over Germany	

The Schweinfurt-Regensburg bomber raids of August 17 and October 14, 1943, were part of the Combined Chiefs of Staff (CCS) bomber offensive initiated in June 1943. U.S. Army Air Forces (USAAF) leaders were determined, despite concerns about their effectiveness, to prove the efficacy of largely unescorted daylight, so-called precision bombing raids, and the ability of strategic bombing to win the war.

The raids were designed to destroy five ball-bearing factories at Schweinfurt and the Messerschmitt aircraft complex at Regensburg. The mission was assigned to Major General Ira Eaker's Eighth Army Air Force in England. Both targets were far beyond the normal range of the USAAF's Boeing B-17 Flying Fortress strategic bomber. Regensburg, to be attacked by the 3rd Bombardment Group, was more than 500 miles from the English coast, while Schweinfurt, to be struck by the 1st Bombardment Group, was nearly 400 miles distant. German fighters would thus have ample opportunity to attack the bomber streams both coming and going. Once they had dropped their bombs, the Regensburg bombers were to fly on to North Africa. Eighteen squadrons of USAAF Republic P-47 Thunderbolts and 16 squadrons of Royal Air Force (RAF) Supermarine Spitfires could provide protection only about 40 percent of the way.

Early morning fog on August 17 disrupted the plan for simultaneous attacks. Of the 3rd Bombardment Group's 146 B-17s, 122 reached their target; they dropped 250 tons of bombs on Regensburg. Four hours later, 184 of the 1st Bombardment Group's original 230 bombers dropped 380 tons of bombs on Schweinfurt. Of the 376 B-17s that took off, following aborts 361 crossed the Dutch coastline. Sixty (36 over Regensburg and 24 over Schweinfurt) were shot down, but 11 of the 301 bombers that made it to base were damaged beyond repair, and another 162 received some damage. The overall loss rate, including aircraft that had to be written off, was 19 percent. The Eighth Air Force lost 408 aircrew, 100 of them killed. U.S. gunners claimed to have downed 228 German fighters; actual losses were 27.

The raid did have some success. Nearly half of the machine tools in the Regensburg assembly plant were destroyed. Although the plant was back in production in less than four weeks, fighter production losses were on the order of 800 to 1,000 planes. Unknown at the time, the raid also destroyed the jigs for the fuselage of the Messserschmitt Me-262 jet fighter. German managers later speculated that this loss delayed the production of this aircraft by four critical months. At Schweinfurt, ball-bearing production suffered a temporary 50 percent drop-off. Double shifts, however, soon made up for this deficiency.

A belated attempt to renew the assault on Schweinfurt on October 14, the so-called Black Thursday raid, cost the Americans 60 of 291 aircraft and more than 600 aircrew. Again, the raid had only limited success. This raid left 133 planes so badly damaged that it took four months to bring the Eighth Air Force back to anything approaching full strength. The Germans lost perhaps 35 fighters.

German minister of armaments and munitions Albert Speer believed that the Allies could have won the war in 1944 had they continued raids against the ball-bearing industry. Speer held in his memoirs that raids such as that at Schweinfurt could well have proven fatal if continued at a high level. The USAAF could not sustain such raids, though; they were simply too costly. The Eighth Air Force was losing some 30 percent of its strength each month, ensuring that few crews made it to the 25 missions necessary for rotation back to the United States. The loss rates for the bombers were totally unsustainable, and the attacks proved to Allied leaders that deep raids were impossible without long-range fighter escort.

The Schweinfurt-Regensburg raids did force the USAAF to address a host of long-standing problems, including navigation and bombing procedures. The raids also sparked a crash program for mass production of a long-range fighter, hitherto inexplicably low on the list of military priorities. That aircraft appeared in the North American Aviation P-51 Mustang, probably the best all-around piston-engine fighter of the war. Mounting six .50-caliber machine guns and capable of a speed of 440 miles per hour (mph), it outclassed the Bf-109 in maneuverability and in speed by at least 50 mph. The P-51 Mustang could also carry 2,000 pounds of bombs. The British and Americans had been slow to utilize drop tanks. An obvious range extender for fighter aircraft, drop tanks had been utilized by the Japanese early on in operations against the Philippines. The P-51's range was 810 miles, but with two 75-gallon drop tanks it had a round-trip range of 1,200 miles; a further 85-gallon internal tank extended this to 1,474 miles, and even with two drop tanks it could reach 400 mph and more. The Allies now had an aircraft with the range of a bomber and the speed and maneuverability of a fighter. The North American P-51 and the Republic P-47 Thunderbolt, another fine fighter and rugged ground-support aircraft, arrived in the European theater at the end of 1943. With drop tanks they could protect the bombers to and from their targets.

The air war thus turned dramatically. In February 1944 the Allies carried out a series of massive raids against German aircraft factories and strikes against Berlin, forcing German fighters aloft so they could be destroyed.

References

Middlebrook, Martin. *The Schweinfurt-Regensburg Mission.* New York: Scribner, 1983.

Neillands, Robin. *The Bomber War: The Allied Air Offensive against Nazi Germany.* New York: Overlook, 2001.

Verrier, Anthony. *The Bomber Offensive.* New York: Macmillan, 1969.

Battle of the Atlantic

Date	1939–1945	
Location	Atlantic Ocean	
Opponents (* winner)	*British, Americans, Canadians, other nations	Germans, Italians
Commander	Various	Vizeadmiral Karl Dönitz
Approx. # Troops	Some 3,500 merchant ships; 175 warships; hundreds of aircraft	783 submarines; a few surface warships and armed merchant raiders; unknown number of aircraft
Importance	The longest campaign of the war; victory by the western Allies is enables if Britain to survive	

The Battle of the Atlantic, actually a campaign extending for the duration of World War II (1939–1945), was one of the key contests of the entire war. Without victory here, Britain would have been forced to sue for peace, and no invasion of the European continent via the English Channel would have been possible. The Germans waged the battle with some surface raiders, the most notorious of which was the battleship *Bismarck* (sunk on May 27, 1941), but chiefly they employed submarines. Italian submarines also took part. The decisive point came in the spring of 1943.

The Battle of the Atlantic was a grim no-holds-barred struggle. Vessels were torpedoed without warning and often at night. Chances of crew survival were slight, especially in the case of tankers, the primary U-boat targets. Death might come with the explosion of a torpedo striking the ship or from subsequent internal blasts. Crewmen might be trapped below decks as the mortally wounded ship sank. Burning oil extending hundreds of yards from a vessel lengthened the odds of survival. If there was time to man the lifeboats, crew members might find themselves face to face with the U-boat that had sunk them as it surfaced to survey the destruction. Some U-boat captains provided assistance, but there were also reports of lifeboats and survivors in the water being gunned down. Other ships in the convoy could not stop to assist survivors, lest they themselves become targets.

On the outbreak of war, the Allies had promptly reinstituted the convoy system of World War I (1914–1918). Convoys were predicated on reducing the number of

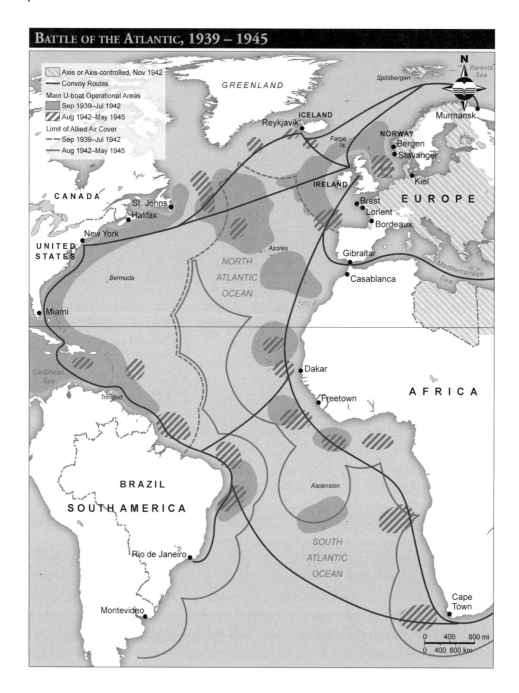

BATTLE OF THE ATLANTIC, 1939 – 1945

targets and the assumption that the more targets there were, the more likely they were to be found. In the convoys, numbers of merchant ships traveled together, with escorting destroyers and destroyer escorts patrolling the flanks. The U-boats would still get their kills, but the percentage of losses was significantly less, and the attackers ran the risk of being hunted down and sunk by the escorting surface warships.

Early in the war commander of German submarines Vizeadmiral Karl Dönitz had few boats. German leader Adolf Hitler had wanted a balanced navy, and Grossadmiral Eric Raeder had been busy building just that. For the German Navy at least, the war came three or four years too early. Germany began the war with 56 U-boats, only a slight improvement from the numbers of August 1914. Despite a shift from surface ship construction to building U-boats, only 37 new U-boats were commissioned in the first year of the war; the earlier plan had been to build 100 in that time frame.

It was 1941 before the U-boat construction program really got going. Although 230 new U-boats were under construction in April, only 32 were available for operations that month. Dönitz asserted that he would have won the Battle of the Atlantic in 1941 or 1942 had he possessed, at the beginning of the war, the 300 U-boats he deemed necessary. It is probably a false claim, for a higher rate of sinking of merchantmen would certainly have forced the Allies to shift military assets to the struggle, including long-range aircraft to Coastal Command, earlier than was the case.

Dönitz's submarines also lacked effective radar until near the end of the war, and they struggled—at least in the first year—with defective torpedoes. Dönitz believed that this cost at least two U-boats in premature explosions and that faulty magnetic torpedo detonators prevented the sinking of the British battleships *Ark Royal* and *Nelson.*

Dönitz developed new tactics, the most important of which was the *Rudeltaktik* (Wolf Tactic, known to the Allies as the Wolf Pack). Groups of up to 15–20 submarines would spread out along the Atlantic sea-lanes. Merchantmen traveling alone would be immediately attacked; in the event of a convoy sighting, the submarine would shadow it and radio for reinforcements. The closest U-boats would then converge for a night surface attack, which would maximize confusion for the defenders and minimize the possibility of submarine detection. The submarines would then submerge and reorganize for a second attack.

To enable his submarines to remain on station for longer periods, Dönitz sent out milk-cow supply submarines. The German Navy's B-Dienst intelligence service also broke the British convoy codes, enabling Dönitz to direct his boats to where he believed enemy ships would be. The Germans also used aircraft, particularly the long-range Focke-Wolfe Fw-200, with considerable effectiveness against Allied convoys in the eastern Atlantic within range of German air bases. Yet Dönitz was handicapped because Luftwaffe commander Reichsmarschall Hermann Göring would not provide planes to reconnoiter at sea, and Hitler often ordered the U-boats to undertake missions for which they were not designed.

The British received an important assist in May 1941 when the U.S. Navy began escorting convoys between the United States and Iceland. In June 1941 Canada created the Canadian Escort Force for the same purpose. Indeed, the Royal Canadian Navy (RCN) played a key role in the struggle. Comprising only 6 destroyers and 5 minesweepers at the beginning of the war, the RCN grew by war's end to 2 light carriers, 2 light cruisers, 15 destroyers, 60 frigates, 118 corvettes, and many other vessels. Virtually all these ships were committed to the Battle of the Atlantic.

By June 1941 the Germans had sent to the bottom some 5.7 million tons of Allied shipping, with British shipyards able to launch only 800,000 replacement tons. Large Italian submarines, a number of them operating out of Bordeaux, also sank 500,000 tons of shipping in the course of the war. A significant increase in U-boat strength enabled the Germans to virtually control the Atlantic for more than a year after America's entry into the war.

Beginning in February 1942 in Operation PAUKENSCHLAG (DRUMBEAT), Dönitz sent 19 U-boats to the U.S. Atlantic coast. These found easy pickings, with tankers and other ships sailing alone and the U.S. shoreline brightly illuminated at night. The U-boats sank 81 ships. Finally the United States organized coastal convoys, and in May Dönitz redirected his submarines southward. Dönitz was then aided by the initiation of British and American convoys in the Arctic to the Soviet Union, which diluted their ability to protect convoys in the Atlantic. He also dispatched some large U-boats into the South Atlantic and the Indian Ocean, but supply problems and attacks by surface ships led to their recall. Dönitz was aided by the dispersal of Allied warships to protect the initiation of British and American convoys in the Arctic to the Soviet Union.

By August 1942 Dönitz had 300 submarines at his disposal. The effect of this increase was augmented when, the month before, Germany changed its naval codes. This opened the critical period in the struggle for control of the Atlantic.

In January 1943 Hitler, displeased by the lack of results from his capital ships, sacked Raeder and appointed Dönitz to head the navy. Dönitz intensified the U-boat war, and early in the year the toll of Allied shipping falling prey to submarines rose precipitously. By March, Britain had food reserves sufficient only for three months. By May, half of the world's 5,600 merchant ships of 1939 had been lost. But large, fast, unescorted converted luxury liners could outrun U-boats and make the trip safely, as could heavily protected troop transports.

Although experts disagree, the turning point in the Battle of the Atlantic probably came with Royal Navy commander Peter W. Gretton's ONS-1 convoy. From April 28 to May 6, 1943, Gretton's 46 merchant ships steamed across the North Atlantic, dueling with 51 U-boats. Gretton lost 13 of his ships, but 7 U-boats were sunk (5 by escorts and 2 by aircraft).

The Allies were on the offensive thereafter. Coastal Command aircraft, equipped with lightweight 10-centimeter radar and working in conjunction with Royal Navy corvettes, attacked U-boats entering and leaving French bases in the Bay of Biscay. In May 1943 Dönitz lost 38 U-boats, a dozen more than were built; at the same time only 41 merchantmen were lost. In June the U.S. Navy Tenth Fleet began operating hunter-killer teams in the Atlantic, and in October 1943 the Allies acquired air bases in the Azores from Portugal.

Aircraft proved vital; they could deflect German bomber attacks and do battle with surfaced submarines before they could dive. One solution was to send fighter aircraft along with a convoy, and the British equipped a number of merchantmen with a forward catapult that held a modified Hurricane fighter. After launch and intercept, the fighter would try to make landfall or else land in the water.

A far more satisfactory solution was to fit a flight deck to a merchant ship hull. The German cargo-passenger ship *Hannover,* taken in the West Indies in March 1940, became the first escort carrier, entering service in June 1941 as the flush-deck aircraft carrier *Audacity,* with six fighters. Additional escort carriers appeared in the form of U.S.-built conversions on C-3 hulls from the Maritime Commission: the *Archer* and the Avenger-class ships.

Originally contracted by the Royal Navy, they were transferred under Lend-Lease and entered service in the first half of 1942. Designed for 15 aircraft each, these escort carriers (CVEs or Jeep carriers) were slow (16.5 knots), but they proved invaluable. U.S. CVE captains had complete freedom of action to mount hunt-and-kill missions. Teams composed of an escort carrier and half a dozen destroyers or new destroyer escorts sank 53 U-boats and captured another; they were probably the single most important U.S. contribution to the struggle against the U-boats.

Long-range aircraft were essential in closing the Mid-Atlantic gap, but the RAF's preoccupation with strategic bombing meant that Coastal Command possessed few aircraft suitable for this purpose. Bomber Command's air marshal Arthur Harris finally made air assets available. The U.S. Consolidated PBY Catalina and PB2Y Coronado and the British Short Sunderland flying boats proved invaluable, as did long-range B-24 Liberator and British Lancaster bombers.

Finally, in August 1944 RAF Bomber Command Squadron 617 (the "Dam Busters") began attacks with specially designed Tallboy bombs against the concrete-reinforced U-boat pens of the Bay of Biscay. U-boats in port were now vulnerable, and in the last year of the war 57 U-boats were destroyed by bombing, compared with only five in the previous five years. This shows what might have been accomplished had the bombers been directed against the submarines earlier. Indeed, after March 1943 aircraft were probably the chief factor in the defeat of the U-boats. Between March 1943 and May 1945 a total of 590 U-boats were destroyed, compared to only 194 in the previous three and a half years of war. Of these, 290 were by aircraft, 174 by ships, and the remainder through a combination of the two or other causes.

In the first few months of 1945, Dönitz sent to sea new snorkel-equipped U-boats that were able to operate submerged while at the same time taking in air from the surface. During January to April these sank some 253,000 tons of Allied shipping, most of it in waters around the British Isles. The Allies countered with hunter-killer teams of destroyer escorts and escort carriers. The last German submarine sinking of an Allied merchant ship occurred on May 6, 1945.

In the 69-month Battle of the Atlantic, the longest campaign of the war, German U-boats sank 2,850 Allied and neutral merchant ships, 2,520 of them in the Atlantic and Indian oceans, as well as many warships, from aircraft carriers to destroyers and smaller ships. The Germans lost 1 large battleship, 1 pocket battleship, some armed merchant raiders, and 650 U-boats, 522 of them in the Atlantic and Indian oceans.

References

Doenitz, Karl. *Memoirs: Ten Years and Twenty Days.* Translated by R. H. Stevens in collaboration with David Woodward. Annapolis, MD: Naval Institute Press, 1990.

German, Tony. *The Sea Is at Our Gates: The History of the Canadian Navy.* Toronto: McClelland and Stewart, 1990.

Middlebrook, Martin. *Convoy.* New York: William Morrow, 1977.

Padfield, Peter. *Dönitz: The Last Führer, Portrait of a Nazi War Leader.* New York: Harper and Row, 1984.

Y'Blood, William T. *Hunter-Killer: U.S. Escort Carriers in the Battle of the Atlantic.* Annapolis, MD: Naval Institute Press, 1983.

Battle for Tarawa

Date	November 20–24, 1943	
Location	Tarawa Atoll in the Gilbert Islands, central Pacific Ocean	
Opponents (* winner)	*Americans	Japanese
Commander	Marine Major General Holland M. Smith	Rear Admiral Shibasaki Keiji
Approx. # Troops	18,000	4,700
Importance	The first amphibious landing against a heavily defended coast since Gallipoli during World War I, it is, in terms of percentage of casualties, one of the bloodiest battles in U.S. military history but it yields valuable lessons for subsequent amphibious operations	

The November 1943 capture of Tarawa in the Gilbert Islands was the first amphibious landing against a heavily defended coast since the Gallipoli Campaign during World War I (1914–1918). In terms of percentage of casualties, the Battle for Tarawa was one of the bloodiest battles in U.S. military history but provided valuable lessons for subsequent amphibious operations.

Following the American victory on Guadalcanal in February 1943, Admiral Chester W. Nimitz, commander of U.S. forces in the Central Pacific, readied the Fifth Fleet for a strike in the Central Pacific. Commanded by Vice Admiral Raymond A. Spruance, the Fifth Fleet included 8 carriers, 7 battleships, 10 cruisers, and 34 destroyers. Rear Admiral Richmond K. Turner's Fifth Amphibious Force lifted U.S. Marine Corps major general Holland M. "Howling Mad" Smith's V Amphibious Corps. In addition to carrier-based naval aircraft, the Seventh Army Air Force provided support.

Bodies of American dead on the beach at Tarawa in the Gilbert Islands. 0f 5,000 marines in the initial assault, 1,500 were killed or wounded on November 20, 1943. (National Archives)

The 16 Gilbert atolls, ringed with coral reefs and at the time Japan's farthest eastern outpost, straddled the equator. The Japanese defense centered on Tarawa and Makin, some 100 miles apart. Betio, Tarawa's biggest island, contained a small airfield from which Japanese planes could threaten Allied shipping lanes between the United States and Australia. The invasion planners allocated 18,000 marines to Tarawa.

Beginning in mid-November 1943, U.S. Navy warships converged on the islands. U.S. Army Air Forces bombers attacked, followed by naval gunfire from battleships and cruisers and strikes by navy aircraft. Army forces landed on Makin on February 20 and secured it in four days.

The capture of Tarawa was not so easy. The citadel of its defense was Betio Island, only two miles long and several hundred yards across. The Japanese had built some 400 concrete pillboxes, bunkers, and strong points covered with logs and sand that were impervious to all but a direct hit. They also had 8-inch guns and had placed mines in gaps in the coral reefs and ringed the island with barbed wire.

On the morning of November 20 the U.S. Marine Corps 2nd Division went ashore. As they did so, the 4,700 Japanese defenders, commanded by Rear Admiral

Shibasaki Keiji, opened fire. Inadequate reconnaissance had failed to disclose inner coral reefs just below the surface of the water. Although the amtracs (amphibious tractors) carrying the first wave of assaulting troops could cross the reefs and most reached the beach, landing craft with the remainder of the men hung up on them. The marines were thus forced to wade hundreds of yards through waist-deep water while under heavy Japanese fire.

Of 5,000 marines landed the first day, 1,500 were killed or wounded. The next day the divisional reserve landed. With no possibility of maneuver in such a small area, advance was slow and by frontal assault. Gradually the marines drove the defenders into the eastern part of the island. Most of them were killed in a suicidal November 22–23 night attack that was shattered by Marine artillery and naval gunfire. The Japanese lost 4,690 men on Tarawa; the marines took only 17 Japanese prisoners, although 129 Korean laborers were captured as well. The marines suffered 985 killed and 2,193 wounded. The casualties shocked Americans at home, and there were even calls for a congressional investigation.

The Americans learned important lessons from the operation. These included the need for better reconnaissance, more effective naval gunfire support (especially plunging fire to destroy fortifications), and additional flamethrowers, demolition charges, amphibious tractors, and infantry firepower. The Battle for Tawara became a symbol of U.S. Marine Corps gallantry.

References

Alexander, Joseph H. *Utmost Savagery: The Three Days of Tarawa.* Annapolis, MD: Naval Institute Press, 1995.

Graham, Michael B. *Mantle of Heroism: Tarawa and the Struggle for the Gilberts, November, 1943.* Novato, CA: Presidio, 1993.

Gregg, Charles T. *Tarawa.* New York: Stein and Day, 1984.

Wright, Derrick. *A Hell of a Way to Die: Tarawa Atoll, 20–23 November 1943.* London: Windrow and Greene, 1997.

Battle of Anzio

Date	January 22–May 25, 1944	
Location	Anzio and Nettuno on the western coast of Italy	
Opponents (* winner)	*Americans, British	Germans
Commander	Major General John Lucas; Major General Lucian K. Truscott	Generaloberst Eberhard von Mackensen
Approx. # Troops	Ultimately 110,000	More than 100,000
Importance	An opportunity thrown away by the western Allies; after 125 days and major commitment of resources, the Allied forces here do eventually break free	

Fighting in Italy that followed the Allied invasion of early September 1943 was some of the most bitter of World War II (1939–1945) and at times resembled World War I (1914–1918) trench warfare. German generalfeldmarschall Albert Kesselring had charge of German forces in Italy and made skillful use of the ideal defensive terrain. The central mountainous spine of the Apennines rises above 10,000 feet, with lateral spurs running east and west. Between these there are deep valleys with wide rapidly flowing rivers. In 1943 the few north-south roads were confined to 20-mile strips adjacent to the Adriatic and Tyrrhenian coasts, where the bridges were dominated by natural strong points.

Kesselring formed German divisions in southern Italy into the Tenth Army under Generaloberst Heinrich von Vietinghoff. Following successful Allied landings by British general Sir Bernard Montgomery's Eighth Army at Calabria and Taranto and by U.S. lieutenant general Mark Clark's Fifth Army at Salerno, Vietinghoff succeeded in holding up the Fifth Army at the rain-swollen Volturno River by blowing its bridges. Skillful German delaying actions elsewhere allowed them time to bring up reinforcements and consolidate behind a formidable defensive line known as the Gustav Line (also known as the Winter Line). The Gustav Line was some 10 miles deep and ran from the mouth of the Garigliano River on the Gulf of Gaeta west along its swift-running tributary, the Rapido River, and then over the mountains to the Adriatic north of the Sangro River.

The Fifth Army eventually got across the Volturno but soon found itself crowded into a small attack zone along the Rapido. German resistance, difficult terrain, constant rain or snow, and a morass of mud all produced a stalemate on the ground by year's end. The town of Cassino, astride the main road from Naples to Rome, was the hub of the German defenses.

The Allies tried to outflank the Gustav Line by landing north of it at Anzio on the west coast of Italy, just 25 miles from Rome. British prime minister Winston Churchill was the plan's chief advocate. The Allies hoped to divert German units from the Gustav Line, allowing a breakout there and permitting the two Allied pincers to converge on Rome. Anzio turned out to be an incredible opportunity thrown away.

General Clark had overall command of the Anzio operation, but VI Corps commander U.S. major general John Lucas led the actual invasion force. The landing began on January 22, 1944. The invaders consisted principally of British major general W. R. C. Penney's 1st Division on the left flank and U.S. major general Lucian K. Truscott's 3rd Infantry Division on the right. U.S. colonel William O. Darby's 509th Parachute Infantry Battalion had the task of securing the port of Anzio.

Code-named Operation SHINGLE, the landing proceeded virtually unopposed. By the end of the day more than 36,000 men, 3,000 vehicles, and large quantities of supplies had come ashore at a cost of only 13 dead, 97 wounded, and 44 missing or captured. Unfortunately for the Allies, 1 of those captured was carrying a copy of the operation plan.

Two days before the invasion, the Allies launched their planned diversionary strike against Cassino. Kesselring immediately rushed two reserve divisions south from Rome to Cassino. Consequently, when the Anzio invasion occurred there were no German reserves to meet a swift Allied thrust to Rome. Although Lucas did get valuable amounts of supplies ashore quickly, which enabled the Allies to beat back subsequent German counterattacks, he was overly cautious at first and failed to take advantage of the temporary German weakness to secure the critical nearby Alban Hills. Although Colonel Reuben Tucker's U.S. 504th Parachute Regiment was available for that purpose, Clark had vetoed an airborne drop. The 504th Parachute Regiment came ashore by landing ship tank to fight as infantry.

After the successful landings, nothing went right for the Allies. The chief reason for the failure of the Anzio operation was insufficient resources in the initial assault. Landing craft and other assets from Italy had been sent to prepare for the upcoming Normandy invasion. Lacking adequate resources at Anzio, the Allies would have been better off to have mounted a decisive operation along the Gustav Line.

The Anzio beachhead soon developed into a precarious situation where the Germans constantly rushed up more men, ultimately committing Generaloberst Eberhard von Mackensen's entire Fourteenth Army there, which soon threatened to drive the Allied forces into the sea. Ultimately the Allies were forced to commit more than 110,000 men to the beachhead. The most famous comment on the situation was provided by Winston Churchill: "I had hoped that we were hurling a wild cat onto the shore, but all we got was a stranded whale" (Trevelyan, *Rome '44: The Battle for the Eternal City,* 144).

The more aggressive 3rd Infantry Division commander, U.S. major general Lucian K. Truscott, took over from Lucas as VI Corps commander in late February, but extremely cold weather and stiff German resistance led to a 125-day stalemate. Not until May 25 and after more than 40,000 casualties were the Allied able to break out from Anzio and drive on Rome.

References

Blumenson, Martin. *Anzio: The Gamble That Failed.* New York: Cooper Square, 2001.

———. *General Lucas at Anzio.* Washington, DC: U.S. Army Center of Military History, 1990.

D'Este, Carlo. *Fatal Decision: Anzio and the Battle for Rome.* New York: HarperCollins, 1991.

Graham, Dominick, and Shelford Bidwell. *Tug of War: The Battle for Italy, 1943–1945.* New York: St. Martin's, 1986.

Lamb, Richard. *War in Italy, 1943–1945: A Brutal Story.* New York: St. Martin's, 1993.

Morris, Eric. *Circles of Hell: The War in Italy, 1943–1945.* New York: Crown Publishers, 1993.

Trevelyan, Raleigh. *Rome '44: The Battle for the Eternal City.* New York: Viking, 1982.

Normandy Invasion

Date	June 6, 1944	
Location	Coast of Normandy, France	
Opponents (* winner)	*Americans, British, Canadians, Free French, Poles, Norwegians	Germans
Commander	U.S. General Dwight D. Eisenhower (overall commander); British General Bernard Montgomery (ground forces); British Admiral Bertram H. Ramsay (naval forces)	Generalfeldmarschall Karl Rudolf Gerd von Rundstedt; Generalfeldmarschall Erwin Rommel
Approx. # Troops	175,000	380,000
Importance	Secures the Western Allies a lodgment in France, making possible their subsequent liberation of that country	

At the Tehran Conference in November 1943, British prime minister Winston Churchill, U.S. president Franklin D. Roosevelt, and Soviet premier Joseph Stalin agreed to a major invasion of Europe via the English Channel as well as a landing in southern France and a major offensive by the Soviets on the Eastern Front. The Germans were well aware that the Western Allies would attempt a cross-Channel invasion. Festung Europa (Fortress Europe) and its coasts of Holland, Belgium, and France bristled with German fortifications and booby traps. In mid-1942 the German Todt Organization began erecting Atlantic coast defenses and during the next two years expended some 17.3 million cubic yards of concrete and 1.2 million tons of steel on thousands of fortifications. The Germans also strongly fortified the Channel ports, which Adolf Hitler ordered turned into fortresses.

The Allies knew that they would likely not be able to count on the immediate use of any French ports, and in one of history's greatest military engineering achievements, thousands of laborers worked in Britain over many months to build two large artificial harbors. Known as Mulberries, these were to be hauled across the Channel from Britain and sunk in place; they were to ease resupply and allow the invaders to temporarily bypass the German-held ports. The Mulberries were of immense importance to the Allied cause.

In a close near-seamless cooperation, British and French staff officers worked out precise and elaborate plans for a mammoth invasion of the Cotentin Peninsula in Normandy. U.S. general Dwight D. Eisenhower had overall responsibility, while British admiral Bertram H. Ramsay commanded the naval operation, code-named NEPTUNE, and British general Bernard Montgomery exerted overall command of the land forces. The object of the operation was "to secure a lodgement on the continent, from which further offensive operations can be developed." In the weeks

NORMANDY INVASION, 1944

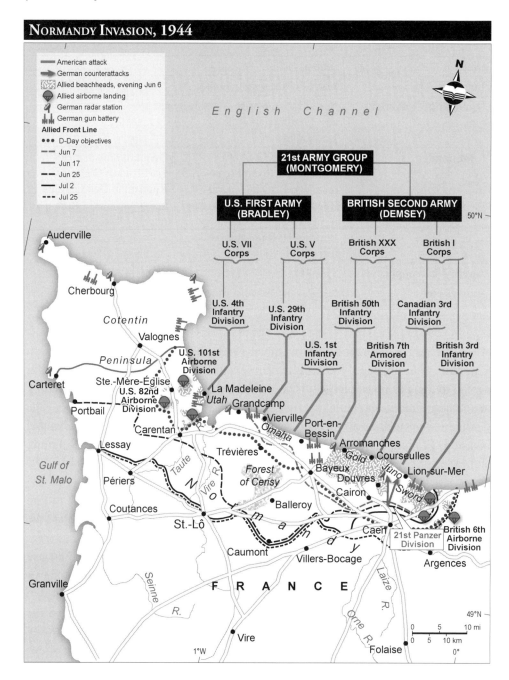

leading up to the landing, Allied air forces carried out a massive bombing campaign to isolate Normandy.

The landing was to be preceded by a night drop of three divisions of paratroops: the British 6th Division and the U.S. 82nd and 101st divisions. The lightly armed paratroopers, operating in conjunction with the French Resistance, had the vital assignment of securing the flanks of the lodgement and destroying key transportation choke points to prevent the Germans from reinforcing the beaches. The German 21st Panzer and 12th SS Panzer divisions were positioned just outside Caen. If they could reach the beaches, they would be able to strike the amphibious forces from the flank and roll them up.

The amphibious assault would occur early the next morning after the airborne assault. Five infantry divisions were to come ashore along a 50-mile stretch of coast, divided into five sectors. The designated units and their beaches were, from west to east, the U.S. 4th Infantry Division, Utah; the U.S. 1st Infantry, Omaha; the British 50th Infantry, Gold; the Canadian 3rd Infantry, Juno; and the British 3rd Infantry, Sword.

The Normandy invasion proved to be a vast undertaking. The airborne forces alone required 1,340 C-47 transports and 2,500 gliders. Ten thousand aircraft secured the skies, while naval support for the invasion numbered 138 bombarding warships, 221 destroyers and other convoy escorts, 287 minesweepers, 495 light craft, and 441 auxiliaries. In addition, some 4,000 landing ships and other craft of various sizes participated.

General Eisenhower faced a difficult decision, given terrible weather in the days leading up to the landing. Informed by his chief meteorologist that a break in the weather should occur, Eisenhower decided to proceed. The weather actually worked to the Allies' advantage, for the Germans did not expect a landing in such poor conditions.

The French Resistance was informed by radio code of the imminent attack, and the airborne forces took off. The drops occurred on schedule on the night of June 5–6, but thick cloud banks over Normandy that caused pilots to veer off course to avoid midair collisions, German antiaircraft fire, jumpy flight crews, and Pathfinders who were immediately engaged in firefights on the ground and unable to set up their beacons all led to premature drops and to paratroopers being scattered all over the peninsula. Some even fell into the Channel, where they were dragged down by their heavy equipment. Gliders crashed into obstacles, and they and the paratroopers came down in fields that had been deliberately flooded by the defenders. Much equipment was thus lost. Nonetheless, the wide scattering of forces caused confusion among the Germans as to the precise Allied objectives. Airborne officers collected as many men as they could, and these improvised units were soon moving on the objectives, most of which were secured.

Success was likely if the Allies could establish a bridgehead large enough to build up their strength and overcome the German defenders. Once they broke out, the Allies would have the whole of France for maneuver. Their armies were fully mechanized, and the bulk of the defending German forces were not. German generalfeldmarschall Erwin Rommel, who had charge of the coastal defenses, understood that the German defense was doomed unless it could destroy the invaders on the beaches. He told Hitler, "If we don't manage to throw them back at once, the invasion will succeed in spite of the Atlantic Wall."

Hitler failed to understand this, however, and indeed welcomed the invasion as a chance to get at and destroy the British and U.S. forces. In Britain they could not be touched; in France they could be destroyed. "Let them come." he said. "They will get the thrashing of their lives."

The only real possibility for German success was the rapid introduction of Panzer reserves, but this was fatally delayed by two factors. The first was Allied air superiority of 30 to 1 over Normandy, including large numbers of ground-support aircraft, especially the Republic P-47 Thunderbolt and the North American P-51 Mustang. The second was Hitler's failure to immediately commit available resources. He was convinced that the invasion at Normandy was merely a feint and that the main thrust would come in the Pas de Calais sector.

Allied deceptions played a key role in deluding the Germans. Every German agent in Britain was dead, jailed, or working for British intelligence. The British actually controlled the entire German spy network in the United Kingdom and used it to feed disinformation to the Germans. In Operation FORTITUDE in particular, the British orchestrated two deceptions of immense importance to the success of the invasion.

FORTITUDE NORTH suggested an invasion of Norway by a bogus British "Fourth Army" headquartered at Edinburgh, Scotland. To convince the Germans, the British employed radio nets and also created large numbers of decoy barges of canvas, wood, and wire; dummy gliders; and inflatable rubber tanks and trucks. Some German reconnaissance aircraft were then permitted to fly over these. This deception and perceived threat to his northern flank caused Hitler to shift some 400,000 men to Norway.

FORTITUDE SOUTH, on the other hand, was designed to convince Hitler that the landing at Normandy (Operation OVERLORD) was only a diversion and that the major invasion would indeed occur later in the closest Channel crossing point, the Pas de Calais. The Allies created the "First U.S. Army Group" under General George Patton, still without command following an incident in which he had slapped soldiers suffering from combat fatigue in Sicily. The Germans expected Patton to command any Allied invasion of Europe. The U.S. First Army Group, a formation of 18 divisions and four corps headquarters, contributed nothing to the initial invasion, however.

Both deceptions involved feeding small bits of information to the Germans, some of it through the Double-Cross System and then letting the Germans draw the proper conclusions. The British plan worked to perfection. Not until late July did Hitler authorize the movement of the Fifteenth Panzer Army from the Pas de Calais to Normandy. The deception effectively immobilized 19 German divisions east of the Seine. Although units of the Fifteenth Army were moved west to Normandy before that date, they arrived piecemeal and thus were much easier to defeat.

The Normandy Invasion began with some 2,700 vessels, manned by 195,000 naval officers and sailors, that transported 130,000 troops to France, along with 2,000 tanks, 12,000 other vehicles, and 10,000 tons of supplies. At about 5:30 a.m. on June 6, 1944, the bombardment ships opened up against the invasion beaches, engaging the German shore batteries. The first U.S. assault troops landed 30 to 40 minutes later, while the British landing craft were ashore 2 hours later.

The landing was in jeopardy only on Omaha Beach, where because of rough seas only 5 of 32 amphibious DD (duplex drive) tanks reached the shore. Support artillery was also lost when DUKW amphibious trucks were swamped by the waves. Some landing craft were hit and destroyed, and those troops of the 1st Infantry Division who gained the beach were soon pinned down by withering German fire. U.S. First Army commander Lieutenant General Omar N. Bradley even considered withdrawal.

At 9:50 a.m. the gunfire support ships opened up against the German shore batteries, and Allied destroyers repeatedly risked running aground to provide close-in gunnery support to the troops ashore; several destroyers actually scraped bottom. It was nearly noon before the German defenders began to give way. The 1st Infantry Division overcame German opposition with sheer determination, reinforced by the knowledge that there was no place to retreat.

The landings on the other beaches were much easier, and the Allies suffered surprisingly light casualties overall for the first day: 10,000–12,000 men. A recent study suggests that a night landing would have produced fewer casualties. The Allies had employed these with great success in the Mediterranean, but Montgomery believed that overwhelming Allied air and naval power would make a daytime landing preferable.

One million men came ashore within a month. Unfortunately for the Allies, during June 19–20 a Force 6–7 storm severely damaged Mulberry A in the American sector. It also sank well over 100 small craft and drove many more ashore, bringing to a halt the discharge of supplies. Vital ammunition stocks had to be flown in. Mulberry A was abandoned, but a strengthened Mulberry B provided supplies to both armies until the end of the war.

The Allied ground offensive meanwhile proceeded slower than expected. By ordering his armies to fight for every inch of ground rather than withdraw along phased lines as his generals wanted, Hitler at first delayed the Allied timetable. His decision greatly speeded up the Allied advance at the end, however, and ensured that the resultant defeat would be costly. Complete Allied air superiority devastated the Germans by day, forcing them to move at night.

The Normandy countryside proved to be ideal defensive terrain for the Germans. Over the centuries the dividing lines between individual fields had been allowed to grow up into tangled hedgerows. This *bocage* resisted passage and slowed the Allied advance to a crawl. On June 17 and 18 the Germans blocked Montgomery's efforts to take Caen. U.S. major general J. Lawton Collins's U.S. VII Corps had more success on the Allied right, gradually pushing across the base of the Cotentin Peninsula. On June 18 VII Corps turned north to liberate the important port of Cherbourg, while the remainder of Bradley's army maintained an aggressive defense. Cherbourg fell on June 27, but the defenders destroyed the harbor facilities, and it took U.S. major general Lucius Clay six weeks to get them back in operation.

Not until the end of July were the Allies able to break out. In Operation COBRA (July 25–31), Bradley's U.S. First Army forced the German line west of Saint-Lô, with Collins's VII Corps making the main effort. Following a carpet-bombing operation, Collins's tanks and infantry rolled through the German left flank. Patton had arrived in France on July 6, and two days after the start of COBRA he took command of VIII Corps.

On August 1 the U.S. command was reorganized. Bradley moved up to command the 12th Army Group, Lieutenant General Courtney Hodges assumed command of the First Army, and Patton's Third Army was activated. In the British zone of operations, Montgomery's mostly British Commonwealth 21st Army Group consisted of Lieutenant General D. G. Crerar's Canadian First Army and Lieutenant General Miles C. Demsey's Second British Army.

The Third Army scored the greatest success. The static warfare of the previous two months had finally passed into the mobile warfare at which Patton excelled. The weather was also dry, and the flat terrain of northern France was ideal tank country. Patton was certainly the outstanding general of the campaign for France. The Third Army soon had parlayed the local breakthrough of COBRA into a theater-wide breakout and in a single month had liberated most of France north of the Loire.

References

Blair, Clay. *Ridgway's Paratroopers: The American Airborne in World War II.* Garden City, NY: Dial, 1985.

Hartcup, Guy. *Code Name Mulberry: The Planning, Building and Operation of the Normandy Harbours.* London: David and Charles, 1977.

Hesketh, Roger. *Fortitude: The D-Day Deception Campaign.* New York: Overlook, 2000.

Keegan, John. *Six Armies in Normandy: From D-Day to the Liberation of Paris, June 6th–August 25th, 1944.* New York: Viking, 1982.

Lewis, Adrian R. *Omaha Beach: A Flawed Victory.* Chapel Hill: University of North Carolina Press, 2001.

Masterman, J. C. *The Double-Cross System in the War of 1939–1945.* New Haven, CT: Yale University Press, 1972.

Battle of the Philippine Sea

Date	June 19–21, 1944	
Location	Philippine Sea	
Opponents (* winner)	*Americans	Japanese
Commander	Vice Admiral Marc A. Mitscher	Vice Admiral Ozawa Jisaburo
Approx. # Troops	112 ships, including 15 carriers (7 fleet and 8 light); 956 aircraft	55 ships, including 9 aircraft carriers (5 fleet and 4 light); 473 carrier aircraft and some 300 land-based aircraft
Importance	This largest battle involving aircraft carriers in history destroys what remains of the Japanese naval air arm	

The Battle of the Philippine Sea during World War II (1939–1945) was the largest engagement between aircraft carriers in history. In June 1944 in Operation FOR-AGER, U.S. Pacific forces moved against the Japanese-held Mariana Islands in the central Pacific. Securing the Marianas would provide bases from which long-range Boeing B-29 Superfortress strategic bombers could strike Japan.

Steaming from Eniwetok 1,000 miles to the east, the U.S. V Amphibious Corps of 530 warships and auxiliaries, lifting more than 127,000 troops, proceeded to Saipan. Admiral Raymond Spruance had overall command. His Fifth Fleet and its chief strike force, Vice Admiral Marc A. Mitscher's Task Force (TF) 58, provided protection for the landing and V Amphibious Corps' ships. TF-58 included 15 carriers (7 fleet and 8 light), 7 battleships, 8 heavy cruisers, 12 light cruisers, 69 destroyers, and 956 aircraft.

The Japanese anticipated the U.S. move, and commander of the Combined Fleet Admiral Toyoda Soemu ordered Vice Admiral Ozawa Jisaburo to prepare a plan to lure U.S. warships, once they moved against the Marianas, into a decisive battle in the Philippine Sea. The Japanese designed this operation, code-named A-GO, to offset somewhat their inferiority in the air by employing land-based aircraft. For the engagement, the Japanese deployed some 90 percent of their surface naval strength: 9 aircraft carriers (5 fleet and 4 light), 5 battleships, 11 heavy cruisers, 2 light cruisers, 28 destroyers, and 473 aircraft.

Ozawa's forces were inferior to those of the Americans in every category except heavy cruisers. However, the Japanese planned to supplement their naval air arm with some 500 land-based aircraft on Yap, Guam, Tinian, and the Palaus. Nearly 100 bombers were ready to fly from Yokosuka if needed. Ozawa hoped to employ his longer-range aircraft to attack the U.S. carriers on their approach. When his own carriers were within range, he would launch a second strike and then land and rearm these aircraft on Guam to attack the American ships in a third strike before they returned to their carriers.

The Japanese aircraft carrier *Zuikaku* (center) and two destroyers under attack by U.S. Navy carrier aircraft during the Battle of the Philippine Sea, June 20, 1944. Although the *Zuikaku* was hit by a bomb, it managed to survive the battle and recover the few remaining Japanese aircraft. (U.S. Naval Historical Center)

On June 15 the 2nd and 4th Marine divisions went ashore on Saipan. Upon learning of the U.S. assault, Vice Admiral Ozawa immediately moved his ships into the Philippine Sea. Spruance, warned of their arrival by the U.S. submarine *Flying Fish,* on the afternoon of June 16 decided to postpone the invasion of Guam and detach 5 heavy and 3 light cruisers and 21 destroyers from the fire-support groups at Saipan to augment TF-58. This left 7 battleships, 3 cruisers, and 5 destroyers to protect the Saipan beachhead. On June 18 he concentrated the Fifth Fleet under Mitscher's tactical command some 180 miles due west of Tinian to search for the Japanese ships.

The resulting June 19–21, 1944, Battle of the Philippine Sea was the first fleet battle between the United States and Japan in two years and turned out to be pivotal. The Japanese employed 55 ships, and the Americans employed 112.

Events went badly for the Japanese early on. Ozawa's ship dispositions were faulty and exposed his carriers to submarine attack. The U.S. submarine *Albacore* sank the *Taiho,* Japan's newest and largest carrier (and Ozawa's flagship), and the submarine *Cavalla* sank the fleet carrier *Shokaku.* Misled about the damage to Japanese land aircraft and unaware that most of them had been destroyed in strikes by planes from Mitscher's carriers, Ozawa believed that he could still count on heavy assistance from Guam.

On the morning of June 19 Ozawa launched four different attack waves against the American ships. Mitscher's fighters and antiaircraft fire downed most of them in what the Americans later referred to as the "Great Marianas Turkey Shoot." The Japanese carriers launched 324 planes but recovered only 56. Other Japanese planes were shot down over Guam or crash-landed there. The Americans lost only 30 aircraft. No U.S. ships were sunk, and only a few sustained damage. Meanwhile, Mitscher's planes attacked Guam and Rota to neutralize the Japanese airfields there. By 6:45 p.m. the battle was effectively over.

Spruance was not aware of Ozawa's exact location and therefore refused Mitscher's suggestion that he move west, as he was concerned that the Japanese might be able to get between his ships and the Saipan landing sites. Mitscher sent out search missions during the morning and early afternoon of June 20, but not until 4:00 p.m. did the Americans definitively locate the Japanese ships at the extreme range of U.S. attack aircraft. Mitscher realized that an attack this late in the day would mean recovering the planes at night and that a number of them might run out of fuel and have to ditch, but he sent 216 aircraft against Ozawa's ships nonetheless.

The U.S. planes arrived at the Japanese ships just before dark and sank the carrier *Hiryu* and two tankers and damaged other vessels. The attack cost the United States 20 planes, but the Japanese lost 21. The homeward-bound U.S. aircraft were forced to find their carriers in the dark. Mitscher ignored the possibility of Japanese submarine attack, however, and lit his carriers. Still, 80 aircraft ran out of gas and either ditched or crash-landed. Destroyers later picked up most of the aircrews, leaving U.S. personnel losses for the day at 16 pilots and 33 crewmen. Spruance pursued the Japanese ships until the early evening of June 21, but he was slowed by the need of his destroyers to take on fuel. Ozawa meanwhile had accelerated his own withdrawal.

The Battle of the Philippine Sea remains controversial for its command decisions. Some historians have criticized Spruance for failing to push westward against the Japanese on the night of June 18–19, which might have yielded a more favorable launch position for Mitscher's aircraft. Mitscher also has been criticized for his failure to send out night searches on June 19–20 that might have located the Japanese ships sooner and allowed an early strike on June 20.

Nonetheless, the Battle of the Philippine Sea was a major defeat for Japan. Air combat and operational losses cost the Japanese approximately 450 aviators. Unable to replace either the carriers or the trained pilots, the vaunted Japanese naval air arm ceased to be a factor in the war. In the Battle of Leyte Gulf that October, the remaining Japanese carriers, bereft of aircraft, served as decoys.

Saipan was declared secured on July 9. This event so shocked Japanese leaders that the cabinet resigned on July 18. Guam was taken during July 21–August 10, and Tinian was taken during July 25–August 2, both after heavy Japanese resistance. Even while the fighting was in progress, U.S. Navy construction battalions

(Cbs, known as Seabees) were at work building runways and preparing facilities for the B-29s that would strike Japan.

References

Dull, Paul S. *A Battle History of the Imperial Japanese Navy, 1941–1945.* Annapolis, MD: Naval Institute Press, 1978.

Morison, Samuel Eliot. *History of United States Naval Operations in World War II,* Vol. 8, *New Guinea and the Marianas, March 1944–August 1944.* Boston: Little, Brown, 1953.

Spector, Ronald H. *Eagle against the Sun: The American War with Japan.* New York: Free Press, 1985.

Y'Blood, William T. *Red Sun Setting: The Battle of the Philippine Sea.* Annapolis, MD: Naval Institute Press, 1980.

Operation BAGRATION

Date	June 22–August 29, 1944	
Location	Belarus	
Opponents (* winner)	*Soviets	Germans
Commander	Marshal Georgi Zhukov	Generalfeldmarschall Ernst Busch; Generalfeldmarschall Walter Model
Approx. # Troops	2,330,000	Approximately 500,000
Importance	Results in the destruction of German Army Group Center	

As the Western Allies drove east through France after the Normandy breakout, the Red Army advanced on the Eastern Front. In January 1944 the Soviets liberated Leningrad, and by the end of April they had reached the borders of Estonia and Latvia. In the south they recaptured Ukraine and were in position to threaten Romania and Hungary. On May 1, Soviet premier Joseph Stalin announced his plan for a great summer offensive that would clear the central part of the front in Belorussia (present-day Belarus), where German Army Group Center still held much Soviet territory. For their Belorussian Offensive the Soviets deployed the 1st Baltic Front (Army Group) and the 1st, 2nd, and 3rd Belorussian fronts, supported by the Dnieper Flotilla and the First Polish Army attached to the 1st Belorussian Front. In all the Soviets utilized some 2.33 million men. Marshal of the Soviet Union Georgi Zhukov had overall command, and the offensive was timed to coincide with the Normandy Invasion.

German leader Adolf Hitler's insistence on holding all captured territory regardless of cost or strategy prevented consolidation of the German lines and ensured that each withdrawal, when it finally occurred, would be more costly. Hitler had already replaced his capable southern group commanders, generalfeldmarschalls Paul von Kleist and Erich von Manstein, for withdrawing contrary to his wishes. Soviet deception now helped convince Hitler that the main blow would fall in the south, aimed at Romania and Hungary, and he transferred units south from Army Group Center to Army Group North Ukraine.

Army Group Center commander Generalfeldmarschall Ernst Busch, however, was convinced that the main Soviet attack would occur in his sector. Army Group Center, with only 500,000 men and few reserves, was thinly spread over a 1,400-mile front. Busch was kept from securing accurate intelligence, however, by Soviet air supremacy and strict radio silence in the days before the offensive.

At dawn on June 22, 1944, the third anniversary of the German invasion of the Soviet Union, the Soviets began their Belorussia Offensive, code-named Operation BAGRATION for Prince Peter Ivanovic Bagration, who had been mortally wounded in the 1812 Battle of Borodino. The 1st Baltic Front struck north of Vitebsk, and by nightfall the Soviets had driven seven miles. On June 23 the 3rd Belorussian Front attacked south of Vitebsk, while the 2nd Belorussian Front drove forward in the vicinity of Orsha. The next day, June 24, the 1st Belorussian Front thrust against the southern portion of the salient.

The Soviets employed massive amounts of conventional artillery (estimated at 400 tubes per mile of front). They also utilized the BM-13 Katyusha multiple rocket launcher. Known as the "Stalin Organ" and mounted on rails in the back of a truck, it could fire a ripple salvo of 16 fin-stabilized 132-millimeter rockets and be reloaded within 6–10 minutes. The Red Army also enjoyed a tremendous advantage over the Germans in numbers of tanks and aircraft. Large numbers of U.S. trucks, which had been shipped to the Soviet Union under Lend-Lease, gave the Red Army great mobility. The few German aircraft available were simply unable to halt the Soviet ground advance or provide adequate intelligence.

With this vast superiority in numbers, the Soviets smashed through the German defenses and penetrated rear areas. Busch pleaded with Hitler to allow him to withdraw to hold a shorter front, but Hitler refused. By the time he relented and authorized the Third Panzer Army to withdraw from Vitebsk, it was too late. Vitebsk fell on June 25, and by June 28 the Third Panzer Army had been largely destroyed. The Fourth Army to the south struggled to hold Minsk, and the German Ninth Army farther south was cut off. Appalled yet refusing to recognize his own responsibility for the disaster, on July 3, the same day that Minsk fell, Hitler sacked Busch and replaced him with Generalfeldmarschall Walter Model, then commanding Army Group North Ukraine.

On July 7, having surrounded much of the Fourth Army, the Soviets entered Minsk. A week later the 1st Ukrainian and 1st Belorussian fronts attacked the northern portion of German Army Group North Ukraine, creating a deep pocket in the Brody area that bagged 42,000 Germans. In the north the Soviets broke through the Finnish Mannerheim Line, and on July 20, 1944, the same day as the famous attempt on Hitler's life, they captured Viipuri.

Beginning on July 10 the Soviets drove into Poland on an ever-widening front, thrusting toward Warsaw. Model managed to check the 1st Belorussian Front just east of Warsaw, but the 1st Ukrainian Front took Lwów (Lemberg, today L'viv in Ukraine) on July 27 and reached the Vistula River on August 7. The long advance having strained their logistics capability, the Soviets then paused to regroup.

The Soviets had smashed Army Group Center, destroying 17 German divisions and 3 brigades; 50 additional German divisions lost more than half their strength. The German Army's official figure of losses was about 300,000 men, or 44 percent of those ultimately engaged, but this may be low. Soviet losses were also high: more than 178,000 dead or missing (8 percent of the total force involved) and more than 587,000 sick or wounded.

The destruction of Army Group Center was a considerable achievement but has been largely ignored by Western historians of the war. The Soviets came up against the bulk of the German Army, for at no time from June 1941 until the end of the war was less than three-quarters of German manpower committed on the Eastern Front.

References

Adair, Paul. *Hitler's Greatest Defeat: The Collapse of Army Group Center.* London: Brockhampton, 1998.

Dunn, Walter S. *Soviet Blitzkrieg: The Battle for White Russia, 1944.* Boulder, CO: Lynne Rienner, 2000.

Battle of Leyte Gulf

Date	October 23–26, 1944	
Location	Leyte Gulf west of Leyte Island, the Philippines	
Opponents (* winner)	*Americans, Australians	Japanese
Commander	Vice Admiral Thomas C. Kinkaid; Admiral William Halsey, Jr.	Vice Admiral Ozawa Jisabuto; Vice Admiral Kurita Takeo; Vice Admiral Nishimura Shoji; Vice Admiral Shima Kiyohide
Approx. # Troops	218 ships (216 U.S. and 2 Australian)	64 ships
Importance	History's largest naval engagement, it witnesses the largest guns ever fired at sea, the last clash of battleships, and the first use of Kamikazes; the battle largely destroys the Japanese Navy as an effective fighting force	

The Battle of Leyte Gulf was history's largest naval engagement. The 282 vessels involved (216 U.S., 2 Australian, and 64 Japanese) surpassed the 250 ships of the 1916 Battle of Jutland. The Battle of Leyte Gulf involved nearly 200,000 men and took place over an area of more than 100,000 square miles. The battle saw all aspects of naval warfare as well as the use of the largest guns ever at sea, the last clash of the dreadnoughts, and the introduction of kamikaze aircraft.

In July 1944 U.S. president Franklin Roosevelt met at Honolulu with his two major Pacific theater commanders to decide on the next target after the conquest of the Mariana Islands. Commander of Southwest Pacific Forces General Douglas MacArthur argued strongly for a return to the Philippines; Central Pacific commander Admiral Chester W. Nimitz, supported by chief of naval operations Ernest J. King, wanted to secure Taiwan. Both plans would place U.S. forces astride the Japanese oil lifeline from the Netherlands East Indies, but Roosevelt sided with MacArthur primarily for political reasons. The next target would be Okinawa rather than Taiwan.

On October 20 more than 132,000 men of the U.S. Sixth Army went ashore on the island of Leyte in the Philippines. Warned by the preliminary bombardment, the Japanese put into effect their contingency plan. The Naval General Staff in Tokyo had actually developed four plans under the SHŌ (VICTORY) code name. Operation SHŌ-1 covered defense of the Philippine archipelago and involved the entire Combined Fleet.

Japanese naval air strength had been severely reduced in the June 1944 Battle of the Philippine Sea, and during October 12–14 U.S. carrier planes and U.S. Army B-29 heavy bombers attacked Japanese airfields on Formosa, Okinawa, and the Philippines. These strikes wiped out much of the Japanese land-based aviation and denied the Japanese Navy badly needed support. This alone probably doomed the Japanese plan. The Japanese did add extra antiaircraft guns to their ships in an attempt to offset their lack of airpower, but offensively they had to rely on naval gunnery and some 335 land-based planes in the Luzon area.

The Japanese hoped to destroy sufficient U.S. shipping to break up the amphibious landing. The plan had four elements. A decoy force would attempt to draw the U.S. fleet north, while two elements struck from the west, on either side of Leyte, to converge on the landing area in Leyte Gulf and destroy the shipping there. At the same time, shore-based Japanese aircraft were to carry out attacks. At best the plan was a long shot.

On October 18 the Japanese intercepted American messages regarding the approaching Leyte landings, and Toyoda initiated SHŌ-1. The original target for the fleet engagement was October 22, but logistical difficulties delayed it to October 25.

Vice Admiral Ozawa Jisabuto's decoy Northern Force (Third Fleet), which consisted of the heavy carrier *Zuikaku,* 3 light carriers, 2 hybrid battleship-carriers, 3 cruisers, and 8 destroyers, sortied from Japan. Ozawa had only 116 planes flown by half-trained pilots. Japanese submarines off Formosa were ordered south, toward the eastern approaches to the Philippine archipelago, and shortly before October 23 what remained of the Japanese 2nd Air Fleet began to arrive on Luzon.

The strongest element of the Japanese attack was the 1st Diversion Attack Force. It reached northwest Borneo on October 20, refueled, split into two parts, and moved

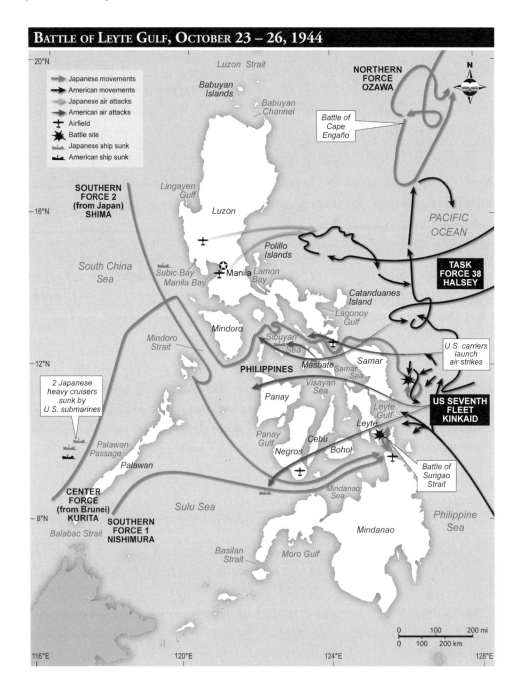

Battle of Leyte Gulf, October 23 – 26, 1944

Legend:
- Japanese movements
- American movements
- Japanese air attacks
- American air attacks
- ✚ Airfield
- ✷ Battle site
- Japanese ship sunk
- American ship sunk

NORTHERN FORCE OZAWA

Battle of Cape Engaño

SOUTHERN FORCE 2 (from Japan) SHIMA

Luzon Strait

Babuyan Islands

Babuyan Channel

Lingayen Gulf

Luzon

Polillo Islands

Subic Bay
Manila Bay
Manila

Lamon Bay

PACIFIC OCEAN

TASK FORCE 38 HALSEY

Catanduanes Island

Lagonoy Gulf

South China Sea

Mindoro

Mindoro Strait

Sibuyan Sea

Masbate

Samar Sea

Samar

U.S. carriers launch air strikes

PHILIPPINES

2 Japanese heavy cruisers sunk by U.S. submarines

Visayan Sea

Panay

Leyte Gulf

Leyte

US SEVENTH FLEET KINKAID

Palawan Passage

Panay Gulf

Negros

Cebu

Bohol

Palawan

CENTER FORCE (from Brunei) KURITA

Sulu Sea

Mindanao Sea

Battle of Surigao Strait

Philippine Sea

SOUTHERN FORCE 1 NISHIMURA

Balabac Strait

Basilan Strait

Moro Gulf

Mindanao

0   100   200 mi
0   100   200 km

116°E   120°E   124°E   128°E

20°N
16°N
12°N
8°N

toward Leyte two days later. The Center Force under Vice Admiral Kurita Takeo contained the bulk of Japanese attack strength, including the superbattleships *Musashi* and *Yamato*. With their 18.1-inch guns, these 70,000-ton behemoths were, at the time, the largest warships ever built. Kurita also had 3 older battleships, 12 cruisers, and 15 destroyers. Center Force would pass to the north of Leyte, through San Bernardino Strait. Vice Admiral Nishimura Shoji's Southern Force (C Force) of

2 battleships, 1 heavy cruiser, and 4 destroyers struck eastward to force its way through Surigao Strait, south of Leyte and north of Mindanao. The Southern Force was trailed by the Second Diversion Attack Force, commanded by Vice Admiral Shima Kiyohide, with 2 heavy and 1 light cruisers and 4 destroyers. Shima's force was late joining Nishimura's force and followed it into Surigao Strait.

Opposing the Japanese were two U.S. Navy fleets: Vice Admiral Thomas C. Kinkaid's Seventh Fleet, operating under General MacArthur's Southwest Pacific Command, and Admiral William F. Halsey's Third Fleet, under Nimitz at Pearl Harbor. Leyte was the first landing to involve two entire U.S. fleets and the first without unified command, which had unfortunate consequences for U.S. forces. The Seventh Fleet was split into three task groups. The first consisted of Rear Admiral Jesse Oldendorf's 6 old battleships, 16 escort carriers, 4 heavy and 4 light cruisers, 30 destroyers, and 10 destroyer escorts. The other two elements were amphibious task groups carrying out the actual invasion.

The Seventh Fleet had escorted the invasion force to Leyte and now provided broad protection for the entire landing area. Because most of Halsey's amphibious assets had been loaned to Kinkaid, the Third Fleet consisted almost entirely of Vice Admiral Marc Mitscher's Task Force (TF) 38 of 14 fast carriers (more than 1,000 aircraft) organized into four task groups containing 6 battleships, 8 heavy and 13 light cruisers, and 57 destroyers. The Third Fleet's orders called for it to secure air superiority over the Philippines, protect the landings, and maintain pressure on the Japanese. If the opportunity to destroy a major part of the Japanese fleet presented itself or could be created, this was to be the Third Fleet's primary task.

U.S. forces detected both western Japanese strike forces early on. The Battle of Leyte Gulf was actually a series of battles, the first of which was the October 23–24 Battle of the Sibuyan Sea. Early on October 23 the U.S. submarines *Darter* and *Dace* discovered Kurita's Center Force entering Palawan Passage from the South China Sea and alerted Admiral Halsey, whose Third Fleet guarded San Bernardino Strait. The submarines sank two Japanese heavy cruisers, the *Atago* (Kurita's flagship) and *Maya,* and damaged a third. Kurita transferred his flag to the *Yamato,* and his force continued east into the Sibuyan Sea where, beginning on the morning of October 24, TF-38 launched five air strikes against it.

The first wave of carrier planes concentrated on the *Musashi.* The *Musashi* took 19 torpedoes and nearly as many bombs before finally succumbing with the loss of half of its crew of nearly 2,200 men. The all-day air attacks also damaged several other Japanese vessels. At 2:40 p.m. on October 25 U.S. pilots reported that Kurita had reversed course and was heading back west; Halsey assumed that this part of the battle was over. He did issue a preliminary order detailing a battle line of battleships known as TF-34 to be commanded by Vice Admiral Willis A. Lee. Admiral Kinkaid was aware of that signal and assumed that TF-34 had been established.

Japanese land-based aircraft from the 2nd Air Fleet harassed a portion of TF-38. Most of the Japanese planes were shot down, but they did sink the light carrier

Princeton and badly damaged the cruiser *Birmingham*. Unknown to Halsey, however, after nightfall Kurita's force changed course again and resumed heading for San Bernardino Strait.

Warned of the approach of the Japanese Center Force, Kinkaid placed Oldendorf's 6 old Seventh Fleet fire-support battleships (all but 1 a veteran of Pearl Harbor), flanked by 8 cruisers, across the mouth of Surigao Strait to intercept Center Force. He also lined the strait with 39 patrol torpedo (PT) boats and 28 destroyers.

The October 24–25 Battle of Surigao Strait was a classic example of crossing the "T" in naval warfare. Nishimura's force was annihilated. While the battleships often get the credit for the Surigao Strait victory, it was U.S. destroyers that inflicted most of the damage. Two converging torpedo attacks sank the battleship *Fuso* and three destroyers. The Japanese then encountered Oldendorf's battle line, whereupon all Japanese warships except the destroyer *Shigure* were sunk. Nishimura went down with his flagship, the battleship *Yamashiro*.

Shima's force, bringing up the rear, was attacked 30 minutes later by PT boats, which crippled a light cruiser. Shima attempted an attack, but his flagship collided with one of Nishimura's sinking vessels. Oldendorf's ships pursued the retreating Japanese. Another Japanese cruiser succumbed to attacks by land-based planes and those of Rear Admiral Thomas L. Sprague's escort carriers. The rest of Shima's force escaped when Oldendorf, knowing that his ships might be needed later, turned back.

During the night of October 24–25 Kurita's force, hoping to join that of Nishimura in Leyte Gulf, moved through San Bernardino Strait and turned south. In the most controversial aspect of the battle, near midnight Halsey had left San Bernardino Strait unprotected to rush with all available Third Fleet ships after Admiral Ozawa's decoy fleet, which had been sighted far to the north. Several of Halsey's subordinates registered reservations about his decision, but the admiral would not be deterred. Compounding the error, Halsey failed to inform Kinkaid, who assumed that TF-34 was protecting the strait.

Halsey's decision left the landing beaches guarded only by the Seventh Fleet's Taffy 3 escort carrier group, commanded by Rear Admiral Clifton A. F. Sprague. Taffy 3 was one of three such support groups operating off Samar. Sprague had six light escort carriers, three destroyers, and four destroyer escorts.

Fighting off Samar erupted at about 6:30 a.m. on October 24, as Taffy 3 found itself opposing Kurita's 4 battleships, including the giant *Yamato;* 6 heavy cruisers; and 10 destroyers. The aircraft from all three Taffy groups now attacked the Japanese. Unfortunately, the planes carried only fragmentation bombs for use against land targets; they put up a strong fight nonetheless, dropping bombs, strafing, and generally harassing the powerful Japanese warships. Sprague's destroyers and destroyer escorts also joined the fight. Their crews skillfully and courageously attacked the much more powerful Japanese warships, launching torpedoes and laying down a smokescreen to try to obscure the escort carriers. These combined attacks forced several Japanese cruisers to drop out of the battle.

Kurita basically lost his nerve. By 9:10 a.m. Kurita's warships sank the escort carrier *Gambier Bay,* the only U.S. carrier ever lost to gunfire, and also sank the destroyers *Hoel* and *Johnston* and the destroyer escort *Samuel B. Roberts.* Kurita believed that he was being attacked by aircraft from TF-38, and just when he might have had a crushing victory, at 9:11 he ordered his forces to break off the attack, his decision strengthened by the fact that the southern attacking force had been destroyed. Kurita hoped to join Ozawa's force to the north but changed his mind and exited through San Bernardino Strait. The four ships lost by Taffy 3 were the only U.S. warships sunk by Japanese surface ships in the Battle of Leyte Gulf.

At 9:40 p.m. Kurita's ships reentered San Bernardino Strait. As the Japanese withdrew, they were attacked by aircraft from Rear Admiral John S. McCain's task force from Halsey's fleet, which sank a destroyer. Meanwhile, Admiral Sprague's escort carriers and Oldendorf's force returning from the Battle of Surigao Strait came under attack from land-based kamikaze aircraft, the first such attacks of the war. These sank the escort carrier *St. Lo* and damaged several other ships.

Earlier, at about 2:20 a.m. on October 25, Mitscher's search planes from Halsey's force located Ozawa's northern decoy force. At dawn the first of three strikes was launched in what became known as the Battle of Cape Engaño. Ozawa had sent most of his planes to operate from bases ashore and thus had only antiaircraft fire with which to oppose the attack. While engaging Ozawa, Halsey learned of the action off Samar when a signal came in from Kinkaid at 8:22, followed by an urgent request eight minutes later for fast battleships.

At 8:48 Halsey ordered Vice Admiral McCain's Task Group (TG) 38.1 to make "best possible speed" to engage Kurita's Center Force. TG-38.1 was en route from the Ulithi to rejoin the other elements of TF-38. As TG-38.1 had more carriers and planes than any of the three other task groups in Halsey's force, detaching it made good sense. Several minutes later Halsey was infuriated by a query from Nimitz at Pearl Harbor: "WHERE IS RPT WHERE IS TASK FORCE THIRTY-FOUR RR THE WORLD WONDERS." At 10:55 Halsey ordered all six fast battleships and TG-38.2 to turn south and steam at flank speed, but they missed the battle. After the war Kurita admitted his error in judgment; Halsey never did. In fact, Halsey said that his decision to send the battleships south to Samar was "the greatest error I committed during the Battle of Leyte Gulf."

By nightfall U.S. aircraft, a submarine, and surface ships had sunk all 4 of Ozawa's carriers as well as 5 other ships. In effect this blow ended Japanese carrier aviation. But the battle of annihilation that would have been possible with the fast battleships had slipped from Halsey's grasp. Still, of Ozawa's force only 2 battleships, 2 light cruisers, and 1 destroyer escaped. Including retiring vessels sunk on October 26 and 27, Japanese losses in the battle were 29 warships (4 carriers, 3 battleships, 6 heavy and 4 light cruisers, 11 destroyers, and a submarine) and more than 500 aircraft. Japanese personnel losses were some 10,500 seamen and aviators dead. The U.S. Navy lost only 6 ships (1 light carrier, 2 escort carriers, 2 destroyers, and 1 destroyer escort) and more than 200 aircraft. About 2,800 Americans were killed and another 1,000 wounded. The Battle of Leyte Gulf ended the Japanese fleet as an organized fighting force.

References

Cutler, Thomas J. *The Battle of Leyte Gulf, 23–26 October 1944.* New York: HarperCollins, 1994.

Field, James A., Jr. *The Japanese at Leyte Gulf: The Shō Operation.* Princeton, NJ: Princeton University Press, 1947.

Morison, Samuel Eliot. *History of United States Naval Operations in World War II,* Vol. 12, *Leyte.* Boston: Little, Brown, 1975.

Potter, E. B. *Bull Halsey.* Annapolis, MD: Naval Institute Press, 1985.

Woodward, C. Vann. *The Battle for Leyte Gulf.* New York: Macmillan, 1947.

Battle of the Bulge

Date	December 16, 1944–January 16, 1945	
Location	Ardennes Forest region of Belgium, France, and Luxembourg	
Opponents (* winner)	*Americans, British, Canadians	Germans
Commander	General Dwight D. Eisenhower; General Omar N. Bradley; Lieutenant General Courtney Hodges; Lieutenant General George S. Patton	Generalfeldmarschall Karl Rudolf Gerd von Rundstedt; Generalfeldmarschall Walther Model; SS Oberstgruppenführer Josef "Sepp" Dietrich
Approx. # Troops	655,000	500,000
Importance	This largest battle of the war for the U.S. Army hastens the defeat of Germany	

By the autumn of 1944 during World War II (1939–1945) Germany's fate was largely sealed. The Western Allies were driving on Germany from the west, and the Soviets were closing from the east. German leader Adolf Hitler, however, rejected the rational course for his people of surrender. Deaf to all reason, his alternative was a desperate gamble. The resulting month-long German Ardennes Offensive, popularly known as the Battle of the Bulge, only speeded the German military defeat.

With the Eastern Front static for several months and the Allied offensive in the West gaining ground, in September 1944 Hitler conceived of a sudden offensive in the Ardennes region to take the Western Allies by surprise, break their front, and recapture the Belgian port of Antwerp. Hitler hoped at the least that such an attack would purchase three to four months to deal with the advancing Soviets. Commander of German forces in the west Generalfeldmarschall Gerd von Rundstedt thought that the plan was unrealistic, as did other high-ranking officers. However, Hitler refused to budge, and substantial German forces were transferred from the Eastern Front for what turned out to be the largest battle fought on the Western Front in the war and the largest single engagement ever for the U.S. Army.

Hitler could not have selected a better location for his attack than the Ardennes. Allied forces there were weak because General Dwight D. Eisenhower, Allied Expeditionary Force supreme commander, had deployed most of his strength northward and southward. The timing could not have been better for the Germans either, as poor weather initially restricted the use of Allied airpower. German security was excellent, Hitler having restricted all communication to secure land lines, which Ultra radio intercepts could not pick up.

The Western Allies were complacent because Ultra revealed nothing of the German plans and because they believed that only they could launch an offensive. Telltale signs were disbelieved. In an exceptional achievement, the Germans secretly marshaled 410,000 men, 1,420 tanks and assault guns, 2,600 artillery pieces and rocket launchers, and just over 1,000 combat aircraft. While this force was considerably greater than the Allied forces in the Ardennes, it was also dwarfed by what the Allies could ultimately bring to bear.

In the predawn darkness and fog of December 16, 1944, the Germans began their offensive, catching the Allies by surprise. Initially, 12th Army Group commander General Omar N. Bradley and his subordinate, Third Army commander Lieutenant General George S. Patton, did not believe it to be a major operation. Eisenhower did, and on its second day he ordered the battle-weary 82nd and 101st Airborne divisions to the front from a reconstitution camp in France. Traveling in trucks, the 101st Airborne Division arrived at midnight on December 18 near the important road hub of Bastogne. This small Belgian town would play a key role in the battle.

The attacking German force of 24 divisions, moving against 3 divisions of Lieutenant General Courtney Hodges's First Army, soon drove a bulge in the American lines, which gave the battle its name. The Battle of the Bulge is more a campaign of a series of smaller battles, each lasting a week or more, with the whole extending over a month. The German penetration eventually extended some 50 miles deep and 70 miles wide.

On December 22 four German soldiers under a white flag walked toward an American outpost near Bastogne. They carried an ultimatum addressed to "the U.S.A. commander of the encircled town of Bastogne." This message called on the American commander (Brigadier General Anthony McAuliffe, in the absence of Major General Maxwell D. Taylor) to save his troops with an "honorable surrender." McAuliffe's response to the Germans was one of the most memorable statements of the war: "To the German Commander: Nuts. The American commander."

German forces flowed around Bastogne, heading northwest toward the Meuse. Generalfeldmarschall Walther Model, commander of Army Group B and charged with carrying out the offensive, sought to have the Fifth Panzer Army make the main effort. Hitler, ignorant of the situation on the ground, insisted that this be done by SS Oberstgruppenführer Josef "Sepp" Dietrich's Sixth Panzer Army.

On the north shoulder of the bulge, the U.S. 1st Infantry Division dug in. The Americans massed 348 artillery pieces that shattered the German attack. In the center, units fighting mostly in isolated formations stood firm, impeding the German advance. Patton's Third Army rushed to the rescue from the south. Patton had ordered his staff to prepare for just such a contingency, and he assured an unbelieving Eisenhower that he could wheel his army 90 degrees and strike north into the bulge with three divisions in only two days. Patton accomplished this feat in one of the most memorable mass maneuvers of the war.

Other Allied resources were also diverted to the Ardennes fighting. Then on December 23 the weather changed along the front, clearing the sky, freezing the ground, and making the terrain passable for armor. Allied aircraft quickly filled the skies, and transports parachuted supplies into Bastogne, where the defenders were down to only 10 rounds per gun. On Christmas Day the German tanks ground to a halt, out of fuel, while U.S. 2nd Armored Division gunners had a turkey shoot at Celles, almost at the German objective of the Meuse, in which they destroyed 82 German tanks. On December 26 the 4th Armored Division of Patton's Third Army lifted the siege of Bastogne.

Unfortunately, 21st Army Group commander British field marshal Bernard L. Montgomery had elected to remain on the defensive, overruling U.S. VII Corps commander Major General J. Lawton Collins's plan to cut off the bulge by striking from each shoulder. Finally, though, the Allies attacked midway up the salient, although this obviated the chance to surround the Germans. Patton held that timidity on the part of Eisenhower and Montgomery allowed the bulk of the German attackers to escape.

On January 1, 1945, as part of the offensive, the Germans mounted an air attack on Allied air bases in Belgium. Operation BODENPLATTE (BASE PLATE) destroyed 500–800 Allied aircraft, most of them on the ground, but also saw about 300 German aircraft shot down and 214 trained pilots lost, many to Allied antiaircraft fire.

On the ground the Battle of the Bulge dragged on to the middle of January. Hitler had already ordered part of the participating Panzer divisions transferred east, but before these resources could arrive the Soviets began their last great offensive. By the end of January the U.S. First Army and Third Army had reached the German frontier and reestablished the line of six weeks before.

The Battle of the Bulge had been fought and won largely by American forces. Of the 600,000 U.S. troops involved, 19,000 were killed, about 47,000 were wounded, and 15,000 were taken prisoner. Of the 55,000 British engaged, casualties totaled 1,400, of whom 200 were killed. The Germans, employing nearly 500,000 men in the battle, sustained nearly 100,000 killed, wounded, or captured.

Both sides suffered heavy equipment losses, about 800 tanks on each side, and the Germans lost virtually all their aircraft committed. But the Western Allies could quickly make good their losses, while the Germans could not. In effect, all Hitler had accomplished was to hasten the end of the war.

References

Cole, Hugh M. *The United States Army in World War II: The European Theater of Operations; The Ardennes: Battle of the Bulge.* Washington, DC: U.S. Government Printing Office, 1965.

Dupuy, Trevor N. *Hitler's Last Gamble: The Battle of the Bulge, December 1944–January 1945.* New York: HarperCollins, 1944.

Eisenhower, John S. D. *The Bitter Woods.* New York: Putnam, 1969.

Forty, George. *The Reich's Last Gamble: The Ardennes Offensive, December 1944.* London: Cassell, 2000.

MacDonald, Charles B. *A Time for Trumpets: The Untold Story of the Battle of the Bulge.* New York: William Morrow, 1985.

Dresden Bombing

Date	February 13–15, 1945	
Location	Dresden, in Saxony, eastern Germany	
Opponents (* winner)	*British, Americans	Germans
Commander	British Air Chief Marshal Sir Arthur Harris	Unknown
Approx. # Troops	1,300 aircraft (773 British; 527 American)	Fighter aircraft and antiaircraft guns
Importance	Although justified by Allied planners at the time, the attack is later seen as excessive and an example of the horrible cost of war for civilians	

The bombing of Dresden, carried out in response to a Soviet request of its Western allies to strike German communications targets in order to prevent the movement of German troops east and mounted by the Royal Air Force (RAF) Bomber Command and the U.S. Strategic Air Forces, became the locus of arguments regarding the strategic bombing campaign and specifically the area bombing of German cities. Certainly it was one of the most destructive air assaults in history.

Later claims to the contrary, in February 1945 Dresden contained many important industrial and transportation targets and was defended, although many of its antiaircraft artillery guns had been sent eastward against the Soviets. British prime minister Winston Churchill supported the attack, although he later tried to distance himself from the operation and the plan to break German civilian morale with a massive Allied air assault on Berlin and refugee centers. There was some American

View of Dresden, Germany after it was fire-bombed by British and American aircraft in February 1945. The bombing of Dresden remains one of the most destructive, and controversial, air attacks in history. (Library of Congress)

unease about the attack, but this was not sufficient to halt it.

Head of Bomber Command Air Chief Marshal Sir Arthur Harris planned the attack and did not shrink from the task or later responsibility for it. Dresden, the capital of Saxony, was a major industrial and communications center and the largest German city yet untouched by bombers. Of particular significance were Dresden's major railways that moved men and supplies east.

Dresden was one of Europe's most beautiful cities, known as the "Florence of the Elbe." The city was also largely composed of wooden structures. Its prewar population was 650,000 people, but in February 1945 the city was choked with refugees from the fighting in the East and from other bombed German cities.

Harris planned the attack carefully. It consisted of two waves of Lancaster bombers, the first of 244 planes and the second, three hours later, of 529 planes. Because of the long distance the planes would have to fly to attack the target and return, bomb loads were minimal: about 7,000 pounds versus 12,000–13,000 pounds per plane carried for attacks against the Ruhr that involved a much shorter range. Most planes carried one cookie, or thin-walled blast bomb, that was in sections and could be up to 6,000 pounds, with the remainder in incendiaries.

Bomber Command struck on the night of February 12–13, 1945. Following the RAF strikes, for the next two days 527 U.S. Army Air Forces B-17 bombers attacked Dresden in daylight. Over a three-day period 1,299 Allied planes dropped 2,431 tons of high explosives and 1,476 tons of incendiaries.

The raging inferno at Dresden was visible 200 miles away. Much of the city was laid waste, particularly the Altstadt, or "Old Town," the nonindustrial part of the city. Estimates of dead vary widely, from a low of 8,200 all the way to a wildly exaggerated 250,000, which was encouraged by Soviet and East German propaganda after the war. British Holocaust denier and historian David Irving later recanted his claim of 135,000 dead, but this figure was subsequently cited in many history books. The number of dead will never be known with certainty because of the refugees in the city and the fact that many bodies were completely incinerated.

The best estimate is between 25,000 and 40,000 deaths, which still makes it one of the most destructive air raids in history.

When news of the bombing reached Britain, there was considerable public outcry over the destruction of such a beautiful city when the war seemed almost over. American air leaders were worried by similar reactions in the United States. Secretary of War Henry Stimson ordered an investigation of the "unnecessary" destruction but was satisfied by the resulting report explaining the background of the operation. Nonetheless, the controversy contributed to the Allied decision to suspend strategic bombing in April.

Public impressions of the excesses of Dresden were reinforced by Kurt Vonnegut's novel *Slaughterhouse Five* and the movie it inspired. The bombing of Dresden has become one of the most commonly evoked images to illustrate the excesses and horror of the conventional bombing of cities.

References

Bergander, Gotz. *Dresden im Luftkrieg.* Cologne: Bohlan Verlag, 1977.

Crane, Conrad C. *Bombs, Cities, and Civilians: American Airpower Strategy in World War II.* Lawrence: University Press of Kansas, 1993.

Irving, David. *The Destruction of Dresden.* New York: Ballantine, 1965.

Konnegut, Kurt. *Slaughterhouse Five.* New York: Delta, 1969.

Smith, Melden E., Jr. "The Bombing of Dresden Reconsidered: A Study in Wartime Decision Making." Unpublished PhD dissertation, Boston University, 1971.

Taylor, Frederick. *Dresden.* New York: HarperCollins, 2004.

Battle for Iwo Jima

Date	February 19–March 24, 1945	
Location	Iwo Jima Island in the Ogasawara or Bonin group, halfway between the Mariana Islands and Japan (some 700 miles from Tokyo).	
Opponents (* winner)	*Americans	Japanese
Commander	Marine Lieutenant General Holland M. Smith; Marine Major General Harry Schmidt	Lieutenant General Kuribayashi Tadamichi
Approx. # Troops	60,000 marines	21,000 (14,000 army; 7,000 navy)
Importance	This test of U.S. Marine Corps amphibious doctrine and practice secures a base for fighter aircraft and emergency landing point for bombers in the U.S. air campaign against Japan.	

The Battle for Iwo Jima is perhaps the best-known battle of the Pacific theater in World War II (1939–1945). The battle was the penultimate test of U.S. Marine

Corps amphibious doctrine and practice in the war. By the end of 1944, American forces had wrested control from Japan of the Mariana Islands of Guam, Saipan, and Tinian. These islands provided air bases from which Boeing B-29 strategic bombers could strike the Japanese home islands. En route to Japan, the big bombers passed in the vicinity of Iwo Jima ("Sulphur Island").

Iwo Jima, the central island in the Ogasawara (or Bonin) volcanic islands halfway between the Mariana Islands and Japan, is some 700 miles from Tokyo. Porkchop-shaped Iwo Jima's most distinctive feature is Mount Suribachi, a 548-foothigh dormant volcano at the narrow southern end of the island. In 1945 Iwo Jima boasted three airstrips and was considered a vital link in the Japanese defense of the home islands. Fighter aircraft based on Iwo Jima attacked the B-29s as they flew to and from Japan. U.S. control of the island would end this threat and allow it to serve as an emergency stopping point for B-29s as well as a base for longrange U.S. fighters to accompany the bombers. U.S. planners considered the capture of both Iwo Jima and Okinawa essential steps toward the invasion of Japan. Iwo Jima was the first target.

The Japanese had long anticipated a U.S. invasion. They evacuated the island's small civilian population and assigned to its defense some 14,000 army and 7,000 navy personnel. Lieutenant General Kuribayashi Tadamichi commanded the defenders, and during the course of a six-month period he oversaw construction of an elaborate system of subterranean fortifications that turned the island of volcanic rock, steep ravines, and caves into a formidable defensive bastion of concrete and steel.

Kuribayashi assumed that the Americans would get ashore. He prohibited banzai charges and ordered his men to stay in their defensive positions and not reveal themselves until the Americans were ashore and then to work to inflict maximum casualties on the attackers while they fought to the last man.

Beginning in August 1944, Iwo Jima was subjected to attack by U.S. heavy bombers from the Marianas; after December 8 it was struck daily. U.S. warships also shelled the island. In all, 6,800 tons of bombs and 22,000 rounds of 5- to 16-inch shells were hurled against Iwo Jima prior to the invasion in the heaviest preliminary bombardment of the Pacific War. Even so, this was less than some wanted.

Fifth Fleet commander Admiral Raymond A. Spruance had overall command of the Iwo Jima operation. Vice Admiral Richmond Kelly Turner commanded the Fifth Amphibious Force transporting Fleet Marine Force commander Lieutenant General Holland M. ("Howling Mad") Smith's marines to the island. Major General Harry Schmidt would head the V Amphibious Corps once it was ashore.

For three days prior to the invasion, eight battleships, five heavy cruisers, and a number of destroyers rained shells on Iwo Jima. Then at 6:45 a.m. February 19 the landing began. The initial assault was made by the 4th and 5th Marine divisions, with the 3rd Division as a floating reserve. Altogether, 60,000 marines were committed to the operation. The landing, accompanied by naval gunfire, was deceptively easy, and optimists predicted that Iwo Jima would be secured in a few days.

Aerial view of the U.S. Marine Corps invasion of Iwo Jima, February 19, 1945. Mount Suribachi looms in the background. (Bettmann/Corbis)

Most of the Japanese defenders survived the bombardment and shelling in their deep underground shelters, however. Once the marines were crowded onto the landing beaches, the Japanese opened a withering fire. Movement was difficult in the light volcanic ash, and the marine positions were easily visible to the Japanese observation posts on Mount Suribachi. Although close naval gunfire support and strikes by naval aircraft allowed the marines to hold a beachhead, the subsequent fighting was foot by foot.

On the second day of the battle the marines took the first airstrip. On the morning of February 23 they took the second airstrip, scaled Mount Suribachi, and planted a U.S. flag on its summit. Nonetheless, fighting continued for another month.

The Japanese made their last stand in what became known as "Bloody Gorge." Only 700 yards in length, it took 10 days to clear. Through March 26, U.S. losses for the marines and navy personnel were 6,812 killed and 19,189 wounded, 30 percent of the entire landing force and 75 percent of the infantry regiments of the 4th and 5th divisions. The battle produced 27 Medals of Honor, 5 in a single day.

There was also a cost at sea. Japanese kamikaze aircraft struck and damaged the aircraft carrier *Saratoga,* causing the loss of 42 aircraft, the deaths of 123 crewmen, and another 192 casualties. Kamikazes also sank the escort carrier *Bismarck*

Sea, with the loss of 218 men. Another escort carrier, a cargo ship, and a landing ship tank were also damaged.

Most of the Japanese fought to the end. Only 216 were taken alive. The marines counted 20,703 Japanese dead. Through May the U.S. Army's 147th Infantry Regiment, which took over from the marines, counted an additional 1,602 Japanese killed and 867 taken prisoner.

Was taking the island worth the cost? From March to August 1945, 2,251 B-29s made forced landings there, and many of these aircraft would otherwise have been lost. Iwo Jima also served as an important base for air-sea rescue operations to retrieve B-29 crews forced to ditch at sea. Long-range Republic P-47 Thunderbolts and North American P-51 Mustangs of VII Fighter Command were also soon flying from Iwo Jima, accompanying the B-29s to Japan and back. The fighters enabled the big bombers to mount midlevel daytime raids in addition to low-level night attacks. With the fighters along, losses of Japanese interceptors increased dramatically, while those of the B-29s continued to decline.

References

Alexander, Joseph H. *Closing In: Marines in the Seizure of Iwo Jima.* Washington, DC: History and Museums Division, Headquarters, U.S. Marine Corps, 1994.

Bradley, James. *Flags of Our Fathers.* New York: Bantam, 2000.

Wright, Derrick. *The Battle for Iwo Jima, 1945.* Phoenix Mill, UK: Sutton, 1999.

Tokyo Raid

Date	March 9–10, 1945	
Location	Tokyo, Japan	
Opponents (* winner)	*Americans	Japanese
Commander	Major General Curtis LeMay	Unknown
Approx. # Troops	334 B-29 bombers	Japanese night fighters and antiaircraft guns
Importance	History's single most destructive air attack	

The attack on Tokyo in March 1945 was the single most destructive air raid in world history. U.S. Army Air Forces (USAAF) strategic bombing of the Japanese home islands began in June 1944, when the four-engine Boeing B-29 Superfortress entered service flying from bases in China. Basing the B-29s in China proved unsatisfactory for a number of reasons. All supplies for the planes, including bombs and even fuel, had to be flown in from India over the so-called Hump of the Himalayas, an extremely difficult and time-consuming operation. Then too, Chinese Nationalist troops were unable to protect the B-29 airfields. No sooner were the fields in operation than Japanese troops attacked and took them.

Another solution was at hand. In July and August 1944 U.S. forces captured Saipan, Guam, and Tinian in the Mariana Islands. Even as these were being cleared of their last Japanese defenders, naval construction brigades (CBs, or Seabees) were at work building runways and support facilities for Brigadier General Haywood S. "Possum" Hansell's XXI Bomber Command. Soon the XXI Bomber Command's B-29s were striking Japan.

The initial B-29 raids from the Marianas were of 150–200 planes per strike, with the 1,200-mile flight to Tokyo and return taking up to 16 hours in the air. USAAF planners had called for precision bombing, but this proved impossible from 30,000 feet. Jet streams threw the planes off course, and ice forming on windshields and wings reduced aircraft performance. The B-29s also flew unescorted and had to pass twice over the Japanese island of Iwo Jima. By December 1944 the B-29 loss rate per mission was averaging 6 percent (the maximum permissible was 5 percent), lowering both morale and crew efficiency.

The raids did have an effect on Japan, however. The strain of frequent air alerts reduced Japanese worker efficiency and lowered the morale of the entire population. The concentration of U.S. bombing attacks on aircraft factories also forced their dispersal, bringing about a decline in actual production.

XXI Bomber Group, nominally under Lieutenant General Nathan Twining's Twentieth Air Force, actually answered to USAAF commander General Henry H. "Hap" Arnold and the Joint Chiefs of Staff (JCS) in Washington, D.C., and Arnold was displeased with the unit's progress. In January 1945 Arnold replaced Hansell with Major General Curtis LeMay, who had enjoyed success commanding XX Bomber Command in India. LeMay was determined to repeat his performance in the Marianas.

Arnold's staff in Washington instructed LeMay to give first priority to attacks on cities rather than industrial targets. In February and March 1945 LeMay developed new tactics. He decided to replicate British air chief marshal and head of Bomber Command Sir Arthur "Bomber" Harris's strategy of area bombing at night. This would take advantage of the Japanese failure to develop an effective night fighter. The B-29s were to fly low, stripped of all armament except the tail gun to increase payloads. They would be loaded with incendiary rather than high-explosive bombs and would drop their loads from only 5,000–8,000 feet.

LeMay's first great firebombing raid was against Tokyo, the Japanese capital, on the night of March 9–10. In the most destructive raid in the history of warfare, a total of 334 B-29s flying at 7,000 feet dropped 1,667 tons of incendiary bombs on a city largely of wooden structures. Widespread firestorms destroyed 15 square miles of central Tokyo, including 267,171 houses. Japanese sources cite 83,793 confirmed dead and 40,918 injured. More than 100,000 people were rendered homeless. The success of the Tokyo raid was repeated four times over the next 10 nights.

Over the next months B-29s hit the largest Japanese cities. Of 64 major cities, 63 were struck. Only the cultural center of Kyoto was spared. Up to 300,000 Japanese died in these attacks. B-29 losses dropped dramatically, to 1.4 percent, in part because of the U.S. capture of Iwo Jima and its use as a fighter field and emergency landing point for crippled B-29s. By August 1945 Japan's cities were burned-out shells. Targets were so scarce that the big U.S. bombers were used to drop mines in the Inland Sea, shutting down what was left of Japanese shipping and helping bring the Japanese nation to starvation levels. Under these conditions and with the dropping of the atomic bombs on Hiroshima and Nagasaki, Japanese leaders decided to surrender.

References

Coffey, Thomas M. *Iron Eagle: The Turbulent Life of General Curtis LeMay.* New York: Crown Publishers, 1986.

Hata Ikuhiko, Sase Morimasa, and Tuneishi Keiichi, eds. *Sekai Senso Hanzai Jiten* [Encyclopedia of Crimes in Modern History]. Tokyo: Bungei-Shunju, 2002.

Johoji Asami. *Nihon Boku Shi* [History of Japanese Air Defense]. Tokyo: Hara Shobo, 1981.

Kerr, E. Bartlett. *Flames over Tokyo: The U.S. Army Air Forces' Incendiary Campaign against Japan, 1944–1945.* New York: Donald I. Fine, 1991.

Battle for Okinawa

Date	April 1–June 21, 1945	
Location	Okinawa in the Ryukyu group between Kyushu, the southernmost island of Japan, and Taiwan	
Opponents (* winner)	*Americans	Japanese
Commander	Lieutenant General Simon Bolivar Buckner; Major General Roy S. Geiger; Major General John R. Hodge	Lieutenant General Ushijima Mitsuru
Approx. # Troops	180,000 men (in the Tenth Army invasion force)	130,000
Importance	The largest and most complicated of the Pacific Theater's amphibious operations, it secures the base for the projected land invasion of the Japanese home islands	

The capture of Okinawa was the final preliminary to an invasion of the Japanese home islands. Located in the Ryukyu group of islands between Kyūshū, the southernmost island of Japan, and Taiwan (Formosa), Okinawa is about 60 miles long and at most 18 miles wide. Taken by Japan in 1875, Okinawa is mountainous in the north and south and level and cultivated in the central portion. If the United States could take the island, it would sever Japanese communications with southern China, but the principal reason was to secure a staging area for the projected invasion of Japan. Okinawa offered suitable air bases, anchorages, and staging grounds for such a vast undertaking.

The operation, code-named ICEBERG, fell to Admiral Raymond Spruance's Fifth Fleet. The lifting force consisted of 1,213 vessels of 45 different classes and types in Vice Admiral Richmond Kelly Turner's Task Force (TF) 51. The vessels ranged from 179 attack transports and cargo ships to 187 landing ship tanks. This does not include the covering force of 88 ships of Vice Admiral Marc Mitscher's TF-58 or the 22 ships of TF-57, a British component commanded by Vice Admiral H. B. Rawlings.

The land assault force for what would be the Pacific theater's largest and most complicated amphibious operation was U.S. Army lieutenant general Simon Bolivar Buckner's Tenth Army of some 180,000 men. It consisted of Major General Roy S. Geiger's III Marine Amphibious Corps (1st, 2nd, and 6th Marine divisions) and Major General John R. Hodge's XXIV Army Corps (7th, 27th, 77th, and 96th Infantry divisions).

Tokyo had begun strengthening Okinawa at the end of March 1944 with the activation of the Thirty-second Army (Ryukus). By October 1944 it contained four divisions (9th, 24th, 62nd, and 28th divisions on Sakishima) plus other units. Altogether, Japanese commander on Okinawa Lieutenant General Ushijima Mitsuru commanded about 130,000 men, including the 20,000-man Okinawan Home Guard. The Japanese constructed a formidable defensive system, particularly on the southern part of the island.

In the second half of March 1945 U.S. forces sought to isolate Okinawa by striking Japanese air bases on Kyūshū and the Sakishima island group between Formosa and Okinawa. Army heavy bombers also hit Formosa and the Japanese home island of Honshu. During these operations the ships, especially the aircraft carriers, came under heavy Japanese kamikaze attacks. Named for the Divine Wind (Kamikaze), a 13th-century typhoon that saved Japan from invasion by Kublai Khan's fleet, kamikazes were first utilized by the Japanese during the Battle of Leyte Gulf, when they sank the escort carrier *St. Lô* and badly damaged other ships.

During March 18–19, 1945, Allied ships off Okinawa came under a heavy kamikaze attack. The carrier *Franklin* took two bomb hits on its flight deck that nearly incinerated the upper decks. Heroic efforts by the crew saved the carrier, but the attacks led to the loss of 724 men, the highest casualty rate of any surviving U.S. Navy vessel in any war. The carrier *Wasp* was also hit by a kamikaze but was saved thanks only to new fire-fighting techniques.

During March 14–31 air attacks and naval shelling proceeded against Okinawa. Then beginning on March 23, the 77th Infantry Division secured the outlying Kerama Islands. This provided anchorages and artillery positions for the invasion force and led to the destruction of some 300 small Japanese suicide boats.

On the morning of Easter Sunday, April 1, the Americans went ashore on Okinawa proper, landing on the west-coast Kadena beaches. Some 16,000 troops came ashore in the first hour, and 50,000 had come ashore by the end of the day. Once again the initial assault was deceptively easy, as the Japanese did not contest the beaches but instead chose to fight in the more populous interior.

The U.S. Marine Corps III Amphibious Corps on the left (1st and 6th divisions) now turned north. The corps met relatively little opposition in clearing the northern area by April 13 and nearby Ie Shima Island during April 16–20. The U.S. Army XXIV Corps swung south. The main landing was facilitated by a demonstration against the southern end of the island by the Marine Corps 2nd Division. The 27th and 77th Infantry divisions were held in reserve. Ushijima now had the majority of his 24th and 62nd divisions in the rugged southern end of the island, where they could mount a determined defense.

It was at this point, beginning on April 7, that the Japanese launched their first major kamikaze assault, aimed at driving the Allied fleet from Okinawa. Some 121 kamikazes and 117 additional orthodox aircraft swept in on the amphibious force. The Americans claimed 383 of the attackers shot down, but 2 U.S. destroyers and 4 smaller ships were sunk and 24 other vessels damaged.

The Allies countered by extending their destroyer screen to 95 miles from Okinawa. The destroyers provided early warning of the attacks but also became easy targets for the kamikazes. From April 6 until July 29 Japanese suicide attacks pounded the destroyer screen, and 14 destroyers were sunk. Through June 10 the Japanese had launched nearly a dozen mass kamikaze raids of between 50 and 300 planes each against the invasion fleet. During the two months that the U.S. Navy was off Okinawa, the navy underwent 2,482 kamikaze attacks. The kamikazes were eventually defeated by new defensive formations that provided maximum antiaircraft fire protection to the carriers and by crushing Allied air superiority.

The largest kamikaze was actually a battleship, the *Yamato*. Departing Japan on April 6 on a one-way mission to Okinawa to attack the invasion fleet and then be beached as a stationary fort, the giant battleship and its escort force of 1 cruiser and 8 destroyers were intercepted on April 7 by 180 U.S. carrier aircraft 200 miles from Okinawa and were sunk in a furious assault of nearly four hours. Only 269 officers and men were rescued; 3,063 aboard the *Yamato* died. U.S. planes also sank 1 light cruiser and 4 escorting destroyers, killing another 1,187 officers and men. U.S. losses in the attack came to 10 aircraft and 12 men.

Meanwhile in fighting on land, XXIV Corps met stiff resistance in the south. Japanese defenders were well dug in along a series of east-west ridge lines across the island, and they incorporated Okinawan burial caves in their successive, mutually supporting positions. The U.S. advance soon ground to a halt.

On April 22 the 1st Marine Division took up position on the right of the line; it was joined there later by the 6th Marine Division. The marines then came up against the main Japanese defensive line, with the heart of its defense at Shuri Castle. On May 4 the Japanese mounted a desperate counterattack that made some headway before it was blunted. On May 18 the marines took Sugar Loaf Hill, the western portion of the Shuri Line. Four days later the Japanese withdrew seven miles south to a new line.

Final operations occurred in June, but on June 18 Buckner was killed by a Japanese shell while at a forward observation post, the highest-ranking U.S. officer lost to hostile fire in the war. Geiger then took command. He was the only U.S. marine ever to command a field army, and he directed the final days of fighting.

Although pockets of resistance remained, Geiger declared the island secure on June 21. The Americans took only 7,400 Japanese prisoners. General Ushijima committed ritual suicide. The Japanese suffered 92,000–94,000 military dead. The Battle for Okinawa was a bloodbath for both sides, the costliest battle for the Americans in the Pacific theater. The U.S. Army lost 12,520 dead and 36,631 wounded. The marines suffered 2,938 dead and 13,708 wounded. The navy lost 4,907 men killed and 4,874 wounded and was the only service in the battle for which dead exceeded wounded; this was a total higher than all the other wars fought by the U.S. Navy put together. The navy also lost 38 ships sunk and 368 damaged. In the campaign for Okinawa the Japanese lost, to all causes, 6,810 aircraft. Civilians on Okinawa especially suffered. Of the preinvasion population of 450,000, perhaps 94,000 died. At considerable cost, the United States had secured the staging base for the invasion of Japan.

References

Gow, Ian. *Okinawa, 1945: Gateway to Japan.* Garden City, NY: Doubleday, 1985.

Leckie, Robert. *Okinawa: The Last Battle of World War II.* New York: Viking, 1995.

Millot, Bernard. *Divine Thunder: The Life and Death of the Kamikazes.* Translated by Lowell Blair. New York: McCall, 1970.

Inoguchi Rikihei and Nakajima Tadashi, with Roger Pineau. *The Divine Wind: Japan's Kamikaze Force in World War II.* New York: Bantam Books, 1978.

Battle for Berlin

Date	April 16–May 2, 1945	
Location	Berlin, Germany	
Opponents (* winner)	*Soviets	Germans
Commander	Marshal Georgi K. Zhukov; Marshal Ivan S. Konev; Marshal Konstantin Rokossovsky	Chancellor Adolf Hitler; Generalleutnant Hellmuth Reymann; General der Artillerie Helmuth Weidling; General der Infanterie Hans Krebs
Approx. # Troops	1,500,000	45,000
Importance	In the last major campaign of World War II, the Soviets secure the German capital city but at great human cost	

The Battle for Berlin between German and Soviet forces was the last major campaign of World War II (1939–1945) in Europe. The battle remains controversial, because with the advent of the Cold War, many Americans believed that U.S. forces should have taken the city in advance of the Soviets. If Washington was not thinking in geopolitical terms, the Kremlin certainly was. Soviet leader Joseph Stalin was determined to capture the German capital.

Berlin, the administrative capital of German chancellor Adolf Hitler's Third Reich, extended over some 900 square miles and was Germany's largest city. It was also the most important industrial and commercial city on the European continent. A major communications and transportation hub, it contained important electrical and armaments factories.

Berlin was at first untouched by the fighting, with food rationing the major problem facing its inhabitants. In August 1940 following the chance bombing of London by the German Luftwaffe, however, the Royal Air Force (RAF) carried out a raid on Berlin. A respite followed until March 1943, and then there was another pause. Between November 1943 and March 1944, however, RAF Bomber Command conducted 16 raids on the German capital. These attacks came to an end when the bombers were reallocated to prepare for the Normandy Invasion. During the offensive, Bomber Command flew 9,111 sorties, dropped 31,000 tons of bombs, and lost 497 aircraft, with more than 3,500 British aircrew killed or captured. On the German side, nearly 10,000 civilians were killed, and 27 percent of the built-up area of Berlin was destroyed. Somehow Berliners managed to carry on amid the ruins, and the goal of defeating Germany by airpower was not realized.

In early 1945 Soviet forces were poised to drive on Berlin, but following the February 1945 Yalta Conference that assigned Berlin within the Soviet occupation zone of Germany, Stalin ordered Red Army forces south to push into Austria, which was not covered by the Yalta Agreement.

In early March 1945 U.S. forces crossed the Rhine River at Remagen. In the West the Germans now had fewer than 60 understrength and poorly equipped divisions to oppose 85 well-equipped Allied divisions. With U.S. forces making solid progress, General Dwight D. Eisenhower, Allied Expeditionary Force supreme commander, ordered General Omar N. Bradley's 12th Army Group to make the main thrust through central Germany, ignoring Berlin. The Ninth Army would encircle the Ruhr, while the remainder of Field Marshal Sir Bernard Montgomery's 21st Army Group would cover Bradley's drive by moving northeast to secure the Province of Schleswig-Holstein in the German North Sea region and the Baltic port of Lübeck, cutting off German forces in Denmark and Norway. Lieutenant General Jacob Devers's 6th Army Group meanwhile would advance down the Danube to secure the so-called Alpenfestung (Alpine Fortress, also known as the "National Redoubt"), a phantom German defensive bastion. On April 1 elements of the First Army and the Ninth Army met at Paderborn, encircling the Ruhr. Ten days later the Ninth Army reached the Elbe near Magdeburg.

Early in 1945 Soviet forces had entered Czechoslovakia and Hungary and began driving into Germany from the east. While telling Eisenhower that he considered the German capital of no importance, Stalin concentrated his resources and goaded his commanders toward capturing Berlin. U.S. forces might have taken both Berlin and Prague. Indeed, airborne forces were poised for an assault on the German capital. British prime minister Winston Churchill, who wanted to "shake hands with the Russians as far east as possible," advocated such a move. He believed that Berlin might be used as a bargaining chip to ensure that the Soviets lived up to their pledges in Eastern Europe.

General Eisenhower was unimpressed. Throughout the war, U.S. leaders paid little attention to geopolitical objectives. Their focus was on winning the war as quickly as possible with the least cost in American lives. Eisenhower, who was in any case distracted by the National Redoubt, said that he had no interest in the capital, which he considered a political rather than a military objective. High casualty estimates for taking the city (Lieutenant General Omar Bradley posited a cost of 100,000 men) also deterred him. Thus, although U.S. forces, including the 82nd Airborne Division, were readied for such an assault, the task was left to the Soviets.

Stalin deliberately concealed U.S. ambivalence concerning a ground assault on Berlin from his front commanders, marshals Ivan S. Konev and Georgi K. Zhukov. By early February, Zhukov's 1st Belorussian Front (Army Group) and Konev's 1st Ukrainian Front had completed the initial phase of their advance into Germany. The Soviets had surrounded large German troop concentrations at Breslau and Posen. Zhukov's troops were across the Oder, 100 miles from the capital. Konev's forces threatened the German capital from the southeast. To defend Berlin, Hitler, who returned to the city in mid-January, had only the remnants of his Third Panzer Army and Ninth Army, now constituting Army Group Vistula. Soviet forces meanwhile exacted a horrible revenge on eastern Germany, murdering and raping tens of thousands of civilians. Total casualties ranged into the millions.

Zhukov might have pushed on to the capital in another few weeks had Stalin not ordered a halt, not because of supposed logistical problems but instead the result of the February 1945 Yalta Agreement and Stalin's decision to push into Austria. Hitler ordered that Berlin be held "to the last man and the last shot."

On March 8, alarmed by the American crossing of the Rhine the day before, Stalin summoned Zhukov to Moscow to discuss the Berlin offensive. The rapid progress of the Western Allies eastward set off alarm bells in Moscow, and the Soviet military staff rushed plans for an offensive to take the German capital. On March 31 Stalin ordered the offensive to begin. Zhukov would make the principal effort, while Konev provided left-flank support and Marshal Konstantin Rokossovsky's 2nd Belorussian Front on the lower Oder moved on Zhukov's right flank. Altogether the three fronts comprised some 1.5 million troops, 6,250 armored vehicles, and 7,500 aircraft. Opposing them were the German Ninth Army and Third Panzer Army, which could muster only 24 understrength divisions with 754 tanks and few aircraft.

Zhukov's frontal assaults on Berlin's defenses from the east failed, and on April 18 Stalin ordered him to go around Berlin from the north while Konev encircled the city from the south. Hitler ordered his Ninth Army to stand fast on the Oder, thus facilitating Konev's move. On April 20, Hitler's birthday, Konev's tanks reached Jüterbog, the airfield and key ammunition depot south of Berlin. That same day Hitler allowed those of his entourage who wished to do so to leave the city. He pledged that he would remain.

The Soviets completed the encirclement of the city on April 25. That same day, elements of Bradley's 12th Army Group linked up at Torgau, on the Elbe, with forces from Konev's 1st Ukrainian Front that Stalin had diverted to prevent a push by the Western Allies into eastern Germany. Hitler attempted to organize the Ninth Army as a relief force for Berlin, but it too was surrounded and soon destroyed. Although German General der Infanterie Walther Wenck's Twelfth Army tried to relieve the city from the west, it was too weak to accomplish the task.

The defense of Berlin fell to miscellaneous German troops—unfortunate enough to be pushed back there—and to old men and boys hastily pressed into the task. On April 30, with the defenders' ammunition nearly depleted and the defenses fast crumbling, Hitler committed suicide. Soviet troops took the Reichstag building in the center of the city that day. On May 2 General der Infanterie Hans Krebs, chief of the German General Staff, surrendered Berlin. Given their country's suffering in the war, Soviet soldiers hardly needed encouragement to destroy the German capital and symbol of Nazism; they committed widespread atrocities in Berlin both during and following its fall.

Bradley's estimate of the cost of taking the city was in fact low. According to one source, the Battle for Berlin produced a staggering total of 352,475 Soviet casualties (78,291 dead), an average of 15,325 a day.

On May 3 U.S. elements of Montgomery's 21st Army Group linked up with Rokossovsky's 2nd Belorussian Front at Wismar. Malinovsky's 2nd Ukrainian Front moved from Hungary into Austria and Czechoslovakia and was preparing to link up with U.S. lieutenant general George S. Patton's Third Army, advancing down the Danube near Linz. On May 7 Hitler's designated successor as chief of state, Grossadmiral Karl Dönitz, surrendered all German forces unconditionally to the Allies. After nearly six years of fighting, the war was over in Europe.

References

Beevor, Antony. *The Fall of Berlin, 1945.* New York: Viking, 2002.

Read, Anthony, and David Fisher. *The Fall of Berlin.* New York: Norton, 1992.

Gavin, James M. *On to Berlin: Battles of an Airborne Commander, 1943–1945.* New York: Viking, 1978.

Krivosheev, G. F., ed. *Soviet Casualties and Combat Losses in the Twentieth Century.* London: Stackpole Books, 1997.

Hiroshima Bombing

Date	August 6, 1945	
Location	Hiroshima, Honshū island, Japan	
Opponents (* winner)	*Americans	Japanese
Commander	Lieutenant Colonel Paul Tibbets	Unknown
Approx. # Troops	B-29 bomber *Enola Gay*	Antiaircraft defenses, fighter aircraft
Importance	The first use of an atomic bomb in history, it changes warfare forever; it also helps make it possible for Emperor Hirohito to justify a Japanese surrender	

In light of heavy U.S. casualties in the capture of the islands of Iwo Jima and Okinawa (26,500 and 75,600 killed or wounded, respectively), it is easy to see why members of the Joint Chiefs of Staff (JCS) were reluctant to invade the Japanese home islands, which the Japanese planned to defend with 1 million troops, 3,000 kamikaze aircraft, and 5,000 suicide boats. With the invasion scheduled for November 1, 1945, and well aware of the probable high cost, the JCS pressed President Franklin D. Roosevelt at the February 1945 Yalta Conference to get the Soviet Union into the war against Japan.

Following the successful test firing of an atomic bomb at Alamogordo, New Mexico, on July 16, 1945, sharp debate occurred among advisers to U.S. president Harry S. Truman over employing the new weapon. Although some key advisers, including de facto JCS chairman Admiral of the Fleet William Leahy, were opposed, most favored its use. Employing the bomb was not then seen as the threat to world peace that it is today. The terror threshold had probably already been passed in the firebombing of Japanese cities. By 1945 it was total war, and the assumption was always that the bomb would be used if it became available.

Proponents of employing the atomic bomb argued that it would in all likelihood bring the war to a speedy end and save many American lives. If this occurred, the United States would not have to share occupation of Japan with the Soviet Union. The atomic bomb was thus seen as essentially a psychological weapon to influence Japanese political leaders rather than a military tool. The bomb might also deter Soviet leader Joseph Stalin from future aggression. Truman said that he never regretted his decision to employ the bomb, which was in any case strongly supported by the great majority of the American people.

Revisionist historians hold that the Japanese government was trying desperately to leave the war and that employing the bomb was therefore unnecessary, but recently available intercepts of Japanese diplomatic messages indicate that Tokyo had not yet reached the decision to surrender when the first bomb was dropped.

Emperor Hirohito and his chief advisers still hoped for a negotiated settlement, and a last decisive battle might force the Allies to grant more favorable peace terms. Historian Ray Skates concluded that the first phase of the invasion of Japan, the conquest of the island of Kyūshū planned for November 1945, would have taken two months and resulted in 75,000–100,000 U.S. casualties. Such losses would not have affected the outcome of the war, but they might indeed have brought the political goals sought by the Japanese leaders.

Even if the bomb had not been employed, an invasion of Japan might not have been necessary. The United States would have continued the strategic bombing campaign, which by August 1945 had largely burned out the Japanese cities. The nation was close to starvation, with caloric intake at an average of only 1,680 daily, and even this reduced food supply was highly dependent on railroad distribution. Destruction of the railroads might have been the final straw bringing a Japanese decision for peace even without the bomb.

Ironically, not employing the atomic bomb would in all likelihood have delayed the surrender and brought a significantly higher cost in Japanese lives than dropping the bombs did. One estimate is that during the war the Japanese lost 323,495 dead on the home front, the vast majority of these to air attack. Continued strategic bombing would have sharply increased this total, and many others would simply have died of starvation. In effect, dropping the bomb resulted in a net saving of lives, both Japanese and American.

Following Japanese rejection of the Potsdam Proclamation on July 26 that threatened total destruction if unconditional surrender was not accepted, President Truman authorized use of the atomic bomb. The bomb was loaded on the Boeing B-29 Superfortress Enola Gay of the specially trained 509th Composite Group of the Twentieth Army Air Force. Lieutenant Colonel Paul Tibbets was the aircraft commander. The bomb consisted of a core of uranium isotope 235 shielded by several hundred pounds of lead, all encased in explosives designed to condense the uranium and initiate a fission reaction. Nicknamed "Little Boy," the bomb possessed a force equivalent to 12,500 tons (12.5 kilotons) of TNT.

The Enola Gay departed Tinian at 2:45 a.m. on August 6. Two B-29s assigned as observer aircraft followed. The bomb was armed in the air shortly after 6:30. The flight to Japan was uneventful. Weather planes informed Tibbets that the primary target, Hiroshima, was clear for bombing.

The port city of Hiroshima is located in southern Honshu and in August 1945 served as the headquarters of the Japanese Second Army. Hiroshima was also a major supply depot. The city of some 250,000 people had not yet suffered heavily in the American bombing offensive.

The Enola Gay arrived over Hiroshima at an altitude of 31,600 feet. An air-raid alert had sounded, and most people in the city had taken cover. Realizing that there were only a few planes overhead, many people then came back out in the open and were thus without protection when the bomb detonated. The Enola Gay dropped the bomb at 8:15:17 a.m. local time. After a descent of nearly six miles, it detonated 43 seconds later, some 1,890 feet over a clinic and about 800 feet from the aiming point, Aioi Bridge.

The initial fireball expanded to 110 yards in diameter and generated heat in excess of 300,000 degrees Centigrade. Core temperatures reached more than 50 million degrees. At the clinic directly beneath the explosion, the temperature was several thousand degrees.

The immediate blast destroyed almost everything within two miles of ground zero. The resultant mushroom cloud rose to 50,000 feet and was observed by B-29s more than 360 miles away. After 15 minutes, the atmosphere dropped radioactive black rain, adding to the death and destruction.

Four square miles of Hiroshima disappeared in seconds, including 62,000 buildings. About 100,000

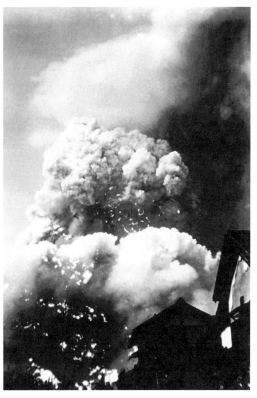

The cloud from the explosion of the Atomic bomb over Hiroshima on August 6, 1945, two minutes after the blast. The bomb killed some 100,000 Japanese outright. (Corel)

Japanese died outright, another 40,000 were injured, and 171,000 were left homeless. About one-third of those killed instantly were soldiers. Most elements of the Japanese Second General Army were at physical training on the grounds of Hiroshima Castle when the bomb exploded. Barely 900 yards from the explosion's epicenter, the castle and the people there were vaporized. Radiation sickness added to the death toll over several years. This was, however, less carnage than inflicted in the March firebombing of Tokyo.

The bombing mission changed the nature of warfare but did not end the war. Truman released a statement on August 7 describing the weapon and calling on Japan to surrender but without result. On August 8 the Soviet Union declared war on Japan, Stalin honoring to the day his pledge at Yalta to enter the war against Japan "two or three months after the defeat of Germany." That same day the Soviets invaded and quickly overran Manchuria. The next day, August 9, a second atomic bomb fell. The primary target of Kokura was obscured by smoke and haze, and the bomb was dropped on the secondary target, the seaport and industrial city of Nagasaki with a population 230,000 people. Hills protected portions of the city, so less than half of Nagasaki was destroyed. The blast there claimed about 70,000 dead, either killed outright or dying later from radiation, and injured as many more.

After prolonged meetings with his advisers, Emperor Hirohito made the decision for peace. Braving possible assassination by fanatics determined to fight to the end, Hirohito communicated the decision over the radio on August 15. On September 2 the final terms of surrender were signed aboard the battleship *Missouri* in Tokyo Bay, and the Japanese islands came under the rule of a U.S. army of occupation under General Douglas MacArthur.

References

Frank, Richard B. *Downfall: The End of the Japanese Empire.* New York: Random House, 1999.

Maddox, Robert James. *Weapons for Victory: The Hiroshima Decision Fifty Years Later.* Columbia: University of Missouri Press, 1995.

Pacific War Research Society, The. *The Day Man Lost: Hiroshima, 6 August 1945.* Tokyo: Kodansha International, 1972.

Skates, John Ray. *The Invasion of Japan: Alternative to the Bomb.* Columbia: University of South Carolina Press, 1998.

Thomas, Gordon, and Max Morgan-Witts. *Enola Gay.* New York: Stein and Day, 1977.

Battle of Huaihai

Date	November 7, 1948–January 10, 1949	
Location	Modern Xuzhou, northeastern China	
Opponents (* winner)	*Chinese Communists	Chinese Nationalists
Commander	Deng Xiaoping	General Liu Zhi
Approx. # Troops	600,000	500,000
Importance	This catastrophic Nationalist military disaster hastens the collapse of the Jiang Jieshi (Chiang Kai-shek) government.	

Immediately after the end of World War II (1939–1945), civil war erupted in China between the Guomindang (GMD, Nationalist) government and supporters of the Chinese Communist Party (CCP). The roots of the Chinese Civil War of 1945–1949 went back to the 1920s. Established in 1921, the CCP initially cooperated with the GMD, but GMD leader Jiang Jieshi (Chiang Kai-shek) feared rising CCP influence and came to regard the Communists as a greater threat to his government than the Japanese, who by the early 1930s established their control over Manchuria and were expanding their influence in northern China. Between 1930 and 1934 Jiang waged a series of campaigns against the CCP base in Jiangxi (Kiangsi) Province, the last of which forced the Communists into their famous Long March. Under Mao Zedong (Mao Tse-tung), they retreated some 6,000 miles to Shaanxi (Shensi) Province in remote northwestern China.

In the December 1936 Sian (Xi'an) Incident, however, some of his own generals forced Jiang to agree to form a united anti-Japanese front with the Communists, but this relationship was an uneasy one at best. During the Second Sino-Japanese War of 1937–1945 the Communists greatly expanded their own military forces and came to control northwestern China. In late 1940 the Communists launched the Hundred Regiments campaign against the Japanese, but the better-equipped Japanese Army defeated them. The Communists then adopted guerrilla tactics, which provoked savage Japanese reprisals but established the CCP as a staunch opponent of Japanese rule.

In late 1941 GMD forces attacked and defeated the Communist New Fourth Army in the lower Changjiang (Yangtze) Valley, marking the end of GMD-CCP collaboration. Thanks to substantial American Lend-Lease aid, GMD forces possessed superior equipment and were far better funded, but Jiang's abandonment of much of China to Japanese control, his reliance on a defensive strategy, and rampant corruption in his government and army all sapped popular support. Meanwhile, CCP attention to the plight of the peasants and their exemplary behavior (in sharp contrast to GMD forces) and effective CCP leaders in their Yenan (Yan'an) base in Shaanxi garnered wide popular support.

With the end of the war in August 1945, the Communists had some 900,000 men under arms and controlled an area with a population of 90 million people. Fighting between the CCP and the GMD broke out almost immediately. Soviet forces that had occupied Manchuria at the end of the war turned over captured Japanese arms and equipment to the Communists. U.S. efforts to reform Jiang's administration and encourage reconciliation between the GMD and the CCP, which included the dispatch of former army chief of staff General George C. Marshall to China during 1946–1947, proved unsuccessful.

Since late 1946 the Nationalists had been seizing key towns in Manchuria. In the spring of 1947 the Soviets withdrew, and GMD forces openly attacked Chinese Communist troops there, winning control of that region in late May. That same month the Communists renamed their military forces the People's Liberation Army (PLA).

Although Jiang ignored American advice, the United States provided massive financial assistance and military hardware to the GMD government. Chronic inflation and corruption both worked against the GMD, while CCP introduction of land reform garnered much peasant support. Although the Communists used guerrilla tactics with great success, in mid-May 1947 CCP general Lin Biao (Lin Piao) and his New Fourth Army opened a major offensive in northeastern China. Six weeks later another large army commanded by Liu Bocheng (Liu Po-ch'eng) moved southwest across the Huang He (Huang Ho, Hwang Ho, Yellow River) into Shandong (Shantung) Province. That offensive culminated in the September 14–20 Battle of Jinan (Tsinan) and the capture of 80,000 GMD troops. In September 1948 Lin began a massive campaign in Manchuria with 700,000 men, taking Shenyang (Mukden) in Liaoning Province on November 2. The Nationalists lost some 380,000 men in the Manchurian campaign as well as vast quantities of weapons and equipment.

GMD forces controlled a cross-shaped area in east-central China that contained two major rail lines running east-west from the Yellow Sea through the city of Xuzhou (Hsü-chow) in Jiangsu (Kiangsu) Province to Kaifeng in Shandong and north-south from Jinan through Xuzhou to Nanjing (Nanking) in Jiangsu. At Kaifeng and Xuzhou the Communists opened their largest major offensives of 1948. The great engagement here became known as the Battle of Huai-Hai for the Huai River and the Longhai (Lung-hai) Railroad that roughly parallels the river. It is also sometimes known as the Battle of Xuzhou.

Ultimately each side committed about 600,000 men to the battle. The GMD had complete air superiority, but poor communications with ground forces rendered its air forces largely ineffective. General Bai Chongxi (Pai Chung-hsi) commanded GMD forces consisting of four army groups: the 2nd, 7th, 13th, and 16th. The 13th Army Group was at Xuzhou, and the 7th Army Group to the east was at the juncture of the Longhai Railroad and the Grand Canal. The 2nd Army Group was to the west along the railroad to Kaifeng, while the 16th Army Group was situated to the south along the rail line to Pengpu (Peng-pu) on the Huai River. General Chen Yi (Ch'en Yi, Ch'en I), commander of the New Fourth Army, had overall command on the Communist side.

The battle opened on November 7, 1948, with Chen's New Fourth Army attacking from the east against the GMD 7th Army Group, while General Liu Bocheng's Central Plains Army drove from the west against the GMD 2nd Army Group. Liu's troops drove GMD forces back into Xuzhou and then swung south to link up with Chen's army and cut off a GMD retreat to the Huai. Liu's rapid advance and further Nationalist defections led to encirclement of the 7th Army Group about 30 miles each of Xuzhou.

Jiang, who had taken personal charge of operations, now ordered 15 divisions of his 2nd and 16th Army groups to relieve the surrounded 7th Army Group, but they were slow to respond. The GMD 7th Army Group surrendered on November 22. Only about 3,000 of its original strength of 90,000 men escaped. Meanwhile, on November 16 Communist People's Liberation Army (PLA) forces surrounded the GMD 13th Army Group at Xuzhou.

Jiang then ordered relief columns of the 12th Army Group and the Eighth Army to advance from the south to assist the escape of the 13th Army Group. Poor leadership again plagued the Nationalists, with the two relief columns unable to join before they came under PLA attack. Liu's PLA forces struck from the east against the 12th Army Group, while Chen's troops fell on the GMD Eighth Army.

Jiang decided to abandon Xuzhou. The 13th Army Group left Xuzhou on December 1, but inept leadership led to it and remnants of other Nationalist forces, altogether about 200,000 men, being surrounded at Yongcheng (Yung-ch'eng) five days later. Jiang's last effort was to commit his Sixth Army from Pengpu, but its advance ground to a halt under fierce PLA guerrilla attacks. Morale in the trapped 12th Army Group was at a nadir, and many men simply defected. The battle ended with the surrender of the last GMD units on January 10, 1949. Total Nationalist casualties, including those who defected or were taken prisoner, came to about 327,000 men, or more than half of the Nationalist force engaged.

This defeat broke the back of the Nationalist forces and removed the principal GMD defensive line north of the Changjiang River, opening the way to Nanjing. Communist troops began to cross the Changjiang on April 20. They took Nanjing two days later.

On January 21, 1949, Jiang resigned as president of Nationalist China. The next day, following a long siege, Beijing (Peking) in Hebei (Hopeh) Province, China's symbolic capital, surrendered to the Communists. The PLA took captured Guangzhou (Canton) in Guangdong (Kwangtung) in southern China in October. On October 1, 1949, in Beijing, Mao proclaimed the new People's Republic of China.

References

Dreyer, Edward L. *China at War, 1901–1949.* New York: Longman, 1995.

Fairbank, John K., and Albert Feuerwerker, eds. *The Cambridge History of China,* Vol. 13, *Republican China, 1912–1949, Part 2.* Cambridge: Cambridge University Press, 1986.

Liu, F. F. *The Military History of Modern China, 1924–1949.* Princeton, NJ: Princeton University Press, 1956.

Westad, Odd Arne. *Decisive Encounters: The Chinese Civil War, 1946–1950.* Stanford, CA: Stanford University Press, 2003.

Pusan Perimeter Defense and Breakout

Date	August 5–September 23, 1950	
Location	Rectangular area 100 miles north to south and 50 miles east to west in far southeastern Korea around the port city of Pusan	
Opponents (* winner)	*United Nations Command	North Koreans
Commander	Lieutenant General Walton H. Walker	Lieutenant General Kang Kon; General Kim Chaek
Approx. # Troops	156,500	98,000?
Importance	A masterful example of mobile defensive warfare, it staves off defeat of the United Nations Command forces	

The battle for the Pusan Perimeter was one of history's great mobile defensive operations. It was certainly the longest, largest, and most complex mobile defense in U.S. military history. On June 25, 1950, Korean People's Army (KPA, North Korean Army) forces invaded the Republic of Korea (ROK, South Korea), unleashing the Korean War (1950–1953). The goal of Kim Il Sung, leader of the Democratic

People's Republic of Korea (DPRK, North Korea), was to conquer the People's Republic of Korea (ROK, South Korea) in a matter of weeks before the United States, should it choose to intervene, could influence the outcome. U.S. president Harry S. Truman committed U.S. forces, and on June 27, while the Soviet Union was boycotting its sessions, the Security Council of the United Nations (UN) voted to ask UN member states to furnish "every assistance" to South Korea. On June 30 Truman authorized U.S. Far Eastern commander General Douglas MacArthur to employ all available forces in Korea.

The four U.S. divisions in Japan comprising Lieutenant General Walton H. Walker's Eighth Army were all below authorized strength. Training levels were low, equipment was worn and dated from World War II (1939–1945), and there were serious shortages in weapons. By cannibalizing the 7th Division though, MacArthur was able to get first the 24th Infantry Division and then the 25th Infantry Division and 1st Cavalry Division to Korea within two weeks.

The war was going badly for the outnumbered and outgunned South Korean forces and their 500 U.S. military advisers. Seoul fell on June 28, and South Korean forces were forced to abandon most of their equipment north of the Han River when bridges on the southern edge of that city were blown prematurely. On July 5 U.S. Task Force Smith went into battle at Osan, 50 miles south of Seoul. Numbering only 540 U.S. troops, the task force was expected to stop an entire KPA division spearheaded by T-34 tanks but was speedily overwhelmed. Meanwhile, a United Nations Command (UNC) came into being. Washington insisted on a U.S. commander, and on July 10 Truman appointed MacArthur to head the new UNC.

U.S. troops did not perform well initially. Lack of training as well as faulty equipment and shortages impacted morale and fighting ability. Difficult terrain, primitive logistics, poor communication, and refugees choking the roads probably did more to delay the KPA advance than did American infantry. From the Battle of Osan, South Korean and U.S. 24th Division forces suffered an unbroken string of reverses: Chŏnan on July 6–8, Chŏngju on July 10, Chochiwŏn on July 11–12, the Kŭm River on July 15–16, and Taejŏn on July 19–20. On July 25 the 1st Cavalry Division was forced to yield Yongdong. Slowly but surely the defenders were being driven back toward the South Korean port of Pusan.

Walker's mission was to trade space for time to build up his forces and hold until the UNC could build up its strength. By the end of July, however, the Eighth Army was out of space, and on July 29 Walker issued his famous "Stand or Die" order. Holding Pusan was critical, but if Walker's forces withdrew too far they would have insufficient depth in which to maneuver and mass forces for an eventual breakout. Walker ordered his forces behind the Naktong River and by August 4 had established what became known as the Pusan Perimeter (also known as the Naktong Perimeter), which consisted of a rectangle, approximately 100 by 50 miles, in the southeastern corner of Korea around Pusan.

Over the next month the Eighth Army was reinforced with the 5th Regimental Combat Team (RCT), the 1st Marine Provisional Brigade, regiments of the 2nd Infantry Division, and the British 27th Infantry Brigade. Walker also had the five surviving Republic of Korea Army (ROKA, South Korean Army) divisions. On the west his defensive line ran along the Naktong River except for the southernmost 15 miles, where the river turned east away from the line. The northern boundary ran through the mountains from Naktong-ni to Yonngdong on the east coast and the sea.

Walker enjoyed the advantage of interior lines and an effective logistics network. Pusan was the key. Korea's chief seaport, it boasted modern facilities capable of handling 30 oceangoing vessels simultaneously with a daily discharge capacity of up to 45,000 tons (during the campaign the daily average was about 28,000 tons). Walker also had the advantage of rail lines linking Pusan with Miryang, Taegu, and Pohang.

Walker positioned his U.S. divisions along the Naktong. The 25th Infantry Division was located in the south, the 24th Infantry Division was in the center, and the 1st Cavalry Division was to its north. The ROKA 1st Division held the north until the line turned to the east. Across the northern flank of the line the ROKA 6th Division held the western portion, the 8th Division and Capital divisions held the center, and the 3rd Division held the eastern end. U.S. Army doctrine called for an infantry division to hold no more than a 9-mile-wide front, but along the Pusan Perimeter frontages ran 20–40 miles.

By mid-August, Walker could call on more than 500 tanks, a 5 to 1 advantage over the KPA. Walker also had the U.S. Navy and the U.S. Air Force, key elements in the ultimate victory. U.S. Navy ships close offshore provided accurate and highly effective gunfire support on the perimeter's flanks. The U.S. Fifth Air Force enjoyed complete air supremacy, meaning that Walker could move assets within the perimeter without regard to cover and concealment. This enhanced the UNC's mobility advantage, while the KPA was also prey to regular air attack and was forced to move largely at night.

Initially, 11 KPA divisions, commanded by Lieutenant General Kang Kon, faced UNC forces. From south to north along the Naktong they were the 6th (with the attached 83rd Motorcycle Regiment), 4th, 3rd, 2nd, 15th, and 1st divisions. In the north from west to east the KPA deployed its 13th, 8th, 12th, and 5th divisions and the 766th Independent Infantry Regiment. The bulk of the 105th Armored Division remained in reserve. In mid-August elements of the newly formed KPA 7th Division entered the southern end of the line north of the 6th Division, and the 9th Division and elements of the 10th Division joined the line south and north, respectively, of the 2nd Division. While intelligence estimates at the time gave a different picture, the UNC actually held a slight numerical advantage of some 92,000 to 70,000 men, although many of Walker's troops were manning the logistics infrastructure.

Between August 5 and September 9 KPA forces attacked the Pusan Perimeter along four widely separated axes, all of which followed natural approach corridors. The southern route ran through Chindong-ni to Masan, 30 miles from Pusan. A northern corridor extended from the Naktong to Miryang. Another route ran through Taegu, the largest city within the perimeter and a vital crossroads. The final avenue ran south from Angang-ni through Kyongju to Pusan.

KPA forces had the initiative and could concentrate superior numbers at the selected points of attack, while Walker was obliged to spread his troops across the entire front, shifting individual regiments as required. None of his divisional commanders had ever commanded divisions in combat, so Walker had to train them on the job.

On August 9 Walker launched a division-sized limited-objective attack (Task Force Kean) on his southern flank, but stubborn KPA resistance blocked it. Between August 5 and 18 the KPA launched a series of attacks along the other three avenues. Although the attackers registered gains, all the drives were halted thanks to Walker's skillful shifting of assets and the arrival of reinforcements.

On August 27 the KPA launched its second offensive over the same avenues. This time the attacks were well coordinated and hit simultaneously. By September 3 Walker was fighting in five different locations at the same time. American casualties during the first two weeks of September 1950 were the heaviest of the war, yet Walker was able to shift his reserves inside the ever-shrinking perimeter and prevent any major breakthroughs. On September 9 General Kang Kon was killed in a land mine explosion and was replaced by Genereal Kim Chaek as commander of KPA forces. On September 12 the KPA offensive reached its culminating point and stalled. The Eighth Army now numbered about 84,500 troops, while the ROKA numbered 72,000 troops.

When the U.S. X Corps of two divisions landed at the port of Inchon on September 15, well behind the bulk of the KPA, UNC forces were still locked in battle along the Pusan Perimeter. The next day the Eighth Army began its attempt to break out. Hampered by insufficient river-crossing equipment and a severe shortage of artillery ammunition, the breakout was not achieved until September 23, when KPA forces began a withdrawal. The allies followed, and on the morning of September 27 just north of Osan, lead elements of the Eighth Army linked up with the U.S. 31st Infantry Regiment of the 7th Infantry Division of X Corps.

The battle for the Pusan Perimeter was over. The single biggest flaw for the KPA was its inability to achieve the necessary mass at a decisive point. Its only hope had been to achieve overwhelming mass at one point, punch through the thinly held UNC lines, and drive on Pusan, but the KPA had failed to do this. Only 20,000 to 30,000 of KPA troops along the Pusan Perimeter ever returned to North Korea. The defenders paid a high price as well. Between July 5 and September 16, Eighth Army casualties totaled 4,280 killed in action, 12,377 wounded, 2,107 missing, and 401 confirmed captured.

References

Appleman, Roy E. *South to the Nakong, North to the Yalu.* Washington, DC: Office of the Chief of Military History, 1961.

Blair, Clay. *The Forgotten War: America in Korea, 1950–1953.* New York: Times Books, 1987.

Ent, Uzal W. *Fighting on the Brink: Defense of the Pusan Perimeter.* Paducah, KY: Turner Publishing, 1996.

Hoyt, Edwin P. *The Pusan Perimeter.* New York: Stein and Day, 1984.

Robertson, William G. *Counterattack on the Naktong, 1950.* Fort Leavenworth, KS: Combat Studies Institute, 1985.

Inchon Landing

Date	September 15, 1950	
Location	Port of Inchon, west coast of Korea near Seoul	
Opponents (* winner)	*United Nations Command	North Koreans
Commander	General Douglas MacArthur; Major General Edward M. Almond	General Choi Yong Kun
Approx. # Troops	40,000	Some 1,000 in Inchon
Importance	Turns the tide of war with the capture of Seoul and the severing of North Korean supply lines to the Pusan Perimeter in the south	

The amphibious assault at Inchon by U.S. forces was General Douglas MacArthur's masterstroke that turned the tide of the Korean War (1950–1953). By mid-July 1950, even as Republic of Korea Army (ROKA, South Korean) and U.S. troops were fighting to defend the vital port of Pusan from attacks by the Korean People's Army (KPA, North Korean Army), United Nations Command (UNC) commander General MacArthur prepared to present the Democratic People's Republic of Korea (DPRK, North Korea) with a two-front war. He was confident that the Eighth Army could hold the Pusan Perimeter, and he began diverting resources for an invasion force.

MacArthur selected Inchon. Korea's second-largest port, it was only 15 miles from Seoul, the capital of the Republic of Korea (ROK, South Korea). This area was the most important road and rail hub in Korea and was also a vital link in the main KPA supply line south. Cutting it would starve KPA forces facing the Eighth Army. Kimpo Airfield near Inchon was one of the few hard-surface airfields, and the capture of Seoul would be a serious psychological blow for the North Koreans. Planning for the invasion, code-named Operation CHROMITE, began on August 12.

Only MacArthur favored Inchon. The Joint Chiefs of Staff (JCS) and most of MacArthur's subordinate commanders opposed it. Tidal shifts there were among the highest in the world. At ebb tide the harbor turned into mudflats, and the navy would have only a three-hour period on each tide to enter or leave the port. The channel was narrow and winding; one sunken ship would block all traffic. There were no beaches, only 12-foot seawalls that would have to be scaled.

MacArthur rejected suggestions for other sites and, on August 28, received formal JCS approval for the landing, to be carried out by X Corps. Activated on August 26 and commanded by Major General Edward M. Almond, X Corps was composed principally of Major General Oliver P. Smith's 1st Marine Division and Major General David G. Barr's 7th Army Division. Vice Admiral A. D. Struble commanded Joint Task Force (JTF) 7 for the landing; Rear Admiral James Doyle, who developed the landing plan, was second-in-command. More than 230 ships took part in the operation. The armada, carrying nearly 70,000 men, was a makeshift affair and included ships from many countries. Planes from 4 carriers provided air support over the landing area. Thirty-seven of 47 landing ship tanks in the invasion were hastily recalled from Japanese merchant service and manned by Japanese crews.

Although loading was delayed by Typhoon Jane on September 3, deadlines were met. On September 13 JTF-7 force was hit at sea by Typhoon Kezia, although no serious damage resulted. JTF-7 reached the Inchon narrows just before dawn on September 15, the fifth day of air and naval bombardment by four cruisers and six destroyers.

At 6:33 a.m. as MacArthur observed events from the bridge of the *Mount McKinley*, the 5th Marines went ashore to capture Wolmi-do, the island controlling access to the harbor. Resistance was light. At 2:30 p.m. cruisers and destroyers began a shore bombardment of Inchon, and at 5:31 the first Americans climbed up ladders onto the seawall. The marines sustained casualties on D day of 20 dead, 1 missing, and 174 wounded. The next day as they drove on Seoul, the Eighth Army began a breakout along the Pusan Perimeter in extreme southeastern Korea. On September 18 the 7th Infantry Division began landing at Inchon, and on September 21 a remaining marine regiment disembarked. The Inchon and Pusan forces made contact on September 26 at Osan. Seoul fell on the afternoon of September 27.

Victory in the Inchon-Seoul campaign greatly increased MacArthur's self-confidence. The KPA was so badly beaten that he was certain the war for Korea had been won and that the conflict was just a matter of mopping up. His assessment proved incorrect.

References

Field, James A., Jr. *History of United States Naval Operations: Korea.* Washington, DC: Naval History Division, 1962.

Heil, Robert Debs, Jr. *Victory at High Tide: The Inchon-Seoul Campaign.* Baltimore: Nautical and Aviation Publishing Company of America, 1979.

Montross, Lynn, and Nicholas Canzona. *U.S. Marine Corps Operations in Korea,* Vol. 2, *The Inchon-Seoul Operation.* Washington, DC: United States Marine Corps Historical Branch, 1955.

Changjin Reservoir Campaign

Date	October–December 1950	
Location	Changjin (Chosin) Reservoir in northeastern Korea	
Opponents (* winner)	*Americans	Chinese
Commander	U.S. Marine Corps Major General Oliver P. Smith	General Song Shilun
Approx. # Troops	20,000	120,000
Importance	One of the most masterful military withdrawals in modern history	

The battle for the Changjin (Chosin) Reservoir during the Korean War (1950–1953) was followed by one of the most masterly withdrawals in military history. Following the landing of Major General Edward M. Almond's X Corps of the United Nations Command (UNC) at Inchon on September 15, 1950, Lieutenant General Walton H. Walker's Eighth Army broke out from the Pusan Perimeter. UNC forces recaptured Seoul and then invaded the Democratic People's Republic of Korea (DPRK, North Korea). UNC commander General Douglas MacArthur ordered X Corps transferred by sea from Inchon on the west coast to the port of Wonsan on the east coast, while the Eighth Army remained in the west to move into northwestern Korea.

In the drive to the Yalu River that MacArthur expected would end the war, the Eighth Army and the reinforced X Corps in northeastern Korea would be separated by a 20–50 mile gap formed by the Taebaek Range. MacArthur assumed that this terrain would not allow Communist forces to conduct large-scale operations.

X Corps arrived off Wonsan on October 19 but remained a week at sea until mines were cleared from the port, which meanwhile had been taken by Republic of Korea Army (ROKA, South Korean Army) forces by land. The delay in resuming the offensive permitted Korean People's Army (KPA, North Korean Army) forces time to regroup and allowed the Chinese to bring troops into North Korea.

Almond's plan for X Corps called for the ROKA I Corps to drive up the coast to the Siberian border of the Soviet Union. Major General David W. Barr's U.S. 7th Division would advance to Hyesanjin. The 1st Marine Division would remain in the Wonsan-Hungnam area and protect X Corps' rear area and lines of communication until relieved by the 3rd Infantry Division from Japan. The marines would then move to the Changjin Reservoir and then continue northward to the Manchurian border, depending on the situation.

On October 24 MacArthur ordered the offensive to begin. Victory seemed imminent. In eastern Korea the ROKA I Corps started the 26th Regiment of its 3rd Division up the road to the Changjin Reservoir without waiting for the 1st Marine Division. On October 25 about halfway to the reservoir, the 26th Regiment encountered Chinese People's Volunteer Army (CPVA) troops and was halted by them and KPA tanks. As in northwestern Korea, the Chinese then suddenly halted operations and broke contact.

Despite the confirmation of Chinese troops, MacArthur ordered the advance to continue. On October 26 the ROKA Capital Division captured the industrial center of Chŏongjin, only 65 miles from the Siberian border. To its west, elements of the U.S. 7th Division drove toward the Pujon Reservoir but on November 8 ran into CPVA troops on its southern end.

The 17th Regiment of the 7th Division took Kapsan on November 14 and Hyesanjin on November 21. Leaving strong detachments to hold the mountain passes east of the reservoir leading to the areas to the rear of his division, Barr consolidated his division in the Hyesanjin-Samsu-Kapsan area.

In late October the 3rd Infantry Division arrived at Wonsan and set up a 100-mile defensive perimeter from south of Wonsan to north of Hamhung. This action freed the 1st Marine Division, and on October 30 Almond ordered it to relieve the ROKA troops on the road to the Changjin Reservoir. The 60-mile road from Hamhung to Changjin climbs some 4,000 feet, and at the beginning of the steepest stretch of road, near Sudong, CPVA units set up a blocking position.

The 1st Marine Division, spearheaded by Colonel Homer Litzenberg's 7th Regiment, set out on November 1. The next morning the 7th Regiment relieved the ROKA troops and promptly ran into the Chinese blocking position. The 7th Regiment then bivouacked for the night. Shortly after midnight on November 3 the CPVA 124th Division struck; by daylight it had secured a dominating position overlooking a bridge separating two of the three U.S. battalions. U.S. Marine Corps air support combined with determined ground action and artillery fire drove off the Chinese, killing about 700 and wounding many more. On November 4 the 7th Regiment took Sudong. On November 10 the regiment moved through the pass to Koto-ri, only seven miles from its objective of Hagaru-ri.

The weather now turned bitter cold. On the night of November 10–11, winds of 35 miles an hour and temperatures of 8 degrees below zero; several hundred men collapsed from cold over the next days. In these circumstances Litzenberg and 1st Marine Division commander Major General Oliver P. Smith were in no hurry to push on to Hagaru-ri. Smith was sufficiently concerned to communicate his doubts directly to U.S. Marine Corps commandant General Clifton P. Cates. Smith was especially worried about the nearly 100-mile gap between his own division (the left flank of X Corps) and the Eighth Army to the west. He therefore worked to improve and secure his supply line and to concentrate his division in the Hagaru-ri area before pushing on to the Yalu.

The marines took what remained of Hagaru-ri on November 14. That night temperatures dropped to 15 degrees below zero, and snow fell. The 7th Regiment took up defensive positions around Hagaru-ri, and work soon began on an airstrip there to supplement supply by road and to provide a means of evacuating sick and wounded. Engineers also improved the road for trucks. The 7th Marine Regiment took over responsibility for maintaining the supply line to Hamhung, while Colonel Lewis B. Puller's 1st Marine Regiment in the vicinity of Hamhung protected the rear from harassment by Communist guerrillas.

Smith deliberately delayed compliance with X Corps' orders to push on to the Yalu as quickly as possible. He did order the 7th Regiment to secure a blocking position at Yudam-ni, some 15 miles from Hagaru-ri over a high mountain pass. He also pushed his 5th Regiment up the east side of the reservoir toward the Manchurian border in accordance with orders. But these moves were deliberately slowed. Smith halted his 7th Regiment on the Hagaru-ri side of the pass until he could close his 1st Regiment into a supporting position. This caution undoubtedly saved his division from annihilation in the weeks to follow.

MacArthur was unconcerned by the Chinese. He believed that if they were to intervene in force, they would be destroyed by artillery fire and bombing. The Joint Chiefs of Staff (JCS) was concerned but also reluctant to impose its will on its field commander. MacArthur did, however, agree to a recommendation by his operations staff for a shift in X Corps' axis of attack to the northwest, thereby threatening the flank and rear of any Chinese units that might try to turn the east flank of the Eighth Army. X Corps was now to secure the reservoir and town of Changjin and then drive northwest with two divisions to cut the Chinese Manpojin–Kanggye–Mupyong-ni supply route. In the revised plan, the 1st Marine Division would attack along the Hagaru-ri–Mupyong-ni axis while the 7th Division protected its right flank by assigning a regimental combat team to take Changjin. Almond set the advance to begin on November 27.

MacArthur expected to crush what remained of Communist forces in a great pincer movement of the Eighth Army and X Corps, but within 24 hours of the resumption of the Eighth Army's offensive on November 24 the situation changed dramatically. The next night the Chinese struck in force, devastating the three divisions of the ROKA II Corps. Eighteen Chinese divisions now smashed into Walker's open right flank, forcing the Eighth Army's withdrawal. This caught X Corps exposed and vulnerable; its southernmost element, the 7th Marine Regiment at Yudam-ni, was almost 90 miles northeast of the bulk of the Eighth Army near Kunu-ri.

The Chinese struck X Corps on November 27 and ultimately fed 12 divisions totaling 120,000 men of their Ninth Army Group commanded by General Song Shlun into the battle in northeastern Korea. MacArthur now agreed that Almond's first task should be to extricate the 1st Marine Division and the two battalions of the 7th Division cut off in the Changjin Reservoir area. He ordered Almond to withdraw as far as necessary to prevent being flanked and to concentrate in the Hamhung-Hungnam area. The JCS in Washington, with President Harry S. Truman's concurrence, approved this shift to the defensive.

With the bulk of the 7th Division well to the north, Almond placed under Smith's command the 31st Regimental Combat Team, known as Task Force MacLean for its commander, Lieutenant Colonel Allan D. MacLean. It consisted of only two battalions and supporting artillery, all east of the reservoir. Following MacLean's capture on November 29, Lieutenant Colonel Don C. Faith Jr. headed the task force, which became Task Force Faith.

Almond ordered Smith to withdraw his 5th and 7th Marine regiments from Yudam-ni and to work with Barr to rescue Task Force Faith. The assembled units were then to fight their way out down the Hagaru-ri–Koto-ri supply route to Hungnam. ROKA divisions would also withdraw, while the U.S. 3rd Infantry Division covered the concentration of X Corps in the Yonpo–Hungnam–Hamhung area.

Generals Barr and Smith agreed that no relief force could reach the retreating marines and Task Force Faith until they gained Hagaru-ri, held by only a battalion of the 1st Marine Regiment and a mix of marine and army service troops. Smith feared that Task Force Faith could not hold out until he could concentrate at Hagaru-ri, and he ordered Faith to fight his way out, promising close air support. At the same time the 5th Marines would withdraw from Yudam-ni to Hagaru-ri.

The 13-day retreat of nearly 80 miles began on December 1. The marines came out in an orderly single column, despite Chinese resistance and movement over narrow snow-covered roads and below-zero weather. They reached Hagaru-ri largely intact with minimum loss in equipment, bringing out with them some 1,500 casualties.

Weakened by two days of attacks by an entire CPVA division, Task Force Faith had a more difficult time. Before starting out, Faith ordered his artillery and excess supplies destroyed along with all but 22 vehicles, sufficient to carry his 600 wounded. Task Force Faith immediately encountered Chinese resistance, but what happened next was not anticipated. U.S. pilots, miscalculating their bomb runs, dropped napalm on the front of Faith's column and scattered its leading companies. Faith got the column moving again but then was mortally wounded leading a flanking attack against a Chinese roadblock. With many of the trucks broken down, Faith's successor, Major Robert E. Jones, had to make the difficult decision to leave behind many of his wounded.

That night the remnants reached Hudong-ni, halfway to Hagaru-ri, but the Chinese controlled the village, and efforts to dislodge them failed. Jones tried to run the vehicles with the wounded through, but the Chinese shot the drivers in the lead vehicles and raked the remainder with fire. The men who remained now scattered, most of them toward the frozen ice of the reservoir. A small task force of army troops, accompanied by tanks, tried to break through from Hagaru-ri to Hudong-ni without success. The Chinese did not make a strong effort to pursue the escaping troops across the ice, and they did aid the wounded in Hudong-ni. Still, of 2,500 men in Task Force Faith, only slightly more than 1,000 made it to Hagaru-ri, and only 385 of these were fit to fight. Reequipped, these latter joined other army units there in a provisional battalion. The airstrip at Hagaru-ri proved vital to operations, enabling the evacuation of 4,316 casualties and flying in 537 replacements.

To the south, attempts to open the road between the 1st Marine Regiment's base at Koto-ri and Hagaru-ri suffered a serious setback. The 41st Commando Battalion of the British Royal Marines, commanded by Lieutenant Colonel Douglas S. Drysdale, had recently arrived in Korea and had yet to see combat. Ordered to join the U.S. marines, it received 30 tanks and a company of the U.S. Army's 31st Infantry Regiment. Known as Task Force Drysdale, this 900-man force set out for Hagaru-ri, ordered to get there "at all costs." On November 29 it encountered Chinese troops who were well dug in in what came to be known as Hell Fire Valley. About 300 were captured, and many more were wounded, including Drysdale. Only 300 men made it to Hagaru-ri. The remaining survivors fell back on Koto-ri. The UNC controlled the air, however, and Chinese ground formations were devastated in air strikes.

The next stage of the withdrawal, to Koto-ri, began on December 6. When correspondents met General Smith at Hagaru-ri and queried him about the withdrawal, he told them, "Gentlemen, we are not retreating. We are merely advancing in another direction." It took a day and a half to cover 11 miles through snow under incessant Chinese attack. Smith again regrouped his forces for the 10 additional miles to Chinhung-ni, now held by units of the 3rd Division, freeing up the 1st Battalion of the 1st Marine Regiment and enabling it to strike north and aid the marine column coming from Koto-ri.

On December 8 a destroyed bridge over the gorge in Hwangchoryong Pass blocked the marines. Special prefabricated bridge-building equipment was dropped by parachute into Koto-ri and then laid across the gorge. On December 9 the advance resumed. On the afternoon of December 11 the last elements of Smith's command passed through the 3rd Infantry Division perimeter around the Hamhung-Hungnam area.

This withdrawal must be considered one of the most masterly operations of its kind in the history of war. During October 26–December 11, 1950, the 1st Marine Division suffered 704 killed in action or died of wounds, 187 missing, and 3,489 wounded, for a total of 4,380 battle casualties. In addition, there were 6,000 non-battle casualties, most from frostbite. Marines remember the withdrawal with pride, while the Chinese remember it with the admission that they now understand the impact of modern automatic weapons, artillery, and airpower. The campaign in northeastern Korea did tie down 12 Chinese divisions, which otherwise could have been utilized against the Eighth Army.

The UNC now evacuated northeastern Korea. Covered by substantial naval air assets, this had already begun when the marines reached Hungnam. Some 3,600 men, 200 vehicles, and 1,300 tons of cargo came out by air, while 105,000 U.S. and ROKA troops, 350,000 tons of cargo, and 17,500 vehicles were lifted off by sea, along with some 98,000 Korean refugees who did not want to remain. The evacuation involved more than 100 ships. When it was completed on Christmas Eve, engineers blew up the Hungnam waterfront with explosive charges. North Korea, half empty and devastated by the fighting, was left to the Communists.

References

Appleman, Roy E. *East of Chosin: Entrapment and Breakout in Korea.* College Station: Texas A&M University Press, 1987.

Hopkins, William B. *One Bugle, No Drums: The Marines at Chosin Reservoir.* Chapel Hill, NC: Algonquin Books, 1986.

Meid, Pat, and James M. Yingling. *U.S. Marine Operations in Korea, 1950–1953: Operations in West Korea.* Washington, DC: U.S. Marine Corps Historical Branch, 1972.

Montross, Lynn, and Nicholas A. Canzona. *U.S. Marine Operations in Korea, 1950–1953,* Vol. 3, *The Chosin Reservoir Campaign.* Washington, DC: U.S. Marine Corps Historical Branch, 1957.

Russ, Martin. *The Chosin Reservoir Campaign, Korea 1950.* New York: Fromm International, 1999.

Battle of Dien Bien Phu

Date	November 20, 1953–May 7, 1954	
Location	Dien Bien Phu, northwestern Vietnam	
Opponents (* winner)	*Vietnamese (Viet Minh forces)	French and allied Vietnamese
Commander	General Vo Nguyen Giap	Brigadier General Christian Marie Ferdinand de la Croix de Castries
Approx. # Troops	49,500	16,500
Importance	Heralds the end of the Indochina War	

The Battle of Dien Bien Phu was one of the most important of the entire 20th century, signaling the end of the Indochina War and Western colonialism in Asia. The French refusal to reach accommodation with Vietnamese nationalism and efforts to restore their pre–World War II position in Indochina led to the beginning of fighting there in December 1946 between French forces and the Vietnamese nationalists, the Viet Minh, led by veteran Communist Ho Chi Minh. The French soon restored control in the cities, but the Viet Minh took to the jungles and waged a growing guerrilla war. Despite increasing quantities of U.S. aid to the French, the Viet Minh steadily controlled more and more territory, especially Tonkin in the northern part of the country.

The war was lost for all practical purposes for the French in the autumn of 1949, when the Communists triumphed in China. This provided the Viet Minh with both a sanctuary and a supply base. The French also lost the battle for the hearts and minds of the people by failing to grant genuine authority to their alternative "State of Vietnam."

In early 1954 Viet Minh commander General Vo Nguyen Giap prepared to invade Laos. French commander in Indochina General Henri Navarre's response was Operation CASTOR, which entailed the establishment of an air base in the village of Dien Bien Phu in far northwestern Vietnam. Muong Thanh was the name of the village in tribal Tai, while Dien Bien Phu is Vietnamese for the French name of "Seat of the Border County Prefecture." Navarre claimed that the base would serve as a blocking position astride the chief Viet Minh invasion route into northern Laos, but he actually hoped to use Dien Bien Phu as bait to draw Viet Minh forces into battle, whereupon he would destroy them with superior artillery and airpower.

Located in an obscure valley some 200 miles by air from Hanoi, Dien Bien Phu boasted a small airstrip. On November 20, 1953, 2,200 French paratroopers dropped into the valley and easily defeated the small Viet Minh garrison there. Navarre assumed that Giap would commit at most one division against Dien Bien Phu. Should this prove incorrect, the French commander was confident that the garrison could be evacuated. Leaving the Viet Minh in control of the high ground surrounding the base, however, was courting disaster.

Colonel Christian Marie Ferdinand de la Croix de Castries (promoted to brigadier general during the battle) commanded French forces at Dien Bien Phu. His men were entirely dependent on air supply by some 75 C-47s Dakotas. The French could also call on 48 B-26 and Privateer bombers, 112 Bearcat and Hellcat fighter-bombers, and a few helicopters. De Castries set up his central command post in the village itself. Around it he ordered the construction of a series of strong points: Beatrice, Gabrielle, Anne-Marie, Dominique, Huguette, Françoise, Elaine, and Isabelle. This last post, three miles to the south, was separated from the others. Easily cut off, Isabelle also tied down a third of the French forces.

By mid-March the French had nearly 11,000 men in the valley, a third of them ethnic Vietnamese. Ultimately the French committed 16,544 men to Dien Bien Phu. Fortifications were totally inadequate, as the French assumed that their artillery could quickly knock out any Viet Minh artillery.

Giap accepted the challenge of trying to dislodge the French at Dien Bien Phu, but there was strong political pressure on him to do so. A diplomatic conference of the great powers was set to begin in Geneva, and a major Viet Minh victory might bring negotiations there that would end the war. Giap committed not one but four divisions to the effort, assembling some 49,500 combat troops and 31,500 support personnel.

The siege opened on March 13, 1954, with a heavy Viet Minh bombardment. Although the French added 4,000 men during the battle, Giap more than offset this with manpower increases of his own; he also steadily improved his artillery. Tens of thousands of porters dragged the guns there. The Viet Minh actually deployed more artillery pieces (20–24 105-millimeter [mm] howitzers, 15–20 75-mm howitzers, 20 120-mm mortars, and at least 40 82-mm mortars, along with 80 Chinese-crewed 37-mm antiaircraft guns, 100 antiaircraft machine guns, and 12–16 six-tube Katyusha rocket launchers) than did the French (four 155-mm howitzers, 24 105-mm howitzers, and four 120-mm mortars). The Viet Minh also fired more artillery rounds than did the French.

On the very first night of the siege, March 13–14, the Viet Minh took Beatrice. Gabrielle fell two days later. The Viet Minh also shelled the airstrip, destroying or driving its aircraft away and knocking out its radio-direction beacon. C-47 transports still flew in supplies and took out wounded but at great risk. The last flight in or out of Dien Bien Phu occurred on March 27. During the battle the Viet Minh shot down 48 French planes and destroyed another 16 on the ground.

Heavy casualties forced Giap to shift from costly human-wave tactics to classic siege warfare. The Viet Minh built miles of zigzag trenches that inched ever closer to the French lines. Their final assault occurred on May 6, and the last French troops surrendered the next evening. A plan to rescue the garrison or break out came too late. The French sustained some 20,000 casualties in the battle (2,242 killed, 3,711 missing, and 6,463 wounded as well as 6,500 taken prisoner and forces lost in relief operations); the Viet Minh lost at least 22,900 (7,900 killed and 15,000 wounded). The Viet Minh sent their prisoners off on foot on a 500-mile trek to prison camps, from which fewer than half returned.

The outcome of the battle allowed French politicians to shift the blame for the defeat in Indochina to the French Army and extricate France from the war. The Geneva Conference did hammer out a settlement for Indochina, but the settlement proved to be only a truce. Within a few years the fighting resumed, but this time the Americans had taken the place of the French.

References

Fall, Bernard B. *Hell in a Very Small Place: The Siege of Dienbienphu.* Philadelphia: Lippincott, 1966.

Roy, Jules. *The Battle of Dienbienphu.* New York: Harper and Row, 1965.

Simpson, Howard R. *Dien Bien Phu: The Epic Battle America Forgot.* Washington, DC: Brassey's, 1994.

Battle of the Ia Drang Valley

Date	October 19–November 20, 1965	
Location	Ia Drang Valley of west central Vietnam	
Opponents (* winner)	*Americans	North Vietnamese
Commander	Lieutenant Colonel Harold G. Moore; Lieutenant Colonel Robert Tully; Lieutenant Colonel Robert McDade	Political Commissar La Ngoc Chau
Approx. # Troops	1,000	2,000
Importance	The first major land battle between U.S. Army and People's Army of Vietnam (PAVN, North Vietnamese Army) forces in the Vietnam War	

The Battle of the Ia Drang Valley, also known as the Plei Mei Campaign, was the first major ground confrontation between U.S. and People's Army of Vietnam (PAVN, North Vietnamese Army) forces during the 1965–1972 American ground war phase of the Vietnam War (1955–1975). By June 1965 the U.S.-backed Army of the Republic of Vietnam (ARVN, South Vietnamese Army) was in desperate straits, losing the equivalent of an infantry battalion a week. Military Assistance Command Vietnam (MACV) commander General William Westmoreland therefore decided to hit PAVN forces first, always his preferred strategy. To carry this out, he committed to battle an entirely new formation, the 1st Cavalry Division (known as the 1st Cav).

The 1st Cav relied on the helicopter. Indeed, the Vietnam War is sometimes known as the Helicopter War, and during the conflict U.S. Army, Marine Corps, Air Force, and Navy helicopters flew 36,125,000 sorties: 3.932 million attacks, 7.547 million assaults (troop landings), 3.548 million cargo sorties, and 21.098 million reconnaissance, search and rescue, and other missions. In the course of the war U.S. forces lost 10 helicopters over the Democratic Republic of Vietnam (DRV, North Vietnam) and 2,066 in the Republic of Vietnam (RVN, South Vietnam) to hostile fire and an additional 2,566 to nonhostile causes. U.S. Army aviators suffered the highest per capita casualty ratio of any U.S. military contingent in the war.

The U.S. Army embraced the helicopter when the 1947 Key West Agreement gave the U.S. Air Force control of most fixed-wing military aircraft. Although vulnerable to ground fire, helicopters proved invaluable in a wide range of roles in Vietnam, including reconnaissance, liaison, troop lift, resupply, and medevac (medical evacuation). To utilize the helicopter to its fullest potential, the army created a new type of division and a new concept, known as air mobility, that seemed ideally suited to a war such as the one in Vietnam, which had few roads, many rice paddies, and an abundance of jungle.

The 11th Air Assault Division (Test) therefore became the 1st Cavalry Division (Airmobile). The 1st Air Cavalry Division, as it was formally known, was entirely airmobile. Although it would take a number of lifts to move the entire 1st Cav, all of its 16,000 men and equipment, including artillery, could be transported by its 435 helicopters.

When the 1st Cav arrived in Vietnam in August 1965, Westmoreland considered breaking the division up into its component brigades and stationing them at various locations around South Vietnam. Division commander Major General Harry W. O. Kinnard strongly objected, and Westmoreland agreed to assign the 1st Cav intact to a base area just north of Route 19 where the road passed through the village of An Khe. The division set up its base there in September 1965.

Meanwhile, U.S. intelligence had identified a PAVN troop concentration in South Vietnam's western Central Highlands. PAVN forces there had been operating out of Cambodia to attack U.S. Special Forces camps in the Central Highlands and seize them prior to a drive to the sea down Route 19 that would split South Vietnam in two. PAVN brigadier general Chu Huy Man, commander of PAVN units on the western plateau, planned to lay siege to the Special Forces camp at Plei Mei with its 12 Americans and some 400 indigenous mountain people, known as Montagnards. Man hoped thereby to provoke a reaction by a road-bound ARVN relief force, which he would then ambush and destroy. Once he had accomplished this, Man planned to assault Pleiku City, permitting an advance down Route 19 toward the city of Qui Nhon and the coast.

Man positioned his three regiments around the 2,500-foot-high Chu Pong massif on the Cambodian border and then on October 19 attacked the Plei Mei camp. Following a week-long battle, the attack and resulting ambush of an ARVN relief force both failed thanks in large part to U.S. air support and air-lifted artillery. Mid-October operations by units of the 1st Cav provided intelligence on PAVN dispositions, and Westmoreland decided on a spoiling attack. This decision resulted in the October 23–November 20 battle in the Ia Drang Valley, a forested area just east of the Chu Pong massif. The Battle of the Ia Drang Valley was the first major battle of the war between PAVN and U.S. Army units and one of the war's bloodiest encounters.

On October 27 Westmoreland committed a brigade of the 1st Cav to a search-and-destroy operation. For two weeks there was sporadic but light contact between the opposing sides. This changed dramatically on November 14. Over the next four days savage fighting erupted over landing zones (LZs) X-Ray and Albany. The battle began when the first troopers of some 450 men comprising Lieutenant Colonel Harold G. Moore's 1st Battalion of the 7th Cavalry Regiment landed at LZ X-Ray almost on top of two PAVN regiments of 2,000 men. Outnumbered and in unfamiliar terrain, the Americans fought desperately. Elephant grass, tall anthills, and small trees all obstructed fields of fire.

PAVN political commissar La Ngoc Chau temporarily commanding the PAVN 66th Regiment, although under intense U.S. artillery fire and air bombardment, tried to outflank the U.S. forces at X-Ray to the south. Moore was able to get his men in line just in time, although one of his platoons advanced too far, and PAVN forces cut off and almost destroyed it. Moore requested assistance and received B Company of the 2nd Battalion of the 7th Cavalry Regiment, employing it in reserve that night.

Chau resumed the attack at dawn on November 15, and Lieutenant Colonel Robert Tully's 2nd Battalion of the 5th Cavalry Regiment marched overland to provide much-needed support. In bitter and sometimes hand-to-hand combat the Americans drove back all the PAVN attacks. The Americans also rescued the survivors of the cutoff platoon as 15 B-52 bombers from Guam initiated six days of ARC LIGHT (the code name for air attacks by the big bombers against targets inside South Vietnam) strikes on the Chu Pong massif. It was the first time in the war that B-52s were employed in a tactical role in support of ground troops.

Two additional batteries of artillery meanwhile arrived at LZ Columbus, bringing to 24 the number of guns providing support to the beleaguered Americans at X-Ray. That night the PAVN 66th Regiment withdrew.

Early on November 16 Chau launched a last attack, which the Americans easily repulsed. Lieutenant Colonel Robert McDade's 2nd Battalion of the 7th Cavalry Regiment arrived that day, and the Americans retrieved their own dead and counted those of the PAVN 66th Regiment. The Americans tallied PAVN losses at 634 killed, but estimates placed the total number at 1,215 killed, or 10 times the 1st Cav losses. That same day, Moore's battalion was lifted to Camp Holloway at Pleiku. Tully's 2nd Battalion of the 5th Cavalry Regiment and McDade's 2nd Battalion of the 7th Cavalry Regiment remained at X-Ray.

On November 17 McDade's battalion, with A Company of the 1st Battalion of the 7th Cavalry Regiment attached, was ordered to march two miles toward LZ Albany and reestablish contact with PAVN units. At the same time, Tully's battalion was to march overland to the fire base at LZ Columbus. McDade's men were moving to LZ Albany, strung out in a 500-yard column in high elephant grass and jungle, when they walked into a three-battalion PAVN ambush.

Chau ordered his men to get as close to the Americans as possible in order to avoid U.S. artillery fire and air support. The ensuing two-hour firefight devolved into a series of small combats in which all unit cohesion was lost. In late afternoon B Company of the 1st Battalion of the 5th Cavalry Regiment arrived overland from LZ Columbus and fought its way into LZ Albany to assist McDade's troopers. At dusk B Company of the 2nd Battalion of the 7th Cavalry Regiment also arrived. In the predawn hours of November 18, Chau withdrew his men across the border into Cambodia. PAVN losses are unknown, but the Americans sustained 155 killed and another 124 wounded.

The month-long Battle of the Ia Drang Valley campaign, which the PAVN official history of the war refers to as the Plei Me Campaign, ended on November 20. During that period the 1st Cav lost 305 killed (the PAVN claimed that 1,700 Americans and 1,370 "puppet troops" had been "eliminated from the field of combat"). The PAVN official history gives no casualty figures for its side in the campaign, but the Americans estimated total PAVN losses at 3,561, less than half of these confirmed.

Both sides claimed victory. The PAVN learned that they could survive high-tech American weapons and the new helicopter tactics. They also learned that they could minimize casualties by keeping their troops close to U.S. positions in what PAVN commander General Giap referred to as the "grab-them-by-the-belt" tactic. The North Vietnamese leadership was not unduly concerned about the lopsided casualty totals, believing that even with losses of 10 to 1 they would eventually wear down American resolve.

The Americans believed that they had prevented a decisive PAVN success before the U.S. deployment could be completed and that they had successfully demonstrated the air mobility concept. Westmoreland saw their impressive kill ratio advantage as proof that the war could be won through attrition by carrying the conflict to the PAVN in search and destroy operations. *Time* magazine selected General Westmoreland as its Man of the Year for 1965.

References

Coleman, J. D. *Pleiku: The Dawn of Helicopter Warfare in Vietnam.* New York: St. Martin's, 1988.

Davidson, Philip B. *Vietnam at War: The History, 1946–1975.* New York: Oxford University Press, 1988.

Military History Institute of Vietnam, The. *Victory in Vietnam.* Translated by Merle L. Pribbenow. Lawrence: University Press of Kansas, 2002.

Moore, Harold G., and Joseph L. Galloway. *We Were Soldiers Once . . . and Young.* New York: Random House, 1992.

First and Second Battles of Khe Sanh

Date	April 24–May 12, 1967; January 20–April 8, 1968	
Location	Khe Sanh support base, extreme northwestern Quang Tri Province, South Vietnam	
Opponents (* winner)	*Americans, South Vietnamese	North Vietnamese
Commander	U.S. Marine Corps Colonel David E. Lownds	General Tran Quy Hai
Approx. # Troops	7,000? (6,000 marines, plus Vietnamese)	20,000–30,000
Importance	One of the signature battles of the Vietnam War, it diverts U.S. and South Vietnamese attention to the periphery, away from the impending Communist Tet Offensive	

Two important battles were fought at Khe Sanh in northern South Vietnam during the Vietnam War (1955–1975). This strategically insignificant base with an air strip was located in western Quang Tri Province, about six miles east of Laos and 14 miles south of the demilitarized zone (DMZ) separating the Democratic Republic of Vietnam (DRV, North Vietnam) and the Republic of Vietnam (RVN, South Vietnam) along the 17th Parallel. U.S. forces established the base to monitor People's Army of Vietnam (PAVN, North Vietnamese Army) infiltration from North Vietnam through Laos into South Vietnam. U.S. Military Assistance Command (MACV) commander General William C. Westmoreland hoped that an enlarged Khe Sanh could block communist movement along Route 9 and serve as a jumping-off point for any invasion of Laos.

To control nearby infiltration routes, U.S. marines were ordered to take three communist-held hills. The fighting was intense, even hand to hand, but at the end

U.S. Marine Corps artillery firing in defense of Khe Sanh. Two battles were fought in 1967 and 1968 for control of the base located in far northwestern South Vietnam close to the borders with Laos and North Vietnam. (National Archives)

of these hill fights, later known as the First Battle of Khe Sanh (April 24–May 12, 1967), the marines had suffered 160 killed and 746 wounded. They claimed 570 confirmed PAVN and Viet Cong (VC, indigenous South Vietnamese communist forces) dead and another 589 probably dead.

The First Battle of Khe Sanh was only part of PAVN commander General Vo Nguyen Giap's peripheral strategy to draw U.S. and Army of the Republic of Vietnam (ARVN) forces away from the population centers before a general communist offensive. In September PAVN forces crossed the DMZ to attack a U.S. Marine Corps outpost at Con Thien, firing some 3,000 shells and rockets in support of their infantry assault. Westmoreland responded with a bombing campaign dubbed SLAM (Seek, Locate, Annihilate, and Monitor). At Con Thien alone, B-52s dropped 22,000 tons of bombs. This was apart from ordnance delivered by fighter bombers, naval gunfire, and ground artillery. The success of SLAM success convinced Westmoreland that with adequate bombing and aerial resupply, U.S. outposts could survive even when outnumbered.

Other communist-initiated peripheral battles occurred at Loc Ninh (70 miles north of Saigon) during October 29–November 3, 1967, and at Dak To (280 miles north of Saigon) during November 3–22, 1967. The fight at Dak To was one of the biggest battles of the war. In it, the allies lost 347 dead. U.S. losses alone were 287 killed, 985 wounded, and 18 missing in action. The official count of PAVN dead was 1,200. Still, according to North Vietnamese leader Ho Chi Minh's earlier statements, 4:1 was a readily acceptable loss ratio.

During these battles Giap had forced U.S. and ARVN troops into fighting in terrain and circumstances of his choosing, and his units had gained experience in larger unit combat against the Americans. PAVN forces also enjoyed the advantage of short supply lines into Laos and North Vietnam, and they could withdraw when they chose. By the end of 1967 the first phase of Giap's plan was complete, and some U.S. ground strength had been dispersed in the north away from the populated centers. In these circumstances the communists launched their general offensive throughout South Vietnam during Tet (the Vietnamese New Year) in late January 1968. The goal of the offensive was to administer a major defeat to ARVN and U.S. forces that would spark a general uprising of the South Vietnamese population against the South Vietnamese government and the Americans.

In January 1968 attention turned again to the marine base at Khe Sanh, the final battle in Giap's peripheral strategy. While it was in progress, this Second Battle of Khe Sanh inspired frequent comparisons to the 1954 Battle of Dien Bien Phu during the Indochina War. Although surrounded by hills that could conceal PAVN artillery, Khe Sanh was not in a bowl such as Dien Bien Phu; indeed, Khe Sanh's location on a plateau gave the defenders the advantage of high ground against an assault.

For 77 days, from January 20 until April 8, some 20,000–30,000 PAVN troops in four divisions commanded by Major General Tran Quy Hai attacked Khe Sanh and the high terrain around it. The Second Battle of Khe Sanh is sometimes referred to as the Siege of Khe Sanh, but the base was never cut off from U.S. aerial resupply. In their attacks, PAVN forces employed a dozen or so PT-76 amphibious tanks, one of only two instances in which they used tanks prior to 1972.

The defenders were equally split between the base and the hill positions around it. The defense centered on 6,000 marines supported by artillery and a small contingent of Army Special Forces. An ARVN Ranger battalion also fought at Khe Sanh. Westmoreland had insisted on this as a sign of allied solidarity.

Fighting erupted at the base on January 20 when a reinforced marine patrol made heavy contact. The next day PAVN troops attempted to take the high ground of Hill 861. Alerted by a deserter, the marines drove back the attackers in hand-to-hand combat. That same day 82-millimeter (mm) mortar rounds and 122-mm rockets rained down on Khe Sanh, hitting the main ammunition dump that blew up in spectacular fashion.

The first major ground attack against the base came on February 8, but the defenders repulsed it at a cost of 150 PAVN troops and 21 U.S. marines dead. Over the next weeks the attackers concentrated on a relentless artillery barrage from 82-mm and 120-mm mortars, 122-mm rockets, and 130-mm and 152-mm artillery pieces. PAVN forces fired an average of 2,500 rounds a week into an area barely 330 by 600 yards in size. This caused few casualties among the sandbagged and dug-in defenders, however. The last major land offensive action occurred during February 29–

March 1 and was directed principally against the ARVN 37th Ranger Battalion. With heavy supporting fire the Rangers turned back three separate PAVN attacks.

Khe Sanh got the attention of the American public. This otherwise obscure fortress became the focus of daily newspaper and television reports, stirring fears of a repetition of the Battle of Dien Bien Phu. U.S. president Lyndon B. Johnson even had a terrain model of the base erected in the White House War Room and insisted that the Joint Chiefs of Staff (JCS) sign a declaration stating their belief that Khe Sanh would hold.

Westmoreland was determined not only to hold the base but also to inflict a major defeat on a massed enemy. Toward that end he planned to employ massive airpower. Westmoreland came up with the operation's name, NIAGARA, "to invoke an image of cascading shells and bombs." Aided by electronic sensors, Operation NIAGARA was intended to destroy PAVN forces and interdict supply lines to the fortress. A wide range of aircraft flew around the clock to provide air support, and the area around the base became one of the most heavily bombed targets in history, much of it resembling the surface of the moon.

On average, 350 tactical fighter-bombers, 60 B-52s, and 30 light observation or reconnaissance aircraft operated daily near the base during the battle. While tactical aircraft attacked to within 400 yards of the defender's positions, B-52s flying at 30,000 feet—which up to that time had always bombed targets only beyond 3,000 yards of friendly positions—now struck to within 1,000 yards of them. Some bombs fell even closer. The B-52s also devastated PAVN staging areas and depots.

In all, the Seventh Air Force flew 9,961 sorties and dropped 14,233 tons of bombs. The 1st Marine Air Wing flew another 7,078 sorties and dropped 17,015 tons of ordnance, while the U.S. Navy flew 5,337 sorties and dropped 7,941 tons of bombs. The total represented one-fifth of all ordnance dropped by the United States in the Pacific theater in all of World War II (1939–1945).

U.S. airpower was also vital in supplying the base. Lockheed C-130 Hercules and Fairchild C-123 Provider transport aircraft, along with U.S. Marine Corps Boeing CH-46 Sea Knight and U.S. Army Boeing CH-47 Chinook and Bell UH-1E Iroquois helicopters regularly ran a gauntlet of communist antiaircraft fire to bring in supplies and evacuate wounded. On February 10 a C-130 was destroyed while unloading fuel. After that C-130 landings were suspended, although these aircraft continued to resupply the base using parachute drops or a hook-and-line system for extracting pallets in flight (LAPES, for Low Altitude Parachute Extraction System).

PAVN forces withdrew from the vicinity of Khe Sanh beginning on March 6, but MACV declared the siege officially ended on April 8 when, in Operation PEGASUS, allied units pushed in by land and relieved the marine defenders. The official MACV casualty count for the Second Battle of Khe Sanh was 205 marines killed and more than 1,600 wounded, although one reliable source at the base placed the actual death toll at closer to 475. This figure does not include those killed in collateral actions, ARVN Ranger casualties on the southwest perimeter, the 1,000–1,500 Montagnards who died during the fighting, or the 97 U.S. and 33 ARVN killed in the relief effort. MACV's official count of PAVN dead was 1,602, but Westmoreland put the number at between 10,000 and 15,000.

Each side saw the Second Battle of Khe Sanh largely as a test of wills and the opportunity to inflict a major psychological defeat. The true measure of Khe Sanh's strategic importance, however, can be seen in the fact that U.S. forces abandoned the base in June 1968. Controversy still surrounds the battle and what Giap actually intended there.

References

Pisor, Robert. *The End of the Line: The Siege of Khe Sanh.* New York: Norton, 1982.

Nalty, Bernard C. *Air Power and the Fight for Khe Sanh.* Washington, DC: USAF/HO, U.S. Government Printing Office, 1973.

Prados, John, and Yay W. Stubbe. *Valley of Decision.* Boston: Houghton Mifflin, 1991.

Shulimson, Jack. *U.S. Marines in Vietnam, 1966.* Washington, DC: U.S. Marine Corps, 1982.

Westmoreland, William C. *A Soldier Reports.* New York: Doubleday, 1976.

Israeli Air Strikes, Six-Day War

Date	June 5, 1967	
Location	Airfields in eastern Egypt	
Opponents (* winner)	*Israelis	Egyptians; Syrians; Jordanians
Commander	Major General Mordechai Hod	Unknown
Approx. # Troops	Nearly 200 aircraft	Nearly 450 aircraft
Importance	This preemptive strike secures Israeli air supremacy and virtually decides the war at its very beginning	

The Arab-Israeli war of 1967, known to history as the Six-Day War, began on the morning of June 5, 1967. For all intents and purposes, it was over by noon on the first day as a result of the preemptive attack by the Israeli Air Force. This aerial offensive remains one of the most stunning successes in modern warfare. In a mere three hours, the Israelis achieved air superiority by destroying much of the Egyptian Air Force on the ground. Attacks against Egypt were followed by sorties against targets in Syria, Jordan, and western Iraq, thus ensuring that Israeli ground operations could go forward unimpeded.

The Six-Day War resulted from Israeli alarm over bellicose moves by the Arab states of Egypt, Syria, Jordan, and Iraq. Syria stepped up border clashes with Israeli forces in 1966, and Egyptian president Gamal Abdel Nasser ordered a blockade of the Strait of Tiran, massed troops on the Egyptian-Israeli border, and secured the removal of the United Nations (UN) peacekeeping troops. Syria and

Jordan had also mobilized their forces, and Iraqi forces had begun moving to Jordan.

Israel had previously announced that it would go to war under any of those conditions. The Israel Defense Forces (IDF) was heavily outnumbered in terms of men and equipment, however. Figures vary widely, but one estimate is as follows: manpower, mobilized strength of 230,000 for Israel to 409,000 for Egypt, Syria, Jordan, and Iraq; tanks, 1,100 for Israel to 2,437 for the Arab states; artillery, 260 for Israel to 649 for the Arab states; naval vessels, 22 for Israel to 90 for the Arab states; and aircraft (all types), 354 for Israel to 969 for the Arab states. The Arab states were handicapped by not having any unified plan, however.

Israeli minister of defense Moshe Dayan, IDF chief of staff Lieutenant General Itzhak Rabin, and Premier Levi Eshkol determined that war was inevitable and decided that Israel should launch a preemptive attack. Defense against an Arab air attack would be difficult because Israel was so small that early warning systems would not provide sufficient time for Israeli fighters to scramble. Tel Aviv was 25 minutes flying time from Cairo but only 4.5 minutes from the nearest Egyptian airbase at El Arish. For whatever reason, Nasser did not believe that the Israelis would strike first, despite his announced eagerness for battle.

The Israeli air attack relied on accurate, timely, and precise intelligence information. The plan called for a first strike against Egypt, the most formidable of Israel's opponents. IDF fighters would take off from airfields all over Israel and fly under radio silence and at low altitude to avoid radar west out over the Mediterranean, and they would then turn south to strike Egyptian airfields as simultaneously as possible. Rather than attacking at dawn, the IDF strikes were timed to coincide with the return of Egyptian pilots to base from their morning patrols, when most Egyptian pilots would be having breakfast.

The Israeli Air Force (IAF), one of the best-trained air forces in the world, was well prepared for its mission. Aircrews had been thoroughly briefed as to objectives and procedures. IAF ground crews were also highly trained and able to reduce turnaround time between missions to a minimum. The operation was daring in that it would employ almost all Israeli bomber and fighter aircraft, leaving only a dozen fighters behind to fly defensive combat air patrols.

The IAF achieved complete tactical surprise. Commanded by Major General Mordechai Hod, its aircraft went into action at 7:45 a.m. (8:45 a.m. Cairo time). One unexpected development was that Field Marshal Ali Amer, the United Arab Republic (UAR) commander in chief, and his deputy, General Mamoud Sidky, were in the air, flying from Cairo to inspect units in the Sinai, when the attacks occurred. Unable to land in the Sinai they returned to Cairo, and for 90 minutes two key UAR commanders were out of touch with their units and unable to give orders.

The first wave struck 10 Egyptian airfields, hitting all of them within 15 minutes of the scheduled time. On their final approach to the targets, the Israeli aircraft climbed to become suddenly visible on radar and induce Egyptian pilots to attempt to scramble in the hopes of catching the pilots in their aircraft on the ground. Only four Egyptian aircraft, all trainers, were in the air at the time of the first strikes, and all were shot down. Subsequent waves of Israeli attacking aircraft, about 40 per flight, arrived at 10 minutes intervals. These met increased Egyptian opposition, mostly antiaircraft fire. Only 8 Egyptian MiGs managed to take off during the strikes, and all were shot down.

In all, the IAF struck 17 major Egyptian airfields with some 500 sorties in just under three hours, destroying half of Egyptian Air Force strength. Most of the Egyptian aircraft were destroyed by accurate Israeli cannon fire, but the Israeli planes also dropped 250-, 500-, and 1,000-pound bombs. Special bombs with 365-pound warheads, developed to crack the hard-surface concrete runways, were dropped on Egyptian airfields west of the Suez Canal, but none of these were employed against the Sinai airfields, which the Israelis planned for subsequent use by their own aircraft. During the war Egypt lost a total of 286 aircraft: 30 Tupolev Tu-16 heavy bombers, 27 Ilyusian medium bombers, 12 Sukhoi Su-7 fighter bombers, 90 MiG-21 fighters, 20 MiG-19 fighters, 75 MiG-17/15 fighters, and 32 transport planes and helicopters.

Later that same day, June 5, Israeli aircraft struck Syria and Jordan. Israeli leaders had urged King Hussein of Jordan to stay out of the war. He desired to do so but was under heavy pressure to act and hoped to satisfy his allies with minimum military action short of all-out war. Jordanian 155-millimeter "Long Tom" guns therefore went into action against Tel Aviv, and Jordanian aircraft attempted to strafe a small airfield near Kfar Sirkin. The Israeli government then declared war on Jordan.

Following an Iraqi air strike on Israel, IAF aircraft also struck Iraqi air units based in the Mosul area. In all during the war, the Arabs lost a total of 390 aircraft of their prewar strength of 969 aircraft of all types (Egypt, 286 of 580; Jordan, 28 of 56; Syria, 54 of 172; Iraq, 21 of 149, and Lebanon 1 of 12). IAF losses were only 32 aircraft shot down of 354 at the beginning of the war; only 2 of these were lost in aerial combat.

With its opposing air forces largely neutralized, the IAF could turn to close air support and other missions in support of Israeli mechanized ground forces, which had begun operations in the Sinai simultaneously with the initial air attacks. Israeli's success in the war was complete. On June 7 Israel and Jordan accepted the UN Security Council call for a cease-fire. The UN also brokered a cease-fire on June 9 between Israel and Egypt. Israel accepted immediately, while Egypt accepted the next day. A cease-fire was also concluded with Syria on June 10.

On the Israeli side the Six-Day War claimed some 800 dead, 2,440 wounded, and 16 missing or taken prisoner. Arab losses, chiefly Egyptian, were estimated at 14,300 dead, 23,800 wounded, and 10,500 missing or taken prisoner. Tank losses were 100 for Israel and 950 for the Arabs.

The war immensely increased the territory controlled by Israel. Israel now possessed all of the Sinai east of the Suez Canal from Egypt, the east bank of the Jordan River and the city of Jerusalem from Jordan, and the Golan Heights from Syria. Whether these acquisitions would enhance or impede the chances for peace in the Middle East remained to be seen.

References

Hammel, Eric. *Six Days in June: How Israel Won the 1967 Arab-Israeli War.* New York: Scribner, 1992.

Oren, Michael. *Six Days of War: June 1967 and the Making of the Modern Middle East.* Oxford: Oxford University Press, 2002.

Rubenstein, Murray, and Richard Goldman. *Shield of David: An Illustrated History of the Israeli Air Force.* Englewood Cliffs, NJ: Prentice-Hall, 1978.

Van Creveld, Martin. *The Sword and the Olive: A Critical History of the Israeli Defense Force.* New York: PublicAffairs, 1998.

Weizman, Ezer. *On Eagle's Wings: The Personal Story of the Leading Commander of the Israeli Air Force.* New York: Macmillan, 1976.

Battle of Hue

Date	January 31–February 24, 1968	
Location	City of Hue in northern South Vietnam	
Opponents (* winner)	*South Vietnamese, Americans	*North Vietnamese and Communist South Vietnamese
Commander	Brigadier General Ngo Quang Truong; U.S. Marine Corps Brigadier General Foster LaHue	General Tran Van Quang
Approx. # Troops	12,000	16,000?
Importance	The most costly battle of the Communist Tet Offensive	

The 1968 struggle to control Hue was one of the biggest battles of the Vietnam War (1955–1975). In November 1967 commander of U.S. forces in Vietnam General William C. Westmoreland returned to Washington with a glowing report on the progress of the war. President Lyndon B. Johnson asked that he make his views public, and Westmoreland did so in a speech to the National Press Club on November 21. He also told a *Time* magazine interviewer that "I hope they try something, because we are looking for a fight."

With U.S. attention in Vietnam focused on peripheral fights, especially at Khe Sanh, leaders of the People's Army of Vietnam (PAVN, North Vietnamese Army) and Viet Cong (VC, for Vietnamese Communists) prepared their most ambitious military venture to date, which would change the course of the war although not as intended. PAVN commander General Vo Nguyen Giap planned to draw U.S. forces away from the populated areas and then mount a widespread military offensive to bring a popular uprising against the government of the Republic of Vietnam (RVN, South Vietnam) and the Americans.

The leadership of the Democratic Republic of Vietnam (DRV, North Vietnam) selected the Lunar New Year celebrations of Tet for the general offensive. As this was the most important holiday of the year, during Tet both sides traditionally observed a cease-fire. South Vietnamese military units would be at low strength, with many men at home for celebrations and to worship at family shrines. Guerrillas found it easy to slip undetected among the crowds traveling to their ancestral homes. Many were disguised as Army of the Republic of Vietnam (ARVN, South Vietnamese) soldiers and even secured rides on American military vehicles.

The Tet Offensive lasted from January 31 until February 25. There was precedent for an attack during Tet in Emperor Quang Trung's 1789 victory over the Chinese. Contrary to popular myth, the U.S. headquarters, the Military Assistance Command Vietnam (MACV), was not caught completely by surprise by the offensive. Military intelligence, especially in III Corps, determined from a variety of sources that PAVN and VC units were moving from the border areas and concentrating around the cities. Commander of II Field Force Lieutenant General Frederick C. Weyand, alarmed by increased communist radio traffic around the South Vietnamese capital of Saigon and an unusually low number of enemy contacts in the border areas, convinced Westmoreland on January 10 to pull additional U.S. combat battalions back in around the capital. It was one of the critical decisions of the war, because when the offensive began there were 27 U.S. battalions (instead of the planned 14) in the Saigon area.

Where MACV erred was in surmising the timing and scale of the attack. Westmoreland's chief of intelligence Brigadier General Philip B. Davidson believed that PAVN and VC forces would strike either just before or just after Tet, but MACV's chief error was underestimating the size of the offensive. As Davidson put it to Westmoreland later, "Even had I known exactly what to take place, it was so preposterous that I probably would have been unable to sell it to anybody. Why should the enemy give away his major advantage, which was his ability to be elusive and avoid heavy casualties?" Westmoreland believed that communist forces had been severely wounded during the peripheral battles of the preceding autumn and winter, and he and Davidson could not conceive of a communist offensive of such magnitude directed against the cities.

With tension mounting, however, Westmoreland visited with both President Nguyen Van Thieu and ARVN chief of the Joint General Staff General Cao Van Vien and tried to convince them to end the cease-fire over Tet altogether or to shorten it from 48 to 24 hours. They agreed only to reduce the cease-fire to 36 hours and to keep at least 50 percent of ARVN duty troops on full-alert status.

During the early morning hours of January 30 PAVN and VC forces struck a number of cities in the Central Highlands. Apparently the offensive had originally been set for the night of January 29–30 but was then moved back 24 hours, and these units,

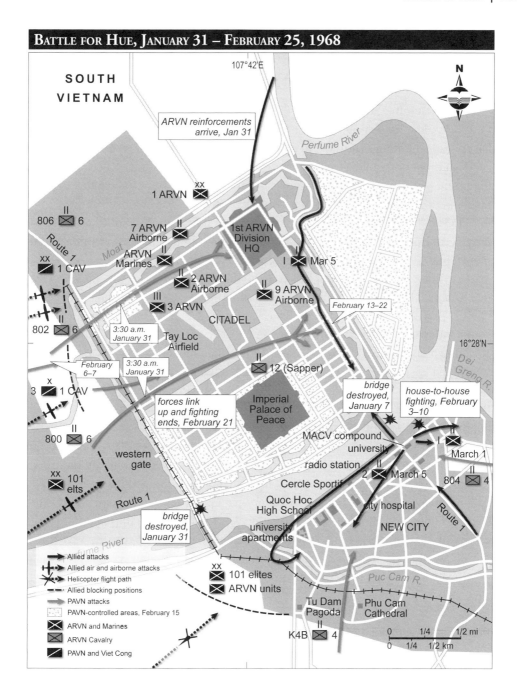

BATTLE FOR HUE, JANUARY 31 – FEBRUARY 25, 1968

SOUTH
VIETNAM

107°42'E

Perfume River

ARVN reinforcements
arrive, Jan 31

1 ARVN XX

806 II 6

Route 1

Moat

7 ARVN Airborne II

1st ARVN
Division
HQ

XX 1 CAV

ARVN Marines II

I Mar 5

2 ARVN Airborne II

9 ARVN Airborne II

February 13–22

3 ARVN III

CITADEL

802 II 6

3:30 a.m.
January 31

Tay Loc
Airfield

16°28'N

Dei Greng R.

February
6–7

3:30 a.m.
January 31

12 (Sapper) II

bridge
destroyed,
January 7

house-to-house
fighting, February
3–10

x
3 II 1 CAV

forces link
up and fighting
ends, February 21

Imperial
Palace of
Peace

II

800 II 6

western
gate

MACV compound
university

I

March 1

101
elts XX

radio station

Cercle Sportif

2 II March 5

804 II 4

Route 1

Quoc Hoc
High School

city hospital

Route 1

bridge
destroyed,
January 31

university
apartments

NEW CITY

Puc Cam R.

Allied attacks
Allied air and airborne attacks
Helicopter flight path
Allied blocking positions
PAVN attacks
PAVN-controlled areas, February 15
ARVN and Marines
ARVN Cavalry
PAVN and Viet Cong

101 elites XX

ARVN units

Tu Dam
Pagoda

Phu Cam
Cathedral

K4B II 4

0   1/4   1/2 mi
0   1/4   1/2 km

all in the same communist command area (Military Region 5), apparently were not notified of the change in plans. The bulk of the attacks began the next night, January 30–31, when communist forces struck 36 of 44 provincial capitals, 5 of 6 autonomous cities, 64 of 242 district capitals, and about 50 hamlets. In the vital strategic area around Saigon, roughly a 30-mile zone around the capital known as the Saigon Circle, the communists committed the equivalent of more than two divisions.

In Saigon, communist sappers actually penetrated the U.S. embassy. More important, the attackers blew up part of the large Long Bình ammunition storage dump and captured all of Bien Hoa City. Most of the fighting inside the Saigon Circle was over in a matter of days.

This was not the case in Cholon, the Chinese district of the capital. Here ARVN forces shouldered the brunt of the effort. Most of Cholon was cleared by March 7, but sporadic fighting continued in the capital for the remainder of the month.

At Hue the communists made a large investment of resources because of the important psychological impact that securing the former imperial capital and cultural-intellectual center of Vietnam would have for the war but also because holding Hue might bring with it control of the two northernmost South Vietnamese provinces. Eight PAVN and VC battalions took part in the initial assault, but communist manpower grew during the battle to 20 battalions.

The assault on Hue began in the early hours of January 31, 1968. ARVN brigadier general Ngo Quang Truong, commanding the excellent 1st Infantry Division at Hue, played a key role. U.S. advisers considered Truong the top senior ARVN commander, one of the few who had won his position by ability rather than political influence or bribery. Truong sensed that something was afoot and that Hue, which had been spared in previous offensives, might be a target. He ordered a full alert for his troops, although many soldiers had already departed on leave during the Tet truce. He also sent out his reconnaissance company to patrol the western approaches to the city, the most likely communist route of advance. Shortly after midnight on January 30–31 the reconnaissance company spotted two battalions of the PAVN 6th Regiment moving toward the city and notified Truong by radio.

The North Vietnamese expected to be welcomed by the people once they had captured the city and had planned a victory parade for later in the day. Many were in dress uniform, complete with unit patches. Truong's leadership and the heroic efforts of his men upset the communist timetable and ensured that the PAVN and the VC would have to fight in broad daylight.

Aided by heavy ground fog, most communist forces reached their attack positions, albeit late. When the battle began at 3:40 a.m., signaled by a rocket barrage, many citizens believed that the noises they heard were merely gunshots and traditional loud firecrackers announcing the arrival of the Lunar New Year. Most of Hue City was soon in communist hands, but thanks to the bravery of an ARVN company, the 1st Division Headquarters in the northern corner of the Citadel held out. The communists also failed to take the MACV compound in southern Hue but only by the thinnest of margins. Although Westmoreland had placed all U.S. forces on full alert, word had not reached Hue, and U.S. personnel there had taken no extra precautions.

By dawn a large communist flag flew over the Citadel. It was not until that afternoon that two companies of the 1st Marine Division, the closest U.S. troops, arrived from Phu Bai, seven miles away. Other units, U.S. and ARVN, were fed into the battle as they became available, but communist ambushes prevented many units from reaching the city. There were also no heavy weapons available, and there was no resupply for a week.

Fighting focused on the Citadel, the center of imperial power of pre-French Vietnam built by Emperor Gia Long in the early 19th century. With its 26-foot-high walls, some as thick as 40 feet and running 2,700 yards on a side, the Citadel had been modeled after the Imperial City at Peking (Beijing). The Citadel proved to be a formidable obstacle.

U.S. and ARVN forces were at first reluctant to use artillery and airpower for fear of destroying the Citadel and other historic structures in Hue. Eventually they had no choice, and these heavy weapons were called in on February 12. The fighting for Hue was house to house and reminiscent of that in Germany at the end of World War II. Not until February 24, however, did ARVN troops raise the South Vietnamese flag over the Citadel. By the end of the battle half of Hue lay in ruins, and an estimated 116,000 civilians were homeless out of a population of 140,000. The battle claimed 142 U.S. marines, 74 U.S. Army troops, and 384 ARVN dead. The allies claimed a body count of 5,113 communists.

There was another horrible legacy of the Battle of Hue. During their occupation, the communists had rounded up all "enemies of the people," including government officials, teachers, and even some children. Some 5,000 people simply disappeared. Weeks after the battle, mass graves were discovered containing the bodies of at least 3,000, many with their hands tied behind their backs and some showing signs of having been buried alive. The remaining missing were never found.

This communist atrocity deserves to be remembered, alongside the U.S. My Lai Massacre. The atrocity at Hue helped rally support for the South Vietnamese government from among the South Vietnamese people and led to a false belief in Washington that any communist victory in South Vietnam would be accompanied by a bloodbath.

There was heavy fighting elsewhere but not on the scale of Hue. Overall the Tet Offensive was a major communist military defeat. North Vietnamese leaders had not realized their goals. There was no crushing defeat of allied forces in South Vietnam, and the PAVN had paid a horrendous price, suffering losses at a greater rate than those sustained by the Japanese in their fanatical charges in World War II. The U.S. estimated losses for the PAVN and the VC during January 29–February 11 at 32,000 killed and 5,800 captured, or close to half the force committed. ARVN and allied killed were 2,082, and U.S. losses were 1,001. Civilian deaths reached 12,600. By the end of February after PAVN and VC forces had been completely routed, MACV estimates of their dead grew to 37,000.

There also had been no general rallying of the civilian population to the communist cause, no general uprising. Much to the relief of the Americans, ARVN fought well; none of its units had broken or defected. Westmoreland noted that the South Vietnamese armed forces, militia, and National Police deserved the major share of credit in turning back the offensive. If anything, the Tet Offensive stimulated support for the South Vietnamese government, especially with revelations of the butchering of civilians at Hue.

The South Vietnamese government took steps to care for the refugees and to bolster the ARVN by drafting 18- and 19-year-olds. But the government faced staggering problems after the Tet Offensive, particularly in caring for what official figures admitted to be some 627,000 newly homeless people. Pacification efforts had also suffered a serious blow in the withdrawal of troops from the countryside to defend the cities.

The American public perceived the Tet Offensive very differently. The early reporting of a smashing communist victory went largely uncorrected in the media. Also, many of those who shaped public opinion now came out forcefully against the war. After the Tet Offensive, U.S. policy focused not on winning the war but on seeking a way out.

References

Hammel, Eric. *Fire in the Streets: The Battle for Hue, Tet 1968.* New York: Dell, 1992.

Nolan, Keith W. *Battle for Hue: Tet 1968.* Novato, CA: Presidio, 1983.

Oberdorfer, Dan. *Tet!* New York: Doubleday, 1971.

Smith, George W. *The Siege at Hue.* Boulder, CO: Lynne Rienner, 1999.

Warr, Nicholas. *Phase Line Green: The Battle for Hue, 1968.* Annapolis, MD: Naval Institute Press, 1997.

Battle of Golan Heights

Date	October 6–22, 1973	
Location	Golan Heights on the Syrian-Israeli border	
Opponents (* winner)	*Israelis	Syrians
Commander	Major General Yitzhak Hofi	Major General Yousef Chakour
Approx. # Troops	12,000 men	60,000 men
Importance	The Israelis prevent the Syrians from possibly winning the war and now are able to threaten Damascus	

This major land and air battle during the October 1973 Arab-Israeli war known as the War of Atonement, the Yom Kippur War (since it began on the Jewish holy day of Yom Kippur), and the Ramadan War saw some of the largest tank engagements in history. The Golan Heights is located on the 45-mile border between Syria and Israel. This volcanic lava plateau of about 480 square miles is bordered by Mount Hermon on the north, the upper Jordan River Valley of the Sea of Galilee to the west, the Yarmouk (Yarmük, Yarmuk) Valley on the south, and the Ruqqad stream

An Israeli Centurion tank moving up to the battle zone in the Golan Heights during the Yom Kippur War, October 1973. Although the battle was a close-run thing, the ability of the Israelis to bring up reserve units quickly was a key factor in their ultimate victory. (Israel Government Press Office/Haris Eitan)

to the east. Israeli forces had captured the Golan from Syria in the 1967 Six-Day War, thus gaining security for its northern settlements from sporadic Syrian bombardment.

On October 6, 1973, Egypt and Syria launched a surprise attack on Israel. Egyptian president Anwar Sadat had sought the war even though he knew that Egypt had not reached military parity with Israel and might suffer another defeat. Sadat believed that Israel was satisfied with the existing territorial conditions and would make no concessions unless it came under pressure from the Great Powers to do so. One means of achieving movement on that front was the threat of a wider Middle East war.

On the Sinai front, the war began with a massive Egyptian air attack and artillery bombardment of the Israeli fortifications of the Bar Lev Line, on the eastern side of the Suez Canal. The Israelis were taken by surprise, and Egyptian forces got across the canal on October 6–7. They then repulsed an Israeli counterattack on October 8, inflicting heavy aircraft losses with antiaircraft guns and surface-to-air missiles (SAMs). The Egyptians then consolidated, with Egyptian commander General Ahmed Ismail Ali rejecting calls for renewed offensive action into the Sinai.

Appeals from the hard-pressed Syrians in the north eventually led to a renewal of the Egyptian offensive to draw off Israeli strength, especially airpower, from that front. On October 14, however, Israeli forces halted the new Egyptian offensive. They then crossed the canal, expanded a bridgehead there, and were pushing to the Gulf of Suez when a cease-fire went into effect on October 24.

Three hundred miles to the north, Syrian forces sought to recapture the Golan Heights and drive on Jerusalem. Syrian Army major general Yousef Chakour commanded a force of some 60,000 men, assisted by Iraqi, Moroccan, and Jordanian units. They were formed into two armored divisions (600 tanks) and two infantry divisions (another 300 tanks). The Syrians also had some 140 artillery batteries, including long-range 130-millimeter (mm) and 154-mm guns. Opposing them, Israeli major general Yitzhak Hofi's Northern Command numbered some 12,000 troops, 177 tanks, and 11 artillery batteries. The Syrian attack, timed to coincide with that of the Egyptians in the south, began with air strikes, but with the exception of one important outpost, Israeli forces were not taken by surprise. Israeli intelligence had accurately detected the massive Syrian buildup, and Israeli forces here were on full alert. Tank crews were in hull-down positions behind earthen barricades, with the infantry in their fighting positions.

At the very start of the war on the northern front, four helicopters delivered Syrian commandos to the back of the fortified Israeli observation post (OP) on Mount Hermon that provided an excellent view of the Golan Heights and the Damascus Plateau. The two-platoon Israeli garrison there was taken by surprise, with most of the soldiers at prayer. Within a few minutes most of the defenders were dead, and some of those who surrendered were subsequently butchered by their captors.

The main Syrian attack by four divisions occurred on three axes against two Israeli brigades in defensive positions. Israeli mobilization was excellent. Reservists were soon on the scene, but it took time to ready their equipment and tanks for action and bring them forward. Nonetheless, within a day the Israeli 7th Armored Brigade brought the northernmost thrust, by the Syrian 7th Infantry Division, to a halt, destroying most of the Syrians' tanks there in the process. The Israelis also repulsed an attack by the Syrian 3rd Tank Division, which was to pass through the 7th Infantry Division.

The two southern Syrian thrusts nearly entered the Jordan River Valley, however. At Rafid during October 6–7, the Syrian 5th Mechanized Division broke through and nearly destroyed the Israeli 188th Armored Brigade. Reinforced by the 1st Tank Division, the 5th Mechanized Division pushed to the western escarpment of the Golan, where it halted for logistical purposes as much as from the actions of Israeli reserve units now fed into the fighting. If the Syrians could pass beyond the escarpment, they could cross the Jordan River and Galilee, cutting Israel in two. The Israeli troops realized what was at stake. If they were not successful, the Syrians would spill into the valleys that contained the defenders' families.

Israeli F-4 Phantoms and A-6 Skyhawks had gone into action immediately following the first Syrian attacks, striking the clusters of Syrian tanks, armored personnel carriers, and artillery pieces. Some 1,500 tanks of the two sides were crammed into a relatively small space, and the Golan Heights became one vast graveyard of armored vehicles (especially the Syrian T-55 tanks) and abandoned guns.

Many of the Israeli jets also fell prey to SAMs and mobile antiaircraft guns, and a number of the Israeli M-48 Patton and A41 Centurions were knocked out. Only Israeli close air support, the rapid arrival of Israeli reserves who were fed immediately into the battle, and unimaginative Syrian attacks prevented the Syrians from overrunning the Israeli positions and retaking the southern Golan on the second day of fighting.

During October 8–9 the Israelis counterattacked in the south, assisted by the 7th Armored Brigade brought down from the northern Golan. On October 9 the Israeli 7th Brigade halted a Syrian thrust north of Kuneitra, and the next day the Israelis mounted a major counteroffensive north of the Kuneitra-Damascus Road, with three of their divisions pushing the Syrian 5th Mechanized and 1st Tank divisions back to and beyond the prewar Israeli-Syrian border.

Beginning on October 12, the Israelis withdrew some units south to fight on the Sinai front. Nonetheless, by October 14 the Israelis had created a salient inside Syria some 10 miles deep and 30 miles wide and only 25 miles from Damascus. The Israelis held there during October 15–19 against fierce Syrian and allied counterattacks. On October 15 the Israelis repulsed the Iraqi 3rd Armored Division and then on October 19 halted another Arab counterattack against the salient, this one spearheaded by Jordanian units. The Israelis held these positions until the ceasefire of October 24. On October 22 following failed assaults on October 8 and 21, Israeli helicopter-borne paratroopers took the Syrian OP on Mount Hermon, above the original Israeli position, while Israeli infantry retook the original Israeli OP.

The constrained area of the Golan Heights and the large forces involved made for fierce fighting and heavy losses on both sides. Israel lost nearly 800 men dead and 250 tanks, along with a number of aircraft carrying out air support to the troops on the ground; the Syrians, however, sustained perhaps 8,000 men killed, 1,150 tanks destroyed, and 118 aircraft lost. While the Israelis had secured 200 square miles of additional territory, tenacious Syrian fighting in the war brought an end to Israeli contempt for the Syrian Army. The Battle of Golan Heights also revealed the vulnerability of both tanks and aircraft to new missile weapons. In the end, the battle had again secured Israel's northern border. Today the Golan Heights remains under Israeli control.

References

Asher, Jerry, and Eric Hammel. *Duel for the Golan.* New York: William Morrow, 1987.

Barker, A. J. *Arab-Israeli Wars.* New York: Hippocrene Books, 1981.

Herzog, Chaim. *The War of Atonement: October, 1973.* Boston: Little, Brown, 1975.

Persian Gulf War and the Liberation of Kuwait

Date	January 17–March 3, 1991	
Location	Kuwait	
Opponents (* winner)	International coalition headed by the United States	Iraqis
Commander	General H. Norman Schwarzkopf	Iraqi President Saddam Hussein
Approx. # Troops	540,000	500,000?
Importance	Iraqi forces are driven from Kuwait	

On July 17, 1990, President Saddam Hussein, Iraqi dictator since 1979, threatened military action against Kuwait for its overproduction of oil quotas that had helped drive down the world price. Iraq was heavily in debt as a consequence of the Iran-Iraq War (1980–1988) and thus wanted the price of oil to be as high as possible. Hussein sought concessions on the vast sums that Iraq owed to Kuwait for loans during the war. He also wanted to secure control of Bubiyan and Warbah islands to improve Iraqi access to the Persian Gulf and to end what he claimed was Kuwaiti slant-drilling into the major Iraqi Rumaila oil field. Undergirding all this was Iraq's long-standing claim that Kuwait was an Iraqi province.

In mid-July 1990 American spy satellites detected Iraqi forces massing along the Kuwait border. U.S. policy was unclear, and Washington had tacitly supported Iraq in its war with Iran, providing intelligence information; however, for some time Washington had been concerned over Iraq's expanding nuclear industry and its development of chemical and biological weapons, which had been employed in the war against Iran as well as against Kurds within Iraq itself.

U.S. ambassador to Iraq April Glaspie delivered mixed messages on behalf of the George H. W. Bush administration that seemed to allow Hussein operational freedom in the Persian Gulf. The Iraqi dictator probably believed that any move against Kuwait would not be challenged by the United States, certainly not by war. For its part, the U.S. State Department did not believe that Hussein would actually mount a full-scale invasion. Washington expected at most only a limited incursion to force the Kuwaitis to accede to Iraq's demands to increase the cost of oil. Clearly, Washington underestimated Hussein's ambition.

On August 2, 1990, four elite Iraqi Republican Guard divisions invaded Kuwait and moved to seize key military installations, including air bases as well as airports. Another division of commandoes and special forces employed small craft and helicopters to assault Kuwait City. The invasion caught the Kuwaitis by surprise. Despite the tensions leading up to the invasion, the Kuwaiti government had not expected an invasion, and its far smaller forces were not on alert. Within two days the Iraqis had seized full control, and on August 8 Iraq formally announced the annexation of Kuwait as its 19th province.

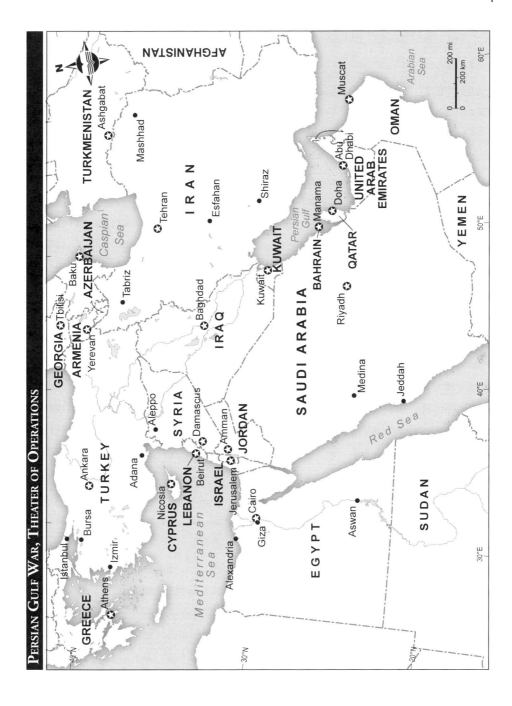

PERSIAN GULF WAR, THEATER OF OPERATIONS

President Bush had immediately convened the National Security Council, the Central Intelligence Agency (CIA), and the military leadership headed by chairman of the Joint Chiefs of Staff (JCS) General Colin Powell. U.S. Central Command (CENTCOM) commander General H. Norman Schwarzkopf was also present. Washington was concerned about Kuwait but also about the stranglehold that Iraq might now have over Kuwait's neighbor Saudi Arabia, which had the world's largest oil reserves. Bush and others of his generation saw Hussein's aggression as a challenge akin to that of Adolf Hitler and made much of the supposed contrast between dictatorship (Iraq) and democracy (Kuwait). Powell and other officers who had fought in Vietnam, however, resisted waging another unpopular war in a faraway country. Most certainly, the Pentagon overestimated Iraq's military prowess.

On August 2 the United Nations (UN) Security Council passed Resolution 660 condemning the Iraqi invasion. Its Resolution 661 of August 6 called for sanctions against Iraq. On August 8 President Bush ordered the deployment of forward forces to Saudi Arabia in Operation DESERT SHIELD. The air, ground, and naval units were sent to bolster the Saudis and to demonstrate U.S. resolve in support of diplomacy.

The buildup of forces was massive. CENTCOM directed the U.S. effort. The U.S. Army provided the bulk of the forces, including armor, infantry, and airborne units from the United States and Europe. The marines also contributed two divisions, while offshore there were two carrier battle groups with full complements of aircraft and a U.S. Marine Corps fleet force. The U.S. Air Force deployed several wings of combat aircraft as well as transports and support units.

President Bush deserved considerable credit for forging an impressive international coalition and then holding most of the Arab states in it by keeping Israel out. Allied support arrived in the form of an armored division and two armored brigades from Britain and a light armored division from France. Saudi Arabia, Syria, and Egypt also provided troops, and Czechoslovakia sent a chemical decontamination and detection unit. Altogether the force in theater numbered some 665,000 troops. Opposing them, Hussein in January 1991 deployed an Iraqi force of some 546,700 men, 4,280 tanks, 2,880 armored personnel carriers, and 3,100 artillery pieces.

When Hussein refused to yield, Operation INSTANT THUNDER began early on the morning of January 17, 1991. INSTANT THUNDER was a massive air offensive directed at targets in Baghdad and throughout Iraq. The operation commenced with Stealth bombers and fighters and cruise missiles destroying the Iraqi air defense network. Large numbers of Iraqi aircraft were destroyed on the ground, and Hussein ordered the remaining aircraft to fly to Iran. In retaliation, Hussein launched Scud missiles against targets in Saudi Arabia and Israel in an attempt to draw Israel into the war and split the coalition of Arab states against him.

Washington responded by dispatching Patriot antiaircraft missiles from Germany to Israel. Much was made at the time of the ability of the Patriots to intercept and destroy Scuds en route to target, but after the war this claim was shown to be largely false. A major objective of the air campaign was to eliminate the highly mobile Scud force, but this was not achieved. At the same time, airpower inflicted tremendous casualties on the dug-in Iraqis, and the capital of Baghdad came under heavy attack. The Fairchild A-10 "Warthog" ground-attack aircraft proved highly effective against Iraqi armor, destroying several hundred tanks during the course of the war.

With his forces now being seriously degraded by coalition airpower and determined to begin what he threatened would be "the mother of all battles," Hussein ordered his commanders to attack across the Saudi border. Only at Khafji did such a battle occur, but during January 29–31 it was beaten back by Saudi and Qatari forces and U.S. marines supported by artillery and airpower.

When Hussein then rejected President Bush's ultimatum that he immediately evacuate Kuwait or face invasion, at 4:00 a.m. on February 24 Iraqi time (February 23 in the United States) Schwarzkopf began the ground war, Operation DESERT STORM. The air campaign had been most effective in destroying targets along Hussein's defensive lines. Coalition forces now executed simultaneous drives along the coast and broke the western edge of the Iraqi flank, rolling up Hussein's troops into a pocket along the Euphrates River and the Red Sea. As the marines moved up along the coast toward Kuwait City, they were hit in the flank by Iraqi armor. In the largest tank battle in U.S. Marine Corps history, the marines, supported by airpower, easily defeated this force in a battle that was fought in a surrealist day-into-night atmosphere caused by the smoke of burning oil wells set afire by the retreating Iraqis.

As the marines prepared to enter Kuwait City preceded by a light Arab force, Iraqi forces laden with booty fled north in whatever they could steal. Thousands of vehicles and personnel were caught in the open on the highway and were pummeled by airpower and artillery along what became known as the "Highway of Death." Schwarzkopf was upset, however, by the slow pace of VII Corps (140,000 men in five divisions, 32,000 wheeled vehicles, and 6,600 tracked vehicles), the inner left-flank hook. Its commander, General Frederick Franks Jr., pled lack of adequate intelligence information on Iraqi dispositions and the need to maintain supply lines. Instead of pushing forward as quickly as possible as Schwarzkopf had urged, Franks insisted on hitting the Iraqis with the maximum strength of his armor divisions in position.

When the fist struck, it was with devastating effect. In the major opening engagement, VII Corps came up against an Iraqi rear guard of 300 tanks covering the withdrawal north toward Basra of four Republican Guard divisions. The Soviet-supplied Iraqi T-72 tank guns were inaccurate at more than .9 mile (1,500 meters); the U.S. M-1 Abrams, however, could bring the Iraqi tanks under fire at 1.8 miles (3,000 meters). The Iraqi force was wiped out at a cost of 1 American dead. As VII Corps closed to the sea, Lieutenant General Gay E. Luck's XVIII Airborne Corps (115,000 men, 21,000 wheeled vehicles, and 4,300 tracked vehicles) to its left, which had a much larger distance to travel, raced to reach the fleeing Republican Guard divisions before they could escape the trap to Baghdad. Hostilities were declared at an end at 8:01 a.m. on February 28 local time.

In the 100-hour ground war, coalition forces had liberated Kuwait and had killed, wounded, or taken prisoner tens of thousands of Iraqis. The war was then stopped. President Bush wanted to keep Iraq intact against a resurgent Iran, and General Powell had no taste for the further slaughter of Iraqis, especially given how images of the Highway of Death might have played on television screens around the world. In arguing against continuation of the war against a beaten opponent, Powell used the words "un-American" and "unchivalrous." Iraq thus escaped with its best Republican Guard troops largely intact.

Schwarzkopf, who at the time declared himself satisfied with the decision, entered a cease-fire agreement that allowed the beaten Iraqis to fly their armed helicopters. This enabled the Iraqi government to crush anti-Hussein resistance in the country. The cease-fire of March 3 at Safwan airfield also established a no-fly zone for Iraqi fixed-wing aircraft north of the 36th Parallel to protect the Kurds. No such prohibition protected the Shiite Muslims in southern Iraq.

The Persian Gulf War, including the air portion, had lasted 43 days and was among the most lopsided conflicts in history. Iraq lost 3,700 tanks, more than 1,000 other armored vehicles, and 3,000 artillery pieces. The coalition lost 4 tanks, 9 other combat vehicles, and 1 artillery piece. The coalition sustained 500 casualties (150 dead), many of these from accidents and friendly fire. Iraqi casualties totaled between 25,000 and 100,000 dead, with the best estimates being around 60,000. The coalition also took 80,000 Iraqis prisoner. Perhaps an equal number simply deserted. The war was a remarkable renaissance of American forces from the 1970s, yet predictions that Hussein would soon be overthrown proved unfounded, which paved the way for a new and more costly conflict, the Iraq War, that began in 2003.

References

Gordon, Michael R., and Bernard E. Trainor. *The Generals' War.* Boston: Little, Brown, 1995.

Scales, Robert H., Jr. *Certain Victory: The U.S. Army in the Gulf War.* Washington, DC: Brassey's, 1997.

Schwarzkopf, H. Norman. *It Doesn't Take a Hero.* New York: Bantam Books, 1992.

Iraq War

Date	March 19–May 1, 2003	
Location	Baghdad, Iraq	
Opponents (* winner)	*Coalition of Americans, British, Australians	Iraqis
Commander	U.S. General Tommy Franks	Iraqi President Saddam Hussein
Approx. # Troops	300,000	375,000
Importance	President Saddam Hussein is driven from power, but the United States and its coalition partners find themselves fighting a long, drawn-out insurgency	

Following the cease-fire of March 3, 1991, that ended the Persian Gulf War (Operation DESERT STORM), Iraqi dictator Saddam Hussein reestablished his authority, putting down both the Shia in the south and the Kurds in the north. The United States had encouraged both to rebel against the central government during the war, and as many as 50,000 Shia may have perished in the subsequent repression. Hussein also began a program of draining the swamps populated by the southern Marsh Arabs to better control that restive group.

Hussein further defied United Nations (UN) inspection teams by failing to account for and destroy all of his biological and chemical weapons, the so-called weapons of mass destruction (WMDs). Stymied, the UN withdrew its inspectors. The United States and Britain continued to enforce the no-fly zone set by the cease-fire north of the 36th Parallel and then a southern no-fly zone set in 1992 at the 32nd Parallel and in 1993 extended to the 33rd Parallel, from which Iraqi fixed-wing aircraft were prohibited in order to protect the Kurds and the Shia. U.S. and British aircraft struck Iraqi ground radars and antiaircraft positions that on occasion fired on their aircraft.

Increasingly, the administration of U.S. president George W. Bush, elected in November 2000, adopted a tough attitude toward Iraq. This followed the Al Qaeda terrorist attacks of September 11, 2001, against the World Trade Center in New York and the Pentagon in Washington, D.C., that brought the deaths of some 3,000 civilians. After the Taliban government of Afghanistan refused Washington's demands to hand over members of Al Qaeda and especially its leader, Osama bin Laden, U.S. forces invaded Afghanistan. They and opposition Northern Alliance (Afghan) forces easily overthrew the Taliban.

In a speech to the U.S. Congress, President Bush then asserted his intention to root out international terrorism and to confront those states that supported it. He noted in particular an "Axis of Evil" of Iraq, Iran, and the Democratic People's Republic of Korea (DPRK, North Korea). Under U.S. and British pressure, the UN Security Council unanimously passed Resolution 1141 calling on Iraq to reveal

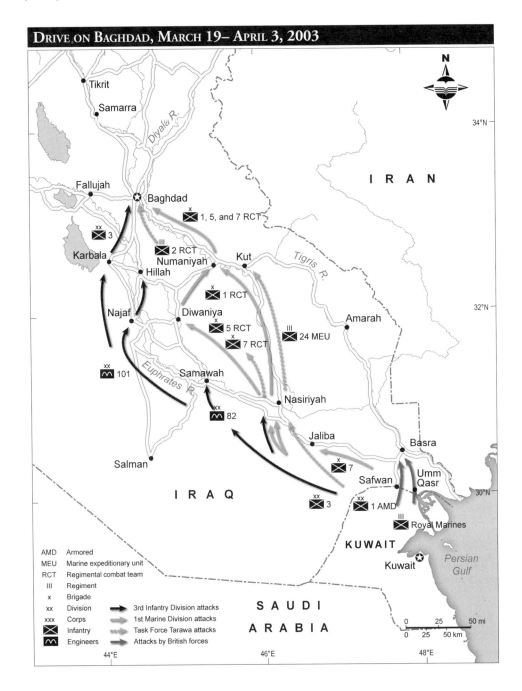

DRIVE ON BAGHDAD, MARCH 19– APRIL 3, 2003

information regarding WMDs and for UN inspectors to report progress to the Security Council. The resolution also threatened force unless Iraq fully complied.

Iraq claimed that it had nothing to hide—no WMDs—but the UN inspections went slowly, and a frustrated President Bush, supported by British prime minister Tony Blair, demanded military action against Iraq. A coalition of France, Germany, and Russia blocked U.S. and British efforts to secure such a resolution in the UN, however. Bush and Blair then decided to go it alone. President Bush sought and won a congressional mandate authorizing the use of force if the president deemed it necessary.

Bush defended the war as necessary to locate and destroy WMDs and to end a claimed link between the Iraqi government and Al Qaeda. Misgivings voiced by lower-level experts at the State Department and the Central Intelligence Agency (CIA) never reached the president or were brushed aside. Certainly there was a rush to war from his principal advisers, including Vice President Dick Cheney and Secretary of Defense Donald Rumsfeld, who confidently saw a democratic Iraq as an irresistible force for change in the Middle East. No serious consideration seems to have been given to the risks involved, particularly the bitter rivalries among the religious and ethnic factions within Iraq. Both Cheney and Rumsfeld asserted that U.S. forces would be welcomed as liberators.

An allied buildup had been under way for some time in Kuwait. More than 300,000 men and women were deployed in theater under coalition commander U.S. Army general Tommy Franks, head of U.S. Central Command (CENTCOM). Unlike DESERT STORM, however, there was no broad grouping of powers arrayed with the United States, and Saudi Arabia refused use of its bases for air strikes against Iraq. Some of the Persian Gulf states, notably Kuwait and Qatar, did cooperate, but coalition forces were drawn chiefly from the United States, Britain, and Australia.

Washington experienced a major setback when the Turkish parliament, despite promises of up to $30 billion in financial assistance, refused to allow U.S. forces to use Turkish territory to open up a northern front, a key component of the U.S. military plan. Three dozen ships laden with equipment for the U.S. 4th Infantry Division (30,000 troops) lay off Turkish ports but never were able to unload. Only after the war began were they redirected through the Suez Canal to Kuwait. In consequence, the 4th Infantry Division became part of the follow-on force. A disinformation campaign to the effect that the Turkish military would pressure Ankara to allow U.S. forces to operate from Turkey apparently proved successful, as Hussein retained two regular Iraqi divisions north of Baghdad. These troops took no part in combating the coalition offensive.

A preinvasion air campaign began on the night of March 19, 2003, just hours after the expiration of President Bush's ultimatum to Hussein, with a cruise missile strike against a purported meeting of the Iraqi leadership in Baghdad. The strike failed to decapitate the Iraqi government as intended, however. On succeeding nights, Baghdad was repeatedly hit from the air with cruise missile attacks and with air strikes by B-1, B-2, and B-52 bombers against key headquarters and command and control targets. This shock-and-awe air campaign employed 70 percent smart (guided) aerial weapons and 30 percent dumb (unguided) munitions, as opposed to only 10 percent smart weapons during the 1991 Persian Gulf War. Also in contrast to 1991, a good many of the air strikes occurred away from the capital.

Even before March 19, coalition U.S., British, and Australian special forces had deployed into Iraq for both reconnaissance and strike roles. One of their missions was to destroy Iraqi watch posts on the southern border. Special forces also secured key bridge and crossing points across the Tigris and Euphrates rivers.

On March 20 the coalition invasion ground force of 100,000 troops moved into southern Iraq from Kuwait in what became known as Operation IRAQI FREEDOM. The few Iraqi missiles launched at coalition staging areas in particular and Kuwait City in general were almost all downed by improved Patriot antimissile missiles. The coalition ground forces moved north on three axes: the U.S. Army V Corps to the west, the U.S. Marine Corps 1st Expeditionary Force in the center, and British forces to the east. The Iraqi capital of Baghdad, a city of 5 million people, lay 300 miles to the north.

In the west the offensive was led by Black Hawk and Apache helicopters, with the 7th Armored Cavalry Regiment the leading ground element followed by the 3rd Infantry Division and follow-on units of V Corps. The western offensive made the most rapid progress, largely because it swung west and moved through sparsely populated areas. In the center part of the front, the 1st Marine Expeditionary Force skirted to the west of the Euphrates River, through the city of Nasiriyah, and then on to Najaf and Karbala. On the eastern part of the front the British had the task of securing the port of Umm Qasr and Iraq's second-largest city, Basra, with its largely Shia population of 500,000. It was not clear how the Shia would react following their abandonment in 1991. After clearing the channel for mines, a British ship docked at Umm Qasr with the relief supplies.

Airpower played a key role in the coalition advance. In northern Iraq, aircraft ferried troops and supplies into the Kurdish-controlled zone, opening a front there against the Iraqi Army but also against Ansar al-Islam, a militant Islamic group with a base camp and training facilities at Kalak on the Iranian border. Coalition airpower dominated the skies, with Iraqi aircraft and helicopters rarely even getting off the ground. Helicopter gunships and the A-10 Thunderbolt "Warthog" tank-buster proved highly effective. Another important factor was the ability of coalition troops to fight at night, whereas the Iraqis could not.

The marines were successful in seizing the oil fields north of Basra—some 60 percent of the nation's total production—and the key refineries. A few wellheads were set afire and some equipment was damaged, but overall damage was slight.

Meanwhile, the British were at Basra. Wishing to spare the civilian population and hoping for an internal uprising, they did not move into the city proper until the night of April 2. They imposed a loose blockade and, to demoralize the defenders, carried out a series of raids into the city to destroy symbols of the regime, such as Baath Party headquarters and images of Hussein. At the same time they distributed relief supplies to win over the civilian population.

As U.S. Special Forces secured airfields in western Iraq, on the night of March 26 1,000 members of the 173rd Airborne Brigade dropped into Kurdish-held terri-

Helicopters played a key role in the Persial Gulf and Iraq wars. The AH-64A Apache is a state-of-the-art attack helicopter capable of providing close air support and defeating a wide range of targets, often at night and in adverse weather. (Department of Defense)

tory in northern Iraq to operate in conjunction with lightly armed Kurdish forces, open a northern front, and threaten the key oil-production center of Mosul. Baath Party terror cells carried out attacks on civilians, including in Basra, while the so-called Saddam Fedayeen (or "technicals," irregulars often wearing civilian clothes) carried out attacks employing civilian vehicles mounting machine guns and rocket-propelled grenades against supply convoys plying the lines of communication north from Kuwait. Near Najaf, Iraqi missiles destroyed two M1 Abrams tanks, the first time this had been accomplished, but the 7th Cavalry Regiment secured bridges south of the town, completing its encirclement.

A week into the war, the coalition advance north stalled in an operational pause because of a *shamal* (strong sandstorm) on March 26; fierce U.S. Army and Marine Corps firefights for Nasiriyah, Najaf, and other places; and the need to protect lengthy logistical lines now under increasing Iraq attack. Friendly fire incidents remained a nagging problem. There were more casualties from these (including two aircraft, one British and one U.S., shot down by Patriot missiles and a Patriot battery engaged by a U.S. aircraft) than during the Persian Gulf War.

The Iraqi leadership now repositioned the six elite Republican Guard divisions around the city of Baghdad. Reportedly Hussein had drawn a so-called Red Line, beyond which the coalition would not be allowed to cross and within which he would employ WMDs. This seemed increasingly possible with coalition discoveries of caches of gas masks and atropine and when some Iraqi Republican Guard troops with gas masks were taken prisoner. As the Baghdad and Medina Republican Guard divisions moved to take up new positions south of Baghdad, they came under heavy coalition air attack, seriously degrading their fighting ability.

The coalition advance quickened again during April 1–2. U.S. troops were within 50 miles of Baghdad, and U.S. secretary of state Colin Powell (who had been chairman of the Joint Chiefs of Staff [JCS] during the Persian Gulf War) traveled to Ankara and secured Turkish government approval for coalition equipment to be moved through Turkey to troops on the Northern Front. On April 3 U.S. forces reached the outskirts of Baghdad and during the next two days secured Saddam International Airport, some 12 miles from the city center. Because of the speed of the advance, the airport was taken with minimal damage to its facilities. When the surrounding territory was secured, the airport became a major coalition staging area. The general Iraqi population seemed to sense the shift of momentum and an imminent coalition victory. Advancing troops reported receiving friendly receptions from civilians and increasing surrenders of Iraqi troops.

By April 5 the 3rd Infantry Division was closing on Baghdad from the southwest, the marines were closing from the southeast, and the 101st Airborne Division was repositioning to move in from the north. Baghdad in effect came under a loose blockade in which civilians were allowed to depart, and sanctuaries were created for civilians and surrendering Iraqi forces. On that day also, the 2nd Brigade of the 3rd Infantry Division pushed through downtown Baghdad in a three-hour-long operation, inflicting an estimated 1,000 Iraqi casualties. This was a powerful psychological blow to Hussein's regime, which had claimed that U.S. forces were nowhere near the city and that the regime still controlled the international airport. The operation showed that coalition forces could move at will and led to an exodus of Baath Party officials and Iraqi Army personnel, who now joined ordinary citizens trying to escape.

The U.S. raid was repeated during April 6–7. In a fierce firefight on April 6, U.S. forces killed an estimated 2,000–3,000 Iraqi soldiers for only 1 killed of their own. U.S. forces also toppled a large statue of Hussein and occupied one of his presidential palaces. Also on April 6 the first C-130 aircraft landed at the renamed Baghdad International Airport, and the coalition announced that it was providing 24-hour air cover over Baghdad to protect U.S. forces there.

On April 7 three 3rd Infantry Division battalions remained in the city, while the next day U.S. Marine Corps elements moved into southeastern Baghdad, securing a military airfield. With the 101st Airborne coming in from the west and then fanning out to the north and the 3rd Infantry Division moving in from the southeast, the ring around the capital was closed. By that day there was at least a brigade in the city.

On April 9 resistance in Baghdad collapsed as civilians, assisted by U.S. marines, toppled another large statute of Hussein. Sporadic fighting continued in parts of the city, however, as diehard Baath loyalists sniped at U.S. troops, but Iraqi government central command and control had ended.

The next day, April 10, a small number of Kurdish fighters, U.S. Special Forces, and 173rd Airborne Brigade troops liberated Kirkuk. They quickly took control of the northern oil fields from the Kurds to prevent any possibility of Turkish intervention. The next day Iraq's third-largest city, Mosul, fell when Iraq's V Corps commander surrendered some 30,000 men. Apart from some sporadic shooting in Baghdad and massive looting there and in other cities, the one remaining center of resistance was Hussein's ancestral home of Tikrit.

On April 12 the 101st Airborne relieved the marines and the 3rd Infantry Division in Baghdad, allowing them to deploy northwest to Tikrit. The battle for Tikrit failed to materialize. Hussein's stronghold collapsed, and on April 14 coalition forces entered the city. That same day the Pentagon announced that major military operations in Iraq were at an end; all that remained was mopping up. President Bush officially proclaimed victory on May 1.

The United States had suffered 138 deaths: 114 from combat and 24 from other causes. The British sustained 42 dead, 19 of them from accidents. Estimates of Iraqi casualties vary widely, from at least 2,320 Iraqi military dead and 7,000 taken prisoner (there were many more desertions) as well as civilian dead of from 1,500 to 10,000 or more.

As it turned out, resistance to the occupation continued in the form of guerrilla warfare on the part of Iraqis, abetted by foreign fighters (fedayeen) who viewed this as a holy war of Islam against the West. U.S. and coalition forces remained in occupation of Iraq and continued to suffer casualties from this insurgency into at 2010, indeed far more losses than they had sustained up to May 1. The long-term consequences of the war remain quite unclear.

References

Cordesman, Anthony H. *The Iraq War: Strategy, Tactics, and Military Lessons.* Washington, DC: Center for Strategic and International Studies, 2003.

Franks, Tommy. *American Soldier: General Tommy Franks.* New York: HarperCollins, 2004.

Keegan, John. *The Iraq War.* New York: Knopf, 2004.

Murray, Williamson, and Robert H. Scales Jr. *The Iraq War: A Military History.* Cambridge: Belknap Press of Harvard University Press, 2003.

Bibliography

Adair, Paul. *Hitler's Greatest Defeat: The Collapse of Army Group Center.* London: Brockhampton, 1998.

Adcock, Frank Ezra. *The Roman Art of War under the Republic.* 1940; reprint, New York: Barnes and Noble, 1960.

Akram, A. I. *The Sword of Allah, Khalid bin al-Waleed: His Life and Campaigns.* Rawalpindi, Pakistan: National Publishing House, 1970.

Alexander, Joseph H. *Closing In: Marines in the Seizure of Iwo Jima.* Washington, DC: History and Museums Division, Headquarters, U.S. Marine Corps, 1994.

———. *Utmost Savagery: The Three Days of Tarawa.* Annapolis, MD: Naval Institute Press, 1995.

Allen, Gardner W. *A Naval History of the American Revolution,* Vol. 1. Cambridge, MA: Houghton Mifflin, 1913.

Allsen, Thomas. *Mongol Imperialism.* Berkeley: University of California Press, 1987.

Anderson, David. *The Spanish Armada.* New York: Hempstead, 1988.

Anderson, Fred. *Crucible of War: The Seven Years' War and the Fate of Empire in British North America, 1754–1763.* New York: Knopf, 2000.

Anderson, M. S. *Peter the Great.* New York: Longman, 1996.

Anderson, R. C. *Naval Wars in the Levant, 1559–1853.* Liverpool: University Press of Liverpool, 1952.

Anna, Timothy E. *The Fall of the Royal Government in Peru.* Lincoln: University of Nebraska Press, 1979.

Appleman, Roy E. *East of Chosin: Entrapment and Breakout in Korea.* College Station: Texas A&M University Press, 1987.

———. *South to the Nakong, North to the Yalu.* Washington, DC: Office of the Chief of Military History, 1961.

Archer, C., ed. *The Wars of Independence in Spanish America.* Wilmington, DE: Scholarly Resources, 2000.

Armstrong, Karen. *Jerusalem: One City, Three Faiths.* New York: Knopf, 1996.

Arnold, James R. *Grant Wins the War: Decision at Vicksburg.* New York: Wiley, 1997.

———. *Marengo and Hohenlinden: Napoleon's Rise to Power.* Lexington, VA: James R. Arnold, 1999.

Arrian [Lucius Flavius Arrianus]. *The Campaigns of Alexander.* Translated by Aubrey de Selincourt. East Rutherford, NJ: Penguin, 1976.

Asbridge, Thomas. *The First Crusade: A New History.* New York: Oxford University Press, 2005.

Asher, Jerry, and Eric Hammel. *Duel for the Golan.* New York: William Morrow, 1987.

Ashley, James R. *Macedonian Empire: The Era of Warfare under Philip II and Alexander the Great, 359–323 B.C.* Jefferson City, NC: McFarland, 1998.

Ashley, Maurice. *The Battle of Naseby and the Fall of King Charles I.* Stroud, Gloucestershire, UK: Alan Sutton, 1992.

———. *Charles II: The Man and the Statesman.* New York: Praeger, 1971.

Asprey, Robert B. *The German High Command at War: Hindenburg and Ludendorff Conduct World War I.* New York: William Morrow, 1991.

Bābur. *The Babur-nama in English: Memoirs of Babur.* Translated by Annette Susannah Beveridge. London: Luxac, 1921.

Balász, György, and Károly Szelényi. *The Magyars: The Birth of a European Nation.* Budapest: Corvina, 1989.

Baldwin, Marshall W., ed. *A History of the Crusades,* Vol. 1, *The First Hundred Years,* edited by Kenneth M. Setton. Madison: University of Wisconsin Press, 1969.

Ballard, Michael B. *Pemberton: A Biography.* Jackson: University Press of Mississippi, 1991.

Balyuzi, H. M. *Muhammed and the Course of Islam.* Oxford: G. Ronald, 1976.

Barber, Richard. *Edward Prince of Wales and Aquitaine.* London: Allen Lane, 1978.

Barker, A. J. *Arab-Israeli Wars.* New York: Hippocrene Books, 1981.

———. *The Bastard War: The Mesopotamian Campaign of 1914–1918.* New York: Dial, 1967.

———. *Townshend of Kut: A Biography of Major-General Sir Charles Townshend K.C.B., D.S.O.* London: Cassell, 1967.

———. *The War against Russia, 1854–1856.* New York: Holt, Rinehart and Winston, 1970.

Barker, John. *Justinian and the Later Roman Empire.* Madison: University of Wisconsin Press, 1966.

Barker, Thomas M. *Double Eagle and Crescent: Vienna's Second Turkish Siege and Its Historical Setting.* Albany: State University of New York Press, 1967.

Barnes, Timothy D. *Constantine and Eusebius.* Cambridge: Harvard University Press, 1981.

Barnett, Correlli. *The Swordbearers: Supreme Command in the First World War.* Bloomington: Indiana University Press, 1963.

Barrow, G. W. S. *Robert Bruce and the Community of the Realm of Scotland.* Berkeley: University of California Press, 1965.

Barthorp, Michael. *Heroes of the Crimea: The Battles of Balaclava and Inkerman.* London: Blandford, 1992.

———. *War on the Nile: Britain, Egypt, and the Sudan, 1882–1898.* Poole, UK: Blandford, 1984.

Bauer, Jack. *The Mexican War, 1846–1848.* New York: Macmillan, 1974.

Baumgartner, Richard. "Relentless Mechanized Assault." *Military History* 3(4) (February 1987): 34–41.

Baxter, James Phinney. *The Introduction of the Ironclad Warship.* New York: Archon Books, 1968.

Beales, Derek. *The Risorgimento and the Unification of Italy.* New York: Barnes and Noble, 1971.

Bearss, Edwin C. *The Vicksburg Campaign.* 3 vols. Dayton, OH: Morningside, 1995.

Beeching, Jack. *The Galleys at Lepanto.* New York: Scribner, 1983.

Beevor, Antony. *The Fall of Berlin, 1945.* New York: Viking, 2002.

———. *Stalingrad: The Fateful Siege, 1942 1943.* New York: Viking, 1998.

Bennett, Martyn. *The Civil Wars in Britain and Ireland, 1638–1651.* London: Blackwell, 1997.

Benson, Douglas. *Ancient Egypt's Warfare.* Ashland, OH: Book Masters, 1995.

Bergander, Gotz. *Dresden im Luftkrieg.* Cologne: Bohlan Verlag, 1977.

Bertaud, Jean Paul. *Valmy: La Démocratie en Armes.* Paris: Julliard, 1970.

Billows, Richard A. *Antigonos the One-Eyed and the Creation of the Hellenistic State.* Berkeley: University of California Press, 1990.

Black, Jeremy. *Culloden and the '45.* New York: St. Martin's, 1990.

———. *War for America: The Fight for Independence, 1775–1783.* Stroud, Gloucestershire, UK: Alan Sutton, 1991.

Blair, Clay. *The Forgotten War: America in Korea, 1950–1953.* New York: Times Books, 1987.

———. *Ridgway's Paratroopers: The American Airborne in World War II.* Garden City, NY: Dial, 1985.

Blond, Georges. *The Marne.* Translated by H. Eaton Hart. 1966; reprint, London: Prion Books, 2002.

Blumberg, Arnold. *A Carefully Planned Accident: The Italian War of 1859.* Selinsgrove, PA: Susquehanna University Press, 1990.

Blumenson, Martin. *Anzio: The Gamble That Failed.* New York: Cooper Square, 2001.

———. *General Lucas at Anzio.* Washington, DC: U.S. Army Center of Military History, 1990.

Bodin, Lynn E. *The Boxer Rebellion.* London: Osprey, 1996.

Boyle, J. H. *China and Japan at War, 1937–1945: The Politics of Collaboration.* Stanford, CA: Stanford University Press, 1972.

Bradbury, Jim. *The Battle of Hastings.* Stroud, Gloucestershire, UK: Sutton, 1998.

———. *Philip Augustus, King of France, 1180–1223.* London: Longman, 1998.

Braddon, Russel. *The Siege.* New York: Viking, 1970.

Bradford, Alfred S., ed. *Philip II of Macedon.* Westport, CT: Praeger, 1992.

Bradford, Ernie. *The Cruel Siege: Malta, 1565.* London: Wordsworth Editions, 1999.

———. *Thermopylae: Battle for the West.* New York: McGraw-Hill, 1980.

Bradley, James. *Flags of Our Fathers.* New York: Bantam, 2000.

Braudel, Fernand. *The Mediterranean and the Mediterranean World in the Age of Philip II.* 2 vols. New York: Harper and Row, 1972.

Bridge, Anthony. *Suleiman the Magnificent: Scourge of Heaven.* New York: Dorset, 1987.

Brockman, Eric. *The Two Sieges of Rhodes: The Knights of St. John at War, 1480–1522.* New York: Barnes and Noble, 1995.

Browning, Robert. *Byzantine Empire.* New York: Scribner, 1980.

Bruce-Jones, Mark. *Clive of India.* New York: St. Martin's, 1975.

Brusilov, A. A. *A Soldier's Note-Book.* 1930; reprint, Westport, CT: Greenwood, 1971.

Bryant, Anthony. *Sekigahara, 1600.* London: Osprey, 1995.

Buckley, John. *The Theban Hegemony.* Cambridge: Harvard University Press, 1980.

Burn, A. R. *Persia and the Greeks: The Defence of the West, c. 546–478 BC.* Stanford, CA: Stanford University Press, 1984.

Burne, Alfred H. *The Crécy War.* 1955; reprint, Westport, CT: Greenwood, 1976.

Burns, Thomas S. *Barbarians within the Gates of Rome.* Bloomington: Indiana University Press, 1994.

Busch, Noel F. *The Emperor's Sword: Japan vs. Russia in the Battle of Tsushima.* New York: Funk and Wagnalls, 1969.

Buttinger, Joseph. *The Smaller Dragon: A Political History of Vietnam.* London: Atlantic, 1958.

Caesar, Gaius Julius. *Seven Commentaries on the Gallic War.* New York: Oxford University Press, 1996.

———. *War Commentaries of Caesar.* Translated by Rex Warner. New York: New American Library, 1960.

Cameron, Averil, and Stuart G. Hall. *Eusebius: Life of Constantine.* Oxford, UK: Clarendon, 1999.

Campbell, N. John M. *Jutland: An Analysis of the Fighting.* London: Conway Maritime, 1998.

Caracciolo, Mario. *L'Italia e i suoi Alleati nella Grande Guerra. Con Nuovi Documenti.* Milan: Mondadori, 1932.

Carrasco, David. *Montezuma's Mexico.* Niwot: University of Colorado Press, 1992.

Carter, John M. *The Battle of Actium: The Rise and Triumph of Augustus Caesar.* London: Hamilton, 1970.

Carver, Michael. *El Alamein.* London: Batsford, 1962.

Cary, M. *The History of the Greek World: From 323 to 146 B.C.* London: Methuen, 1932.

Casali, Luigi, and M. Galandra. *La battaglia di Pavia: 24 Febbraio 1525.* Pavia: Luculano, 1984.

Cassar, George. *Beyond Courage: The Canadians at the Second Battle of Ypres.* Ottawa: Oberon, 1985.

Caulaincourt, Armand de. *With Napoleon in Russia: Memoirs of General de Caulaincourt, Duke of Vicenza.* New York: William Morrow, 1935.

Caven, Brian. *The Punic Wars.* New York: Barnes and Noble, 1980.

Chandler, David G. *The Campaigns of Napoleon.* New York: Macmillan, 1966.

———. *Jena 1806: Napoleon Destroys Prussia.* London: Osprey, 1993.

———. *Marlborough as Military Commander.* London: Batsford, 1973.

Chapelle, Howard I. *The History of the American Sailing Navy: The Ships and Their Development.* New York: Norton, 1949.

Churchill, Winston S. *Marlborough: His Life and Times,* Vol. 2. London: Harrap, 1934.

———. *The Second World War,* Vols. 2 and 4. Boston: Houghton Mifflin, 1949, 1950.

———. *The World Crisis,* Vol 2. New York: Scribner, 1923.

Clark, G. N. *The Seventeenth Century.* Oxford, UK: Clarendon, 1950.

Cleaves, Freeman. *Old Tippecanoe: William Henry Harrison and His Time.* New York: Scribner, 1939.

Clot, Andre. *Suleiman the Magnificent.* London: Saqi Books, 1992.

Clowes, William Laird. *The Royal Navy: A History from the Earliest Times to 1900.* 4 vols. London: Sampson Low, Marston, 1897–1900.

Coddington, Edwin B. *The Gettysburg Campaign: A Study in Command.* New York: Scribner, 1984.

Coffey, Thomas M. *Iron Eagle: The Turbulent Life of General Curtis LeMay.* New York: Crown Publishers, 1986.

Cole, Hugh M. *The United States Army in World War II: The European Theater of Operations; The Ardennes: Battle of the Bulge.* Washington, DC: U.S. Government Printing Office, 1965.

Coleman, J. D. *Pleiku: The Dawn of Helicopter Warfare in Vietnam.* New York: St. Martin's, 1988.

Connaughton, Richard Michael. *The War of the Rising Sun and the Tumbling Bear: A Military History of the Russo-Japanese War.* London: Routledge, 1991.

Connelly, Owen. *Blundering to Glory: Napoleon's Military Campaigns.* Rev. ed. Wilmington, DE: Scholarly Resources, 1999.

Conroy, Robert. *The Battle of Manila Bay: The Spanish-American War in the Philippines.* New York: Macmillan, 1968.

Contamine, Philippe. *War in the Middle Ages.* Translated by Michael Jones. New York: Basil Blackwell, 1984.

Cook, J. M. *The Persian Empire.* New York: Schocken Books, 1983.

Cook, M. A., ed. *A History of the Ottoman Empire to 1730.* New York: Cambridge University Press, 1976.

Cook, Tim. *No Place to Run: The Canadian Corps and Gas Warfare in the First World War.* Vancouver: University of British Columbia Press, 1999.

Cooper, Bryan. *The Ironclads of Cambrai: The First Great Tank Battle.* London: Cassell, 2002.

Corbett, Julian S., and Henry Newbolt. *Naval Operations: History of the Great War, Based on Official Documents,* Vol. 3. London: Longman, 1923.

Cordesman, Anthony H. *The Iraq War: Strategy, Tactics, and Military Lessons.* Washington, DC: Center for Strategic and International Studies, 2003.

Cowley, Robert. "The Somme: The Last 140 Days." *MHQ: Quarterly Journal of Military History* 7(4) (Summer 1995): 74–87.

Cracroft, James E., ed. *Peter the Great Transforms Russia,* Lexington, MA: D. C. Heath, 1991.

Craig, Gordon A. *The Battle of Königgrätz: Prussia's Victory over Austria, 1866.* Westport, CT: Greenwood, 1975.

Craig, William. *Enemy at the Gates: The Battle for Stalingrad.* New York: Dutton, 1973.

Crane, Conrad C. *Bombs, Cities, and Civilians: American Airpower Strategy in World War II.* Lawrence: University Press of Kansas, 1993.

Craven, Brian. *The Punic Wars.* New York: Barnes and Noble, 1992.

Creasy, Edward S. *The Fifteen Decisive Battles of the World: From Marathon to Waterloo.* New York: Heritage, 1969.

Crook, Malcom. *Toulon in War and Revolution: From the Ancient Regime to the Restoration, 1750–1820.* Manchester, UK: Manchester University Press, 1991.

Cutler, Thomas J. *The Battle of Leyte Gulf, 23–26 October 1944.* New York: HarperCollins, 1994.

Dancocks, Daniel G. *Welcome to Flanders Fields, the First Canadian Battle of the Great War: Ypres, 1915.* Toronto: McClelland and Stewart, 1988.

Darrieus, Henri, and Jean Quéguiner. *Historique de la Marine française (1815–1918).* Saint-Malo, France: Éditions l'Ancre de la Marine, 1997.

David, Daniel. *The 1914 Campaign.* New York: Military Press, 1987.

Davidson, Philip B. *Vietnam at War: The History, 1946–1975.* New York: Oxford University Press, 1988.

Davies, Norman. *White Eagle, Red Star: The Polish Soviet War, 1919 1920.* New York. St. Martin's, 1972.

Davis, Burke. *The Campaign That Won America: The Story of Yorktown.* New York: Dial, 1970.

Davis, Paul K. *100 Decisive Battles: From Ancient Times to the Present.* Santa Barbara, CA: ABC-CLIO, 1999.

De Beer, Gavin. *Hannibal: The Struggle for Power in the Mediterranean.* London: Thames and Hudson, 1969.

DeKay, James Tertius. *Monitor.* New York: Walker, 1997.

Delbruck, Hans. *Warfare in Antiquity.* Translated by Walter J. Renfore Jr. Lincoln: University of Nebraska Press, 1990.

D'Este, Carlo. *Fatal Decision: Anzio and the Battle for Rome.* New York: HarperCollins, 1991.

Déveria, G. *Histoire des Relations de la Chine avec L'Annam-Vietnam du XVIe au XIXe Siècle.* Paris: Ernest Leroux, 1880.

Diaz del Castillo, Bernal. *The Discovery and Conquest of Mexico, 1517–1521.* Translated by A. P. Maudslay. New York: Harper, 1928.

Dillon, Richard. *We Have Met the Enemy: Oliver Hazard Perry, Wilderness Commodore.* New York: McGraw-Hill, 1978.

Divine, David. *The Nine Days of Dunkirk.* New York: Norton, 1959.

Dodge, Theodore Ayrault. *Gustavus Adolphus.* London: Greenhill Books, 1992.

———. *Hannibal: A History of the Art of War among the Carthaginians and the Romans Down to the Battle of Pydna, 168 B.C.* Mechanicsburg, PA: Stackpole Books, 1994.

Doenitz, Karl. *Memoirs: Ten Years and Twenty Days.* Translated by R. H. Stevens in collaboration with David Woodward. Annapolis, MD: Naval Institute Press, 1990.

Donner, Fred. *The Early Islamic Conquests.* Princeton, NJ: Princeton University Press, 1981.

Dorn, Frank. *The Sino-Japanese War, 1937–41: From Marco Polo Bridge to Pearl Harbor.* New York: Macmillan, 1974.

Dowling, Timothy. *The Brusilov Offensive.* Bloomington: Indiana University Press, 2008.

Dreyer, Edward L. *China at War, 1901–1949.* New York: Longman, 1995.

Duby, Georges. *The Legend of Bouvines.* Berkeley: University of California Press, 1990.

Duffy, Christopher. *Austerlitz.* London: Archon, 1977.

———. *Borodino: Napoleon against Russia, 1812.* New York: Scribner, 1973.

———. *The Military Experience in the Age of Reason.* New York: Atheneum, 1988.

———. *The Military Life of Frederick the Great.* New York: Atheneum, 1986.

Duffy, James P. *Lincoln's Admiral: The Civil War Campaigns of David Farragut.* New York: Wiley, 1997.

Dull, Paul S. *A Battle History of the Imperial Japanese Navy, 1941–1945.* Annapolis, MD: Naval Institute Press, 1978.

Dunn, Walter S. *Soviet Blitzkrieg: The Battle for White Russia, 1944.* Boulder, CO: Lynne Rienner, 2000.

Dupuy, Trevor N. *Hitler's Last Gamble: The Battle of the Bulge, December 1944–January 1945.* New York: HarperCollins, 1944.

Durant, Will. *The Age of Faith.* New York: Simon and Schuster, 1940.

———. *Caesar and Christ,* Vol. 3, *The Story of Civilization.* New York: Simon and Schuster, 1944.

Eastman, Lloyd E. *Seeds of Destruction: Nationalist China in War and Revolution, 1937–1945.* Stanford, CA: Stanford University Press, 1984.

Eby, Cecil D. *The Siege of the Alcazar, Toledo: July to September 1936.* London: Bodley Head, 1966.

Edgerton, Robert B. *Death of Glory: The Legacy of the Crimean War.* Boulder, CO: Westview, 1999.

Edmunds, R. David. *The Shawnee Prophet.* Lincoln: University of Nebraska Press, 1983.

Eisenhower, John S. D. *The Bitter Woods.* New York: Putnam, 1969.

———. *So Far from God: The U.S. War with Mexico, 1846–1848.* New York: Random House, 1989.

Elleman, Bruce A. *Modern Chinese Warfare, 1785–1989.* New York: Routledge, 2001.

Ellul, Joseph. *The Great Siege of Malta.* Siggiewi, Malta: Ellul, 1992.

Elting, John R. *Swords around a Throne: Napoleon's Grande Armée.* New York: Free Press, 1988.

Elton, Geoffrey. *England under the Tudors.* New York: Routledge, 1991.

Ent, Uzal W. *Fighting on the Brink: Defense of the Pusan Perimeter.* Paducah, KY: Turner Publishing, 1996.

Erickson, Edward J. *Ordered to Die: A History of the Ottoman Army in the First World War.* Westport, CT: Greenwood, 2001.

Erickson, John. *The Road to Stalingrad: Stalin's War with Germany.* New York: Harper and Row, 1975.

Esherick, Joseph W. *Origins of the Boxer Rebellion.* Berkeley: University of California Press, 1987.

Evans, David C., and Mark R. Peattie. *Kaigun: Strategy, Tactics, and Technology in the Imperial Japanese Navy, 1887–1941.* Annapolis, MD: Naval Institute Press, 1997.

Everest, Allan S. *The War of 1812 in the Champlain Valley.* Syracuse, NY: Syracuse University Press, 1981.

Fadeyev, Aleksandr. *Leningrad in the Days of the Blockade.* Westport, CT: Greenwood, 1971.

Fairbank, John K., and Albert Feuerwerker, eds. *The Cambridge History of China,* Vol. 13, *Republican China, 1912–1949, Part 2.* Cambridge: Cambridge University Press, 1986.

Falco, Giorgio. *The Holy Roman Empire.* Westport, CT: Greenwood, 1980.

Falk, Stanley L. *Seventy Days to Singapore.* New York: Putnam, 1975.

Fall, Bernard B. *Hell in a Very Small Place: The Siege of Dienbienphu.* Philadelphia: Lippincott, 1966.

Falls, Cyril. *Caporetto 1917.* London: Weidenfeld and Nicolson, 1971.

Farris, W. W. *Heavenly Warriors: The Evolution of Japan's Military, 500–1700.* Cambridge: Harvard University Press, 1992.

Farwell, Bryon. *Queen Victoria's Little Wars.* New York: Harper and Row, 1985.

Fernández-Armesto, Felipe. *Ferdinand and Isabella.* New York: Taplinger, 1975.

———. *The Spanish Armada: The Experience of War in 1588.* London: Oxford University Press, 1988.

Ferrero, Guglielmo. *The Gamble: Bonaparte in Italy, 1796–1797.* London: Walker, 1961.

Ferrill, Arthur. *The Fall of the Roman Empire: The Military Explanation.* London: Thames and Hudson, 1986.

Fezensac, Montesquieu. *The Russian Campaign, 1812.* Translated by Lee B. Kennett. Athens: University of Georgia Press, 1970.

Fiddick, Thomas C. *Russia's Retreat from Poland, 1920: From Permanent Revolution to Peaceful Coexistence.* New York: St. Martin's, 1990.

Field, James A., Jr. *History of United States Naval Operations: Korea.* Washington, DC: Naval History Division, 1962.

———. *The Japanese at Leyte Gulf: The Shō Operation.* Princeton, NJ: Princeton University Press, 1947.

Finley, M. I., ed. *The Greek Historians: The Essence of Herodotus, Thucydides, Xenophon, Polybius.* New York: Viking, 1959.

Fischer, David Hackett. *Washington's Crossing.* New York: Oxford University Press, 2004.

Fitz-Enz, David G. *Plattsburg, the Final Invasion: The Decisive Battle of the War of 1812.* New York: Cooper Square, 2001.

Fleming, Peter. *The Siege at Peking: The Boxer Rebellion.* New York: Dorsey, 1990.

Foltz, Richard C. *Mughal India and Central Asia.* Karachi, Pakistan: Oxford University Press, 1998.

Foreman, Laura. *Napoleon's Lost Fleet: Bonaparte, Nelson, and the Battle of the Nile.* New York: Discovery Books, 1999.

Forty, George. *The Reich's Last Gamble: The Ardennes Offensive, December 1944.* London: Cassell, 2000.

Fox, Robin Lane. *The Search for Alexander.* Boston: Little, Brown, 1980.

France, John. *Western Warfare in the Age of the Crusades, 1000–1300.* Ithaca, NY: Cornell University Press, 1999.

Frank, Richard B. *Downfall: The End of the Japanese Empire.* New York: Random House, 1999.

———. *Guadalcanal: The Definitive Account of the Landmark Battle.* New York: Random House, 1990.

Franks, Tommy. *American Soldier: General Tommy Franks.* New York: HarperCollins, 2004.

Freeman, Edward. *The History of the Norman Conquest of England.* Chicago: University of Chicago Press, 1974.

Freidel, Frank. *The Splendid Little War.* Boston: Little, Brown, 1958.

Friedman, Lawrence J., and David Curtis Skaggs. "Jesse Duncan Elliott and the Battle of Lake Erie: The Issue of Mental Stability." *Journal of the Early Republic* 10 (Winter 1990): 493–516.

Friend, Jack. *West Wind, Flood Tide: The Battle of Mobile Bay.* Annapolis, MD: Naval Institute Press, 2004.

Friendly, Alfred. *The Dreadful Day: The Battle of Manzikert, 1071.* London: Hutchinson, 1981.

Fuchida, Mitsuo, and Masatake Okumiya. *Midway, the Battle That Doomed Japan: The Japanese Navy's Story.* Annapolis, MD: Naval Institute Press, 1955.

Fuller, J. F. C. *A Military History of the Western World.* 2 vols. New York: Funk and Wagnalls, 1954, 1995.

Furguson, Ernest B. *Chancellorsville, 1863: The Souls of the Brave.* New York: Knopf, 1992.

Gabba, Emilio. *Republican Rome, the Army, and the Allies.* Translated by P. J. Cuff. Oxford: Basil Blackwell, 1976.

Gabriel, Richard, and Donald Boose. *The Great Battles of Antiquity.* Westport, CT: Greenwood, 1994.

Gallagher, Gary W., ed. *Antietam: Essays on the 1862 Maryland Campaign.* Chapel Hill: University of North Carolina Press, 1999.

Gardiner, Robert, ed. *Fleet Battle and Blockade: The French Revolutionary War, 1793–1797.* London: Chatham, 1996.

———, ed. *Nelson against Napoleon: From the Nile to Copenhagen, 1798–1801.* London: Chatham, 1997.

Gascoigne, Bamber. *The Great Moghuls.* New York: Harper and Row, 1971.

Gates, David. *The Spanish Ulcer: A History of the Peninsular War.* New York: Norton, 1986.

Gaunt, Peter. *Oliver Cromwell.* Oxford, UK: Blackwell, 1996.

Gavin, James M. *On to Berlin: Battles of an Airborne Commander, 1943–1945.* New York: Viking, 1978.

Gelb, Norman. *Dunkirk: The Complete Story of the First Step in the Defeat of Hitler.* New York: William Morrow, 1989.

German, Tony. *The Sea Is at Our Gates: The History of the Canadian Navy.* Toronto: McClelland and Stewart, 1990.

Gernet, Jacques. *A History of Chinese Civilization.* New York: Cambridge University Press, 1994.

Geyl, Pieter. *The Netherlands in the Seventeenth Century: Part One, 1609–1648.* London: Ernest Bern, 1966.

Gibbon, Edward. *The Decline and Fall of the Roman Empire, 1185–1453.* New York: Modern Library, 1983.

———. *The History of the Decline and Fall of the Roman Empire,* Vols. 3, 4, and 6. Edited by J. B. Bury. London: Methuen, 1909–1912.

Gies, Frances. *Jean of Arc: The Legend and the Reality.* New York: Harper and Row, 1981.

Gil, Moshe, and Ethel Broido. *A History of Palestine, 634–1099.* Cambridge: Cambridge University Press, 1997.

Gilbert, Martin. *The First World War: A Complete History.* New York: Henry Holt, 1994.

Gillingham, J. *Richard I.* 2nd ed. New Haven, CT: Yale University Press, 2000.

Gilpin, Alec R. *The War of 1812 in the Old Northwest.* East Lansing: Michigan State University Press, 1958.

Giono, Jean. *The Battle of Pavia, 24 February 1525.* London: Peter Owen, 1965.

Glantz, David M., and Jonathan M. House. *When Titans Clashed: How the Red Army Stopped Hitler.* Lawrence: University Press of Kansas, 1995.

Gliddon, Gerard. *1914.* Stroud, Gloustershire, UK: Sutton, 1997.

Goedicke, Hans, ed. *Perspectives on the Battle of Kadesh.* Baltimore: Halgo, 1985.

Goldsworthy, Adrian. *The Punic Wars.* London: Cassell, 2000.

Gordon, G. A. H. *The Rules of the Game: Jutland and British Naval Command.* Annapolis, MD: Naval Institute Press, 1996.

Gordon, Michael R., and Bernard E. Trainor. *The Generals' War.* Boston: Little, Brown, 1995.

Gore, Terry L. *Neglected Heroes: Leadership and War in the Early Medieval Period.* Westport, CT: Praeger, 1995.

Gow, Ian. *Okinawa, 1945: Gateway to Japan.* Garden City, NY: Doubleday, 1985.

Graham, Dominick, and Shelford Bidwell. *Tug of War: The Battle for Italy, 1943–1945.* New York: St. Martin's, 1986.

Graham, Michael B. *Mantle of Heroism: Tarawa and the Struggle for the Gilberts, November, 1943.* Novato, CA: Presidio, 1993.

Grant, Michael. *The Army of the Caesars.* New York: Scribner, 1974.

———. *History of Rome.* New York: Scribner, 1978.

———. *The Jews in the Roman World.* New York: Scribner, 1973.

———. *Julius Caesar.* New York: M. Evans, 1992.

Great Britain, Dardanelles Commission. *The Final Report of the Dardanelles Commission.* London: HMSO, 1919.

Green, David. *Blenheim.* New York: Scribner, 1974.

Green, Peter. *Alexander of Macedon, 356–323 B.C.: A Historical Biography.* Berkeley: University of California Press, 1991.

———. *Armada from Athens.* Garden City, NY: Doubleday, 2003.

———. *The Greco-Persian Wars.* Berkeley: University of California Press, 1996.

Greene, Jack, and Alessandro Massignani. *Ironclads at War: The Origin and Development of the Armored Warship, 1854–1891.* Conshohocken, PA: Combined Publishing, 1998.

———. *Rommel's North Africa Campaign, September 1940–November 1942.* Conshohocken, PA: Combined Publishing, 1999.

Gregg, Charles T. *Tarawa.* New York: Stein and Day, 1984.

Gregory of Tours. *History of the Franks.* Translated by Ernest Brehaut. New York: Columbia University Press, 1916.

Grousaset, Rene. *The Empire of the Steppes: A History of Central Asia.* New Brunswick, NJ: Rutgers University Press, 1970.

Grove, Eric. *Big Fleet Actions: Tsushima, Jutland, Philippine Sea.* London: Arms and Armour, 1995.

Guilmartin, J. F. *Gunpowder and Galleys.* New York: Cambridge University Press, 1974.

Guingand, Francis de. *Operation Victory.* London: Hodder and Stoughton, 1946.

Gure, Leon. *The Siege of Leningrad.* Stanford, CA: Stanford University Press, 1962.

Gurval, Robert Alan. *Actium and Augustus: The Politics and Emotions of Civil War.* Ann Arbor: University of Michigan Press, 1995.

Guy, John. *Tudor England.* New York: Oxford University Press, 1990.

Haber, L. F. *The Poisonous Cloud: Chemical Warfare in the First World War.* New York: Oxford University Press, 1986.

Habib, Irfan, ed. *Akbar and His India.* Oxford: Oxford University Press, 1997.

Haig, Wolseley, ed. *The Cambridge History of India,* Vol. 3. Delhi: S. Chand, 1965.

Hainsworth, Roger, and Christine Churches. *The Anglo-Dutch Naval Wars, 1652–1674.* Phoenix Mill, Stroud, UK: Sutton, 1998.

Hall, Richard. *The War at Sea in the Ironclad Age.* London: Cassell, 2000.

Hamilton, General Sir Ian. *Gallipoli Diary.* New York: George H. Doran, 1920.

Hamilton, Nigel. *Monty: The Battles of Field Marshal Bernard Montgomery.* New York: Random House, 1994.

Hamilton-Williams, David. *Waterloo: New Perspectives.* London: Arms and Armour, 1993.

Hammel, Eric. *Fire in the Streets: The Battle for Hue, Tet 1968.* New York: Dell, 1992.

———. *Guadalcanal, Decision at Sea: The Naval Battle of Guadalcanal, November 13–15, 1942.* Pacifica, CA: Pacifica Press, 1988.

———. *Six Days in June: How Israel Won the 1967 Arab-Israeli War.* New York: Scribner, 1992.

Hammond, Nicholas G. L. *Alexander the Great: King, Commander, and Statesman.* 3rd ed. London: Bristol Classical Press, 1996.

———. *Philip of Macedon.* London: Duckworth, 1994.

Hanák, Péter, ed. *The Corvina History of Hungary: From Earliest Times until the Present Day.* Translated by Zsuzsa Béres. Budapest: Corvina Books, 1988.

Harder, Harry. *Italy in the Age of the Risorgimento, 1790–1870.* New York: Longman, 1983.

Harries, Meirion, and Susie Harries. *Soldiers of the Sun: The Rise and Fall of the Imperial Japanese Army.* New York: Random House, 1991.

Harrington, Peter, and Frederick A. Sharf. *Omdurman, 1898: The Eye-Witnesses Speak.* London: Greenhill Books, 1898.

Harris, R. W. *Clarendon and the English Revolution.* Stanford, CA: Stanford University Press, 1983.

Hartcup, Guy. *Code Name Mulberry: The Planning, Building and Operation of the Normandy Harbours.* London: David and Charles, 1977.

Harvey, L. P. *Islamic Spain, 1250 to 1500.* Chicago: University of Chicago Press, 1990.

Hata Ikuhiko, Sase Morimasa, and Tuneishi Keiichi, eds. *Sekai Senso Hanzai Jiten* [Encyclopedia of Crimes in Modern History]. Tokyo: Bungei-Shunju, 2002.

Hayward, Joel S. A. *Stopped at Stalingrad: The Luftwaffe and Hitler's Defeat in the East, 1942–1943.* Lawrence: University Press of Kansas, 1998.

Healy, Mark. *Cannae, 216 B.C.: Hannibal Smashes Rome's Army.* London: Osprey Military, 1994.

Hearn, Chester G. *Mobile Bay and the Mobile Campaign: The Last Great Battle of the Civil War.* Jefferson, NC: McFarland, 1993.

Heil, Robert Debs, Jr. *Victory at High Tide: The Inchon-Seoul Campaign.* Baltimore: Nautical and Aviation Publishing Company of America, 1979.

Henderson, Nicholas. *Prince Eugene of Savoy.* New York: Praeger, 1965.

Herbert, Frederick William von. *The Defense of Plevna, 1877.* Ankara, Turkey: Ministry of Culture, 1990.

Hermanns, William. *The Holocaust: From a Survivor of Verdun.* New York: Harper and Row, 1972.

Herodotus. *The History of Herodotus.* Edited by Manuel Komroff. Translated by George Rawlinson. New York: Tudor Publishing, 1956.

Herwig, Holger H. *The First World War: Germany and Austria-Hungary, 1914–1918.* New York: St. Martin's, 1997.

Herzog, Chaim. *The War of Atonement: October, 1973.* Boston: Little, Brown, 1975.

Hesketh, Roger. *Fortitude: The D-Day Deception Campaign.* New York: Overlook, 2000.

Hess, Earl J. *Pickett's Charge: The Last Attack at Gettysburg.* Chapel Hill: University of North Carolina Press, 2001.

Hewitt, H. J. *The Black Prince's Expedition of 1355–1357.* Manchester, UK: University of Manchester Press, 1958.

Hibbert, Christopher. *Agincourt.* New York: Dorset, 1978.

———— *Wolfe at Quebec.* London: Longmans, Green, 1959.

Hignett, C. *Xerxes' Invasion of Greece.* Oxford: Oxford University Press, 1963.

Hilditch, A. Neville. *The Stand of Liège.* London: Oxford University Press, 1915.

Hillgarth, J. N. *The Spanish Kingdoms, 1250–1516.* 2 vols. Oxford, UK: Clarendon, 1976–1978.

Hofschroer, Peter. *1815, the Waterloo Campaign: The German Victory, from Waterloo to the Fall of Napoleon.* Harrisburg, PA: Stackpole Books, 1999.

Holmes, Richard. *The Western Front.* London: BBC Books, 1999.

Holt, Mack P. *The French Wars of Religion, 1562–1629.* Cambridge: Cambridge University Press, 1995.

Holt, P. M., Ann K. S. Lambton, and Bernard Lewis. *The Cambridge History of Islam,* Vol. 1. Cambridge: Cambridge University Press, 1970.

Holzer, Harold, and Tim Mulligan. *The Battle of Hampton Roads: New Perspectives on the USS MONITOR and CSS VIRGINIA.* New York: Fordham University Press, 2006.

Hopkins, William B. *One Bugle, No Drums: The Marines at Chosin Reservoir.* Chapel Hill, NC: Algonquin Books, 1986.

Horne, Alistair. *The Fall of Paris: The Siege and the Commune, 1870–1871.* New York: Doubleday, 1965.

———. *How Far from Austerlitz? Napoleon, 1805–1815.* New York: St. Martin's, 1997.

———. *The Price of Glory: Verdun, 1916.* New York: Penguin, 1993.

Hoskins, Janina. *Victory at Vienna: The Ottoman Siege of 1683, a Historical Essay and a Select Group of Readings.* Washington, DC: Library of Congress, 1983.

Hough, Richard. *The Fleet That Had to Die.* New York: Viking, 1958.

———. *Nelson: A Biography.* London: Park Lane, 1980.

Hough, Richard, and Denis Richards. *The Battle of Britain: The Greatest Air Battle of World War II.* New York: Norton, 1989.

Hourtoulle, F. G. *Jena-Auerstadt: The Triumph of the Eagle.* Paris: Histoire and Collections, 1998.

Howard, Michael. *The Franco-Prussian War.* New York: Routledge, 2001.

Howarth, David. *1066: The Year of the Conquest.* New York: Viking Penguin, 1977.

———. *Trafalgar: The Nelson Touch.* New York: Atheneum, 1969.

———. *Waterloo: A Near Run Thing.* Conshohocken, PA: Combined Books, 1997.

Hoyt, Edwin P. *Blue Skies and Blood: The Battle of the Coral Sea.* New York: S. Eriksson, 1975.

———. *The Pusan Perimeter.* New York: Stein and Day, 1984.

Hsu, Immanuel C. Y. *The Rise of Modern China.* New York: Oxford University Press, 1970.

Hugill, J. A. C. *No Peace without Spain.* Oxford, UK: Kensal, 1991.

Humble, Richard. *Napoleon's Peninsular Marshals: A Reassessment.* New York: Taplinger Publishing, 1974.

Inber, Vera. *Leningrad Diary.* New York: St. Martin's, 1971.

Innes, Hammond. *The Conquistadors.* New York: Knopf, 1969.

Inoguchi Rikihei and Nakajima Tadashi, with Roger Pineau. *The Divine Wind: Japan's Kamikaze Force in World War II.* New York: Bantam Books, 1978.

Inouye Jukichi. *The Japan-China War: The Naval Battle of Haiyang.* Yokohama, Japan: Kelly and Walsh, 1895.

Irving, David. *The Destruction of Dresden.* New York: Ballantine, 1965.

———. *The Rise and Fall of the Luftwaffe: The Life and Death of Field Marshal Erhard Milch.* Boston: Little, Brown, 1974.

Irving, Washington. *Mahamet and His Successors.* Madison: University of Wisconsin Press, 1970.

Israel, Jonathan I. *The Dutch Republic and the Hispanic World, 1606–1661.* Oxford, UK: Clarendon, 1982.

James, D. Clayton. *The Years of MacArthur,* Vol. 2, *1941–1945.* Boston: Houghton Mifflin, 1975.

James, Robert Rhodes. *Gallipoli: The History of a Noble Blunder.* New York: Macmillan, 1965.

James, William M. *The British Navy in Adversity: A Study of the War of American Independence.* London: Longmans, Green, 1926.

———. *The Naval History of Great Britain,* Vol. 6. London: Richard Bentley, 1859.

Johoji Asami. *Nihon Boku Shi* [History of Japanese Air Defense]. Tokyo: Hara Shobo, 1981.

Jones, A. H. M. *The Herods of Judea.* Oxford, UK: Clarendon, 1967.

Jones, J. R. *The Anglo-Dutch Wars of the Seventeenth Century.* New York: Longman, 1996.

———. *Marlborough.* New York: Cambridge University Press, 1993.

Judah, Tim. *The Serbs: History, Myth, and the Destruction of Yugoslavia.* New Haven, CT: Yale University Press, 1997.

Jukes, Geoffrey. *Kursk: The Clash of Armour.* New York: Ballantine Books, 1968.

Junt, Metin, and Christine Woodhead, eds. *Suleyman the Magnificent and His Age: The Ottoman Empire in the Early Modern World.* New York: Longman, 1995.

Kaegi, Walter E. *Byzantium and the Early Islamic Conquests.* New York: Cambridge University Press, 1992.

Kagan, Donald. *The Peloponnesian War.* New York: Viking, 2003.

Kar, H. C. *Military History of India.* Calcutta: Firma KLM, 1980.

Keay, John. *The Honourable Company.* New York: Macmillan, 1994.

Keegan, John. *The Face of Battle: A Study of Agincourt, Waterloo & the Somme.* New York: Vintage Books, 1977.

———. *The Iraq War.* New York: Knopf, 2004.

———. *Six Armies in Normandy: From D-Day to the Liberation of Paris, June 6th–August 25th, 1944.* New York: Viking, 1982.

Kennedy, Hugh. *Muslim Spain and Portugal: A Political History of al-Andalus.* London: Longman, 1997.

Kenyon, John. *The Civil Wars of England.* London: Weidenfeld and Nicolson, 1989.

Keppie, L. J. F. *The Making of the Roman Army.* London: Batsford, 1984.

Kern, Paul Bentley. *Ancient Siege Warfare.* Bloomington: Indiana University Press, 1999.

Kernan, Alvin. *The Unknown Battle of Midway.* New Haven, CT: Yale University Press, 2005.

Kerr, E. Bartlett. *Flames over Tokyo: The U.S. Army Air Forces' Incendiary Campaign against Japan, 1944–1945.* New York: Donald I. Fine, 1991.

Ketchum, Richard M. *Saratoga: Turning Point of America's Revolutionary War.* New York: Henry Holt, 1997.

———. *The Winter Soldiers: The Battles for Trenton and Princeton.* New York: Anchor Books, 1975.

Kinross, Lord [John Patrick]. *The Ottoman Centuries: The Rise and Fall of the Turkish Empire.* New York: William Morrow, 1977.

Kiriakopoulos, G. C. *The Nazi Occupation of Crete, 1941–1945.* Westport, CT: Praeger, 1995.

Kishlansky, Mark A. *The Rise of the New Model Army.* Cambridge: Cambridge University Press, 1979.

Kitchen, Kenneth A. *Pharaoh Triumphant: The Life and Times of Ramses II.* Warminster, UK: Aris and Philips, 1982.

Knecht, R. J. *Renaissance Warrior and Patron: The Reign of Francis I.* Cambridge: Cambridge University Press, 1994.

Knightly, Charles. *Flodden: The Anglo-Scottish War of 1513.* London: Almark Publishing, 1975.

Konnegut, Kurt. *Slaughterhouse Five.* New York: Delta, 1969.

Konstam, Angus. *Pavia, 1525: The Climax of the Italian Wars.* London: Osprey, 1996.

———. *Poltava 1709: Russia Comes of Age.* New York: Praeger, 2005.

Kraff von Dellmensingen, Konrad. *Der Durchbruch am Isonzo.* 2 vols. Stalling: Oldenburg, 1926.

Krivosheev, G. F., ed. *Soviet Casualties and Combat Losses in the Twentieth Century.* London: Stackpole Books, 1997.

Lacouture, Captain John. "Disaster at Savo Island." *Naval History* 6(3) (Fall 1992): 11–15.

Lamb, Harold. *Cyrus the Great.* Garden City, NY: Doubleday, 1960.

Lamb, Richard. *War in Italy, 1943–1945: A Brutal Story.* New York: St. Martin's, 1993.

Lambert, Andrew, ed. *Steam, Steel and Shellfire: The Steam Warship, 1815–1905.* Annapolis, MD: Naval Institute Press, 1993.

Lander, J. R. *The Wars of the Roses.* New York: St. Martin's, 1990.

Lane-Poole, Stanley. *Medieval India under Mohammedan Rule.* 1903 reprint, New York: Krause, 1970.

La Pierre, Laurer L. *1759: The Battle for Canada.* Toronto: McClelland and Stewart, 1990.

Large, David Clay. "Guernica: Death in the Afternoon." *MHQ: Journal of Military History* 1(4) (Summer 1989): 8–17.

Larrabee, Harold A. *Decision at the Chesapeake.* London: William Kimber, 1965.

Lavery, Brian. *Nelson and the Nile: The Naval War against Bonaparte, 1798.* London: Chatham, 1998.

Lazenby, J. F. *Hannibal's War: A Military History of the Second Punic War.* Norman: University of Oklahoma Press, 1998.

Leckie, Robert. *Okinawa: The Last Battle of World War II.* New York: Viking, 1995.

Lendon, J. E. "Roman Siege of Jerusalem." *MHQ: Quarterly Journal of Military History* 17(4) (Summer 2005): 6–15.

———. *Soldiers and Ghosts: A History of Battle in Classical Antiquity.* New Haven, CT: Yale University Press, 2005.

Le Thanh Khoi. *Histoire de Viet Nam des origines à 1858.* Paris: Sudestasie, 1981.

Lewis, Adrian R. *Omaha Beach: A Flawed Victory.* Chapel Hill: University of North Carolina Press, 2001.

Lewis, Michael A. *Armada Guns: A Comparative Study of English and Spanish Armaments.* London: Allen and Unwin, 1961.

Liddell Hart, Basil. *Scipio Africanus: Greater Than Napoleon.* New York: Da Capo, 1994.

Lindley, Augustus. *Ti-Peng Tien-kwoh: The History of the Ti-Ping Revolution.* New York: Praeger, 1970.

Liu, F. F. *The Military History of Modern China, 1924–1949.* Princeton, NJ: Princeton University Press, 1956.

Lloyd, Christopher. *The Capture of Quebec.* New York: Macmillan, 1959.

———. *St. Vincent and Camperdown.* New York: Macmillan, 1963.

Lord, Walter. *The Miracle of Dunkirk.* New York: Viking, 1982.

Lowry, Thomas P. *The Attack on Taranto: Blueprint for Pearl Harbor.* Mechanicsburg, PA: Stackpole Books, 1995.

Loxton, Bruce. *The Shame of Savo.* Annapolis, MD: Naval Institute Press, 1997.

Ludendorff, Erich. *Ludendorff's Own Story: August 1914–November 1918.* 2 vols. New York: Harper, 1919.

Lumpkin, Henry. *From Savannah to Yorktown: The American Revolution in the South.* Columbia: University of South Carolina Press, 1981.

Lundstrom, John. *The First Team: Pacific Naval Air Combat from Pearl Harbor to Midway.* Annapolis, MD: Naval Institute Press, 1990.

Lunt, James. *John Burgoyne of Saratoga.* New York: Harcourt, Brace, Jovanovich, 1975.

Lynch, John. *The Spanish-American Revolutions.* New York: Norton, 1986.

———. "Valmy." *MHQ: Quarterly Journal of Military History* 5(1) (Autumn 1992): 88–96.

Lyons, M., and D. Jackson. *Saladin: The Politics of Holy War.* Cambridge: Cambridge University Press, 1982.

MacDonald, Charles B. *A Time for Trumpets: The Untold Story of the Battle of the Bulge.* New York: William Morrow, 1985.

MacDonald, Cullum. *The Lost Battle: Crete 1941.* New York: Free Press, 1993.

Macdonald, Lyn. *1915: The Death of Innocence.* New York: Henry Holt, 1995.

———. *Somme.* London: Michael Joseph, 1983.

Maddox, Robert James. *Weapons for Victory: The Hiroshima Decision Fifty Years Later.* Columbia: University of Missouri Press, 1995.

Mahan, Alfred Thayer. *The Major Operations of the Navies in the War of American Independence.* Boston: Little, Brown, 1913.

Mahon, John K. *The War of 1812.* Gainesville: University of Florida Press, 1972.

Maier, Klaus. *Guernica 26.4.1937: Die deutsche Intervention in Spanien und der "Fall Guernica."* Freiburg, Germany: Rombach, 1975.

Malcolm, Noel. *Kosovo: A Short History.* New York: New York University Press, 1998.

Mallonée, Richard. *Battle for Bataan: An Eyewitness Account.* New York: I Books, 2003.

Manceron, Claude. *Austerlitz: The Story of a Battle.* Translated by George Unwin. New York: Unwin, 1968.

Manstein, Erich von. *Lost Victories.* Edited and translated by Anthony G. Powell. Chicago: Henry Regnery, 1958.

Manz, Beatrice Forbes. *The Rise and Fall of Tamerlane.* Cambridge: Cambridge University Press, 1989.

Marder, Arthur. *From Dreadnought to Scapa Flow: The Royal Navy in the Fisher Era, 1904–1919,* Vol. 3. London: Oxford University Press, 1967.

Marichal, Paul, ed. *Mémoirs de Marsechal de Turenne.* Paris: Librairie Renouard, 1914.

Marozzi, Justin. *Tamerlane: Sword of Islam, Conqueror of the World.* New York: Da Capo, 2006.

Marsden, E. W. *The Campaign of Gaugamela.* Liverpool: Liverpool University Press, 1964.

Martin, Christopher. *The Boxer Rebellion.* London: Aberlard-Schuman, 1968.

Martin, Colin, and Geoffrey Parker. *The Spanish Armada.* New York: Norton, 1988.

Mason, Philip. *A Matter of Honour.* London: Jonathan Cape, 1974.

Mason, R. H. P., and J. G. Caiger. *History of Japan.* New York: Free Press, 1972.

Masterman, J. C. *The Double-Cross System in the War of 1939–1945.* New Haven, CT: Yale University Press, 1972.

Matthews, Herbert L. *Half of Spain Died: A Reappraisal of the Spanish Civil War.* New York: Scribner, 1973.

Mattingly, Garrett. *The Armada.* Boston: Houghton Mifflin, 1959.

Maude, F. N. *The Jena Campaign, 1806.* London: Greenhill, 1998.

May, Robin, and Gerry Embleton. *Wolfe's Army.* London: Osprey, 1997.

McGraw, Donner F. *The Early Islamic Conquests.* Princeton, NJ: Princeton University Press, 1981.

McKay, Derek. *Prince Eugene of Savoy.* London: Thames and Hudson, 1977.

McNeill-Moss, Geoffrey. *The Siege of Alcazar: A History of the Siege of the Toledo Alcazar, 1936.* New York: Knopf, 1937.

McPherson, James M. *Crossroads of Freedom: Antietam.* New York: Oxford University Press, 2002.

McPhillips, Martin. *The Battle of Trenton.* Parsippany, NJ: Silver Burdett, 1984.

Means, Philip A. *The Fall of the Inca Empire and the Spanish Rule in Peru, 1530–1780.* New York: Gordian, 1971.

Meid, Pat, and James M. Yingling. *U.S. Marine Operations in Korea, 1950–1953: Operations in West Korea.* Washington, DC: U.S. Marine Corps Historical Branch, 1972.

Melegari, Vezio. *The Great Military Sieges.* New York: Crowell, 1972.

Mercer, Patrick. *"Give Them a Volley and Charge!": The Battle of Inkerman, 1854.* Staplehurst, UK: Spellmount, 1998.

Meretskov, K. A. *Serving the People.* Moscow: Progress Publishers, 1971.

Middlebrook, Martin. *Convoy.* New York: William Morrow, 1977.

———. *First Day on the Somme.* New York: Norton, 1972.

———. *The Schweinfurt-Regensburg Mission.* New York: Scribner, 1983.

Military History Institute of Vietnam, The. *Victory in Vietnam.* Translated by Merle L. Pribbenow. Lawrence: University Press of Kansas, 2002.

Millar, Ronald William. *Death of an Army: The Siege of Kut, 1915–1916.* Boston: Houghton Mifflin, 1970.

Millett, Allan R. "Caesar and the Conquest of the Northwest Territory: The Wayne Campaign, 1792–95." *Timeline: A Publication of the Ohio Historical Society* 14 (1997): 2–21.

Millot, Bernard. *The Battle of the Coral Sea.* Annapolis, MD: Naval Institute Press, 1974.

———. *Divine Thunder: The Life and Death of the Kamikazes.* Translated by Lowell Blair. New York: McCall, 1970.

Moberly, F. J. *The Campaign in Mesopotamia, 1914–1918.* 3 vols. Nashville, TN: Battery Press, 1997–1998.

Montross, Lynn, and Nicholas A. Canzona. *U.S. Marine Operations in Korea, 1950–1953,* Vols. 2 and 3. Washington, DC: U.S. Marine Corps Historical Branch, 1955, 1957.

Moore, Harold G., and Joseph L. Galloway. *We Were Soldiers Once . . . and Young.* New York: Random House, 1992.

Moore, William. *Gas Attack: Chemical Warfare, 1915 to the Present Day.* New York: Hippocrene Books, 1987.

Moorehead, Alan. *Gallipoli.* New York: Harper and Row, 1956.

Morillo, Stephen, ed. *The Battle of Hastings: Sources and Interpretations.* Rochester, MN: University of Rochester Press, 1996.

Morison, Samuel Eliot. *History of United States Naval Operations in World War II.* 15 vols. Boston: Little, Brown, 1947–62.

Morley, J. W., ed. *The China Quagmire: Japan's Expansion on the Asian Continent, 1933–1941.* New York: Columbia University Press, 1983.

Morris, Eric. *Circles of Hell: The War in Italy, 1943–1945.* New York: Crown Publishers, 1993.

Morrison, J. S. *Greek and Roman Oared Warships.* Oxford: Oxbow Books, 1996.

Morrissey, Brenden. *Yorktown, 1781: The World Turned Upside Down.* London: Osprey, 1997.

Morselli, Mario A. *Caporetto 1917: Victory or Defeat?* London: Frank Cass, 2001.

Morton, Louis. *United States Army in World War II: The War in the Pacific; Fall of the Philippines.* Washington, DC: Office of the Chief of Military History, United States Army, U.S. Government Printing Office, 1953.

Murdoch, Adrian. *Rome's Greatest Defeat: Massacre in the Teutoburg Forest.* Stroud, Gloucestershire, UK: Sutton, 2006.

Murfin, James V. *The Gleam of Bayonets: The Battle of Antietam and Robert E. Lee's Maryland Campaign, September 1862.* Baton Rouge: Louisiana State University Press, 2004.

Murnane, William J. *The Road to Kadesh.* Chicago: Oriental Institute, 1990.

Murphey, Rhoads. *Ottoman Warfare, 1500–1700.* New Brunswick, NJ: Rutgers University Press, 1999.

Murray, Williamson, and Robert H. Scales Jr. *The Iraq War: A Military History.* Cambridge: Belknap Press of Harvard University Press, 2003.

Nafziger, George. *Napoleon at Leipzig: The Battle of the Nations, 1813.* Chicago: Emperor's Press, 1996.

Nalty, Bernard C. *Air Power and the Fight for Khe Sanh.* Washington, DC: USAF/HO, U.S. Government Printing Office, 1973.

Nardo, Don. *The Battle of Zama: Battles of the Ancient World.* San Diego: Lucent Books, 1996.

Neillands, Robin. *The Bomber War: The Allied Air Offensive against Nazi Germany.* New York: Overlook, 2001.

Nelson, James L. *Benedict Arnold's Navy: The Ragtag Fleet That Lost the Battle of Lake Champlan but Won the American Revolution.* New York: McGraw-Hill, 2006.

Nelson, Paul D. *Anthony Wayne: Soldier of the Early Republic.* Bloomington: Indiana University Press, 1985.

———. "Anthony Wayne's Indian War in the Old Northwest, 1792–1795." *Northwest Ohio Quarterly* 56 (1984): 115–140.

Nelson, Richard B. *The Battle of Salamis.* London: William Luscombe, 1975.

Newman, Peter. *The Battle of Marston Moor, 1644.* Chichester, UK: Anthony Bird, 1981.

Nicolle, David. *The Age of Tamerlane.* London: Osprey, 1996.

———. *Armies of the Ottoman Turks, 1300–1774.* London: Osprey, 1992.

———. *The Mongol Warlords: Genghis Khan, Kublai Khan, Hulegu, Tamerlane.* London: Brookhampton, 1998.

———. *Yarmuk 636 A.D.: The Muslim Conquest of Syria.* Osprey Campaign Series #31. London: Osprey, 1994.

Nolan, Keith W. *Battle for Hue: Tet 1968.* Novato, CA: Presidio, 1983.

Norwich. John Julius. *Byzantium: The Decline and Fall.* New York: Knopf, 1996.

Oberdorfer, Dan. *Tet!* New York: Doubleday, 1971.

O'Connell, D. P. *Richelieu.* New York: World Publishing, 1968.

O'Connor, Richard. *The Boxer Rebellion.* London: Robert Hale, 1974.

Oren, Michael. *Six Days of War: June 1967 and the Making of the Modern Middle East.* Oxford: Oxford University Press, 2002.

Ortzen, Len. *Guns at Sea: The World's Great Naval Battles.* London: Cox and Wyman, 1976.

Pacific War Research Society, The. *The Day Man Lost: Hiroshima, 6 August 1945.* Tokyo: Kodansha International, 1972.

Pack, S. W. C. *The Battle for Crete.* London: Ian Allan, 1973.

Padfield, Peter. *Dönitz: The Last Führer, Portrait of a Nazi War Leader.* New York: Harper and Row, 1984.

———. *Guns at Sea.* New York: St. Martin's, 1974.

Palmer, Alan. *Napoleon in Russia: The 1812 Campaign.* New York: Simon and Schuster, 1967.

Palmer, Dave R. *1794: America, Its Army, and the Birth of the Nation.* Novato, CA: Presidio, 1994.

Parker, Geoffrey. *The Dutch Revolt.* Rev. ed. London: Penguin Books, 1990.

———. *The Thirty Years' War.* New York: Military Heritage Press, 1988.

Parker, Harold. *Three Napoleonic Battles.* Durham, NC: Duke University Press, 1983.

Parkinson, Roger. *Summer, 1940: The Battle of Britain.* New York: David McKay, 1977.

Parkman, Francis. *Montcalm and Wolfe.* New York: Atheneum, 1984.

Parshall, Jonathan, and Anthony Tully. *Shattered Sword: The Untold Story of the Battle of Midway.* Washington, DC: Potomac Books, 2005.

Parsons, James Bunyan. *Peasant Rebellions of the Late Ming Dynasty.* Tucson: University of Arizona Press, 1970.

Paschall, Rod. *The Defeat of Imperial Germany, 1917–1918.* Chapel Hill, NC: Algonquin Books, 1990.

Pfanz, Harry W. *Gettysburg: Culp's Hill and Cemetery Hill.* Chapel Hill: University of North Carolina Press, 1993.

———. *Gettysburg: The Second Day.* Chapel Hill: University of North Carolina Press, 1987.

Piekalkiewicz, Janusz. *Moscow: 1941, The Frozen Offensive.* Novato, CA: Presidio, 1981.

Pierson, Peter. "Lepanto." *MHQ: Quarterly Journal of Military History* 9(2) (1997): 6–19.

Pisor, Robert. *The End of the Line: The Siege of Khe Sanh.* New York: Norton, 1982.

Pitt, Barrie. *1918: The Last Act.* New York: Ballantine Books, 1963.

Plutarch. *The Lives of the Nobles: Grecians and Romans.* Translated by John Dryden, revised by Arthur Hugh Clough. New York: Modern Library, 1979.

Pope, Alexander, trans. *The Iliad of Homer.* New York: Heritage, 1943.

Pope, Dudley. *Decision at Trafalgar.* Philadelphia: Lippincott, 1960.

———. *The Great Gamble.* London: Weidenfeld and Nicolson, 1972.

Potter, E. B. *Bull Halsey.* Annapolis, MD: Naval Institute Press, 1985.

Prados, John, and Yay W. Stubbe. *Valley of Decision.* Boston: Houghton Mifflin, 1991.

Prago, Albert. *The Revolutions in Spanish America.* New York: Macmillan, 1970.

Prange, Gordon W., with Donald M. Goldstein and Katherine V. Dillon. *At Dawn We Slept: The Untold Story of Pearl Harbor.* New York: McGraw-Hill, 1981.

———. *Miracle at Midway.* New York: McGraw-Hill, 1982.

———. *Pearl Harbor: The Verdict of History.* New York: McGraw-Hill, 1986.

Prata, Nicholas C. *Angels in Iron.* Huntingdon Valley, PA: Arx Publishing, 1997.

Preble, John. *Culloden.* New York: Atheneum, 1962.

Prescott, William H. *The History of the Conquest of Peru.* 1847; reprint, New York: New American Library, 1961.

Prestwick, Michael. *The Three Edwards: War and State in England, 1272–1377.* New York: St. Martin's, 1980.

Priest, John M. *Antietam: The Soldier's Battle.* New York: Oxford University Press, 1994.

Proctor, Raymond L. *Hitler's Luftwaffe in the Spanish Civil War.* Westport, CT: Greenwood, 1983.

Rabb, Theodore K. *The Thirty Years' War.* 2nd ed. Lanham, MD: University Press of American, 1981.

Rady, Martyn. *From Revolt to Independence.* London: Hodder and Stoughton, 1990.

Read, Anthony, and David Fisher. *The Fall of Berlin.* New York: Norton, 1992.

Reddaway, W. F. *Frederick the Great and the Rise of Prussia.* New York: Greenwood, 1969.

Reuter, Timothy. *Germany in the Early Middle Ages.* London: Longman, 1991.

Richá, Pierre. *The Carolingians.* Translated by Michael I. Allen. Philadelphia: University of Pennsylvania Press, 1993.

Richman, Irving Berdine. *Adventures of New Spain: The Spanish Conquerors.* New Haven, CT: Yale University Press, 1929.

Ridley, Ronald T., ed. and trans. *Zosimus: New History.* Canberra: Australian Association for Byzantine Studies, 1982.

Ries, Karl, and Hans Ring. *The Legion Condor: A History of the Luftwaffe in the Spanish Civil War, 1936–1939.* London: Schiffer, 1992.

Riley-Smith, Jonathan, ed. *The Oxford Illustrated History of the Crusades.* New York: Oxford University Press, 1997.

Ritter, Gerhard. *Frederick the Great: A Historical Profile.* Berkeley: University of California Press, 1968.

Robert, P. E. *History of British India.* London: Oxford University Press, 1952.

Roberts, Michael. *Gustavus Adolphus.* 2 vols. 2nd ed. New York: Longman, 1992.

Robertson, William G. *Counterattack on the Naktong, 1950.* Fort Leavenworth, KS: Combat Studies Institute, 1985.

Rodgers, William Ledyard. *Naval Warfare under Oars, 4th to 16th Centuries: A Study of Strategy, Tactics and Ship Design.* Annapolis, MD: Naval Institute Press, 1940, 1967.

Rogers, R. *Latin Siege Warfare in the Twelfth Century.* Oxford, UK: Clarendon, 1992.

Rommel, Erwin. *The Rommel Papers.* Edited by B. H. Liddell Hart. London: Collins, 1953.

Roskill, Stephen. *Churchill and the Admirals.* London: William Collins, 1977.

Ross, Charles. *The Wars of the Roses.* London: Thames and Hudson, 1976.

Rothenberg, Gunther E. *The Army of Francis Joseph.* West Lafayette, IN: Purdue University Press, 1976.

———. *Napoleon's Great Adversaries: The Archduke Charles and the Austrian Army, 1792–1814.* Bloomington: Indiana University Press, 1982.

Rowse, A. L. *Bosworth Field and the Wars of the Roses.* New York: Macmillan, 1966.

Roy, Jules. *The Battle of Dienbienphu.* New York: Harper and Row, 1965.

Rubenstein, Murray, and Richard Goldman. *Shield of David: An Illustrated History of the Israeli Air Force.* Englewood Cliffs, NJ: Prentice-Hall, 1978.

Rudorff, Raymond. *War to the Death: The Siege of Saragossa, 1808–1809.* London: Hamish Hamilton, 1974.

Runciman, Steven. *Byzantine Civilization.* New York: Barnes and Noble, 1994.

Russ, Martin. *The Chosin Reservoir Campaign, Korea 1950.* New York: Fromm International, 1999.

Sadler, John. *Flodden, 1513: Scotland's Greatest Defeat.* London: Osprey, 2006.

Salisbury, Harrison E. *The 900 Days: The Siege of Leningrad.* New York: Harper and Row, 1969.

———. *The Unknown War.* New York: Bantam Books, 1978.

Samson, George. *A History of Japan, 1334–1615.* Stanford, CA: Stanford University Press, 1961.

Sandler, Stanley. *The Emergence of the Modern Capital Ship.* Newark: University of Delaware Press, 1979.

Scales, Robert H., Jr. *Certain Victory: The U.S. Army in the Gulf War.* Washington, DC: Brassey's, 1997.

Schlüter, W. "The Battle of the Teutoburg Forest: Archaelogical Research at Kalkriese near Osnabrück." *Journal of Roman Archaeology,* Supp. 32 (1999): 125–159.

Schofield, Brian B. *The Attack on Taranto.* London: Allan, 1973.

Schom, Alan. *Trafalgar: Countdown to Battle, 1803–1805.* New York: Oxford University Press, 1990.

Schwarzkopf, H. Norman. *It Doesn't Take a Hero.* New York: Bantam Books, 1992.

Scott, Robert McNair. *Robert the Bruce, King of Scots.* New York: Carroll and Graf, 1996.

Sears, Stephen W. *Chancellorsville.* Boston: Houghton Mifflin, 1996.

———. *Landscape Turned Red: The Battle of Antietam.* New York: Ticknor and Fields, 1983.

Sekunda, Nick, and John Warry. *Alexander the Great: His Armies and Campaigns, 332–323 B.C.* London: Osprey, 1988.

Sells, A. Lytton. *The Memoirs of James II: His Campaigns as Duke of York, 1652–1660.* Bloomington: Indiana University Press, 1961.

Seth, Ronald. *Caporetto: The Scapegoat Battle.* London: Macdonald, 1965.

Seward, Desmond. *The Hundred Years' War: The English in France, 1337–1453.* New York: Atheneum, 1978.

Sherwell, Guillermo. *Antonio José de Sucre.* Washington, DC: Byron S. Adams, 1924.

Showalter, Dennis. *Tannenberg: Clash of Empires.* Hamden, CT: Archon, 1991.

Shulimson, Jack. *U.S. Marines in Vietnam, 1966.* Washington, DC: U.S. Marine Corps, 1982.

Sibourne, William. *History of the Waterloo Campaign.* London: Greenhill Books, 1990.

Sima Qian. *Record of the Great Historian: Han Dynasty I.* Translated by Barton Watson. New York: Columbia University Press, 1993.

Simpson, Howard R. *Dien Bien Phu: The Epic Battle America Forgot.* Washington, DC: Brassey's, 1994.

Singletary, Otis. *The Mexican War.* Chicago: University of Chicago Press, 1960.

Singleton, Frederick Bernard. *A Short History of the Yugoslav Peoples.* New York: Cambridge University Press, 1998.

Sire, H. J. A. *The Knights of Malta.* New Haven, CT: Yale University Press, 1996.

Skaggs, David Curtis. "The Battle of Lake Erie." In *Great American Naval Battles,* edited by Jack Sweetman, 64–84. Annapolis, MD: Naval Institute Press, 1998.

———. *Oliver Hazard Perry: Honor, Courage, and Patriotism in the Early U.S. Navy.* Annapolis, MD: Naval Institute Press, 2006.

———. *Thomas Macdonough: Master of Command in the Early U.S. Navy.* Annapolis, MD: Naval Institute Press, 2003.

Skaggs, David Curtis, and Gerard T. Altoff. *A Signal Victory: The Lake Erie Campaign, 1812–1813.* Annapolis, MD: Naval Institute Press, 1997.

Skates, John Ray. *The Invasion of Japan: Alternative to the Bomb.* Columbia: University of South Carolina Press, 1998.

Skrjabina, Elena. *Siege and Survival: The Odyssey of a Leningrader.* Carbondale: Southern Illinois University Press, 1971.

Smith, Digby. *1813, Leipzig: Napoleon and the Battle of the Nations.* London: Greenhill Books, 2001.

Smith, Gene A. *Iron and Heavy Guns: Duel between the Monitor and Merrimac.* Abilene, Texas: McWhiney Foundation Press, 1998.

Smith, George W. *The Siege at Hue.* Boulder, CO: Lynne Rienner, 1999.

Smith, Melden E., Jr. "The Bombing of Dresden Reconsidered: A Study in Wartime Decision Making." Unpublished PhD dissertation, Boston University, 1971.

Smith, Peter C. *Midway, Dauntless Victory: Fresh Perspectives on America; Seminal Navy Victory of 1942.* Barnsley, UK: Pen and Sword Maritime, 2007.

Smithers, A. J. *Cambrai: The First Great Tank Battle, 1917.* London: Leo Cooper, 1992.

———. *Taranto, 1940: "Prelude to Pearl Harbor."* Annapolis, MD: Naval Institute Press, 1995.

Sokol, Edward D. *Tamerlane.* Lawrence, KS: Coronado, 1977.

Speck, W. A. *The Butcher: The Duke of Cumberland and the Suppression of the 45.* Oxford, UK: Blackwell, 1981.

Spector, Ronald H. *Admiral of the New Empire: The Life and Career of George Dewey.* Baton Rouge: Louisiana State University Press, 1974.

———. *Eagle against the Sun: The American War with Japan.* New York: Free Press, 1985.

Spiers, Edward M., ed. *Sudan: The Reconquest Reappraised.* London: Frank Cass, 1998.

Stanley, George F. G. *War of 1812: Land Operations.* Ottawa: National Museums of Canada and Macmillan, 1983.

Starr, Chester G. *The Roman Imperial Navy, 31 B.C.–A.D. 324.* New York: Barnes and Noble, 1960.

Steindorff, George, and Keith Seele. *When Egypt Ruled the East.* Chicago: University of Chicago Press, 1957.

Steward, Desmond. *The Wars of the Roses.* New York: Viking, 1995.

Stone, Norman. *The Eastern Front, 1914–1917.* New York: Scribner, 1975.

Stoye, John. *The Siege of Vienna.* New York: Holt, Rinehart, and Winston, 1965.

Strachan, Hew. *The First World War,* Vol. 1, *To Arms.* New York: Oxford University Press, 2001.

Strauss, Barry. *The Battle of Salamis: The Naval Encounter That Saved Greece—and Western Civilization.* New York: Simon and Schuster, 2004.

Suetonius. *The Twelve Caesars.* Translated by Michael Graves. London: Penguin, 1957.

Sumner, B. H. *Russia and the Balkans, 1870–1880.* Oxford: Oxford University Press, 1937.

Sumption, Jonathan. *The Hundred Years' War: Trial by Battle.* Philadelphia: University of Pennsylvania Press, 1988.

Sutherland, Daniel E. *Fredericksburg & Chancellorsville: The Dare Mark Campaign.* Lincoln: University of Nebraska Press, 1998.

Sutherland, N. M. *The Huguenot Struggle for Recognition.* New Haven, CT: Yale University Press, 1980.

Sweetman, John. *Tannenberg, 1914.* London: Cassell, 2002.

Sword, Wiley. *President Washington's Indian War: The Struggle for the Old Northwest, 1790–1795.* Norman: University of Oklahoma Press, 1985.

Symonds, Craig. *Confederate Admiral: The Life and Wars of Franklin Buchanan.* Annapolis, MD: Naval Institute Press, 1999.

Syrett, David. *The Royal Navy in American Waters, 1775–1783.* Aldershot, UK: Scolar Press, 1989.

Tacitus. *The Annals of Imperial Rome.* Translated by Michael Grant. London: Penguin, 1974.

The Taiping Revolution. Peking: Foreign Languages Press, 1976.

Takushiro Hatsutori. *Daitoa Senso Zenshi* [Complete History of the Greater East Asian War]. Tokyo: Hara Shobo, 1965.

Tarn, W. W. *Alexander the Great.* Cambridge: Cambridge University Press, 1948.

Taylor, Frederick. *Dresden.* New York: HarperCollins, 2004.

Tebbel, John W. *The Battle of Fallen Timbers, August 20, 1794.* New York: Franklin Watts, 1972.

Teng Ssu-Yü. *New Light on the History of the Taiping Rebellion.* New York: Russell and Russell, 1966.

Terraine, John. *A Time for Courage: The Royal Air Force in the European War, 1939–1945.* New York: Macmillan, 1985.

Thomas, David. *Nazi Victory: Crete 1941.* New York: Stein and Day, 1973.

Thomas, Gordon, and Max Morgan-Witts. *Enola Gay.* New York: Stein and Day, 1977.

Thomas, Hugh. *The Spanish Civil War.* New York: Harper and Brothers, 1961.

Thompson, E. A. *A History of Attila and the Huns.* Oxford, UK: Clarendon, 1948.

Thucydides. *History of the Peloponnesian War.* Translated by Rex Warner. New York: Penguin, 1984.

Tilley, John A. *The British Navy and the American Revolution.* Columbia: University of South Carolina Press, 1987.

Townsend, Peter. *Duel of Eagles.* London: Butler and Tanner, 1991.

Townshend, Sir Charles V. F. *My Campaign in Mesopotamia.* London: Thornton Butterworth, 1920.

Tracy, Nicholas. *Nelson's Battles: The Art of Victory in the Age of Sail.* Annapolis, MD: Naval Institute Press, 1996.

Trask, David F. *The War with Spain.* New York: Macmillan, 1981.

Travers, Tim. "The Somme: The Reason Why." *MHQ: Quarterly Journal of Military History* 7(4) (Summer 1995): 62–73.

Treadgold, Warren. *Byzantium and Its Army, 284–1081.* Stanford, CA: Stanford University Press, 1995.

Tregaskis, Richard. *Guadalcanal Diary.* New York: Random House, 1943.

Trevelyan, Raleigh. *Rome '44: The Battle for the Eternal City.* New York: Viking, 1982.

Truong Buu Lam. *Resistance, Rebellion, and Revolution: Popular Movements in Vietnamese History.* Singapore: Institute of Southeast Asian Studies, 1984.

Tuchman, Barbara W. *The Guns of August.* New York: Macmillan, 1962.

Tucker, Spencer C. *Handbook of 19th Century Naval Warfare.* Annapolis, MD: Naval Institute Press, 2000.

———. *Tanks: An Illustrated History of Their Impact.* Santa Barbara, CA: ABC-CLIO, 2004.

Tunstall, Brian. *Naval Warfare in the Age of Sail: The Evolution of Fighting Tactics, 1650–1815.* Edited by Nicholas Tracy. London: Conway Maritime, 1990.

Turnbull, Stephen. *Battles of the Samurai.* New York: Arms and Armour, 1987.

———. *The Samurai: A Military History.* New York: Macmillan, 1977.

Twitchett, Denis, and Michael Lewis. *The Cambridge History of China,* Vol. 1. New York: Cambridge University Press, 1986.

Tyerman, Christopher. *Fighting for Christendom: Holy War and the Crusades.* New York: Oxford University Press, 2005.

Van Creveld, Martin. *The Sword and the Olive: A Critical History of the Israeli Defense Force.* New York: PublicAffairs, 1998.

Vandervort, Bruce. *Wars of Imperial Conquest in Africa, 1830–1914.* London: UCL Press, 1998.

Vasiliev, Alexander Alexandrovich. *History of the Byzantine Empire, 324–1453.* Madison: University of Wisconsin Press, 1990.

Velikovsky, Immanuel. *Ramses II and His Time.* New York: Doubleday, 1978.

Verbruggen, J. F. *The Art of Warfare in Western Europe during the Middle Ages.* Amsterdam: North Holland, 1977.

Verney, Peter. *The Battle of Blenheim.* London: Batsford, 1976.

Verrier, Anthony. *The Bomber Offensive.* New York: Macmillan, 1969.

Viet Chung. "Recent Findings on the Tay Son Insurgency." *Vietnamese Studies* 81 (1985): 30–62.

Walder, David. *The Short Victorious War: The Russo-Japanese Conflict, 1904–5.* New York: Harper and Row, 1973.

Wallace-Hadrill, J. M. *The Fourth Book of the Chronicle of Fredegar with Its Continuations.* London: Nelson, 1960.

Walter, Francis X. *The Naval Battle of Mobile Bay, August 5, 1864.* Birmingham, AL: Prester Meridian, 1993.

Ward, Christopher. *The War of the Revolution.* 2 vols. New York: Macmillan, 1952.

Warner, Denis, and Peggy Warner. *Disaster in the Pacific: New Light on the Battle of Savo Island.* Annapolis, MD: Naval Institute Press, 1992.

———. *The Tide at Sunrise: A History of the Russo-Japanese War, 1904–1905.* New York: Charterhouse, 1974.

Warner, Marina. *Joan of Arc: The Image of Female Heroism.* New York: Knopf, 1981.

Warr, Nicholas. *Phase Line Green: The Battle for Hue, 1968.* Annapolis, MD: Naval Institute Press, 1997.

Warry, John. *Warfare in the Classical World.* New York: Salamander Books, 1993.

Wawro, Geoffrey. *The Austro-Prussian War: Austria's War with Prussia and Italy in 1866.* New York: Cambridge University Press, 1996.

———. *The Franco-Prussian War: The German Conquest of France in 1870–1871.* New York: Cambridge University Press, 2003.

Wedgwood, C. V. *The Thirty Years' War.* London: Jonathan Cape, 1944.

Weir, Alison. *The Wars of the Roses.* New York: Ballantine Books, 1995.

Weizman, Ezer. *On Eagle's Wings: The Personal Story of the Leading Commander of the Israeli Air Force.* New York: Macmillan, 1976.

Werth, Alexander. *Russia at War, 1941–1945.* New York: Dutton, 1964.

Westad, Odd Arne. *Decisive Encounters: The Chinese Civil War, 1946–1950.* Stanford, CA: Stanford University Press, 2003.

Westmoreland, William C. *A Soldier Reports.* New York: Doubleday, 1976.

Westwood, J. N. *A New Look at the Russo-Japanese War, 1904–1905.* Boulder, CO: NetLibrary, 1999.

———. *Witnesses of Tsushima.* Tokyo: Sophin University, 1970.

White, Colin. "The Bombardment of Alexandria." *Mariner's Mirror* 66 (1980): 31–49.

———. *1797: Nelson's Year of Destiny.* Stroud, UK: Sutton, 1998.

White, Jon Manchip. *Cortés and the Downfall of the Aztec Empire.* London: Hamish Hamilton, 1971.

Whitman, John W. *Bataan: Our Last Ditch: The Bataan Campaign, 1942.* New York: Hippocrene Books, 1990.

Whittacker, C. R. *Frontiers of the Roman Empire.* Baltimore: Johns Hopkins University Press, 1994.

Wilson, Dick. *When Tigers Fight: The Story of the Sino-Japanese War, 1937–1945.* New York: Viking, 1982.

Winschel, Terrence J. *Vicksburg: Fall of the Confederate Gibraltar.* Abilene, TX: McWhiney Foundation Press, 1999.

———, ed. *Triumph and Defeat: The Vicksburg Campaign.* Campbell, CA: Savas, 1998.

Winston, Richard. *Charlemagne: From the Hammer to the Cross.* Indianapolis: Bobbs-Merrill, 1954.

Winter, Denis. *Haig's Command: A Reassessment.* New York: Viking, 1991.

Wood, James B. *The Army of the King: Warfare, Soldiers, and Society during the Wars of Religion in France, 1562–1676.* Cambridge: Cambridge University Press, 1996.

Woodward, C. Vann. *The Battle for Leyte Gulf.* New York: Macmillan, 1947.

Woodworth, Steven E. *Beneath a Northern Sky: A Short History of the Gettysburg Campaign.* Wilmington, DE: Scholarly Resources, 2003.

Woolrych, Austin. *Battles of the English Civil War.* London: Batsford, 1961.

Wright, Derrick. *The Battle for Iwo Jima, 1945.* Phoenix Mill, UK: Sutton, 1999.

———. *A Hell of a Way to Die: Tarawa Atoll, 20–23 November 1943.* London: Windrow and Greene, 1997.

Xenophon. *Cyropaedia.* Translated by Walter Miller. Cambridge: Harvard University Press, 1979.

Y'Blood, William T. *Hunter-Killer: U.S. Escort Carriers in the Battle of the Atlantic.* Annapolis, MD: Naval Institute Press, 1983.

———. *Red Sun Setting: The Battle of the Philippine Sea.* Annapolis, MD: Naval Institute Press, 1980.

Yeh Wen-hsin, ed. *Wartime Shanghai.* New York: Routledge, 1998.

Young, Peter. *Naseby, 1645: The Campaign and the Battle.* London: Century, 1985.

Young, Peter, and Richard Holmes. *The English Civil War.* London: Eyre Methuen, 1974.

Yung, Louise. *Japan's Total Empire: Manchuria and the Collapse of Wartime Imperialism.* Berkeley: University of California Press, 1998.

Zabecki, David T. *Steel Wind: Colonel Georg Bruchmüller and the Birth of Modern Artillery.* Bridgeport, CT: Praeger, 1994.

Zamoyski, Adam. *The Battle for the Marchlands.* New York: Columbia University Press, 1981.

Ziemke, Earl F., and Magna E. Bauer. *Moscow to Stalingrad: Decision in the East.* Washington, DC: U.S. Government Printing Office, 1987.

Index